PER

RE

ZURICH TAX HANDBOOK 2015–16

Gerald A. Mowles
and Tony Foreman

BBL&G

Pearson Education Limited
Edinburgh Gate
Harlow CM20 2JE
United Kingdom
Tel: +44 (0)1279 623623
Web: www.pearson.com/uk

First published in Great Britain in 2015 (print and electronic)

Pearson Education is not responsible for the content of third-party internet sites.

ISBN: 978-1-292-09878-4 (print)
       978-1-292-09879-1 (PDF)
       978-1-292-09880-7 (ePub)

British Library Cataloguing-in-Publication Data
A catalogue record for the print edition is available from the British Library

No responsibility for loss occasioned to any person acting or refraining from action as a result of the material in this publication can be accepted by Zurich, the author or publishers. The views and opinions of Zurich may not necessarily coincide with some of the views and opinions expressed in the book which are solely those of the authors and no endorsement of them by Zurich should be inferred.

10 9 8 7 6 5 4 3 2 1
19 18 17 16 15

Print edition typeset b
Printed in Great Brita

NOTE THAT ANY P

FINANCE ACT 2015 AND OTHER CHANGES

(including changes planned for Finance Act 2016)

SCOTLAND

In June 2015, HMRC published a Memorandum of Understanding between it and Revenue Scotland, which sets out arrangements between HMRC and the Scottish Government for setting up and operating the Scottish rate of income tax.

See also 34.10 on the definition of a Scottish taxpayer who will be liable for the Scottish rate of income tax from 2016–17 onwards.

CHAPTER 2 SELF-ASSESSMENT

Alternative to annual tax returns

The Government intends to replace tax returns with digital accounts which will incorporate information already provided to HMRC.

CHAPTER 3 HMRC AND YOU

Accelerated Payment Notices (see 3.6.2)

Provisions in FA 2014 allow HMRC to require payment of tax from users of schemes which have been registered under the DOTAS regulations. The Chancellor has decided to continue this policy and HMRC expects to issue another 21,000 APNs in 2015.

Penalties (see 3.5)

FA 2015 has introduced enhanced penalties for offshore tax evasion.

Relying on an adviser (see 3.5.3)

The Tax Tribunal held that it was quite reasonable for a taxpayer to rely on professional advice in not disclosing aspects of a tax avoidance scheme.

Disclosure facilities (see 3.6.4–3.6.6)

The Government has decided to close the Liechtenstein Disclosure Facility and the Crown Dependency Disclosure Facilities earlier than previously indicated. These will close on 31 December 2015. A new and less generous facility will then apply for approximately 18 months.

CHAPTER 4 EMPLOYMENT INCOME

P11D limit to be abolished from 2016–17 (see 4.4.9)

The distinction between employees earning less than £8,500 per annum and P11D employees will no longer apply from 6 April 2016.

Company car benefits (see 4.5)

There are new taxable figures for 2015–16.

Beneficial loans (see 4.7)

The official rate for 2015–16 is 3%.

Armed forces early departure scheme (see 4.16)

Termination payments under this scheme will be exempt.

Testimonials

At present, sportsmen who benefit from testimonial matches are not generally taxed. The Government is reviewing this exemption.

CHAPTER 5 DISGUISED REMUNERATION

Disguised fee income to be taxed (see 5.6 and 7.6.1)

Investment managers are to be charged income tax on disguised fee income.

CHAPTER 7 SELF-EMPLOYMENT

Farmer's averaging (see 7.9.1)

The current two-year period for averaging farm profits is to be increased to five years from April 2016.

Foreign entity classification (see 7.7.2)

A decision by the Supreme Court in *IRC v George Anson* indicates that members of US Limited Liability Corporations are to be taxed as members of a partnership. This is in conflict with previous HMRC practice.

CHAPTER 8 INCOME FROM PROPERTY

Let property campaign (see 3.6.7 and Chapter 8)

HMRC is operating a let property campaign, which is an opportunity for landlords who owe tax through letting out residential property, in the UK or abroad, to get up to date with their tax affairs under the best possible terms.

CHAPTER 9 INCOME FROM SAVINGS

0% band for savings income up to £5,000 (see 9.1)

Where an individual's other income is covered by the personal allowance, he or she can have savings income of up to £5,000 without paying tax.

CHAPTER 10 OTHER INCOME

Miscellaneous losses (see 10.8.1)

There are new restrictions on relief for miscellaneous losses.

CHAPTER 12 PERSONAL ALLOWANCES

Married couples and civil partners (see 12.2.3)

It is now possible to transfer unused allowances provided that neither spouse is a higher rate taxpayer.

Personal savings allowance

From 2016–17, basic rate taxpayers will have a £1,000 personal savings allowance and higher rate taxpayers will have a £500 allowance.

CHAPTER 13 CAPITAL GAINS TAX

Non-residents and UK property (see 13. 3, 13.20 and 14.5)

Non-residents can now be charged CGT on UK residential property. Returns are required within 30 days.

CGT and wasting assets (see 13.4.2 and 13.16.1)

The exemption does not apply to wasting assets used in a trade. From 18 March 2015, this includes a trade carried on by someone other than the owner of the wasting asset.

CHAPTER 16 COMPUTATION OF BUSINESS PROFITS

Whether expenditure is wholly and exclusively for business (see 16.1.5)

In *Healy* [2015] TC 04425 the First-tier Tribunal (FTT) dismissed a taxpayer's claim to deduct expenditure incurred renting a three bedroom flat near the London theatre in which he was performing. The FTT found that the expenditure was incurred for the dual purpose of enabling him to perform his duties as an actor and to receive visitors in London and as the latter of these was a non-business purpose and there was no identifiable part or proportion of the expenditure incurred wholly and exclusively for the purposes of the trade the whole expense was disallowable.

Flood defence expenditure (see 16.1)

FA 2015 provides a specific tax deduction for this.

Annual investment allowance (see 16.2.7)

The AIA will be £200,000 from 1 January 2016.

CHAPTER 17 CAPITAL GAINS TAX AND BUSINESS TRANSACTIONS

Entrepreneurs' relief (see 17.7)

Restrictions now apply where gains arise from associated disposals or from the sale of goodwill to a company.

See also the new definition of 'trading company.' Investment companies which hold shares in joint venture companies no longer qualify.

Entrepreneurs' relief can now be due where deferred gains are brought into charge on the disposal of EIS investments.

Entrepreneurs' relief must be claimed within a period which ends one year after the 31 January filing date for the tax return which reports the disposal.

CHAPTER 18 TAX AND COMPANIES

New rate of corporation tax (see 18.4)

The small companies rate has been abolished. The standard rate of corporation tax is now 20%.

CT relief for late interest payments (see 18.5.5)

Relief will in future be available on the accruals basis

Acquisition of goodwill (see 18.6)

There is no relief under the intangibles legislation where goodwill is acquired from a connected person on or after 3 December 2014. From 8 July 2015, no relief is due even where the goodwill is acquired from a vendor who is not a connected person.

Controlled foreign companies (see 18.10.2)

From 8 July 2015, companies cannot relieve losses against a charge on profits arising from CFCs. For accounting periods which straddle 8 July 2015 CFC profits will need to be apportioned on a just and reasonable basis.

R&D credit (see 18.16.1)

SMEs can get relief on 230% of their expenditure on research and development.

CHAPTER 22 OUTLINE OF VAT

VAT registration (see 22.4.1)

The threshold is now £82,000.

CHAPTER 23 NATIONAL INSURANCE CONTRIBUTIONS

Exemption from Employer NICs for wages paid to apprentices (see 23.1.7)

No employer contributions are due from 6 April 2015 on wages paid to apprentices under the age of 21. From 6 April 2016, the age limit will be increased to 25.

New regime in the future for the self-employed (see 23.2 and 23.4)

The Government proposes to abolish Class 2 contribution for the self-employed and replace Class 4 contributions with a new scheme that will provide additional pension benefits.

CHAPTER 25 TAX EFFICIENT INVESTMENT

Help to buy ISAs (see 25.1.4)

There is a new Government subsidy for first time buyers saving through an ISA.

ISA benefits for the surviving partner (see 25.1)

The Government intends that a widow or widower should be able to cash in an ISA that they have inherited without suffering a tax charge.

Enterprise Investment Scheme changes (see 25.4)

There are proposed new limits on the age of the company and the number of employees; and exceptions for knowledge intensive companies.

Entrepreneurs' relief can now be due where deferred gains are brought into charge on the disposal of EIS investments.

Social Venture Trusts (see 25.8)

These are a new type of VCT.

CHAPTER 26 PENSIONS

Lifetime Allowance (see 26.1.2)

The Lifetime Allowance will reduce from £1.25 million to £1 million from 6 April 2016. Transitional protection will be available.

Withdrawals of income from a money purchase scheme (see 26.2)

A member can now draw on his pension pot as he wishes, without restriction.

Annuities payable to a spouse or a dependant (see 26.2.3)

These are tax free where the member dies before attaining age 75. Note that this exemption applies only to annuities which came into payment on or after 6 April 2015.

Sale of annuities

The Government is considering changes whereby people who have taken out an annuity may be able to sell that annuity for a lump sum.

Tighter rules on recycling of lump sums (see 26.2.8)

Tax charges can arise where tax free lump sums of more than £7,500 are used to fund pension contributions.

CHAPTER 28 LIFE ASSURANCE

Partial withdrawals from an insurance bond (see 28.3.3)

A recent case shows the consequences of not taking professional advice – fortunately the Tribunal allowed rectification.

CHAPTER 30 INHERITANCE TAX

Deeds of variation (see 30.4.6)

The IHT treatment of deeds of variation is under review.

Death from wounds suffered in active service (see 30.11.2)

From 3 December 2014, the IHT exemption for a member of the armed forces whose death is caused or hastened by injury on active service has been extended to members of the emergency services and humanitarian aid workers responding to an emergency situation.

There is an exemption from IHT for medals and decorations awarded to members of the armed forces. This has been extended to cover medals awarded to members of the emergency services. Also, the exemption now extends to all awards made by the Crown for services and achievements in public life.

CHAPTER 31 THE TAXATION OF TRUSTS

Periodic charge (see 31.5.14)

Special rules may govern the way in which the periodic charge is calculated for relevant property trusts created on or after 10 December 2014 or where property is added to pre 10 December 2014 trusts. The changes are intended to remove any advantage being obtained by a series of trusts being created on different days.

CHAPTER 33 ANTI-AVOIDANCE LEGISLATION

B share schemes (see 33.4)

New legislation has been introduced to counteract arrangements which offered investors a choice between an income and a capital return.

CHAPTER 34 RESIDENCE

Scottish taxpayers (see 34.10)

The definition of Scottish taxpayers who will be liable for the Scottish rate of income tax from 2016–17.

CHAPTER 35 THE INCOME AND CAPITAL GAINS OF FOREIGN DOMICILIARIES

Special charge (see 35.3)

The £50,000 special charge has been increased to £90,000 for non-doms who have been resident in the UK for 17 of the last 20 tax years

What constitutes a remittance (see 35.4)

Securing loans on foreign income and gains may be treated as a constructive remittance.

CHAPTER 36 STAMP TAXES

Rates of SDLT (see 36.2)

There are new bands from 4 December 2014.

Changes to ATED (see 36.4)

The threshold for ATED was reduced to £1 million from 1 April 2015 and will be further reduced to £500,000 with effect from 1 April 2016.

Scotland (see 36.5)

Land and Buildings Transfer Tax.

Wales (see 36.6)

There is a proposed new tax for Welsh land transactions.

JULY 2015 BUDGET: CHANGES FOR 2016–17 AND BEYOND

In the week that this edition of the Tax Handbook was passed for press, the first Conservative Budget in almost two decades took place.

Recently Budgets have been seen as cautious and prudent, in effect tinkering with legislation, whereas this Budget has in mind more fundamental changes, and envisages a new tax regime which will gradually be rolled out over the next five years.

Key proposals in George Osbourne's July 2015 Budget are as follows:

CHAPTER 8 INCOME FROM PROPERTY

Wear and Tear allowance for furnished lettings (see 8.2.12)

In 2016–17, the Government will introduce a new allowance for residential landlords to provide relief for the cost of replacing furnishings (except those properties that qualify as furnished holiday lettings). This will be a replacement for the existing 10% 'wear and tear' allowance that will no longer be available.

Interest (see 8.2.13)

From 2017–18, tax relief on the finance costs incurred on residential property (other than properties which are used for furnished holiday lettings) will be restricted to basic rate tax relief.

The measure will be introduced on a phased basis over four years: 25% of the total finance costs will be restricted to basic rate tax relief in 2017–18, 50% in 2018–19, 75% in 2019–20, rising to a restriction on 100% of the finance costs to basic rate from 2010–21.

Rent-a-room relief (see 8.4)

This relief will be increased from £4,250 to £7,500 for 2016–17.

CHAPTER 9 SAVINGS INCOME

Dividends from UK and foreign companies (see 9.8–9.10)

The taxation of dividends will change from 2016–17, with the abolition of the dividend tax credit, the introduction of a dividend tax allowance and a change to the income tax rates applicable to dividends.

A 10% notional tax credit currently applies to dividends paid by UK companies and some foreign companies. This reduces the effective rate of income tax on the dividend to 0% at the basic rate, 25% at the higher rate and 30.56% at the additional rate. From 6 April 2017, the notional tax credit will no longer apply.

A dividend tax allowance will be introduced which will exempt the first £5,000 of dividend income a year.

Dividend income in excess of this will be taxed at 7.5% at the basic rate, 32.5% at the higher rate and 38.1% at the additional rate.

CHAPTER 12 ALLOWANCES AND TAX CREDITS

Personal allowance (see 12.1)

The Government has committed itself to increasing the income tax personal allowance from £10,600 in 2015–16 to £11,000 in 2016–17 and £11,200 in 2017–18.

CHAPTER 18 TAX AND COMPANIES

Corporation tax (see 18.1–18.4)

The current 20% rate of corporation tax will be reduced to 19% from 1 April 2017 and to 18% from 1 April 2020.

CHAPTER 26 PENSIONS

Annual allowance (see 26.4)

From 2016–17, a restriction will apply to the tax relief available on pension contributions made by individuals who have income above £150,000. The £40,000 allowance will be reduced on a tapering basis of £1 of relief lost for every £2 of income over £150,000, subject to a minimum annual allowance of £10,000.

CHAPTER 30 INHERITANCE TAX AND INDIVIDUALS

Deemed UK domicile for IHT purposes (see 30.1)

From 6 April 2017, a foreign domiciled individual who has been resident in the UK for 15 of the last 20 tax years will be treated as if he were domiciled in the UK. This status will then remain until such time as he has been non-resident for five tax years.

In addition, an individual who had a UK domicile at birth will be regarded as domiciled in the UK if he is resident in the UK.

Changes to definition of UK situs property (see 30.1)

The Government have unveiled plans to bring indirectly owned UK residential property within the scope of Inheritance Tax. This will apply to UK property owned via a non-UK company or partnership by a foreign domiciled individual.

This radical change is to take effect from 6 April 2017.

Nil rate band (see 30.1.1)

The Government plans to introduce an additional nil rate band when a residence is passed on death to children, grandchildren or great grandchildren ('direct descendants'). The additional amount will be £100,000 in 2017 to 2018, £125,000 in 2018 to 2019, £150,000 in 2019 to 2020, and £175,000 in 2020 to 2021. The additional nil rate band will then increase in line with the Consumer Price Index from 2021 to 2022 onwards.

The additional amount will be reduced by £1 for every £2 by which the deceased person's estate exceeds £2 million.

Any unused nil-rate band will be transferred to a surviving spouse or civil partner.

The additional nil rate band will also be available when a person downsizes or ceases to own a home on or after 8 July 2015 and assets of an equivalent value are passed on death to direct descendants.

CHAPTER 35 THE INCOME AND CAPITAL GAINS OF FOREIGN DOMICILIARIES

Deemed UK domicile for long-term residents

From 6 April 2017, a foreign domiciled individual who has been resident in the UK for 15 of the last 20 tax years will be treated as if he were domiciled in the UK for all purposes of income tax and capital gains tax. His worldwide income will be subject to UK tax, whether or not it is remitted to the UK.

Foreign domiciliaries who have set up an offshore trust before they become deemed domiciled here under the 15 year rule will not be taxed on trust income and gains that are retained in the trust and such excluded property trusts will have the same IHT treatment as at present (subject to the new rule for UK residential property held through offshore companies and similar vehicles). However, such long-term residents will, from April 2017, be taxed on any benefits, capital or income received from any trusts on a worldwide basis.

Foreign domiciliaries whose domicile of origin was in the UK

An individual who had a UK domicile at birth will be regarded as domiciled in the UK if he is resident in the UK. New rules will also apply to trusts set up while such individuals were not UK domiciled if they are UK resident on or after 6 April 2017. In these circumstances, the individual will be taxed on all income and gains arising in such trusts under the same rules as any other UK domiciliary. The IHT treatment of such trusts will also be the same as for UK tax payers who have never lost their UK domicile.

CONTENTS

ACKNOWLEDGEMENTS

Once again this book is in no small part a reflection of what colleagues, other professionals, clients and HMRC have taught us over the years even when we have been unwilling students.

As ever we are most grateful to our outside contributors Paul Cullen, Mike Evans, Tim Buss, and David Ford, and to our BBL colleagues Linda Smith in London and Nicholas Tarrant in New York.

Once again we thank our Editor, Linda Dhondy, for patiently managing the process by which our manuscript has been turned into a proper book and to Christopher Cudmore at Pearson for inviting us back.

Lastly though never least to our families for all their support behind the scenes.

1

INTRODUCTION: PRINCIPLES OF TAX PLANNING AND HOW TO USE THIS BOOK

This chapter contains the following sections:

(1) Introduction

Managing your tax affairs

(2) General strategy
(3) Planning points if you are employed
(4) If you are thinking of becoming self-employed
(5) If you are already in business

Good housekeeping

(6) Ensure that all important deadlines are kept

1.1 INTRODUCTION

Why read a book on tax? Almost certainly because you want to have a better understanding of how taxes are assessed and administered in general, and how they can be made as painless as possible in your particular case. The hope is that this book will help empower you so that you can deal with your filing obligations (or better understand when you may need to instruct a professional), stay on top of your tax affairs and identify tax planning opportunities.

MANAGING YOUR TAX AFFAIRS

Managing your tax affairs and planning ahead are inextricably connected: you cannot plan in an effective way unless you are on top of your responsibility to file returns and you are aware of the deadlines. In recent years, HMRC has been given sweeping powers to investigate and to impose penalties for late filing and/or late payment as well as the potential to withhold participation in certain beneficial tax regimes where your filing record has been poor. It is therefore more important than ever before to ensure you meet your obligations in good time.

1.2 GENERAL STRATEGY

There is no easy solution to the question of how to pay less tax – if only there were! And there are plenty of ways of getting it wrong and increasing your tax problems. However, you should not go too far wrong if you bear in mind the following advice:

1 Carry out some background research

Your tax affairs need to be taken seriously. It is important to fill out your tax return in a meticulous way. You should carefully read the notes issued with the tax return and, if there are areas on which you are not quite sure, you should seek advice, either from HMRC itself by calling the Self-Assessment Helpline number 0300 200 3310, or from a practising accountant.

2 Deal with your self-assessment return issued in April 2015

You need to submit your 2015 (2014–15) Self Assessment (SA) tax return by either 31 October 2015 (paper filers) or 31 January 2016 (online filers), and settle your outstanding tax by 31 January 2016. If you fail to do this, you automatically become liable for interest and penalties. You may not receive a tax return form or a notice to make a return, but you still have a duty to notify HMRC by 5 October following the end of the tax year, if you need to make a return of income or gains for that year.

3 Check on back years

Mistakes do happen, and in the past you may have failed to claim all the allowances to which you were entitled. You should therefore carry out a periodic check or 'audit' to ensure that you (and family members, eg your minor children or elderly dependent relatives) have claimed all the tax allowances and reliefs to which you – and they – are entitled. The time limits for claiming repayments from earlier years is four years.

Year of assessment	Time limit
2011–12	5 April 2016
2012–13	5 April 2017
2013–14	5 April 2018

If you find that mistakes have occurred in relation to your tax for 2011–12, you need to file a repayment claim by 5 April 2016. If you do not, the overpaid tax will be lost to you forever.

4 Steer clear of tax evasion

Arguably this should be point number 1.

Before you commit yourself to any course of action, make sure that you would be happy for all the facts and documentation to be laid out before the Inspector of Taxes. If a scheme or arrangement relies on non-disclosure, you may be getting involved in tax evasion. People who are found out become liable for interest and punitive penalties and are sometimes prosecuted.

Tax evasion is illegal; tax avoidance *is* legal but may still lead to problems with HMRC (see below).

5 Take professional advice

Unless your affairs are extremely straightforward, you could probably do with a financial 'health check' from time to time, ie a discussion with an accountant or tax adviser to go over your affairs to look at how you might improve your situation and pay less tax. A good accountant should be able to more than cover the fees charged by pointing out ways in which you can reduce personal taxes or avoid penalties.

If your affairs are more complex, you probably need to take professional advice regularly. It also makes sense for a tax accountant or adviser to take over the detailed work of preparing your tax return, agreeing payments and making sure that deadlines are not missed.

6 Plan ahead

Part of practical tax planning is to anticipate what could change in the future. For example, it may be that you are likely to sell your present home in two or three years' time when you reach retirement. If you have let the property in the past, you need to look into the position now to see whether there could be a CGT charge when you sell it and, if there is a potential problem, what steps you might take to mitigate it. If you are going to sell your business when you retire in a few years' time, you need to find out what tax may be payable and what you can do to reduce this.

7 Take all taxes into account

It is important to be aware that steps you might take to avoid one tax will have consequences for other taxes, and may even result in an increase in the amount you pay overall. For example, you may be able to obtain a tax deduction if you set aside part of your home for work. However, if a couple of rooms are set aside exclusively for business purposes, this may affect your main residence exemption and could result in a CGT charge when you sell the property. There may well be ways in which you could both have your cake and eat it, but you need to look into the fine detail of the rules concerning the main residence exemption.

Whilst looking at the income and capital taxes effects of any tax planning or business structuring you intend to implement, the transactional taxes can tend to be forgotten, and you should always ensure you find out the VAT and SDLT consequences before proceeding.

8 Be flexible

It makes no sense to invest in a savings plan because the return is free of tax if the plan is not suited to your personal requirements and the capital is tied up for, say, ten years but you require access to liquid funds within a shorter timescale. You should bear in mind that circumstances may change. It may therefore be unwise to put all your spare investments into a trust for the benefit of your children if your own situation might change for the worse. In recent years, many individuals have suffered unexpected demands on their capital and some people are now regretting that they gave away capital that they thought was surplus to their requirements.

9 Do not forget the rules might change

Tax legislation is subject to a review at least once a year in the Chancellor's Budget. One only has to look at recent changes to the rules relating to relief for interest, company cars, charitable giving, foreign domiciliaries, residence (and so the list goes on) to realise that tax law is in constant flux and changes often leave taxpayers, their advisers and sometimes even HMRC staff, trailing behind. The 'cap' on tax reliefs which came in from 2013–14 caused terrible problems for people whose finances were based on getting tax relief for very large amounts of interest or business losses.

Before you carry out any tax planning that will affect your situation in future years, put down on paper how much the various tax reliefs are worth to you and the extent to which you could rearrange your affairs if the law were changed and the reliefs curtailed or abolished.

Court decisions constantly result in changed interpretations or sometimes HMRC simply decides to interpret the legislation in a different way. It could be unwise to rely too heavily on tax breaks afforded by the present rules. An example is HMRC's attack on situations where a husband and wife took out profits from a company in the form of dividends and the spouse who contributed most to the business took what HMRC regarded as an unrealistically low salary (see 33.6.3). HMRC suddenly picked up on this and demanded extra tax for past years, which the individuals concerned had thought to be long since settled. The taxpayers eventually won their case, after a lengthy battle, but at only at the cost of years of stress and uncertainty.

10 If it sounds too good to be true, it probably is . . .

All professional advisers complain that clients invariably know someone who assures them that, quite legitimately, he or she is paying virtually no tax at all. Be wary of advice given over a 'gin and tonic': very often, your helpful friend does not really understand all the ramifications of his or her own affairs, let alone yours. Worse still, some of the schemes put forward often turn out to involve evasion (which is illegal) rather than avoidance. Even where there is some substance to what is being said, your friend's or colleague's situation may be quite different from yours. For example, someone who advises you that he or she pays no tax on his or her earnings from work carried out outside this country may have a foreign domicile (see Chapter 35) and so be entitled to reliefs that are not available to you as a UK domiciliary.

11 Bear in mind the anti-avoidance provisions

One definition of tax avoidance is that it involves 'really smart people doing things that would be absolutely dumb if it were not for the tax advantages'. Unfortunately, Governments do not see the funny side. The tax legislation now contains extensive anti-avoidance provisions intended to make sure that you cannot save tax by carrying out transactions in a roundabout way. In particular, much of this legislation is already aimed at preventing a person from converting income into capital gains and in view of the current differential in tax rates for income and capital, further action can be expected if there is widespread abuse in this area. There are also provisions aimed against the use (or, to be more specific, the abuse) of settlements. In the main, you will be assessed on income arising to trustees of a settlement if you created that settlement and there is any way in which you, your spouse or registered civil partner, or minor children may benefit under the settlement.

If you are considering taking steps for tax planning that you hope will help you to escape tax, but that are contrary to the spirit of the legislation, you need to take a particularly close look at the anti-avoidance provisions. This is a situation where it is normally imperative to take professional advice.

12 Artificial tax avoidance schemes are likely to be challenged

Using unacceptably artificial avoidance schemes is like playing with fire (your wallet may well require urgent medical attention as a result). The Government has naturally encouraged HMRC to challenge tax avoidance schemes with the utmost vigour. It has also reinforced HMRC's information powers by requiring tax advisers to register tax avoidance schemes. Someone who uses a tax scheme must therefore expect wide-ranging and searching questions from the taxman. If there is significant money at stake, you are likely to be dragged through the courts. If you lose in the High Court, or one of the superior courts, you will normally have to bear HMRC's legal costs on top of your own costs – and of course the underpaid tax, interest and, potentially, penalties.

The last Labour Government introduced income tax and CGT charges that operated 'retroactively' rather than retrospectively (see pre-owned assets (33.8) and trusts and main residence exemption (33.14)), although that distinction may not be apparent to those caught by these measures. The coalition Government introduced retrospective legislation in FA 2012 aimed at tax avoidance schemes used by Barclays Bank and it is likely that similar tactics will be used if further examples of widespread or endemic avoidance are discovered in future. This is a trend that tips the balance of risk versus reward even further against tax avoiders. During the Election, Conservative and Labour competed with one another in promising that they would ensure that in future HMRC will come down even more heavily on tax avoiders.

See also the *Ramsay* doctrine (33.19) on the way that the courts will ignore purely artificial steps inserted for tax avoidance purposes. The introduction of the General Anti-Abuse Rule (see 33.20) represents another fundamental shift in the rules of the game – the odds are very much against you in relation to artificial schemes entered into after the FA 2013 received royal assent and GAAR came into operation.

If you have used a tax avoidance scheme in the past, you should seek professional advice to ensure that the year concerned is now closed (see 3.4.12 on HMRC's powers to issue a discovery assessment where relevant facts were not fully disclosed). If the scheme is still being challenged, you need an up-to-date prognosis as to the chances of HMRC succeeding.

1.3 PLANNING POINTS IF YOU ARE EMPLOYED

Whether you are a company director, a senior executive, a manager or an ordinary employee, there are still legal ways in which you may be able to reduce your tax liabilities.

1.3.1 Claim expenses

It is important to claim all genuinely allowable expenses (see 4.3). There are fixed deductions for workers in certain industries (eg nurses, dental nurses, midwives and radiographers can now claim £100 pa, uniformed police officers can claim £140 pa and pharmacists £60 pa without having to produce any receipts).

If you have to belong to a professional institute in connection with your job, the subscription is normally an allowable expense. If you are required to provide certain equipment yourself (eg a fax machine at home), make sure you put in a claim for the expenses associated with it, and claim capital allowances. If you have to use your own car for business trips, consider claiming mileage allowances (see 4.4.12).

1.3.2 Keep records

If you are required to travel extensively, especially overseas, keep a note of your itinerary and the expenses you incur. By doing this, you will be well placed to answer any queries from the Inspector and you should be able to demonstrate that there is no benefit-in-kind provided all the expenses are business related.

Again, if you need to use your own car in the course of your employment, find out whether your employer pays the authorised mileage rates (see 4.4.12). If it does not, or if the mileage payments exceed the authorised rates, you need to keep a detailed note of your business and private mileage so that any benefit-in-kind can be calculated. Under SA, keeping good records is no longer simply a matter of 'good housekeeping' but a necessity (see 3.3.2 and 3.6).

1.3.3 Reduce car scale benefits and consider cash options

The taxable benefit has been increased each year. If you have a company car, but your employer would be prepared to give you cash instead, you should check that having the car still makes sense. You need to work out the after-tax value of having a company car and compare this with your after-tax position if you were to run your own car and claim approved mileage allowances when you use it for business (see 4.4.12).

1.3.4 Go for benefits that do not attract NIC

The cost of traditional benefits packages became much more onerous for employers because of the imposition of the Class 1A NIC charge at 13.8% (see 23.1.8). Why not suggest a package of benefits that are not subject to Class 1A NIC, such as approved share schemes?

1.3.5 Other tax-efficient benefits

If you have any influence over the way your remuneration package is made up, take account of the fact that some benefits are more tax efficient than others. For example, it is well worth having an interest-free loan of up to £10,000 since no benefit-in-kind is assessed whatsoever. Indeed it may be worth considering the idea of a loan above this limit as the tax charge may be more favourable than the commercial options. The benefit of having the use of a company flat can compare favourably with the cost of providing accommodation personally (see 4.8).

1.3.6 Pension schemes

Pension benefits are particularly attractive as they are not normally taxable. If you do not need all your salary to cover your living costs, it may well be attractive if you can reach a 'deal' with your employer so that it makes contributions towards your pension instead of giving you a larger annual pay rise. If your employer has gone to the trouble of setting up a pension scheme for you, make sure that you get the maximum possible benefit from it. Recent changes in legislation mean that anyone who employs more than five employees can be *required* by the employees to offer a pension scheme.

Quite separately from this, do carefully consider the merits of making additional voluntary contributions; but again, remain aware of the £40,000 annual allowance (and potential tax charges for exceeding this limit). If you are not in a company pension scheme, you are most strongly advised to start a personal pension scheme or at least review your retirement planning strategy. See generally Chapter 26.

1.3.7 'Disguised' remuneration

See Chapter 5 on disguised remuneration. Company directors and senior executives have in the past often been offered the opportunity to be rewarded with an interest in an employee benefit trust (EBT) or employer financed retirement benefit scheme (EFRBS). Successive governments have considered that such structures have been abused, so from 6 April 2011, legislation on disguised remuneration made it virtually impossible to reward employees in this way without incurring an up-front PAYE charge.

If you already have funds accruing in an EBT or EFRBS, you really should seek professional advice as a matter of urgency, as the rules are highly complex and can operate in a draconian manner, catching situations which appear to be innocent of any avoidance motive.

1.3.8 Share incentives

Company directors and senior executives are often offered an opportunity to acquire shares in their company. However, there are various pitfalls that can apply if you acquire shares through a non-approved scheme (see 6.2), so you need to seek professional advice. You need to plan ahead; for example, there can be situations where you can elect to pay tax up front on the receipt of restricted shares and this can be a sensible course of action if it results in any future capital growth being subject to only 28% (or even 18% or 10%) CGT. Also, if you have been given approved share options in the past (see 6.3), consider how you will reap the benefit in a way that involves the least CGT cost.

Approved schemes offer significant advantages (see Chapter 6). The all-employee share scheme provides total exemption from tax after five years; Enterprise Management Incentive (EMI) options are designed to provide larger equity profits that may – in certain circumstances – be taxed at just 10% rather than at the normal 28% rate.

It is particularly important to take advice if you are offered the opportunity to subscribe for shares on a partly-paid basis as a particularly punitive tax charge can arise on a sale of such shares (see 6.4).

You should also take advice if you are offered a chance to participate in a management buy-out (MBO) as there are a number of tax considerations (see 6.8 and 11.5.3) of which you should be aware.

1.4 IF YOU ARE THINKING OF BECOMING SELF-EMPLOYED

1.4.1 Will HMRC accept that you are self-employed?

The first question to address is whether HMRC is likely to accept that you are self-employed. If the main thing that you have to sell is your time, and you are subject to supervision in the way in which you carry out your work, you may well be regarded as an employee. It cuts no ice that your contract may state that you are self-employed.

One reason why HMRC will look into this so closely is that, if you are self-employed, you will be able to claim tax relief for certain expenditure that is not allowable as a deduction for employees. So you should take all possible steps to ensure that your claim for self-employed status can stand up to scrutiny by HMRC (see 7.2).

In theory, the risk of HMRC's reclassifying a self-employed person as an employee lies with the employer. If its view is eventually upheld, the employer is liable to pay Class 1 NIC and HMRC may well require it to pay over the tax that the employer ought to have withheld under PAYE as well. Where this happens, the consequences can be disastrous. In law, an employer is precluded from collecting arrears of Class 1 NIC by deducting them from subsequent payments to the individual concerned. In other words, if the employer does not get it right first time round, it cannot correct its mistake later on. Similarly, the primary responsibility for deducting tax under PAYE and paying it over to HMRC lies with the employer. HMRC is normally reluctant to get into time-consuming disputes with the employee and will simply demand the tax from the employer, leaving it to make any adjustment by agreement with the employee. Nevertheless, most self-employed individuals also have a vested interest in HMRC's accepting that they are genuinely self-employed. If a dispute arises with someone to whom you provide services, he or she is unlikely to want to deal with you again in the future, certainly not on a self-employed basis.

1.4.2 Keep HMRC informed

Once you start to be self-employed, your best interests are safeguarded by keeping HMRC advised about what you are doing. You are legally obliged to make your existence known to your local tax district by either completing a form available at www.hmrc.gov.uk/startingup or by calling on 0300 200 3504. This will enable you to register both with HMRC for tax purposes, and to pay Class 2 NIC.

Where a new business commences, a penalty is potentially payable where there is a failure to notify that event to HMRC by 31 January following the end of the tax year in which the liability to pay Class 2 NIC first occurred. The amount of the penalty is geared to the amount of the 'potential lost revenue', ie the amount of contributions which were due from commencement to 31 January following the first year of assessment (ie a maximum of 22 months' contributions, for an April start-up), even where these are later paid when notifying HMRC of the liability. The gearing of the penalty to the lost contributions closely follows the model used for income tax errors under Schedule 24, FA 2007 although the issue here is a failure to notify rather than a misdeclaration. So, it is more important than ever before to ensure that you register with HMRC in good time.

An Inspector of Taxes, like anyone else, is likely to be more inclined to be reasonable if treated with civility and respect, rather than irritated by the fact that he or she constantly has to chase you for information.

There are various other practical matters. You have a statutory duty to register your business for VAT if you have exceeded (or are likely to exceed) the registration threshold.

HMRC's website gives plenty of helpful advice on what to do (see also 22.4.1). You will also find other useful advice about starting your business, including employing people.

HMRC also issues a starter pack for new employers, which can be obtained by visiting www.hmrc.gov.uk.

1.4.3 Should you employ your spouse or civil partner?

Depending on the type of business you carry on, it may be appropriate for you to employ your spouse or civil partner, or even to have him or her as a business partner (see 1.5.4). This may be a particularly good idea if he or she would otherwise have little or no taxable income. However, if you employ your spouse or civil partner, do not pay an unrealistic salary. HMRC will challenge any situation where the salary is disproportionate. Its argument is that you will be due a deduction only for a reasonable rate of remuneration paid to him or her in return for actual services and expertise provided.

Do be careful on this; in principle you could suffer double taxation if you get it wrong since your spouse will still be taxed on his or her full salary, even if only part of that salary is allowed as a deduction in arriving at your business profits for tax purposes. Alternatively, where the work done by your spouse or civil partner is truly not commensurate with the payments made and he or she has no 'capital' interest in the business and does not share in the risks, this may be open to attack under the settlement provisions, and potentially, the amounts paid could be taxed on you, at your marginal tax rates, instead. This is an area in which it would be prudent to take professional advice. Problems will also arise if you are deemed to be paying your spouse or civil partner (or yourself) too little; you should also obtain advice on the implications of the minimum wage legislation.

1.4.4 Provide for tax

Finally, when you commence self-employment, do think ahead and make provision for the tax payments that you will need to make over the next 18 months to two years. Get into the habit of setting aside part of your income each month so that you will have something in hand to pay HMRC when the time comes. Under self-assessment, the first tax payment can often be crippling as it represents a payment of tax for your first year plus a 50% payment on account for the next tax year.

Example – 50% payment on account

> S becomes self-employed during the tax year to 5 April 2015 and draws up his accounts on a fiscal year basis. He was formerly an employee who paid all his tax under PAYE and was therefore not required to make payments on account. On 31 January 2017, S will have to pay a balancing payment for all of the tax due for the year to 5 April 2016 plus a payment on account in respect of the year to 5 April 2017 equal to 50% of the 2015–16 tax.

1.4.5 Take advice on IR35 and managed services companies

If you are setting up a limited company to supply your services, bear in mind that the company may have to pay over PAYE tax on notional salary that you have not actually taken out. The legislation is aimed at individuals who provide their services via intermediary companies (or partnerships) and who would otherwise be regarded as employees of the end customer. The effect of the rules is that your company is required to account for tax on its income from 'relevant engagements' as if that income was your earnings subject to PAYE. See 21.3 on this. The coalition Government tasked the Office of Tax Simplification (OTS) with looking at the IR35 provisions to see if they could be simplified or replaced. However the Government decided that it could not put substantial tax revenue at risk and therefore decided to retain IR35 and to achieve simplification by making improvements to the way in which it is administered.

These improvements were intended to:

- provide greater pre-transaction certainty, including a dedicated Helpline staffed by specialists;
- provide greater clarity by publishing guidance on those types of cases HMRC views as outside the scope of IR35;
- restrict reviews to high risk cases carried out only by specialists teams; and
- promote more effective engagement with interested parties through an IR35 Forum to monitor HMRC's new approach.

There were also rules which were intended to prevent the use by individuals of managed services companies to avoid PAYE. A number of promoters are still selling schemes that purport to skirt around the managed service companies' legislation. You are advised to be very wary of these – they are, almost without exception, disclosable to HMRC and in the writer's experience often do not work as advertised in any case.

1.4.6 VAT

Research the VAT implications relating to your business. Check regularly to make sure you comply with registration requirements (see 22.4.1). The onus is on you to notify HMRC if you exceed the VAT registration threshold. Make sure that you charge VAT where appropriate and allow for VAT in costings. VAT is a transaction tax, not a tax on profit, so forgetting VAT can be costly and putting mistakes right can often wipe out any profit.

1.5 IF YOU ARE ALREADY IN BUSINESS

1.5.1 Keep good records

Much of the above applies to the same extent if you have already been in business for a number of years. In many businesses, some figures have to be estimated·(eg the extent to which a trader's telephone bill relates to business, as opposed to private, calls). There is nothing wrong with estimates, but do try to keep as complete a record as possible, so that the estimate can be supported if HMRC challenges it. For example, where you regularly need to include estimates for business usage, it may be worth separately noting either personal or business usage (whichever will be easier, eg if you know your private use is only in the region of 10% it will be much quicker to note private calls, or mileage, etc rather than noting the business proportion) over a sample period of a month – or during four or five separate weeks spread throughout a year – to be able to show HMRC a representative sample of your private usage, to support the estimates you make.

HMRC's approach to business record checks changed in November 2012.

Under the new approach, taxpayers are contacted by letter if it is thought that they are likely to have inadequate records. HMRC will follow this up with a telephone questionnaire.

If the telephone discussions indicate that there is a risk that inadequate records are being kept, a face-to-face visit will take place. The visit will usually last around two hours.

If the records are found to be inadequate, HMRC will allow time for them to brought up to an adequate standard. A follow-up visit will take place within three months. If this reveals insufficient improvement a penalty of £500 will be charged (£250 if the business is in its first year of trading).

If the Revenue finds that records have been deliberately destroyed, a penalty of £3,000 may be imposed.

You must indicate estimated entries on your SA return. HMRC may enquire into this and the Inspector may well want to go back to previous years if he or she later looks into the position and decides the estimate is unreasonable. The main defence against this would be where the Inspector was already on notice about the way in which estimates were arrived at.

Discovery is a whole topic in itself, but there are certain simple rules to follow regarding disclosures in the 'white space' of the tax return, which should help to protect you from the danger of HMRC making discovery assessments in future (see 3.4.12).

Keep your records: HMRC may call for them up to five years and ten months after the end of the tax year. Remember that this applies to all your tax affairs, not just the records relating to your business.

If you are a partner, keep tabs on the partnership's tax affairs. One of the partners (the 'representative partner') is responsible for filing a partnership return and you will not be able to complete your personal return without reference to this.

1.5.2 Do not cut corners on PAYE

Beware of situations where you should withhold tax, especially where you are paying casual or freelance workers whom HMRC may regard as employees. HMRC has teams of investigators who carry out regular reviews of PAYE compliance.

1.5.3 Take VAT seriously

VAT is a constant source of problems. It is a complex regime, and subject to frequent changes in European, as well as domestic, case law. Whenever you carry out a major transaction you should always ask a VAT specialist for advice. Also, bear in mind that HMRC makes regular control visits to examine accounting records. Penalties can be levied if mistakes are uncovered during visits, so it is well worth having a review carried out in good time for errors to be corrected before a visit.

If you are VAT-registered, you are effectively an unpaid tax collector. Make certain that VAT works for you by taking account of opportunities to improve cash flow. Ideally you should organise matters so that suppliers send you invoices before the end of the return period. Ensure that you take full advantage of recovering input VAT. Consider whether special accounting schemes or flat rate schemes may be best for you (see 22.6).

1.5.4 Remunerating your spouse or civil partner

Think carefully about the salary you pay to your spouse or civil partner. If it is less than you have to pay to an ordinary employee, increase the amount (it must be at least that required under the minimum wage legislation). Consider setting up a pension scheme for your spouse or civil partner, as your contributions will be tax deductible.

Think also about bringing your spouse or civil partner into partnership. This is a complex matter on which it is best to seek professional advice that will take account of the nature of your business, and the time, expertise or capital brought to the business by him or her.

1.5.5 Financing a partnership

There are some interesting possibilities for accelerating tax relief by you and your partners raising personal loans to put money into the firm to enable it to clear borrowings. Suppose your firm makes up accounts to 30 April 2016: interest on the firm's borrowings will be an expense in arriving at 2016–17 taxable profits, whereas interest paid in 2015–16 by the partners on personal loans invested in the partnership business will be a deduction from their taxable income for 2015–16, so you actually get your tax relief one year earlier (see 11.4).

1.5.6 Relief for losses

If your business has not been going well and you have suffered losses, look into the best way you can get relief. In some cases, you may be able to carry back the losses and set them against your other income (see 7.7). In other situations, the choice open to you is to set your losses against your income for the year of the loss, or against the following or preceding year's income, or carry forward the losses to be set against trading income received in later years. Obviously, it will make a great difference if you take relief in a year in which you will otherwise be subject to tax at 40% or 45% rather than in a year in which your other income is relatively low and tax relief will be obtained at only 20%.

1.5.7 Pension schemes (see Chapter 26)

It is particularly important for self-employed individuals to provide for their retirement since they qualify only for the basic State pension and not for S2P.

Contributions to a personal scheme are tax deductible. Furthermore, the scheme is not generally subject to tax and so the fund is likely to grow at a far faster rate than investments that are subject to tax.

Up to 25% of the fund may be taken as a tax-free lump sum. The balance must be used to provide a pension or other taxable income.

1.5.8 If you are a partner in a large professional firm

Make sure that tax relief is due for interest on loans used to finance your investment in the partnership (see 11.4).

You must liaise with your firm's 'nominated partner' to obtain the information required for your SA return (see 7.4). If you incur any expenses, or buy plant and machinery used for the firm's business (eg a fax machine), you must arrange for the appropriate relief to be claimed in the partnership return (see 7.4).

Your firm may be considering conversion into a limited liability partnership (LLP) (see 7.5). The tax legislation makes allowance for this. However, there may be other considerations, for example a bank manager or landlord may be happy to take a guarantee from a normal partnership as he or she knows that each partner is jointly and severally liable, whereas he or she may not be inclined to accept a guarantee from an LLP, where each partner's liability is limited to their share of the capital. Also the rules regarding interest on qualifying loans can give rise to problems where an investment LLP is involved (see 11.4).

1.5.9 Should you transfer your business to a company?

If your business is going very well, you should consider incorporating your business, ie transfer your business to a company. Some general principles are set out in Chapter 20, but once again this is a matter where you would probably be best advised to consult an accountant or tax adviser. You will also have to consider the rules in respect of service companies, discussed at 21.4. Another option is to set up an LLP (see 7.5).

1.5.10 If you already have a private company

A key issue is whether it makes sense to take a smaller salary and take the rest of your income in the form of dividends (which are not subject to NIC). Another issue concerns the ownership of shares; if shares are held by your spouse or civil partner, he or she may pay a lower rate of tax on dividends. However, bear in mind that HMRC is looking at these situations much more closely of late (see 33.6).

You should fund your pension scheme to the maximum extent you can afford. A small self-administered scheme may have much to commend it if you wish to be able to take loan-backs or have the fund buy a property to rent to your company (see 26.3).

Do you see an opportunity to start a new business or extend your company's existing business to a new location? You might establish a subsidiary company but this may not necessarily be the best approach.

Do you need to recruit or retain key managers? If so, consider share schemes because these can have great motivational value and (provided you take suitable professional advice) can be taxed more beneficially than cash bonuses and benefits-in-kind (see 4.13-4.16). Bear in mind that your company may get tax relief for such schemes (see 18.3) and you may also qualify for CGT relief on sales to approved employee trusts (see 13.7).

1.5.11 Plan for retirement and handing the business on

Do plan ahead, both for retirement and for passing on your business in due course to your family. Try not to leave pension funding until the last few years as this will inevitably make it much more expensive.

Key questions need to be addressed in relation to CGT planning: make sure that you take full advantage of entrepreneur's relief, which carries a £10m lifetime allowance.

Will IHT be payable on your death? It may be possible to organise your affairs so that either 100% or 50% business or agricultural property relief will be due, see 30.8-30.9 on this.

Finally, see Chapter 32 on passing on a family business.

GOOD HOUSEKEEPING

1.6 ENSURE THAT ALL IMPORTANT DEADLINES ARE KEPT

It is pointless trying to arrange your affairs tax efficiently unless you get the basics right and keep your affairs tidy. This means watching deadlines for action (eg paying tax) and for making elections.

The most important tax planning deadlines are listed below. Note that this section should be read subject to three cautions:

(1) Most of the deadlines are dates by which returns, payments, claims or elections must be received by HMRC. A document or payment

must be posted a minimum of three working days before the deadline and, because of the danger of postal delays, ideally at least a week. Filing and paying online can provide certainty that your return or payment has been received by the due date and in many instances, is now compulsory.

(2) To keep this checklist to a manageable size, only those deadlines likely to apply to the majority of people have been included; the checklist is not fully comprehensive.

(3) Many deadlines cannot be included because they are fixed by reference to the facts of the individual case. For example, most corporation tax deadlines are fixed by reference to the end of the company's accounting period.

1.6.1 Outstanding deadlines for tax year 2014–15

5 October 2015	To avoid the danger of incurring penalties, individuals with new sources of income in 2014–15 should have notified HMRC by 4pm today if no tax return has been received.
19 October 2015	Amounts agreed under 2014–15 PSAs due for payment – interest starts to run.
31 October 2015	Paper filers: the self-assessment tax return for 2014–15 needs to be filed by this date if it was issued to you before 31 July 2015.
31 January 2016	Online filers: the self-assessment tax return for 2014–15 needs to be filed and 2014–15 tax paid by this date.

1.6.2 Main 31 January 2016 deadlines for tax year 2013–14

Personal tax

(1) Claiming a set-off for industrial buildings allowances on enterprise zone investments made in 2013–14.

(2) Electing for the tests for furnished holiday accommodation to be computed by reference to an average (see 8.5.1).

(3) Claiming relief against income tax for 2013–14 for a loss on the disposal of shares in a qualifying trading company (see 17.2).

Capital gains tax

(1) Claiming that an asset became of negligible value during 2013–14 under s 24(2) TCGA 1992 (see 13.5.9).

(2) Electing under s 138A TCGA 1992 where an earn-out is to be satisfied by the issue of securities (see 17.8).

(3) Electing under s 261B TCGA 1992 for 2013–14 trade losses to be relieved against gains.

(4) Electing under s 261D TCGA 1992 for 2013–14 post-cessation expenses to be relieved against gains.

Business tax

(1) Claiming that a trading loss incurred in 2013–14 should be set against other 2013–14 income under s 64 ITA 2007 (see 7.7).

(2) Claiming that a trading loss incurred in 2013–14 should be set against a capital gain realised in 2013–14 under s 71 ITA 2007 (see 7.7).

(3) Claiming that a trading loss incurred in 2013–14 be carried back, where permitted under the 'new business' rules under s 72 ITA 2007 (see 7.7).

(4) Electing under s 162A TCGA 1992 to disapply CGT incorporation relief (see 17.6.5).

(5) Electing under s 83 CAA 2001 to treat plant or machinery purchased in 2013–14 as a short-life asset for capital allowance purposes (see 16.2).

(6) Electing under s 257 ITTOIA 2005 for post-cessation receipts received in 2013–14 to be taxed for the year the trade was discontinued (see 16.4).

1.6.3 Last chance deadlines for 2011–12

The following claims for 2011–12 must be made by 5 April 2016.

Personal tax

(1) Claiming personal allowances (see Chapter 12).

(2) Claiming relief for interest paid.

(3) Claiming relief for pension contributions paid.

(4) Claiming 'top-slicing' relief in respect of life assurance policy gains (see 28.3.4).

(5) Claiming relief to correct an error or mistake made by the taxpayer that resulted in an excessive assessment being made in the year.

Business tax

(1) Claiming to carry forward trade losses under ss 83 and 88 ITA 2007.

(2) Claiming to carry back terminal losses under s 89 ITA 2007.

Capital gains tax

(1) Claiming roll-over and hold-over relief in respect of disposals (see 17.3 and 17.4).

(2) Claiming a set-off against capital gains assessed in respect of a loss incurred on a qualifying loan to a trader under s 253 TCGA 1992 (see 17.1).

1.6.4 Deadlines for next year's diary

5 April 2016   The deadline for maximising the use of your ISA allowance for 2015–16.

19 April 2016   PAYE/NIC payments due at the Accounts Office by today. Interest chargeable after this date (see 21.1).

19 May 2016   Employers who do not file end-of-year returns by today may be fined (see 21.1).

31 May 2016   Last date for giving a 2015–16 form P60 to each relevant employee.

6 July 2016   Substantial fines may be imposed on any employer who does not submit Form P9D/P11D (returns of benefits, etc provided for employees) by today (see 4.4 and 21.1). Details of benefits shown on P9D or P11D forms must be supplied to each employee.

Deadline for submission of form 42 covering reportable events under the legislation on employment-related securities (see 6.1).

19 July 2016   Due date for payment for 2015–16 Class 1A NIC (see 23.1).

PAYE quarterly payment date for small employers (see 21.1).

31 July 2016   Second interim tax payment for 2015–16 due (see 2.1.4).

2

SELF-ASSESSMENT

This chapter contains the following sections:

(1) Self-assessment (SA)
(2) Filing SA tax returns online
(3) Ten golden rules for dealing with your 2015 tax return
(4) Common errors
(5) Providing additional information

2.1 SELF-ASSESSMENT (SA)

2.1.1 An overview of the SA system

Try not to be put off by the fact that the form and filing instructions seem complicated: HMRC has produced a number of helpsheets and will be only too pleased to clarify anything that is not covered by the notes.

The principle is that by completing the form you should work out your own tax liability and settle what you owe by 31 January each year. However, provided a paper SA return is filed not later than 31 October following the end of the tax year, HMRC will calculate the amount of tax payable for you. Filing online provides instant gratification in that the tax payable is calculated automatically, whenever the return is filed.

2.1.2 'Incentives' to make you comply

The legislation contains a number of 'incentives' to ensure that people comply with their obligations. If a person does not file his or her SA return by the 31 October or 31 January deadline, he or she currently becomes liable for a fixed penalty of £100. If the return has still not been sent in by 31 July (or 30 April for paper returns), there is another £100 fixed penalty. If a return is filed more than 12 months late, further penalties, up to 100% of the amount of tax outstanding (but usually reduced) may be imposed after the return is filed.

In addition to the £100 penalty for submitting a return late, a further penalty of £10 may be applied for each day that the failure continues during the period of 90 days beginning with the date specified in a notice given by HMRC.

These penalties for late submission of the return forms are in addition to surcharges that may be imposed on outstanding tax (see 2.1.7).

If a return is more than six months late, the penalty will be the higher of 5% of any liability to tax which would have been shown in the return in question, and £300. If the failure continues for more than 12 months and the taxpayer has deliberately withheld information which would enable HMRC to assess the tax due, this becomes the greater of 100% of any liability to tax which would have been shown in the return in question, and £300.

If the withholding of the information is deliberate *and* concealed, the penalty is the greater of 100% of any liability to tax which would have been shown in the return in question, and £300. If the withholding of the information is deliberate but not concealed, the penalty is the greater of 70% of any liability to tax which would have been shown in the return, and £300. In any other case, the penalty will be the greater of 5% of any liability to tax which would have been shown in the return, and £300. Higher penalties (up to double the amount of tax due) can be charged where the withheld information concerns offshore matters.

2.1.3 Steps that HMRC will eventually take if you do not file your return

The current rules are that, if an individual continues to be dilatory, HMRC may apply to the Tribunal for more penalties to be imposed of up to £60 per day that the return remains outstanding. As a last resort, HMRC will issue a 'determination' (which it must do within three years of the filing date for the return) which shows the tax that HMRC estimates is due for the year. This tax is then due and payable and the determination may only be set aside by the taxpayer submitting the outstanding tax return. HMRC can take you to court to enforce collection of tax payable under a determination.

Once issued, a determination can only be replaced by the taxpayer filing a return (including a Self Assessment (SA)) within three years from the statutory filing date or 12 months from the issue of the determination if later. Some taxpayers fail to meet these deadlines and do not have a reasonable excuse for doing so. In the past, by concession, HMRC has only collected the sum that would have been due for the period had the taxpayer filed the return on time, rather than the determined amount. HMRC had intended to abolish this concession, which is known as 'equitable liability', but following sustained pressure from tax advisers and professional bodies, it was retained.

2.1.4 The process

The chances are that if you are going to receive a 2015 SA tax return or Notice to Complete a Tax Return (SA316), you would have received it just after the start of the tax year in April. If you do not receive a form and you had a new source of income or capital gains in the year ended 5 April 2015, you should report this to HMRC by 5 October 2015. If you have received the paper form, this must be filed by 31 October 2015, but if you intend to file online you have until 31 January 2016.

If you want HMRC to work out your tax for you or have underpayments collected under PAYE in the following tax year, you need to file your paper return by 31 October 2015. The online filing date is 31 January 2016 and the online system will work out your tax liability, though you will still need to file by 31 December 2015 if you want any tax to be collected by a PAYE adjustment in 2016–17 (see Figure 2.1).

Figure 2.1 – Deadlines

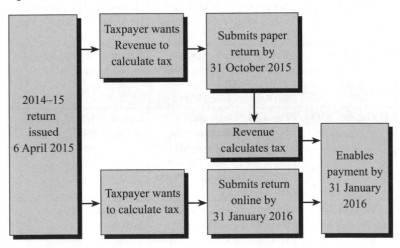

Tax notes

Your tax affairs need to be taken seriously. It is important to fill out the tax return in a meticulous way. You should read the notes issued with the tax return carefully and, if there are areas on which you are not quite sure, seek advice, either from HMRC itself from its website (www.hmrc.gov.uk), by calling the Self-Assessment Helpline number 0300 200 3310, or from a practising accountant or tax practitioner.

Table 2.1 – Diary under self-assessment

Date	Who is affected	What happens
6 April 2015	Everybody who gets a tax return	Paper self-assessment tax return for 2014–15 sent out or form SA316 sent out as a reminder to people who filed online last year.
31 May 2015	Employees	Employer should have given employee P60 for 2014–15 by this date
6 July 2015	Employees who receive expenses and benefits-in-kind (not covered by a dispensation)	Employer should have given employee details of expenses and benefits for 2014–15 by this date
31 July 2015	Some people: HMRC will notify in advance where it applies	Second interim payment on account of 2014–15 tax
5 October 2015	People with new sources of income or capital gains arising in 2014–15, who have not received a return	Report to HMRC by now or risk penalty
31 October 2015	Paper filers who want HMRC to calculate their 2014–15 tax. If you file a paper return after this date you may be charged a £100 fixed penalty	Report to HMRC by now or risk penalty
31 October 2015	Paper filers who pay tax under PAYE and want HMRC to collect any tax due (up to £2,000) through their PAYE code during 2016–17	Send in tax return by now
31 December 2015	Online filers who pay tax under PAYE and want HMRC to collect any tax due (up to £2,000) through their PAYE code during 2016–17	File tax return online now

31 January 2016	Online filers	This is the deadline for filing the online return and paying all the tax due (£100 penalty for those failing to comply)
31 January 2016	Everybody who had an income tax liability for 2014–15 of more than £1,000 and less than 80% of liability not accounted for by tax deducted at source	First interim payment on account in respect of 2016–17 tax
28 February 2016	Everybody who has not paid tax due on 31 January 2016	Automatic 5% surcharge will arise
6 April 2016	Start of new tax year	Paper return or SA316 for 2015–16 will be sent out.

If you read nothing else in this chapter read this!

The UK allows taxpayers more time to file tax returns than many other countries. Compare the US where the tax year ends on 31 December and the individual is required to file the return and pay the outstanding tax by the following 15 April! If the UK imposed the same timetable, the tax form you received in April would need to be filed in July of the same year, not October or even January of the following year. So what are you waiting for? Why wait until after Christmas to file your tax form; risk losing tax papers issued the previous summer; pay interest on missed payments on account; forgo the option to have unpaid tax collected under PAYE in the following tax year (in effect an interest-free loan)? If you organise your filing early you will have time to save for any payment due the following January and, better still, you may be owed a tax refund!

Tax notes

Organise your tax papers early and aim to file early to improve your tax position. You can turn this chore into something constructive as a tax return can serve a similar function to an annual set of accounts. Armed with this information you will be better placed to make informed financial decisions going forward.

2.1.5 Provisional figures, estimates and valuations

The maximum time permitted for completion and submission of a return is 10 months (ie for 2014–15, 6 April 2015 to 31 January 2016) if you file online. Final figures may not always be available by the submission deadline and therefore it may be necessary to estimate these amounts.

HMRC's current policy is that it will accept a return (assuming there are no other problems) where the taxpayer has used a provisional or estimated figure and it will not send back a return just because it does not contain an adequate explanation for why such figures are needed or which does not give a date for the supply of final figures. However, the omission of such explanations or information will be a factor to be taken into account in deciding whether to open an enquiry into the return. Furthermore, HMRC also believes that it is possible for the use of provisional or estimated figures to result in an incorrect return for which a penalty may be charged. This might apply where the taxpayer has not taken reasonable care when calculating the figures or because final figures could have been obtained before the return was sent to HMRC.

There will be situations where an estimated figure is submitted that will not be amended in the future (eg where there is inadequate information to reach a precise figure). If the estimate is considered to be sufficiently reliable to make a complete return (eg where it is based on detailed records for a sample representative period in the case of private proportion expenses such as motoring expenses), it is not necessary to refer specifically to the estimate. However, if the figure is not reliable (eg because the records may have been lost or destroyed), HMRC requires identification of the amount and an explanation of its calculation.

HMRC also draws a distinction between estimates and judgemental figures. A valuation at 31 March 1982 for CGT is a good example of a judgemental figure. That is, there is no right or wrong answer. The figure to be included is basically the taxpayer's best judgement (preferably based on professional valuations) as to the figures, which should be agreed with HMRC. Again, HMRC requires identification of, and details about, the valuation. This may be enquired into during the 12-month enquiry period. HMRC has stated (in SP1/06) that most taxpayers who state that a valuation has been used, by whom it has been carried out, and that it was carried out by a named independent and suitably qualified valuer if that was the case, on the appropriate basis, will be able, for all practical purposes, to rely on protection from a later discovery assessment, provided those statements are true.

2.1.6 Payment of tax

Having filed the SA return, the taxpayer must settle any tax liability for the year concerned. Of course, some income will have borne tax during the course of the year, either under PAYE or for example, a bank may have deducted tax from interest paid. A self-employed person may also have made payments on account of his or her tax liability (see 2.1.8).

2.1.7 Surcharges

If tax is still outstanding after the 31 January payment date, interest is charged and the following surcharges are imposed:

(a) a 5% surcharge on any tax that is unpaid by 28 February after the end of the tax year (a month after the tax fell due);

(b) a further 5% surcharge on any tax still outstanding by 31 July (six months after the date that the tax fell due for payment on 31 January).

Tax notes

Try not to get into this situation but, if you find it impossible to submit your tax return within 30 days of the filing date, make a payment on account of the tax that is owing to keep any surcharge to the minimum.

2.1.8 Payments on account

A person who files an SA return may be required to make payments on account of the tax liability for the current year. Basically, the person should take the total tax liability for the previous year (ie the year covered by the SA return) and deduct CGT and tax withheld at source. If less than 80% of the tax has been deducted at source (ignoring any CGT), and the balance is £1,000 or more, the taxpayer must make equal payments on account on 31 January and 31 July, which together add up to this amount.

Example

A files a SA return for 2014–15 in January 2016. There is tax to pay of £10,000, but £4,500 of this is CGT. A must pay £2,750 on 31 January 2016 as a payment on account for 2015–16 and must make a similar payment on account on 31 July 2016.

Tax notes

You can apply for a reduction in your 2015–16 payments on account if you have reason to believe that your tax liability will be lower than that for 2014–15, but if you turn out to be mistaken you will be charged interest. Penalties may be charged where HMRC contends that the payments on account were improperly reduced, ie where the taxpayer was aware that the tax was due, but merely sought to defer payment until 31 January following the tax year.

2.1.9 Direct recovery of tax debts

The Government plans to introduce powers that will enable HMRC to recover debts of over £1,000 direct from the debtor's bank account.

It is concerned at the amount of tax debts outstanding and the length of time it takes HMRC to collect these. The proposals will enable HMRC to recover tax and tax credits owed by taking the money directly from the debtor's bank or building society account, including ISAs. It is proposed that this power will apply only to debts of more than £1,000 and that a minimum aggregate balance of £5,000 will be left across all accounts.

2.1.10 Return amendments by the taxpayer and HMRC

The taxpayer may within 12 months of the filing date give a notice to HMRC amending an SA return.

HMRC may repair an SA return within nine months of receiving it to correct obvious errors of principle, transpositions of figures and arithmetical errors. HMRC is required to issue a notice of this correction and the taxpayer can then either accept the repair or file an objection.

2.1.11 Tell HMRC to issue a return if you owe tax

(s 7 TMA 1970)

A taxpayer who has not received a return form is still obliged to inform HMRC of any taxable income or gains (other than income taxed under PAYE, income taxed by deduction at source, and income and gains already assessed) within six months of the end of the year of assessment (ie by 5 October following the end of the tax year). Any taxpayer who fails to do so becomes liable to a penalty under Schedule 41, FA 2008:

(a) for a deliberate *and* concealed act or failure, 100% of the potential lost revenue;

(b) for a deliberate but not concealed act or failure, 70% of the potential lost revenue;

(c) for any other case, 30% of the potential lost revenue, ie the tax unpaid at the filing date.

2.2 FILING SA TAX RETURNS ONLINE

Over the years HMRC has tried to encourage people to file their tax returns electronically. The benefits for HMRC are obvious and – as stated on Californian state tax returns – no tree wants to grow up to be a tax return! It is advisable for confidentiality that you use your own personal computer to file online and that you ensure that you have adequate anti-virus software installed on your machine.

You will also have to register at www.hmrc.gov.uk before you can file and will need the following details to hand:

- your UTR – unique taxpayer reference, which is ten digits long;
- your national insurance number;
- your postal code.

Tax notes

Don't leave it too late – the HMRC website advises that: 'It can take 20 working days (this is usually 4 weeks) to complete the registration process.' So ensure that you register in time to meet your filing deadline.

The site asks also for an email address and a password of your choice. Once you have successfully registered, an ID number will be generated on screen and an activation PIN (Personal Identification Number) sent in the post.

The online filing set up process is summarised by HMRC in the steps shown in Figure 2.2.

Figure 2.2 – Steps in the activation process

1	2	3	4	5	6
Terms and conditions	About you	Create password	Note user ID	Enter details	Receive activation code

The following forms can be filed online:

- Self-assessment tax returns SA100 (individuals) and supplementary pages for employment, self-employment; partnership (to report the income you receive as a partner), UK property, capital gains and foreign income can be filed using HMRC's online filing software. Non-UK residents are also able to register to use HMRC online services.
- Amended tax returns (but only for 12 months after the usual filing date for that return).
- Compulsory online filing applies to companies – see Chapter 18 for details. Smaller companies may be able to use HMRC's online filing software, but generally, commercial software will be needed to file online.
- It is necessary to use commercial software in order to file SA800 (partnerships) and SA900 (trusts) forms online, and to file supplementary pages for non-UK residence, trust income, Lloyds underwriting or income earned as a Minister of Religion or Member of Parliament.

The following are not available online:

- non-resident company tax returns (SA700) or self-administered pension schemes returns (SA 970).

The preferential 31 January deadline still applies for individuals', partnerships' and trusts' online filing, ie the tax return for the year ended 5 April 2015 must be filed no later than 31 January 2016. There is a deadline for individuals who wish to have payments of up to £2,000 collected via the PAYE code operated against their earnings in the tax year commencing 6 April 2017. For the 2015 SA, this online deadline is 31 December 2015. If you do miss the 31 October deadline for paper filing it may therefore be worth considering filing online by the December deadline.

There are certain individuals who will be unable to file online eg Members of Parliament. There also continue to be exclusions and 'special cases' for certain returns due to technical issues with the online filing system. In these circumstances the paper form will be accepted within the deadlines that apply to returns filed online, ie the filing deadline is 31 January not 31 October. If your paper return is filed between 1 November and 31 January, due to technical issues, your return should be accompanied by an explanation of the circumstances.

Tax notes

HMRC states the advantages of filing online are that it is: 'secure, accurate and you will get an immediate acknowledgement of receipt, plus you should receive a repayment significantly faster if you are owed money. Our Self Assessment Service checks your Tax Return as you fill it in and automatically calculates your tax for you.'

2.3 TEN GOLDEN RULES FOR DEALING WITH YOUR 2015 TAX RETURN

The SA system requires that you carry out certain tasks by fixed deadlines. If you fail to deal with your tax affairs in a business-like way, you will be charged interest, surcharges and penalties.

The SA tax return may still be unfamiliar but is not as difficult as it seems at first glance. A review carried out by HMRC showed that 30% of returns contained clerical errors that needed correction (eg arithmetical mistakes, figures entered in the wrong columns, etc), but 90% of the mistakes could be readily identified to enable the return to be 'processed' and the taxpayer's details entered on the HMRC computer. The standard return may need to be supplemented by additional schedules so this is probably your first task: to see if you have been sent all the extra schedules that you will need. The tax legislation can be very complicated but HMRC has gone to considerable expense to provide detailed notes and helpsheets that accompany the extra schedules and these should enable you to cope with most straightforward situations.

The next thing to take on board is that HMRC has powers enabling it to check up on taxpayers. Tax officials will be using these powers and will not find it amusing if you are audited and found wanting, even where the shortcomings amount only to carelessness. The HMRC Enquiry Manual makes it quite plain that SA will not be allowed to degenerate into 'pay what you like'. Furthermore, even though there is a set time limit for HMRC to announce that a return will be audited ('selected for enquiry'), it will be able to reopen back years if the taxpayer has omitted key information (this is called 'discovery': see 3.4.12).

Therefore, you are advised to do the following:

(1) Get organised; start to collect together the information you will need (see Table 2.2).

(2) Do not throw anything away for the time being. In fact, you should keep your 2014–15 records until 31 January 2017 (2021 if you run a business or receive rental income). Remember that HMRC's policy is 'process now, check later'. HMRC will be able to open an enquiry into your 2014–15 return by serving a notice within 12 months of the date it receives the SA form – and it will not have to give any justification for doing so.

(3) Do not leave everything until the last minute. There will be an automatic £100 penalty if you are late in filing your return, with additional penalties if the failure continues and in any case, it will be easier to tackle the return while things are fresh in your mind. If there are any gaps in your records, you may be able to reconstruct them by getting down to the task before the trail goes cold.

(4) Do not send in an incomplete return because it will be rejected. If you had benefits-in-kind, such as a company car, you will need to put down a figure for your taxable benefit: just reporting 'per form P11D' or 'as PAYE' is not acceptable.

(5) Start to put cash aside now so that you can settle your 2014–15 tax and make a payment on account for 2015–16 on 31 January 2016. If you are short of funds after Christmas you may find yourself exposed to interest. Worse still, if you are unable to clear your 2014–15 tax by 28 February 2016, you will be liable for an automatic 5% surcharge, with a further 5% charge falling due if the tax remains unpaid by the next 31 July.

(6) Consider filing early. HMRC has given repeated assurances that filing early will not increase the likelihood of your return being selected for enquiry. On a positive note, HMRC will collect underpayments of up to £2,000 via the PAYE system if you submit your paper return by 31 October or online by 30 December. This may be much more convenient than having to make a lump sum payment.

(7) Work on the basis that your return will be selected for enquiry. HMRC selects about 10,000 returns each year randomly; this means

there is a less than 1% chance of being selected, but you are considerably more likely to be selected for random enquiry than to win the National Lottery for instance. Tax offices are also expected to check another 30,000 returns with the selection being made on a more scientific assessment of risk factors.

(8) Remember to tick box 20 if your return contains any estimated or provisional figures. It will probably be in your own best interests to give an explanation of how you have arrived at the figures concerned as this may pre-empt queries from HMRC. It may also afford a degree of protection against HMRC reopening the 2014–15 tax year after the 12-month enquiry deadline by making a 'discovery assessment'.

(9) Think twice about not drawing attention to any assumptions you have made in completing your return where these could be challenged by HMRC. You do not have to follow HMRC's line on everything, especially if you receive professional advice that HMRC's interpretation of the legislation is open to doubt, but you should not be coy about this. From time to time HMRC is shown to be wrong, but HMRC wins more often than it loses. You could be liable for penalties if the courts uphold HMRC's interpretation and it emerges that you had not put all your cards face up on the table. Bear in mind the case of *Langham* v *Veltema,* which is covered at 3.4.12. Consider investing in a certificate of tax deposit to cover exposure to interest if HMRC challenges your interpretation (see 3.4.11).

(10) Finally, get professional advice if your affairs are complicated. DIY tax returns may be a false economy if your situation is non-standard, however hard HMRC has tried to explain the rules in its helpsheets.

Table 2.2 – Information you will need

If you are employed:	
Form P60, ie the annual certificate of pay and tax deducted at source	Your employer should have provided this automatically by 31 May 2015
Taxable figures for any benefits-in-kind (company car, cheap loans in excess of £10,000)	Your employer should have provided this automatically by 6 July 2015
Details of amounts paid to you as approved mileage payments for using your own car for company business (see 4.4.12)	Your HR dept may be able to provide this but you would do better to keep a log of business travel and amounts claimed from your employer

If you changed jobs during the year ended 5 April 2015, details of benefits and pay provided by your previous employer	You may have to ask for this
Advice from your employer as to what to report if you received free shares or exercised (or were given) a share option in 2014–15	Speak to your HR department about this
If you were self-employed:	
You will need to prepare accounts or ask an accountant to do this for you. HMRC requires your details in a set format so that it can use its computer to assist it in identifying cases that should be taken up for enquiry	See 7.1
If you have rental income:	
You should keep an analysis of rents receivable and a note of any bad debts, details of expenditure such as fees paid to managing agents, repair bills and redecoration, replacement of electrical goods and furniture. If you have borrowed to fund your property business, the interest should be an allowable expense	Rent charged for 2014–15 will normally be taxable even if you did not receive it until after the end of the year
If you have income from savings:	
Keep a copy of your bank account statements, your building society passbook and dividend vouchers	Most banks include details of the interest earned on an account, and any tax deducted, on a statement within a couple of months following 5 April
If you had trust income:	
You need form R185, which sets out the amount of income paid to you and the tax deducted at source	
If you have made capital gains:	
You will need any stockbroker's contract notes for sales of shares and copies of the sale contract and completion statement if you made real estate sales. If you gave assets to your children or other family members you may be liable for CGT as if you had sold at market value so seek advice in such situations	The gains are exempt if they totalled less than £11,000. See 13.1.1. Remember that the date of disposal for CGT is the contract date, not the date payment is received.

2.4 COMMON ERRORS

HMRC's Press Office has, over the years, kindly provided us with a note of the more common errors on the SA form:

(1) Not explaining unusual variations – there is an area on the return that allows you to explain variations. By filling in this section you can avoid follow-up requests for extra information to explain any apparent discrepancies.

(2) Misclassifying expenses – any anomalies may trigger a request for further explanation.

(3) Not including relevant supplementary pages – any supplementary pages indicated as relevant must be sent with the return.

(4) Using rounded-up figures or estimates – these can be a sign that a person's affairs have not been properly maintained and could trigger further enquiry.

(5) Not including actual information on the main Tax Return – it is important to provide specific figures where appropriate on the return itself – reference to supplementary sheets or accounts can lead to delays.

(6) Capital expenditure v capital allowances – another common mistake is entering your capital expenditure in the Self-Employment section instead of your capital allowances, resulting in a claim to undue tax relief.

(7) Highlighting 'private use' items – it should be made clear where items have been used for private purposes, and the relevant adjustments made to reflect this.

(8) For paper returns, not signing and dating the return.

Tax notes

Deal with the self-assessment return issued in April 2015. Under self-assessment (SA), you need to submit your tax return either by 31 October 2015 if you file the paper form or 31 January 2016 if you file online and settle your outstanding tax by 31 January 2016. If you fail to do this, you automatically become liable for interest and penalties.

Enabling letters

In recent years HMRC has taken to issuing what are referred to as 'enabling letters' to (amongst other targeted groups) self-employed individuals with turnover of up to £150,000. The letters are not enquiries into the taxpayer's affairs and do not reflect upon the character of either the taxpayer or tax agent, but can be taken as a warning over common areas of inaccuracies and reporting. HMRC's objective in issuing these letters is to ensure that the taxpayer is aware of their obligations.

Typically the letter will highlight the fact that most formal inquiries result in additional tax due together with interest and penalty charges. The following general points will be made:

- read the SA form guidance notes;
- include all business income;
- claim only actual expenses;
- have records that support both income and expenditure;
- file and pay your taxes on time.

The letter then highlights specific areas where errors are likely to occur when reporting self-employed income.

- **Turnover** – taxpayers should ensure that the gross income received and not the net is shown, eg if you are a freelance self-employed consultant and receive a fee subject to deduction of tax, it is the gross figure that needs to be declared. (If you are VAT registered, the VAT element should not be included.) Payments in kind, tips and insurance proceeds for loss or damage to stock should also be included. Conversely, tax credits, business-start up allowance, funds introduced by the taxpayer and proceeds from the sale of a fixed asset need not be included.
- **Goods taken from stock for private use** – goods that a trader takes from trading stock, for the personal use and enjoyment of him or herself and/or members of his or her household, should be credited at market value. The relevant legislation is in ss172A–172F ITTOIA 2005 for income tax and Chapter 10, Part 3, CTA 2009 for corporation tax. In brief, any disposal of trading stock not made in the course of the trade should be dealt with for taxation purposes as if it were a sale at market value.
- **Plant and machinery** – the cost of repairing, but not of buying, equipment is an allowable business expense, although capital allowances may be claimed on the latter (see 16.2).
- **Dual purpose expenditure** – if an expense is for both private and business purposes, it is said to have a duality of purpose. If the two elements are inseparable, no tax relief is due (see 16.1.5). For instance, a claim for everyday clothing, albeit only worn whilst undertaking the duties of the employment or business (*Mallalieu* v *Drummond* and more recently, *S. Williams* TC00397). It was held that there was an intrinsic duality of purpose, because although the clothes were bought to maintain a professional and business-like appearance, the individuals concerned had to wear clothing for the purposes of warmth and decency.
- **Motoring costs** – remember that travel between your home and place of work is not deductible. The object of home to work travel is not to allow you to undertake your business, but to enable you to live away from it.

- **Business trips** – only reasonable costs are allowable. However, attempts by HMRC officers to define 'reasonable costs' by reference to their own, internal, civil service guidelines for incurring travelling and hotel expenditure should be strenuously resisted.
- **Cost of home office** – these should be accurately calculated to reflect only that part of the home which is used for business. Remember that home office expenditure is a double-edged sword in that it might give rise to a capital gains tax charge on disposal (see 14.2.2). In practice, where there is only minor use of the home for business, HMRC will accept a claim of up to £4 per week without detailed enquiry.
- **Salaries** – where sums are paid from the business to the self-employed individual these are effectively drawings and are not deductible. Any payments to spouses, civil partners or minor or young adult children may give rise to the question as to whether any services performed by the family member were commensurate with the salary paid, in allowing them as a deduction. Remember the national minimum wage rules must also be considered.
- **Cost of services** – where provided to friends and family these are non-deductible.

2.5 PROVIDING ADDITIONAL INFORMATION

At the end of the SA form, HMRC has left a number of blank spaces for additional information. You may be tempted to think that this is HMRC's way of giving you enough rope to hang yourself, but in reality it should be grasped as a lifeline. There may be aspects of the form where either you or your tax adviser has relied on a certain interpretation of the tax law. HMRC may not agree with your interpretation but will be unaware of the basis on which you have completed the form unless you draw its attention to this. If this emerges later on, HMRC may seek to re-open your self-assessment and possibly charge interest and penalties. One way of covering yourself is to make appropriate entries in the additional information box, 19 (sometimes referred to as the 'white space'). If you make your assumptions and interpretations explicit, you will protect yourself against HMRC using its discovery powers (see 3.4.12).

Tax notes

Protect yourself against penalties or discovery assessments by making entries on the tax return in the white space.

3

HMRC AND YOU

This chapter contains the following sections:

(1) Understanding your responsibilities and rights
(2) Information available from HMRC
(3) The tax return process
(4) HMRC enquiries into tax returns
(5) What penalties can HMRC impose?
(6) Other initiatives
(7) Remission of tax by HMRC
(8) Error or mistake relief (overpayment relief)
(9) Equitable liability
(10) Complaints and compensation
(11) Revenue Adjudicator
(12) HMRC rulings

3.1 UNDERSTANDING YOUR RESPONSIBILITIES AND RIGHTS

3.1.1 Background

HMRC is increasingly run more like a business. It has limited resources which are becoming more thinly spread, hence must be allocated efficiently to ensure that tax is not lost. At the same time, the Government requires it to operate quality management and to assess its efficiency in terms of 'satisfied customers'.

It is HMRC's stated policy to help taxpayers understand their rights and obligations, get their tax affairs right and pay their tax on time, whilst at the same time tackling those who seek to pay less tax than HMRC believes is due.

3.1.2 The Taxpayers' Charter

The Government decided that HMRC must publish a charter and various consultations took place throughout 2009. Originally titled 'HMRC's Charter', the final document is called 'Your Charter', thereby recognising that the focus of the Charter is the service provided by HMRC to its 'customers'. It sets out standards and values to which HMRC will aspire in dealing with taxpayers and others and what HMRC expects in return. HMRC will have to report annually on progress in meeting those standards.

One practical problem is that the activities undertaken by HMRC are so wide and diverse. They range from the SA system, running the tax credit system, assessing death duties (all these activities relate to private individuals) to administering corporation tax and VAT (often dealing with large companies). HMRC also exists to prevent criminal activities such as smuggling. Can a single charter properly do justice to the standards applicable to dealing with such a diverse range of customers?

3.1.3 HMRC and you in practice

In practice, this means that a taxpayer should attend promptly to correspondence from HMRC and complete tax returns accurately and within a reasonable period. If you find there are some aspects of your tax return that are complex and prevent you from completing the entire form, you should contact the Inspector and explain the reason for the difficulty. In return, HMRC promises to deal with you in a professional, fair and reasonable way, to assume that you are honest unless it has good reason not to and to avoid making unnecessary demands on your time.

3.2 INFORMATION AVAILABLE FROM HMRC

3.2.1 Codes of practice and fact sheets

HMRC has published codes of practice (COPs), some of which are examined in this chapter, explaining its approach and procedures in certain areas of work, which set out the legal rights of taxpayers (and HMRC) and explain what the taxpayer can expect to happen. The COPs (which can be found at www.hmrc.gov.uk/leaflets) include the following:

- COP8   Specialist Investigations (fraud and avoidance). Cases other than suspected serious fraud;
- COP9   Civil investigation into cases of suspected serious fraud;
- COP10   Information and advice;
- COP24   Stamp duty land tax enquiries for individuals;
- COP25   Stamp duty land tax enquiries for companies and partnerships
- COP26   Overpayments of tax credits.

The information provided by COPs is also supplemented by Fact Sheets. These are typically shorter than COPs at around 1–5 pages and are designed to help understand how the changes to HMRC investigation powers brought in by FA 2008 have altered the way HMRC officers check a person's tax position. Links to the fact sheets can be found at www. hmrc.gov.uk/compliance/factsheets.htm. Examples of the Fact Sheets are:

- FS1   General information about compliance checks;
- FS2   Requests for information and documents;
- FS3–5   Visits to business premises;
- FS6–7   What happens when inaccuracies are found and penalties;
- FS13   Publishing details of deliberate defaulters;
- FS14   Managing deliberate defaulters;
- FS15   Self assessment and old penalty rules.

A further fact sheet, *HMRC1 – HM Revenue & Customs decisions – what to do if you disagree* may also be useful.

3.2.2 Statements of practice and extra-statutory concessions

It is extremely important that HMRC operates a uniform interpretation of the tax legislation.

In cases where the legislation is obscure or its precise implication is uncertain, HMRC publishes statements of practice (SPs). These operate as a shield for the taxpayer rather than a sword for HMRC. You can rely on HMRC applying these SPs but they do not affect your statutory rights and, if you believe that HMRC's interpretation is wrong, it is still open to you to appeal to the Tax Tribunal.

HMRC also publishes extra-statutory concessions (ESCs). These apply in cases where the legislation is quite clear but the letter of the law produces an unreasonable result. In effect, HMRC recognises that Parliament could never have intended to impose certain tax liabilities, and ESCs are common sense rules that HMRC applies so as to avoid an unreasonable result. Once again, HMRC publishes these ESCs because it recognises the need to treat all taxpayers alike. In general, unless your circumstances are special, or you are seeking to apply an ESC so as to avoid tax, you can rely on HMRC applying a published ESC if it covers your particular circumstances.

Following the House of Lords decision in *Wilkinson* in 2007, HMRC became concerned that it had been acting outside its powers in making such concessions. It has therefore legislated for a number of these, others are now considered obsolete, and a considerably reduced number remain in operation.

3.2.3 General information available from HMRC

The following information is available from HMRC:

- explanatory leaflets, booklets and help sheets, designed to explain different aspects of the tax system and provide assistance with tax return completion;
- press releases, which announce a proposed change in the law, in HMRC practice or other change;

- the *Revenue & Customs Brief* is a short bulletin giving information on developments and changes of interest, and is generally used to announce changes in policy or to set out the legal background to an issue: they have a six-month life span;
- the *Tax Bulletin* which played a similar role to *Revenue & Customs Briefs* before 2007;
- the internal guidance *Manuals,* which cover HMRC's interpretation of tax law and the operation of the tax system.

Most of the above information is on HMRC's website, www.hmrc.gov. uk which also includes a 'top stories and what's new' section where the latest announcements can be found. The website is valuable for not only the large amount of information it makes available, but also for the speed with which it is updated. As well as providing information, SA return forms and employer's forms can be downloaded. In addition to covering tax generally there are also more specialist areas covering matters such as:

- Construction industry scheme;
- Coming to the UK;
- Starting a business;
- Trusts and estates;
- Tax credits.

HMRC's internal Manuals are largely in the public domain. They are available for reference at www.hmrc.gov.uk/thelibrary/manuals.htm.

The HMRC manuals do not have the force of law, nor can they be used as aids to statutory construction. The manuals merely provide HMRC's interpretation of legally binding statutes, case law and practice. They are, therefore, open to challenge through the courts.

3.3 THE TAX RETURN PROCESS

3.3.1 Processing of tax returns

HMRC has designed the SA return with its own data processing needs in mind. Returns are normally read electronically or figures are input by people who have little or no tax knowledge.

The basic principle adopted by HMRC is 'process now, check later'. The fact that the return is processed does not imply that it has been accepted.

Past experience has shown that many returns need correcting because of arithmetical errors, figures being transposed, amounts being entered in the wrong column, etc. When an HMRC officer identifies such obvious mistakes he or she issues a notice to the taxpayer advising him or her of the correction (or 'repair') needed. The taxpayer can object, but if HMRC does not hear further within 30 days, the correction is deemed to form part of the return. In recent years HMRC has taken a more pragmatic approach to this process by phoning the taxpayer or his or her agent to discuss any simple amendments that show up on the processing of the forms. Routine checking and making corrections must not be confused with HMRC officers carrying out an enquiry or other compliance check (see 3.4).

Tax notes

If you receive a phone call from HMRC it is important that you keep a note of the HMRC officer's name, date of call, topic discussed and any agreement made.

3.3.2 Keeping proper records

Because HMRC operates on a 'process now, check later' basis, you need to keep records to be able to back up the entries on your SA return. The length of time that you need to retain your records depends on whether you have a business or are letting property. If you do, the required period is five years and ten months after the end of the tax year (six years for a company). If you do not have either of these sources of income, the minimum period for retaining your records is normally one year and ten months after the end of the tax year concerned.

The duty to preserve records may be discharged by preserving them in any form, eg on an electronic filing system, or by preserving the information contained in those records.

3.4 HMRC ENQUIRIES INTO TAX RETURNS

3.4.1 HMRC enquiries and other compliance checks

Once HMRC has received a tax return, it has 12 months to issue a notice that it is carrying out an enquiry into a tax return.

When an enquiry is completed, or if no enquiry is opened before the deadline, the position becomes final and HMRC cannot reopen enquiries into that year unless it can show 'discovery', ie that the taxpayer acted negligently or fraudulently or that key information was not made available to HMRC.

Enquiries can be made into partnership returns under the same rules as apply to individual returns, but any amendments to partnership profits then need to be taken through to each partner's tax returns.

Powers introduced in FA 2008 enable HMRC to undertake compliance checks outside of the enquiry regime. These include powers to visit business premises and to demand documents and information. There is no necessity for the tax year in question to have ended, or for an enquiry to be open, although other criteria may need to be met in such circumstances, such as HMRC having reasonable grounds to suspect a discovery exists.

3.4.2 Selection of returns for HMRC enquiries

HMRC has the statutory power to enquire into any tax return without giving a reason. However, because of its limited resources, it has to be selective. It is more likely to look into cases where tax is perceived to be at risk perhaps, for example, because of known intelligence concerning the taxpayer's reliability or, at the other extreme, a new entry appearing on the return when compared to prior years. A number of returns not suspected of being incorrect will also be selected at random each year, although these will be very few as the vast majority of cases will be based on risk assessment.

Even without evidence of inaccuracies, HMRC's employees (and its computer systems) are more likely to choose certain returns for enquiry based on other factors such as:

- returns filed late;
- payments made late;
- returns that include provisional figures;
- cases that involve large capital gains or loss claims;
- changes in accounting date.

3.4.3 HMRC procedure for enquiries

HMRC must give written notice that an enquiry is to be made into an SA return. This notice must be served within 12 months from the date HMRC receives the form.

Historically, HMRC has not given reasons for having opened an enquiry, although it is becoming more open about this issue in the interests of moving matters smoothly forward. In any case it should soon become apparent whether it is initially an enquiry into one particular aspect of the return or a full enquiry under which HMRC is reviewing the entire return and usually requires access to all the taxpayer's records. An aspect enquiry can extend into a full enquiry as HMRC receives information, so the distinction is not completely clear cut.

The opening of an enquiry is not meant to imply that HMRC believes that anything is untoward; merely that it is carrying out checks to test the return's accuracy and reliability.

The Enquiry Manual states repeatedly that HMRC officers should adopt a non-confrontational approach and keep an open mind. HMRC intends that the opening of enquiries should be less contentious, and its aim is to develop a more neutral and less confrontational approach in this area. It is acknowledged that the information initially available in the return and elsewhere is unlikely to be sufficient to establish whether the return is incorrect, and even where it appears incorrect it could be that the information is incomplete, misleading or capable of explanation. The Manual advises officers that unless they are reasonably certain that there have been omissions (and often it will not be possible for them to be certain), they should ask the taxpayer in a neutral way whether there is anything more that he or she has to say, taking account of what has already been said. They should make it clear that no allegations are being made at this point. When HMRC opens an enquiry or compliance check, it will issue details of its code of practice and/or fact sheets as appropriate.

3.4.4 Information required

The HMRC officer is instructed to request informally any information needed, in most cases, rather than using HMRC's formal powers to require the production of the data. A formal notice will, however, be issued for documents and information in the taxpayer's power or possession if he or she has refused to co-operate with the informal request or has failed to comply within the specified timescale. Such a notice must allow the taxpayer a reasonable amount of time to comply; how long is 'reasonable' depends on the particular circumstances, but there is no longer the 30-day minimum period that existed under pre-FA 2008 legislation. The taxpayer may appeal to the Tax Tribunal in some, but not all, circumstances: for example if he or she thinks that the notice is invalid because the data requested is not reasonably required to check his or her tax position. There is no right of appeal against demands for 'statutory records' (broadly, being those records required in order to be able to prepare a complete a correct return) nor is there an appeal mechanism to determine if something is a 'statutory record' in the first place. However, that point may well be covered in any appeal as to the validity of a penalty issued for non-compliance with the statutory notice.

HMRC should only request information and documents that are relevant and reasonably required to determine whether the tax position (which in practice will usually mean the self-assessment return) is correct. Its approach varies according to whether the taxpayer is a business taxpayer (ie a taxpayer who is in self-employment or in receipt of income from property). In the case of a full enquiry into the business taxpayer's affairs, HMRC considers that the following items can be reasonably requested without providing an explanation:

- business records generally;
- cash book, petty cash book, sales and purchase invoices and bank account statements;
- details of how any adjustments made by the accountant have been calculated;
- an analysis of drawings;
- details of any balancing figures or estimates used in the accounts.

Private bank and credit card statements should not normally be required at the initial stage of an enquiry but may be required as matters progress. The advice to officers is that they should not ask to see private bank statements at this early stage unless it can be demonstrated that the statements are relevant to the return and can be reasonably required for checking the return's accuracy.

However, one should not take this for granted. In *Beckwith* v *HMRC*, a carpenter was asked for copies of his private bank statements. He argued that they were not part of his business records but it was found that over 90 business transactions had gone through that account. The tribunal held that the fact that the bank account also contained personal expenditure did not prevent the statements for that account being part of Mr Beckwith's business records.

Where there is a full enquiry into a non-business taxpayer that is a complex case, officers should seek to verify in the first place the income and gains declared by reference to any third-party information held (eg a form P11D). The information requested directly might then comprise:

- dividend vouchers;
- certificates of loan interest paid;
- form PPCC (a certificate confirming payment under a personal pension scheme);
- a detailed CGT computation;
- a copy of a property valuation;
- an account of the precise use made of a company asset, such as a private plane.

In *Long* [2014] TC 03339, the First-tier Tribunal accepted a taxpayer's appeal against an HMRC information notice. It found that because a doctor's private practice business appointments diaries contained no financial information and did not necessarily provide an accurate record of patients seen and services provided and charged for they were not 'reasonably required' in order to check the taxpayer's position.

In aspect cases (where HMRC focuses on just one aspect of the return), the request should, unsurprisingly, concentrate on information relevant to the particular point under review.

3.4.5 Meetings with HMRC

Taxpayers are not obliged to attend any meeting requested by HMRC, but are expected to provide promptly any information considered essential to the enquiry. HMRC believes that meetings allow taxpayers to clarify and explain any points that might have been misunderstood, and to ask questions. The taxpayer will be told if HMRC considers correspondence is an inadequate substitute for a meeting. HMRC has confirmed that the taxpayer should be sent an agenda in advance of such a meeting. The Enquiry Manual states:

An agenda covering the main areas for discussion at a meeting with the taxpayer should always be provided [. . .] It should be case specific but not a detailed list of questions and should not be seen by either party to be exhaustive or restrictive [. . .] It would, however, be unusual for a completely new major agenda item to be introduced at the meeting unless something unexpected is revealed during the course of the meeting.

However, an HMRC officer cannot insist that a taxpayer attends any meeting, and his or her only option in terms of asking questions of the taxpayer face-to-face is to take an appeal to the Tax Tribunal and put his or her questions to the taxpayer during cross-examination (assuming the taxpayer is put forward as a witness).

There is no reason in principle why enquiries should not be conducted entirely through correspondence. The relevant Codes of Practice instruct the HMRC officer to be mindful of the taxpayer's compliance costs and it may be possible to agree with the officer that matters should proceed by way of correspondence without this being viewed as lack of co-operation on the taxpayer's part. It should be borne in mind, however, that a refusal to attend a meeting might, in certain circumstances, be seen as a lack of co-operation when it comes to assessing penalties in the event that the enquiry reveals an under-declaration of tax.

A request for a meeting can often be taken as an indication that the officer, having considered the information initially supplied, has concluded that there are grounds for doubting the return's accuracy or that there are matters that require further detailed enquiry. Officers are instructed that where irregularities are suspected they would need to consider how to give the taxpayer the opportunity to disclose them and to co-operate actively in quantifying them. Whether the taxpayer takes this opportunity could have a bearing on the level of penalty that might be levied on him or her. HMRC officers are instructed to seek early meetings.

3.4.6 Visits to business premises

FA 2008 introduced legislation allowing HMRC to inspect business premises, assets and documents. Although a formal enquiry does not need to be open, it is likely that most visits that are not part of a traditional VAT or PAYE review will take place as part of an enquiry. HMRC's review may well cover several taxes at once, perhaps requiring several officers to visit. Hence, in practice, it will not be straightforward and careful follow-up will be needed if off-the-cuff responses are given.

The legislation provides for only seven days' notice of a visit which does not have to be in writing. It may be that less, perhaps no, notice will be given if the visit is approved internally or by the Tax Tribunal.

Once on the premises, HMRC officers can only inspect those documents which could be required under a formal information notice. They are also only allowed to 'inspect', not to 'search'. HMRC's guidance confirms that this means to inspect by eye rather than by hand, although in practice the distinction is unlikely to be straightforward. HMRC's manuals give examples of a room with various files on the table as requested by the Inspector. In the corner is a filing cabinet. The Inspector cannot go over and open the filing cabinet to see what is in it; that is considered to be searching. However, if, for example, he or she has been told that the invoices backing up the books he or she is reviewing are stored in the filing cabinet then he or she can open it at will to inspect the invoices.

It should also be noted that the new legislation only creates a power to inspect, it does not give HMRC officers any power to interview or to demand answers to questions at all.

When the legislation was drafted it did not preclude HMRC turning up at an individual's home. An amendment was later made so that the power could not be used to visit premises used 'solely' as a dwelling. The key word is, of course, 'solely'. In practice, very few visits will be made to private homes as the legislation also includes the express caveat that visits can be made only 'if the inspection is reasonably required for the purposes of checking that person's tax position'.

In the vast majority of cases how can it be 'reasonably required' that the records are reviewed at home rather than anywhere else, such as at an agent's or the business's main premises? HMRC officers are in fact instructed that, wherever practicable, they should avoid inspecting at a person's home as there will normally be an appropriate alternative location.

In addition to buildings, 'premises' also includes any means of transport. Hence there may be requests for access to those premises, for example for a car boot to be opened, subject to whether those actions constitute a search as opposed to an inspection. In reality HMRC recognises that the definition primarily covers things such as mobile chip vans and market stalls run from vans and its manual instructs that officers should not routinely enter all the transport used in a business. The instructions also state, however, that in certain circumstances, officers may open the door of a delivery van in the business's yard and be allowed to look at the boxes inside; climb inside the van to look at the boxes not visible from outside; and to ask the trader to open any box in order to check the tax position of what is inside.

Finally it is worth noting that, if the taxpayer refuses access or asks that the Inspector leaves, HMRC's instructions are simply to withdraw. The right of refusal of entry is not overridden by the inspection notice. There is normally no penalty for doing this; only if the Tax Tribunal has authorised the visit can a penalty can be levied, for deliberately obstructing an HMRC officer during a visit. Even if a tribunal has authorised the visit but no advance notice has been given there should be no penalty, at least initially. The Government is on record as stating that the new powers must be used reasonably so HMRC will surely have to concede that it is unreasonable to levy a penalty for obstruction if all the taxpayer has asked is that the visit is delayed until such time as he or she can arrange representation to deal with issues that he or she is far from expert in.

3.4.7 Closure of the enquiry

The legislation does not specify any time limit within which HMRC must complete its enquiries. However, any taxpayer who feels that the HMRC officer has had sufficient information may appeal to the Tax Tribunal for it to direct HMRC to bring the enquiry to an end.

When the HMRC officer who has conducted the enquiry has completed his or her investigation, he or she must issue a notice stating this and setting out the conclusions of the correct amount of tax that should be payable for the year in question. Once the notice has been issued, HMRC is debarred from starting new enquiries in relation to that return.

3.4.8 If you cannot reach agreement with HMRC

There will be cases where a HMRC officer and a taxpayer (or professional adviser) will form different conclusions about whether, or how, tax should apply to a particular transaction. In such cases where there is an honest difference of opinion, or even in cases where there is an argument about the actual facts, HMRC does not have the last word. The procedure for resolving such disputes is ultimately to require an appeal to be heard by the Tax Tribunal.

Prior to that, an 'independent' internal review may be offered by the HMRC officer or requested by the taxpayer or his or her adviser. This means that an HMRC officer totally unconnected with the case will review it and then report back with his or her views. Whilst this is clearly not truly independent, such reviews can be useful and the contents of the reviewer's report can be enlightening. Whichever way the review goes, the taxpayer can still appeal to the Tax Tribunal. There is also a procedure for alternative dispute resolution.

3.4.9 Tax Tribunals

The current tribunal system came into force on 1 April 2009. The previous bodies, the General Commissioners and Special Commissioners, have been abolished. Most appeals will initially be heard by the First-tier Tribunal. However, some complex cases may be heard by the Upper Tribunal.

Appeals to the Upper Tribunal may be taken on a decision by a First-tier Tribunal on matters of law, but not on matters of fact. Appeals on decisions of the Upper Tribunal will be heard by the Court of Appeal.

Costs

Both the First-tier and the Upper Tribunal have discretion to award costs in certain limited circumstances. In the main, the First-tier Tribunal will award costs only where the unsuccessful party has acted unreasonably. Where the case heard by the First-tier Tribunal is a complex one, the

Tribunal has the power to award costs but an appellant can opt out of this in advance.

The Financial Secretary to the Treasury stated on 27 March 2009:

> The general rule in the appeal courts is that the losing party risks having to pay the other side's costs, and I do not think it would be right to treat tax cases differently as a matter of course.

> However, HM Revenue and Customs (HMRC) exercise their discretion and are willing in appropriate circumstances, and in particular where it is they who are appealing against an adverse decision, to consider waiving any claim to costs in cases before the Upper Tribunal or the appeal courts, or to consider making other arrangements – this may also extend to cases before the First-tier Tribunal.

> In the minority of cases categorised as complex, where costs can be awarded in the Tax Chamber of the First-tier Tribunal other than for unreasonable behaviour, the appellant can ensure that there is no risk of them bearing HMRC's costs by opting for the costs rules not to apply.

> In considering the exercise of HMRC's discretion, influential factors include the risk of financial hardship to the other party, the involvement of a point of law the clarification of which would be of significant benefit to taxpayers as a whole and the efficient collection and management of revenue for which HMRC have responsibility.

> If HMRC are to come to an arrangement of this nature, they would expect to do so in advance of the hearing and following an approach by the taxpayer involved.

3.4.10 What happens if the SA return is found to be incorrect?

If the outcome of the enquiry is that a taxpayer has paid too much tax, the difference is refunded, together with interest (normally from the due date of payment).

If the enquiry reveals material errors in the taxpayer's favour, he or she is likely to be charged interest from the 31 January filing date. He or she may also be charged a penalty (see below).

3.4.11 Certificates of tax deposit

There is a way of protecting yourself against interest charges that might otherwise arise if HMRC successfully challenges your tax return.

A taxpayer can make deposits with the Collector of Taxes. A certificate is issued and the deposit is held for the general benefit of the individual until such time as he or she surrenders all or part of the certificate to cover tax liabilities.

Where a deposit is used to cover a tax liability, interest on overdue tax no longer runs from the date that the deposit was made. Deposits are therefore commonly used to cover a tax liability that cannot easily be quantified, for example a capital gain on a sale of unquoted shares where a value at 31 March 1982 needs to be negotiated with the Shares Valuation Division.

Interest is credited from the date the deposit is made to the date it is used (or cashed) for a maximum of six years. The interest is taxable. Interest is paid at a lower rate where deposits are encashed rather than used to settle tax liabilities.

3.4.12 Discovery assessments

If errors revealed in an enquiry were also made in previous tax years, HMRC is likely to raise discovery assessments for those years. Such assessments may be made even though the normal time limit for starting an enquiry may have expired. The time limit for raising such an assessment is normally four years after the end of the year in question, rising to six years in cases of failure to take reasonable care (in effect, negligence) and 20 years where the inaccuracy was deliberate (ie fraud).

HMRC may revisit the past in this way only if fresh information comes to light or if it turns out that the taxpayer had negligently or fraudulently withheld that information.

No discovery assessment may be made where HMRC could reasonably have been expected to identify the point at issue from information provided in a SA return. Moreover, information provided in SA returns for the two previous years is also to be taken into account in this connection. It follows that taxpayers should provide HMRC with too much information rather than too little to avoid discovery assessments. The provision of business accounts is particularly useful in this context, although HMRC's guidance notes for taxpayers state that it is not necessary to send them.

The case of *Langham* v *Veltema* (2004) STC 544 sheds interesting light on all this. The taxpayer had bought a property from his company and it did not occur to the Inspector that the valuation needed to be agreed. The Court of Appeal held that a discovery assessment could be made as the return should have contained an explicit reference to the fact that the valuation had not been agreed with HMRC and hence the insufficiency in the amount of tax emanating from the figures returned. Subsequent discovery cases have followed the same line. HMRC's position and guidance on the implications of this case for taxpayers who wish to ensure finality by filing tax returns which draw its attention to potentially contentious aspects is contained in SP1/06.

In *Daniel* v *R & C Commissioners* [2014] TC 03312, the Tribunal dismissed the taxpayer's appeal against a 'discovery' assessment for tax year 1999–2000, on the grounds that he did not work 'full-time abroad' during that year (and so did not fall to be treated as non-resident in accordance with the guidance in IR 20), and that the assessment in question was validly made outside normal time limits.

Protection from discovery

In *HMRC* v *Charlton* [2012] UKUT 770 (TCC), it was held that discovery assessments were invalid because the taxpayers had made sufficient disclosure in their tax returns.

An additional form of protection may be secured by obtaining post-transaction rulings (see 3.12).

3.5 WHAT PENALTIES CAN HMRC IMPOSE?

The four Finance Acts between FA 2007 and FA 2010 brought about fundamental reforms to the various penalty regimes. The reforms were made as follows:

- 2007 – penalties for incorrect returns;
- 2008 – penalties for failure to notify;
- 2009 – penalties for late filing and late payment of tax;
- 2010 – penalties of up to 200% related to offshore bank accounts.

All follow similar principles, with the later Finance Acts building on the format introduced by FA 2007. This section will therefore concentrate on the penalties for incorrect returns which are in practice likely to be the most commonly argued.

3.5.1 The penalty regime

Three conditions must be satisfied before HMRC can charge a penalty:

- a person delivers a return or other document (such as accounts or a document which is likely to be relied upon by HMRC to determine without further inquiry a question about the taxpayer's liability to tax) to HMRC;
- the return or document contains an inaccuracy which amounts to or leads to
  - an understatement of a person's tax liability; or
  - a false or inflated statement of loss by that person; or
  - a false or inflated claim to repayment of tax;
- the inaccuracy was careless or deliberate.

3.5.2 Different types of inaccuracy

These are defined as follows:

- 'careless' if the inaccuracy is due to the taxpayer failing to take proper care;
- 'deliberate but not concealed' if the inaccuracy is deliberate but the taxpayer did not take steps to conceal it;
- 'deliberate but concealed' if the taxpayer made arrangements to conceal a deliberate misrepresentation.

3.5.3 Taking reasonable care

The HMRC manual (the Compliance Handbook) states:

> Where an inaccuracy in a document has been made despite the person having taken reasonable care to get things right, no penalty will be due.

The manual gives examples of situations where a penalty would not be applicable. These include:

- taking a reasonably arguable view of situations that is subsequently not upheld;
- an arithmetical or transposition inaccuracy that is not so large either in absolute terms or relative to overall liability as to produce an obviously odd result or be picked up by a quality check;
- the taxpayer has followed advice from HMRC that subsequently proves to be wrong;
- the taxpayer has acted on advice from a competent tax adviser (having provided that adviser with a full set of accurate facts) which turns out to be wrong.

The manual also instructs HMRC staff that they should treat a person as taking reasonable care where arrangements or systems have been put in place which could reasonably be expected to produce an accurate basis for the calculation of tax.

The guidance in the Compliance Handbook stresses that HMRC officers should accept that it is possible for taxpayers to make simply careless – rather than intentional – errors and that not every error is automatic evidence of a deliberate attempt to pay the wrong amount of tax.

There have, however, been worrying reports of cases where – rather than following the clear guidance in the Compliance Handbook – HMRC has taken a hard line and sought to charge the full, unmitigated, penalty for a deliberate but unconcealed error in inappropriate circumstances. This is one of the situations in which expert advice from a tax investigations specialist can be invaluable as he or she will be able to ensure that not only does HMRC act within the law, but also according to its own guidance.

In *Harding* v *R & C Commrs* [2013] UKUT 575 (TCC), the Upper Tribunal upheld a First-tier Tribunal decision on a penalty for a careless inaccuracy in a tax return ruling that the taxpayer had failed to take reasonable care because he knew, or should reasonably have known, that there was a possibility that a 'severance payment' that he received was taxable.

In *Mariner* [2013] TC 03039, the First-tier Tribunal allowed a taxpayer's appeal against a penalty for a careless or negligent error because the taxpayer had relied on her tax adviser to provide her with proper professional advice and she had no reason to believe that it was wrong.

The Tribunal took a similar line in *Herefordshire Property Company Limited v HMRC* TC04286. HMRC unsuccessfully argued that the taxpayer ought to have sought independent advice on the disclosure of a tax avoidance scheme rather than rely on the firm that advised it on the matter. The Tribunal held that it was quite reasonable for the taxpayer not to have done so.

3.5.4 Penalties – amounts

In cases not covered by the 'reasonable care let-out' the maximum penalties (or 'starting point') are as follows:

Action	Penalty
Careless action	30% potential lost revenue
Deliberate but not concealed	70% potential lost revenue
Deliberate and concealed	100% potential lost revenue

3.5.5 Discounts for disclosure

A taxpayer may identify an error and volunteer it to HMRC. Alternatively he or she may be challenged ('prompted') and decide to come clean. The following discounts may be allowed:

Maximum penalty	Disclosure	Minimum penalty (irreducible minimum)
30%	unprompted	0%
30%	prompted	15%
70%	unprompted	20%
70%	prompted	35%
100%	unprompted	30%
100%	prompted	50%

3.5.6 Discounts depend on the quality of disclosure

The above discounts are not automatic, they depend upon the quality of the taxpayer's disclosure which is, essentially, how co-operative the taxpayer has been.

The HMRC manual tells its staff to take into account three elements:

- **telling** HMRC what is wrong;
- giving HMRC reasonable **help;**
- allowing HMRC **access** to records.

The discount between the maximum and minimum penalty is then allocated as follows:

Element of disclosure	Percentage
Telling HMRC	30%
Helping	40%
Giving access	30%

3.5.7 Penalties for careless mistakes can be suspended

A penalty may be suspended as part of a process of encouraging a person to improve his or her reporting systems. Suspended penalties then become payable if further careless mistakes arise during the suspension period.

3.5.8 Accepting an under-assessment

Knowingly accepting an under-assessment of tax by HMRC is an offence within the 'careless' category and up to a 30% penalty may be charged.

3.5.9 Appeals against penalties

A taxpayer may appeal against a penalty (and/or request an internal review). The appeal will be heard by the Tax Tribunal.

3.5.10 Naming and shaming

HMRC is allowed to publish the names of persons who incur penalties for serious irregularities. This can apply to companies and individuals who have deliberately understated more than £25,000 of tax. The details published will include not only the relevant names and amounts, but also addresses, the business sector, periods affected and any other information considered appropriate by HMRC to make clear the person's identity.

Those who make a full unprompted disclosure or a full prompted disclosure within the required time cannot be named in this way. This is on the basis that the penalty is reduced for the quality of the disclosure to the full extent permitted.

Those who have deliberately evaded a much smaller figure, just £5,000 of tax, will be monitored by HMRC (see 3.6 below) and required to submit returns for up to the following five years showing more detailed tax information, for example, detail of the nature and value of any balancing adjustments within business accounts.

> **Tax notes**
>
> Minimise penalties by co-operating fully in an investigation. Don't make matters worse by digging your heels in if you are in the wrong.

3.6 OTHER INITIATIVES

HMRC has, in recent years, stepped up its efforts to monitor areas it regards as posing risks to the Exchequer, whether in the form of common errors, inadequate records, or more serious and deliberate evasion.

The first initiative is the provision of 'toolkits' covering a number of areas of tax. These toolkits were originally intended for advisers, however, since they only cover certain aspects of each specific area, and given HMRC's views rather than the strict legal position, they will mainly be of use to unrepresented taxpayers to provide general guidance on areas of error that HMRC frequently sees in returns and set out the steps that can be taken to reduce those errors. The toolkits will be updated at least annually, but remember, if your affairs are complex, you are likely to save money in the long run by paying a tax adviser to look after your tax affairs.

HMRC also created 'products' which are suitable for the self-employed, sole traders and small businesses:

- **Keeping records for business** – this is a basic guide, which includes details of where to obtain further information.
- **A general guide to keeping records for your tax return** – this provides more detailed guidance on record-keeping covering what type of records you may have to keep, common problems and examples for different types of business.
- **How to set up a basic record-keeping system** – this guidance gives examples of spreadsheets and information about setting up a record-keeping system.
- **Finding out what records you should be keeping** – the guidance details the records you need to keep and will help you assess how well you are keeping them. If you are thinking of starting a business the guidance provides you with a checklist. If you are established it will give feedback and advice on any improvements you may need to make.

HMRC has commenced pilot business record checks. If HMRC contacts you to arrange a record check, it is likely that it regards your business as being at high risk of having inadequate records, although it will carry out a small number of random checks. It is expected that HMRC officers will visit your business premises to carry out the record checks and they will seek to make an appointment within the following seven days to carry this out. However, some record checks may be carried out over the telephone.

HMRC has legal powers enabling its inspectors to visit your business premises and in some circumstances it does not even require your permission do to so. Therefore, it is vital that you take this process seriously and notify your adviser as soon as you are contacted by HMRC. It should be noted that, although a factsheet issued with the letters in the pilot project refers to the possibility of penalties for poor records, HMRC has confirmed that no such penalties will be levied at all during the pilot period.

It remains to be seen what HMRC's attitude to record-keeping standards will be. It may be that some inspectors – who are of course not accountants or generally experienced in running a business – stick to a rigid checklist of what sort of records ought (in HMRC's opinion) to be kept for a business of a particular size. However, it is hoped that inspectors will be more practical than this and take account of what records are strictly needed for each business in question.

In the consultation document HMRC recognised that a simple 'money in' and 'money out' record may be all that is needed for many small businesses. Examples were given of traders who simply put all receipts into a box, not necessarily knowing which of the expenses were capital, disallowable or deductible as revenue, to be sorted out later, perhaps by the business's accountant. That was described as sufficient, on the basis that those records were capable of being turned into a correct and complete return of taxable business profits. Your adviser will be able to help you tidy up your records and get things in order before a records check visit takes place and, if you wish, can be on hand during the visit to protect your interests. Even if HMRC just wants to do a record check over the phone, it is important to contact a suitably qualified professional for guidance before the check takes place: a telephone interview with HMRC could still lead to a tax penalty.

3.6.1 Deliberate defaulters

HMRC is also monitoring what it refers to as 'deliberate defaulters'. Deliberate defaulters are taxpayers who have deliberately evaded tax in the past, whether by failing to make returns or by deliberately making incorrect entries on returns. HMRC will notify taxpayers who it intends to monitor in this way and tell them what obligations they will have to meet. Those individuals who trigger the rules will be required to supply additional information with their SA returns. This additional burden can last for up to five years and is unlikely to last for less than two.

Whilst in the programme (which HMRC refers to by the acronym of MDD) defaulters will be closely monitored to ensure that all tax obligations are being fully met. Where there is any failure to meet and maintain those obligations or HMRC considers the taxpayer presents a high risk to the Exchequer, further compliance activity will be undertaken in accordance with HMRC's new inspection and information powers. Any further failures to meet tax obligations or continuing deliberate defaults are likely to result in the imposition of penalties and may ultimately lead to criminal proceedings being taken against the defaulter.

3.6.2 Payment of tax in cases involving tax avoidance schemes

Payment of tax can be required from taxpayers involved in planning arrangements which HMRC believes should fail as a result of principles established in related court decisions.

In 2014, HMRC issued accelerated payment notices to some 33,000 individual taxpayers and 10,000 companies, the majority relating to schemes disclosed under the DOTAS regulations.

3.6.3 Dishonest agents

Legislation introduced in FA 2012 allows HMRC to issue a tax agent with a conduct notice if it has determined that they have engaged in dishonest conduct. This notice would be subject to appeal.

Subject to prior approval by the First-tier Tribunal, HMRC would be able to issue a File Access Notice requiring production of the working papers of tax agents found to have engaged in dishonest conduct. Where working papers are no longer in the power or possession of the tax agent, HMRC would be able to request these from a third party.

A civil penalty for dishonest conduct can be imposed of up to £50,000. In cases where full disclosure was not made, HMRC is able to publish details of the penalised tax agent.

3.6.4 Liechtenstein Disclosure Facility

There are special arrangements which remain open until December 2015 for those with accounts or other assets held in Liechtenstein (the Liechtenstein disclosure facility). This provides an opportunity for significant tax savings in certain circumstances. The reason for this is that it was negotiated directly between Liechtenstein and HMRC so its terms are unusual and bespoke rather than general in nature.

A key principle of the Liechtenstein Disclosure Facility (LDF) is that Liechtenstein financial intermediaries (such as banks) must identify any clients who may have a tax liability in the UK, for example if a UK address is somehow linked to the account in question. Those persons must then register for and use the LDF (assuming there is a UK tax problem) otherwise the bank must cease acting. Anyone with an account in Liechtenstein who is already fully UK tax compliant must provide an accountant's certificate to that effect; otherwise the Liechtenstein bank or other financial intermediary must again cease to act entirely.

If anyone has tax to declare that is linked to an offshore account but did not use the previous (now closed) facilities, it may still be possible to use the LDF even if there is currently no link with Liechtenstein. There are various complexities to consider before ascertaining if the beneficial terms of the LDF will be available but, in principle, a Liechtenstein presence can be validly created in order to make a disclosure under the LDF.

If you have not disclosed taxable income, you should take advantage of this facility because much more severe penalties will be imposed if your transgressions emerge later, particularly if they come to light as a consequence of an HMRC investigation, potentially up to 200% under the provisions in FA (No. 1) 2010.

3.6.5 UK/Switzerland Agreement on unpaid tax

The UK and Switzerland entered into an agreement whereby a withholding tax was used from 2013 to clear certain unpaid taxes relating to Swiss bank accounts and certain other assets owned by UK passport holders. The withholding tax did not apply if:

- the individual could show that he or she was not resident in the UK; or
- he or she agreed to the existence of all his or her Swiss accounts being disclosed to HMRC; or
- he or she was not domiciled in the UK and made no remittances to the UK.

If none of these let-outs applied, a withholding was made automatically of between 21% and 41% of the value of the Swiss account as at 31 December 2010. The actual percentage was determined by the length of time that the account has been in existence.

Now that this has been paid, the funds are 'cleared' and no further income tax, capital gains tax, IHT or VAT will be due.

Income earned in future years on Swiss accounts that are not disclosed will suffer withholding at the following rates:

- capital gains 28%,
- dividends 40%,
- interest 48%.

3.6.6 Disclosure facilities for Isle of Man and Channel Islands

From 1 October 2016, the Revenue Authorities in the Isle of Man, Guernsey and Jersey will exchange information with HMRC. In the meantime, there is a disclosure facility which allows taxpayers to settle arrears for a fixed penalty of 10% for years up to 2007–08 and 20% for subsequent years.

3.6.7 Let property campaign

HMRC is operating a let property campaign, which is an opportunity for landlords who owe tax through letting out residential property, in the UK or abroad, to get up to date with their tax affairs under the best possible terms.

The let property campaign is aimed at residential property landlords, ranging from those that have multiple properties to those with single rentals who may owe tax, whether through misunderstanding the rules or deliberate evasion. These landlords are invited to tell HMRC about any unpaid tax on rents, and pay what they owe, including any penalties and interest due. Penalties will be lower than if HMRC come to them first.

The guidance and disclosure form are available at https://www.gov. uk/government/publications/let-property-campaign-your-guide-to-making-a-disclosure

3.7 REMISSION OF TAX BY HMRC

(ESC A19)

HMRC's policy is to give up arrears of tax that have arisen because of its failure to make proper and timely use of information supplied. Remission of tax in this way is normally available where the taxpayer could have reasonably believed that his or her tax affairs were in order and was notified of the arrears more than 12 months after the end of the tax year in which HMRC was informed. Alternatively, in the case of an over-repayment, it is available if the taxpayer was notified after the end of the tax year following the year in which the repayment was made.

3.8 ERROR OR MISTAKE RELIEF (OVERPAYMENT RELIEF)

(s 33 and Schedule 1AB TMA 1970 inserted by Schedule 52, FA 2009)

Sometimes errors are made against the taxpayer and relief can be claimed against any over-assessment to income tax or CGT owing to an error or mistake in a return. However, relief does not extend to an error or mistake in a claim included in the return. Relief will not be available on the grounds of an alleged error in the basis of computation of liability if the return was made on the basis of, or in accordance with, the practice generally prevailing at the time when the return was made.

The term 'error or mistake' includes errors of omission such as the non-deduction of an admissible expense, errors of commission (eg computational or arithmetical errors), errors arising from a misunderstanding of the law and erroneous statements of fact.

The relief is also available for an error or mistake in a partnership statement where the partners claim that their self-assessments were excessive. If the claim results in an amendment to the partnership statement, any necessary amendments to the partners' individual self-assessments are made by notice by the Board of HMRC.

The rules at s 33 TMA were replaced by Schedule 52 FA 2009 in relation to claims made on or after 1 April 2010. The relief is now called overpayment relief. New Schedule 1AB goes into much more prescriptive detail than its predecessor. The gist of the rules has, however, not changed, although eight prescribed circumstances are now listed where such claims will not be entertained. These include cases where the taxpayer knew (or ought to have known) that relief could have been claimed before a certain period expired (such as the tax return amendment window or the time limit to appeal against an assessment) but did not do so.

Relief may be claimed within four years of the tax year to which the return relates.

The FA 2013 amended the legislation on overpayment relief to ensure that:

- a claim will not be prevented by prevailing practice if tax has been charged contrary to EU law;
- the time limit in all mistake cases runs from the period of the mistake.

3.9   EQUITABLE LIABILITY

When HMRC has sought to collect unpaid tax on income and gains for back years, it has sometimes allowed reliefs even though claims have not been made by the appropriate deadlines. This practice was concessionary and was set to cease from 1 April 2010 but it now continues on a statutory basis.

3.10 COMPLAINTS AND COMPENSATION

A taxpayer who is not happy with the way he or she has been treated by HMRC is entitled to complain. In this first instance, it is recommended that the complaint be raised with the person or officer who has been dealing with the case to see if matters can be resolved before entering into the formal complaints procedure. If matters cannot be resolved (or if the complainant does not want to approach the officer who has been working the case) the complaint will be referred to a complaints handler. If this proves unsatisfactory, the complaint should be raised with the Adjudicator; failing that, the case could be referred through the taxpayer's local MP to the independent Parliamentary Ombudsman. Further details of how to complain and who to contact are provided in leaflet C/FS Complaints (www.hmrc.gov.uk/factsheets/complaints-factsheet.pdf), the complaints fact sheet.

If HMRC makes a mistake or causes unreasonable delay, the taxpayer is entitled to an apology, an explanation of what went wrong and, if appropriate, details of the steps taken to ensure the mistake does not happen again. If reasonable and possible, HMRC will also have the mistake corrected.

In addition, the taxpayer may receive some form of financial redress such as the payment of costs incurred by the taxpayer; a (small) payment to reflect the worry and distress caused; and waiving of interest. The redress payments are ex-gratia and HMRC is under no legal obligation to pay them.

3.11 REVENUE ADJUDICATOR

If you are dissatisfied with the treatment you receive from HMRC and have exhausted HMRC's own complaints procedure you can ask an independent body to investigate your complaint. The matter should be referred to:

> The Adjudicator's Office, PO Box 10280, Nottingham NG2 9FF; Tel: 030 0057 1111; Fax: 030 0057 1212; www.adjudicatorsoffice.gov.uk.

If this fails you can ask your Member of Parliament to refer the case to the Parliamentary and Health Service Ombudsman (www.ombudsman.org.uk).

3.12 HMRC RULINGS

There are two types of HMRC rulings: post-transaction and advance rulings.

3.12.1 Post-transaction rulings

Post-transaction rulings are rulings on the application of tax law to a specific transaction after it has taken place. Although ultimately a matter for the courts, HMRC will consider itself bound by its rulings unless material information is withheld.

The following information has to be submitted before a ruling can be obtained:

- the taxpayer's name and tax reference number;
- full particulars of the transaction or event in question;
- copies of all relevant documents with the relevant parts or passages identified;
- the taxpayer's opinion of the tax consequences of the particular transaction along with reasons for that opinion;
- an explanation of the particular point(s) of difficulty that led to the request;
- details of what sections of the Taxes Acts, case law, extra-statutory concessions or statements of practice are considered to be relevant;
- when submitting an application for a transaction for which there is also the disclosure of an avoidance scheme which covers all or part of the transaction, it is important that explicit mention is made of any related disclosures, preferable by including a copy of the disclosure or, where available, by reporting the allocated DOTAS scheme reference number;
- a statement that, to the best of the taxpayer's knowledge and belief, the facts given are correct and all relevant facts have been disclosed;
- full details, including tax reference numbers, of any other parties involved;
- if advice on HMRC's interpretation of tax law is sought, the taxpayer must make it clear that he or she is seeking considered guidance and say how he or she intends to use it, for example by publishing it.

> **Tax notes**
>
> After a tax return is filed, a ruling will only be given up to the deadline for HMRC opening an enquiry. Make use of the post-transaction rulings procedure before you need to file your return so that when you file that particular aspect has been agreed in advance. For example, you may want to agree the value of unquoted shares at the time that you acquired them if that value determines your tax liability under the employment income provisions. Or if you have sold shares in a private company, you may need confirmation that the gain qualifies for entrepreneurs' relief.

3.12.2 Advance clearances

HMRC also has a system for giving clearances and advance transactions rulings to 'business customers'. HMRC aims to provide some certainty for businesses and will, normally within 28 days, provide clearances on areas of material uncertainty arising within four Finance Acts of the introduction of any new legislation (although for years – like 2010–11 – where there is more than one Finance Act, by concession HMRC will provide clearances on areas of material uncertainty arising in Finance Acts for the last four years). Older legislation will also be considered where there is material uncertainty around the tax outcome of a real issue of commercial significance to the business itself, determined by reference to the scale of the business and the impact of the issue upon it.

Similar details to those noted above for non-business clearances must be provided.

3.12.3 Annual statements

Taxpayers receive an annual statement showing how much tax has been deducted from their earnings each tax year and providing a breakdown of how their tax contribution has been spent (for example, on the NHS and welfare payments).

4

EMPLOYMENT INCOME

This chapter contains the following sections:

(1) Basis of assessment
(2) How tax is collected
(3) Allowable expenses
(4) Benefits-in-kind
(5) Company cars
(6) Free use of assets
(7) Beneficial loans
(8) Living accommodation
(9) Miscellaneous benefits
(10) Share incentives
(11) Options to acquire gilts
(12) Options to acquire company assets
(13) Golden hellos
(14) Restrictive covenants
(15) Redundancy payments
(16) Golden handshakes, other termination payments and continuing benefits
(17) Dividends
(18) Designing a 'tax efficient' remuneration package
(19) Specific occupations and trades
(20) Losses

4.1 BASIS OF ASSESSMENT

4.1.1 Introduction

An individual who holds an office or employment is taxed under the Income Tax (Earnings and Pensions) Act (ITEPA) 2003.

Employment income is taxed according to the residence status of the individual concerned. The rules are set out in Table 4.1.

Table 4.1 – Different treatment according to residence/domicile of employee

Individual resident in the UK: tax is due on total remuneration (s 15 ITEPA 2003).

Individual not resident in the UK: tax is due on total remuneration for duties performed in the UK (s 27 ITEPA 2003).

Individual who has recently become resident in the UK where the duties are performed outside the UK: the remittance basis applies for remuneration for overseas workdays where the individual has not been resident in the UK for three years (see 34.4).

Individual resident but not domiciled in the UK where all the duties are performed abroad ('foreign earnings', see 35.4). Tax is due on earnings brought into or enjoyed in the UK (s 26 and s 22 ITEPA 2003).

The remainder of this chapter concentrates on UK resident employees who are taxed under s 15 ITEPA 2003. See Chapter 35 for the taxation of non-UK domiciled individuals.

4.1.2 Receipts basis

(s 10 ITEPA 2003)

The amount that is assessable for a tax year is the amount of earnings chargeable in any year.

4.1.3 Date remuneration is deemed to be received

(s 18 ITEPA 2003)

Special provisions define the date that an individual is deemed to receive remuneration as the earlier of:

(1) the date when payment is actually made; and
(2) the time when the employee becomes entitled to payment.

In the case of directors, the date can be earlier than above, in that payment is deemed to take place on the earliest of (1) and (2); and

(3) the date that sums are credited to the director in the company's accounts or records (whether or not there is any restriction on the right to draw those sums); or
(4) the end of a period if the director's earnings for a period are determined before the period has expired; or
(5) if earnings are not determined until after the end of a period the date when the amount is determined.

The employer is required to operate Pay As You Earn (PAYE) when payment is deemed to have taken place (see 21.1).

4.1.4 Amounts deducted in arriving at pay

(s 713 ITEPA 2003)

Contributions to a payroll giving scheme ('give as you earn') are deducted from an individual's salary in arriving at taxable pay for both PAYE and for assessment purposes. Note that NIC is based on pay before such amounts are deducted (see 23.1).

4.1.5 Distributions from qualifying employee trusts

Finance Act 2014 introduced an exemption from income tax for any relevant bonus payment made after 30 September 2014 to an employee by a qualifying employee-owned company that meets the relevant conditions. A relevant bonus will be a cash award other than regular salary or wages that is paid to all employees on equal terms, although bonuses can be set by an employer by reference to a percentage of salary or length of service or hours worked. The exemption is subject to an annual cap of £3,600 per employee for each qualifying company.

4.2 HOW TAX IS COLLECTED

4.2.1 Tax deductions under PAYE

Earnings paid to directors and employees are subject to PAYE. Earnings for this purpose are all cash payments (salary, wages, bonus, etc) and a limited number of benefits and expense payments.

PAYE code numbers

HMRC issues code numbers that determine the amount of PAYE deductions. Such code numbers are based on the latest information available to HMRC and are intended to ensure that the amounts withheld under PAYE approximate closely to an individual's actual liability. Nevertheless, deduction of tax under PAYE is provisional in that if the actual liability exceeds the amount withheld under PAYE, HMRC may collect the balance either by increased PAYE deductions in subsequent years or by raising an assessment and similarly, overpayments can be recovered by the individual. HMRC may issue 'K codes' under which increased deductions may be taken, of up to 50% of an individual's pay. The principle behind K codes is that notional pay is added to an employee's actual pay, and PAYE is operated accordingly. This is intended to cover the situation where taxable benefits-in-kind exceed a person's allowances.

What the letters in your code mean

L Basic personal allowance.

M one of a married couple who receives the transfer of unused allowances (see 12.2)

N one of a married couple who has surrendered surplus allowances

P Full personal allowance for those aged 65–74.

Y Full personal allowance for those aged 75+.

T Any other items HMRC needs to collect through a tax code or if someone asks HMRC not to use any of the other tax code letters listed. This has also been in use from 2010–11 for those expected to lose some or all of their personal allowances because income is expected to exceed £100,000.

K Total allowances in a code are less than the total deductions. Sections PAYE11095 and PAYE11096 in HMRC's PAYE Manual explain how a K coding works.

BR Tax deducted at the basic rate, currently 20%.

D0 Tax deducted at a flat rate of 40%.

D1 Tax is deducted at the additional rate of tax – currently 45% (most commonly used for a second job or pension)

NT No Tax, usually used for non-UK residents being paid from the UK.

How HMRC tax code is worked out

Step one

Your tax allowances are added up (in most cases this will just be your personal allowance and any blind person's allowance; in some cases it may include certain job expenses).

Step two

Income you have not paid tax on (for example, untaxed interest or part-time earnings) and any taxable employment benefits are added.

Step three

The total amount of income you have not paid any tax on ('deductions') is taken away from the total amount of tax allowances. The amount you are left with is the total tax-free income you are allowed in a year.

Step four

To arrive at your tax code, the amount of tax-free income you are left with is divided by ten and added to the letter that fits your circumstances.

As an example, the tax code 177L means that £1,770 must be taken away from your total taxable income after accounting for untaxed income etc.

How tax is worked out using this code 177L for 2015–16

Pay from employment or pension		£21,840
Minus tax free amount for the year		£1,770
Pay on which tax will be paid		£20,070
On £20,070 the tax payable is		
Basic rate 20%	=	£4,014.00
So tax to be paid in the year	=	£4,014.00

Tax notes

It is important that you pay attention to the tax code being operated against your monthly income to ensure that when you come to filing your tax form there are no surprises. Two areas to watch are as follows:

(1) You start a new job part way through a tax year and you do not have a form P45 from your previous employer and a form P46 is not filed. In previous years, your payroll department would have operated a basic rate (BR) tax code which would have resulted in an underpayment for a higher rate taxpayer and an overpayment for a basic rate taxpayer but rarely the right amount of tax being deducted. Your employer will be required to deduct tax using the 0T code on a non-cumulative basis. Tax code 0T will ensure that tax is deducted at the basic, higher and additional rates where necessary. This is likely to result in you overpaying tax until your code is corrected.

(2) You file an annual SA form but HMRC includes some of your investment income in the code to be operated against your earnings. Consider whether you want to be taxed on this basis, ie paying tax via your coding, or if you would prefer to continue to pay tax via the self-assessment system.

4.2.2 Collection of tax outside PAYE

Where a person is employed by a foreign employer that has no place of business in the UK, PAYE is not normally operated. Tax is payable by the employee as if he or she were self-employed, ie two payments on account based on the previous year's tax bill plus a balancing payment on 31 January following the end of the tax year.

4.2.3 Self-assessment

An employee has until 31 January following the year of assessment to file a return and pay any additional tax due (ie for 2014–15, by 31 January 2016). If the employee wants the tax underpaid (of up to £2,000) to be collected by way of an adjustment in the code operated against his or her salary, he or she is requested to file a paper return by 31 October following the year of assessment (ie for 2014–15, by 31 October 2015). The 31 October filing date is extended to 31 December (ie for 2014–15, by 31 December 2015) for individuals who file their returns online.

Where the taxpayer fails to notify HMRC, and pays any tax due by 31 January, interest, penalties and surcharges may arise (see Chapter 2).

4.3 ALLOWABLE EXPENSES

4.3.1 Strict conditions must be satisfied for expenses to be allowed

(s 327 ITEPA 2003)

The rules governing the amounts that may be deducted for tax purposes from remuneration subject to tax as employment income are extremely strict. The legislation provides for a deduction to be made only in respect of expenses that are wholly, exclusively and necessarily incurred in the performance of the duties of the employment or office.

Wholly, exclusively . . .

The courts have held that the following expenses are **not** deductible for employment income purposes because they are not deemed to have been incurred wholly and exclusively in the performance of the employment duties:

(1) meal expenses paid out of meal allowances;
(2) the rent of a telephone installed for business reasons but not used wholly and exclusively in the performance of duties;
(3) the cost of domestic assistance where the taxpayer's wife is employed;
(4) the cost of looking after a widower's children; and
(5) the cost of ordinary clothing.

. . . and necessarily . . .

The situation often arises that the employer has reimbursed the expense because it is regarded as essential. This is helpful, but not conclusive. HMRC will assess the amount paid to a director or P11D employee (see 4.4.2) but may then seek to disallow the individual's expenditure claim on the grounds that it is not *necessary*. Two of the leading cases won by HMRC involved reimbursed expenditure by journalists on newspapers and other periodicals. The point at issue was whether reading such newspapers was part, or inherent in the performance, of the journalists' duties. The key point here is that it is not the employer's decision that determines the case. The employer may be fully prepared to reimburse the expenditure but HMRC may still argue that it fails to meet the very strict guidelines on what constitutes 'necessary'.

... in the performance of the duties

Other expenses were rejected on the grounds that they were not incurred in the performance of the duties of the relevant employment:

(1) employment agency fees (although entertainers specifically are now entitled to claim a deduction for such expenses of up to 17.5% of their earnings);
(2) a headmaster's course to improve background knowledge;
(3) an NHS registrar's costs of attending training courses that had to be completed so that he could apply for a position as a consultant (*HMRC* v *Decadt* [2007] ER (D) 139)
(4) an articled clerk's examination fees;
(5) travelling costs from home to the place where the employment duties were performed;
(6) expenses paid out of living allowances given to an employee when working away from home;
(7) expenditure by a rugby league player on diet supplements to improve and maintain his fitness (*Ansell* v *Brown* 2001 STC 1166);
(8) expenses incurred by a supply teacher in keeping a room at her home for preparation of lessons, marking, etc (*Warner* v *Prior* 2003 SpC 353);
(9) expenses incurred by a Civil Servant who was allowed to work from home in Norfolk but was required to travel to the department's offices in Leeds each week (*Kirkwood* v *Evans* 2002 STC 231).

Cases where the taxpayer has succeeded

There have been cases where travelling expenses have been allowed because the courts were satisfied that a person's duties started as soon as he or she left home. For example, in *Gilbert* v *Hemsley* [1981] STC 703, a plant-hire company director's duties involved him using his home as a base and travelling to various sites. The court held that once he left home he was travelling in the course of his duties. Similarly, in *Pook* v *Owen* (1969) 45 TC 571 a doctor was 'on call' and his duties started once he was telephoned by the hospital to ask him to attend.

In *HMRC* v *Banerjee* [2010] EWCA Civ 843, a trainee doctor's course costs were allowed because the expenditure on training was held to be incurred solely for the purpose of meeting the requirements of her employment contract.

4.3.2 Expenses that *are* allowable

(ss 333–360 ITEPA 2003)

Certain expenses are specifically allowable, such as the cost of professional subscriptions to an approved body that is relevant to the individual's employment (eg the annual subscription to the Institute of Chartered Accountants or The Law Society – see www.hmrc.gov.uk/list3/list3.pdf). Also, flat rate expenses are given to employees in certain industries to cover expenditure on tools, overalls, special clothing, etc.

Tax notes

HMRC publishes a list of approved bodies whose subscriptions qualify as allowable expenses.

Despite the very restrictive rules outlined in 4.3.1, you may be able to secure a deduction if you pay interest on a loan applied to purchase equipment used in the course of your employment (eg a computer or a fax machine at your home that you use for business purposes). See Helpsheet 340.

In addition to claiming a deduction for loan interest, relief may be due for expenses such as running costs and (in the case of a fax machine) the line rental. Capital allowances may also be due, subject to restrictions if the equipment is used for private purposes as well as for your employment.

At one time, directors or employees could not obtain tax relief for expenditure on items such as directors' and officers' liability insurance, or professional indemnity insurance. Relief from tax and NIC is now specifically due for such premiums. Moreover, tax relief is also available where an employee has to meet his or her own uninsured liability.

The relief for insurance or payment of uninsured liabilities is also available to former employees who incur such expenses within a six-year period after the year in which the employment ceased.

4.4 BENEFITS-IN-KIND

There are two ways in which tax may be charged on benefits:

- FA 2011 provisions on disguised remuneration;
- the general provisions for taxing benefits provided by reason of employment.

4.4.1 Disguised remuneration

Particular care should be taken where benefits are provided, or assets or loans are made available, via a third party such as a trust, as the legislation on disguised remuneration may apply rather than the normal benefit-in-kind provisions. If the disguised remuneration legislation applies, not only will the tax charge be accelerated, it may also be substantially increased as the charge will be on the full capital value of what has been made available, rather than an annual 'usage' value. The disguised remuneration provisions are considered in brief in Chapter 5.

These provisions are extremely complex and if you think you might be affected, it would be advisable to take specialist professional advice, as any errors could prove very costly.

General provisions for taxing benefits in kind

4.4.2 Directors and 'higher paid' employees

(s 201 ITEPA 2003)

For 2016–17 and subsequent years, an employer will be required to submit form P11D in respect of all employees who may then be assessed on the cost to the employer of benefits-in-kind received by them.

For 2015–16 and earlier years, an employee falls within the PIID category only where remuneration, together with benefits and reimbursed expenses, is paid at the rate of £8,500+ pa or where they are directors (see below). Such employees formerly were called 'higher paid' employees!

Example

> A person whose employment began on 1 January 2015 and who had received a salary of £2,000 and reimbursed expenses of £200 by 5 April 2015 would be within the P11D category as the total amount of £2,200 would give an annual rate greater than £8,500.

All reimbursed expenses and other benefits have to be reported on form P11D and count towards the £8,500 pa limit (even though they may be validly incurred for business purposes and ultimately no taxable benefit-in-kind arises) unless a dispensation has been agreed by HMRC (see 4.4.4).

Directors are normally within the P11D regime, regardless of whether their remuneration reaches or exceeds the £8,500 pa limit. Furthermore, individuals who control a company's affairs and take management decisions may be treated as directors, even if they do not hold a formal position with the company and may have another title or job description within the company.

4.4.3 Reporting benefits on form P11D

An employer must provide the employee with details of the taxable amounts for benefits shown on his or her form P11D. This must be done before 6 July following the tax year unless the employee had left employment before the end of the tax year (in which case the employer must provide the information within 30 days of the former employee requesting him or her to do so). The P11D must include the cost of benefits provided by third parties where these were arranged by the employer.

Some employers tax benefits-in-kind via the payroll (in a horrible mutilation of the English language, this is commonly known as 'payrolling' benefits). However, unless prior agreement has been obtained from HMRC, they are currently still required to complete and submit forms P11D, otherwise penalties will be charged. Where employers have taxed some expenses and benefits for some or all of their employees via the payroll and file P11D information online, they are advised to telephone the Employer Helpline at least a week in advance of any online submission of forms P11D, advising HMRC that payrolling has taken place in that year, in order to avoid incorrect processing of the data (ie double charging!). The employer should then complete the *amount made good or from which tax deducted* box (where this box is available for the relevant benefit) and, separately on paper, submit P11D information for other payrolled benefits (where the *amount made good or from which tax deducted* box is not available). These separate P11Ds and lists must be clearly marked 'payrolled'. Form P11D(b) should then be completed as normal. Where paper returns are still being made, all relevant forms must be clearly marked 'payrolled' and form P11D(b) completed as normal.

4.4.4 Dispensations

HMRC may grant a dispensation so that certain reimbursed expenses that would not, in any event, give rise to a tax charge need not be reported on form P11D. This is useful in reducing administration and accounting work and, wherever possible, employers should apply for a dispensation. HMRC will set out expenses covered by it; any expenses not covered must still be reported. Any changes in the method of reimbursing expenses or scales of allowances must be notified to HMRC.

4.4.5 Benefits-in-kind provided by third parties

(s 265 ITEPA 2003)

It is not uncommon for wholesalers and distributors to offer benefits-in-kind to employees of retailers with whom they do business. Subject to certain *de minimis* rules, such benefits are taxable just as if they had been provided by the retailer him or herself. This can also apply in other situations.

However, non-monetary gifts costing no more than £250 received by an employee or his or her family from someone other than his or her employer are generally exempt from income tax. Likewise, no income tax liability usually arises on entertainment that an employee receives from a third party. These exemptions apply only where the gift or entertainment is not provided directly or indirectly by their own employer and, furthermore, where it is not provided as a reward for, or in recognition of, specific services done or to be done by the employee.

Where the third party benefits have not been arranged by the employer, the provider must give the employee details of any taxable benefits by 5 July following the tax year.

4.4.6 Benefits for a director's family

(s 201(2) ITEPA 2003)

A fundamental point is that an assessment may arise even though the director or employee has not personally received a benefit-in-kind. A tax liability may arise if a benefit is made available to a member of the director's or employee's household by reason of his or her employment. HMRC may argue that substantial benefits-in-kind enjoyed by a director's family are provided by reason of the director's employment even though the recipient may also be a company employee. HMRC is especially likely to argue this where a director's spouse or civil partner is employed by the company and receives abnormally large benefits-in-kind for an employee of that particular category.

The legislation defines an individual's family or household as his or her spouse or civil partner; children and their spouses or civil partners; parents, domestic staff, dependants and guests. Note that this definition does not include grandparents, brothers, sisters and grandchildren, although there can be situations where such relatives count as dependants.

4.4.7 Scholarships

(s 213 ITEPA 2003)

There is a general exemption for scholarships, but a scholarship provided to a child by reason of his or her parent's employment is normally treated as a benefit-in-kind of the parent. The benefit is taxable unless it can be shown that the scholarship was not awarded by reason of the employment and 75% of the scholarships awarded by the fund are awarded to children whose parents are not employed by the company.

See *S Kucha* v *HMRC* (TC02769) where a director was taxed on payments to his two sons whilst they were at university.

4.4.8 2014–15 and 2015–16 benefits that may result in a tax charge for non-P11D employees

The general rule for 2014–15 and 2015–16 is that employees not within the P11D category are assessable only on benefits capable of being converted into cash or on any benefits provided by an employer meeting an employee's personal liability. Table 4.2 sets out the position.

Table 4.2 – Treatment of benefits received by non-P11D employees

	Taxable	Non-taxable
Benefits capable of being turned to pecuniary account, ie convertible to cash	✓	
Luncheon vouchers*	✓	
Credit tokens and vouchers	✓	
Transport vouchers (ie any ticket, pass or other document or token intended to enable a person to obtain passenger transport services)	✓	
Living accommodation	✓	
Payment of employees' personal liabilities	✓	
Company cars		✓
Free use of assets		✓
Beneficial loans		✓
Medical insurance		✓

* The tax exemption for luncheon vouchers up to 15p per day was abolished from 6 April 2013.

4.4.9 All employees subject to P11D rules from 2016–17

From 6 April 2016, the distinction between P11D employees and non-P11D employees will be abolished – all employees will be subject to the P11D regime.

4.4.10 Tax treatment of specific benefits when received by a non-P11D employee in 2014–15 and 2015–16

Benefits capable of being converted into cash

Where the benefit is convertible into cash, the measure of assessable benefit is the amount of cash that could be realised. For example, an employee provided with a new suit by the employer would be taxable on its second-hand value.

Credit tokens and vouchers

(s 90 ITEPA 2003)

The taxable amount in respect of credit tokens and vouchers is the cost to the employer of providing them. Vouchers other than cheque vouchers are deemed to be taxable earnings as and when they are allocated to a particular employee, not when they are used by that employee.

Transport vouchers

(s 82 ITEPA 2003)

Specific legislation ensures that season tickets provided by employers are taxable. Once again, the measure of the assessable benefit is the cost to the employer of providing the ticket or voucher.

Living accommodation

(s 97 ITEPA 2003)

The assessable amount is the greater of the property's gross rateable value or the rent payable by the employer, less any amount made good by the employee. Following the abolition of domestic rates, estimated values are used for new or substantially altered properties. No assessable benefit arises where the employee occupies representative accommodation (see 4.4.11).

Payment of employee's personal liabilities

A liability arises where the employer has paid a personal liability of the employee. This would include such items as home heating, lighting bills and water rates, but special rules apply where the employee is in representative accommodation (see 4.4.11).

4.4.11 Benefits not taxable for any category of employees

There are certain benefits that are not usually taxable even for P11D employees. The most widely used tax-free benefits are as set out below.

Retirement benefits

As a general rule, payments by an employer to an approved occupational pension scheme to secure retirement benefits for an employee do not give rise to an income tax liability for that employee, unless the payment causes the lifetime allowance to be exceeded.

Payments by the employer into an 'unregistered' scheme are treated as payments to an employer funded retirement benefits scheme (EFRBS). Previously, no tax or NIC was payable on contributions into the scheme (but neither the employee nor the employer received tax relief on contributions). Instead, when relevant retirement benefits were paid out, the employee (or ex-employee) was subject to tax at his or her marginal rate at that time. Payments out could be free of NIC provided certain strict conditions were met. With the introduction of Part 7A ITEPA, such payments are likely to give rise to an immediate tax charge under the 'disguised remuneration' rules – see Chapter 5.

To secure approval, a registered pension scheme must be established for the sole purpose of providing 'relevant benefits' (ie pensions, death-in-service payments and widows' and dependants' pensions). The pension benefits payable by a registered scheme must not exceed certain limits. Pension schemes are covered in more detail in Chapter 26.

Luncheon vouchers

Non-transferable luncheon vouchers were exempt from income tax up to a limit of 15p per working day. This exemption was abolished from 6 April 2013.

Staff canteen and dining facilities

No taxable benefit-in-kind arises where the canteen, etc is available to all staff. Furthermore, the use of a separate room by directors and more senior staff does not prejudice this exemption, unless the meals provided are superior. HMRC also accepts that facilities provided by a hotel or restaurant for staff to 'eat in' may come within the definition of a 'canteen', provided that the meals are taken at a time or place when they are not being served to the public or where part of the restaurant or dining room is designated specifically as being for staff use only. This relief is available only where it is not linked to relevant salary sacrifice or flexible remuneration arrangements.

Where an employer provides meals in a canteen by giving employees a smart card which is topped up periodically by the employer, but to which the employee can also add funds, this is regarded as the provision of money rather than the provision of free or subsidised meals. Employers should operate PAYE and NIC in these circumstances.

Sports facilities

(s 261 ITEPA 2003)

No taxable benefit arises in respect of the use or availability of sports facilities owned by the employer. HMRC's view is that the exemption is not available for use of facilities that are available to the general public, eg under a corporate subscription to a sports club.

Medical check-ups

The provision of routine health checks or medical screening does not constitute a taxable benefit provided the check-ups are available to all employees or all those employees who have been identified in a health screening as requiring a medical check-up.

The exemption does not apply to payment for any medical treatment which follows such a check-up.

Eye tests and corrective glasses

Employers are required by law to pay for eye tests and corrective glasses where employees use computer screens. HMRC does not charge tax in these circumstances, whether the benefit is provided directly or through the provision of a voucher. However, where spectacles are for general use, but include a special prescription for VDU use, only a proportion of the cost relating to the special prescription will be exempt from tax.

Employee medical expenses

An exemption from income tax and NICs of up to £500 has been introduced for the provision of recommended medical treatment to help an employee return to work after a period of absence through sickness or injury. Relief covers the payment or reimbursement of treatment costs.

Workplace nurseries and crèches

Employees are exempt from income tax on the benefit derived from the use of a workplace nursery provided by the employer. The exemption applies only to nurseries run by employers alone or jointly with other employers or bodies, either at the workplace or elsewhere.

The provision by an employer of cash allowances to employees for childcare, or the direct meeting of an employee's childcare bills by an employer, are at present taxable benefits. An employer can provide a tax free benefit of up to £55 pw by either contracting with an approved childcarer or providing vouchers that the employee can use to pay an approved childcarer. This relief is not available where the benefit is provided through a salary sacrifice arrangement.

Pool cars

(s 167 ITEPA 2003)

No tax charge arises by reason of the use of a pooled car. A car qualifies as a pooled car only if all of the following conditions are satisfied:

(1) It is available for, and used by, more than one employee and is not used ordinarily by any one of them to the exclusion of the others.

(2) Any private use of the car by an employee is merely incidental to its business use.

(3) It is not normally kept overnight at or near the residence of any of the employees unless it is kept on the employer's premises.

These requirements are interpreted strictly. Employers need to be able to demonstrate that the conditions for the car to be a pool car have been met, for instance by keeping detailed mileage records to show when the car was used, by whom and for what journeys.

Note that a car only qualifies as a pooled car by reference to a tax year. There is a danger, therefore, in a car being taken out of pooled use and allotted to a specific employee towards the end of a tax year. As the car now no longer qualifies as a pooled car, any employee who has had the car available for private use during the same tax year may be assessed. So, if the car is ordinarily parked overnight near the home of one of the users, it will not qualify as a pooled car and creates a tax problem for any other employees who use it.

Emergency service vehicles

Emergency service workers in the fire, police and ambulance services are entitled to a specific exemption from the benefit charge which might otherwise arise from having to take their emergency vehicles home when on call.

Disabled employees' travel costs

Assistance with travelling costs between home and work is not taxable where it is given to disabled persons. This includes contributions towards the cost of travel by public transport. A car provided for travel between home and work is not taxed where:

- the employee is severely and permanently disabled; and
- the car has been specially adapted; and
- no private use is made other than travel between home and work.

'Green commuting' facilities

There is no taxable benefit in respect of:

- works buses with a seating capacity of nine or more;
- subsidies to public bus services, provided the employee pays the same fare as other members of the public;
- bicycles and cycle safety equipment made available for employees to get to and from work; and
- workplace parking for bicycles and motorcycles.

For employees who may need to shower and change clothes after arriving at the office because, for example, they cycle or run to work, tax is not chargeable on the free use by employees of changing and shower room facilities at an employer's premises, provided they are generally available to all employees. The employer can also currently provide breakfast on designated 'cycle to work days' without this constituting a taxable benefit, but this latter relief is to be abolished, following a period of consultation.

Late travel

There is also currently an exemption for the cost to an employer of providing transport to get an employee home (after 9 pm) where public transport is not available or it is not reasonable for the employer to expect the employee to use it. The exemption does not apply if the employee has to work late on a regular or frequent basis. There is an overall limit of 60 occasions on which transport can be provided.

The exemption has been extended to cover extra travel costs where car-sharing arrangements temporarily break down. This can include situations where the employee travels home at his or her normal time (eg where the employee whose car he or she shares is unexpectedly kept late).

The OTS has also recommended the abolition of this relief (following a period of consultation).

Employees' rail strike costs

(s 245 ITEPA 2003)

There is a statutory exemption covering the extra costs incurred by employees in getting to work because of a rail strike. The exemption (which may also cover the cost of hotel accommodation near the place of work) means that no tax is payable where the employer meets these expenses.

Homeworking allowance

An exemption is available for payments of up to £4 per week to cover extra expenses where the employee is required to work from home. This mirrors the amount that HMRC will accept for minor use of home by self-employed individuals. Alternatively, employees can reclaim the actual additional costs incurred in working at home but must be prepared to justify any claim.

Relocation expenses

(s 271 ITEPA 2003)

There is an exemption from tax on certain removal expenses borne by an employer when an employee has to change his or her residence to take up a new job within the same organisation, or to take up completely new employment. It is not necessary for the employee to sell his or her former home, but the exemption is available only where it would be unreasonable to expect him or her to work at the new location without moving closer to it. Abortive costs where a particular purchase falls through can be covered by the exemption provided the employee does eventually move house. The exemption is subject to a ceiling of £8,000 for any one move.

Qualifying expenses and benefits must fall into one of the six categories below:

- the employee's sale of their old residence;
- their purchase of a new residence;
- transporting the employee's belongings to the new residence;
- associated travel and subsistence costs;
- domestic goods for the new premises;
- bridging loans.

Payments made to compensate employees for losses on the sale of their former houses are regarded as taxable.

Sometimes employers provide guaranteed selling prices for the employee's former home, either directly or through a relocation agency. These will not come within the exemption.

Gifts by third parties

The exemption for non-monetary gifts by third parties covered at 4.4.5 applies to all categories of employees.

Long service awards

(s 323 ITEPA 2003)

Awards to directors and employees to mark long service are exempt provided the period of service is at least 20 years and no similar award has been given to the employee within the previous ten years. The gift must not consist of cash and the cost should not exceed £50 per year of service. The exemption also applies to gifts of shares in the company that employs the individual or in another group company.

Awards under suggestion schemes

(ss 321–322 ITEPA 2003)

Provided the employee is not engaged in research work, he or she may receive a tax-free payment under a firm's suggestion scheme. Making suggestions should not, however, be regarded as part of the employee's job. The size of the award should be within certain limits, ie £25 or less where the suggestion, although not implemented, has intrinsic value. Where the suggestion is implemented, the amount should be related to the expected net financial benefit to the employer. In any event, any excess over £5,000 is taxable.

Representative accommodation

(s 99 ITEPA 2003)

Living accommodation qualifies as representative accommodation and as such is not treated as a taxable benefit if any one of the following conditions is satisfied:

- it is necessary for the proper performance of the employee's duties that he or she should reside in the accommodation;
- the accommodation is provided for the better performance of the employee's duties and it is customary to provide accommodation for such employees; or
- the employee has to live in the accommodation because of a special threat to his or her security.

Under the first two conditions, if the employee is a director, the exemption is usually only available if he or she (together with his or her associates) holds 5% or less of the company's ordinary share capital and is a full-time working director.

HMRC strongly resists the application of the third exemption to any but the most clear-cut cases. However, in 2004, the Special Commissioners upheld a claim by the late Lord Hanson that he was entitled to the security exemption.

Where the employer pays for heating, lighting, repairs, maintenance, etc, the representative occupiers cannot be assessed, in respect of such benefits, on more than 10% of their earnings from the employment.

The main occupations that satisfy the conditions for exemption are:

- agricultural workers living on farms or agricultural estates;
- lock-gate and level-crossing gatekeepers;

- caretakers who live on the premises for which they are responsible: this only covers those with a genuine full time caretaking job who are on call outside normal working hours;
- stewards and greenkeepers who live on the premises they look after;
- managers of public houses who live on the premises;
- wardens of sheltered housing who live on the premises and are on call outside normal working hours;
- police officers and Ministry of Defence police;
- prison governors, officers and chaplains;
- clergymen and ministers of religion, unless engaged on administrative duties only;
- members of the armed forces;
- members of the Diplomatic Service;
- managers of newspaper shops that have paper rounds;
- managers of traditional off-licences (ie those with opening hours that are the same as for public houses);
- head teachers and teachers at boarding schools who have pastoral responsibility, if the accommodation is at or near the school;
- stable staff of racehorse trainers who live on the premises and certain key workers who live close to the stables.

In addition, provided that the accommodation is necessary for the better performance of their duties, the following two categories can also qualify

(1) veterinary surgeons who live near their practice; and
(2) managers of camping and caravan sites living on or near the premises.

Retraining

(ss 311–312 ITEPA 2003)

Where an employer pays the cost of a course undertaken by a full-time or part-time employee (or former employee) to provide him or her with skills for future employment elsewhere, that cost can be a deductible expense of the employer, and may not be a taxable benefit of the employee. The employee must have completed at least two years' service.

The exemption is normally dependent on the employee leaving his or her job no later than two years after completing the course.

Sandwich courses

(SP4/86, as revised in April 2005)

Where an employer releases an employee to take a full-time educational course at a university, technical college or similar educational institution that is open to the public at large, payments for periods of attendance may be treated as exempt from income tax. There are various conditions that attach to this exemption:

- the course must last for at least one academic year with an average of at least 20 weeks of full-time attendance; and
- the annual rate of payment including lodging, subsistence and travelling allowances, but excluding any tuition fees payable by the employee to the university must not exceed £15,480.

Where the rate of payment exceeds £15,480, the full amount is taxable; where the amount of payment is increased during a course, only subsequent payments are taxable.

Education and training

(ss 255–260 ITEPA 2003)

No tax charge arises on payments made to a provider in respect of the costs of providing 'qualifying education or training' for a fundable employee. Similar relief is available for payment or reimbursement of any incidental costs incurred wholly and exclusively as a result of the employee undertaking the course. The exemption is available only where participation is available on similar terms to all employees.

'Qualifying education or training' is education or training which qualifies for grants under the Learning and Skills Act 2000 and its Scottish equivalent. A fundable employee is one who holds an account qualifying under s 104 Learning and Skills Act 2000 or who is a party to arrangements under s 105 or s 106 of that Act.

4.4.12 Expenses relating to directors and P11D employees

This section deals with problem areas that arise regularly in practice where expenses are paid on behalf of directors and senior employees or where the employer reimburses them.

Travelling expenses

(ss 336–340 ITEPA 2003)

Travel between home and the ordinary place of work does not rank as business travel and therefore will be treated as a taxable benefit-in-kind if it is funded by the employer. Where an individual is 'on call' and assumes the responsibilities of the employment upon leaving home, it may be possible to argue that home to work travel is business, not private travel, but this applies only in exceptional cases. Other travelling expenses are not normally treated as a benefit-in-kind so long as the individual has a 'normal place of work' that he or she attends the majority of the time. The Special Commissioners decided in 2003 that site-based employees of an agency did not meet these requirements (*Phillips* v *Hamilton* 2003 SpC 366).

Where an employee performs incidental duties of the employment at another location and travels there directly to or from his or her home, the expense is usually allowable. However, if the temporary workplace is close to the normal place of work, this will not apply.

If an employee is obliged to attend a place of work for a period that it is reasonable to assume will exceed two years then that is regarded as a permanent workplace from the time that assumption is made.

To secure tax relief on reimbursed travelling expenses, the employee must keep adequate records so as to distinguish business from non-business travel. Ideally, expenses claims to the employer should show the actual cost of such travel and, if the employer is to obtain a dispensation, HMRC will need to be satisfied that such internal controls exist.

Approved Mileage Allowance Payments (AMAP)

There is a statutory scheme of flat-rate allowances for business mileage. The following rates apply.

	Per mile
Cars and vans:	
First 10,000 miles in tax year	45p
Each additional mile	25p
Passengers (including volunteers)	5p
Motorcycles	24p
Bicycles	20p

The employee cannot claim tax relief for interest on a loan used to buy his or her car.

Tax notes

Where an individual is required to use his or her own car for business, and he or she is reimbursed at less than the authorised rates, he or she can claim a deduction equal to the shortfall. Form P87 is designed to be used by employees who make such claims. You should keep a log of your business travel to back up your claim.

In addition to the mileage allowance payment, an employer can also pay up to 5p per passenger per mile free of tax and NICs for fellow employees, including volunteers, carried in the employer's or employee's car or van where the journey constitutes business travel for both driver and passengers. The employee cannot claim any relief if the employer does not pay the passenger rate.

Mileage allowances for business travel in a company car

Where an employer reimburses fuel costs relating to business mileage, the following rates may be paid tax free (rates published 1 June 2015).

	Petrol	*LPG*
1,400cc or less	12p	8p
1,401–2,000cc	14p	9p
Over 2,000cc	21p	14p

The diesel rates are:

1600cc or less	10p
1601–2000cc	12p
Over 2000cc	14p

These rates are normally reviewed twice a year with any changes taking effect on 1 June and 1 December and are published on the HMRC website shortly before the date of change. HMRC will also accept the figures in the table for VAT purposes though employers will need to obtain the relevant fuel receipts from employees in line with current legislation.

Employee car ownership schemes

HMRC has been reviewing employee car ownership schemes that take maximum benefit of the approved mileage allowances and this could lead to a more restrictive approach in future.

Using a bicycle for business

Employees can claim capital allowances on bicycles used for business travel. A tax-free cycling allowance of 20p per business mile can be paid. Where the employer pays less than this rate, the employee can claim a tax deduction for the difference.

Subsistence

HMRC's view is that it is strictly only the extra costs of living away from home that are allowable. If there are continuing financial commitments at home, the whole cost of living away from home is normally allowed. This concession is not available if the employee has no permanent residence, for example an unmarried person who normally lives in a hotel or club and who gives up that accommodation when away on a business trip. There is a specific exemption where an employee performs his or her duties wholly overseas and needs board and lodging abroad to do so.

Personal incidental expenses

There is a statutory exemption for employees' miscellaneous personal incidental expenses when they are required to stay away from home overnight on business. This exemption allows employers to meet expenses of up to £5 a night (£10 if overseas).

Benchmark scale rates for subsistence

HMRC has published benchmark scale rates for employees who incur subsistence expenses while travelling on business but are not away from home overnight. These rates apply only where the following conditions are satisfied:

- the travel must be in the performance of the employee's duties or to a temporary workplace;
- the employee should be absent from his or her normal workplace or home for a continuous period which either exceeds five or ten hours;
- the employee has incurred a cost on a meal after starting the journey.

The scale rates vary between £5 and £15.

Higher rates may be negotiated for a particular set of circumstances or actual sums validly incurred can be claimed instead of scale rates. However, if a higher rate is paid without such an agreement, HMRC says that the excess should be subject to PAYE tax and NIC.

For further details see www.hmrc.gov.uk/briefs/income-tax/brief2409.htm

Travel costs

Site-based employees

A deduction is allowed for the costs of travel to or from any place where attendance at that place is in the performance of the duties of a person's employment. The subsistence costs of site-based employees are also an allowable expense.

This is subject to certain conditions and in particular, if it is reasonable to assume that the worker will be based at the site for two years or longer, no relief is available.

Temporary absence from normal place of work

Where an employee is required to work temporarily at a place other than his or her normal workplace, the deductions for travel expenses described above are available.

Temporary relocation to another office, etc

HMRC has clarified the circumstances in which employees who are temporarily absent from their normal place of work can claim a deduction for travelling and subsistence expenses. Normally an employee is regarded as temporarily absent from his or her normal place of work if:

- the absence is not for more than 24 months; and
- the employee returns to the normal place of work at the end of the period.

If these conditions are satisfied, the employer can pay a subsistence allowance free of tax.

HMRC takes the view that an individual may also qualify if these conditions are expected to be satisfied at the outset but circumstances subsequently change. Relief is available for the period up to the time when it becomes clear that either condition will be breached.

There are special rules for subsistence allowances given to employees of overseas companies who are seconded to work in the UK for periods of up to two years. These rules are dealt with in 35.4.

Overseas travelling expenses

(s 370 ITEPA 2003)

Where some or all of the employment duties are performed abroad, travelling expenses to and from the UK in connection with the carrying out of such duties are specifically regarded as having been necessarily incurred in the performance of the overseas employment. It follows that if those expenses are reimbursed by the employer, no benefit-in-kind arises.

Where an employee travels between places where different jobs are performed, and one or more of these jobs is performed wholly or partly overseas, the expenses incurred in travelling overseas are also deemed to be necessarily incurred in performing the duties carried out overseas, so that once again no benefit-in-kind arises. In many cases, there is dual purpose in travelling and a taxable benefit-in-kind arises on the private element. Consequently, where travel expenses relate partly to a foreign holiday taken at the end of the business trip, there would be a taxable benefit-in-kind.

Similarly, a benefit-in-kind may be assessed on the expense relating to a spouse or civil partner who accompanies a director or employee on a trip unless this is necessary for business purposes.

When he or she is abroad, the maximum allowance to cover an employee's personal incidental expenses is £10 per night.

A director or employee who travels overseas must be able to substantiate a claim that expenses were necessarily incurred for business purposes by producing details of the expenses and the time spent away from home. A brief itinerary should be available where travel is undertaken within the overseas country or countries. HMRC expects that an employer will properly control expenditure and in certain cases may wish to inspect receipted bills or other vouchers.

HMRC has published benchmark scale rates that employers can use to reimburse accommodation and subsistence expenses incurred by employees while visiting various countries. See the HMRC Employment Manual at EIM05255.

Tax notes

Keep records of your travel costs to avoid arguments with HMRC. These records should include details of the purpose of each trip and the business undertaken.

Spouse's travelling and subsistence expenses

HMRC are rarely persuaded that there is a business need for a spouse or civil partner to accompany a director or employee. Where a spouse, civil partner or other member of the family accompanies a director abroad on a business trip, a Board minute stating that it is necessary for the person to accompany the director may assist in attempts to persuade HMRC that no benefit-in-kind arises. However, this is not generally sufficient in itself and it must be shown that the spouse, etc performed tasks that could not be carried out by the director.

It may be possible to show this if the spouse or civil partner has some practical qualification, for example an ability to speak the appropriate foreign language. A relative's expenses may also be allowable where the director or employee is in poor health and to travel alone would be impracticable or unreasonable. Where the individual's presence is for the purpose of accompanying his or her spouse or civil partner at business entertainment functions, the expenses of his or her trip may be disallowed in calculating the employer's tax liability under the entertainment legislation, even if the expenses are not included in the employee's tax liability.

Tax notes

Be prepared for HMRC to contend that the cost of your spouse or civil partner's travel is a benefit-in-kind and collect evidence to show that his or her accompanying you was necessary for business purposes.

Employees working overseas: family visits

(s 371 ITEPA 2003)

Where an employee is abroad for a continuous period of 60 days or more, there is an exemption for amounts borne by the employer in respect of the travelling expenses for visits by the employee's spouse and minor children. The exemption is available for up to two journeys by the same person in each direction in a tax year. There is no relief if the employee bears the expense personally.

Entertaining expenses and allowances

It is not uncommon for directors or employees to have a round-sum allowance to cover such things as travelling, subsistence and entertaining. In the case of travelling and subsistence, the allowance counts as the director's or employee's taxable income charged to PAYE and NIC, but a tax deduction may be claimed in respect of any part of the allowance that can be shown to have been spent for business purposes. It is very important to keep records that enable such claims to be substantiated. It may be better to dispense with entertainment allowances and reimburse the director or employee for properly substantiated expenditure, since no benefit-in-kind should then arise.

The situation is more complex for entertaining expenditure. If an employer reimburses entertaining expenditure or pays an amount that is specifically intended for client entertaining, the expense to the employer is disallowed for tax purposes. The reimbursement or allowance is entered on the director's or employee's P11D, but a deduction may be claimed for expenditure which is for genuine business purposes. If the payment relates to staff entertaining, then it will be a taxable benefit-in-kind and no deduction can be claimed.

Once again, if the employer pays a round-sum allowance for entertaining this must be charged to PAYE and NIC.

Where an employer does make payments for business-related expenses that will ultimately lead to a claim for a tax deduction for the employee, it is advisable to apply for a dispensation so that the expense does not need to be included on forms P11D. This will not normally be available in connection with round sum allowances.

4.5 COMPANY CARS

(s 114 ITEPA 2003)

4.5.1 Car benefits

A more environmentally friendly regime applies for calculating the cash equivalent of the benefit where an employer provides a car to an employee or member of his or her family or household. This is based on the published carbon dioxide (CO_2) emissions figure (in grams per kilometre) for a given car. Since 1 March 2001 that figure has appeared in the car log book. For cars registered between 1 January 1998 and 1 March 2001, the emissions figure can be obtained from a booklet published by:

The Vehicle Certification Agency
1 The Eastgate Office Centre
Eastgate Road
Bristol BS5 6XX
Website: www.vca.gov.uk

The emissions figure is rounded down to the nearest whole 5g below and is then converted to a percentage using the HMRC table (see Table 4.3). The maximum percentage to be applied to the list price of the car is 35%.

Table 4.3 – 2015–16 company car tax benefit-in-kind rates

Vehicle CO_2 g/km	Percentage of car's price taxed
1–50	5
51–75	9
76–94	13
95–99	14
100–104	15
105–109	16
110–114	17
115–119	18
120–124	19
125–129	20
130–134	21
135–139	22
140–144	23
145–149	24
150–154	25
155–159	26
160–164	27
165–169	28
170–174	29
175–179	30
180–184	31
185–189	32
190–194	33
195–199	34
200–204	35
205–209	36
210 or above	37

Cars registered before 1 January 1998 do not have a listed CO_2 emissions figure and the percentage for these vehicles continues to be based on engine size, but with no discounts for age or business use, as follows:

Engine size (cc)	Percentage of car's price taxed
0–1,400	15%
1,401–2,000	22%
2,001 and over	32%

Diesel cars

Add a 3% supplement to the relevant percentage scale charge to arrive at the amount of the car's price to be taxed. This is subject to a maximum charge based upon 37% of the car's list price. The supplement does not apply to diesel hybrid cars.

Automatic cars

These have higher CO_2 emissions.

Disabled employees who need to drive automatic cars

Where an employee is disabled (ie holds a 'blue badge') and can only drive an automatic car, the taxable benefit is taken as that of the 'equivalent manual car', ie the closest non-automatic variant of the car concerned.

Second cars

Second and subsequent cars are charged at the same rate as first cars.

4.5.2 Future changes

From 6 April 2016 the appropriate percentage (AP) used to calculate the company car benefit will increase from 5% to 7% for those company cars emitting 0–50g CO_2/km and from 9% to 11% for those emitting 51–75g CO_2/km.

In addition, the remaining APs will increase by a further 2%, to a maximum of 37%.

The 3% addition for diesel cars will cease to apply from 2016–17.

The Government has also announced that in 2018–19 the APs will again be increased by a further 2% per year, subject to a 37% maximum. However, the AP for company cars emitting 0–50g CO_2/km will increase from 9% to 13% and from 13% to 16% for 51–75g CO_2/km. The differential between these two bands will revert to 2% in 2019–20.

4.5.3 Reductions in the scale benefit

The scale figures are reduced proportionally where an employee was provided with a company car part way through the tax year, or where he or she ceases to have a company car. However, there is no reduction where the car was not available for use because it was being repaired, unless it was incapable of being used for at least 30 consecutive days. Contributions made by an employee for private use of the car can be deducted from the chargeable benefit.

> **Tax notes**
>
> If you are not using your company car while you are away on holiday, your scale benefit would be reduced if your employer required you to hand back your car for this period so that it was not available for your use.

4.5.4 Private petrol

(s 149 ITEPA 2003)

For 2015–16, the fuel scale charge is based on multiplying the relevant CO_2 rate by £22,100. The scale figures apply regardless of the amount of private fuel provided. If any is provided at all, the fuel scale charge is always applied unless the employee reimburses the employer for the full cost. It may well be cost effective for the employee to do this so the position should be reviewed before the start of each tax year.

The charge is reduced if the car is not available for part of the tax year (see 4.5.3), the employee makes good the cost during part of the tax year or where fuel is withdrawn during a tax year and not subsequently reinstated. Care has to be taken as there is no apportionment for days before provision of free fuel commenced.

4.5.5 Car parking spaces

(s 266(1) ITEPA 2003)

The provision of a car parking space at or near the employee's place of work is not treated as a taxable benefit. Where an employee pays for car parking him or herself, he or she cannot claim a deduction for those charges.

4.5.6 Private use of company vans

(s 154 ITEPA 2003)

There is a scale charge for employees who have private use of company vans. An employee may be assessed on a standard amount of £3,150 for 2015–16 in respect of private use of a van irrespective of its age and for 2015–16 an additional charge of £594 applies if the employer provides fuel for private use. Any vehicles in excess of 3.5 tons are exempt from tax altogether (unless the vehicle is used wholly or mainly for the employee's private purposes). From 6 April 2010 to 5 April 2015, the £3,000 charge was reduced to nil for electric vans.

The scale charge is reduced if the van was not available for private use throughout the year. Where an employee has two or more vans made available for private use at the same time, tax is charged on the scale figure for each van. The standard amount is reduced pro rata where the van is only available part of the year. As for company cars, a £1-for-£1 reduction is made for any contributions made by the employee towards the private use. Where a van is shared among several employees, the standard amount is apportioned among the employees.

Private mileage does not include travel from home to work.

It is expected that legislation will be introduced to extend support for zero-emission vans to 5 April 2020 on a tapered basis. In 2015–16 the van benefit rate paid by zero-emission vans is 20% of the rate paid by conventionally fuelled vans, followed by 40% in 2016–17, 60% in 2017–18, 80% in 2018–19 and 90% in 2019–20, with rates equalised in 2019–20. In Budget 2016 the Government will again consult on zero-emission vans.

4.5.7 Congestion charge

No tax charge arises where an employer pays the congestion charge on a company car or van. It does apply where the congestion charge relates to a vehicle that is not owned by the employer unless the travel into London was an expense incurred wholly and necessarily in the performance of the employee's duties.

4.5.8 Hands-free phone kit

HMRC accepts that no additional benefit arises where an employer pays for a hands-free phone kit to be fitted in a company car.

4.6 FREE USE OF ASSETS

(s 203 ITEPA 2003)

A taxable benefit arises where an employer makes an asset available for use by a director or P11D employee. The annual benefit is 20% of the asset's market value when it was first made available for use by the employee. Virtually any asset apart from living accommodation and company cars may be involved including yachts, furniture, television sets and stereo equipment. If the employer rents or hires the asset for a sum in excess of 20% of its original market value, the higher rental charge is substituted as the assessable benefit. A deduction is allowed for any contribution or rental paid by the employee.

A further charge may arise if the ownership of an asset is eventually transferred to the employee. The amount will be determined by either the asset's market value at the time of transfer of ownership or, where a higher figure results, its original cost at the time it was first made available as a benefit for any person, less any amounts already charged as benefits in connection with its availability. Care must be taken that the disguised remuneration provisions are not triggered – Chapter 5 deals with this charge.

Example – Transfer of assets

A company provides an employee with the use of a yacht that costs £40,000, with the employee paying a rental of £2,000 pa. After two years the yacht is sold to the employee for its second-hand market value of £20,000. The assessable benefit would be:

		Benefit £
Year 1:	£40,000 × 20%	8,000
	Less: rental paid	(2,000)
		6,000
Year 2:	£40,000 × 20%	8,000
	Less: rental paid	(2,000)
		6,000
Year 3:	Cost of yacht	40,000
	Less: benefits assessed in Years 1 and 2	(12,000)
	Amounts paid by employee	(24,000)
		4,000

Where an asset previously made available to an individual is transferred to him or her (or to another employee) at a time when its market value is still high, it is possible that the total amount charged as a benefit for tax purposes exceeds the original cost. In other cases, the rules may operate to impose a high benefit charge on the transfer of an asset despite its value having depreciated rapidly during the period of use.

Such rules must therefore be considered carefully when planning the provision of an asset for use by an employee or arranging for its transfer to him or her. It may be that where a tax-efficient remuneration package is desired, transfer of ownership should be avoided where assets have a relatively short useful life.

Example – Ownership of assets

> A company provides employees with the use of suits that remain the property of the company. The suits cost £200 and have a useful life of two years, after which they are scrapped. An employee could therefore have an effective benefit of £200, but would be charged tax on only £40 for each of the two tax years.

4.6.1 Assets where this charge does not arise

In the case of a car, the charge is calculated only by reference to the market value at the time that the car is transferred to the employee. Thus if a car had been purchased for £40,000 and after two years the employee buys it for £20,000, a tax charge will arise only if the £20,000 is less than market value.

Similarly, the tax charge on a transfer to an employee of a computer or bicycle previously made available to him or her, or another employee, is based only on the market value at that time.

4.7 BENEFICIAL LOANS

(s 184 ITEPA 2003)

4.7.1 Type of loans caught

A charge generally arises for directors and P11D employees on the annual value of beneficial loan arrangements. A loan's 'annual value' is taken as interest at the 'official rate' less the amount of interest (if any) paid by the employee. The official rate is now generally set annually in advance. For 2014–15, the official rate was 3.25%. For 2015–16 the rate is 3%. An additional taxable benefit arises if the loan is subsequently written off or forgiven. The beneficial loan provisions can also apply if a loan is made to a member of an employee's family. In some circumstances, the disguised remuneration provisions can create an upfront tax charge on the full capital amount of the loan; see Chapter 5 for details.

Moreover, HMRC can assess benefits where credit has been involved, even though there may be no formal loan. In particular, a director who overdraws his or her current account with the company is regarded as having obtained a loan.

Almost all loans by employers (and persons connected with them) are caught as the legislation deems such loans to have been given by reason of the employment. There is an exception where the employee is related to the employer and it could be shown that the loan was given for family reasons. Loans made by an employer whose business includes lending money to the general public do not give rise to a charge on the employees provided the loans are made on similar terms to those available to the public.

4.7.2 Beneficial loans used for qualifying purpose

No benefit-in-kind charge arises in respect of a cheap loan where the money borrowed has been applied for a qualifying purpose, for example to purchase shares in a close company in which the individual has a material interest or where he or she is employed full time in the conduct and management of the company's business. However, it is possible that a disguised remuneration charge might still apply in these circumstances.

4.7.3 *De minimis* exemption

No benefit-in-kind charge arises for an employee provided that the total of all cheap or interest-free loans does not exceed £10,000. This figure excludes loans used to buy shares in employee-controlled companies (see 11.6).

4.7.4 Employee loans written off

If the loan is written off, the amount forgiven is treated as assessable income for that year even if the company no longer employs the person concerned. The main exception here is if the loan is forgiven on the employee's death – however, despite the relief in s 190 ITEPA, in most cases, the loan write off will be taxable under s 62 ITEPA as general earnings in any case. Where the employee is also a shareholder in a close company, there will be no charge as employment income and instead, the individual is deemed to receive a distribution on their shares.

Some care must be taken if it is decided to clear a loan by making an *ex gratia* or compensation payment to an employee on termination of employment. An income tax liability will arise if the loan is formally written off. However, no liability normally arises if the employee receives a cheque as an *ex gratia* or compensation payment and uses that sum to clear his or her outstanding loan. It is recommended that professional advice be taken in such circumstances.

4.7.5 Further information

HMRC guidance on how loans provided by employers to employees are taxed can be found at www.hmrc.gov.uk/manuals/eimanual/eim26100.htm.

4.8 LIVING ACCOMMODATION

(ss 105–106 ITEPA 2003)

4.8.1 Introduction

The income tax charge that generally applies where an employee is provided with accommodation (unless it is representative accommodation: see 4.4.11) depends on whether the property is rented or owned by the employer.

Where the property is rented by the employer, the assessable amount is the greater of the rent paid and the annual value. In addition, a charge may arise on the annual value of any furniture and fixtures and on any occupier's expenses borne by the company such as water rates, decorations, gardener's wages, etc.

Where an employer purchases a leasehold interest in a property on or after 22 April 2009, and that lease has less than ten years to run, the lease premium may be treated as if it were rent for the period of the lease.

Where the employer owns the property, the assessable amount was originally confined to the gross annual value for rating purposes. Despite the abolition of domestic rates, this treatment continues to apply for properties on existing rating lists (see 4.4.10). For new properties and those where there have been major improvements, HMRC makes an estimate of what the gross annual value (GAV) would have been had rates continued. Over the years, this has meant that the GAV is far less than a market rent. Accordingly, the Government has introduced an additional charge for more expensive properties.

This additional charge arises where the employer paid more than £75,000 to acquire the property. The additional amount assessable is a percentage of the excess of the property's cost over £75,000. The percentage to be applied is the official rate of interest used for beneficial loans (see 4.7) at the beginning of the tax year.

Example – Charge on living accommodation in excess of £75,000

For several years a company director has occupied a property owned by the company that has a gross annual value of £2,000. The cost of the property in 2005 was £95,000. The director will be assessed on the following amount for 2014–15:

	£	£
Gross annual value		2,000
Additional charge:		
Cost in 2005	95,000	
Less:	(75,000)	
	20,000	
Assessment on £20,000 at official rate of 3.25%		650
		2,650

Where a property is unavailable for any part of the year, this will reduce the amount chargeable. It is emphasised that this will not apply merely because an employee chooses not to stay in a property that is available for his or her use.

In addition, the benefit charge is reduced by any rent or expenses reimbursed by the employee.

97

4.8.2 Properties owned for more than six years

Where the company has owned the property for at least six years before it was occupied by the employee and the employee first occupied it after 30 March 1983 then, rather than the cost, the figure taken into account in computing the additional charge is the market value at the time it was first made available to the employee, plus any amounts that had been spent on improving it after the employee took up occupancy and before the start of the tax year.

The actual cost (including improvements) to the employer is still used to determine whether the provisions apply. Consequently, properties where the actual cost was less than £75,000 (including the cost of any improvements) are not within the scope of this additional charge even if their market value exceeds £75,000. Where the actual cost exceeded £75,000, the additional charge is based on the market value.

Example – Charge on living accommodation purchased more than six years ago

In the example in 4.8.1, assume the company has owned the property for more than six years before the director moves in. Also assume that in May 2004, when the director first occupies it, the market value is £225,000. As the original cost of the property exceeded £75,000, the director will be assessed on the following amount for 2014–15:

	£	£
Gross annual value		2,000
Additional charge:		
Market value in 2004	225,000	
Less:	(75,000)	
	150,000	
Assessment on £150,000 at official rate of 3.25%		4,875
		6,875

4.8.3 Possible reductions in taxable amount

It may be possible to reduce the taxable amount where the employee is required to occupy a property that is larger than would normally be needed for his or her own purposes. In *Westcott v Bryan* (1969) 45 TC 476 a director was required to live in a large house so that he or she could entertain customers. He was allowed a reduction in the taxable amount to cover the relevant proportion of the annual value and the running expenses.

Some care is needed if it is intended to claim relief in this way. This claim succeeded because the house was larger than needed for the director and his family. It would not have succeeded had the property merely been more expensive than he would have chosen. It was also helpful that the company directors had approved board minutes setting out their requirement and the business reason for it.

Where part of the property is used exclusively for work, the taxable amount may be reduced on a pro rata basis. Revenue Helpsheet IR202 contains working sheets that enable you to compute your taxable benefits in this situation.

4.8.4 Possible increase in taxable benefit

It is sometimes the case that an employer offers a choice: salary of £x or salary of £y plus a house. In this situation, if the difference between £x and £y calculated along the lines set out in 4.8.1–4.8.2 exceeds the normal benefit-in-kind it may be taxed as additional remuneration.

4.8.5 Holiday accommodation and foreign properties

Some employers buy holiday flats, cottages, etc for use by staff. In practice, generally HMRC apportions the assessable amount for the year among those employees who have occupied the property. However, where only a single employee or director has access to the property, they will usually be liable to pay a benefit charge for the whole year, not just the time that they occupy it.

The assessment can be reduced by letting the accommodation to third parties when directors and employees do not require it.

A practical problem arises with overseas properties. Because there is no rateable value, the benefit is the annual rent that the property would normally command on the open market. Where this applies, there is normally no additional charge based on the excess of the property's cost over £75,000 (see 4.8.1).

4.8.6 Overseas holiday homes held in a single purpose company

It is common for a UK individual who is acquiring a home overseas to set up a company to buy the property. Where the individual is a director, he or she is potentially subject to the tax charge under s 105 ITEPA 2003. FA 2008 provides an exemption from this (with full retrospective effect) as long as the following conditions are satisfied:

- the company must be owned by individuals;
- the company's main activity must be to own the property, any other activity being incidental;
- the property must be the only or main asset of the company;
- the company must not be funded directly or indirectly by a connected company.

4.9 MISCELLANEOUS BENEFITS

Council tax

Where an employer pays council tax on behalf of an employee, this is normally chargeable as part of the employee's remuneration package, resulting in a charge to both income tax and NIC. The one exception to this is where the employee is a representative occupier (see 4.4.11).

Mobile phones

(s 319 ITEPA 2003)

No tax charge arises on the provision of one telephone for each employee. However where an employee has more than one phone, for example a mobile phone plus an iPhone, a charge will arise on the second phone. A charge will also arise if the employer pays for the use of a mobile phone owned by the employee, unless the payment is for business calls only and can be fully substantiated.

No benefit-in-kind arises where an employer pays for a hands-free mobile kit to be fitted in an employee's car provided the employer retains ownership of the kit.

Telephone line rental

HMRC treats the full amount of the rental paid by the employer as a taxable benefit-in-kind even though the phone may be partly (or mainly) used for business calls. The decision in *Lucas* v *Cattell* (1972) 48 TC 353 was that the expenditure on rental had a dual purpose (ie that a phone was intended to be used for both business and personal use) and therefore no part of it was allowable.

Liability insurance and payment of uninsured liabilities

Section 349 provides that employees are not subject to tax on a benefit-in-kind where their employer pays premiums on items such as directors' and officers' liability insurance or a professional indemnity insurance policy. Furthermore, the Act also provides that payment of an employee's uninsured liabilities does not give rise to a benefit-in-kind provided they arise from the employee's work. This is subject to the overriding requirement that the liabilities could have been insured against and this means that those arising from, for example criminal convictions, cannot attract relief.

Medical insurance

The cost of medical insurance is normally assessable on P11D employees. Where the employer has a group scheme, a proportion of the total premiums is related to individual employees. There is an exception in that the premiums are exempt to the extent that they provide cover for an employee working outside the UK.

Club subscriptions

A benefit-in-kind is deemed to arise where an employer pays or reimburses an employee's subscription to a club, even though the employee may only belong to the club to entertain the employer's customers.

In-house tax and financial advice

This is a type of expenditure that HMRC has ignored in the past as the marginal cost of providing such advice is inconsequential, but certain Inspectors of Taxes are now treating this as a benefit-in-kind where there is a cost that can clearly be allocated to particular employees. HMRC will also seek to assess directors on a benefit-in-kind where work on their personal taxation affairs has been carried out by the company's auditors or other external advisers.

Christmas parties and other functions

HMRC does not assess a benefit in respect of 'modest' expenditure on a Christmas or other annual party for staff, provided the party is open to all staff. The limit regarded as modest in this context is £150 per head. If the cost (including VAT) amounts to over £150, the whole amount is taxable, not just the excess. Although this rule is generally attributed to Christmas parties, it may apply to a function at another time of year. The £150 can be used to cover the cost of more than one function.

Legal fees

There may be expenditure incurred for the benefit of the company's business but which nevertheless is deemed to give rise to a benefit-in-kind. A leading case in this connection concerned a company director who was accused of dangerous driving. It was necessary for the company's business that he should not be imprisoned and the company paid his legal expenses. Although the lawyers engaged by the company were more expensive than the director would have used himself, the expenditure by the company was treated as a benefit-in-kind.

Outplacement counselling

(s 310 ITEPA 2003)

The value of outplacement services provided to employees made redundant is exempt from income tax. Such services may include assistance with CVs, job searches, office equipment provisions and advice on interview skills.

Goods and services provided at a discount to the normal price ('in-house benefits')

Where employees are allowed to purchase goods or services from their employer, no tax charge arises provided they pay an amount equal to the employer's cost. The House of Lords eventually decided that 'cost' meant marginal, and not average, cost (*Pepper* v *Hart* [1992] STC 898). This will normally produce a significantly lower benefit.

Following this case, HMRC published a statement of their practice with regard to teachers, employees within the transport industry and other employees who receive goods or services from their employer. It stated that the *Pepper* v *Hart* decision means that:

- rail or bus travel by employees on terms that do not displace fare-paying passengers involves no or negligible additional costs;
- goods sold at a discount that leave employees paying at least the wholesale price involve no or negligible net benefit;
- where teachers pay 15% or more of a school's normal fees, there is no taxable benefit;
- professional services that do not require additional employees or partners (eg legal and financial services) have no or negligible cost to the employer (provided the employee meets the cost of any disbursements).

Employer Financed Retirement Benefit Schemes (EFRBS)

(ss 393–400 ITEPA 2003)

Some employers make contributions to an EFRBS for the benefit of their employees. The creation of an EFRBS must be reported to HMRC under normal rules for reporting the creation of trusts. No taxable benefit charge arose for the years 2006–07 to 2010–11, however from 6 April 2011, an upfront tax charge arises under new Part 7A ITEPA. See Chapter 5 and 26.7 for details.

Making good benefits-in-kind for previous years

The cash equivalent of any benefit chargeable to tax under s 203 ITEPA 2003 is the cost of the benefit 'less so much (if any) of it as is made good by the employee to those providing the benefit'. HMRC accepts that there is no time limit for making good (subject to exceptions mentioned below) and, provided the relevant year's assessment has not been determined, there could be some merit in the person concerned taking further remuneration now and using the net cash left to him or her, after PAYE, to make good benefits provided for earlier years. This could be a particularly good idea where a director of a family company is faced with an income tax assessment plus penalties and interest in respect of prior year incorrect returns because benefits have not been reported properly.

For beneficial loans, however, the cash equivalent can be reduced by a payment in a later year only if the interest is paid under an obligation that existed at the time of the loan.

In a First-tier Tribunal case it was held that a payment by an employee could reduce a car benefit for an earlier year even though the requirement for the payment did not exist in the year concerned (see *P Marshall* v *HMRC* TC02466). This decision has been overridden by FA 2014 which provides that such payments are now deductible only if they are made in the tax year concerned.

4.10 SHARE INCENTIVES

We cover the subject of share incentives in Chapter 6, both from the employee's point of view and from the employer's perspective.

There are many situations where a gift of shares or the exercise of an option gives rise to a liability for the employer to account for PAYE or alternatively, the employee must pay tax through self-assessment. Where this happens, the taxable income should be included in the figure for taxable pay on form P60.

There are also situations where shares are made available through an HMRC approved scheme and no income tax charge will arise on the acquisition of such shares provided the necessary conditions are satisfied.

In the case of other share incentives ('unapproved schemes'), the employee will need to complete a special schedule to his or her tax return (HS305, Employee Share Schemes).

4.11 OPTIONS TO ACQUIRE GILTS

FA 2003 introduced rules that apply to options over other securities such as British Government securities ('gilts'). These rules can now be found in ss 471–487 ITEPA 2003.

A profit on the exercise of such an option will generally be subject to income tax as employment income. Furthermore, the profit will normally be subject to PAYE.

4.12 OPTIONS TO ACQUIRE COMPANY ASSETS

The rules regarding options to acquire shares or other employment-related securities are set out in Chapter 6. The treatment of options involving other assets is quite different. An income tax charge may arise at the time that an option over assets other than securities is granted if the option has a market value. However, if the price at which the option may be exercised is higher than the asset's present market value, it is arguable that the option has little or no value at the time it is granted.

No employment income tax charge would normally arise on the exercise of the option. Furthermore, on a subsequent disposal of the asset there would normally be liability only for CGT on the profit over the amount paid. However, problems may arise if the employee is a shareholder in a close company that grants such an option.

Example – Option to acquire assets

A company director, who is not a shareholder, is granted the option to purchase a house owned by the company for £150,000. She has not occupied it at any time. The house has a market value of only £125,000 at the time the option is granted and the option, therefore, has no real value at that time. When the option is exercised the house has a market value of £250,000 and the director has in effect acquired a capital asset at a discount of £100,000 on its current market value. This discount would not normally be subject to income tax.

4.13 GOLDEN HELLOS

These are payments made to induce a prospective employee to take up employment with the company and are (very) occasionally not taxable. In *Pritchard* v *Arundale* (1971) 47 TC 680, which involved a firm of chartered accountants, a senior partner was approached by a client to leave his practice and become a director of the client's company. In order to induce him to do this, he was given shares in the company that were held to be not a reward for services to be rendered in the future but an inducement to leave his practice and take up the employment. They were therefore not taxable.

In *Vaughan-Neil* v *IRC* [1979] STC 644 a barrister received £40,000 to induce him to give up his practice and join a company as its 'in-house adviser'. Once again it was held that the payment was not taxable. By contrast, in *Glantre Engineering Ltd* v *Goodhand* [1983] STC 1 a payment by an engineering company to induce an employee of a firm of accountants to join them was held to be taxable.

The principles that emerge from these three cases are as follows:

- it must be clear from the facts that the payment is an inducement and not a reward for future services;
- the payment must not be returnable if the person does not take up the employment; and
- it is probably more likely that the payment will be accepted as non-taxable if the recipient has previously been in practice or self-employed rather than an employee of another company.

Shilton v *Wilmshurst* [1991] STC 88 extended these principles by deciding that a payment made by a football club to a footballer about to transfer as an inducement to him to join his new club was taxable. The House of Lords held that an emolument from an employment meant an emolument for being or becoming an employee and therefore would include a sum paid by a third party as an inducement to enter into a contract of employment to perform services in the future. It was not necessary for the payer to have any interest in the performance of those services.

In *Silva* v *Charnock* (2002) SpC 332, the taxpayer had taken a career break to study for an MBA. Her tuition fees cost her £18,000. After getting her MBA, she took a new job and received a signing-on bonus of £18,000. It was held that this was not taxable as it fell within the exemption contained in s 200B ICTA 1988 (now s 250 ITEPA 2003).

4.14 RESTRICTIVE COVENANTS

(s 155 ITEPA 2003)

Where the present, past or future holder of an office or employment gives an undertaking that restricts his or her conduct or activities, any sum paid in respect of that restrictive covenant is treated as remuneration from the office or employment for the year in which the payment is received. This rule applies even where the covenant is not legally valid. In some cases, valuable consideration other than money is given for the restrictive covenant and in such a situation a sum equal to the value of that consideration is treated as having been paid. The payment may not necessarily come from the employer and so a payment to an employee that was made by a major shareholder in a family company may well be caught under these provisions.

4.15 REDUNDANCY PAYMENTS

(s 309 ITEPA 2003)

A statutory redundancy payment made under the Employment Rights Act 1996 is exempt from tax, although it may need to be taken into account in computing the tax payable on a termination payment (see 4.16). HMRC generally treats payments to an employee under a non-statutory redundancy scheme as exempt under SP1/94 where payments are made only on account of redundancy as defined in s 139 of the Employment Rights Act 1996. Further, it is usually expected that payments will be made to all relevant employees and not merely to a selected group of employees and the payments should not be excessively large in relation to earnings and length of service.

In such situations, HMRC is willing to give advance clearance confirming that payments will fall within the exemption. Employers are strongly advised to take advantage of this facility.

In *Mairs* v *Haughey* [1993] STC 569 HMRC sought to tax a payment made to an employee for giving up contingent redundancy rights. HMRC argued that the payment constituted an emolument of the employment, but it was held that a redundancy payment is not an emolument and a lump sum paid in lieu of a right to receive such payment is equally not an emolument.

4.16 GOLDEN HANDSHAKES, OTHER TERMINATION PAYMENTS AND CONTINUING BENEFITS

(s 401 ITEPA 2003)

4.16.1 Introduction

Where a director's or employee's contract of service is terminated, it may be possible for a compensation or *ex gratia* payment to be made that is either wholly or partly tax-free provided the employee is not entitled to the compensation under a contract of service, the anti-avoidance provisions relating to disguised remuneration are not triggered and the payment is not deemed to be a benefit under a retirement benefit scheme. Where the individual receives compensation under a term of his or her employment contract, HMRC's view is that it is taxable in the usual way. A payment made to a director as compensation for accepting a reduced salary or any other variation of his or her service contract is not regarded as a termination payment, and the amount received is normally taxable in full. However, HMRC lost in the case of *Wilson* v *Clayton* where an employer was required by an employment tribunal to reinstate an employee and make a payment of £5,060.

HMRC succeeded in *Allum & Allum* v *Marsh* SpC 446 in arguing that voluntary payments to outgoing directors were, in fact, no more than a payment for past services and therefore taxable in full as earnings.

There is a considerable burden of proof which must be discharged in cases where it is argued that payments which are made to outgoing employees are not taxable. See *D Thomas* v *HMRC* TC02463 where the taxpayer unsuccessfully argued that a payment to him of £37,200 was compensation for the breach of an undertaking that his employment could continue for three years beyond normal retirement date. However, the burden of proof may be easier where the payment is made by someone other than the employer. In one recent case, a payment of $2m to a retired executive by the former owner of a company was held to be a personal gift rather than anything to do with his employment. See *Collins* v *HMRC* TC02088.

4.16.2 Exemptions from the charge under s 401

There are various types of termination payment that are exempt:

(1) Payments made because of termination of employment through death, injury or disability. Disability covers not only a condition arising from a sudden affliction, but also a continuing incapacity to perform the duties of an office or employment because of the culmination of a process of deterioration of physical or mental health caused by chronic illness (see SP10/81).

(2) Terminal grants and gratuities to members of HM forces. This includes payments under the Armed Forces early departure scheme.

(3) Lump sum payments from Commonwealth government superannuation schemes or compensation for loss of career owing to constitutional changes in Commonwealth countries.

(4) A special contribution by an employer into an approved retirement benefit scheme (ie a registered pension scheme).

(5) A lump sum payment where the employment has constituted foreign service that exceeds any of the following limits:

(a) three-quarters of the whole period of service;

(b) the last ten years;

(c) one-half of the period of service provided this amounted to at least 20 years and subject to at least ten of the last 20 years of service being foreign service.

(6) 'Foreign' service is defined as meaning a period of service during which the earnings were not taxable because either the individual was not resident in the UK or the 100% deduction was available because the period spent working overseas exceeded 365 days.

4.16.3 Basic £30,000 exemption

(s 403 ITEPA 2003)

Where a termination payment is not wholly exempt, the first £30,000 can often be paid tax free and only the balance is chargeable. Where an individual receives both statutory redundancy payments and a termination payment, the statutory redundancy payments use up part of the £30,000 exemption and only the balance is available to cover the remainder of the termination payment. Whilst the tax exemption is limited to £30,000, the full amount paid may be exempt from NIC provided it is essentially compensatory in nature.

4.16.4 Employment includes a period of foreign service

The £30,000 exemption may be increased where the employment has included 'foreign service'.

Example – Increased exemption owing to foreign service

> *B* was non-resident in the UK, working overseas from 1993 to 2003. *B* retired in December 2014 and received compensation of £80,000. The exemption is found by using the fraction:
>
> $$\frac{\text{Foreign services}}{\text{Total period of employment}}, \text{ i.e. in this case } \frac{10 \text{ years}}{21 \text{ years}}$$
>
> This fraction is applied to the amount of the golden handshake after deduction of the £30,000 exemption. The taxable amount would be arrived at as follows:
>
> | | £ |
> |---|---:|
> | Compensation | 80,000 |
> | *Less*: 'normal exemption' | (30,000) |
> | | 50,000 |
> | $^{10}/_{21}$ thereof | (23,809) |
> | Taxable amount | 26,191 |

4.16.5 Year for which a termination payment may be taxed

It used to be the case that the timing of a termination payment did not affect the tax liability because it was always treated as taxable income for the year in which the employment was terminated. However, termination payments are now taxed as income of the year in which they are received.

4.16.6 Taxation of continuing payments and benefits

Redundancy and other termination settlements often include provisions for payments to be made or benefits to continue after termination. Such benefits are taxable only as they arise. So, both benefits and payments are taxable in the year when received or enjoyed (not in the year of termination).

Example – Benefits-in-kind following redundancy

> *M* was made redundant on 6 October 2013 and received a lump sum of £20,000 plus a further £20,000 on 6 April 2014. She also continued in the company medical insurance scheme for 18 months at a continuing cost to the employer of £350 in 2013–14 and £650 in 2014–15.
>
> In 2013–14 *M* received a combined redundancy package of £20,350 that is covered by the £30,000 exemption. The £9,650 exemption balance is carried forward to the following year. In 2014–15 she received the balance of the package of £20,650, of which £9,650 is exempt. The medical benefit of £650 is covered by the balance of the exemption as is £9,000 of the cash payment, leaving £11,000 to be taxed at her marginal rate under PAYE.

4.16.7 Certain benefits are not taxed on former employees

(The Employer-Financed Retirement Benefits Schemes (Excluded Benefits for Tax Purposes) Regulations 2007 (SI 2007 No 3537))

No charge arises where an employer continues to provide certain benefits after an employment has ceased. These benefits are:

- living accommodation and related benefits;
- health screening and annual medical check-ups;
- welfare counselling;
- recreational benefits;
- annual parties and similar functions;
- writing of Wills, etc;
- equipment for disabled employees.

4.16.8 *Ex gratia* payments

HMRC have sometimes taxed *ex gratia* payments as relevant retirement benefits under s 393 ITEPA 2003. If this charge arises, the £30,000 exemption is not available. An *ex gratia* payment is normally regarded as a retirement benefit taxable under ss 393–400 only where it is paid in connection with an individual's retirement.

It is possible that the rules on disguised remuneration may have created an upfront tax charge on payments made into an EFRBS, EBT or other structure. In that case, amounts received by the employee will only be taxable under ss 393–400 to the extent that a tax charge has not already arisen.

HMRC has also given guidelines on hypothetical situations. In particular, it regards it as possible for a person to retire from one employment and draw benefits from that employer's EFRBS while taking up employment with a new employer – see Table 4.4, which defines the position for EFRBS purposes. It does not follow that the same treatment will necessarily apply when considering whether a termination payment is taxable as a contribution to an unapproved retirement benefits scheme.

4.16.9 Payments in lieu of notice (PILONs)

PILONs have featured increasingly in employment contracts as employees have tried to formalise their rights and employers have wanted to be able to enforce restrictive covenants and prevent ex-employees using confidential information that they have acquired in the course of their employment. HMRC set out its opinion in a lengthy article in *Tax Bulletin 24* (August 1996). In large measure, HMRC's interpretations have been upheld by the courts (see *EMI Electronics*

Table 4.4 – Guidelines on hypothetical situations

Situation	Retirement position
A long-service employee leaves to take a senior executive position in another company at the age of 60	The employee has retired
A division of the company is sold and the 55-year-old manager responsible for running it leaves to take a job with the purchaser	The manager has retired
A person in his 50s has a heart attack and is advised by his doctor to leave and seek a less stressful position	If the person were re-employed in an entirely different capacity with the same employer or finds employment with another employer, HMRC would generally accept the member had retired early from the original employment (possibly on ill-health grounds or possibly on normal early retirement grounds – depending on scheme rules and exact medical advice). But if the *ex gratia* payment made is purely consolation for loss of health that results in the premature termination of employment, it would not be regarded as made in connection with retirement)
Situation	Retirement position
An employee aged 35 is involved in an accident and suffers disabilities that make it impossible to continue with the job	A lump sum paid on retirement solely by reason of disability from an accident is not taxable as a benefit from an employer-financed retirement benefits scheme
An employee aged 50 leaves to take a job nearer home to be able to nurse her aged parents	Employee has retired

Group Ltd v *Coldicott*). Also see *SCA Packaging Limited* v *HMRC* [2007] EWHC 270.

The term 'PILON' is sometimes used loosely to include payments to employees on 'garden leave'. This is not correct. An employee on garden leave is still an employee: he or she cannot take another job until the end of the notice period. All that has changed is that he or she is not required to carry out any duties. Payments to such an employee are taxable in the normal way and the employer should deduct tax under PAYE.

There are also situations where the employee's service contract actually provides for a PILON, usually at the employer's option. HMRC's view is that where an employer decides to make a PILON, the payment is made under the contract rather than as compensation for the contract having been broken. As such, it remains taxable in full and PAYE deductions should be made.

Rather more controversially, HMRC argues that there may be an implied term to an employment contract where an employer customarily makes PILONs. This is common in certain industries (IT, stockbroking, asset management, etc) where the last thing an employer wants is for an employee who is serving out a notice period to have continued access to confidential information or to clients. You should take professional advice if you are an employer who has a history of regularly making PILONs.

Virtually the only circumstances in which you can be completely confident that a PILON will be treated as a golden handshake is where the payment is a 'one-off' exception to your normal rule, and there is no reference to the possibility of such a payment in the service contract or related documents such as the staff handbook. In this situation, the first £30,000 (including other elements of the termination package) is normally exempt from tax.

4.17 DIVIDENDS

In the past, it was thought that a dividend could not be treated as employment income. The decision by the Court of Appeal in *HMRC v PA Holdings* [2011] EWCA Civ 1414 has shown that this no longer applies. Shares were issued to employees by an employee benefit trust and they then received dividends. It was held that these receipts were employment income. In effect, the Court held that what matters is the character of the receipt in the hand of the recipients rather than the source of the payment made to them. See also the First-tier Tribunal case *Manthorpe Building Products Limited* TC01778.

4.18 DESIGNING A 'TAX EFFICIENT' REMUNERATION PACKAGE

Where an individual has a real degree of influence over the way his or her total remuneration package of salary and benefits is made up, the following should be borne in mind.

(1) Pension schemes are still very tax efficient.
(2) Approved share options are treated more favourably than non-approved options.
(3) The legislation on benefits-in-kind still leaves some scope for manoeuvre.
(4) Golden handshakes are not always taxable.

4.18.1 Advantages of pension funds in general

From a tax perspective, there can be no better medium to long-term investment than a pension scheme. The fact that pension schemes are not subject to tax internally because of the funds' exemption from UK income tax and CGT, combined with the facility to take one quarter of the fund as a tax-free lump sum at retirement, means that the overall return will almost certainly beat any comparable investment. Furthermore, an employer's contribution does not attract NIC.

4.18.2 Employer can contribute up to £40,000 pa

An employer can make contributions of up to £40,000 pa (plus any of the employee's unused allowances for the last three tax years) provided that the contributions do not take the employee's pension fund over the lifetime allowance (see 26.1.2).

4.18.3 Employee shares

With CGT at 28%, or 18% for basic rate taxpayers, an employee share scheme can form part of a very attractive benefits package. However, close attention needs to be given to the rules on special shares (see 6.4). Bear in mind the election at 6.4.7 where restricted shares have only a small initial value as it could be well worth accepting a modest income tax charge upfront in order to ensure that the capital appreciation will be subject only to CGT.

4.18.4 Approved share option schemes

The tax treatment of an individual who exercises an approved share option is significantly better than that for someone who benefits via an unapproved arrangement. Basically, no tax charge arises on the exercise of an approved share option provided that certain conditions have been observed (see 6.4).

The conclusion must be that wherever an individual has a choice, he or she should participate via an approved rather than a non-approved scheme to the maximum extent permitted.

4.18.5 Tax efficient benefits-in-kind

Despite the Government's long-term intention to remove any discrimination between the tax treatment of benefits-in-kind and cash remuneration, there are still certain benefits that are treated favourably for tax purposes. If a person is a company director, or someone else who has a degree of say in the way his or her remuneration package is made up, significant tax benefits can be secured by a judicious choice of benefits-in-kind.

Company cars or cash allowance?

You need to check that you will be better off with a company car as opposed to receiving a cash allowance with which you can buy your own car and then charge for business mileage at the flat-rate mileage allowances (see 4.4.12). Similar considerations apply to car fuel.

It may pay to buy your company car

Because of the high rate of depreciation in the first year, it may be advantageous for a director to arrange for his or her company to purchase a car with a view to its being sold to him or her after it has been used for a period. Provided he or she pays the full market value for the car in its second-hand condition, there will be no tax charge on the difference between the cost of the car to the company and the amount at which the director purchases it. Admittedly, there is a scale benefit for the period the company owns the car, but this is often significantly less than the vehicle's depreciation during the period concerned.

Car fuel

Where an employee or director has a company car, it is clearly beneficial that he or she should have as much free petrol as possible as the scale benefit does not vary according to how much private petrol is provided. However, as the taxable benefit is so high, it is often better for the employee to pay for fuel then claim for reimbursement of business mileage.

Interest-free loans

There is a *de minimis* limit so that, if an individual has a beneficial loan from his or her company, no income tax charge arises unless the loan exceeds £10,000.

Company accommodation

The tax treatment where a director or employee occupies a company property can still be attractive. This is a complex area where you should take professional advice.

4.18.6 Golden handshakes are not always taxable

A termination payment can still be treated favourably, either because of the £30,000 exemption or because it qualifies for total exemption (see 4.16).

4.19 SPECIFIC OCCUPATIONS AND TRADES

4.19.1 Ministers of religion

Ministers treated as office holders

For tax purposes, a minister of religion (which includes include vicars, reverends, priests, rabbis, imams or any other titles given to religious leaders) is generally treated as an employed person unless his or her remuneration does not consist wholly or mainly of stipend or salary. However, different rules can apply for NIC purposes (eg Elim Pentecostal ministers and Roman Catholic priests can be regarded as self-employed because of the absence of a right to remuneration).

No tax on rent-free accommodation

A minister of religion is not normally liable for tax in respect of his or her occupation of a vicarage or other living accommodation provided by the church, charity or ecclesiastical body (references to a 'church' include a mosque, synagogue, temple and so on; 'vicarage' includes any building in which the minister lives and from which the duties of the ministry are performed) for carrying out his or her duties (ss 99, 290 and 351 ITEPA 2003).

The taxable amount where the Church, etc bears costs such as heat and light, cleaning and gardening is limited to 10% of the minister's remuneration after deducting allowable expenses.

Allowable expenses

The following expenses commonly incurred by clergy are allowable deductions under s 336 ITEPA:

- stationery, postage and use of telephone for clerical duties;
- secretarial costs (including wages paid to the minister's spouse for providing such assistance provided this is separate and distinct from work he or she performs as an active member of the church);
- travelling in the course of his or her duties (including 20p a mile for 'business use' of a bicycle);
- cost of repair or replacement of robes;
- communion expenses;
- cost of providing a locum;
- reasonable entertainment on official functions.

White v *Higgingbottom* [1983] STC 143 decided that a clergyman was not entitled to allowances for an overhead projector and screen that he paid for personally.

For further background information, *The Taxation of Ministers of Religion: A Rough Guide* can be downloaded from the Churches' Legislation Advisory Service at www.churcheslegislation.org.uk/publications.

4.19.2 Members of Parliament

As one would expect, there are special rules that apply to MPs, Members of the Scottish Parliament (MSPs) and Members of the Welsh Assembly (AMs). MPs are dealt with by a central HMRC office in Cardiff. They complete a supplementary form SA102(MP), which is available on HMRC's website, together with help notes. HMRC also publishes a leaflet, *MPs, Ministers and Tax* (www.hmrc.gov.uk/freedom/mps-leaflet.pdf).

Salary and allowances

MPs receive allowances for the costs of running an office, having homes both near Westminster and in their constituency, and travelling between both. Members of the cabinet, the Prime Minister and other Ministers of State receive additional amounts, on top of the basic MP's salary, although a number of Ministers have volunteered to cap these amounts in the current economic conditions.

Responsibility for paying MPs' expenses belongs to the Independent Parliamentary Standards Agency (IPSA). IPSA is also responsible for MPs' pay and pensions.

Details of the current guidance for MPs allowances can be accessed via the IPSA website http://parliamentarystandards.org.uk.

Tax notes

HMRC has stated that MPs cannot claim a deduction for:

- mortgage interest on an office or part of a residence used as an office;
- newspapers, books and periodicals;
- charitable subscriptions;
- constituency newsletters and other circulars relating to party political activities, canvassing literature, election expenses or Christmas cards;
- entertaining constituents or others;
- extra costs arising out of late night sittings;
- expenses incurred by spouses or civil partners, eg in deputising for or accompanying MPs;
- accountancy fees incurred in the preparation of the SA tax return or related expenses claims.

4.19.3 University lecturers

Allowable deductions

A lecturer may claim a deduction for annual subscriptions to a learned society such as the Royal Society of Chemistry. Annual subscriptions to bodies such as the Association of Teachers and Lecturers and the National Association of Teachers in Further and Higher Education are also allowable (for details of the professional subscriptions that are allowable see www.hmrc.gov.uk/list3/index.htm).

The cost of academic dress is also an allowable deduction. Where a lecturer is required to demonstrate in a laboratory or do other laboratory based work, the cost of a lab coat, goggles and other protective clothing can also be claimed. For guidance on these, and other expenses, agreed with the Association of University Teachers, by HMRC, see www.hmrc.gov.uk/manuals/eimanual/EIM70705.htm.

Study allowance

Where a lecturer is required to undertake research work, he or she may be able to secure a study allowance reflecting extra expenditure on light and heat and the cost of office equipment such as a photocopier or fax machine. HMRC accepts that giving a deduction for a study does not result in any restriction of the CGT main residence exemption.

Shares in university spin-outs

Some university lecturers may be offered the opportunity to acquire shares in companies that exploit their research (university spin-outs). The acquisition of such shares could give rise to tax charges on employment income under the FA 2003 legislation. FA 2005 added new Chapter 4A to Part 7, ITEPA 2003. This legislation ensures that where intellectual property is transferred from a research institution to a company, the relevant transfer will not give rise to an employment-related security tax charge unless employer and employee choose that treatment. The employee is therefore placed in an enviable position. If the venture fails, he or she will be able to exit without facing a tax liability; if it succeeds he or she will pay CGT on the profit, rather than being caught within the employment-related securities net.

The exemption only applies to the value of intellectual property transferred. In situations where the company has other inherent value, for example as a result of funding, a charge to income tax and NIC could still apply to the element that is not related to the intellectual property.

The relieving provisions apply where the individual acquires shares, or the intellectual property is transferred after 1 December 2004 and the individual acquires his or her shares within a period of six months before and after the date of an agreement under which the university or other research institution transfers intellectual property to the company.

4.19.4 Seafarers

(ss 378–385 ITEPA 2003)

A 100% deduction can be claimed by seafarers where they spend a continuous period of 365 days working outside the UK and they are resident and ordinarily resident in the UK during that period. Section 4 FA (No. 3) 2010 extends this treatment to seafarers who are EU or EEA residents. Journeys starting or ending outside the UK are treated as periods working outside the UK. A day of absence is a day when the seafarer is outside the UK at midnight. Shorter periods can be aggregated to make up a 365-day period provided that UK days in between do not make up more than one half of the combined period.

Although the definition of 'seafarer' is somewhat loose, employees who work on jack-up rigs or similar structures in the offshore oil and gas industry are not treated as seafarers and are therefore not entitled to the 100% deduction.

The Upper Tribunal has recently held that two cruise ship entertainers were self-employed and therefore not entitled to the 100% deduction. The deduction is available only against employment income so this is one of the rare occasions where HMRC have argued that workers are self-employed. See *Pete Matthews and Keith Sidwick* v *HMRC* [2012] UKUT 229 (TCC).

4.19.5 Entertainers

Individuals who are employed as entertainers are entitled to claim a deduction for fees paid to agents of up to 17.5% of their earnings (s 722 ITEPA 2003).

4.20 LOSSES

It is possible for an employee to have a loss. Mr Martin was employed by JLT Risk Solutions. In 2005, he received a £250,000 bonus in return for agreeing to stay with JLT for five years. In 2006–07, Mr Martin gave notice and under the terms of the agreement he became liable to repay £162,500 of his bonus. His salary for 2006–07 was £140,000 so he said that he had suffered a loss for that year of £22,500 and that loss should be relieved by its being set against his other income.

The First-tier Tribunal agreed that this was the correct analysis (see *Martin* v *HMRC* TC02460).

5

EMPLOYMENT INCOME THROUGH THIRD PARTIES: DISGUISED REMUNERATION

This chapter covers the following sections:

(1) Introduction
(2) When a charge arises
(3) Exclusions from the charge on disguised remuneration
(4) Risks for employers
(5) Summary
(6) Disguised fee income

5.1 INTRODUCTION

(ss 554A–554Z20, Part 7 ITEPA 2003)

The Government introduced legislation in 2011 to counteract tax and NIC avoidance by arrangements involving 'disguised remuneration'. Schedule 2 FA 2011 inserted new Part 7A into ITEPA 2003. These provisions took effect predominantly from 6 April 2011, although some had effect from 9 December 2010, and from that date onwards, most payments made to employees via third parties will fall within the new rules.

Much of the publicity surrounding these rules has focused on the use of employee benefit trusts (EBTs) and employer-financed retirement benefit schemes (EFRBS). However, in practice, the legislation is much wider and catches almost all situations where value is created for an employee (or anyone linked with the employee) that is arranged via or involves a third party.

5.2 WHEN A CHARGE ARISES

In the simplest terms, an employer will be liable to pay PAYE and NIC where:

- a step is taken towards creating an arrangement that involves a third party; and
- that arrangement will eventually cause some value to be received by an employee (including former or prospective employees) or a person linked with that individual.

To illustrate how wide the legislation is, a person linked with a current, former or prospective employee is defined as any person that would normally be regarded as connected under UK tax law and extended to cover more distant corporate connections and even common law spouses or civil partners.

It is important to note that it is not necessary for an employee to receive any value for tax charges to be triggered. For example, if an employer places funds on discretionary trust for past, present or future employees that alone would not trigger a charge. However, telling the trustees (the third party) how you would like the funds to be spent in the future, for example via a letter of wishes, or telling employees what level of bonus or share ownership they can look forward to in future would be treated as earmarking the funds and would trigger tax and NIC charges immediately.

The rules are specifically designed to trigger tax charges where EBTs and other similar arrangements have been used in the past to advance value to employees tax-free, such as where amounts are loaned to employees after 9 December 2010 (although HMRC is still challenging pre-9 December 2010 arrangements under the legislation then in force). Under the rules on disguised remuneration, as soon as the funds are put in the hands of a third party and in some way linked to an individual (even verbally), tax and NIC liabilities are created.

Existing arrangements where loans are already in place should not be caught by these new rules. Employers (and employees) should be wary of changing the terms of such arrangements or advancing further sums, as this is likely to bring the arrangement within the rules. HMRC has also stated that it will continue to challenge the tax treatment of loans and other value transfers made from EFRBS before 9 December 2010 under the existing legislation.

Finance Act 2013 contains provisions which impose a charge on temporary non-residents, ie individuals who are not resident for periods of less than five tax years. The amount charged as disguised remuneration is taxed as if it were income of the individual for the year in which he or she resumes UK residence.

5.3 EXCLUSIONS FROM THE CHARGE ON DISGUISED REMUNERATION

As the rules are so widely drafted, it has been necessary for the Government to build in a number of specific exclusions. A list of the more important exclusions is shown below but it should be remembered that each exemption has a number of conditions that will need to be met before it can apply to any given situation:

- an approved SIP, SAYE or CSOP scheme;
- an arrangement, the sole purpose of which is the issue of qualifying EMI options;
- an arrangement, the sole purpose of which is the provision of excluded benefits (broadly on ill health, accidental death or disablement during service or from a relevant life policy);
- a registered pension scheme (note that EFRBS are not registered pension schemes), employee pension contributions or purchases of annuities out of pension scheme rights;
- an arrangement, the sole purpose of which is making authorised member payments from registered pension schemes;
- a transaction that is part of a package of benefits available to over 50% of the employer's employees or employees whose status is comparable on the same terms;
- a commercial loan made in the ordinary course of the lender's business where there is no connection with a tax avoidance arrangement;
- a commercial transaction with the employee in the ordinary course of business where a substantial proportion of the payer's business involves similar transactions with the public, on the same terms and there is no tax avoidance purpose;
- employee car ownership schemes (but only over a four-year term);
- items on which employees are normally exempt from tax (eg work related training).

5.4 RISKS FOR EMPLOYERS

These rules create a considerable risk of triggering PAYE and NIC liabilities where any element of a remuneration package is provided via a third party.

Employers should seek advice where any payment or asset transfer to a third party is contemplated in respect of employees, or where the employer itself undertakes to provide future unapproved retirement benefits, to ensure that the full tax consequences are understood before it is made.

> **Tax notes**
>
> The provisions are extremely complex and if you think you might be affected, it is essential that you take specialist professional advice, as any errors could prove very costly.

5.5 SUMMARY

This legislation is incredibly widely targeted. It can, even with the reliefs and exclusions outlined above, catch far too many innocent transactions. It is also likely to create considerable uncertainty which is contrary to one of the Government's stated objectives for the tax system.

Tax liabilities can arise in circumstances where the employee receives no value at all from the arrangement, either when the taxable 'step' is taken or at any later time. All that is required for the charge to apply is that there is a 'step' that may or may not lead to some form of advantage for the employee later.

If you think you may be affected by this legislation, you need to take professional advice, as errors can be very expensive. See also the HMRC replies to frequently asked questions at www.hmrc.gov.uk/budget-updates/autumn-tax/wms-aa.htm.

5.6 DISGUISED FEE INCOME

FA 2015 contains legislation which can apply to investment managers. The provisions are intended to ensure that annual management fees are taxed as income in situations where partnerships or LLPs are used. They apply to all arrangements where there is an attempt to disguise what is, in substance, an investment management fee so that it is not taxable as income.

Carried interest is excluded from these provisions.

6

SHARE INCENTIVES

This chapter contains the following sections:

(1) Shares acquired at a discount
(2) Non-approved share options
(3) Approved share schemes
(4) Special shares, etc
(5) Split year treatment
(6) The employer's perspective
(7) Some tax planning ideas
(8) Venture capitalists and participants in MBOs

6.1 SHARES ACQUIRED AT A DISCOUNT

6.1.1 Normal tax treatments

Shares offered to an employee at below their market value are normally taxable as employment income. The charge is based on the difference between that market value and the amount, if any, that the employee pays to acquire the shares. This applies regardless of who provided the shares, so that they could come by subscription or from an existing shareholder.

If the shares are given to the employee by a shareholder, he or she is normally treated as if he or she had made a disposal of the shares at their market value, and therefore may be liable for CGT. This would not apply where the employee subscribed for new shares.

A company must report the acquisition of shares by an employee as a 'reportable event' on form 42. This return must be submitted to HMRC by 6 July following the end of the tax year.

> **Tax notes**
>
> You should take advice on your CGT position if you are considering making a gift of some of your shares to an employee.

PAYE must be accounted for if either the shares are readily convertible assets (see 20.1) or trading arrangements are in place. There is then a further liability for PAYE if the individual does not reimburse the company within 90 days of the end of the tax year (until 2014–15, within 90 days of the date on which the shares were acquired).

6.1.2 Shares issued for employee shareholder status

The Growth and Infrastructure Act 2013 provides for employees to give up their employment rights in return for being issued shares. Employee shareholders are deemed to have paid £2,000 for the shares. A gain on a sale of the shares is exempt from capital gains tax (up to a limit of £50,000).

6.2 NON-APPROVED SHARE OPTIONS

6.2.1 Introduction

An income tax charge may arise on the exercise of a share option that was granted by reason of the individual's office or employment.

6.2.2 Non-approved share options

(s 471 ITEPA 2003)

A tax charge may arise on the exercise of the option. The grant of the option is not an event that gives rise to an income tax charge.

Exercise of the option

A person who is subject to tax under s 15 ITEPA 2003 (see 4.1.1) may be subject to an income tax charge when he or she exercises a non-approved share option that has been granted by reason of an office or employment. The charge is not dependent on his or her selling the shares, but arises on any profit or gain that he or she is deemed to have made by exercising the option and thereby acquiring shares at less than their current market value. Normally the profit is simply the difference between the shares' market value at the time the employee exercises his or her option and the price payable under the option, although if he or she paid anything for the option grant, that can be deducted as well.

Example – exercise of share options

A was granted an option to acquire 1,000 shares in XYZ Ltd at a price of £2 per share. After five years have elapsed, he exercises the option and pays £2,000 to acquire the 1,000 shares. By this time the shares have grown in value to £5 per share. *A* will be assessed for the year in which he exercises the option. His profit will be assessed as £3,000, ie:

	£
Market value of 1,000 shares	5,000
Less: amount paid	(2,000)
	3,000

If the employee agrees to pay the employer's NIC on the profit from exercising the option, the employer's NIC is deducted in arriving at the taxable amount.

6.2.3 Employee's residence status

Before 6 April 2008, no charge arose under s 471 unless the employee was resident and ordinarily resident in the UK at the date the option was granted. However, a charge can now arise on the exercise of an option granted on or after 6 April 2008 to an individual who was resident but not ordinarily resident in the UK. It can also arise if an option was granted whilst he or she was not resident in the UK, if the option was granted in contemplation of his or her performing duties after taking up residence in the UK.

The tax treatment of options exercised by an individual who is resident but not ordinarily resident may depend upon whether the option relates to duties performed outside the UK. See further at section 34.3 on this.

An income tax charge still applies where an individual who was resident and ordinarily resident when the option was granted exercises his or her option after he or she has ceased to be resident in the UK. In some cases, the income tax charge may be reduced because of relief due under a double taxation agreement or on general principles.

6.2.4 Other employee share options

(ss 193–197 ITEPA 2003)

In limited circumstances, where no other charging provision applies, if an individual exercises an option that was granted to him or her as an employee at a time when he or she was either not resident in the UK or not ordinarily resident, and retains the shares, an income tax charge may arise on their eventual disposal. The legislation contains deeming provisions that treat the difference between the shares' market value at the time the option is exercised and the amount paid to exercise the option as if it were a loan. On a subsequent sale or disposal of the shares, the loan is deemed to be written off and an income tax charge arises if the individual is UK-resident at that time. If you think you may be in this situation, you should seek professional advice.

6.2.5 Reporting requirements

The grant or exercise of options must be notified on form 42 by 6 July following the end of the tax year.

PAYE must be accounted for on profits from options where the shares are readily convertible assets at the time of exercise. A further charge can arise unless the employee reimburses his or her employer within 90 days (see 21.1.4).

6.2.6 Retrospective legislation on options that form part of tax schemes

Section 443(1A) contains legislation that imposes a charge on certain options granted on or after 2 December 2004.

The legislation contains a 'purpose test' – basically, special rules apply where the right or opportunity to acquire a securities option was granted mainly to avoid tax or NIC. Options caught by this rule are taken out of the tax regime described in 6.3 and are taxed under legislation that applies to convertible securities (see the last part of 6.4.10), which would not otherwise be applicable to options.

HMRC has published the following example of the tax consequences where an option after 1 December 2004 fails the purpose test.

Example of the charge under s 443

> An option to purchase securities is used as part of an avoidance scheme. This brings into play anti-avoidance legislation first enacted in FA (No.2) 2005 that applies where convertible securities are acquired under an avoidance scheme. The application of this legislation means that the individual is taxed on the acquisition of the convertible security and the measure of the tax charge is based on a notional market value which assumes that the entitlement to convert is immediate and unconditional. The effect is to bring into charge the maximum possible gain.

6.3 APPROVED SHARE SCHEMES

(ss 517–526 ITEPA 2003)

6.3.1 Introduction

The types of approved share option schemes for employees are:

- save as you earn share option scheme (SAYE) – 6.3.2;
- share incentive plan (SIP) – 6.3.4;
- company share option plan (CSOP) – 6.3.10; and
- enterprise management incentives (EMI) – 6.3.13.

6.3.2 Approved SAYE-linked share option scheme

These schemes utilise an option for employees to purchase company shares at a price that must not be 'manifestly less' than 80% of their market value at the time the options are granted. The employee is required to take out an SAYE-linked savings scheme (maximum £500 pm) with a bank or building society and may use the proceeds to exercise the share option three, five or seven years later, depending on the rules of the particular scheme. No income tax liability arises on the grant or exercise of the options. CGT is charged on an eventual disposal of the shares. The limit on monthly contributions was £250 up to 2013–14.

6.3.3 Reporting requirements

The grant or exercise of options must be notified on Form 34 by 6 July following the end of the tax year.

Tax notes

SAYE schemes are a 'one way bet'. If the share price goes up, exercise the option. If it goes down, take your cash from the scheme instead.

6.3.4 Share incentive plan (SIP)

(ss 488–515 ITEPA 2003)

These plans may involve one or more of the following elements:

- free shares;
- partnership shares;
- matching shares;
- dividend shares.

The principle is that all employees should participate on similar terms. However, if an employer awards free shares, the award may made be partly or wholly by reference to performance targets. Under the plan, trustees acquire shares in the employing or holding company of a group. No income tax or NIC is payable on the award of shares to individual employees. All income and capital growth that arises while the trustees hold shares will normally be tax-free. The shares must be fully paid-up ordinary shares in a company that is not controlled by another company or shares in a quoted subsidiary of a company that is not a close company (see 18.14).

6.3.5 Free shares

An employee may be awarded free shares with a value of up to £3,600 pa (£3,000 up to 2013–14). The shares may be awarded partly by reference to objective criteria including salary and length of service. In such a case, the highest performance-linked award must not exceed four times the highest award by reference to non-performance linked criteria. In other cases (eg where all awards are by reference to performance), the employer must demonstrate to HMRC's satisfaction that the performance targets are broadly comparable.

Wherever awards are to be made by reference to performance, the targets and other criteria must be communicated to employees in advance.

Performance criteria may be linked to individual, team, divisional or corporate performance.

Free shares must be held by the trustees for a period of between three and five years. Shares can, at the employer's discretion, be awarded so that they will be forfeited if the employee leaves within three years.

Where an employee withdraws from the scheme within three years, income tax and NIC is payable on the shares' market value at the date of withdrawal. Where he or she withdraws between three and five years from an award, the employee is charged on the lower of the shares' initial value or their market value at the time that he or she withdraws.

Where an employment comes to an end because of death, disability or redundancy, the shares may be withdrawn tax free even if this occurs within the three-year period.

6.3.6 Partnership shares

Employees may relinquish up to £1,800 pa of their pay in return for 'partnership shares' (£1,500 up to 2013–14). This is subject to a limit of 10% of earnings. No income tax or NIC arises on salary forgone in this way, but the employing company receives a deduction in arriving at its taxable profits equal to the amount relinquished. The partnership shares cannot be subject to forfeiture, but the scheme rules can require the trustees to repay the sums invested if the employee leaves before acquiring shares.

Where an employee withdraws from the scheme within three years, income tax and NIC is payable on the shares' market value at the date of withdrawal. Where he or she withdraws between three and five years from an award, the employee is charged on the lower of the shares' initial value or their market value at the time that he or she withdraws.

Where an employment comes to an end because of disability or redundancy, the shares may be withdrawn tax free even if this occurs within the three-year period.

6.3.7 Matching shares

If an employer so wishes, matching shares can be awarded to employees on a basis of up to 2:1 (ie matching shares worth up to £3,600 pa can be offered to an employee who relinquished salary of £1,800 in order to 'buy' partnership shares). An award of matching shares may be made on the basis that they are forfeited if the employee leaves within three years or withdraws his or her partnership shares during that period. The tax treatment is similar to that for free shares.

6.3.8 Dividends

The legislation gives employers a choice of whether to offer dividend reinvestment. If dividends are paid out they are taxable income for the employees. However, dividends may be reinvested tax-free up to £1,500 pa.

6.3.9 Reporting requirements

Each year, a form 39 return is required for each approved scheme. The trustees will also receive a Trust SA Return for completion.

6.3.10 Company share option plan (CSOP)

The general principle is that if an employer agrees to abide by relatively strict constraints, he or she can offer employees tax-efficient share options worth up to £30,000 per individual.

6.3.11 Conditions for approval

To receive HMRC approval, the following conditions must be satisfied:

(1) Participation in the scheme must be open only to full-time directors or to full or part-time employees. Part-time directors may not participate in this scheme: HMRC has indicated that it regards a director who works 25 hours pw as full-time. The employer may choose which employees are to be permitted to participate in the scheme.

(2) Where the employer is a close company, no participant must (together with associates) own (or be entitled to acquire as a result of the grant of the option) more than 25% of the company's shares. Furthermore, no individual who has owned more than 25% of the company's shares within the previous 12 months can participate.

(3) The price at which the option is to be exercised must not be 'manifestly less' than the shares' value at the time the option is granted.

(4) There is a limit on the value of shares over which a particular employee may be granted options. The scheme must limit the employee's options to shares with a market value at the time the options are granted that does not exceed £30,000.

(5) The shares issued under the scheme must be fully paid ordinary shares of the company or its parent company. They must be shares either quoted on a recognised stock exchange or in a company not under the control of another company.

(6) Options must not be transferable.

(7) The exemption from income tax applies only to options exercised between three and ten years after they are granted or where the option is exercised within three years because of the individual's employment coming to an end by reason of death, retirement, redundancy, injury or disability.

6.3.12 Reporting requirements

The grant or exercise of options must be notified on form 35 by 6 July following the end of the tax year.

Tax notes

These approved options mean that you are not subject to an income tax charge unless you exercise the option within the first three years. You will be subject to CGT but only when you sell the shares. If you transfer some of the shares to your spouse or civil partner (and you have no other capital gains in the year), you can each realise tax-free capital gains of £11,000 in 2015–16.

6.3.13 Enterprise Management Incentives (EMI)

(ss 527–541 ITEPA 2003)

The main aspects of the EMI option scheme are as follows:

(1) Share options, with a value of up to £120,000 per employee, can be issued to employees. This refers to the value of underlying shares at the time the options are granted.

(2) The total value of shares over which options can be granted by a company or group of companies is £3m.

(3) The price at which options may be exercised may be more or less than market value at the time the options are granted.

(4) The only income tax charge is on exercise of the options and is equal to the difference between the shares' market value at the time of grant (or if lower at exercise) less the exercise price. If the options are granted at market value, no tax is payable.

(5) If the shares are readily convertible assets at the time the option is exercised any tax is collected through PAYE and NIC is charged on the same basis as the income tax charge.

(6) Where the conditions for entrepreneurs' relief are satisfied, see 17.7, the effective rate of CGT may be 10%. The Finance Act 2013 has made major changes here.

The normal requirement that a person selling shares must have a minimum 5% holding (and 5% of voting power) in order to qualify for entrepreneurs' relief was removed from 6 April 2013 where shares are acquired by the exercise of EMI options (or by a share exchange involving shares acquired by exercising such options). Furthermore, the period in which the option is held counts towards the 12-month ownership requirement for entrepreneurs' relief.

Only certain companies can operate the arrangement, and certain employees may be ineligible. A summary of the rules is as follows:

(a) the company must be independent and not under the control of another company;

(b) the company or, where relevant, a group member must be carrying on a qualifying trade defined as for EIS purposes (see 19.3.4) – this trade must be carried on through a permanent establishment in the UK;

(c) its gross assets cannot exceed £30m at the time the options are granted. The £30m test is applied on a consolidated basis where the company is the parent of a group of companies. There is a relieving provision that prevents a company from failing the £30m test simply by reason of its transferring an intangible asset within the group;

(d) the company or group must have fewer than 250 employees;

(e) the employee must be employed for at least 25 hours pw or, if less, 75% of his or her working time;

(f) the option ceases to qualify once the employee no longer meets the 25 hours pw 75% requirement;

(g) the employee must not own or control more than 30% of the shares in the company.

The grant of an EMI option must be notified to HMRC within 92 days.

Where an individual exercises an EMI option, the shares may be restricted shares (see 6.4.2 below). He or she is regarded as automatically making the election described at 6.4.7 if there is no income tax charge under (4) above (as this will always be to his or her advantage).

Where a company is taken over by another company which itself is able to establish an EMI scheme, an individual can surrender his or her options for replacement options in an EMI scheme operated by the new parent company. The value of the shares over which the new options are granted must not exceed the value at the time of the takeover of the shares to which the original options related.

6.3.14 Reporting requirements

The grant of EMI share options must be notified to HMRC no more than 92 days from the date of grant. Adjustments or exercises of options should be notified on form EMI 40 by 6 July following the end of the tax year.

Tax notes

EMI options are the most favourable type of options because they are flexible in that there is no minimum holding period and the share valuation can be agreed with HMRC before the options are granted. Where the conditions for entrepreneurs' relief are satisfied, the rate of CGT may be 10%.

6.4 SPECIAL SHARES, ETC

(ss 417–440 ITEPA 2003)

6.4.1 Background

The legislation on employee shares (also called 'employment-related securities') was substantially amended by Schedule 22, FA 2003, which focused on special shares such as restricted shares and convertible shares. It also dealt with situations where employee shareholders are treated in an especially favourable way.

In the main, the amended rules apply only to securities acquired on or after 16 April 2003 (but note the exception to this for conversion of employment-related securities – see 6.4.10 below).

Sections 6.4.2–6.4.7 below will not apply to events that occur more than seven years after the individual has ceased to be an employee of the company awarding the shares.

Further information is available on HMRC's website (www.hmrc.gov. uk/shareschemes).

6.4.2 Restricted securities

Until 5 April 2008, the charge on restricted securities applied only if the securities were acquired at a time when the employee was resident and ordinarily resident in the UK. It now also applies to restricted securities acquired by employees who are resident but not ordinarily resident in the UK. We cover the treatment of internationally mobile employees at 34.3 and 34.6.1. See also 6.5 on ESC A11 which may apply to income arising in the year in which an individual becomes resident in the UK or in which he or she ceases to be resident.

Sometimes shares or other securities subject to special restrictions, eg in relation to voting rights or freedom to sell are given (ie 'awarded') to employees. The shares may become much more valuable once the restrictions cease to apply. Similarly, shares may be awarded on the basis that they will be forfeited if a target is not met or if the employee leaves within a certain period. In such a situation, the employee only acquires full ownership of the shares when the forfeiture provisions fall away. Forfeiture provisions are really just a special type of restriction on the individual's ownership of his or her shares.

6.4.3 Meaning of 'restrictions'

Restrictions include the following:

- restrictions on dividend rights;
- restrictions on voting rights;
- restrictions on transferability.

The legislation provides that shares are not to be treated as restricted if the only restrictions are that:

- partly-paid shares will be forfeited if outstanding calls are not paid;
- the shares have to be sold if the employee is dismissed for misconduct;
- the shares are redeemable for payment.

For further details, see Figure 6.1.

Figure 6.1 – Does removal of restrictions mean there is an income tax charge?

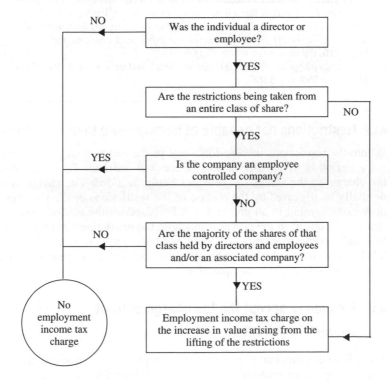

6.4.4 Charge depends on whether the restrictions can apply for more than five years

Schedule 22 made a significant distinction on restrictions that might last for more than five years.

6.4.5 Restrictions capable of lasting more than five years

If the shares or securities are subject to longer-term restrictions, an income tax charge will arise on the award of the shares and a further charge on the restrictions ceasing to apply. This is not a double charge; the amount taxed on the award of the shares is the market value of those shares, taking into account the effect of the restrictions, less anything paid by the employee for the shares. When these restrictions are lifted, the amount taxed is based on the increase in value as a result of lifting the restriction.

Example

> T was given shares on 1 June 2007 that had an open market value of £1,000. However, T will forfeit them if he leaves his employer before 1 July 2016. The effect of this restriction is to depress the value on acquisition to £650 (ie a 35% discount). When the forfeiture provisions cease to apply on 1 July 2016, the shares are worth £5,000.
>
> A tax charge arose for 2007–08 on £650 and arises for 2016–17 on £1,750, ie 35% of £5,000.

6.4.6 Restrictions not capable of lasting more than five years

Where the restrictions involve forfeiture provisions that can apply only for a period of five years or less, there will normally be no income tax charge on the shares or securities being awarded. The charge will normally be triggered by the release of the restrictions or the forfeiture provisions coming to an end and will be based on the market value at that time. Thus, if in the previous example the restrictions had been due to expire within five years, T would not have been taxed on £650 for 2007–08 but he would have been taxed on £5,000 for the year in which the restrictions ceased to be operative.

6.4.7 Election to accept the tax charge upfront

(ss 430–431 ITEPA 2003)

There is an election that is available. The employee can choose to accept a tax charge at acquisition on the full value, ignoring the effect of the restrictions. If he or she adopts this course of action, there will be no further income tax charge on the restrictions being lifted, the employee will have 'taken his or her medicine' upfront.

This election is available regardless of whether the restrictions are capable of remaining in force for more than five years. It must be made within 14 days of the shares being acquired.

> **Tax notes**
>
> Take advice on the value of shares at the time you receive them because it may be better to accept a modest upfront tax charge or even no charge to avoid having to pay tax when the forfeiture provisions expire.

Non-resident employees

From 6 April 2015, with the removal of the residence exclusion at ITEPA03 s421E, Chapter 2 can apply to restricted securities acquired whilst the employee is not resident in the UK and not carrying out duties in relation to a UK employment. However, elections under ITEPA03 ss 425(3), 430 and 431 may not be made unless at the time of the chargeable event (in the case of s 430) or the acquisition (in the case of ss 425(3) and 431), the earnings from the employment are general earnings to which any of the charging provisions of Chapters 4 and 5 of Part 2 applies.

6.4.8 Charge where value is extracted

(s 446A ITEPA 2003)

If value is extracted by artificial means, this will generally give rise to a chargeable event, with income tax and NIC becoming due on the value derived.

6.4.9 Special rules where restrictions are part of a tax-avoidance scheme

There is an exception to the general rule that no employment income tax charge arises on the acquisition of shares which are subject to forfeiture for up to five years (see 6.4.6 above). The legislation imposes a charge where the market value of the shares at the date that the restrictions are lifted has been artificially decreased by things done other than for genuine commercial purposes.

The legislation is drafted in wide terms and can apply where transactions are part of a scheme or arrangement designed to avoid tax or NIC. A charge can also arise where the market value of shares is artificially increased as part of such a scheme or arrangement.

6.4.10 Convertible securities

(s 439 ITEPA 2003)

An income tax charge can arise on the value of any new shares received when a share conversion takes place and the original shares were employment-related securities. It can also arise on an employee selling convertible securities to a third-party or on his or her receiving a payment for relinquishing the conversion rights. The amount charged takes account of any amount already charged on the acquisition of the original shares.

This charge is intended to catch arrangements where an employee receives shares with a low value that are later converted to shares with a much higher value. The charge does not normally arise where the event is triggered by the employee being disabled.

There is some concern that s 439 could apply to a gain realised by a former owner of a company on the completion of an earn-out satisfied by the issue of loan notes or other securities. This is likely to be a problem where the individual is required to remain with the company after selling out and he or she is receiving more than other vendors or where the earn-out is closely linked with his or her personal performance.

FA (No.2) 2005 introduced special rules where convertible securities are acquired as part of a tax avoidance scheme. Income tax may be charged on a notional market value of the option at acquisition, with this value being arrived at on the assumption that the right to convert is immediate and unconditional. The effect is to bring into charge the maximum possible gain.

6.4.11 Additional rights

(s 446K ITEPA 2003)

An income tax charge can arise where the value of employment-related securities is enhanced by means of non-commercial transactions. Once again, this charge can apply even where the individual was not resident and ordinarily resident at the time that he or she acquired the securities in question.

For the charge to apply, the market value of the employment-related securities must be increased by at least 10% by transactions carried out other than for genuine commercial purposes. The taxable amount is the increase in value and this is charged as employment-related income for the year in which the transactions take place.

6.4.12 Sale of shares by an employee at an overvalue

(s 446Y ITEPA 2003)

An income tax charge arises where an employer or connected person purchases employment-related securities from an employee for more than market value. The amount taxed as income is the over-value. Again this is not limited to situations where the employee was resident and ordinarily resident at the time that he or she acquired the securities in question.

6.4.13 Employee can elect to pay employer's NIC

Sections 428A and 442A provide tax relief if an employee bears his or her employer's NIC on a charge relating to restricted or convertible shares. This works in a similar way to the relief where an employer pays the NIC on exercising a non-approved option over readily convertible assets (see 6.2.2).

6.4.14 Partly-paid shares or shares acquired by borrowing from the employer

(s 446Q–U ITEPA 2003)

Where an employee acquires partly-paid shares, he or she is treated as if he or she had received a notional loan. An annual charge may arise on the interest that would have been payable if the 'loan' had carried interest at the official rate (see 4.7).

Where the employer lifts the obligation to pay up the outstanding amount, the employee is deemed to have received employment income for that year (s 446U). Furthermore, a sale of the shares will also normally be treated as a discharge of the obligation so that once again a tax charge arises on the amount of the notional loan.

These provisions could also apply where there is an actual loan, eg a loan from a major shareholder.

Section 446U can apply even though the individual was neither resident nor ordinarily resident at the time that he or she acquired the partly-paid shares if he or she subsequently carried on his or her employment whilst resident in the UK.

Tax notes

In many cases, it may be better for you to make shares fully paid before you sell them to avoid a tax charge under s 446U. This is a situation where you should take professional advice.

6.5 SPLIT YEAR TREATMENT

The residence status of an individual is decided for a complete tax year. When an individual's tax liability is affected by residence the tax year may be split. Liability to UK tax which is affected by residence is computed by reference only to that part of the year when the employee is resident.

HMRC, EIM42850

HMRC has clarified the application of the split year treatment to charges under the employment-related securities legislation. This issue has become more significant since radical reforms to the remittance basis were introduced by FA 2008 (see 34.3).

- **Year of arrival in the UK:** HMRC's view used to be that the split year treatment did not apply to taxable income arising during the year of arrival but before the individual came to the UK. However, it has emerged that many employers, taxpayers and advisers were not aware of this. HMRC therefore stated that the split year treatment would cover income from employment-related securities other than where there is a notional loan charge in respect of shares acquired at an undervalue (see 6.1). This will apply both in relation to past years where a taxpayer's liability has not been finalised, and going forwards (until further notice).

- **Year of departure from the UK:** Previous HMRC guidance had made it clear that ESC A11 did not apply during the year of departure but after the individual left the UK where a charge arose on the notional loan treatment of shares acquired at an undervalue (see 6.1). However, HMRC has reluctantly accepted that it had not made clear that the concession did not cover other tax charges under the employment-related securities legislation. It has therefore confirmed that the split year treatment may apply in the year of departure to prevent a tax liability arising under these other provisions of the employment-related securities legislation. ESC A11 was put on a statutory basis by FA 2014.

6.6 THE EMPLOYER'S PERSPECTIVE

An employer will often not wish to be tied into the 'democratic' aspects of some of the approved schemes, ie the principle that all employees must be allowed to participate on a similar basis (see 6.3). The managing director will often want to reserve the incentive for 'key employees' whose input to the business is likely to make a significant difference to its profitability. Enterprise Management Incentives (6.3.13) are one type of approved scheme that is aimed primarily at such people but there are limits, both to the equity available and the types of companies that can operate an EMI (eg a company that is a subsidiary of another company cannot do so). Other approved schemes contain a much lower ceiling for the value of shares that can be provided without a tax charge (see 6.3.10 on the £30,000 limit for CSOPs).

Employers will also be concerned that additional costs such as employer's NIC are kept to a minimum. If the company is going to receive a corporation tax deduction for the costs of establishing and operating a share scheme, this will reduce the net cost for the employer. See 18.3.2 on the circumstances in which the company may qualify for such relief.

6.7 SOME TAX PLANNING IDEAS

6.7.1 Subscription for shares

In some cases, it may be possible to keep things simple. Instead of having an option, the company pays a cash bonus and the amount that is left after PAYE and NIC is used by the individual to subscribe for new shares. This would make a lot of sense where a company has been set up relatively recently and the shares do not have a great deal of value (even though they are seen as capable of becoming very valuable if the business takes off).

Example

A company pays a bonus of £18,868 to a key employee. After 45% income tax and 2% NIC, he or she is left with £10,000 and uses this to subscribe for shares.

There will generally be some timing differences but overall the company's position could work out as follows:

	£
Bonus	18,868
Employer's NIC	2,604
	21,472
Cash returned to company as subscription for shares	(10,000)
Net cost to company	11,472
Corporation tax relief at 20%	(4,294)*
Effective net cost	7,178

* received nine months after company's year end

6.7.2 Make the election within 14 days

When this method is adopted, it will often be the case that the employee's shares are subject to restrictions and it will therefore be important that the individual and company make an election under s 431 ITEPA 2003 (see 6.4.7) so as to ensure that any future growth in value is subject only to CGT. This election has to be made within 14 days of the shares being issued to the employee.

6.7.3 Use approved schemes where possible

In cases where the shares have significant value, it is advisable to use approved schemes provided these fit in with the commercial objectives. For example, it may be that the controlling shareholders of a long-established company believe that a key manager will be tied into staying with the company in the medium term by being given 5% of the equity. Simply giving him or her the shares would give rise to an immediate income tax charge. Giving him or her an option may therefore be a better idea, especially if the option can be granted under an EMI scheme (see 6.3.13). Such options can be granted over shares worth up to £120,000. Subject to the various conditions being satisfied, the individual need then have no income tax liability on acquiring his or her shares. In due course it may be appropriate for the employee to be given a cash bonus to give him or her sufficient cash to exercise his or her option. Where this happens, the overall effect is exactly the same as if the manager had been given the shares except that he or she will suffer no tax beyond the PAYE on his or her cash bonus.

CSOP and EMI options can be granted selectively, ie the legislation does not require similar options to be offered to other employees.

The company will qualify for a corporation tax deduction for the difference between the amount payable on exercising the option and the market value of the shares at the date of exercise (see 18.3.2).

6.7.4 Consider making loans or issuing partly-paid shares

Suppose that the employing company's shares are not eligible for approved share options or EMI schemes (eg the company may be a subsidiary of another company).

One possible way of designing a tax-efficient share scheme would be for a loan to be made to the employee (possibly from a parent company or another group company as this will be excluded from the 'disguised remuneration' charge under Part 7A ITEPA – see Chapter 5 – unless there is a tax avoidance motive) and for the employee to use this to buy shares, whether by subscribing for new shares or in purchasing existing shares. In such cases, employees must always be given the opportunity to understand that they will be liable to repay the loan at some future time, even if the shares are by then worthless.

No income tax charge will normally arise at the outset provided the shares are not acquired at an undervalue. Once again, an election under s 431 may well be appropriate so that any profit on an eventual sale should be subject only to CGT (see 6.4.7).

No income tax charge will normally be payable on the loan provided interest is charged at a rate no lower than the official rate (see 4.7) or the company is a close company and the employee meets either of the tests set out in 11.5 (ie the employee has a material interest or is engaged full-time in the management of the company's business).

The employee may be better off subscribing for new shares if this will mean that he or she can secure income tax relief under s 131 ITA 2007 in the event of suffering a capital loss (see 17.2).

On a disposal of the shares, an income tax charge may arise on the amount of the loan unless the loan is repaid beforehand (see 6.4.14 on this)

6.7.5 Other possibilities

Recently, unquoted companies have explored the advantages of creating a separate class of growth shares. The idea is that these will have no intrinsic value unless the company is successful after their acquisition. Therefore they cannot give rise to an income tax charge on acquisition. However, if the company grows in value, any gain on these shares may be subject to income tax.

Listed companies have begun to use Joint Share Ownership Plans. These are complex structures that require shares to be jointly acquired by an employee benefit trust and an employee, with the employee's interest having little or no value at acquisition. If set up effectively, they have a similar tax treatment to growth shares.

In both cases, it is advisable to seek professional guidance before entering into such arrangements as they can easily go wrong.

6.8 VENTURE CAPITALISTS AND PARTICIPANTS IN MBOS

A concern for managers involved in MBOs (management buy-outs) is whether they may be subject to an income tax charge on their shares. Similarly, individuals who work for venture capital firms are able to participate in investments, either alongside the fund through 'co-investment schemes' or through a shareholding in the venture capital company, or by being a partner in a limited partnership.

HMRC has published a memorandum setting out a 'safe harbour' whereby such investments will be subject only to CGT rather than income tax if certain conditions are satisfied. See *The memorandum of understanding between the Revenue and the BVCA* online at admin.bvca. co.uk/library/documents/PDF_2.pdf.

7

SELF-EMPLOYMENT

This chapter contains the following sections:

(1) How self-employed individuals pay tax
(2) Are you really self-employed?
(3) Basis of assessment
(4) Partnerships
(5) Limited liability partnerships (LLPs)
(6) Partnership anti-avoidance rules
(7) Partnerships controlled outside the UK
(8) Relief for trading losses
(9) Rules for specific trades and professions

We cover the detailed rules governing the computation of profits for tax purposes in Chapter 16. This chapter focuses on the way in which a self-employed individual should deal with his or her tax affairs once the amount of the taxable profit or loss has been ascertained, usually by an accountant.

7.1 HOW SELF-EMPLOYED INDIVIDUALS PAY TAX

7.1.1 Payment of tax

Unlike employees who suffer deduction of tax from their earnings under PAYE, self-employed individuals pay tax directly to HMRC. Tax payable by them for 2014–15 needed to be paid in two instalments, on 31 January 2015 and 31 July 2015. The amount payable for each instalment was normally half the income tax liability for 2013–14. Any balance of tax for 2014–15 is then payable on 31 January 2016.

If you are in the construction industry scheme (CIS) and are not registered to receive gross payments, the contractor will deduct an amount (currently 20%) before paying you and is then responsible for paying this over to HMRC. You will still need to pay tax and NIC on your income through your tax return, but HMRC will set any deductions that have already been made from your income against this bill.

If you started self-employment fairly recently, and previously over 80% of your tax was collected under PAYE, you may find that you do not have to make instalment payments for 2015–16. However, the system will catch up with you on 31 January 2017 as you will then have to settle the whole of your 2015–16 tax and make the first payment on account for 2016–17.

> **Tax notes**
>
> Bear in mind that self-employed individuals have to pay instalments on account of their tax liability for the year, the first instalment falling due on 31 January within the tax year.

7.1.2 Completing your tax return

You will need to complete a special schedule as part of your SA tax return; this asks for details of the type of business you are carrying on. If your sales for the year ending in 2014–15 did not exceed £81,000, you can complete an abbreviated self-employment schedule (SA103S). You have the option of completing the tax return on the basis of four entries: sales, expenses, capital allowances and profit. Alternatively, a more detailed breakdown of expenses can be provided on the full length form, SA103F.

7.1.3 Ascertaining taxable profits based on accounts

There is no obligation to prepare accounts, although it may well be advisable to do so for other reasons. If accounts have been prepared it is advisable to send them with the SA return (or attach them as a PDF file for online filing), whether or not HMRC wants them, as this limits the scope for HMRC to reopen back years by making 'discovery assessments'.

Very often, accounts are drawn up for other reasons as well (eg for production to banks and other lenders) and it is important to bear in mind that there may need to be adjustments for tax purposes. There are also specific rules that govern the amount of capital allowances that a trader may claim – in broad terms, capital allowances are an adjustment for depreciation or wear and tear on equipment, etc used in the business.

7.1.4 Cash basis

(Chapter 3A ITTOIA 2005)

Key principles are as follows:

- a business whose accounts are prepared on the cash basis does not have to use accounts for a period that is aligned to the fiscal year;
- the cash basis applies to expenses as well as receipts;
- receipts are inclusive of VAT and include refunds of VAT;
- receipts include the value of payments-in-kind and amounts received for damages or insurance claims;
- goods taken for own consumption can be treated as sales at cost;

- the cash basis is optional;
- an election can be made for the cash basis only if turnover is less than the VAT registration limit (£81,000 for 2014–15);
- if a person carries on more than one business, the turnover test has to be satisfied in relation to the combined turnover;
- an election for the cash basis takes effect for the tax year concerned and each subsequent year until the individual opts out or the business's turnover for the preceding tax year exceeded twice the VAT registration limit (ie, using the current figure, £162,000).

7.1.5 Businesses that cannot use the cash basis

The following cannot use the cash basis:

- businesses carried on by companies;
- businesses carried on by LLPs;
- Lloyd's Underwriters;
- businesses which are using the herd basis;
- businesses which are averaging taxable profits.

7.1.6 Restrictions on loss relief

Losses arising to a business which uses the cash basis can be carried forward for only one year. Losses cannot be set against the individual's other income.

7.1.7 Simplified basis for computing expenses

Following a review of small business taxation by the Office of Tax Simplification (OTS), the Government introduced a simplified basis for computing certain expenses for small unincorporated businesses.

7.1.8 Simplified expenses

A flat rate allowance may be claimed for

- motor expenses;
- use of home for business purposes;
- use of premises both as a home and for business.

The flat rate allowances are as follows:

Motor expenses

Cars – 45p per mile for the first 10,000 business miles, 26p per mile thereafter
Motorcycles – 25p per business mile

Use of home for business

The number of hours worked at home is multiplied by the applicable amount. The applicable amount is between £10 and £26 per month, depending on the number of hours worked at home. The flat rate does not include internet or telephone expenses which can be claimed separately.

Premises used both as a home and for business

The private element is taken as:

- one occupant – £350 per month;
- two occupants – £500 per month;
- three or more occupants – £650 per month.

Fixed-rate allowances are not compulsory

It remains open for a trader to claim expenses by reference to actual expenditure.

7.2 ARE YOU REALLY SELF-EMPLOYED?

7.2.1 Introduction

It is not possible to elect to be self-employed; whether you are self-employed is a matter of fact. However, since the Taxes Acts do not define 'self-employment', the rules have evolved through decisions handed down by the courts.

The real distinction between being self-employed and an employee is that there is no 'master-servant' relationship. Yet in practice it is often difficult to discern the dividing line and HMRC may take a different view from the parties concerned. For example, freelance workers may not necessarily be recognised as being self-employed and salaried partners may be classified as employees. At one time, the position could be complicated further in that the Contributions Agency was responsible for assessing liability for NIC and occasionally reached a different conclusion from HMRC. Such grey areas have sometimes resulted in companies treating freelance workers as if they are employees and deducting tax and NIC under PAYE accordingly. This is essentially to protect the employer, as it is HMRC's practice to seek unpaid tax from them in cases where the company has not operated PAYE correctly. As a result, it is very difficult, for example, for workers in the computer industry to secure payment as being self-employed. Similar problems are often experienced by workers in the TV industry, journalists, actors and artistes, and many other industries where freelance workers are required to work 'on-site'.

HMRC has addressed this issue by the introduction of legislation (in April 2000) known colloquially as IR35. These rules are covered in more detail at 21.3 as they deal primarily with individuals who offer their services through a service company. During the consultation period leading up to the introduction of this legislation, HMRC consolidated its statements on the dividing line between being employed and self-employed: see www.hmrc.gov.uk/ir35/index.htm.

The Government recently asked the OTS to review IR35 to see if it could be replaced or improved upon. However, it looks as though we are going to be stuck with it for some time to come, as the Government's conclusion following the review was that it could ill afford to give up on this source of revenue. It is however considering whether the administration of the charge can be simplified.

7.2.2 HMRC's criteria

Guidelines issued by HMRC to clarify employment status (leaflet ES/FS1, www.hmrc.gov.uk/leaflets/es-fs1.pdf) include the following points:

(1) An employee generally does the work in person (and does not hire someone else to do it), working at times and places and in the way specified by the firm for whom the work is done and normally paid at hourly, weekly or monthly rates, possibly including overtime.

(2) A self-employed person may hire and pay others to do the work, or do it personally, in either case specifying the time and the way it is done, providing major items of equipment, being responsible for losses as well as profits and correcting unsatisfactory work in his or her own time and at his or her own expense.

These criteria are only for guidance and in some cases the courts have held that a person who did not fulfil the requirements in (2) above was nevertheless self-employed. Thus, a journalist who worked as a freelance sub-editor at various national newspapers was held by the Special Commissioners to be self-employed even though she carried out all her work at the newspapers' offices. Similarly, a test case sponsored by Equity resulted in the Special Commissioners finding that actors engaged in London West End theatre work were not employees.

First-tier Tribunal (previously Commissioners') decisions, unlike court decisions, do not set binding legal precedents. It was therefore even more important that the Court of Appeal held in *Hall* v *Lorimer* [1994] STC 23 that a TV vision mixer was self-employed even though he failed to satisfy virtually all of the above tests. The taxpayer used extremely expensive equipment provided by the TV companies concerned and his work was controlled rigorously.

The decision in *Castle Construction (Chesterfield)* v *HMRC*, SpC 723 shows how difficult it is for HMRC to show that freelance workers are employees rather than self-employed. See also *HMRC* v *Larkstar Data Ltd.*

Tax notes

Take professional advice if you are a borderline case rather than simply accepting a 'ruling' from HMRC. The rules can work in an unexpected way; for example there are provisions that can treat certain partnership income as if it were employment income subject to PAYE.

7.3 BASIS OF ASSESSMENT

7.3.1 The way in which residence status affects liability

(s 5 ITTOIA 2005)

A person is taxed on the profits of a trade carried on by him or her if he or she is resident in the UK regardless of where that trade is carried on. If he or she is not resident in the UK, he or she is taxed on the profits of the trade if it is carried on in the UK. If part of a trade is carried on in the UK, a non-resident person is taxed on the profits of that part of the trade.

7.3.2 Basis of assessment

The same rules apply for both trades and professions. A self-employed person may draw up accounts to any date he or she chooses; there is no requirement that accounts be made up to 5 April to fit in with the fiscal year (albeit HMRC may encourage him or her to do so). All self-employed individuals are now taxed on the 'current year' (CY) basis.

7.3.3 Current year basis

A business's assessable profits are dealt with on the CY basis. The basic principles of the current year basis are to tax 12 months' profits in each tax year of the business other than the first and last years; and over the life of a business, for profits taxed to equal profits actually earned. The CY basis of assessment is determined by the profits for the accounting year that ends in the year of assessment. Thus a business with a 31 May year end will be assessed for 2014–15 on its profits for the year ended 31 May 2014. Taxable profits for these purposes are those after deducting capital allowances (see 16.2).

Special rules govern the first tax year since there are normally no accounts that end in that tax year (see below).

Opening years

Special rules apply for the opening years:

Tax year	Taxable profits
Year one	the profits from the date of commencement to 5 April following
Year two	the profits in the 12-month accounting period ending in year two (if the period is more than 12 months long, only 12 months worth of profit is included), *or*
	if the period to the accounting date in year two is less than 12 months from commencement, the profits of the first 12 months (apportioned from two sets of accounts), *or*
	if there is no accounting date in year two, the profits of the 12 months to 5 April.
Year three onwards	the profits of the 12 month accounting period ending in the tax year, *or*
	12 months to 5 April if accounts not drawn up to a date in year three and there has been no change of accounting date.

Example – Opening years rules under the CY basis

A started in business on 6 October 2012. Accounts for the year to 5 October 2013 showed profits of £48,000. Profits for the year ending 5 October 2014 are £72,000. *A* will be assessed as follows:

	£
2012–13 'actual' basis	
($^6/_{12}$ × £48,000)	24,000
2013–14 first 12 months' profits	48,000
2014–15 CY basis	72,000

Example – Position where first accounts not drawn up for 12-month period

The precise way in which the opening year rules work is slightly more complicated when there are no accounts for a period of 12 months ending in the second tax year. This is covered by the following examples:

(1) *B* started in business on 1 January 2013. The first set of accounts was made up to 30 April 2013, then to 30 April 2014. *B* will be assessed on profits computed as follows:

2012–13	Profits of period 1 January to 5 April 2013.
2013–14	Profits of first 12 months, ie
	$^4/_4$ profits of period 1 January to 30 April 2013
	Plus $^8/_{12}$ of profits for year ended 30 April 2014.

> (2) C started up on 1 March 2013 and the first set of accounts was made up to 30 April 2014, ie there are no accounts ending in the second tax year. C's assessable profits are:
>
> 2012–13 $^1/_{14} \times$ profits for 14 months ended 30 April 2014.
>
> 2013–14   Profits of first tax year, ie
>
> $^{12}/_{14}$ profits for 14 months ended 30 April 2014.
>
> 2014–15 $^{12}/_{14} \times$ profits for 14 months ended 30 April 2014.

7.3.4 Final year of trading

An individual who ceases to carry on a business is taxed under the CY basis on the profits for a notional period that starts immediately after the basis period for the previous tax year and ends on the date that he or she ceases to trade. This can be illustrated by a case where a person makes up accounts to 30 April. Assume the profits for the year ended 30 April 2014 are £80,000. He or she ceases business on 30 November 2014 and profits for the final seven months amount to £50,000. The assessable income for 2014–15 is his or her profit for the period 1 May 2013 to 30 November 2014, ie £80,000 plus £50,000 (but subject to either overlap or transitional relief: see below).

7.3.5 Overlap relief

Because of the way a new business is assessed under the CY basis for the first two tax years, some profits may be taxed more than once. To compensate for this, and to ensure that over the life of the business tax is paid only on the actual amount of profits, overlap relief is given when the business is discontinued or, in the case of partners, when they leave the firm, and partially, on a change of accounting date closer to 5 April.

If the overlap relief exceeds the taxable profits for the final year, the balance may be treated as an allowable loss and either set against the individual's other income for that year or the preceding year, or carried back against profits of the last three years as terminal loss relief (see 7.7.7).

Example – Overlap relief

> In the first example at 7.3.3, in which A's first accounts end on 5 October 2013, $^{183}/_{365}$ of the first 12 months' profits are assessed twice. Accordingly, a figure of £24,000 is carried forward and is deducted from A's profits for the final year of trading. Thus, if A retires on 5 October 2020 and the final year's profits are £60,000, the assessment for 2020–21 will be as follows:

	£
CY basis	60,000
Less: overlap relief	(24,000)
Taxable profits	36,000

Change of accounting dates

Unless a business – from the date of commencement – draws up annual accounts ending in the period 31 March to 5 April, there will be overlap relief.

Example – Change of accounting dates (1)

G started trading on 1 October 2014. The profit for the first year of trading was £45,000. The basis of assessment for the opening years would be:

2014–15	1 October 2014 to 5 April 2015
2015–16	12 months to 30 September 2015
2016–17	12 months to 30 September 2016

The overlap period is the 187 days to 5 April 2016 that will be assessed both in 2014–15 and 2015–16. The overlap profit is £23,055.

If during the business's lifetime the accounting date were extended to bring it nearer to 5 April, the overlap relief would be utilised in part. The intention of the legislation is to give relief in full when accounts are drawn up on a fiscal year basis, ie for the year to 5 April, so if the accounting reference date is changed to 31 March or 5 April, the relief will be given in full. If the accounting period is shortened, additional overlap relief is created.

Example – Change of accounting dates (2)

G changes his accounting date to 30 April 2018. The profit in the year to 30 September 2017 is £90,000.

2017–18	12 months to 30 September 2017
2018–19	12 months to 30 April 2018

The period of overlap is 1 May 2017 to 30 September 2017. The overlap profit is therefore £37,726 over 153 days, which is combined with the earlier overlap profit to give an overlap profit of £60,781 over 340 days.

If G later extends his basis period towards 5 April, the overlap relief is used: logically, if G were to extend the accounting date to 5 April, all of the relief would be used.

Tax notes

Give consideration to the fact that the value of the relief will diminish in real terms with time. Professional advice should be taken in respect of using this relief during the course of the business by advancing the accounting date towards the following 5 April.

7.3.6 Transitional relief

The current year basis was brought in from 1997–98. Where a trader was in business before that date he is due transitional overlap relief which can generally be set against profits for the year of cessation.

Where the trader made up accounts to 30 April, the transitional relief will be 341/365 × the profits for the year ended 30 April 1997. Unless the trader has already utilised some or all of this relief by adopting a new accounting date which fell later in the tax year, the transitional relief is due for the year that he ceases to carry on the business.

Tax notes

Overlap relief is properly computed on a daily basis, however, HMRC is content to split years in these situations by either months or days providing there is consistency. Transitional relief will be allowed against current profits when the accounting date is moved to a point later in the tax year, or the individual ceases to carry on business.

7.4 PARTNERSHIPS

A partnership's profits are computed in the same way as a sole trader's (see 7.3). However, there are complications.

7.4.1 Salaried partners

A salaried partner is engaged under a contract of employment. His or her profits are normally taxed as employment income. His or her remuneration is treated as a normal employee cost in arriving at the firm's profits. Sometimes partners have a fixed share of profits and it is not always easy to determine whether they are self-employed or salaried partners. The main indicators that a partner is self-employed are that the individual has capital at risk and that he or she is not subject to the control and direction of the other partners.

7.4.2 Treatment of partners under CY basis

Partners assessed individually

Assessments under the CY basis have always been made on individual partners rather than on the firm itself. Each partner is responsible for settling his or her own tax liabilities and is not jointly and severally liable for the total amount of tax (apart from VAT) payable by the partners. There may be a minor exception to this where there are non-resident partners in the firm.

Application of CY basis to partners

Basically, each partner is treated separately and the rules described at 7.3.1–7.3.3 are applied.

Example – How partners' taxable income is computed

K and L start a firm on 6 October 2013. They share profits equally. On 6 January 2015, M joins them and takes a one-third entitlement to profits. Accounts to 5 October 2014 show a profit of £132,000. The accounts for the years to 5 October 2015 and 5 October 2016 show a profit of £240,000 and £300,000 respectively. The position is as follows:

2013–14 K and L are each assessed on the actual basis, ie the firm's profits of £66,000 for 2013–14 ($^6/_{12}$ × £132,000 profits for the year ended 5 October 2014) are divided equally between them, so K and L are each assessed on £33,000.

2014–15 K and L are assessed on their share of the firm's profits for the first 12 months, ie profits of £132,000 are divided equally and each is assessed on £66,000. M is assessed on the actual basis, because 2014–15 is her first tax year as a partner in this firm, so she is assessed on £20,000 ($^3/_{12}$ × her one-third share of the profits for the year ended 5 October 2015).

2015–16 K and L are assessed on the CY basis on their share of the firm's profits for the year ended 5 October 2015, ie £80,000 each. M is assessed on the profits for her first 12 months (ie $^9/_{12}$ × £80,000 plus $^3/_{12}$ × £100,000).

From 2016–17 all three partners are assessed on the CY basis, ie their one-third share of the firm's profits for the year ended 5 October 2016 of £300,000.

Similarly, the provisions on overlap relief are applied separately in relation to each partner. Thus, in the above example, if K retired on 5 October 2016, he would be entitled to overlap relief in arriving at his taxable profits for 2016–17. The other ongoing partners will get their overlap relief only when they retire or the firm changes its accounting date (see below). Their overlap relief is as follows:

	£
K	33,000
L	33,000
M	45,000 ($^3/_{12}$ × £80,000 + $^3/_{12}$ × £100,000).

7.4.3 Partnership interest and other investment income

A partner may be entitled to a share of interest earned by the firm on surplus cash – or indeed any other investment income.

Each partner is assessed on his or her share of such income, but it is assessed on the CY basis. Thus, if a firm makes up accounts to 31 May, the partners will be assessed for 2015–16 on their share of investment income in the firm's accounts for the year ended 31 May 2015 – even though the relevant income may actually have been received during the tax year 2014–15. Overlap relief and transitional overlap relief therefore applies to partnership untaxed investment income such as gross interest or rental income. The exception to this is investment income taxed at source, which is assessable on a tax-year basis, ie bank interest received net.

7.4.4 Partnership tax returns

As well as requiring returns from individual partners, HMRC issues a partnership tax return to the 'nominated partner'. The return requires full details of the firm's profits and capital gains and the way profits (and losses) are divided between the partners.

7.4.5 Expenditure incurred personally by a partner

The legislation requires that all business expenses must be claimed on the partnership return, even where the expenditure is borne by an individual partner (eg his or her car expenses or the purchase of a fax machine for business use at home). HMRC states in Helpsheet HS231 that:

> The only legal basis for giving relief for expenditure that qualifies for capital allowances is as a deduction in the calculation of the profits of the partnership business (unless there is a formal leasing agreement between the partner and the partnership, when the allowances will be due against the leasing income).

However, this does not mean that any legitimate expenditure incurred by a partner – that is any expense that would be allowable if met from partnership funds – can only be relieved if it is formally included in the partnership accounts. Nor does it mean that capital allowances can only be claimed on vehicles, or other assets, that feature in the partnership accounts. Provided that:

- any expenditure, or claim to capital allowances, is correctly calculated for tax purposes; and
- records relevant to those calculations are made and kept as if the expenditure, or assets, were part of the partnership accounts.

HMRC will accept entries in the relevant sections of the Partnership Tax Return that, although based on the partnership accounts, include adjustments for such expenditure, or allowances. But once the adjustments have been made the expenditure will be treated, for all practical purposes, as if it had been included in the partnership's accounts.

7.4.6 Interest paid by partners on personal loans

Where a partner has taken a personal loan to finance buying into the firm or to provide part of its working capital, he or she can claim relief for the interest paid on such borrowings. However, this relief is given by way of a deduction from his or her total taxable income rather than as an expense in computing his or her trading profits (see 11.4).

7.5 LIMITED LIABILITY PARTNERSHIPS (LLPS)

7.5.1 Background

Specific legislation on limited liability partnerships (LLPs) was enacted in 2000. In essence, an LLP is a hybrid. Legally, it takes the form of a body corporate (a company) with its own legal personality, but for tax purposes it may be treated as transparent. Provided the LLP is carrying on a lawful business with a view to profit, its members have always been taxed as if they were partners in a partnership (ie as self-employed). This tax treatment no longer applies where members of a LLP are classified as employees (see 7.6).

Members are assessed on their share of the LLP's profits and capital gains. Unlike a conventional partnership, there is no joint and several liability between the members. Members' liability, in most cases, is limited to the capital contributed to the LLP, together with any further capital they may have agreed to contribute in the event of winding up the LLP. Undrawn profits do not automatically become part of a member's capital contributed (unless otherwise agreed). The member ranks equally with other unsecured creditors for repayment of his or her current account balance. This contrasts with conventional partnerships where the partner is jointly and severally liable for partnership debts other than tax to the full extent of his or her personal assets. An LLP may therefore have attractions as compared with conventional partnerships, but there can also be drawbacks. For example, the LLP is technically a company and has to file accounts and disclose certain financial information, broadly in line with companies of a similar size.

7.5.2 Restriction of loss relief

If a loss arises, there may be a restriction on the member's ability to set the loss against his or her other income. The limit is the amount of capital contributed by the member.

This restriction does not apply where the LLP carries on a profession. Guidance notes on LLPs can be obtained from Companies House (www.companieshouse.gov.uk).

7.6 PARTNERSHIP ANTI-AVOIDANCE RULES

Following consultation and the publication of draft legislation, complex anti-avoidance measures relating to the taxation of partnerships were enacted in FA 2014 and took effect from 6 April 2014.

The measures introduced are intended to combat:

- the disguising of employment relationships through LLPs by making the individual a 'salaried member';
- artificial or contrived allocations of business profits and losses in mixed partnerships where there are individual and non-individual partners; and
- tax-motivated disposals of assets through partnerships.

The necessary statutory amendments to enable the operation of PAYE in respect of income tax payable and the collection of national insurance contributions on behalf of salaried members of LLPs from 6 April 2014 have also been made.

See also 33.8.

7.6.1 Disguised fee income

FA 2015 contains legislation which can apply to investment managers from 6 April 2015. The provisions are intended to ensure that annual management fees are taxed as income in situations where partnerships or LLPs are used. They apply to all arrangements where there is an attempt to disguise what is, in substance, an investment management fee so that it is not taxable as income.

Carried interest is excluded from these provisions.

HMRC issued a Technical Note on this on 29 March 2015.

7.7 PARTNERSHIPS CONTROLLED OUTSIDE THE UK

(ss 857–858 ITTOIA 2005)

A UK resident may be a partner in a partnership controlled outside the UK. His or her earnings from such a partnership are taxable in the same way as if they arose from a partnership controlled in the UK unless he or she is not domiciled in the UK. A foreign domiciled partner's share of profits from a trade (or part of a trade) carried on outside the UK are taxed on the remittance basis, subject to making the relevant election (see 35.2).

7.7.1 Current year basis

A partner in a foreign partnership is assessable on the CY basis (see 7.3.3).

7.7.2 Classification of overseas entities

In practice, it is often not clear whether an overseas legal entity will be treated as a partnership or a company for UK tax purposes. This is so especially where an entity combines some of the characteristics of UK partnerships and companies. HMRC sets out its opinion of the correct tax treatment of various US and European entities in its International Manual (www.hmrc.gov.uk/manuals/intmanual/INTM180000.htm).

7.8 RELIEF FOR TRADING LOSSES

Relief may be available for a loss incurred by an individual in a trade or profession. Relief may also be due for pre-trading expenditure treated as a loss incurred when the trade was commenced (see 16.3). The provisions that govern the relief for trading losses are complex and there are several ways in which it is possible to claim for losses to be utilised.

7.8.1 Carry forward relief against subsequent assessments

(s 83 ITA 2007)

A loss incurred by a sole trader or a partner's share of his or her firm's trading loss may be carried forward and deducted in assessments for later years in respect of the same trade or profession. With the introduction of the CY basis of assessment (see 7.3.3), capital allowances are treated as trading expenses and can therefore increase or create a loss. Where losses are carried forward in this way, they must be used against the assessable profits for the first subsequent year in which profits arise. The loss carried forward in this way may also be relieved against certain income connected with the trade even though it is assessed under different provisions (eg interest earned on temporary investment of trade receipts and dividends from trade investments). There is no limit on the number of years for which a loss may be carried forward provided the same trade is carried on.

The loss must be claimed within four years of the tax year end (ie for a loss arising in 2011–12, by 5 April 2016).

Table 7.2 – Losses under self-assessment for 2013–14

Reference	Description	Deadline
s 64 ITA 2007	Deduction from general income for 2012–13 or 2013–14	31 Jan 2016
ss 261B and 261C TCGA 1992	Deduction from capital gains for 2012–13 or 2013–14	31 Jan 2016
s 72 ITA 2007	Loss in first four years of trade carried back	31 Jan 2016
s 83 ITA 2007	Carry forward against future profits	5 April 2018
s 89 ITA 2007	Terminal loss relief	5 April 2018

7.8.2 Relief against general income

(s 64 ITA 2007)

Where a sole trader or partner incurs a loss and the trade was carried on with a view to profit, the loss may be relieved against his or her general income for the year of assessment in which it was incurred (ie his or her total income for the year). Relief may also be claimed against general income for the preceding tax year. The claim for a loss to be set against his or her general income for the preceding tax year is an alternative to the claim for the loss to be relieved against income of the year of loss. In other words, either the loss may be set against income of the current year (with any balance being set against income of the previous year) or the individual may forgo the chance to set the loss against his or her income for the current year and set the full amount against income of the preceding year.

Where an individual takes relief for trading losses against his or her general income, he or she must use up the losses to the extent to which he or she has taxable income. It is not possible for a claim to be made to restrict the amount of losses so as to enable sufficient income to be left to make use of personal allowances. On the other hand, the legislation permits the deduction of certain items before arriving at the general income against which trading losses can be offset. These items include relief for allowable expenses for employment income purposes, retirement annuity and personal pension contributions, interest relief and relief for donations to charities by deed of covenant or Gift Aid.

Relief for losses against other income must be claimed within 22 months of the end of the tax year in which the loss arises (ie one year after the filing date for the return relating to that year of assessment) so that a 2013–14 loss must be claimed by 31 January 2016.

Cap on tax reliefs for 2013–14 and subsequent years

A claim for losses to be set against an individual's other income may be affected by the cap on tax reliefs – see 11.14.

7.8.3 Relief by aggregation

Where the profits of different accounting periods are time apportioned (eg on commencement of a business), a loss may be relieved by aggregation with a profit. This situation could arise if a first period of trading were less than 12 months.

Example – Loss relief by aggregation

W started business on 1 January 2014. She made a loss of £6,000 for the period ended 30 September 2014 and a profit of £24,000 for the year ended 30 September 2015. Relief by aggregation would produce the following result:

Profits assessable 2013–14	Nil
Profits assessable 2014–15	Nil
Profits assessable 2015–16	£24,000

This is because the first 12 months' trading would be deemed to produce a net loss computed as follows:

	£
Loss for period 1 Jan to 30 Sept 2014	(6,000)
3/12 of profit for year ended 30 Sept 2015	6,000
	Nil

If a loss is set against other income, it cannot also be relieved by aggregation. Thus, if W had claimed relief for the £2,000 loss that she had incurred in 2013–14, only the balance of the loss for the period ended 30 September 2014 which relates to the period 6 April to 30 September 2014 could be taken into account in arriving at the profits of the first 12 months' trading. The 2014–15 assessment would then be £2,000.

Example – Loss set against other income

Y commenced trading on 5 August 2014. He has a loss during the nine months ended 5 May 2015 of £36,000. He has profits for the year ended 30 April 2016 of £60,000.

If the 2014–15 loss was used by being set against Y's other income, the taxable income would be:

		£
2014–15		Nil
2015–16	Profits of first 12 months:	
	9 months ended 5 May 2015	(4,000)
	3/12 × profits for year ended 5 May 2016	15,000
		11,000
2016–17	CY basis profits for year ended 5 May 2016	60,000

Contrast this with the situation where relief for the loss is obtained by aggregation:

2014–15		Nil
2015–16	Loss for 9 months to 5 May 2015	(36,000)
	3/12 × Profits for year ended 5 May 2016	15,000
	Loss carried forward	(21,000)
2016–17	Profits assessed on CY basis	60,000
	Less: loss brought forward	(21,000)
		39,000

7.8.4 Losses arising from a business taxed under CY basis

Under the CY basis (see 7.3.3), losses are attributed to a tax year in the same way as profits are assessed. This means that once the business has got past the opening years, a loss will be treated as arising in the tax year in which the trader's accounting period ends. Losses for the opening years are computed on exactly the same basis as profits.

7.8.5 Losses in early years of a trade

(s 72 ITA 2007)

In certain circumstances, relief may be claimed against an individual's general income for the three years of assessment preceding the year in which the loss is incurred. Relief is given against income for the earliest year first.

There are certain preconditions for a loss to be claimed in this way:

(1) The loss must arise during the first four tax years in which the business is carried on.

(2) Where a trade is acquired from a spouse or civil partner, the four years run from the date the spouse first commenced trading (unless the trade is taken over on the spouse's death).

(3) The trade must be carried out on a commercial basis and with a reasonable expectation of profits.

The claim for a 2013–14 loss must be made by 31 January 2016, to be relieved in this way.

Tax notes

Many new businesses take time before generating substantial profits. In the past you might have been in a job that paid well and a large part of your earnings was taxed at 40% or 45%. Carrying back losses in this way could enable you to recover tax paid at higher rates whereas setting the losses against your income for the current year or carrying them forward may give you only limited benefit.

7.8.6 Relief for trading losses against capital gains

(ss 261B and 261C TCGA 1992)

An individual who has incurred a trading loss may claim to have it set against any capital gains that arise in the same or preceding year. It is not possible to claim relief for losses in this way without first having made a claim for relief for the loss to be set against the individual's general income for the year (see 7.8.1 for the time limit for making such a claim).

Tax notes

If you have a substantial loss, you should look into the possibilities for relieving it against capital gains. However, this is generally a 'last resort', especially as trading losses which are used in this way attract a maximum rate of relief of 28% as opposed to the 40% or 45% relief which may be achieved by setting losses against income that would otherwise be taxed at the top rate.

7.8.7 Terminal loss relief

(s 89 ITA 2007)

Where a trade, profession or vocation is permanently discontinued, a loss incurred during the last 12 months can be deducted from the profits charged to tax in the three tax years before the final year. The relief can include a claim for the loss arising in the tax year in which the cessation takes place as well as a proportion of the loss for the previous tax year.

Capital allowances for the final tax year may also be claimed, as can an appropriate proportion of the preceding year's capital allowances, representing the allowances due for the period beginning 12 months before the cessation.

The terminal loss may be carried back against profits from the same trade for the three tax years immediately preceding the year of cessation. The relief is given against the latest year's profits first.

If interest and dividends would have been included as trading profits (except for the fact that they were subject to deduction of tax at source), the terminal loss may be set against such income.

7.8.8 Anti-avoidance provisions

Losses from limited partnerships

(ss 104 to 106 ITA 2007)

Limited partnerships have, in the past, been widely used in tax avoidance arrangements. The House of Lords decided in *Reed* v *Young* [1986] STC 285 that a limited partner could be entitled to loss relief for an amount that exceeded his or her actual liability under the Limited Partnership Act. This led to specific legislation to limit the amount of loss relief to the capital that is 'at risk'. Any losses incurred beyond this amount must be carried forward to be set against any future share of profits received by the limited partner from the firm. The s 104 provisions apply to individuals who are limited partners or members of a joint venture arrangement under which their liability is limited to a contract, agreement, guarantee, etc.

'Non-active partners'

A partner who devotes less than ten hours a week to the partnership business cannot secure relief against other income for losses that exceed the capital he or she has contributed to the firm. Losses that exceed this capital must be carried forward and used only to offset profits from the firm for a later year. This rule came into effect on 10 February 2004.

Further legislation that came into effect on 2 March 2007 prevents any sideways relief where participation in the partnership forms part of tax avoidance arrangements. Furthermore, even where no such avoidance arrangements are present, FA 2007 restricts the tax relief available to non-active partners to £25,000 a year. The perceived abuse occurred where a non-active partner contributed capital to a partnership to take advantage of tax losses.

'Non-active sole traders'

As a result of the numbers of individuals switching from taking part in loss-making partnership arrangements to sole trader structures, following the FA 2007 anti-avoidance legislation, similar provisions were introduced from 12 March 2008 for sole traders who devoted less than ten hours a week to a loss-making business. Once again, loss relief against other income is restricted to £25,000 (and sideways relief is excluded altogether where the business forms part of tax avoidance arrangements). These provisions do not apply to Lloyd's Names or qualifying film expenditure.

Loss relief for film partnerships, etc

FA 2004 contained anti-avoidance provisions aimed at individuals who participate in partnerships only for tax planning purposes. We deal with these provisions at 25.8.

7.8.9 Loss relief where business transferred to a company

(s 86 ITA 2007)

Where a business has been carried on by an individual (either as a sole trader or in partnership) and is transferred to a company, it is possible for any unused trading losses to be relieved against his or her income from the company in subsequent years. This relief is available only if the business is transferred to a company wholly or mainly in return for an allotment of shares and then only if the individual has retained ownership of those shares throughout the tax year concerned. In practice, HMRC is unlikely to withhold relief provided the individual has retained at least 80% of the shares.

7.8.10 Losses from an overseas partnership

(s 95 ITA 2007)

A UK resident partner's share of profits from a trading partnership that is managed or controlled abroad are taxed under s 852 ITTOIA 2005 (formerly Schedule D Case V). If a loss should arise, relief is calculated in the same way as for a loss incurred in a UK trade, profession or vocation. Relief for such losses is then given in the same way as relief is given for UK trading losses, except that where a loss is to be set against other income, the loss can be deducted only from:

- profits from other foreign trades;
- foreign pensions and annuities where a 10% deduction is available;
- foreign emoluments taxed as employment income.

7.9 RULES FOR SPECIFIC TRADES AND PROFESSIONS

7.9.1 Farmer's averaging

(ss 221–225 ITTOIA 2005)

It is possible for a farmer to make a claim under which his or her profits of two consecutive years of assessment are averaged. This election cannot be made where the profits of the lower year exceed three-quarters of the other year's profits.

Where the profits of the lower year are no more than 70% of the higher year's profits, the results of the two years are simply averaged. Where the profits of the lower year are between 71% and 75% of the higher year, averaging is done as follows:

Take three times the difference between the two years' profits	A
Deduct 75% of the profits for the higher year	(B)
	C

The resulting figure (C) is taken away from the taxable profits for the higher year and added to the profits for the lower year, to give the assessable profit for each year.

The averaging period will be extended from two to five years in FA 2016.

7.9.2 Farming losses

Restrictions in s 67 ITA 2007 may apply to losses suffered by farmers. The legislation may prevent a farming loss being set against the individual's other income where he or she has suffered losses for each of the preceding five tax years. This period may be extended to 11 years for thoroughbred horse breeders (see *Taxline* 1991/71) – this concession (which dates from a 1982 meeting of the then Inland Revenue and the Thoroughbred Breeders Association) applies to breeding of all thoroughbred horses (not just racehorses). The restriction will also not be applied where it can be shown that no reasonably competent farmer would have expected to have made a profit until after the period end. It should be noted that the loss position is considered before being adjusted for capital allowances.

When dealing with a farming business being carried through a partnership the losses available to a non-active partner are restricted by s 26 ITA 2007.

8

INCOME FROM UK PROPERTY

This chapter contains the following sections:

(1) Basis of assessment and administration
(2) How to calculate your taxable profit
(3) Lump sums deemed to be rent (premiums)
(4) 'Rent-a-room' relief
(5) Furnished holiday accommodation
(6) 'Buy to let' investments
(7) Capital allowances on investment properties
(8) Losses
(9) Mineral royalties
(10) Woodlands
(11) Property investment companies
(12) VAT considerations
(13) Interest earned on trust funds for service charges and sinking funds

8.1 BASIS OF ASSESSMENT AND ADMINISTRATION

8.1.1 All rental activities treated as single business

All rental income received by an individual from UK properties is assessed under s 264 ITTOIA 2005, whether the property is let unfurnished or furnished. All income and expenses are brought together in a single business of letting UK property. Income and expenses on overseas properties are totally excluded when computing the profits of an individual's UK property business and deficits on overseas properties cannot be offset against profits that fall into the other category.

The income from a UK property business is determined using normal commercial accountancy principles, on an accruals, rather than a cash, basis. Expenses are allowed if they satisfy the test that the expense is incurred wholly and exclusively for business purposes and this rule applies to interest (including overdraft interest) just as for any other expense.

8.1.2 Exceptional types of rental income

Rental income includes ground rents. It also includes 'other receipts from an estate' in land such as charges levied by a landlord in return

165

for maintaining a block of flats and payments made to a landowner for sporting rights. It does not include admission charges made by hotels, boarding houses, theatres, etc, since the profits of such businesses are chargeable to tax as trading income.

Income from taking in lodgers is generally treated as trading income rather than UK property business income. However, see 8.4 on 'rent-a-room' relief.

8.1.3 Property income assessed on fiscal year basis

An individual must report income on a tax-year basis, ie accounts must be drawn up to 5 April.

8.1.4 Partnership income dealt with separately

Rental income received by a partnership is treated as a separate source. If the partnership does not have any trading income, the rental income is assessed on a fiscal-year basis, irrespective of the date to which the partnership draws up accounts. In contrast, if the partnership also has some trading income, its UK property income is assessed on the same basis. Thus, if a trading partnership had a 30 April year end, the partners will be assessed for 2015–16 on their share of the partnership's UK property income for the year ended 30 April 2015.

8.1.5 UK property income is investment income

(ss 118, 120 ITA 2007)

Although all UK rental income is treated as arising from a single business of letting property, the income is still treated as investment income. Any losses can only be carried forward for offset against UK property income and cannot be set against the individual's other income for the year. There are exceptions; where capital allowances are available, the lower of the net capital allowances and the loss itself may be set against other income, and for deficits arising from letting agricultural properties, the deficit may be set against other income (see below).

8.1.6 Husband and wife

Income from properties held in joint names by married couples or civil partners is normally taxed 50:50.

Where the ownership of the properties is not 50:50, an election can be made on form 17 so that the rental income is divided according to the way in which the property is owned beneficially.

It is possible for a property to be held in the name of one party but owned beneficially by another (eg a husband holds the property as bare trustee for his wife or children). The fact that the person holds the property as bare trustee needs to be evidenced by a deed. In such a situation, the rental income is taxed as the beneficial owner's income.

8.1.7 Record keeping

A landlord is required to maintain complete records of all expenses incurred and income received from his property business. These records must be kept for five years and 10 months after the end of the tax year to which they apply.

Where the property is let as furnished holiday accommodation (see 8.5), the number of days that each property is let to a particular tenant should be recorded.

8.2 HOW TO CALCULATE YOUR TAXABLE PROFIT

The legislation requires that landlords should calculate their income and expenses in accordance with normal accountancy principles but subject to the same specific rules that apply for computing trading profits (see Chapter 16).

You should study the notes and help sheets issued by HMRC to enable landlords to complete their SA tax returns. HMRC's guide to the SA return sets out the normal treatment of certain common expenses.

8.2.1 Pre-letting expenditure

The cost of renovating a property to bring it into a fit condition for letting is regarded as capital expenditure. It should be added to the capital cost of the property rather than deducted from the rental income.

Other pre-letting expenses such as minor repairs to the property (eg such as replacing locks, painting and cleaning) can be deducted from the rents received in the first tax year of the letting business if the following conditions are met:

- the costs are incurred within seven years of the start date for the business;
- the expenses would have been deductible if they had been incurred after the property rental business started.

However, the property must be in a habitable condition before these repairs are carried out, and in a fit state to let out. The landlord needs to be able to show that the property was in a fit state to be let before such expenditure was incurred.

8.2.2 Rent receivable

HMRC confirms in its manuals that you do not bring rent into a year's tax computation merely because you receive it, or it is due to be paid to you, in the year. Equally, you do not exclude rent merely because you receive it outside, or it is due outside, the tax year. You bring in the proportion of rent earned in the year from the tenants' use of the property in the year. You exclude the proportion earned from the tenant's right to use the property outside the year. So, you may need to make an adjustment where rent is receivable, say, quarterly, either in advance or in arrears. Incidentally, HMRC's notes to the SA return point out that rental income includes receipts-in-kind as well as in cash.

However, see 8.2.14 regarding the use of a cash basis in preparing accounts and returns.

8.2.3 Bad debts

A landlord can claim a deduction for rent that is due to him or her but has not been paid where the debt is clearly irrecoverable. A deduction can also be claimed for doubtful debts. Such a deduction is available only where the landlord has taken all reasonable steps to recover the debt. Furthermore, if the outstanding rent is collected in a later tax year, he or she should bring the recovery into his or her accounts as a receipt for his or her rental income for that year.

No deduction is available for a general bad debt reserve (ie a landlord cannot deduct 5% of the outstanding rents due to him or her at the year end just to be on the safe side). Tax relief is available for provisions for doubtful debts only if the provisions relate to specific debts and the facts relating to each debtor have been taken into account. Furthermore, as HMRC literature makes clear, you cannot deduct a bad or doubtful debt merely because the tenant is always a slow payer. There has to be good reason for thinking the debt is likely to be bad.

8.2.4 Rent-free periods

HMRC's approach follows the accounting principles set out in SSAP21. If the landlord, for example, grants a lease for a five-year period with no rent being payable in year one and rent of £10,000 being payable in years two to five, the landlord should spread the total amount of rent receivable over the five years (ie £40,000) and bring into his or her accounts one-fifth of that total income for each year of the lease. In other words, the treatment reflects the substance of the transaction; in essence there is not really a rent-free year at all since the £40,000 payable over the first five years is rent for the whole of that period.

8.2.5 Expenses

Expenses should also be brought into account on normal accountancy principles. This means that a landlord should deduct any allowable expenses that relate to work done, or goods or services supplied to him or her, for a particular year. There is no requirement that the supplier should have been paid during the tax year. Thus if you have raised a loan for the purchase or improvement of repairs of properties that are let out, you can claim relief for interest that has accrued up to 5 April even though the bank or building society may debit interest on a different basis (eg at 30 June and 31 December).

Expenses are deductible only if they meet the 'wholly and exclusively' rule (ie expenditure that is part business/part private is not allowable). For example, the cost of travelling to Wales to supervise repairs to a holiday cottage is not an allowable deduction for tax purposes if the landlord also takes a holiday while there (ie the visit had a dual purpose). But where a definite part or proportion of an expense is wholly incurred for business purposes, that part may be deducted. This may well arise where a landlord lives in part of the property that is rented out: here, a proportion of the insurance premium relating to the property as a whole may be deducted in arriving at the landlord's UK property income. Remember that where expenditure is partly for business and partly for personal use, you have to complete a specific box on the SA return.

A landlord may use his own car to visit properties or tenants. He may also work from home on paperwork and administration of the property business. He may use the fixed rate deductions to calculate the appropriate motor expenses and use of home deductions to include in the property letting accounts (see 7.1.8).

8.2.6 Repairs, maintenance and renewals

Examples of common repairs normally deductible in computing income for tax purposes are:

- exterior and interior painting and decorating;
- stone cleaning;
- damp and rot treatment;
- mending broken windows, doors, furniture and machines such as cookers or lifts;
- re-pointing;
- replacing roof slates, flashing and gutters.

Improvements are generally treated as capital expenditure. However, if the replacement of a part of the 'entirety' is like-for-like, or the nearest modern equivalent, HMRC generally accepts the expenditure is allowable revenue expenditure. For example, HMRC has confirmed that the cost of replacing worn out single-glazed windows with double glazing may be an allowable expense in computing UK property income (see *Tax Bulletin* 59). Substantial repairs carried out shortly after a landlord has occupied a property to put it into a fit state are generally disallowed as constituting capital expenditure.

The *Jenners* case (see 16.1.9) means that a specific and scientifically calculated provision for the cost of repair work to be carried out in the future might be allowable. You need to take specialist advice on whether making such a provision accords with the generally accepted accountancy principles set out in FRS12.

8.2.7 Energy saving allowance

Until 5 April 2015, landlords of residential property were allowed a deduction for expenditure of up to £1,500 per dwelling on the installation of the following energy saving items:

- loft insulation;
- cavity wall insulation;
- solid wall insulation;
- draught proofing;
- hot water system insulation;
- floor insulation.

The maximum deduction for a tax year was £1,500, but the way in which this limit applies depends on when the expenditure was incurred.

Originally, the limit applied to all the expenditure incurred in relation to a building, irrespective of how many separate dwellings there were in the building and how many possibly eligible claimants there might be for the building, ie only one £1,500 allowance was available, even if the property contained ten eligible flats.

The limit applied to all expenditure incurred in relation to each separate dwelling. So if there are three flats in a building, relief of up to £4,500 per tax year could be available. The relief was also available to corporate landlords who let residential property.

8.2.8 Refurbishing business premises in disadvantaged areas

Business Premises Renovation Allowances (BPRA) were originally introduced for an initial period of five years. The Government decided in 2011 that the allowance should be retained until at least 2017.

The BPRA provides relief against the cost of renovating business property which has been empty for at least one year in designated 'disadvantaged areas'. The whole of Northern Ireland qualifies. The capital costs of such renovations would normally not be relieved immediately, but the relief means that a 100% allowance should be available.

Relief is claimed on page 2 of the 'UK Property' supplementary SA form in Box 31 with any balancing charge shown in Box 29. For details on the computation of capital allowances and balancing charges generally see 16.2.

8.2.9 Renewals

The landlord can claim the cost of replacing furniture, furnishings and machinery. However, expenditure on renewals is not available where the landlord claims the standard 10% wear and tear allowance (see 8.2.12).

Where expenditure on renewals is claimed, the landlord should bring into account of his or her income any amounts received for items that have been scrapped or sold. Also, expenditure on renewals should not normally include the cost of items that represent a significant improvement or addition to the furniture and furnishings, etc previously made available to the tenant.

8.2.10 Legal and professional costs

HMRC's view is as follows:

Non-allowable expenses

(1) Expenses in connection with the first letting or subletting of a property for more than one year (including eg legal expenses, such as the cost of drawing up a lease, agents' and surveyors' fees and commission).
(2) Any proportion of the legal, etc costs that relate to the payment of a premium on the renewal of a lease.
(3) Fees incurred in obtaining planning permission or on the registration of title when buying a property.

Allowable expenses

(1) Expenses for granting a lease of a year or less.
(2) The normal legal and professional fees incurred on the renewal of a lease, provided it is for less than 50 years (HMRC confirmed in its property income manual (at PIM2205) that the costs of granting a lease to a new tenant are normally allowable provided the replacement lease follows closely on the previous one and is broadly similar in terms).
(3) Professional fees incurred:
    (a) in evicting an unsatisfactory tenant, with a view to re-letting;
    (b) on an appeal against a compulsory purchase order; and
    (c) in drawing up accounts.

8.2.11 Costs of services provided, including wages

A landlord who provides any service to a tenant (eg gardening, the provision of a porter, cleaning, etc) can claim the cost of these services, provided they are incurred wholly and exclusively for the purposes of the letting.

8.2.12 10% wear and tear allowance

(ESC B47)

A landlord who lets a dwelling-house as furnished accommodation can claim (instead of claims on a renewals basis) an allowance amounting to 10% of the rent received after deducting charges or services that would normally be borne by the tenant but are, in fact, borne by the landlord (eg council tax). This allowance, known as 'wear and tear allowance', is accepted by HMRC as broadly covering the cost of normal renewals of furniture.

Furnished accommodation is accommodation containing all the furniture and fittings that a tenant needs in order to occupy the property. Partly furnished accommodation does not attract the wear and tear allowance.

The wear and tear allowance does not apply where rent-a-room relief is claimed (see 8.4).

The wear and tear allowance does not cover expenditure on integral fixtures such as bathroom fittings, immersion heater and central heating boiler, air conditioning etc. Such expenditure can often be claimed as a repair or replacement.

A landlord who lets non-residential property (eg offices) can normally claim capital allowances for any items provided (eg furniture).

8.2.13 Interest

For many years, it was understood by most tax advisers, and virtually all HMRC staff, that relief for mortgage interest could only be set against

Table 8.1 – Computing your 2014–15 property income (straightforward situation)

For each property, bring in the rental income that relates to the tax year (ie if rent is receivable on 25 March 2015 for the quarter ending 24 June 2015, include a proportion for the period 25 March to 5 April 2015).

Deduct

- charges made by an agent for rent collection and management;
- any rent you have to pay on the property (eg ground rent);
- any service charges you have to pay (particularly likely to apply if you are letting out a flat);
- insurance premiums paid for the period covered by the tax year: if you pay insurance for a calendar year, include $3/12$ of the premium for 2016 + $9/12$ of the premium for 2014;
- repairs and similar expenses (eg gardening) incurred in the tax year. Note that the expense need not actually have been paid in the tax year so long as it is clear that it relates to the tax year;
- interest on borrowings used to finance the original purchase of a property, improvements or repairs or against the value of the property at the time that it was brought into the UK property business.

Aggregate all the income and expenses for your different properties – except for properties not let on a commercial basis (any deficit on such properties will almost certainly not be allowable). Add in any lump sums taxable as premiums (see 8.3).

rental income to the extent that it related to interest paid on loans used to *purchase* the property that was being let. We all thought relief was not available on any subsequent borrowings except to the extent that the money was borrowed to finance capital improvements. However, HMRC's updated *Business Income Manual,* (at BIM45700) contradicts this. The relevant section states:

> Mr A owns a flat in central London, which he bought ten years ago for £125,000. He has a mortgage of £80,000 on the property. He has been offered a job in Holland and is moving there to live and work. He intends to come back to the UK at some time. He decides to keep his flat and rent it out while he is away. His London flat now has a market value of £375,000.
>
> The opening balance sheet of his rental business shows

Mortgage	£80,000	Property at MV	£375,000
Capital account	£295,000		

> He renegotiates his mortgage on the flat to convert it to a buy-to-let mortgage and borrows a further £125,000. He withdraws the £125,000, which he then uses to buy a flat in Rotterdam.
>
> The balance sheet at the end of Year 1 shows

Mortgage		£205,000	Property at MV	£375,000
Capital account				
brought forward	£295,000			
Less Drawings	£125,000			
carried forward		£170,000		

> Although he has withdrawn capital from the business, the interest on the mortgage loan is allowable in full because it is funding the transfer of the property to the business at its open market value at the time the business started. The capital account is not overdrawn.

(Source: HMRC BIM 45700)

8.2.14 Use of cash basis

The HMRC Property Income Manual states at PIM1101.

> The 'earnings basis' treatment of receipts and expenses as outlined above follows ordinary commercial accountancy methods. Accruing income and expenses in this way gives the correct measure of business profits. However, rental business profits based on cash received and paid in the tax year may not be materially different from the strict earnings basis profits where:
>
> - rental incomings fall due at frequent intervals (say weekly or monthly), and
> - business expenses are paid at similarly short intervals.

We are, therefore, prepared to accept the use of a 'cash basis' (profits based on the cash paid and received in the year) provided all the following conditions are met:

- the case is small; by 'small' we mean where, for any year, the total gross receipts of a rental business (before allowable expenses are deducted) don't exceed £15,000, and
- the 'cash basis' is used consistently, and
- the result is reasonable overall and does not differ substantially from the strict 'earnings basis'.

Source: HMRC

8.2.15 HMRC guidance

The following HMRC helpsheets contain useful information (https://www.gov.uk/self-assessment-forms-and-helpsheets):

- HS223 – Rent a room for traders
- HS252 – Capital allowances and balancing charges
- HS263 – Calculating foreign tax credit on income
- HS264 – Remittance basis.

HMRC also publishes a Property Rental toolkit designed to help reduce the incidence of common errors in tax returns: http://www.hmrc.gov.uk/agents/toolkits/property-rental.pdf. The toolkit consists of a checklist of the areas relating to property letting which HMRC finds give rise to problems. The toolkit also includes links to its more detailed guidance on those issues.

8.3   LUMP SUMS DEEMED TO BE RENT (PREMIUMS)

(s 277 ITTOIA 2005)

8.3.1   Introduction

A landlord faced with the choice of letting a property for five years at £10,000 pa, or taking a lump sum in return for granting a lease for five years at an annual rent of £100, would regard the two transactions as very similar in their overall consequences. The purpose behind the tax legislation that deals with lump sums (or 'premiums') is to ensure that the tax treatment of both transaction types is similar in nature. The principle is that a proportion of a premium received by a landlord for granting a lease of less than 50 years should be taxed as if it were rent.

The following sections apply only where the person who receives the premium is the landlord, ie a person who continues to hold a superior interest in the property. An outgoing tenant who assigns the whole of his or her interest in the property for a lump sum is not regarded as receiving a premium for income tax purposes.

8.3.2 How premiums are apportioned between income and capital

(s 277 ITTOIA 2005)

The rule is that the full amount of the premium is treated as rent except for 2% for every complete year of the lease after the first year. For example, if a ten-year lease is granted for a premium of £25,000, the amount subject to tax as income is 82% of £25,000, ie £20,500. See Table 8.2.

Table 8.2 – Extract from Revenue helpsheet

Working sheet for chargeable premiums – leases up to 50 years		
Premium	**A**	£
Number of complete periods of 12 months in the lease, ignore the first 12 months	**B**	£
50 minus box B	**C**	£
Box C divided by 50	**D**	£
Box A multiplied by Box D	**E**	£
Copy box E to box 20.		

Source: HMRC

8.3.3 Payments in kind

(s 278 ITTOIA 2005)

It is provided that if a tenant is required to carry out work as a term of his or her lease, the whole of the benefit accruing to the landlord is deemed to be a premium receivable at the commencement of the lease.

8.3.4 Deemed premiums

(s 281 ITTOIA 2005)

Any lump sum paid by a tenant to vary the lease can be treated as a premium receivable at the time the contract for the variation is entered into.

Example – Deemed premium

A is the landlord of a property used as offices and let on a 15-year lease. It is a term of the lease that the tenant should not use the premises for any other purpose.

The tenant secures planning consent to use the property for light industrial use. He makes a payment to A of £12,000 in Year 4 to induce him to vary the lease so that the property can be used for industrial purposes. A is deemed to receive a premium in Year 4. The taxable amount is:

	£
	12,000
Less: (10 × 2%)	(2,400)
	9,600

Similarly, if A had received a lump sum to induce him to waive the relevant term in the lease, the lump sum would be treated as a premium.

8.3.5 Sale with right to repurchase the property

(s 284 ITTOIA 2005)

Where the freehold or leasehold of a property is sold subject to a condition that at a future date the purchaser may be required to sell it back to the vendor at a lower price, the vendor must treat the excess of the sale price over the repurchase price as a premium. The excess, or notional premium, is reduced by 2% for each complete year between the date of sale and the date of resale less one year, the balance is taxed as income from property.

A similar rule applies where a vendor sells a property but retains an option to repurchase it.

8.4 'RENT-A-ROOM' RELIEF

(ss 309, 784–802 ITTOIA 2005)

Special relief is available to an individual who receives payment for letting furnished accommodation in a qualifying residence. The relief provides total exemption from income of £4,250 pa unless sums accrue to another person in respect of lettings of furnished accommodation in the same property, in which case the exemption is reduced to £2,125, regardless of the number of other people (ie if three people qualified in respect of the same property, the limit for all three would be £2,125 each).

A qualifying residence is a residence that is the individual's only or main residence at some time in the basis period for the year of assessment in relation to the lettings. If the receipts would otherwise be brought into account in calculating the profits of a trade, the 'income period' in s 786(1)(b) is the basis period for the tax year. Otherwise the income period is the tax year. 'Residence' means a building (or part of a building) occupied or intended to be occupied as a separate residence.

Rent-a-room relief is available automatically unless the taxpayer elects otherwise or the gross sums received exceed the £4,250 limit.

Where the gross sums received exceed the £4,250 limit for the year of assessment (or the £2,125 limit where some other person receives income from furnished lettings within the same property), the taxpayer may elect for his or her profits or gains for the basis period to be treated as equal to the excess. For example, if a taxpayer has gross rent of £5,000, he or she may compute his or her taxable income as £750 or he or she can compute it in the normal way by reference to the expenses actually incurred.

Need for caution

HMRC has commented on the suggestion that rent-a-room relief might be available where part of an individual's residence is let to a company for use as an office (or for some other trade or business purpose). HMRC's view is that the relief is available only where the person paying rent uses the premises for residential purposes.

8.4.1 Revenue leaflets

For further information on rent-a-room relief, obtain leaflet HS223, *Rent-a-Room for Traders*.

8.5 FURNISHED HOLIDAY ACCOMMODATION

(s 322–328 ITTOIA 2005)

8.5.1 Definition

Furnished holiday lettings (FHL) in the UK and other EEA countries can qualify for special tax reliefs (see 8.5.4).

The qualifying conditions were altered from April 2011 onwards.

In order for property to qualify as a FHL property, it has to be available for commercial letting as holiday accommodation for 210 days a year (previously 140 days) and actually let for 105 days (previously 70 days). However, to cater for fluctuations in lettings from year to year, it will be possible for owners to elect for continuation of a qualifying holiday letting to cover a break of one or two years where the letting thresholds are not reached (see period of grace below).

Lettings during the year for periods exceeding 31 days should not amount to more than 155 days.

8.5.2 Averaging

The tests can be satisfied by averaging:

Where a person has a number of units of accommodation that are let for holiday purposes:

- each of them must separately satisfy the availability condition and the pattern of occupation condition, but
- if some are individually let for less than 105 days, the landlord is allowed to apply the letting condition to the average rate of occupancy of the units.
- A unit cannot be used more than once in the same period in a claim for averaging treatment.

Example – Illustrating the averaging rule

Joe lets four holiday cottages, and all would otherwise qualify as furnished holiday lettings. The actual letting periods are:

No 1	190 days
No 2	138 days
No 3	170 days
No 4	50 days
Total	548 days
Average 548 ÷ 4 =	137 days

By averaging the four all will qualify. Without averaging, No 4 would not qualify.

Source: HMRC

8.5.3 Period of grace

In addition to the option to use averaging to help meet the occupation threshold, there is also the possibility of making an election for a period of grace.

A period of grace election allows you to treat a year as a qualifying FHL year where you genuinely intended to meet the occupancy threshold but were unable to do so. In the year before the first year you want to be treated as a qualifying FHL year, the property must have reached the occupancy threshold, either on its own or because of an averaging election. If, in the following year the property still does not meet the occupancy threshold then providing an election has been made for the earlier year, that year can also be treated as a qualifying FHL year.

Example – Period of grace

Mr X lets a property which would otherwise qualify as a FHL. The actual lettings periods are:

Year	Days	Election	Qualifies
2014–15	110	None needed	Yes
2015–16	73	Yes	Yes
2016–17	80	Yes	Yes
2017–18	106	None needed	Yes

Mr X qualifies in all four years.

If the property still does not meet the required letting level in the fourth year (after two years being treated as qualifying), then the property is no longer a FHL property.

Genuine intention to let

The property must meet the availability threshold (and the pattern of occupation test). You must be able to show that there was a genuine intention to let the property in the year for which a period of grace election is made. For example, where you have marketed a property to the same or greater level than in successful years, this might be used as evidence of a genuine intention to let.

If the lettings are cancelled due to unforeseen circumstances, for example, because of extreme adverse weather conditions, then it is likely that you would be able to say that there had been a genuine intention to let.

8.5.4 Reliefs available

A qualifying FHL is regarded as a trade for CGT purposes and, therefore, qualifies for various CGT reliefs. For example, on selling a FHL, the owner can claim rollover relief on reinvesting the gain or, in some circumstances, entrepreneurs' relief (ER). These tax advantages will continue but only if the new letting thresholds are met.

The following reliefs will be available if a property is treated as being let as furnished holiday accommodation.

Profits classified as earned income

Profits are treated as earned income. This is not dependent on the owner taking any active involvement in the lettings: the whole activity can be dealt with by an agent where desired.

Relief for interest

Interest on loans used to purchase the property and to finance the lettings should qualify as an expense incurred in the trade. In some cases, the inclusion of such interest may give rise to a loss for tax purposes.

Capital allowances for plant and machinery

Equipment, furniture and furnishings may attract capital allowances: see 16.2.

Relief for pre-trading expenditure

Expenditure incurred before the business of letting such properties actually commences may be allowed as a loss incurred at the point in time when the lettings commence, as pre-trading expenditure (see 16.3).

Relief for losses

FHL losses arising after April 2011 may only be set off against future profits from FHL businesses and losses from qualifying UK and overseas FHL must be segregated. Previously, losses arising from FHL businesses were treated as trading losses and set against other profits, income and gains of the owner.

Capital gains tax

Roll-over relief may be available (see 17.4).

The property is regarded as a business asset for entrepreneurs' relief (see 17.7).

Inheritance tax

In some circumstances, a furnished holiday letting business can qualify for 100% IHT business property relief, making it easy to pass such an asset to members of the family. In the past, HMRC generally allowed relief where the lettings were short term, and the owner, either him or herself or through an agent such as a relative, was substantially involved with the holidaymakers in terms of their activities on and from the premises.

HMRC has, in recent years, reconsidered its approach. In particular it now looks much more closely at the level and type of services, rather than who provided them.

8.6 'BUY TO LET' INVESTMENTS

8.6.1 General principles

The tax legislation does not recognise the term 'buy to let' investments but in practice the tax treatment of such investments falls within certain clearly defined rules:

(1) Interest paid on a buy to let mortgage can be offset against other UK property income if it exceeds the rent from the property.

(2) A buy to let investment will not attract roll-over relief unless it is to be let as furnished holiday accommodation (see 8.5 above).

8.6.2 Cashbacks

A feature in recent years has been the receipt by buy to let investors of cashbacks from developers. Sometimes the cashbacks have been conditional on the purchase going through by a given date. There are instances where the lender was not advised of the cashbacks and SDLT has been paid on the full price. In such cases, the cashback might have covered the purchaser's deposit so that the lender had effectively made a 100% loan against the discounted price.

No tax charge should arise on the receipt of the cashback (see SP4/97) as this is an ordinary discount to a retail customer.

8.6.3 Deficit situations

In the current market, with initial fixed-rate mortgage periods coming to an end, many over-stretched buy to let investors may face a situation where their borrowing costs exceed their rental income. Income tax legislation now gives no sideways relief for such losses against the investor's other income except in so far as the loss arises from capital allowances.

A possible solution would be for the investor to sell some or all of the properties to a company and raise new loans, which he or she lends on to the company to enable it to pay for the properties. The money received from the company could then be used to clear all or some of the investor's original borrowings. Interest paid on the individual's new loans could be relieved against his or her other income (see 11.5). The company would generally pay tax at the small companies' rate (currently 20%). However, the main problem with this strategy will be if the properties have fallen in value and their current value is substantially less than the investor's outstanding borrowings. Also, SDLT will be payable and the long-term CGT implications may not be attractive (the company's acquisition cost will be the market value of the properties at the time that it bought them).

There is no easy solution or 'quick fix' for this situation. If you find yourself in this boat, seek advice from an accountant.

8.7 CAPITAL ALLOWANCES ON INVESTMENT PROPERTIES

8.7.1 Introduction

Capital allowances are usually given when HMRC assesses the profits of a trade. It is also possible to qualify for capital allowances in respect of expenditure on investment properties, for example where a landlord installs a lift, air-conditioning, electrical equipment etc, or incurs capital expenditure on a flat over a shop (see 16.2.14). Plant or machinery provided for use in residential property is otherwise excluded. The allowances must first be set against the income of a defined class (see below), but any surplus of allowances may be set against the individual's other income for that year or the following tax year.

8.7.2 Expenditure that may attract allowances

The following are often installed by landlords and generally qualify as plant:

- electrical, cold water, gas and sewerage systems designed to meet the particular requirements of a trader to whom the building is let;
- water-heating systems;
- powered systems of ventilation, air cooling or air purification;
- lifts, hoists and moving walkways;
- sprinkler systems and fire alarms;
- burglar alarm systems;
- thermal insulation (deduction of £1,500 per dwelling house or capital allowances on all other buildings used for any qualifying business purpose).

8.7.3 Purchase of second-hand buildings

A landlord who acquires a building can often claim capital allowances for the plant contained in it (see 16.2.18).

8.7.4 Capital allowance rates

- Integral fixtures. The writing down allowances for plant that is contained in a building (ie a fixture) is currently 8%.
- Annual investment allowance. The first £500,000 of expenditure each year by businesses on most plant and machinery currently attracts tax relief in full. The limit may be changed from 1 January 2016.
- General plant and machinery. The main rate of writing down allowances is 18%.

8.8 LOSSES

8.8.1 No offset against other income

A loss realised on let property cannot normally be set against the taxpayer's other income for the same tax year. The loss can only be carried forward for relief against future property income profits.

An individual's property profits or losses cannot be combined with or set against profits from let property held by a partnership or a trust.

8.8.2 Exceptions

However, if the loss is created by capital allowances on equipment used for the property trade, or when initial allowances are claimed under the Business Premises Renovation Allowance (see 8.2.8), that loss can be set against the taxpayer's other income for the same tax year.

8.8.3 Deficiency on agricultural property

(s 120 ITA 2007)

Where an estate consists of or includes agricultural land, a deficiency may be set against any UK property income. Any balance that cannot be relieved in this way may be set against the individual's other income for the year, or the following tax year.

'Agricultural land' is defined as land, houses or other buildings in the UK occupied wholly or mainly for husbandry purposes. 'Estate' means any land and buildings managed as one estate. Where only part of the estate is used for husbandry, only a proportion of any deficiency can be relieved in this way.

8.9 MINERAL ROYALTIES

(ss157, 319, 340–343 ITTOIA 2005; ss201–203 TCGA1992)

Mineral royalties are normally received net of tax at the basic rate. However, only part of the royalties is taxable as income. Where the recipient is resident or ordinarily resident in the UK, one-half of the mineral royalties is treated as capital gains rather than income. Only 50% of any management expenses or other sums normally deductible in computing property income may be set against the part of the mineral royalties treated as income, and no deduction of any kind is allowed from the 50% of the receipt charged to CGT.

When the mineral lease comes to an end, the person may claim a capital loss as if he or she had disposed of the land at its market value at that time. The loss may be set against capital gains for the year in which the mineral lease expires or against capital gains taxed on mineral royalties during the preceding 15 years.

Mineral royalties is defined as including rents, tolls, royalties and other periodic payments relating to the winning and working of minerals (other than water, peat and topsoil) under a lease, licence or other agreement.

8.10 WOODLANDS

Profits or gains arising from the occupation of woodlands are exempt and woodlands are not chargeable as UK property income.

8.11 PROPERTY INVESTMENT COMPANIES

This is covered in Chapter 27.

8.12 VAT CONSIDERATIONS

Do not overlook VAT: it is possible to register many rental businesses for VAT purposes and this can mean you will recover input tax. However, doing this will mean you will have to charge VAT on the rent (see 22.3.7). Also, VAT will have to be charged when you sell the property. The treatment of VAT on property interests is a complex area, and one in which it is essential to take professional advice.

8.13 INTEREST EARNED ON TRUST FUNDS FOR SERVICE CHARGES AND SINKING FUNDS

Many landlords, or their agents, are required to hold service charges and sinking fund payments made by tenants and leaseholders. In general, these monies are held on trust, ie if the building were destroyed or for some other reason the money never had to be used, it would have to be returned to the tenants.

Interest earned on these funds used will normally be taxed at the basic rate of 20%.

9

SAVINGS INCOME

This chapter contains the following sections:

Interest income received gross

(1) Bank and building society interest
(2) Other interest income
(3) Loans to individuals and other private loans
(4) Gilts and loan stocks

Interest received net of tax

(5) Rate of tax deducted at source

Interest-type income

(6) Accrued income scheme
(7) Deeply discounted securities

Dividends from UK companies

(8) Dividends
(9) Sundry receipts treated as dividends

Overseas interest and dividend income

(10) Foreign interest and dividends

Exchange-traded funds

(11) Tax treatment of exchange-traded funds

Apart from dividends, income from savings is always taxed at 20% unless the taxpayer is an individual liable for higher rate or additional rate tax (or whose non-savings income is insufficient to exhaust the starting rate band, ie it is less than the personal allowance plus £2,880 in 2014–15 and £5,000 in 2015–16). Dividends are subject to their own rates of tax of 10% for basic rate taxpayers, 32.5% for higher rate taxpayers and 37.5%

for additional rate taxpayers. The top rate (together with the 45% rate on non-dividend income) applies where an individual's taxable income is over £150,000 a year.

Savings income is taxed as the highest part of income, with dividends forming the highest part, so an individual with 2014–15 employment income of £149,000 and savings income of £20,000 (including dividends of £5,000) will pay tax on his or her savings income as follows: dividends of £5,000 at 37.5% (less a notional tax credit at 10%); other savings income, £14,000 at the 45% rate and £1,000 at the 40% rate.

INTEREST INCOME RECEIVED GROSS

9.1 BANK AND BUILDING SOCIETY INTEREST

9.1.1 Interest receivable without tax deducted at source

The National Savings Bank (NSB) always pays interest without deduction of tax. Interest on an NSB investment account or from deposit bonds, income bonds or capital bonds is subject to deduction of tax at source.

Interest payments by UK banks or building societies on deposit accounts are normally subject to deduction of tax at source unless the depositor completes form R85. This form requires the depositor's full name, address, date of birth and national insurance number and contains a declaration that the depositor is unlikely to be liable for income tax. The form may now be submitted if you believe that your total income will be less than £15,600. Form R85 cannot be used to enable NSB interest to be paid without deduction of tax.

Interest payments used to be made without deduction of tax on certificates of deposit (qualifying time deposits) provided the deposit is for at least £50,000 and the bank or building society takes the deposit for a fixed period (which must not exceed five years). Interest may also be paid without deduction of tax on deposits where no certificate of deposit has been issued, but the depositor would be entitled to a certificate if he or she called for one to be issued. However, tax is deducted at source from taxable interest paid on new 'qualifying time deposit' accounts opened since 6 April 2012.

Interest may also be received without tax being deducted at source from loans to individuals; deposits held by a solicitor and on certificates of tax deposit (see 9.2).

9.1.2 How the taxable amount is arrived at

The assessable income is the actual income that arises during the tax year, ie the CY basis. This means that for the current tax year 2015–16 the assessable income is the income received for the year ending 5 April

2016. Similarly for the 2014–15 SA form, the income declared is that received in the year ended 5 April 2015.

9.1.3 Date of receipt

Interest is regarded as received when it is credited to the account. Occasionally, cases arise where an individual is required to make a deposit with a bank as a condition of the bank advancing money to a company. In some situations, he or she is precluded from making withdrawals from the deposit account as long as the company's borrowings are outstanding. The courts have held that an individual who has a deposit account subject to such a block may nevertheless be taxed on interest credited to that account. Furthermore, there is no relief if he or she never receives the interest because the company goes into liquidation and the bank appropriates the money outstanding to his or her credit on the deposit account.

9.1.4 Minor children's accounts

A parent who gifts capital to his or her unmarried, minor, child's account is generally charged tax on interest credited to it, unless the total income from that gift does not exceed £100 (see 33.6.4 on aggregation of minor children's income in general).

9.1.5 Rate of tax on income from savings

All interest income counts as income from savings. Tax is charged at 20% unless the recipient is liable for the higher or additional rates or is only liable for tax at the lower rate.

Example

B received interest of £15,000 in the year ended 5 April 2015. She is single and has other income of £12,000, so she is not subject to higher rate tax. She will pay tax on the interest as follows:

	£
Non-savings income	12,000
Savings income	15,000
	27,000
Less: allowance	(10,000)
	17,000
Basic rate tax on £17,000 @ 20%	3,400
Less:	
Basic rate tax deducted at source	3,000
£15,000 @ 20%	
Tax due	400

9.1.6 Holocaust victims' bank accounts: compensation

Compensation paid by banks on dormant accounts opened by Holocaust victims and frozen during World War II is exempt from tax.

9.2 OTHER INTEREST INCOME

9.2.1 Interest payable by a solicitor

Interest may be received without deduction of tax from client's accounts held by a firm of solicitors or accountants. Such income is taxed under s 369 ITTOIA 2005.

9.2.2 Interest receivable on compulsory purchase monies

Where a property is the subject of a compulsory purchase order (CPO) that goes to appeal, and the amount payable is increased, interest is generally payable on the increase. This is regarded as income for the year in which the entitlement arises, ie when the CPO appeal is settled by agreement or on appeal and the interest is received. This principle is not affected by the fact that the interest may have accrued over several years and may be calculated using six-monthly rests.

9.2.3 Certificates of tax deposit

Interest is credited to an individual who has invested in certificates of tax deposit that are either applied to cover tax payable by assessments or are encashed. The interest is taxable and is income for the year of receipt.

9.2.4 Exempt interest

Interest paid by HMRC on over-payments of tax (called 'repayment supplement') is not subject to tax for individuals. However, interest paid by Customs in respect of official error is taxable.

9.2.5 Interest awarded by the courts

This may be exempt. The treatment turns on whether the court order or arbitration award provides for payment of interest as such (taxable) or is merely an element taken into account in arriving at the amount to be awarded (which is capital and not taxable income).

Where an investor receives compensation for being mis-sold an investment, part of what he or she receives may be interest (see *Tax Bulletin 72* August 2004).

9.3 LOANS TO INDIVIDUALS AND OTHER PRIVATE LOANS

Interest on a private loan to an individual or trust is generally received without deduction of tax. Interest paid by cheque is received when the sum is credited to the recipient's account, not when the cheque is received. Interest is not assessable where an individual waives the interest before it falls due for payment, provided he or she receives no consideration for the waiver.

9.4 GILTS AND LOAN STOCKS

Interest payments on British Government Securities ('gilts') will usually be received gross.

Interest payments on loan stocks issued by companies are normally subject to deduction of basic rate tax at source.

INTEREST RECEIVED NET OF TAX

9.5 RATE OF TAX DEDUCTED AT SOURCE

(Chapters 2 and 15, Part 15 ITA 2007)

Interest payments made by UK banks and building societies are normally subject to deduction of tax at source (for exceptions see 9.1.1).

Interest paid on local authority loan stocks and company loan stocks and debentures is subject to deduction of tax, as indeed is all interest paid by UK companies to persons other than group companies. Because such income is income from savings, tax is deducted at 20%.

Certain unit trusts that invest only in bank deposits or gilts are treated as 'transparent' so that distributions of income are treated as interest rather than dividends. Once again, 20% tax is withheld at source.

INTEREST-TYPE INCOME

9.6 ACCRUED INCOME SCHEME

(Part 12 ITA 2007)

References are given below to specific sections, but in order to fully understand the taxation of accrued income, the whole of Part 12 ITA 2007 will need to be considered, as in many cases a concept is now dealt with across five or six different – and non-consecutive – sections of the legislation.

9.6.1 Introduction

An individual who sells a gilt or fixed-interest loan stock may sell either cum- or ex-interest. In the former case, the buyer receives the next interest payment; in the latter, the seller receives the next interest payment even though it is paid after he or she has sold the gilt or loan stock. In practice, gilts, etc, are quoted on an ex-interest basis from six weeks or so before interest is due for payment.

The price at which a gilt or loan stock is sold generally reflects an adjustment for accrued interest. For example, if a gilt pays interest every six months, a person who sells at the end of month 4 will receive a price that reflects four months' accrued interest. Conversely, a person who sells at the end of month 5 would normally sell on an ex-interest basis and the purchaser would take a deduction for one month's interest (as the seller would receive this).

9.6.2 Accrued income taxable

The accrued income scheme may apply where the nominal value of gilts or loan stocks held at any point in the year exceeds £5,000. It brings into charge the interest credited to sellers of gilts and loan stocks. The interest deemed to accrue on a daily basis is treated for tax purposes as if it had been received by the seller. The amount of any adjustments in the other direction (interest received but not earned over the period of ownership) is deducted and the net amount charged to tax on the CY basis.

Example

C subscribes £30,000 for a new Government Stock, 4.5% Treasury Stock 2042 issued on 1 August 2014. He holds the stock for 86 days and then sells it to *D*, who holds the stock at 1 February 2015 when the first six months' interest is payable. *C* will be assessable for income tax purposes on £317, ie $^{86}/_{183}$ × £675 (the half-yearly interest payable on the stock). *D* will be entitled to a deduction of the same amount in computing his taxable income. His position will therefore be as follows:

	£
D receives six months' interest of	675
He or she deducts 'rebate interest'	(317)
Taxable income	358

9.6.3 Types of securities within accrued income scheme

(s 619 ITA 2007)

The scheme applies to acquisitions and disposals of virtually all types of fixed interest securities by UK-resident individuals. The securities must be loan stock and not shares, but the scheme may apply to foreign securities as well as to UK loan stocks.

Savings certificates, certificates of deposit and zero coupon bonds are excluded. Bills of exchange and Treasury bills are not regarded as securities because they are within the definition of certificates of deposit (see 9.2.3), which are also excluded.

9.6.4 Types of disposal that may be caught

(s 620 ITA 2007)

The scheme applies to transfers. This term is widely defined in ITA 2007 and includes:

(1) a sale (s 620(1)(a));
(2) an exchange (s 620(1)(a)) or a conversion of securities (s 620(1)(b));
(3) a gift (s 620(1)(a));
(4) any transfer other than under (1)–(3) above (s 620(1)(b));
(5) a change in the true ownership where a person entitled to securities becomes a trustee in relation to them (s 651).

9.6.5 Year of assessment

(s 617 ITA 2007)

The assessment is made for the tax year in which the interest period ends, ie if a loan stock pays interest on 30 April, a disposal of the stock on a cum-interest basis on 5 April 2015 produces taxable income for 2014–15.

9.6.6 Calculation of accrued amount and rebate amount

(s 628 ITA 2007)

Where transactions go through the London Stock Exchange, the accrued and rebate amounts are calculated by the broker and appear on the contract note. Where the transaction does not go through the market, the calculation is made in the same way.

If there is more than one transaction in 'securities of the same kind', the accrued and rebate amounts can be netted off. This term is interpreted strictly: £5,000 4.75% Treasury Stock 2020 is 'of the same kind' as £10,000 4.75% Treasury Stock 2020, but is not 'of the same kind' as some other issue of Treasury stock.

Separate calculation is necessary of all accrued and rebate amounts. Relief is given for a rebate amount against the next interest received on that security or, if a transfer intervenes, against the accrued amount. Thus it is possible for a rebate amount in one tax year to be set against interest received in the next.

9.7 DEEPLY DISCOUNTED SECURITIES

(s 427 ITTOIA 2005)

9.7.1 Introduction

The legislation may also bring sums deemed to be interest income into charge.

A loan stock may be issued at a discount, or be redeemable at a premium. In either case, the borrower undertakes that when the loan is repaid the borrower will receive more than the amount originally paid on the issue of the stock. A typical situation is where a loan stock is issued at £80 for every £100 nominal and when the loan stock is redeemed the investor is entitled to receive £100. There are no provisions for the payer to deduct tax from the discount.

The discount or premium is charged to tax where the loan stock is within the definition of a deeply discounted security and the company that issues the bond is a UK company. If the issuer is an overseas company, the discount is treated as foreign interest income.

9.7.2 Definition of 'deeply discounted security'

(s 430 ITTOIA 2005)

A loan stock is not a deeply discounted security (DDS) just because it is issued at a discount; it must be issued at a deep discount. A discount is regarded as a deep discount only where it exceeds 0.5% for every year of the loan stock's intended life (up to a maximum of 30), or where the discount exceeds 15% in total.

The following cannot be deeply discounted securities (s 432):

- shares in a company;
- gilt-edged securities that are not strips;
- life assurance policies;
- capital redemption policies.
- securities (which might otherwise be DDS) issued under the same prospectus where the preponderance of the securities so issued are not DDS; and
- 'excluded indexed securities'.

Examples – Deeply discounted security

> (1) A five-year loan stock is issued at £95 for every £100 nominal. This is a deeply discounted security because the discount exceeds 0.5% pa.
> (2) A 35-year loan stock is issued at £80 for every £100 nominal. This is a deeply discounted security, even though the discount is less than 0.5% pa, because it exceeds 15% in total.

9.7.3 Events that give rise to a tax charge

(ss 437–439 ITTOIA 2005)

A disposal of a deeply discounted security can give rise to a tax charge. The whole of the profit is taxable as if it were interest.

Example – Disposal of deep discount security

> A bond is issued at £82, redeemable at £100 after two years. This reflects a compound interest rate of approximately 10.5% since $82 \times (^{110.5}/_{100})^2 = 100$. If the holder sells for £93 after 12 months, he or she will be assessed on the difference between £82 and £93, ie £11. If the purchaser holds the bond until it is redeemed in Year 2 he or she will be chargeable on the redemption profit of £18 as income for that year.

9.7.4 Stripped gilts

(ss 443–452, 452A–452G and 453–456 ITTOIA 2005)

There is one exception to the general rule that individuals and trustees are taxed on discounted securities only when a disposal takes place. Where a stripped gilt is held, it is necessary to revalue it at the end of each tax year and the owner must pay tax on any increase in value as if it were income. These rules also apply to strips of non-UK government securities.

DIVIDENDS FROM UK COMPANIES

9.8 DIVIDENDS

9.8.1 Taxable for year in which they fall due for payment

(ss 383–385 ITTOIA 2005)

The dividends that need to be reported on a tax return, and that are income for a tax year, are the dividends that were due for payment in the year. If you have shares in a company that declared a dividend that was payable on 5 April 2015, you must report the dividend as 2014–15 income. This is not affected by the fact that you may not receive the dividend payment until early in the next tax year.

The period for which the dividend is paid is also not relevant. A final dividend for a company's year that ended on 31 December 2014 would be income for 2015–16 if it was paid in, say, June 2015.

Dividends from UK companies carry a tax credit (see 9.8.2).

9.8.2 Rate of tax on dividends received from UK companies

A shareholder is entitled to a tax credit of one-ninth of the dividend. This credit is non-refundable.

An individual whose income is within the basic rate band does not have to pay any additional tax on UK dividends; the tax credit is treated as covering his or her liability. Higher rate taxpayers pay a special 32.5% rate on dividends and are able to set the tax credit against this. In practice, this means that the effective rate of higher rate tax is 25% of the actual dividend receipt. Additional rate taxpayers pay tax on dividends falling within the additional rate band at a rate of 37.5%.

9.8.3 Dividends paid by unit trusts

Dividends from unit trusts are normally treated in the same way as dividends from companies except in regard to 'equalisation'. This is an amount paid to holders of units who have acquired them since the last dividend was paid. The equalisation payment is not taxable as income but is instead treated as a return of capital.

Unit trusts that invest in gilts and corporate bonds are treated differently (see 9.5).

9.8.4 Dividends paid by Real Estate Investment Trusts

REIT distributions should not be included in the figure entered in a tax return for UK dividends because they are instead treated as rental income. Basic rate tax is withheld at source and this tax can be reclaimed by recipients who are not liable for tax (ie their non-savings income is less than £15,600 for 2015–16).

9.8.5 Stock dividends

(s 409 ITTOIA 2005)

A company may make a 'scrip' or bonus issue so that shareholders receive new shares in proportion to their existing shareholdings. This is not taxable income because in reality all that has happened is that the company has subdivided its share capital by issuing new shares.

In contrast to this, a company may offer shareholders the choice between a cash dividend and additional shares to a similar value. This is called a 'stock dividend' and is taxable income.

'Enhanced scrip dividends' are a special type of stock dividend where the company offers a premium to shareholders who take stock rather than cash and makes prior arrangements to enable the shareholders to dispose of the shares that they have acquired by taking the stock alternative.

9.8.6 How stock dividends are assessed

(SP A8 and s 412 ITTOIA 2005)

A shareholder who accepts extra shares in lieu of a cash dividend is normally treated as if he or she had received a dividend equal to the cash that he or she could have taken. Tax is deemed to have been paid at 10%.

A slightly different treatment applies where the value of the shares taken as the stock dividend differs from the cash dividend by 15% or more. In such a case, the shareholder is deemed to have received a dividend equal to the shares' value at the date of issue. The shareholder may therefore be required to pay higher rate tax on the 'grossed up' value of the dividend or the shares. However, HMRC has said it is normally prepared to use the amount of the cash dividend when the difference between the market value of the share capital and the cash dividend is no more than one or two percentage points greater than 15%.

Example – Taxation of dividends

E is a 40% taxpayer. He was entitled to a dividend of £2,100 or extra shares in X plc. He took the shares. If the shares were worth £1,900, he will nevertheless be charged higher rate tax on £2,100 (the dividend he could have taken) plus an amount equal to the tax credit; the amount charged to higher rate tax for 2014–15 is £2,333 (£2,100 grossed up for the 10% tax credit).

If the shares were worth £2,600 when they were issued, he would be charged higher rate tax on £2,600 'grossed up', ie £2,889.

9.8.7 Consequences for CGT of taking a stock dividend

In the example in 9.8.6, E's acquisition value for CGT purposes of the shares that he acquires through the stock dividend is the market value of the shares before grossing up. Where the market value rule does not apply, the base cost for CGT is the cash that would have been received had the dividend been taken (£2,100 above) before the inclusion of the 10% notional tax credit.

9.8.8 Demerger dividends

(ss 1075–1080 CTA 2010)

A dividend may take the form of an issue of shares formerly held by the company in a subsidiary. Where the necessary HMRC clearances have been obtained, such a dividend is treated as capital and not as taxable income. The documentation issued by the company normally states that clearance has been obtained from HMRC and that the demerger is an exempt distribution.

9.8.9 Other dividend income

See 9.9 on sundry receipts from UK companies that are treated as distributions. See also 9.10.1 on dividends paid by foreign companies that are treated as income from savings.

9.9 SUNDRY RECEIPTS TREATED AS DIVIDENDS

9.9.1 Deemed dividends

(s 1000 CTA 2010)

There are various transactions that can count as a distribution, particularly where a person holds shares in a close company (see 18.14). From the recipient's point of view, a distribution is for all practical purposes the same as a dividend.

9.9.2 Interest at more than commercial rate

(s 1000E CTA 2010)

Interest paid to a shareholder may constitute a distribution in so far as it exceeds a normal commercial rate.

9.9.3 Issue of redeemable shares

(s 1000C CTA 2010)

An issue to shareholders of redeemable preference shares (or other redeemable shares) counts as a distribution. The redeemable shares' value at the date they are issued is treated as if it were a dividend paid in cash at that time. This rule does not apply where the redeemable shares are issued for new consideration.

9.9.4 Bonus issue following repayment of share capital

(s 1000H CTA 2010)

Where a company has repaid share capital in the past, a subsequent bonus issue is treated as a dividend paid to the shareholders who receive the bonus shares. These shareholders may not be the same people whose shares were previously bought back by the company, but this does not make any difference to the way in which the current shareholders are taxed on receipt of a bonus issue of shares in these circumstances.

9.9.5 Benefits-in-kind provided to shareholders

(ss 1000(2), 1064 CTA 2010)

Where shareholders in a close company (see 18.14) are provided with benefits-in-kind, they may be assessed as employment income. If the shareholders are not employed by the company, it is not possible for HMRC to assess benefits-in-kind in this way. In these circumstances, the company may be deemed to have made a distribution equal to the value of the benefits-in-kind concerned.

9.9.6 Assets transferred by or to close company

(s 1020 CTA 2010)

A deemed distribution may arise where assets are transferred from the members of a company to the company at a price that exceeds their market value, or company assets are transferred to shareholders at a price that is less than market value.

9.9.7 Purchase by company of its own shares

(ss 1033–1043 CTA 2010)

The general rule is that where a company buys back its shares, the amount paid by the company is treated as a distribution in so far as it exceeds the shares' original issue price, except as noted below (see 9.9.8).

The amount treated as a distribution is not affected by the shares' value at the time they were acquired by an individual. Consequently, where a person has acquired shares by inheritance or bought them from an existing shareholder, his or her acquisition value may exceed the original issue price (ie the amount paid to the company in return for the shares being issued). In the event of a purchase of own shares by a company, it is the issue price that is important.

Example – Purchase by company of own shares

F acquires 1,000 shares in Y Ltd for £10,000. The shares were originally issued at their par value of £1 per share. It subsequently transpires that F cannot get on with the company's directors. If her shares are bought back by the company at £9 per share, F is deemed to have received a distribution of £8,000, even though she has actually made a capital loss.

9.9.8 Relief under ss 1033–1043 CTA 2010

In certain circumstances it may be possible for a company to purchase its own shares without the transaction being treated as giving rise to a distribution. Clearance must be obtained from HMRC that the purchase of own shares is for the benefit of the company's trade. The conditions that must be satisfied are:

- the company is an unquoted trading company or the unquoted holding company of a trading group, and
- the redemption, repayment or purchase is made wholly or mainly for the purpose of benefiting a trade carried on by the company or any of its 75% subsidiaries,
- it does not form part of a scheme or arrangement, one of the main purposes of which is to enable the owner of the shares to participate in the profits of the company without receiving a dividend, or the avoidance of tax, and the other requirements set out in ss 1034–1043 (so far as applicable) are met.

Alternatively, s 1033 may apply where shares are being bought back within two years of the shareholder's death and the reason for this is that the personal representatives would not otherwise be able to pay the IHT due on the estate.

OVERSEAS INTEREST AND DIVIDEND INCOME

9.10 FOREIGN INTEREST AND DIVIDENDS

Interest on bonds issued by overseas governments or companies is received without deduction of UK tax.

9.10.1 Foreign interest and dividends

Prior to the enactment of ITTOIA 2005, non-UK income was generally assessable under Schedule D, Cases IV and V. ITTOIA 2005 takes a different approach to charging such income to tax, so that for 2005–06 onwards each type of non-UK income previously within Case IV or V is charged to tax under the provisions charging the equivalent type of UK income.

9.10.2 How the taxable amount is computed

Income is taxed on the CY basis.

A point to watch with all foreign investments is that income tax is charged on the interest credited or dividends received, without reference to any exchange gain or loss on the money deposited or invested.

Tax notes

With foreign investments, income tax is charged on the interest credited or dividends received, without taking into account any exchange gain or loss.

Example – Foreign currency deposit account

In June 2014, *F* deposited £10,000 with a foreign bank. At the then exchange rate of £1=20 units of foreign currency, that sum was credited as 200,000 units. In June 2015, when the exchange rate was £1=25 units, interest of 30,000 units was credited to the account. In June 2016, *F* closes the account, receiving back her original capital, the interest credited in June 2015 and a further 20,000 foreign currency units as interest to close. By then the exchange rate was £1=30 units, so the sterling equivalent of the 250,000 units was only £8,333.

In commercial terms, *F* has suffered a loss of £1,667, but for tax purposes she received interest of £1,200 in June 2015 (30,000 units at £1=25) and £667 in June 2016 (20,000 units at £1=30) and income tax must be paid on that interest. She has also made a capital loss of £3,534, calculated as follows:

			£	£
Proceeds of	250,000	Units		8,333
	200,000	units cost (June 2014)	10,000	
	30,000	units cost (June 2015)	1,200	
	20,000	units cost (June 2016)	667	
Capital loss				11,867
				(3,534)

Unfortunately, that capital loss may only be used by set-off against capital gains on the disposal of other assets. If *F* has no such gains, she cannot utilise the loss and so has paid tax on a profit of £1,867 when she has in fact made an overall loss of £1,667.

9.10.3 Double tax relief

Relief may be claimed for foreign tax withheld from the interest or dividends. This credit will be restricted to the amount of UK tax due on the income source, and if the foreign tax does not meet the full amount of tax due this shortfall will be payable.

Example – Relief by credit

G has UK earnings of £17,500 in 2014–15 and foreign income from property of £3,000 on which foreign tax of £500 has been paid. She is entitled to a personal allowance of £10,000.

(a)	Tax on total income	£	
	Earnings	17,500	
	Income from property	3,000	(foreign tax £500)
		20,500	
	Personal allowance	10,000	
	Taxable income	10,500	
	Tax on £10,500 @ 20%	2,100	

(b)	Tax on total income less foreign income		
	Earnings		17,500
	Personal allowance		10,000
	Taxable income		7,500
	Tax on £7,500 @ 20%		1,500

The difference in tax between (a) and (b) is £600. The foreign tax is less than this and the full credit of £500 is available against the UK tax payable. If the foreign tax had been £750, the credit would be limited to £600 and the balance of £150 would be unrelieved.

9.10.4 Retention tax

Countries in the EU, and most offshore territories, introduced a system during 2005 whereby a person who is not resident there and who is in receipt of interest must either agree to his or her identity being revealed to the revenue authorities of the country where he or she resides or have 20% retention tax withheld at source. The retention tax is then paid over to the revenue authority of the country in which the person is resident but without the person's identity being disclosed.

The fact that interest has suffered retention tax does not alter the person's obligation to include the income on his or her tax return. Conversely, a person is allowed a credit for tax withheld in this way. If, exceptionally, he or she is not liable for the 20% tax, HMRC will repay this.

9.10.5 Foreign dividends not treated as savings income

Remittance basis users who bring foreign dividends into the UK and who are liable for higher rates will be taxed at 40% or 45% and not at the 32.5% or 37.5% rates.

9.10.6 Stock dividends and other peculiarities

(s 410 ITTOIA 2005)

As explained in 9.8.5, an investor who opts to take a stock dividend (ie additional shares in lieu of a cash dividend) from a UK company is taxed as if he or she had received an equivalent amount in cash. This rule does not apply where a non-UK resident company declares a stock dividend.

A higher or additional rate taxpayer offered the choice between a stock and a cash dividend is therefore usually better off taking the stock dividend. However, this assumes that the additional shares offered are worth at least as much as the cash option and that they are readily saleable. As always, the 'tax-saving' tail must not be allowed to wag the 'sensible investment policy' dog. Moreover, in one court case it was suggested that, if stock dividends are taken year after year, and the shares so obtained are sold to provide the shareholder with an income, then income tax may be charged on that income. HMRC is unlikely to take this view unless a substantial amount of money is at stake.

In some situations, payments by an overseas company may escape income tax where an equivalent payment by a UK company would be taxable as a dividend. The most common situation where this occurs is where a payment by an overseas company is treated under the relevant foreign law as a partial return of the shareholders' original investment. Such distributions are treated as capital even though a similar payment by a UK company would be treated as taxable income. This is an area where you will need to take professional advice.

9.10.7 Reporting untaxed income from abroad

If you have foreign dividends or interest, you will need to tick the box at Q5 on the second page of your tax return and complete a special schedule for foreign income.

9.10.8 Taxation of foreign dividends

Owners of foreign shares are entitled to a non-repayable tax credit of one-ninth of the dividend to align the treatment with that of dividends paid by UK companies. The notional tax credit covers any basic rate liability. Higher, or additional, rate taxpayers are charged at a rate of 32.5% or 37.5% respectively on the dividend and tax credit in the same way as if they had received a UK dividend.

This treatment did not apply where an individual owned 10% or more of the shares in the foreign company but from 22 April 2009, the availability of tax credits was extended to include offshore funds (provided that distributions from the fund are not treated as interest) and to some investors with shareholdings of 10% or more (see 9.10.9 below).

9.10.9 Taxation of foreign dividends paid by companies based in DTA countries

From 22 April 2009, however, a non-repayable tax credit can be available to individuals on *all* dividends from non-UK companies. However, where the recipient has a shareholding of 10% or more, the company must be resident in a 'qualifying territory' (ie a territory which has agreed a double taxation agreement with the UK with a non-discrimination article).

Also from 22 April 2009, all dividends from offshore funds attract the non-repayable tax credit provided the fund concerned is largely invested in equities. However, where the fund is substantially invested in interest bearing assets, individuals in receipt of distributions from such funds will be treated as having received interest instead.

EXCHANGE-TRADED FUNDS

9.11 TAX TREATMENT OF EXCHANGE-TRADED FUNDS

These are a type of collective investment scheme that have become increasingly popular. An investor in such a fund gets an income and capital return that exactly matches the index chosen, whether that be the FTSE 100 share index, an index based on an overseas stock exchange or an index that reflects all the Investment Grade $ Corporate Bonds etc. Furthermore, the charges are usually rather less than those charged by managers of tracker unit trusts.

The tax treatment will generally follow the legal structure. Many exchange-traded funds are Luxembourg or Irish open-ended companies. As such, distributions of income are normally treated as dividends. No tax will normally be withheld from such dividends.

However, distributions from exchange-traded funds invested in loan stocks may be treated as interest in the hands of an investor.

The realisation of an investment in an exchange-traded fund will give rise to a capital gain or loss. Bear in mind that an investor in an exchange-traded fund which is invested in qualifying corporate bonds may have a capital gain on realising his or her investment whereas no capital gain would have arisen if he or she had realised direct investments in such bonds.

10

OTHER INCOME

This chapter contains the following sections:

Untaxed income from abroad

(1) Foreign real estate income
(2) Alimony and maintenance payments
(3) Investment in overseas partnerships
(4) Double tax relief
(5) Foreign pensions

Miscellaneous investment income

(6) Sale of certificates of deposit
(7) Gains from roll-up, and other offshore, funds

Miscellaneous income

(8) Miscellaneous income
(9) Taxation of commission, cashbacks and discounts

Income received net of tax

(10) Annuities, trust income, etc

UNTAXED INCOME FROM ABROAD

10.1 FOREIGN REAL ESTATE INCOME

(s 265 ITTOIA 2005)

It is not unusual for a UK resident to have bought – or inherited – a villa or flat abroad. It is less usual to own commercial premises, but the tax rules are the same. In addition, the same rules apply to properties bought under 'timeshare' arrangements.

Tax notes

If you have untaxed income from abroad, a special schedule of your SA tax return must be completed. Advice on which form needs to be completed can be obtained by calling the number on the front of your tax form or by consulting a practising tax accountant.

10.1.1 How income is computed

In calculating the assessable rent, the landlord may deduct expenses paid: for example, repairs, redecoration, insurance, maid service, gardening, management fees and advertising. If the landlord sometimes uses the property him or herself, then an apportionment of these expenses must be made in the same way as for a UK property (see 8.2).

There are three important differences between the tax treatment of rent from real property in the UK and rent from property abroad:

(1) The 'rent-a-room' scheme (see 8.4) applies only to residential properties in the UK; this exemption cannot be claimed against rents from an overseas property.

(2) The special rules allowing the provision of furnished holiday accommodation to be treated as a trade (see 8.5) apply only where the relevant property is situated in the EEA.

(3) If the rental income statement for an overseas property shows a deficit for a year (ie if expenses excluding interest paid exceed rent received), that deficit may be carried forward and deducted from the rent received in respect of the same property in the next year (and the deduction may be rolled forward indefinitely until there is rental income against which it can be set). However, no other form of loss relief is available. In particular, the deficit may not be set against rents received from other properties, whether in the UK or abroad. Interest payments can be deducted even if the interest is paid overseas.

10.1.2 Accounts

In the past, rental income statements should have been drawn up to 5 April, but in practice HMRC often accepted statements drawn up to any convenient date. For example, the rental statement for the calendar year will often have been taken as the measure of the income for the tax year. This is no longer acceptable and it is necessary to report the income that has actually arisen in the tax year ie on a receipts rather than a cash basis.

One possible complication is that income may be received, and expenses incurred, in either UK or local currency. In practice, HMRC accepts any reasonable basis of currency conversion. For example, if a local agent collects the rents, disburses local expenses and remits a net sum to the landlord, that net amount may be converted at the spot rate for the day it was remitted. However, HMRC expects the same basis of conversion to be retained from one year to the next.

10.2 ALIMONY AND MAINTENANCE PAYMENTS

(s 727 ITTOIA 2005)

A UK resident may receive maintenance or alimony payments from a spouse, former spouse or civil partner, or a parent resident abroad. This income is almost always exempt from tax.

10.3 INVESTMENT IN OVERSEAS PARTNERSHIPS

(s 95 ITA 2007)

A UK resident may be a sleeping partner in a business carried on abroad. For example, an individual might provide the finance for his or her son to set up in business abroad in return for a share of the profits. It may be difficult to tell whether the parent has become a sleeping partner in the son's business or has made a loan at interest to the son. If the parent is entitled to a stated proportion of profits (say, one-quarter), then he or she is certainly a sleeping partner; if he or she is entitled to a fixed annual sum, he or she may be a sleeping partner or may simply have made a loan. In practice, since both interest and a sleeping partner's profit share are taxed in the same way, it will not normally be necessary to decide this.

The important question is whether the UK resident is a sleeping or an active partner. If he or she is an active partner, the partnership business is likely to be carried on at least partly within the UK, in which case complex questions arise that are outside the scope of this book and specialist advice should be sought.

If the sleeping partner is entitled to a fixed sum, at annual or other intervals, and that sum is stated in a foreign currency, then each instalment must, for tax purposes, be converted into sterling at the spot rate for the date it falls due. If he or she is entitled to a stated proportion of profits, and the business accounts are prepared in a foreign currency, the appropriate profit figure must be converted into sterling at the spot rate for the last day of the accounting period. If the sleeping partner is obliged to bear a share of a trading loss, that loss may be relieved against overseas trading and pension income, but not against overseas investment income or any UK income. In most cases, therefore, it is relieved by deducting the loss amount from the partnership profit share assessable for a later year.

10.4 DOUBLE TAX RELIEF

(s 18 TIOPA 2010)

Foreign tax paid can be deducted from the UK tax charged on the same income.

Example – Double tax relief

D, a basic rate taxpayer, receives an interest payment of £1,000 from abroad, on which the foreign tax is £150. The UK tax position is:

	£
Gross interest	1,000
Foreign tax deducted or paid	(150)
Net receipt	850
UK tax at 20% of £1,000	200
Less: foreign tax paid	(150)
UK tax to be paid	50
After-tax income	800

If D were liable for tax at only 10%, credit for the foreign tax would bring his UK tax liability down to nil, but he would not be entitled to reclaim the surplus foreign tax of £50.

10.4.1 An important practical point

Relief for overseas tax is not given unless the individual can prove that he or she has indeed paid the tax. It is not sufficient simply to demonstrate that tax is payable under foreign law: the claimant must be able to show that he or she has indeed paid that tax by producing an official receipt or tax deduction certificate. In some jurisdictions it can be a lengthy and difficult process to obtain such certificates.

10.4.2 Foreign tax adjustments

HMRC must be notified if an amount of foreign tax paid is later adjusted and this means that too much credit has been allowed as double taxation relief. Failure to notify HMRC within one year of an adjustment results in a taxpayer becoming liable to a penalty (not exceeding the tax underpaid) because of the claim that has proved to be excessive.

If a foreign tax adjustment means that you have not claimed enough you are under no statutory duty to report this, but it is clearly in your own interests to do so.

10.5 FOREIGN PENSIONS

(s 573 ITEPA 2003)

Certain foreign pensions are taxable as foreign income:

- pensions paid by a person outside the UK;
- pensions paid on behalf of a person outside the UK;
- voluntary pensions paid by a person outside the UK.

Foreign pensions are taxed as follows:

(a) pensioner is resident, ordinarily resident and domiciled in the UK – 90% of the pension is charged to tax;

(b) pensioner is resident but not ordinarily resident in the UK – the pension is assessed on the remittance basis by reference to sums brought into the UK;

(c) pensioner is resident and ordinarily resident, but not domiciled, in the UK – the pension may be taxed on the remittance basis in 2008–09 and subsequent years if the individual makes a claim to be taxed on that basis (and pays the £30,000 remittance basis charge if applicable).

Foreign pensions are taxed on the CY basis.

Nazi compensation pensions

(s 642 ITEPA 2003)

Annuities and premiums paid under German or Austrian law to victims of Nazi persecution are exempt from income tax. These are pensions paid because of serious damage to the individual's health; they are also exempt from tax in Germany and Austria.

In addition, some payments to victims or their heirs from dormant bank accounts are also exempted from tax.

MISCELLANEOUS INVESTMENT INCOME

10.6 SALE OF CERTIFICATES OF DEPOSIT

(s 551 ITTOIA 2005)

A certificate of deposit is a document that entitles the holder to receive the amount held on deposit. An owner of such a deposit can assign it to someone else. Where this is done for valuable consideration, the profit is taxable as income.

At one time it was possible to avoid having taxable income by assigning ownership of a deposit without there being a certificate of deposit. Profits on such transactions are now also caught as income taxable under s 551. They are not treated as income from savings. This income should be reported on the SA form as part of the answer to Q15 on page 3.

10.7 GAINS FROM ROLL-UP, AND OTHER OFFSHORE, FUNDS

(Offshore Funds (Tax) Regulations 2009)

The rules relating to the treatment of UK investors in offshore funds have been amended on several occasions over the years since they were first introduced in 1984.

The current regime took effect for the purposes of income tax for the tax year 2009–10 and subsequent tax years.

The purpose of both the original and the replacement offshore funds tax regimes remains the same, and they work by charging realisations of an interest in an offshore fund investment to tax as income rather than as chargeable gains, unless certain conditions are met.

The previous tax regime for UK investors in offshore funds, worked on the basis that if an offshore fund did not distribute at least 85% of its income then, on disposal of interests in the fund, UK investors would be charged to tax on income rather than on chargeable gains. This was to prevent any roll-up of income in an offshore fund being subject only to tax on chargeable gains rather than being charged to tax as income, as would be the case for income arising on investments in UK funds.

The 2009 regime moved away from the requirement that income is distributed, to a basis where the CGT treatment will instead apply if an offshore fund's income is reported to UK investors in such a way that UK investors are charged to tax on their share of the 'reported income' of the fund, regardless of whether that income is distributed to them or accumulated in the fund. Funds will either be 'reporting funds' or 'non-reporting funds'.

The definition contained within s 40A FA 2008, detaches the tax definition of an offshore fund from the regulatory definition and instead bases the tax definition on certain characteristics of the fund.

The key features of the new regime for offshore funds rules include:

- a new tax definition of an offshore fund;
- a facility for an advance election to be a 'reporting fund';
- a requirement (for reporting funds) to report fund income to UK investors rather than the requirement to actually distribute the income;
- the consideration of only one 'layer' of funds for reporting funds;

- revised rules to deal with breaches of conditions, in particular to deal with occasions of minor or inadvertent breaches; and
- treating investments in non-reporting funds in the same way as under the old regime for investments in non-distributing funds.

Reporting funds

UK investors must make a return of their income to include both the actual distributions received, as well as the 'reported income' (ie their proportionate share of the fund's reportable income in excess of the sums distributed). They will be liable to income or corporation tax as appropriate on the total of those sums.

In most cases, providing the fund in question has been a reporting fund for the entire period that an investor has held their interest, then on any subsequent disposal of that interest the investor will be subject to tax on any chargeable gain (or loss) arising, subject to some transitional arrangements.

Non-reporting funds

UK investors in non-reporting funds remain chargeable to income or corporation tax on any distributions the fund actually makes to them. Alternatively, if the fund is transparent for income purposes then the investor will be chargeable to tax on income arising on the underlying investments. On disposal of an interest in a non-reporting fund, UK investors will be subject to tax on any gains arising as if those gains were income – that is, on an 'offshore income gain' (OIG). There are detailed rules relating to the calculation of OIGs and their effect on chargeable gains computations.

10.7.1 Two special cases

There is an exception to the OIG tax charge where non-reporting funds are invested almost entirely in unlisted trading companies and gains arise on the disposal of such non-reporting funds.

Fiscally transparent funds will be outside the scope of legislation which treats holdings in certain funds as loan relationships (for corporate investors). This will have the effect that corporate holders will 'look through' all transparent offshore funds for tax purposes including those that are mainly invested in interest bearing assets. The loan relationships rules will therefore apply directly to the underlying assets where relevant. These changes account for the effect of equalisation arrangements in the calculation of reportable income where an offshore reporting fund operates equalisation arrangements.

10.7.2 Gains realised by foreign domiciliaries

A gain from a disposal of an offshore fund by a person of foreign domicile may be taxed on the remittance basis if this is claimed (see Chapter 35).

Tax notes

Investments in reporting offshore funds are treated in the same way for capital gains tax purposes as shares or units in unit trusts.

MISCELLANEOUS INCOME

10.8 MISCELLANEOUS INCOME

(ss 261, 575, 579, 609, 614, 687 ITTOIA 2005)

Tax is charged under ITTOIA 2005.

Post-cessation receipts (see 16.4) are charged as miscellaneous income, as are gains from roll-up funds, profits under the accrued income scheme and gains on foreign life policies. Furthermore, where tax is charged under various anti-avoidance provisions (see Chapter 33) the amounts charged to tax are normally miscellaneous income.

In addition, profits from certain 'one-off' or isolated business activities in the nature of a trade have been charged as miscellaneous income. Thus, the following were held by the courts to be this type of income:

- commission for guaranteeing overdrafts;
- underwriting commission on share issues;
- insurance commission;
- receipts for the use of copyright material;
- payments made to the wife of a train robber for their life story;
- profits realised by an 'angel', ie a person who sponsored a play and was entitled to a share of the profits.

Miscellaneous income can be earned income or investment income.

10.8.1 Miscellaneous income losses

(s 872 ITTOIA 2005)

For years up to 2014–15 losses from activities that would be taxed as miscellaneous income can be set against any profits assessable as miscellaneous income, whether or not the profits arise from the same activity. However, they cannot be set against other types of income such as employment income or savings income.

New anti-avoidance provisions took effect from 6 April 2015. Miscellaneous income losses may now be relieved only against *relevant* miscellaneous income, ie the same sort of miscellaneous income.

10.9 TAXATION OF COMMISSION, CASHBACKS AND DISCOUNTS

10.9.1 Commission on insurance products, etc

HMRC published SP4/97 on the taxation of commission, cashbacks and discounts, further commenting on this subject in its business income manual; BIM40655 onwards and BIM64600 onwards. HMRC has offered its assurances to the 'ordinary retail customer' that there normally will be no tax liabilities on rebated commissions or discounts. However, the position is more complex with regard to insurance products. SP4/97 states:

Life insurance and personal pensions

Qualifying life insurance policies

36 Where commission in respect of a policy holder's own qualifying life insurance policy is received, netted off or invested, that policy will not be disqualified as a result of entitlement to that commission if the contract under which commission arises is separate from the contract of insurance. In practice, HMRC will not seek to read two contracts as one in a way that would lead to the loss of qualifying policy status.

37 Where a policy holder pays a discounted premium in respect of his or her own policy, the premium payable under the policy will be the discounted premium. It is this amount that must be used for the purposes of establishing whether the relevant qualifying rules are met.

Calculation of chargeable event gains in respect of life policies, capital redemption policies and life annuity contracts

38 Chargeable event gains are computed by reference to the premiums or lump sum consideration paid. The amount paid will be interpreted as follows –
   – where a policy holder pays a gross premium and receives commission in respect of that policy, the chargeable event gain is calculated using the gross amount paid without taking the commission received into account;
   – where an amount of commission is received or due under an enforceable legal right and subsequently invested in the policy, that amount is included as a premium paid when calculating the chargeable event gain (but see 10.9.2 below);

- where a policy holder nets off commission from an insurer in respect of his or her own policy from the gross amount of premium payable and the commission is not taxable as income on the policy holder, the chargeable event gain is calculated using the net amount paid to the insurer;
- where a policy holder pays a discounted premium, the chargeable event gain is calculated using the discounted amount of premium paid;
- where extra value is added to the policy by the insurer (for example by allocation of bonus units), the premium for the purpose of calculating the chargeable event is the amount paid by the policy holder without taking the extra value into account.

Tax relief in respect of personal pension contributions

39 Tax relief for contributions to personal pension schemes is due in respect of 'a contribution paid by an individual'. The amount of the contribution will be interpreted as follows where the contract under which the commission arises is separate from the personal pension scheme contract

- where a contributor pays a gross contribution and receives commission in respect of that contribution, tax relief is given on the gross amount paid without taking the commission received into account;
- where an amount of commission is received by, or is due under an enforceable legal right to, the contributor and subsequently invested in the personal pension that gave rise to the commission, tax relief is given on that amount;
- where a contributor deducts commission in respect of his or her own pension contribution from the gross amount payable, relief is due on the net amount paid;
- where a contributor pays discounted contributions, tax relief is due on the discounted amount paid;
- where extra value is added to the policy by the insurer (for example by allocation of bonus units), relief is due on the amount paid by the contributor without taking the extra value into account.

40 If commission were to be rebated to the contributor under the same contract as the personal pension contract, this would be an unapprovable benefit (since it would involve leakage of the pension fund to the member) which would jeopardise the tax-approved status of the arrangement.

41 The consequences of paying commission on transfers between tax-approved pension schemes may be different from those outlined if such payment is effectively a benefit not authorised by the rules of the pension scheme.

Source: HMRC

The statement also encompasses HMRC's two previous press releases by stating that:

(1) other commission rebates to ordinary customers will not be taxed; and
(2) cashbacks offered by banks and building societies as an inducement to take out a mortgage will not be regarded as chargeable to CGT.

10.9.2 Limit imposed by FA 2007

Since 21 March 2007, certain commission rebates on insurance bonds (single premium insurance policies) have had to be taken into account in computing chargeable gains on the encashment of the bond. This treatment is required where:

(1) premiums paid to the insurance company exceed £100,000 in a given year; and
(2) the bond is surrendered, matures or is assigned before three tax years have elapsed.

10.9.3 Payments arising from trade or employment

If a cashback is received in the course of either the recipient's business or employment, the cashback may be chargeable as income.

The income tax consequences of the statement of practice are that employees who receive commission arising from, and discounts in connection with, goods, investments or services sold to third parties are assessable regardless of whether the commission is passed on by them to the customer and whether the commission is paid by the employer or anyone else.

HMRC takes the view that PAYE will apply in any situation where the commission, etc falls to be taxed as employment income.

10.9.4 Trail commission

HMRC issued a Tax Brief (04/13) setting out its views that cash payments to investors are 'annual payments' from which basic rate tax should be withheld under s 683 ITTOIA 2005. HMRC also believes that payment in kind in the form of extra units is an annual payment.

Investors who have received trail commission payments should enter the gross amount of the commission payment in Box 16 of the main tax return, and the amount of tax deducted in Box 18.

Tax is not being pursued in relation to similar payments in earlier years.

Trail commission paid to an ISA or a SIPP will not normally be taxable but payments to an individual relating to ISA or SIPP investments will be taxable.

INCOME RECEIVED NET OF TAX

10.10 ANNUITIES, TRUST INCOME, ETC

10.10.1 Annuities

(s 422 ITTOIA 2005)

Annuities paid by an insurance company are dealt with at 28.5. Where an annuity is payable by an individual or a private company, the payer must deduct tax at the 20% basic rate.

Example – Annuity income received net of basic rate tax: 2014–15

M sells his business to N for a cash sum plus an annuity of £10,000 a year payable by N out of the business profits. In 2014–15, N paid M £8,000 (£10,000 less tax at 20%).

(1) M may set any available personal allowances against the annuity, so that if he is aged 67, is single and has other income of £8,000, the position will be:

	£	£
Annuity (gross amount)		10,000
Personal allowance not used to cover other income		(2,500)
Taxable amount		7,500
Tax payable £7,500 at 20%	1,500	
Less: tax withheld at source	(2,000)	
HMRC will repay	500	

(2) If M's other income is sufficient to utilise both his personal allowances and the lower rate band, there will be no repayment. If he is a higher rate taxpayer, he will have to pay additional tax on the annuity, as follows:

	£
Higher rate tax on annuity (40% of £10,000)	4,000
Less: Already paid by deduction	(2,000)
Additional tax payable	2,000

(3) The buyer, N, can obtain relief for the annuity paid to M not as a trading expense, but as a deduction in computing total taxable income.

(a) If he is only a basic rate taxpayer, he obtains the relief to which he is entitled by keeping for himself the £2,000 difference between the gross amount of the annuity and the £8,000 actually paid to M.

(b) If he is a higher rate taxpayer, additional relief is given by not charging higher rate tax on an amount equal to the gross annuity paid – a process usually referred to as 'extending the basic rate band'.

(4) Suppose N's profits are £50,000, he has no other income and is entitled only to the basic personal allowance of £10,000. If he did not have to pay the annuity, his tax position would be:

	£
Income	50,000
Personal allowance	(10,000)
Tax payable on	40,000
£31,865 charged at 20%	6,373
£8,135 charged at 40%	3,254
£40,000	9,627

(5) As he does have to pay the annuity, the basic rate band is extended by the gross amount of that annuity (£10,000), so the position becomes:

	£
£40,000 charged at 20%	8,000

This is a reduction of £1,627 and so overall the position is:

	£
Gross annuity	10,000
Net payment to M	(8,000)
Basic rate tax relief	2,000
Reduction in tax payable by assessment	1,627
Total tax relief	3,627

If N has more income within the 40% band, the total tax relief might be £4,000 (ie 40% of £10,000). Where N is an additional rate taxpayer, relief is not given at 45%. Section 10(6) ITA 2007 mentions only two circumstances in which the higher rate band, as well as the basic rate band, will be extended – Gift Aid and pension contributions.

10.10.2 Income from trusts

Income paid to a beneficiary of a fixed interest trust is normally taxed at source at 20%. However, tax will sometimes have been charged on the trustees at other rates, eg dividends will carry a 10% tax credit. In such a situation, the beneficiary will have a credit for basic rate tax on that element of his or her income from the trust that represents income that has borne 20% tax and a 10% tax credit on dividend income which he or she has received from the trust.

Income payments to discretionary beneficiary in 2014–15 and 2015–16 carry a credit of 45%. In practice, a beneficiary will normally receive a form R185, which sets out his or her income from the trust and the tax withheld.

10.10.3 Estates of deceased persons

(ss 649–656 ITTOIA 2005)

When someone dies, it takes time for his or her executors or personal representatives to identify all his or her assets, pay all his or her debts, settle any IHT liability and work out the best way of dividing the estate between those entitled (eg one beneficiary may want to take specific investments, another may prefer cash). During this time, known as the administration period, it is quite likely that income will be received by the executors or personal representatives, both on the deceased's existing investments and, for example, as interest on a bank account into which the executors have paid money collected on behalf of the estate.

The executors or personal representatives must pay tax on all income received. Items such as share dividends and bond interest are received net of tax and this tax will cover the executors' liability. Income from savings is taxed at 20%. Other income is also subject to tax at the basic rate and, where no tax has been withheld at source (eg rental income), the executors will need to go through the self-assessment procedures.

The executors or personal representatives must therefore pool income on which tax has been paid. That pool must be divided between the beneficiaries in accordance with the terms of the deceased's Will, or of the laws of intestacy if he or she left no Will.

Example – Tax treatment of estate income

The gross income from an estate for 2014–15 is £200, on which the executors have paid tax of £40. The deceased's son is, under the Will, entitled to half that income. He will receive a cheque for £80 plus a certificate, signed by the executors, confirming that tax of £20 has been paid to HMRC. The son's income for tax purposes is £100, but he is treated as having already paid basic rate tax on that £100. If he has personal allowances or other reliefs available, he can obtain (from HMRC) a repayment of some or all of the £20 tax paid; if he is a higher or additional rate taxpayer, he will have to pay over to HMRC the difference between basic and higher or additional rate tax.

10.10.4 Allocation of estate income to particular tax years

Payments made to beneficiaries out of the income of the residue of an estate are taxable as income for the year of payment. If, following death, income which accrued before death is taken into account both in determining the value of the estate for the purposes of IHT, and in calculating the residuary income of the estate for a tax year, a reduction is made in the residuary income of the estate for that tax year in ascertaining the extra liability, if any, of a person with an absolute interest in the whole or part of the residue.

11

ALLOWABLE DEDUCTIONS

This chapter contains the following sections:

(1) Alimony and maintenance
(2) Loans used to purchase an annuity from an insurance company
(3) Loans to purchase investment property
(4) Loans to invest in partnerships
(5) Loans to invest in close companies
(6) Loans to invest in employee-controlled companies
(7) Loans to purchase plant and machinery
(8) Alternative finance 'products'
(9) Gift Aid
(10) Gift of listed shares and securities
(11) Gift of land and buildings
(12) Tainted charity donations
(13) Annuities, etc
(14) Cap on tax reliefs
(15) Life assurance premiums
(16) Community Investment Tax Credit (CITC)

11.1 ALIMONY AND MAINTENANCE

No relief is normally given for any payments whatsoever made after 5 April 2000. The remaining relief is of limited relevance as it is only available where one of the parties to the agreement under which the payments are made was born before 6 April 1935. For those who qualify, an allowance of up to £3,220 can be claimed for 2015–16. Relief is given at 10%.

11.2 LOANS USED TO PURCHASE AN ANNUITY FROM AN INSURANCE COMPANY

(ss 353(1A), (1AA) and (1AB) ICTA 1988)

MIRAS relief, abolished from 6 April 2000, was given for interest on loans taken out before 9 March 1999, by individuals already aged 65 or over, and secured on the borrower's main residence, where at least 90% of the loan on which the interest was payable was used to buy an annuity for the remainder of his or her life. Interest payable on this type of loan continues to attract relief at 23% despite the general abolition of MIRAS and the reduction in the basic rate to 20%.

11.3 LOANS TO PURCHASE INVESTMENT PROPERTY

Interest on loans used to acquire a property that is let out may be allowed in computing the rental income assessable for tax purposes (see Chapter 8).

11.4 LOANS TO INVEST IN PARTNERSHIPS

(s 398 ITA 2007)

Tax relief may be obtained on loan interest which is paid in a tax year provided that the loan has been used to invest in a partnership that is not an investment LLP. Interest on qualifying loans may be set against the individual's general income, ie relief is not confined to an offset against income from the partnership.

11.4.1 Conditions for relief

It does not matter that such loans may be secured by way of a mortgage against the partner's main residence; the availability of relief depends on the purpose for which the loan is raised, not the way in which the lender secures its position. Relief is basically available where the loan is applied:

- in purchasing a share in a partnership; or
- in contributing capital to a partnership or advancing money to a partnership where the money advanced is used wholly for the purposes of the partnership's trade, profession or vocation; or
- in paying off another loan the interest on which would have been eligible for tax relief.

However, there are further conditions that must be satisfied. The borrower must be a member of the partnership throughout the period in which the interest accrues (and not just as a limited partner). Also, he or she must not have recovered any capital from the partnership since raising the qualifying loan.

11.4.2 Recovery of capital

(s 399(3) ITA 2007))

If, at any time after the application of the proceeds of the loan, a partner recovers capital from the partnership, he or she is deemed to have used the money withdrawn to repay the qualifying loan on which he or she is claiming interest relief. This applies whether or not the proceeds are actually used in this manner. It is therefore advisable to segregate the partners' capital and current accounts in the partnership's books so that any withdrawal can be clearly identified.

Tax notes

Relief is due for interest which is paid in a year. Interest that is 'rolled-up' will not normally be eligible for relief until it is actually paid.

11.4.3 Property occupied rent-free by partnership

Where a partner takes out a loan to purchase property occupied by the partnership for business purposes and the interest is paid by the partnership, technically no deduction is due to the partnership because the interest is not its liability but the partner's. However, in practice, the interest paid can be treated as rent so that it then becomes allowable as a deduction. In the partner's hands, the rent is taxable but the interest paid is allowed as a deduction in arriving at the amount taxable as income from property.

11.4.4 Incorporation of partnership

(ss 409(1), 409(2) and 410 ITA 2007)

Where a partnership business is transferred to a limited company in return for shares, any qualifying loan in existence at the time continues to attract tax relief provided the conditions for relief in 11.5 below would be met if a new loan was taken out.

11.4.5 Tax planning: withdrawing partnership monies and replacing working capital by raising qualifying loans

Where a partner has a surplus balance on either his or her current or capital account with a partnership and he or she does not already have a qualifying loan, he or she may withdraw the balance due to him or her (with his or her partners' consent), use the money to pay off non-qualifying borrowings and then borrow further funds to introduce capital into the partnership and obtain tax relief.

Example – Replacement capital

B is a partner in the XYZ partnership. She has a credit balance of £100,000 in her capital account. Outside the partnership, she has bought a yacht for her private use with the help of a £40,000 loan from her bank and she has a house mortgage of £20,000. *B* could withdraw £60,000 from her capital account in the partnership and use the money to make the following repayments:

	£
Yacht bank loan	40,000
Building society	20,000
	60,000

Once these transactions have been completed, *B* could borrow £60,000 as a loan (not overdraft) and use the funds to reintroduce capital into the partnership with full tax relief on the interest payable. Professional advice should be sought well in advance before setting up this sort of loan.

11.4.6 Raising qualifying loans to replace partnership borrowings

Another situation where it may be appropriate to restructure existing borrowings is where the partnership has taken a loan, typically to purchase another business or the property from which the business is carried on. In this situation, each partner is normally required to borrow privately his or her share of the partnership loan and introduce the monies raised into the partnership. The partner can then personally claim tax relief on the interest paid as a charge on his or her income.

The partnership collects the monies raised by each partner's loan and uses the funds to redeem the partnership loan. As a result, each partner's share of profits becomes correspondingly higher because no interest is now payable by the partnership. However, the situation redresses itself because the higher profits must be used to finance the private borrowing.

Rearranging matters in this way can provide significant cash-flow benefits because relief is available for interest up to one year earlier than where the borrowings remain within the partnership. For example, if the partnership makes up its accounts to 30 April, interest paid on partnership borrowings in the year to 5 April 2016 will normally attract tax relief in 2016–17 (ie as an expense in arriving at the partnership profits for its year falling in 2016–17), whereas replacing these borrowings with qualifying loans raised by the partners will mean that the interest attracts tax relief against their income for the tax year 2015–16.

11.5 LOANS TO INVEST IN CLOSE COMPANIES

(ss 392–395 ITA 2007)

Where interest is paid on a loan used to purchase ordinary shares in a close company, or in lending money to such a company that is used for the purposes of the close company's business, the interest may be eligible for tax relief. For the definition of a close company, see 18.14.1. Once again, relief is dependent on the way the loan is used, not on the way it is secured; the borrower may therefore have a qualifying loan that is secured by way of a mortgage on his or her home.

Interest on such a loan may be set against the individual's general income, ie relief is not restricted to an offset against income from the close company.

Tax notes

Interest on a qualifying loan may be set against any of your taxable income; it does not have to be set against the income from the close company first.

Relief is due for the year in which the interest is paid, not for the year in which it accrued.

11.5.1 Conditions for relief where the loan is used to buy shares

Relief is dependent upon conditions being satisfied by the borrower, the company and in relation to the shares that are acquired.

Conditions applicable to the borrower

(1) The borrower, either alone or together with certain associates, owns a material interest in the close company (defined broadly as more than 5% of the ordinary share capital).

(2) The borrower holds less than 5% of the ordinary share capital, but works for the greater part of his or her time in the actual management or conduct of the company or an associated company (a works manager, a production manager or a company secretary would normally satisfy this condition).

Conditions applicable to the company

The company must exist wholly or mainly for one of the following purposes:

(a) To carry on a trade or trades on a commercial basis.
(b) To make investments in land or property let commercially to unconnected parties.
(c) To hold shares or securities or make loans to 'qualifying companies' or an intermediate company, all of which are under its control. A qualifying company is one that is under the close company's control and satisfies the conditions at (a) and (b) above.
(d) To co-ordinate the administration of two or more qualifying companies.

If the company holds property, the individual must not reside in it unless he or she has worked for the greater part of his or her time in the actual management or conduct of the company.

For these purposes, a close company may be a company which is resident in the EEA rather than (as before 2014–15) just in the UK.

Conditions applicable to the shares being acquired

A loan used to buy shares is a qualifying loan only if the shares are ordinary share capital. 'Ordinary share capital' includes any shares in the company other than fixed rate preference shares.

Tax notes

Tax avoidance legislation in FA 2009 counters arrangements designed to generate a certain (or almost certain) financial profit for individuals through the availability of income tax deductions for loan interest. These provisions apply to interest payable on loans taken out to finance various forms of investment (such as an interest in a close company or a partnership) where the availability of interest relief means that, taking this into account, the investor cannot fail to make a post-tax profit from the overall arrangements.

11.5.2 Close EIS companies

(s 161(2) ITA 2007)

Loan interest relief is not available in respect of shares issued under the Enterprise Investment Scheme.

11.5.3 Company ceases to be close after loan taken out

Relief can continue to be due for interest paid on a loan even though the company has ceased to be a close company provided the other conditions remain satisfied. For example, the individual must either have a material interest or be employed full-time in the management of the company or an associated company. This is often relevant where management form a company in a management buy-out (MBO) and it ceases to be close after outside institutions inject further share capital.

11.5.4 Close company taken over on share-for-share basis

Where an individual has borrowed to invest in a close company and that company is taken over by another close company on a share-for-share basis, his or her loan can continue to be a qualifying loan provided all the other conditions are satisfied.

11.5.5 Close company shares sold

If you sell the shares in a close company, and you have a loan that was used to finance the purchase of the shares, the loan interest ceases to qualify for relief from the date of disposal. Interest charged by a bank on the subsequent redemption of the loan does not attract income tax relief.

Furthermore, if you give away shares, you may also be regarded as having 'recovered capital'. This means you may cease to be eligible for relief on interest paid on your borrowings.

11.5.6 Borrowing to lend money to a close company

Relief is also available under s 392 if you borrow to lend money to a close company in which you have a material interest, or are a full-time director or manager, and the company uses the money in its business.

Once again, the loan ceases to be a qualifying loan to the extent that you recover capital from the company. There is a trap here in that a gift or other disposal of shares may constitute a 'recovery of capital' even though the money you have lent to the company has not been withdrawn.

Tax notes

You should make sure that your bank debits you for accrued interest just before you sell or give away the shares because interest charged after that date will not attract tax relief.

11.6 LOANS TO INVEST IN EMPLOYEE-CONTROLLED COMPANIES

(ss 396, 397 ITA 2007)

It is also possible for an individual to establish a qualifying loan where he or she uses it to buy shares in an employee-controlled company, even if it is not a close company. The conditions that need to be satisfied for a loan to qualify under this provision are:

- during the year of assessment in which the interest is paid, the company must either become employee-controlled for the first time or be employee-controlled for at least nine months;
- the individual or his or her spouse or civil partner must be a full-time employee throughout the period commencing with the application of the loan and ending with the date on which the interest is paid: he or she can also continue to obtain relief for interest paid within 12 months of his or her having ceased to be an employee;
- the shares must be acquired before, or not later than 12 months after, the date on which the company first becomes an employee-controlled company; and
- the individual must not have recovered any capital from the company during the period from applying the loan proceeds to paying the interest.

The legislation requires that the company be unquoted and resident only in the UK (or, for 2014–15 onwards, in the EEA) and either a trading company or the holding company of a trading group. A company is 'employee-controlled' if more than 50% of its ordinary share capital and voting power is owned by full-time employees or their spouses or civil partners. If a full-time employee owns more than 10%, the excess is disregarded. For this purpose, a spouse or civil partner's holding is attributed to the employee unless the spouse or civil partner is also a full-time employee.

11.7 LOANS TO PURCHASE PLANT AND MACHINERY

(ss 388–391 ITA 2007)

Where a partner incurs capital expenditure on the purchase of plant and machinery used for the partnership's business purposes and eligible for capital allowances, he or she can claim tax relief on interest paid if the plant is financed by a loan. The relief is available only in the tax year in which the loan is taken out and the following three tax years.

Example – Use of loans to purchase plant and machinery

A partner borrowed £10,000 at 10% pa on 6 October 2014 to buy a van that is used for the partnership's business. His private use is agreed at 25%. Interest relief is available on £375 in 2014–15 and on £750 for the following three tax years.

Similar relief is available for employees who are required to purchase plant for use in carrying out their duties but the relief is not available for loans used to buy a car, van or motor cycle.

Tax notes

If you have realised some capital and are in a position to clear some of your borrowings, it will generally be best to repay non-qualifying loans where you get no tax relief for the interest.

11.8 ALTERNATIVE FINANCE 'PRODUCTS'

Where an individual enters into a shariah compliant contract with an Islamic bank or financial institution, he or she will not pay interest. However, the transactions may have similar economic consequences. For example, a diminishing musharaka contract is in essence a partnership arrangement which involves a buyer and a bank jointly purchasing a property. The buyer pays rent to the bank on its share of the property. The buyer also gradually acquires the bank's share and, as he or she does so, the rent payable to the bank reduces because the bank owns a smaller proportion of the property. In economic terms, the musharaka contract has the same consequences as a repayment mortgage.

The object of the tax legislation on alternative finance contracts is to provide a level playing field, ie the same tax relief should be obtained in respect of the bank's charges as would be available if those charges were interest. For example, in the case of a diminishing musharaka contract, the rent paid to the bank would attract relief if the property were let or used for business purposes.

11.9 GIFT AID

11.9.1 Introduction

(s 414 ITA 2007)

Gift Aid is a way in which the Government seeks to encourage taxpayers to support charities.

Example – Gift Aid donation

In 2014–15, *A* gives £800 to a recognised charity. Under the Gift Aid scheme, it will be treated as a donation of £1,000, from which basic rate tax of £200 has been deducted. The charity can claim that tax from HMRC, so it will receive a total of £1,000.

If *A* is a basic rate taxpayer that is the end of the story: he has paid over £800 that HMRC has 'topped up' to £1,000. If *A* is a higher rate taxpayer, he may claim higher rate relief on the gift, calculated as follows:

	£
Gross donation made	1,000
Tax relief at 40%	400
Less: deducted when gift made	(200)
Reduction in *A*'s own tax liability	200

If *A* is not a taxpayer at all, HMRC will require him to make good the £200 it has paid to the charity.

If *A* is a 45% taxpayer in 2014–15, he will be able to claim tax relief at his highest marginal rate of tax. Relief can also be obtained against tax on an individual's capital gains if his income tax liabilities are insufficient to cover the Gift Aid donation.

11.9.2 Carrying back relief

It is possible to carry back Gift Aid donations made. The amount that may be carried back is the amount of donations made by the time the individual submits his or her tax return, ie payments made up to 31 January 2016 can be set against the 2015 tax liability.

An individual will need to make a formal carry-back election either on the tax return when filing or as a stand alone claim. The deadline for making this election is the date that he or she files his or her tax return or (if earlier) 31 January following the year to which the donations are being carried back.

Tax notes

Carrying back Gift Aid donations will mean that you get the benefit of the higher rate relief 12 months earlier than if you simply take the relief for the year of payment. It could also be beneficial if you were a higher rate taxpayer for the previous year but only a basic rate taxpayer for the year of payment.

The case of *John Cameron* v *HMRC* TC00415 highlights a potential pitfall with claims to carry-back donations. Mr Cameron had made a claim to carry back Gift Aid contributions made in 2006–07 to 2005–06 on an amended 2006 tax return, having submitted his tax return for the year in question in good time. The Tribunal judge reluctantly concluded that the relief was not due (although in the judge's view this ran contrary to the principles of common sense and fairness) because the claim had not been made by the date that Mr Cameron delivered his original return, and the legislation is worded in such a way that a claim made on an amendment to the return for a year cannot be valid.

11.9.3 Qualifying donations

Several conditions must be satisfied under the Gift Aid scheme:

(1) The recipient must be a recognised charity or a community amateur sports club. Many appeal funds and societies established for the public benefit are not technically charities. In case of doubt, intending donors should ask for evidence of charitable status or should consult:

Charity Commission Direct

PO Box 1227

Liverpool L69 3UG

Web: www.charity-commission.gov.uk

By way of exception, four bodies that technically are not charities are deemed to be charities for Gift Aid purposes: the British Museum, the National History Museum, the National Heritage Memorial Fund and the Historic Buildings and Monuments Commission for England.

(2) The gift must be of money: it is not possible to claim Gift Aid relief for donated works of art, or even for goods (eg clothing or blankets) to be used to assist distressed people. Also, it is not possible to give money on condition that it is used to buy something from the donor, a member of his or her family, or a company in which he or she has an interest.

(3) The gift may be made in cash, by cheque or bank transfer, or by credit card. However, HMRC does not accept that writing-off an existing loan to the charity is equivalent to a gift of money.

(4) There is no minimum or maximum donation.

(5) Any reciprocal benefit received from the charity (by the donor or a member of his or her family) must fall within prescribed limits.

11.9.4 Permissible benefits for Gift Aid donors

A charity may wish to give a token of its appreciation to donors for their donations. Modest benefits received in consequence of making a donation will not stop the donation from qualifying as a Gift Aid donation, provided their value does not exceed certain limits. If the benefits exceed the permitted limits, the donations cannot qualify as Gift Aid donations.

If a charity wishes to provide benefits to donors it should consider whether the proposed benefits fall within the limits in the donor benefit rules.

The benefit limit which applies for donations over £10,000 is £2,500 or 5% of the donation (whichever is lower).

11.10 GIFT OF LISTED SHARES AND SECURITIES

Individuals who make gifts to charity of listed shares and securities are able to claim relief in calculating their taxable income. The relief applies where listed shares or securities are given or sold at undervalue to a charity. The shares must be listed on a recognised stock exchange in the UK or overseas. A gift of AIM shares can qualify.

The deduction is equal to the market value of the shares or securities on the date of the gift (inclusive of the incidental cost of disposal) less any consideration received for or in consequence of the gift.

Example – Giving shares to charity

C, a basic rate taxpayer, gives listed shares with a market value of £10,000 to a charity. The shares show an unrealised gain of £9,000. C obtains income tax relief at 20% on £10,000 and gains of £9,000 escape tax at 18%: giving total tax relief of £3,620). If C was a higher rate taxpayer, this would increase to £6,520.

Note that the deduction is given only against income, not against capital gains.

Anti-avoidance

There is anti-avoidance legislation to prevent the abuse of this relief by the donor having a right to repurchase the shares at less than market value.

In recent years, a number of avoidance schemes exploiting the Gift Aid provisions have been disclosed to, or discovered by, HMRC. These schemes sought to exploit the rules which enable a charity to claim a repayment of tax at the basic rate on a qualifying donation by an individual, with the individual claiming relief for the donation on the difference between the higher and basic rates of tax.

One scheme depended upon a circular series of payments. It starts with the charity purchasing, say, gilts of £100,000 which pass through a third party to an individual taxpayer for perhaps £10. The taxpayer is expected to make a sale for £100,000 and pass the money to the charity. There is an option that ensures the gilts will be returned to the charity if it does not receive a cash gift of £100,000 within one or two days.

In these circumstances, HMRC does not accept that the charity is entitled to a repayment of tax or that Gift Aid relief is due to the individual.

In addition, there have been a number of schemes that seek to generate Gift Aid (and gift of shares) tax relief claims. A cash donation to a nominated charity is made and in return shares are received from an unnamed non-UK 'philanthropist'. These shares are claimed to be worth many times the amount of the cash donation but are in companies listed on a stock exchange that is not recognised by HMRC. The shares are then donated to the nominated charity.

No Gift Aid is due on the cash donation because the donor receives a benefit (the shares) that is in excess of the donation. No relief is due on the gift of shares because the requirement that the shares are listed on a stock exchange recognised by HMRC is not met.

Section 31 and Schedule 7 FA (No.1) 2010 introduced rules to block tax avoidance schemes that exploit the rules for tax relief on gifts of qualifying investments to charities under Chapter 3, Part 8 ITA 2007.

The anti-avoidance deals with gifts of certain shares, securities and land. The avoidance depends on the donor receiving tax relief at their highest marginal rate of tax on the full market value of the qualifying investments at the date of the gift where:

- the donor acquired the investments at below market value as part of a scheme or arrangement, or
- the market value of the investment is artificially inflated at the date of the gift to charity.

The new rules adjust the amount of relief to the donor to the economic cost of acquisition of the gift, to the donor, where:

- the qualifying investment gifted to the charity (or anything from which the investment derives) was acquired within four years of the date of disposal; and
- where the main purpose, or one of the main purposes, of acquiring the qualifying investment was to dispose of it to a charity and claim the tax relief.

Income tax relief in addition to CGT exemption

No CGT arises on a gift of shares to charity, so the donor's 40% income tax relief may be in addition to a significant saving of CGT that would apply if he or she were to sell the shares.

Tax notes

Bear in mind that in the same way that no capital gain is recognised on a gift to charity, no loss is allowed. Therefore, if you are making a gift of shares ensure first that there would be a chargeable gain if you actually disposed of the shares. If not, then a better option would be to actually sell the shares and realise the capital loss. You can then make a cash donation to the charity. This would be especially beneficial if you had other chargeable gains arising during the tax year.

11.11 GIFT OF LAND AND BUILDINGS

Tax relief is available to a person who makes a charitable donation in kind by transferring land or buildings to the charity as gift or sale at an undervalue. The donor is allowed to deduct the value of land or buildings in arriving at his or her taxable income. The relief is basically the same as that for gifts of listed shares; therefore, the same considerations apply, including the anti-avoidance provisions introduced in FA (No.1) 2010. Note that again the deduction is given only against income, not against capital gains.

11.12 TAINTED CHARITY DONATIONS

Anti-avoidance legislation on substantial donors was introduced in 2006 and was designed to address the perceived abuse of charitable tax reliefs. The legislation was re-cast in 2011.

The tainted charity donations rules apply only to donors who enter into arrangements to obtain an advantage from a charity. Where this applies it is the donor who will be penalised rather than the charity.

The FA 2011 removed the entitlement to tax reliefs where a person makes a relievable charity donation (meaning a donation eligible for tax relief) which is a tainted donation.

A tainted donation exists if Conditions A, B *and* C are met:

A. The donor (or persons connected with the donor) enters into arrangements (either before or after the donation is made) and it is reasonable to assume that the donation would not have been made and the arrangements would not have been entered into independently of one another.
B. The main purpose, or one of the main purposes of the person entering into the arrangements, is to obtain an advantage either directly or indirectly from the charity to which the donation is made or a connected charity.
C. The donor is not a company wholly owned by one or more charities, at least one of which is the charity to which the donation is being made.

11.13 ANNUITIES, ETC

(ss 447–452 and 900 ITA 2007, s 727 ITTOIA 2005)

11.13.1 Introduction

Most annuities are payments under deed of covenant, ie a written promise to pay another person a certain sum of money each year (or each week, month, quarter, etc), either for a fixed number of years or for a period determined by events (eg until the payer's or the payee's death).

At one time, all deeds of covenant operated so as to transfer taxable income from the payer to the payee, so that the payer's taxable income was reduced by the amount of the covenanted payment and the payee's similarly increased. This could save a great deal of money where (as would usually be the case) the payee was subject to a lower rate of tax than the payer. As a result, deeds of covenant were often used to redistribute income around a family. Inevitably this led to anti-avoidance legislation that gradually became all-embracing and the position now is that, generally, the payer does not obtain a deduction from income, and the recipient's income does not include the covenanted amount.

11.13.2 Business purchase and partnership annuities

There are still two categories of payments where the gross payment is deducted in arriving at net income. For a basic rate taxpayer the tax deducted is effectively the income tax relief but a higher rate taxpayer is entitled to the benefit of the difference between the basic rate and the higher rate. This only applies where the payment is one that requires the deduction of income tax at the basic rate:

- patent royalties where the payment arises in the UK, and
- payments made for commercial reasons in connection with the individual's trade, profession or vocation – this would include annuities paid by a partnership to former partners. Again, the payment must arise in the UK and the recipient must be subject to UK tax on the amount.

For details of such annuities, see 10.10.1.

11.14 CAP ON TAX RELIEFS

11.14.1 Basic outline

The Finance Act 2013 introduced a cap on the amounts that may be deducted in arriving at an individual's taxable income.

The cap is the greater of £50,000 or one quarter of the individual's adjusted total income. Adjusted total income is the amount of an individual's total income for the year increased by the amounts of any payroll giving deductions and reduced by the gross amount of pension contributions which are allowable for tax purposes. The cap applies for 2013–14 onwards.

The policy behind the legislation is to put a limit on reliefs which do not themselves contain a cap such as pension contributions. It is not intended that the cap should apply to amounts which are deductible in arriving at the taxable profit from a given business activity or to prevent brought forward losses being offset against profits from the same trade or business.

11.14.2 Reliefs which are subject to the cap

The following reliefs are subject to the cap:

- qualifying loan interest (see 11.4–11.6);
- trading losses which are set against an individual's total income, either for the year of the loss or for an earlier year (see 7.7.2). However, this restriction of relief does not apply to losses arising from overlap relief (see 7.3.5) or the Business Premises Renovation Allowance (see 16.2.14);
- relief for post-cessation expenses (see 16.4);
- employment loss relief (see 4.20);
- income tax relief for capital losses on shares in unquoted trading companies (see 17.2).

11.14.3 Charitable donations are not subject to the cap

Gift Aid donations (see 11.9) and gifts of quoted shares or property to a charity (see 11.10 and 11.11) are not subject to the cap.

11.14.4 EIS and VCT reliefs

Reliefs for investments which qualify for the Enterprise Investment Scheme (see 25.4), the Seed Enterprise Investment Scheme (see 25.5) and venture capital trusts (see 25.7) are not subject to the cap.

11.15 LIFE ASSURANCE PREMIUMS

(ss 266, 274 ICTA 1988)

The relief was abolished on 6 April 2015.

11.16 COMMUNITY INVESTMENT TAX CREDIT (CITC)

The Community Investment Tax Credit (CITC) scheme applies to investments in accredited Community Development Finance Institutions (CDFIs). The relief is intended to stimulate private investment in disadvantaged communities by providing a tax incentive to individuals and companies investing in not-for-profit and profit-seeking enterprises in or for those communities.

The tax relief is worth up to 25% of the value of the investment in the CDFI and is spread over five years, starting with the year in which the investment is made.

The relief for a year should normally be claimed on the tax return for that year, page 2 of the Additional Information schedule to the SA form. However individual investors who have received a tax relief certificate may also request a change to their PAYE code number, or claim a reduction in their self-assessment payments on account.

12

ALLOWANCES AND CHILD TAX CREDIT

This chapter looks at allowances and tax credits that may be claimed by taxpayers under the following sections:

(1) Personal allowances
(2) The basic personal allowance
(3) Married couple's allowance
(4) Pensioner couples
(5) Blind persons
(6) Time limits
(7) Child tax credit

12.1 PERSONAL ALLOWANCES

(ss 35–37 ITA 2007)

Income tax is not charged on the whole of a person's taxable income. In calculating the amount on which tax must be paid, he or she may claim a personal allowance that depends on his or her individual circumstances (eg age).

Personal allowances may, in most circumstances, be claimed by anyone resident in the UK. There is no minimum age requirement so that, for example, a new born baby is entitled to a personal allowance. Sometimes it is possible, through the use of trusts or settlements, to redirect part of a family's income to a child, so that it may (being covered by his or her personal allowance) be enjoyed tax free (although the scope for transferring taxable income in this way has been whittled down by a succession of complex anti-avoidance provisions: see 33.6.4).

British subjects and certain other categories of people not resident in the UK may also claim personal allowances. However, Commonwealth citizens are no longer entitled to claim UK personal allowances in these circumstances.

12.2 THE BASIC PERSONAL ALLOWANCE

(s 35 ITA 2007)

Subject to income limits (see 12.2.3), every individual resident in the UK is entitled to the basic personal allowance – often called the 'single person's allowance', a throwback to the days when there was also a 'married man's allowance' and 'wife's earned income relief'. See 12.2.3 below concerning changes to personal allowances for individuals with income of £100,000 or more, and 35.13 concerning the restriction of allowances for non-UK domiciliaries claiming the remittance basis.

The allowance for 2014–15 was £10,000 and for 2015–16 it is £10,600. If the individual is born or dies part way through a year of assessment, the allowance is not scaled down.

Example – Death during tax year

Suppose *D* died at the end of September 2015, by which time he had earned only half his annual salary. His tax bill for 2015–16 would be:

	£
Salary	20,000
Professional subscription paid	(135)
	19,865
Personal allowance	(10,600)
Tax payable on	9,265
£9,265 charged at 20%	1,853

Because the PAYE scheme assumes that personal allowances will be used in equal monthly (or weekly) instalments over the year, D will have had the benefit of only part of his £10,600 allowance whilst he was alive and there will therefore be a tax overpayment up to the date of death. On request, HMRC will therefore repay his executors the excess tax deducted.

12.2.1 Higher allowances for the over-65s

(ss 36 and 37 ITA 2007)

Higher allowances have been given to those who have attained age 65 and are of limited means. The 2014–15 allowance was £10,500 for those between ages 65 and 74 and £10,660 for those aged 75+. The 65–74 allowance was effectively phased-out in 2015–16 and the amount of the 75+ allowance was not increased for 2015–16.

Furthermore, the increased allowance is not given to an individual who attained 65 after 5 April 2013.

The higher allowance is given where the individual was alive on the first day of the tax year and would have achieved age 65 or 75 within the tax year had he or she not died.

The allowances were designed to assist only those of limited means. The 2014–15 allowance is reduced by £1 for every £2 by which the individual's 'total income' exceeds £27,000, until it falls back to the level of the standard allowance for the under-65s.

Within this band, every £2 of income can cost 30p in tax (20p on the £2 itself, plus 10p on the £1 of allowances withdrawn). This is an effective percentage rate of 30%.

'Total income' means income after deducting qualifying interest, allowable losses, gift aid payments and gifts of shares or property to charity (see 11.10 and 11.11).

12.2.2 Personal allowances for individuals with high income

For individuals with income over £100,000 per annum, the personal allowance is reduced by £1 for every £2 of total income over £100,000 per annum. 'Total income' is as defined in 12.2.1 above. The effect of this is that the basic personal allowance will be reduced to nil where an individual's net income for 2015–16 is over £121,200. This limit applies irrespective of age.

For individuals with income over £150,000 per annum, a 45% tax rate applies to taxable non-dividend income above £150,000 per year.

A 37.5% dividend tax rate applies where taxable income is over £150,000 per annum and dividend income falls into the 'additional' (over £150,000) rate band (after gains, savings and dividend income are treated as the 'top slice' of income).

12.2.3 Transfer of unused allowances

For 2015–16 and future years, a married person, or one in a civil partnership, can transfer 10% of their personal allowance to their spouse or civil partner. This is allowed only where neither the transferor or the recipient are liable for higher rate tax.

12.3 MARRIED COUPLE'S ALLOWANCE

This relief was abolished with effect from 6 April 2000 for those born on or after 6 April 1935, though it is still available for 2014–15 to married couples and civil partners where either spouse or civil partner was born before 6 April 1935 – see 12.4 below.

12.4 PENSIONER COUPLES

(ss 42–46 ITA 2007)

The married couple's allowance is still available if either spouse or civil partner was born before 6 April 1935. The allowance for 2015–16 is £8,355 (£8,165 for 2014–15). Relief is restricted to 10%. The allowance is subject to claw-back if the individual's income exceeds £27,700 (£27,000 for 2014–15) (see 12.2.1). However, a minimum allowance of £3,220 (£3,140 for 2014–15) is due even where the income exceeds the limit (including where income exceeds the £100,000 limit).

There is a choice for those married prior to 5 December 2005. The s 45 rules allow the husband (where he or his wife was born before 6 April 1935) to claim the allowance however, he can elect for the s 46 rules to apply instead. Section 46 applies to couples married on or after 5 December 2005 and civil partners (and those who elect for it to apply) and the allowance is given to the higher earning spouse or civil partner.

12.4.1 Pensioner couples: transfer of excess allowances

(s 47–53 ITA 2007)

The whole of a higher, age-related married couple's allowance may be transferred to the wife if the husband has insufficient income to use it himself (where a s 45 claim has been made) or alternatively, the higher earning partner may elect under s 47 to transfer the allowance (for s 46 claims). Where either claim has been made, the couple can jointly elect (under s 48) to share the allowance between them in the desired proportions. An election to do this must be lodged with HMRC before the start of the first tax year for which it is to have effect, or during that year if the marriage takes place during the year, or within the first 30 days of the tax year in which it is to take effect if HMRC is given prior notice. Civil partners can also make such elections.

12.5 BLIND PERSONS

(ss 38–40 ITA 2007)

A person who is blind may claim a special, additional personal allowance of £2,290 (£2,230 for 2014–15). A person counts as 'blind' if:

- he or she lives in England or Wales and his or her name appears on the local authority's register of blind persons; or
- he or she lives in Scotland or Northern Ireland and is so blind that he or she cannot perform any work for which eyesight is essential.

This definition means that a person resident abroad can never, for tax purposes, count as blind – an odd rule which is strictly enforced by HMRC.

A person who becomes blind during a year of assessment may claim the full blind person's allowance for that year.

12.5.1 Married couples

If both spouses or civil partners are blind, each may claim a separate blind person's allowance.

A blind person with insufficient income to use all his or her personal allowances may be able to transfer the whole or part of his or her blind person's allowance to his or her spouse or civil partner (whether or not he or she also is blind). This election must be made within four years of the end of the tax year to which it relates. However, the transfer of the pensioners' married couple's allowance will take priority, so a transfer of blind person's allowance is only possible for pensioners where the husband or higher earning spouse or civil partner's income was insufficient to use his or her basic personal allowance and the blind person's allowance itself.

Example – Blind married couple

G, who is sighted, earns £15,000 a year. His wife, H, who is blind, has a pension of £7,000. The position for 2014–15 is:

H	£	£
Pension		7,000
Basic personal allowance	10,000	
Blind person's allowance	2,230	
		(12,230)
Excess, part transferable to husband*		5,230
G		
Salary		15,000
Basic personal allowance	10,000	
Transferred excess from wife*	2,230	
		(12,230)
Tax payable on		2,770
£2,770 charged at 20%		554

* capped at £2,230 as the personal allowance was non-transferable.

12.6 TIME LIMITS

As noted at 12.2, subject to the income limit, every individual resident in the UK is automatically entitled to the basic personal allowance.

These allowances must be claimed within four years of the end of the year to which they relate, for example a claim in respect of blind person's allowance relating to the year ended 5 April 2012 must be made by 5 April 2016.

In general, most claims for allowances are made annually in the tax return. However, where a claim is overlooked or a formal return is not issued, a claim can be made to the taxpayer's tax office, normally in writing, though in certain circumstances phone claims will be accepted.

12.7 CHILD TAX CREDIT

12.7.1 Child tax credit

As its name suggests, the child tax credit is meant to support families with children and can be claimed if you have responsibility for a child.

The credit, which can be claimed in addition to any child benefit or working tax credit, is available for the support of:

- a child until 1 September following their 16th birthday;
- a person aged 16–18 who
  - is in full time education, up to and inclusive of A levels or their equivalent (NVQ3/Scottish Highers); or
  - if not in education has no job/training place and has registered with the Careers or Connexions Service.

The 'child' must not be claiming income support or tax credits and must not be serving a custodial sentence of more than four months.

12.7.2 Tax charge

An income tax charge applies to individuals earning more than £50,000 and receiving child benefit or living with a partner who receives this benefit.

The effect is that, where a single parent, or one or both spouses or co-habiting partners, earns £60,000 or more per year, the child benefit received will be reduced to nil. Where the single parent or highest earning spouse/partner earns between £50,000 and £60,000, the benefit is reduced by 1% for every £100 above which his or her earnings exceeds £50,000. So, for example, a single person or chief bread winner with income of £55,000 will effectively only receive half of the normal child benefit available.

The charge is collected through self-assessment and PAYE. Child benefit claimants are able to elect not to receive child benefit and will then not be subject to the charge. The earnings amount used to test liability to the charge is the individual's adjusted net income, which is the same measure used in determining eligibility for personal allowances for individuals with income over £100,000.

13

CAPITAL GAINS TAX

This chapter contains the following sections:

(1) Outline of CGT
(2) CGT and the self-assessment form
(3) Who is subject to CGT?
(4) What assets are chargeable assets?
(5) Which types of transaction may produce a chargeable gain?
(6) Hold-over relief where a gift is a chargeable transfer for IHT purposes
(7) Amount to be brought in as disposal value
(8) What costs are allowable?
(9) Assets held at 31 March 1982
(10) Other acquisition values
(11) Working out your capital gain
(12) Assets that have attracted capital allowances
(13) How gains are computed on quoted securities
(14) Unquoted shares
(15) When may a chargeable gain arise on foreign currency?
(16) Special rules for disposals of chattels
(17) Specific rules that apply to disposals of land and investment properties
(18) Disposal of foreign property
(19) Gains and losses on second-hand insurance policies
(20) Non-resident and disposals of UK residential property

Unless otherwise stated, the statutory references are to the Taxation of Chargeable Gains Act (TCGA) 1992.

13.1 OUTLINE OF CGT

Capital gains are assessed for a tax year. Under self-assessment the due date for payment of the tax is 31 January following the tax year (ie for gains arising in the year ended 5 April 2015, tax is payable by 31 January 2016). There is no requirement to make payments on account: indeed capital gains do not form part of the payment on account calculation (see 2.1.8).

The way that chargeable gains are computed is quite different from the rules that determine assessable income for tax purposes. At present different rates of CGT apply for basic and higher rate taxpayers (see 13.1.4) although both pay at a rate of 10% where entrepreneurs' relief is available (see 17.7).

13.1.1 Annual exemption

(s 3 TCGA 1992)

You are not liable for CGT unless you make gains of more than the annual exemption, which for 2015–16 is £11,100. The exemptions for the previous four years are:

Tax year	£	Tax year	£
2014–15	11,000	2012–13	10,600
2013–14	10,900	2011–12	10,000

13.1.2 No gain/loss on spouse or civil partner transactions

(s 58 TCGA 1992)

Provided a couple has not separated permanently, there can be no chargeable gains on any assets transferred from one spouse or civil partner to the other, whether by gift or sale. The asset is treated as passing across on a no-gain/no-loss basis, with the recipient acquiring it at his or her spouse or civil partner's cost. There is an exception to this rule in respect of the transfer of an asset that becomes part of the trading stock used in the spouse or civil partner's business.

13.1.3 Losses

(ss 16, 16ZA–ZC, 16A TCGA 1992)

Capital losses may arise as well as capital gains. The normal rule is that capital losses cannot be offset against an individual's income but must be offset against gains arising in the same year with any excess loss carried forward against capital gains of future years. Losses arising from transactions involving connected persons may only be set against gains arising from transactions with the same person.

Where gains and losses are made in the same year, the individual can decide against which gains they are set so that they can be used in the most tax-efficient way (eg where gains are liable at different rates within the same tax year – see 13.1.4 – the taxpayer can ensure that his or her loss is set against the gain suffering the highest rate of tax).

Brought-forward losses do not need to be set against gains that are covered by the annual exemption. However, current year losses must be set against capital gains before using the annual exemption.

> **Tax notes**
>
> If you have already realised gains in the current tax year, and these will be covered by the annual exemption, it may pay to defer sales that will produce CGT losses until next tax year. You will then be able to carry the losses forward in full to offset against future gains.

13.1.4 Rate of tax

(s 4 TCGA 1992)

Once the gains for the year have been computed (net of any losses), the annual exemption is deducted. For basic rate taxpayers, the net amount is taxed at 18% (subject to special rules for non-UK domiciliaries – see Chapter 35). The CGT rate is now 28% for higher and additional rate taxpayers.

Where a basic rate taxpayer realises chargeable gains that, when added to his or her income for the year, exceed the basic rate tax band for that year, the excess gains are taxed at 28%.

Note that for disposals of business assets, entrepreneurs' relief may apply and reduce the rate of tax to 10% – see 17.7.

13.1.5 Trading losses

If relief for trading losses has been claimed against income from other sources for the year, any balance of unrelieved loss may be set against capital gains for that year, or against income and capital gains of the preceding tax year.

A formal claim must be lodged with HMRC by one year and ten months after the tax year of loss, ie a claim to utilise a 2013–14 trading loss must be made by 31 January 2016. Similar claims can be made for losses arising from letting furnished holiday accommodation, from post-cessation expenditure or from post-employment deductions (see 8.5 and 16.5).

13.2 CGT AND THE SELF-ASSESSMENT FORM

An individual is required to complete the CGT pages of the SA form if:

- there is CGT to pay;
- total proceeds for the tax year are more than four times the annual CGT exemption, ie for 2014–15 is £44,000;
- chargeable gains exceed the annual exemption and are reduced by losses;
- a CGT relief is to be claimed;
- a CGT election is being made;
- CGT losses are being claimed (a loss cannot be used in later years unless it has been claimed).

13.3 WHO IS SUBJECT TO CGT?

An individual's residence and domicile status may have a crucial bearing on CGT liability.

13.3.1 Significance of residence status

(s 2 TCGA 1992)

An individual is normally subject to the CGT legislation only if he or she is resident or ordinarily resident in the UK for the year in which relevant disposals take place. Residence and ordinary residence are determined in the same way as for income tax (see 34.2). There are three exceptions:

(1) Where a non-resident and non-ordinarily resident person carries on a trade or profession through a branch or agency in the UK, CGT may be charged on a disposal of assets used in that branch despite the fact that normally that individual would be outside the charge on capital gains.

(2) Non-residents can be charged capital gains tax for gains realised after 5 April 2015 from a disposal of a UK residential property (see 13.20 and 14.5).

(3) An individual who has been non-UK resident for a period of less than five complete tax years is regarded as a temporary non-resident and he or she may be taxed on his or her return to the UK. This applies only where the individual had been resident or ordinarily resident in the UK during at least four of the seven tax years prior to ceasing to be resident (see further at 13.3.2 and 34.5.4).

13.3.2 Individual non-resident for part of tax year

There is a split-year treatment for the years of arrival and departure. An individual who leaves the UK and is treated on departure as not resident and not ordinarily resident here is not charged to CGT on gains from disposals made after the date of departure.

Provided that an individual is not caught by the five year rule for temporary non-residents (see below), HMRC will treat an individual who comes to live in the UK and is treated as resident here for any year of assessment from the date of arrival as chargeable to CGT only in respect of chargeable gains from disposals made after arrival.

HMRC will assess capital gains where an individual has returned to the UK during the year in question and was non-resident for less than five complete tax years. In such a case, capital gains and losses realised in the period of non-UK residence on disposals of assets held at the time of departure, will be treated as accruing in the tax year in which he or she resumes UK residence.

13.3.3 Foreign domicile may make an important difference

(s 12 TCGA 1992 – see 35.1 on domicile)

An individual who is resident (or ordinarily resident) and domiciled in the UK is subject to CGT on a worldwide basis (ie on gains realised both in the UK and abroad). By contrast, a non-UK domiciled individual can elect for a special tax treatment called the 'remittance basis' (although he or she may have to pay £30,000 (or even £90,000) for this privilege, see 35.2). Under the remittance basis, the individual will be charged tax on gains from disposals of foreign assets only if the proceeds are brought into (or, as the legislation puts it, the gains are 'remitted' to) the UK. There are more details on the CGT treatment of foreign domiciled individuals in 35.16.

13.4 WHAT ASSETS ARE CHARGEABLE ASSETS?

13.4.1 Assets within the scope of CGT

(s 21 TCGA 1992)

Gains on virtually all types of assets are potentially subject to CGT, subject to certain stated exceptions. Section 21(1) TCGA 1992 states:

> All forms of property shall be assets for the purposes of this Act, whether situated in the UK or not, including:
>
> (a) options, debts and incorporeal property generally, and
> (b) any currency other than sterling, and
> (c) any form of property created by the person disposing of it, or otherwise coming to be owned without being acquired.

The asset need not be transferable or capable of being assigned. The term 'any form of property' is all-embracing. For example, the courts have held that CGT was due on an employer's right to compensation from an employee who wished to be released from his service agreement. In another case, the right to compensation for property expropriated by the USSR in 1940 was held to be a form of property and therefore an asset for CGT purposes. Similarly, the High Court held in *Zim Properties Ltd v Proctor* [1985] STC 90 (see ESC D33) that the right to bring an action before the courts constitutes an asset that can be turned to account by the potential litigant negotiating a compromise and receiving a lump sum.

The conclusion therefore is that virtually all forms of property that can yield a capital sum are subject to CGT unless they are specifically exempt.

13.4.2 What assets are specifically exempt?

The following are the main categories of exempt assets:

- main private residence (see 14.1) [s 222];
- chattels that are wasting assets, unless used in a business (see 13.16) [s 44];
- chattels where the sale consideration is less than £6,000: there is some alleviation of the charge when more than £6,000 is received (see 13.16) [s 262];
- decoration for valour as long as sold by the original recipient [s 268];
- foreign currency acquired for personal expenditure outside the UK, including money spent on the purchase or maintenance of any property situated outside the UK [s 269];
- foreign currency bank accounts held by individuals, trustees and personal representatives (new exemption from 6 April 2012);
- winnings from betting (eg the pools, horses, bingo and lotteries) [s 51];
- compensation or damages for a wrong or injury suffered in a profession or vocation [s 51]; certain compensation from foreign governments for property lost or confiscated [by concession];
- debts, where disposed of by the original debtor [s 251];
- National Savings certificates and non-marketable securities, ie those that cannot be transferred or are only transferable with a Minister of the Crown or National Debt Commissioner's consent [s 121];
- gilt-edged securities and qualifying corporate bonds (QCBs) and any options to acquire or dispose of such investments [s 115]: a QCB is a loan stock that is not convertible and is not a deeply discounted security (see 9.7);
- shares held in NISAs (see 25.1) and PEPs (now obsolete) [s 151];
- shares issued by way of business expansion schemes after 18 March 1986 (provided the BES was not withdrawn) where the shares are sold, etc by the original subscriber or their spouse or civil partner;
- shares that qualified for income tax relief issued under an Enterprise Investment Scheme (see 25.4) provided the EIS relief has not been withdrawn;
- shares in a Venture Capital Trust (see 25.7);
- motor cars, unless not suitable for use as a private vehicle or commonly used for the carriage of passengers [s 263]; and veteran and vintage cars;
- woodlands [s 250];
- gifts to charities and for national purposes to any one mentioned in Schedule 3 IHTA 1984 [s 257];
- works of art where they are taken by HMRC in lieu of death duties such as IHT [s 258];
- gifts to housing associations; a claim is made by both transferor and the association [s 259];

- mortgage cash-backs: HMRC accepts that mortgagees who receive cash inducements from banks and building societies are not liable to CGT on such receipts;
- compensation for mis-sold personal pensions taken owing to disadvantageous advice given between 29 April 1988 and 30 June 1994;
- compensation or damages paid as a capital sum because of a right to take court action – ESC D33. Note that from 27 January 2014, the exemption does not automatically apply unless the compensation is £500,000 or less;
- life assurance policies, but only where the policy is disposed of by the original owner or beneficiaries or by a person who acquired it by way of a gift from a person who had not him or herself acquired it by purchase [s 210] (see 13.19 and 28.3.10).

Where an asset is exempt, no gain is assessable. Unfortunately, it follows that no relief is normally given for losses (losses on a disposal of shares in an EIS are an exception to this general rule).

13.5 WHICH TYPES OF TRANSACTION MAY PRODUCE A CHARGEABLE GAIN?

13.5.1 Introduction

The most obvious type of disposal is an outright sale with immediate settlement of the proceeds due, but there are many other transactions that count as a disposal for CGT purposes, for example:

- outright sale (possibly with payment by instalments);
- conditional sale;
- exercise of an option;
- exchange of property;
- compulsory acquisition of asset by local authority, etc;
- sums payable as compensation or proceeds under an insurance policy;
- gifts or sales at undervalue;
- asset destroyed or becoming of negligible value.

The liability to CGT is determined by the tax year in which the date of disposal falls.

13.5.2 Outright sale

(s 28 TCGA 1992)

The date of disposal is the day on which the unconditional contract is entered into, which may be different from the date the vendor receives payment.

Sale with payment by instalments

The date of disposal is fixed by the time the parties enter into an unconditional contract. It may be possible to pay CGT arising from such transactions as the instalments come in, over a period of up to eight years (provided the instalments are spaced over a period of more than 18 months: s 280 TCGA 1992). HMRC operates a concession where a vendor grants a mortgage to a purchaser who defaults and the vendor takes back the asset in satisfaction of the sums due to him. The disposal is effectively treated as if it had never happened (see ESC D18).

13.5.3 Conditional sale

(s 28 TCGA 1992)

A conditional sale is a contract that does not take effect until a stated condition is satisfied.

Example – Conditional sale

D agrees to purchase E's shares in XYZ Ltd provided the local authority grants planning permission over land owned by XYZ by April 2016. Under this type of agreement, E remains the legal owner of her shares until the condition is satisfied. If the local authority does not in fact grant planning permission, D is under no obligation to buy E's shares.

The date of disposal under such contracts is the day the condition is satisfied and the contract becomes unconditional; in the above example, the date planning permission is granted.

13.5.4 Exercise of an option

(ss 144, 144ZA–144ZD, 144A TCGA 1992)

A 'call' option is a legally binding agreement between the owner of an asset and a third party under which the owner agrees to sell the asset if the other party decides to exercise his or her option. The purchase price payable upon the exercise of the option is normally fixed at the outset; this constitutes one of the terms of the option.

A 'put' option is one where the other party agrees to buy the asset if the owner decides to exercise an option requiring him or her to do so.

The grant of either type of option does not constitute a disposal of the asset concerned. This happens only when the option is exercised and the day on which this happens is the date of disposal.

In some cases, payment is made for the option to be granted. This is treated as a disposal of a separate asset unless the option is subsequently exercised.

13.5.5 Exchange of property

An agreement to exchange an asset for another is a disposal of the old asset and an acquisition of the new asset. If there is any cash adjustment, this must also be brought into account. For example, if *F* exchanges his holding in ICI for *G*'s shareholding in Glaxo, *F* is treated as if he has disposed of the ICI shares for the market value of the Glaxo shares at the time of the exchange. This type of transaction commonly occurs where an individual transfers portfolio investments to a unit trust in return for units.

There is an important exception to the rule that an exchange constitutes a disposal, which may apply where a shareholder takes securities offered on a company takeover. Provided certain conditions are satisfied, the exchange does not count as a disposal and the securities issued by the acquiring company are deemed to have been derived from the original shares, with the shareholder carrying forward his or her original acquisition value.

Example – Exchange of shares on company takeover

> *H* holds 1,000 shares in XYZ plc that he acquired in 1998 for £9,000. Another company, ABC plc, makes a takeover bid and offers all XYZ shareholders a share exchange whereby they receive one ABC share (worth £30 each) for every two XYZ shares that they own. The offer document confirms that agreement has been obtained from HMRC that s 136 TCGA 1992 applies.
>
> If *H* accepts, he will receive 500 ABC shares worth £15,000, but he will be deemed to have acquired them in 1998 for £9,000. No disposal is deemed to have occurred on the share exchange.

13.5.6 Compulsory acquisition of asset

(s22 TCGA 1992)

The transfer of land to, for example, a local authority exercising its compulsory purchase powers is a disposal for CGT purposes. In some cases, once the compulsory purchase order (CPO) has been served, contracts are drawn up and the land is transferred under the contract. The rules in relation to outright sales and conditional sales apply.

Where the CPO is disputed, the date of disposal is normally the earlier of:

- the date on which compensation for the acquisition is agreed or otherwise determined; and
- the date on which the local authority enters the land in pursuance of its powers.

13.5.7 Sums payable as compensation or proceeds under an insurance policy

(s 22 TCGA 1992)

In some cases, an asset (eg a building) may be destroyed or damaged and a capital sum received as compensation. In such cases, the asset is deemed to have been disposed of at the date the capital sum is received. Similarly, where a capital sum is received from an insurance policy following such damage, receipt of insurance monies is treated as constituting a disposal.

Section 268A exempts the disposal of the right to receive the whole or any part of a qualifying payment in respect of National-Socialist persecution, or the disposal of an interest in any such right for periods from 6 April 1996.

Section 268B covers the receipt of compensation from the following territories:

- the Baltic States under the UK-USSR 1969 agreement;
- the former Soviet Union under the UK–USSR 1986 agreement;
- Czechoslovakia under the UK–Czech 1982 agreement;
- the Czech Republic and Slovakia under their domestic legislation;
- China under the UK–China 1987 agreement;
- the former East Germany under the domestic legislation of Germany;
- Uganda under that country's domestic legislation;
- Iraq and the Persian Gulf under United Nations resolutions;
- Grenada under that country's domestic legislation;
- Portugal under that country's domestic legislation.

A relevant compensation award is an award or distribution made under an Order in Council made under the Foreign Compensation Act 1950, or arrangements established by the government of a territory outside the UK that are equivalent in effect to such an Order.

13.5.8 Gifts and sales at undervalue

(s 17 TCGA 1992)

A gift is treated as a disposal at market value (except where it is from one spouse or civil partner to the other: see 13.1.2). In some specific situations capital gains may be held over (see 13.6). For example, hold-over relief may be available where the gift involves business property (see 17.4) or is a lifetime chargeable transfer for IHT purposes, such as a gift to a discretionary trust (see 30.12) – but not a PET (see 30.6.1).

Such a gift often constitutes a transaction between connected persons: see also 33.12.

13.5.9 Asset destroyed or becoming of negligible value

(s 24 TCGA 1992)

The total destruction or entire loss of an asset constitutes a disposal. This could be physical destruction (eg by fire) or legal/financial destruction (eg bankruptcy or winding-up).

The legislation also permits a person to elect that he or she should be treated as having disposed of an asset that has become of negligible value. Normally, a capital loss will arise on such an occasion.

'Negligible value' is interpreted by HMRC as meaning 'considerably less than small'. For example, HMRC will only agree that shares, loan stock and other securities are of negligible value on being satisfied that the owner is unlikely to recover anything other than a nominal amount on the liquidation of the company. The mere fact that shares have been suspended or de-listed by a stock exchange is not regarded as sufficient. See the recent FTT cases of *Roger Dyer and Jean Dyer* v *HMRC* TC03073 and *Robert Brown* v *HMRC* TC03118.

The legislation provides that a disposal is deemed to take place in the year during which HMRC agrees that the asset has become of negligible value (HMRC publishes a list of shares that it agrees are of negligible value at www.hmrc.gov.uk/cgt/negvalist.htm). However, HMRC permits a claim to take effect up to two tax years prior to the claim provided the asset was of negligible value in the prior year (see s 24(2)).

In practice it is not always beneficial for an individual to claim the benefit of s 24(2), or indeed for a claim to be made, until such time as there are gains against which the loss can be set (see 13.1.3).

Tax notes

Because the date of disposal is linked to the date that you submit a negligible value claim, you can choose to defer the loss to a later year if this will be beneficial.

HMRC does not accept that a claim may be made by someone who acquired his or her shares from a spouse or civil partner at a time when the shares were already of negligible value.

13.6 HOLD-OVER RELIEF WHERE A GIFT IS A CHARGEABLE TRANSFER FOR IHT PURPOSES

(s 260 TCGA 1992)

Where a gift or a sale at undervalue is a chargeable transfer for IHT purposes, and the donee is UK resident, the donor and donee can elect for any gain to be held over. This generally means that the asset is deemed to pass across to the donee on a no gain/no loss basis, with the donee inheriting the donor's acquisition cost. This relief is not available for transfers of assets to settlor interested trusts after 9 December 2003. The definition of a settlor-interested trust includes trusts under which the settlor's minor, unmarried children can benefit.

Section 260 relief is not available where the gift is a potentially exempt transfer for IHT purposes (see 30.6) but another type of hold-over relief may be available if the property being transferred is business property (see 17.4). You should obtain a copy of Helpsheet IR295 if you make such a chargeable transfer. Section 260 was extended to cover the various situations encountered on making transfers to and from trusts for bereaved minors (s 71A) and '18-25 trusts' (s 71D) with effect from 22 March 2006.

The held-over gain becomes chargeable if the donee ceases to be resident within six years.

Tax notes

The right to transfer shares to a (non-settlor interested) family trust without having to pay CGT is crucially important. Transfers to such trusts can save IHT but without hold-over relief the CGT consequences would often be unattractive.

13.7 AMOUNT TO BE BROUGHT IN AS DISPOSAL VALUE

13.7.1 Market value

(s 17 TCGA 1992)

The general rule is that market value must be used unless the transaction is at arm's length. In the straightforward situation where a contract is entered into with a third party on a commercial basis, the disposal proceeds are the actual sale proceeds. An individual is not penalised because he or she has made a bad bargain and sold an asset for less than it is really worth. However, if the bargain is not at arm's length and the individual deliberately sells the asset for an amount less than its true value, the legislation requires market value to be substituted. If the disposal is to a connected person, for example a relative or the trustee of a family settlement or a family company, there is an automatic assumption that the bargain is not at arm's length and market value is always substituted for the actual sale proceeds if the two amounts are different. There are three exceptions:

- transactions between spouses and civil partners (see 13.1.2);
- gifts to charities and similar bodies (see 13.4.2);
- situations where a hold-over election can be made (see 13.6 and 17.4).

> **Tax notes**
>
> Take advice if you are intending to give (or sell) assets to a connected person otherwise you may end up paying a lot of tax on notional sale proceeds.

13.7.2 Contingent liabilities

(s 49 TCGA 1992)

There may be occasions where the sale contract may require part of the proceeds to be returned at some time in the future. This is known as a sale with 'contingent liabilities'.

Suppose a vendor receives £150,000 for the disposal of a plot of land, but is under an obligation to return £60,000 in certain circumstances. Will the capital gain be charged on sale proceeds of £150,000 or £90,000? In fact, s 49 provides that in these circumstances the capital gain must be computed in the first instance without any deduction for the contingent liability, ie £150,000. However, if and when the vendor is required to refund part of the sale proceeds because the contingent liability has become an actual liability, the CGT assessment is adjusted accordingly.

13.7.3 Contingent consideration: quantifiable

(s 48 TCGA 1992)

In a similar way, it is possible that the contract may provide that additional sums may be payable if certain conditions are satisfied in the future. If it is possible to put a value on the further amount of consideration that is 'contingent' (ie payable only if certain conditions are satisfied), the full amount that might be received is brought into account at the date of disposal without any discount. If the conditions are not satisfied, so that the further amounts are never received, an adjustment is made later to the CGT assessment.

13.7.4 Contingent consideration: unquantifiable

The position is different where the contingent consideration cannot be ascertained at the date of disposal (this is normally the situation where the contingent consideration may vary and is not a fixed amount). Basically, the legislation requires that the market value of the right to receive the future consideration should be regarded as the disposal proceeds. The difference between this amount and the amount eventually received forms a separate CGT computation for the year in which the final amount of the actual contingent consideration is determined. The treatment of contingent consideration, especially variable contingent consideration, is fairly complex. It normally arises in relation to either land or shares in private companies. See also 17.8 on earn-outs.

Tax notes

A sale for contingent consideration can be a tax minefield and it is essential to take professional advice.

13.7.5 Deduction for amounts charged as income

(s 37 TCGA 1992)

In some cases the disposal of an asset may give rise to an income tax charge. Where this happens, the amount taken into account in arriving at taxable income is deducted from the sale proceeds and only the balance is brought into account for CGT purposes. This commonly arises where a private company buys back its own shares and the transaction is treated as a distribution (see 9.9.7).

13.8 WHAT COSTS ARE ALLOWABLE?

13.8.1 Certain specific types of expenditure

The legislation permits only a limited range of expenses to be deducted in computing capital gains and losses. Section 38(1) TCGA 1992 states:

The sums allowable as a deduction from the consideration in the computation of the gain accruing to a person on the disposal of an asset shall be restricted to:

(a) the amount of value of the consideration, in money or money's worth, given by the individual or on his or her behalf wholly and exclusively for the acquisition of the asset, together with the incidental costs to the individual of the acquisition or, if the asset was not acquired by the individual, any expenditure wholly and exclusively incurred by him or her in providing the asset,

(b) the amount of any expenditure wholly and exclusively incurred on the asset by the individual or on his or her behalf for the purpose of enhancing the value of the asset, being expenditure reflected in the state or nature of the asset at the time of the disposal, and any expenditure wholly and exclusively incurred by the individual in establishing, preserving or defending title to, or to a right over, the asset,

(c) the incidental costs of making the disposal.

13.8.2 The cost of the asset

The asset's market value at 31 March 1982 must be substituted for actual cost if the asset was held at that date (see 13.9).

13.8.3 Incidental costs of acquisition

These are limited to:

- fees, commission or remuneration paid to a surveyor, valuer, auctioneer, accountant, agent or legal adviser;
- transfer/conveyancing charges (including stamp duty); and
- advertising to find a seller.

13.8.4 Enhancement expenditure

The legislation permits a deduction to be claimed in respect of expenditure incurred in order to enhance the asset's value provided such expenditure is reflected in the state or nature of the asset at the time of disposal. The latter condition excludes relief for improvements that have worn out by the time the asset is disposed of. Certain grey areas are worth mentioning:

- Initial expenditure by way of repairs to newly acquired property that is let may be allowable if no relief has been given in computing UK property income.
- Expenditure means money or money's worth; it does not include the value of personal labour or skill.

Tax notes

HMRC will charge tax on notional sale proceeds if you give an asset away but it will not give relief for notional expenditure where you carry out the improvement work yourself.

13.8.5 Expenditure incurred in establishing, preserving or defending legal title

The case law concerned with the allowable nature of this expenditure hinges on the interrelationship between the words 'incurred', 'establishing', etc. The High Court held in *IRC* v *Richards' Executors* (1971) 46 TC 626 that the cost of making an inventory and providing a valuation for a grant of probate was allowable under this head (see SP2/04).

13.8.6 Incidental costs of disposals

The following expenses may be deductible under this head:

- fees, commission or remuneration for the professional services of a surveyor, valuer, auctioneer, accountant, agent or legal adviser;
- transfer/conveyancing charges (including stamp duty);
- advertising to find a buyer;
- any other costs reasonably incurred in making any valuation or apportionment for CGT purposes, including in particular expenses reasonably incurred in ascertaining market value where this is required. Professional costs incurred in getting a valuation agreed with HMRC are not allowable.

Tax notes

The costs of getting a valuation at 31 March 1982 are allowable in arriving at your capital gain but the valuer's charges for negotiating with HMRC and arriving at an agreed valuation are not allowable. You need to establish in advance what fees are likely to be incurred in such negotiations.

13.8.7 Part disposals

(s 42 TCGA 1992)

Where a person disposes of part of an asset, the cost is apportioned between the part disposed of and the part retained by the formula $[A \div (A + B)]$ where A is the consideration received or deemed to have been received and B is the market value of the part retained.

Example – Part disposals

B holds 1,000 shares in XYZ Ltd that cost him £10,000. The company is taken over and he receives cash of £5,000 and convertible loan stock issued by the acquiring company worth £15,000 (assume that in this particular case no capital gain arises in respect of the loan stock because it is issued on the occasion of a takeover and the necessary clearances have been obtained from HMRC). B's acquisition value will be apportioned as

$$£10,000 \times \frac{5,000}{(5,000 + 15,000)} = £2,500$$

ie the proportion of acquisition value that relates to the part sold. £7,500 is treated as the acquisition value of the part retained, ie it will be taken into account in computing any gain or loss as and when the loan stock is sold.

13.8.8 Small capital receipts

(s 122 TCGA 1992)

There are occasions where the formula [A ÷ (A + B)] does not have to be used, and the amount received is simply deducted from the owner's acquisition value. The most common situation where this arises is where a shareholder sells his or her entitlement under a rights issue, normally on a nil-paid basis. Provided the amount received is small as compared with the asset's value, the receipt can be deducted from the owner's acquisition value. 'Small' in this context, (as interpreted by HMRC in IR Int. 157) can mean 5% or less of the value of the asset, or a receipt of £3,000 or less whether or not falling within the 5% test; exceptionally, taxpayers may suggest different limits in the context of their particular circumstances (see *O'Rourke* v *Binks* [1992] BTC 460).

> **Tax notes**
>
> Small capital proceeds received are deducted from the allowable cost on the eventual disposal of the asset.

13.8.9 Capital sums applied in restoring assets

(s 23 TCGA 1992)

Under normal circumstances, an asset is regarded as having been disposed of for CGT purposes if it is lost or destroyed. However, where a capital sum is received from such an asset (eg insurance policy proceeds), the owner may claim that the asset is not treated as disposed of if at least 95% of the capital sum is spent in restoring the asset.

13.9 ASSETS HELD AT 31 MARCH 1982

(s 35 and Schedules 2 and 3, TCGA 1992)

The general rule is that where assets were held at 31 March 1982, it is to be assumed that they were sold on that date and immediately reacquired at their market value at that time. This is known as 'rebasing'.

> **Tax notes**
>
> For disposals made on or after 6 April 2008, there are no exceptions to this rule.

13.10 OTHER ACQUISITION VALUES

13.10.1 Assets acquired via inheritance or family trust

(ss 62, 71 and 274 TCGA 1992)

Where a person inherits an asset, he or she is generally deemed to have acquired it for its market value at the date of the testator's death (ie probate value). There is one exception to this: it is possible to claim a form of relief from IHT where quoted securities have gone down in value after the person has died (see 30.11.3). Where such relief has been claimed for IHT, a corresponding adjustment is made so that the person taking the assets concerned is deemed to have acquired them not at probate value, but at the value actually brought into account for IHT purposes after taking account of the fall in value.

Where assets have been acquired from a trust, the beneficiary's acquisition value is normally the market value at the time the asset is transferred to him or her. However, the acquisition value may be lower than this where the trustees have claimed hold-over relief (see 17.4).

13.10.2 Deemed acquisition value where income tax charged

(ss 120 and 141 TCGA 1992)

Where a person is subject to an income tax charge on earnings under ITEPA 2003 when he or she acquires an asset (eg where an individual exercises a non-approved share option), he or she is deemed to have acquired it for an amount equal to the value taken into account in computing the income tax charge on him or her. Similarly, where a person acquires shares by way of a stock dividend (ie where there is a choice between a cash dividend or further shares issued by a UK company), the shares are deemed to be acquired for a consideration equal to the amount brought into account for income tax purposes by reason of the stock dividend (see further 9.8.6).

13.11 WORKING OUT YOUR CAPITAL GAIN

Table 13.1 can be used as a 'pro forma' when calculating capital gains or losses.

Table 13.1 – Computing your 2013–14 capital gains

Sale proceeds (consider whether the market value provisions may apply) – see 13.7).	A	
Deduct incidental costs of disposal (see 13.8.6).	B	
Net sale proceeds (A – B).		C
If the asset was acquired after 31 March 1982, enter cost.	D	
Amount of any enhancement expenditure.	E	
If the asset was owned at 31 March 1982, enter value at 31 March 1982 (see 13.9).	F	
Enter the amount of enhancement expenditure – if 31 March 1982 value is entered at F or G, include only post-31 March 1982 enhancement expenditure.	G	
Enter the total of figures entered in any of D and E, or F and G		H
Capital gain (C – H).		I

13.12 ASSETS THAT HAVE ATTRACTED CAPITAL ALLOWANCES

No CGT loss arises on a disposal of an asset whose cost has attracted capital allowances (see 16.2). On the other hand, the cost is fully deductible if the disposal gives rise to a gain.

The Special Commissioners have held that a loss on a disposal of units in an enterprise zone property trust is an allowable loss even though the individual had received 100% capital allowances. This decision was on the basis that the units were a distinct asset that was separate from the underlying properties on which the capital allowances arose. See *Smallwood* v *HMRC* 2005 SpC 509 and [2007] EWCA Civ 462.

13.13 HOW GAINS ARE COMPUTED ON QUOTED SECURITIES

'Quoted securities' means shares, loan stock, warrants, etc that are dealt in on the London Stock Exchange and other similar stock exchanges recognised by HMRC as having similar rules and procedures to the London exchange. This section deals with the tax treatment of transactions such as:

- sale of part of a shareholding;
- bonus issues and rights issues;
- takeovers and mergers.

13.13.1 Identification rules

Specific rules apply where a person sells part of his or her holding in securities of the same class. Securities are treated as being of the same class if they are treated as such under stock exchange practice. For example, all ICI ordinary shares are securities of the same class, whereas BP ordinary shares are not and form a different class.

Shares sold are identified as follows:

- with acquisitions on the same day;
- with acquisitions made within 30 days after;
- with acquisitions being treated as having come out of a pool. All acquisitions of shares of the same class are treated as forming a single pool, with shares coming out at average cost.

Different identification rules applied in 2007–08 and in earlier years, see the 2008–09 *Tax Handbook* at 12.15.

Special election for shares acquired under an employee share scheme

There is one exception to the 'same day' rule. Where an employee acquires shares from more than one employee share scheme and sells some of those shares all on the same day, the employee can elect as to which shares have been sold.

13.13.2 Takeovers and mergers

There is a special relief that may apply where a company issues shares or securities in order to take over another company or takes a 25% stake in the target company. The shareholders who accept this offer will not be treated as making a disposal provided they meet one of the following requirements:

- together with persons connected with them, they do not hold more than 5% of the company's share capital; or
- HMRC is satisfied that the share exchange is a bona fide commercial transaction that is not entered into with a view to tax avoidance.

In *Snell* v *HMRC* 2006 SpC 532, it was held that an exchange of shares for loan notes had a tax avoidance motive because the taxpayer intended to take up residence in Jersey before cashing in the loan notes and it was clear from the contemporaneous records that he had deliberately chosen to take loan notes rather than cash to enable him to defer the gain until after his UK residence had ceased.

So far as quoted securities are concerned, the position is generally straightforward. The offer document forwarded to shareholders normally states whether clearance has been obtained from HMRC under s 138

TCGA 1992 confirming that s 135 TCGA 1992 applies. Provided this is the case, no capital gain will arise on the exchange of shares for securities issued by the company making the takeovers.

What happens if there is a mixture of shares and cash?

Suppose a shareholder in X plc is offered a share in Y plc plus cash of £1 in exchange for every share that he or she holds in X plc. If he or she accepts this offer there will be a part disposal. The value of the new Y plc shares on the first day of trading is taken and the following computation is required:

Amount received via cash element Take proportion of cost of holding in X plc	A
$\dfrac{\text{Cash received}}{(\text{Cash} + \text{Value of Y plc shares})} \times \text{Cost}$	B
Capital gain/(loss) on cash element	C

What happens if there is a mixture of shares and loan stock?

Suppose the shareholder in X plc had instead accepted an offer of one share in Y plc plus £1.25 loan stock. Assume that when the new Y plc shares were first traded they had a price of £2 and the loan stock was traded at £80 for every £100 nominal. The cost of the two types of new securities would be determined as follows.

Example – Takeover by mixture of shares and loan stock

Apportioned to Y plc shares:

$$\frac{\text{Value of Y shares}}{\text{Value of Y shares} + \text{Y loan stock}}$$

ie $\dfrac{£2}{£2 + £0.80} \times \text{Cost of X shares} = \text{Deemed cost of Y shares}$

Apportioned to Y plc loan stock:

$$\frac{\text{Value of loan stock}}{\text{Value of loan stock} + \text{Shares}}$$

ie $\dfrac{£0.80}{£0.80 + £2} \times \text{Cost of X shares} = \text{Deemed cost of Y loan shares}$

This division of the cost of the original holding in X plc will be relevant as and when there is a disposal of either the Y plc shares or loan stock.

Tax notes

The part disposal rules can produce some unexpected results if one part of the 'package' subsequently increases in value quite substantially. This happened when BT demerged O_2: the way that a BT shareholder's cost was divided between BT and O_2 shares reflected the respective values of the BT and O_2 shares at the time of the split. The O_2 shares then increased in value far more than the BT shares.

13.13.3 Special rules where share exchange involves qualifying corporate bonds

(s 116 TCGA 1992)

Loan stock is often a type of qualifying corporate bond (QCB), ie an exempt asset for CGT purposes (see 13.4.2). The offer document sent to shareholders on a company takeover normally draws attention to whether the loan stock falls into this category. In the past, an investor who took QCBs was entitled to entrepreneurs' relief on a subsequent disposal if he or she fulfilled the conditions at the time of the takeover. This contrastsed with the treatment of non-QCBs. This anomaly was rectified from 3 December 2014 (see 17.7.7).

As a matter of fact, the deferred gain is triggered by any kind of disposal of the QCBs. For example, a gift of the loan stock causes the deferred gain to become chargeable. Indeed, a chargeable gain could even arise on a deemed disposal such as would apply if the company that had issued the loan stock went into liquidation.

13.14 UNQUOTED SHARES

There are some special features to the way in which gains on unquoted shares are computed. Other aspects follow the principles already covered in this chapter. For example, the identification rules where a person disposes of part of a shareholding of unquoted shares are exactly the same as for quoted securities (see 13.13.3).

There are also practical considerations that do not arise in relation to quoted securities such as the need to negotiate a valuation of the shares at 31 March 1982.

In the case of gifts, the value used for CGT purposes is normally the value of the asset taken by the acquirer, not the reduction in value for the person making the disposal. From this point of view, CGT works differently from IHT.

13.14.1 Shares held at 31 March 1982

Inevitably, the market value of shares held at 31 March 1982 will be the subject of negotiation with HMRC's Shares Valuation Division and professional advice should be taken. The shares' value will reflect factors such as the nature of the company, its assets and the size of the shareholding. See www.hmrc.gov.uk/shareschemes/shares-valuation.htm.

The general approach adopted by the SVD is to determine the value of the unquoted shares and securities by reference to a completely hypothetical market. It is assumed that any prospective purchaser will have available all of the information that a prudent purchaser of the asset might reasonably require when proposing to purchase it from a willing vendor by private treaty and at arm's length. Open market value must be assumed and the yardstick is always the requirement of the willing and prudent purchaser and not the wishes, etc of the directors of the private company.

The company's underlying assets are largely irrelevant if a person has only a relatively small minority shareholding; they may be a more important consideration if an individual has control. Therefore, a quite different valuation might be placed on shares that form, say, a 7% shareholding from a 51% shareholding that gives the owner control. In the former case the valuers will be looking at factors such as the level of dividends paid in the past and the likelihood of such dividends being paid in the future. At the other extreme, a 51% shareholder would place great value on a 7/51 part of his or her shareholding as a disposal of such shares would lead that shareholder to lose voting control over the company.

On a practical note, it is possible to enter into negotiations with HMRC in advance of filing your SA tax return. If you wish to reduce any uncertainty to the minimum by trying to agree 31 March 1982 values before filing your return, ask HMRC for form CG34.

13.15 WHEN MAY A CHARGEABLE GAIN ARISE ON FOREIGN CURRENCY?

There is an exemption for foreign currency provided it was acquired for an individual's personal expenditure abroad. In all other situations, foreign currency is a chargeable asset and a gain (or loss) will arise when the currency is disposed of. A disposal may take place on the foreign currency being spent, converted into another foreign currency, or converted into sterling. In each of these situations, the sterling equivalent of the foreign currency at the date of acquisition is compared with the sterling equivalent at the date of disposal.

In theory, each separate bank account denominated in foreign currency counts as a separate asset. In practice, HMRC permits taxpayers to treat all bank accounts containing the particular foreign currency as one account (see SP10/84 and M03/2010). Anti-avoidance was introduced from 16 December 2009 to prevent losses from accruing to remittance basis taxpayers where amounts on foreign currency bank accounts have been taken into account for income tax purposes and, due to the operation of s 37, there has been no genuine economic loss.

13.16 SPECIAL RULES FOR DISPOSALS OF CHATTELS

(s 262 TCGA 1992)

A chattel is defined by the legislation as a tangible, movable asset. Examples are a picture, a silver teapot and a first edition of a famous novel.

13.16.1 Chattels that are wasting assets

(s 45 TCGA 1992)

Special rules apply to chattels that fall within the definition of 'wasting assets'. These are assets with a useful life expectancy of less than 50 years. They are exempt regardless of the amount of the sale proceeds. Equally, there is no relief for any losses realised on their disposal.

This exemption is not available for an asset on which the owner was entitled to capital allowances because it had been used in a trade.

This restriction can now apply where the trade is carried on by a company rather than by the owner of the chattel.

13.16.2 Other types of chattel

(s 262 TCGA 1992)

A gain arising on the disposal of a chattel not covered by the exemption in 13.16.1 is exempt only if the sale proceeds do not exceed £6,000. However, there is a form of marginal relief under which, if the sale proceeds are more than £6,000, the maximum chargeable gain cannot exceed five-thirds of the excess. For example, if a picture costing £900 is sold for £6,900, the chargeable gain cannot exceed 5/3 × £900 ie £1,500.

In some cases the marginal relief will not help, for example if the sale proceeds were £6,900, but the picture had cost £5,800, the chargeable gain would be computed on normal principles.

Losses

A capital loss may arise on the disposal of a chattel. Where the sale proceeds are less than £6,000, the loss must be calculated on the basis that notional sale proceeds of £6,000 were received. For example, if an uninsured antique table costing £10,000 is destroyed by fire, the proceeds are taken to be £6,000, not nil.

Assets forming a set

Several chattels may be deemed to form a single asset, for example a set of antique chairs and a table. Where these are sold to the same person, or to persons acting in concert, they may be regarded as the disposal of a single asset. This rule may apply even though the sales take place at different times. As a consequence, gains that would otherwise be exempt because of the £6,000 limit may be brought into charge.

For example, someone may own four antique chairs each worth £6,000. If they were to be sold one at a time to the same person, the total sale would be regarded as the sale of a single asset for £24,000 and the £6,000 exemption would not apply.

13.17 SPECIFIC RULES THAT APPLY TO DISPOSALS OF LAND AND INVESTMENT PROPERTIES

13.17.1 Will the gain be subject to income tax?

Speculative or short-term transactions in land may well give rise to a claim by HMRC that the individual is dealing in land and therefore the transaction is subject to tax as trading income. Whether a trade is being carried on is a matter of fact. HMRC may cite the following 'badges of trade' in support of an assessment as trading income:

- evidence that an asset was acquired with a view to its being resold in the short term;
- a large part of the purchase price being financed by borrowings, especially short-term borrowings such as an overdraft;
- the taxpayer has a background of similar transactions or has special expertise that assists in achieving a profit on disposal of the asset.

In *Kirkby* v *Hughes* [1993] STC 76, the court held that the taxpayer was carrying out a trade and the following were regarded as badges of trade:

- the properties were larger than would be expected for sole occupancy;
- the periods of occupancy were short;
- another property was purchased while the taxpayer was still resident in the first without any clear intention of selling the first;
- there was no proof that the taxpayer had intended to acquire the first house as a personal asset.

Quite separately from the above, Chapter 3, Part 13 ITA 2007 may enable HMRC to assess a gain to income tax as miscellaneous income. Chapter 3, Part 13 may apply where a capital gain is realised and UK land:

- was acquired with the sole or main object of realising a gain on its disposal; or

- is developed with the sole or main object of realising a gain on the disposal of it when developed.

There are also circumstances where disposal of shares in a company that owns land may give rise to an income tax charge (see 33.2.3).

Chapter 3, Part 13 can apply whether or not the person is UK-resident. Furthermore, the capital gain may be received by a third party such as a company and yet still give rise to an assessment under these provisions if an individual has transferred the opportunity of making a gain to the third party. Moreover, the rules can also apply to one or more transactions that form a scheme and any number of transactions may be regarded as constituting a single arrangement or scheme if a common purpose can be discerned in them, or if there is other sufficient evidence of a common purpose.

The main disadvantage for a UK resident who is assessed to income tax on gains from land is the differential in the tax rates applying to income and gains and that he or she cannot deduct the annual exemption. Also, the fact that gains are assessed as income may mean that the individual cannot make use of capital losses that have been brought forward from earlier years or have arisen during the same year on other transactions. On the other hand, where an individual has borrowed to acquire the land, he or she may be able to deduct the interest in calculating the gain for income tax purposes, whereas no deduction is normally available for CGT purposes.

The main circumstances where HMRC is likely to argue that these rules apply is where the individual concerned is a builder, developer or estate agent or has entered into a large number of land transactions or the amounts involved in a particular transaction are substantial.

13.17.2 Specific points on computation of gains on transactions involving land

(Schedule 8 TCGA 1992)

Wasting assets

Where a person disposes of a wasting asset the individual's cost or acquisition value may need to be restricted. This applies where a person disposes of a leasehold interest in land and the lease has less than 50 years to run at the date of disposal. Table 13.2 shows how the cost of a lease must be adjusted.

Table 13.2 – Depreciation of leases

Years	Percentage	Years	Percentage	Years	Percentage
50 (or more)	100	33	90.280	16	64.116
49	99.657	32	89.354	15	61.617
48	99.289	31	88.371	14	58.971
47	98.902	30	87.330	13	56.167
46	98.490	29	86.226	12	53.191
45	98.059	28	85.053	11	50.038
44	97.595	27	83.816	10	46.695
43	97.107	26	82.496	9	43.154
42	96.593	25	81.100	8	39.399
41	96.041	24	79.622	7	35.414
40	95.457	23	78.055	6	31.195
39	94.842	22	76.399	5	26.722
38	94.189	21	74.635	4	21.983
37	93.497	20	72.770	3	16.959
36	92.761	19	70.791	2	11.629
35	91.981	18	68.697	1	5.983
34	91.156	17	66.470	0	0

The fraction of the cost of the lease which is not allowed is given by the fraction

$$\frac{P(1) - P(2)}{P(1)}$$

where

$P(1) =$ the percentage derived from the table for the duration of the lease at acquisition

$P(2) =$ the percentage derived from the table for the duration of the lease at the time of disposal

Example – Wasting assets

E purchases a 48-year lease in 2000 for £10,000. In 2008 she spends £2,000 on improvements that affect the value of the lease. She disposes of it with 33 years left in 2015. Her allowable expenditure is therefore as follows:

$$\text{Original cost } £10,000 \times \frac{(99.289 - 92.280)}{99.28} = £706$$

$$\text{Additional } £2,000 \times \frac{(95.457 - 90.280)}{95.457} = £108$$

$$= \underline{£814}$$

Total allowable expenditure = £12,000 − 814 = £11,186

Enhancement expenditure

It commonly happens that a person has spent money over the years on improvements. This expenditure can be taken into account provided the improvements are reflected in the state of the property when it is sold.

Where such enhancement expenditure occurred after 31 March 1982, the expenditure is added to the acquisition value.

Enhancement expenditure prior to 31 March 1982 may be taken into account only if the total of original cost and pre-31 March 1982 enhancement expenditure exceeds the market value at 31 March 1982.

13.18 DISPOSAL OF FOREIGN PROPERTY

13.18.1 Gains must be computed in sterling

Just as a chargeable gain may arise on the disposal of foreign currency, there may similarly be a currency gain on the disposal of certain foreign assets, such as a house or flat in a foreign country. Where overseas assets are disposed of, it is not correct to calculate the gain or loss in terms of the foreign currency and then convert that gain or loss into sterling at the time of the disposal. Instead, the following formula should be used:

Market value of foreign currency received at sale (converted at exchange rate applying at that time)	X
Deduct sterling equivalent of cost of asset on acquisition (converted at exchange rate applying at the time of acquisition)	Y
Chargeable gain	Z

Example – Disposal of foreign property

> G acquired a property in the USA in 1987 for $600,000 (exchange rate $2:£1) and sold it in 2014 for $720,000 (exchange rate $1.6:£1). The gain would be computed as follows:
>
> | | £ |
> |---|---|
> | Sale proceeds | |
> | (proceeds converted at $1.6:£1) | 450,000 |
> | *Less:* cost at the conversion rate applicable at date of purchase | (300,000) |
> | Chargeable gain | 150,000 |
>
> This can produce some unexpected consequences. Suppose that G had borrowed the purchase price in $. When she repaid the mortgage on selling the property, she might well be left with no cash in hand. In fact, the profit on the sale of the property in sterling terms was matched by the increase in the sterling value of her mortgage debt. However, there is no CGT relief for this increase and the gain of £150,000 would still be chargeable.

13.18.2 Relief for foreign tax

(ss 277–278 TCGA 1992)

Many overseas countries reserve the right to charge CGT on the disposal of real estate situated in that country, whether or not the owner is resident there. Where a UK resident has had to pay foreign tax in these circumstances, he or she may claim double tax relief. In effect, the overseas country's tax is available as a credit against the UK tax.

Example – Relief for foreign tax

> H has a property in Italy that cost 160m lire (at the time of purchase this was the equivalent of £90,000). The property is sold for 120,000 euros and there is a chargeable gain for UK tax purposes of £50,000 (assume that Italian CGT of £7,000 is payable). If H's £50,000 gain is chargeable to tax at 28%, the position would be:
>
> | | £ |
> |---|---|
> | UK CGT | 14,000 |
> | *Less:* double tax relief | (7,000) |
> | UK CGT actually payable | 7,000 |
>
> However, there is no relief for any excess. Thus, if H had unrelieved losses brought forward such that his UK tax had been only £6,500, there would be no relief for the balance.

Sometimes there will be a liability for foreign tax, but no capital gains for UK tax purposes.

Example – Foreign CGT only

> *J* disposes of a property in Sierra Leone at a £40,000 loss in sterling terms. However, there was a gain in terms of local currency and the tax bill in Sierra Leone is £10,000. *J* can claim a deduction for this amount as if it were a deduction from his sale proceeds, and this would mean that his loss for UK CGT purposes would be increased from £40,000 to £50,000.

13.18.3 Foreign gains that cannot be remitted

(s 279 TCGA 1992)

Where a person realises a gain on the disposal of assets situated abroad, but is genuinely unable to transfer that gain to the UK because of restrictions imposed abroad or because the foreign currency is not convertible, the amount of the gain may be omitted from assessment for the year in which it arose. Instead, the gain will be assessed to CGT only when it becomes remittable. Claims for this relief to apply must be made within four years of the end of the tax year in which the gain was realised.

13.19 GAINS AND LOSSES ON SECOND-HAND INSURANCE POLICIES

An insurance policy will normally be an exempt asset for CGT purposes. However, there is an exception for some second-hand policies.

13.19.1 Is a second-hand insurance policy a chargeable asset for CGT purposes?

A second-hand insurance policy is a chargeable asset for CGT purposes if the person making the disposal acquired it by purchase (as opposed to receiving it as a gift). Furthermore, a second-hand policy is also a chargeable asset where it is received as a gift from a person who acquired it by purchase.

There are special rules for more complex situations where policies have at any stage been bought second-hand. However, these rules still allow exemption in three circumstances. The policy will not constitute a chargeable asset where consideration is given only on transfers between:

- spouses or civil partners;
- former spouses under the terms of a divorce settlement;
- two companies within a group of companies.

13.19.2 **Computation of CGT losses**

Where a second-hand insurance policy is sold, the amount brought into account in computing taxable income is excluded from the consideration used in computing a CGT gain (or loss). In practice, this used to produce substantial CGT losses. From 9 April 2003, the CGT loss is restricted to the economic loss, which will generally be negligible.

13.20 **NON-RESIDENTS AND DISPOSALS OF UK RESIDENTIAL PROPERTY**

FA 2015 has introduced a charge on non-resident persons who realise a capital gain from the disposal of a residential property in the UK.

13.20.1 **Calculation of the chargeable gain**

In the absence of any elections, the gain will be arrived at by rebasing the property to its market value at 6 April 2015 so that only the gain realised over that value is subject to tax.

The owner has the option to time apportion the whole gain over the period of ownership.

13.20.2 **Rate of tax**

Individuals and trustees will pay tax at 28%, non-resident companies will pay tax at 20%.

13.20.3 **Reporting the gain and payment of tax**

On a disposal of a UK residential property after 5 April 2015, a non-resident person will need to report the disposal to HMRC on-line by completing a new NRCGT return and will usually have to pay the CGT due within 30 days of completion of the sale. However, non-residents who already file a UK self-assessment return will have the option of deferring payment of the CGT until their normal end of year tax payment date.

Non-resident vendors who file SA tax returns still need to report the disposal on the NRCGT return within 30 days of sale. They are required to file a nil return on a relevant disposal even if no CGT is due.

14

YOUR MAIN RESIDENCE

This chapter contains the following sections:

(1) Main residence exemption
(2) Possible restrictions on exemption
(3) Living in job-related accommodation
(4) Treatment where property not occupied throughout whole ownership period
(5) New rules for non-residents
(6) Passing on the family home – CGT considerations
(7) Anti-avoidance provisions
(8) Stamp duty land tax

It is important to note that the main residence exemption is a complex topic, to which entire books have been devoted. The following chapter is a quick overview of some of the quirks and pitfalls in the legislation, but is not intended to be comprehensive nor is it a substitute for professional advice where substantial sums are at stake.

14.1 MAIN RESIDENCE EXEMPTION

14.1.1 Basic conditions that must be satisfied

(s 222 TCGA 1992)

There is a total exemption from CGT where a gain is realised by an individual on the disposal of a property that has been his or her sole or main residence throughout the period of ownership. The legislation also provides exemption for land that forms part of the property (the garden or grounds) up to the 'permitted area'. The permitted area is always at least 0.5 of a hectare (approximately one acre), but may be more where the land is required for the reasonable enjoyment of the property (see 14.1.3).

Tax notes

The same rules that exempt the gain also deny the loss, so if you are unfortunate enough to make a loss on your qualifying residence then it will not be an allowable loss for CGT purposes.

Married couples or civil partners living together can have the exemption in respect of only one property between them for a particular period. Note that the exemption can also apply to a property outside of the UK.

14.1.2 Occupation test

(s 223(2) TCGA 1992; ESC D49)

A delay of up to 12 months between a property being acquired and the owner taking up residence does not prejudice the exemption; the property is still treated as if it were his or her main residence. The 12-month period can be extended by up to a further 12 months if it can be shown that there were good reasons for the owner not taking up residence, for example, the need to carry out alterations or building work, or where there was an unavoidable delay in the owner being able to dispose of his or her previous residence.

The last three years of ownership are treated as qualifying for the exemption, whether the owner lives in the property or not, provided the property has previously at some time been his or her main residence (see also 14.2.4).

14.1.3 The permitted area

The legislation also provides exemption for an area of gardens or grounds larger than 0.5 hectare if it can be shown that it was 'required for the reasonable enjoyment' of the property as a residence. If the taxpayer and HMRC cannot agree on this, the First-tier Tribunal can determine the matter.

Relevant factors here include considerations such as the extent to which other similar properties have gardens or grounds larger than 0.5 hectare, the need for an area of land to provide either privacy or a buffer between the property and, for example, a motorway, and the need to have room for other facilities and amenities appropriate to the property.

The last-mentioned factor is often the most difficult to argue with HMRC, which relies on a judgment by Du Parcq J in a 1937 compulsory purchase case, the so-called *Newhill* case [1938] 2 All ER 163:

'Required' . . . does not mean merely that the occupiers of the house would like to have it, or that they would miss it if they lost it, or that anyone proposing to buy the house would think less of the house without it . . . 'Required' means . . . that without it there will be such a substantial deprivation of amenities or convenience that a real injury will be done to the property owner . . .

HMRC's interpretation is not free from doubt, as the CGT legislation is worded differently from the compulsory purchase legislation, but *Longson* v *Baker* [2001] STC 6 lent support to HMRC. Mr Longson had used land for equestrian pursuits, but the High Court upheld the Commissioners' decision that, while it might have been convenient for him to be able to stable his horses and exercise them on land attached to his home, the facility was not required for the reasonable enjoyment of the property.

This is an area where it is essential to take professional advice.

14.1.4 What is 'the residence'?

There have been several cases concerning property where servants occupy a part of the premises.

In *Batey* v *Wakefield* [1981] STC 521 the property consisted of the main house and a caretaker's lodge. The caretaker/gardener and his wife (who was the owner's housekeeper) occupied the lodge rent free. The main house and the lodge were separated by the width of a tennis court. The Court of Appeal upheld the taxpayer's claim that his residence consisted of the main house and all related buildings that were part and parcel of the property and were occupied for the purposes of the owner's residence.

Yet in *Lewis* v *Rook* [1992] STC 171 the Court of Appeal decided against a taxpayer who claimed the exemption should cover a gardener's cottage located some 170 metres away, as it was not within the same curtilage as the taxpayer's house. Following that decision, HMRC, has set out its views in its CGT manual at CG64245 *et seq*. This area is complex and specialist advice should be taken if substantial sums are involved.

14.2 POSSIBLE RESTRICTIONS ON EXEMPTION

14.2.1 Exemption not available where the owner joined in a hold-over claim

(s 226A TCGA 1992)

No exemption is due where an individual acquired his interest in the property from a trust after 9 December 2003 and a hold-over election was made under s 260 TCGA 1992.

14.2.2 **Part of property used for business purposes**

(s 224(1) TCGA 1992)

If part of the property has been used exclusively for the purposes of a trade, business, profession or vocation, the exemption does not cover the part of the gain attributable to that part. This restriction does not apply where the relevant rooms are used for part business/part personal reasons. So, if a journalist's living room doubles up as a workroom from which he or she carries on his or her business, there is no restriction under this provision.

14.2.3 **Part of property let out**

(s 223(4) TCGA 1992)

A similar restriction may apply where the owner has let out part of his or her home. Thus, if the owner had let approximately one-third of the house, the exemption would normally be confined to two-thirds of the gain on disposal. This rule may be overridden if the lettings are of residential accommodation: the gain on the part of the property let out in this way may still be exempt up to the lesser of:

- the exemption on the part of the property occupied by the owner; and
- £40,000.

Tax notes

Civil partners or spouses who own a property jointly can each claim a letting exemption of up to the lesser of their exempt gain or £40,000 against their share of the gain on the let property.

The period during which the property was let which may qualify for the additional exemption can be before or after the period during which the property was the owner's main residence.

14.2.4 **Expenditure incurred with view to gain**

(s 224(3) TCGA 1992)

The exemption is not available if a gain arises from the purchase of property made wholly or partly for the purpose of realising a gain.

Example – Expenditure with a view to gain

> K, a partner, lived in a flat owned by his firm. He was offered the opportunity to buy it for £75,000. He accepted because he knew he could fairly quickly find a buyer at £120,000. He sold it, and realised a gain of £45,000. HMRC is likely to argue that the gain is a chargeable gain because of s 224(3). Similarly, a person who holds a leasehold interest and acquires the freehold because it will enable a better price to be obtained may suffer a restriction under s 224(3) if HMRC can show that this was the only purpose of buying the freehold.

Some guidance on the circumstances in which HMRC may seek to deny exemption on these grounds can be found in its manuals at CG65200 onwards. In particular, where it is clear that an individual who is a builder or property developer has purchased a property to renovate and resell, occupying a property while it is renovated prior to sale will not change the fact that any profit on the sale is likely to be regarded by HMRC as trading income so the main residence rules will not apply. See HMRC's manuals at CG65214.

A number of cases have been heard by the First-tier Tribunal in recent years; in *Springthorpe* [2010] UKFTT 582 (TC), the taxpayer's occupation was held to be for the purpose of renovating the property with a view to letting it. The Tribunal decided that the appellant's occupation was not occupation of the property as his residence. Instead, the evidence produced indicated that he had not definitely made up his mind, when doing the renovation work, whether to sell, let or live in the house when it was completed. Accordingly, the Tribunal concluded that, to the extent that the Mr Springthorpe did occupy the property, he did so for the purpose of renovating the property rather than occupying it as his home which he expected to occupy with some degree of continuity. Thus the quality of his occupation and his intentions in respect of his occupation of the property did not satisfy the test in s 222 TCGA.

Favell [2010] UKFTT 360 (TC) was also decided against the taxpayer. The First-tier Tribunal, dismissing the appeal, said that the question of whether the taxpayer's occupation was sufficient to make him resident was one of fact and degree for the tribunal to decide in the light of the nature, quality, length and circumstances of the taxpayer's occupation.

In this case, the taxpayer had not discharged the burden of proof required to demonstrate that he occupied the property as his only or main residence at any time. There was a complete absence of objective documentary evidence to show that the taxpayer resided at the property. In the circumstances the tribunal was not satisfied that the taxpayer had occupied the property at the relevant time.

In *Moore* [2010] UKFTT 445 (TC), the First-tier Tribunal (dismissing the appeal) said that, in order to be a person's 'residence' for the purpose of s 222, a property had to be that person's home and a place where he lived. Although an occasional and short residence might suffice, there had to be an assumption of permanence and a degree and expectation of continuity in order to turn mere occupation into residence (following *Sansom v Peay (HMIT)* (1976) 52 TC 1, *Frost (HMIT) v Feltham* (1980) 55 TC 10 and *Goodwin v Curtis (HMIT)* [1998] BTC 176).

A similar conclusion was reached in the First-tier Tribunal case of *Harte v HMRC* TC01951 where it was found that short periods of occupation did not have the necessary degree of permanence. Mr Harte had inherited a property. He and his wife stayed there occasionally but they never put any of the bills into their own names. They did not entertain or have friends to stay there. They used the furniture that was there when Mr Harte inherited the property and did not bring in any of their own furniture, pictures or ornaments. They did not have any work carried out on the property.

In each case, the taxpayer had not demonstrated the necessary *quality* of occupation. In *Springthorpe,* during the period of supposed residence, the kitchen had no units, and although electricity and water supplies were connected throughout the period of the renovations, bills were minimal and the gas supply had been turned off and was only reconnected once a central heating system had been installed. An exemption from Council Tax had been obtained on the grounds that the works required were such that the property was uninhabitable, and there were no proper lavatory or washing facilities.

In *Favell,* the appellant had no documentary evidence (bills, bank statements, correspondence, etc) to show that he had occupied the property. Mr Favell did not notify any official body (eg his bank, utilities, etc) that he had moved to the property. All his official correspondence continued to be sent to his previous address. Accordingly, the Tribunal decided that he had not discharged the burden of proof required to demonstrate that he had occupied the property but noted that, had Mr Favell been able to establish such proof, it would have been minded to hold that his seven months' occupation did in fact amount to residence.

In the third case, *Moore,* again no documentary evidence had been retained and the appellant admitted that he had no furniture apart from a bed and a cooker at the property between the relevant dates. The Tribunal held that Mr Moore had not proved that he registered as a resident of the property for council tax purposes, water rates purposes or DVLA purposes, and noted that he could not produce any insurance or telephone bills demonstrating that he had in fact taken up occupation. The fact that his girlfriend – later his wife – had refused to live in the property, instead remaining at the second property throughout added weight to the Tribunal's finding that he had occupied the property for the purposes of renovating it for subsequent letting, but not for the purposes of residing there.

Tax notes

Interestingly, in the case of *Jones* v *Wilcock (SP C 92), [1996] SSCD 389*, HMRC successfully argued that a property had not been purchased for trading purposes and was, therefore, able to prevent the owners claiming a loss made on the same property because it was, in reality, their main residence.

14.2.5 Sale of part of gardens

Special care is needed if it is decided to sell surplus land for development. In *Varty* v *Lynes* [1976] STC 508 the taxpayer had owned and occupied a house and the garden was less than one acre (the permitted area at that time). He sold the house and part of the garden in June 1971. Slightly less than 12 months later, he sold the rest of the garden to a builder and realised a substantial gain because he had secured planning permission in the meantime. He was assessed on the gain on the land sold to the builder. The High Court decided that the main residence exemption did not apply. Brightman J held that the exemption for the garden or grounds could apply only in relation to garden or grounds occupied as such by the owner at the date of sale.

HMRC subsequently stated that it would invoke this only where land was sold with development value. Therefore, the following principles should be borne in mind:

(1) A sale of land out of a parcel of land greater than 0.5 hectare may be vulnerable even where the owner remains in occupation. The fact that the owner continues to live in the property suggests that the surplus land was not required for the reasonable enjoyment of the property.

(2) A sale of land with development value at the same time as the owner ceases to live in the property is not open to attack in the same way as in *Varty* v *Lynes*.

(3) A sale of land with development value after the owner has moved out is likely to result in a tax charge.

The case of *Henke & Another* v *HMRC* SpC 550 is also helpful on practical issues where land adjoining an individual's home is sold off for development.

14.2.6 What happens where there are two homes?

An individual may live in two (or more) properties without necessarily owning both (or all) of them. HMRC's view is that a person has two residences if, for example, he or she owns a large house in Yorkshire and rents a modest flat in London where he or she lives during the week.

If necessary, the First-tier Tribunal will decide which of an individual's two or more residences is his or her main residence. The test is not necessarily where the individual lives most of the time, and it is often not clear in a particular case what view the Tribunal might take.

14.2.7 Taxpayer's right of election

(s 222(5) TCGA 1992)

Fortunately, the owner can settle the matter by formally electing one property to be treated as his or her main residence. As we have seen from revelations concerning MPs, it is possible for you to elect for a property which is not actually your main residence. However, you must have lived in the property. The election is conclusive, see *Ellis v HMRC* TC02426.

The election may be varied from time to time (known in the Press as 'flipping'), but only in relation to the last two years prior to the variation.

There is a time limit for a notice under s 222(5) of two years. HMRC's view has been that the time limit refers to the point in time the individual starts to have a second residence. This interpretation was upheld by the High Court in *Griffin v Craig Harvey* [1994] STC 54.

There is one circumstance in which HMRC will accept an election outside the two-year time limit. ESC D21 provides:

> Where for any period an individual has more than one residence, but his [or her] interest in each of them, or in each of them except one, is such as to have no more than a negligible capital value on the open market (eg a weekly rented flat or accommodation provided by an employer) the two-year time limit will be extended where the individual was unaware that such a nomination could be made. In such cases the nomination may be made within a reasonable time of the individual becoming aware of the possibility of so doing, and it will be regarded as effective from the date on which the individual first had more than one residence.

14.2.8 Two adjacent flats

A situation in which you should take professional advice is if you occupy two flats as a combined home. HMRC's manuals confirm that the two flats can sometimes be regarded as constituting a single residence where certain conditions are satisfied. One condition is that the flats are contiguous. Another condition is that the two flats are in the same block. However, even if you satisfy both these conditions you may still not qualify. Furthermore, you should be prepared for HMRC to resist such a claim, at any rate in the first instance.

14.3 LIVING IN JOB-RELATED ACCOMMODATION

14.3.1 Meaning of job-related accommodation

Job-related accommodation is defined as accommodation provided for an individual or spouse or civil partner by reason of the individual's employment where:

- it is necessary for the proper performance of the individual's duties that he or she should live there; or
- it is provided for the better performance of his or her duties and the employment is one where employers customarily provide accommodation; or
- the accommodation is provided as part of the special security arrangements for the employee's safety.

14.3.2 Right to nominate a property

(s 222(8) TCGA 1992)

Where an individual is required to live in job-related accommodation, a house owned by that individual and intended to be occupied as his or her residence in due course is treated as if it were his or her residence. Such a house may, therefore, qualify for exemption even if the owner had let it and never actually occupied it personally before disposing of it, provided it is nominated by the individual as his or her only or main residence.

14.3.3 Similar provisions for self-employed individuals

A self-employed individual who is required to live at or near his or her place of work (eg a publican) can nominate a property under s 222(8) for eventual use as his or her main residence. This also applies if his or her spouse or civil partner is required to occupy such premises. Only his or her residence in job-related accommodation after 6 April 1983 can qualify under this heading.

14.4 TREATMENT WHERE PROPERTY NOT OCCUPIED THROUGHOUT WHOLE OWNERSHIP PERIOD

14.4.1 Proportion of gain may be exempt

The s 222 main residence exemption is not necessarily an 'all or nothing' test. The legislation makes provision for a proportion of the capital gain to be exempt where the necessary conditions are satisfied for part of the period of ownership. The exempt proportion of the gain is normally:

$$\frac{\text{Period of qualifying use}}{\text{Total period of ownership}} \times \text{Gain}$$

Example – Incomplete period of occupation

A property was acquired in March 1975 but was not the owner's main residence until March 1988. Thereafter it was the owner's sole residence. It was sold in March 2012 for a gain of £360,000. The exempt proportion of the gain would be:

$$\frac{24}{30} \times £360,000 = £288,000.$$

14.4.2 Periods prior to 31 March 1982 ignored

A period of non-qualifying use is ignored if it is prior to 31 March 1982.

14.4.3 Final period of ownership

(s 223(2) TCGA 1992)

Provided the property has at some time qualified as the owner's main residence, the last three years of ownership has also qualified for exemption. This still applies if the property is let or another property is nominated as the individual's main residence for all or part of that three-year period. It also applies even where the period when the property was occupied as the individual's main residence was before 31 March 1982. This relief is intended to ensure taxable gains do not arise on the sale of a main residence at times when – as at present – it may take some time sell a property.

The three-year period has been reduced to 18 months where a property is sold after 5 April 2014. However, this reduction does not apply where contracts were exchanged in 2013–14 and completed in 2014–15.

14.4.4 Periods spent working abroad

(s 223(3)(b) TCGA 1992)

If, during a period when a property is (or is nominated as) an individual's main residence, the owner has to work abroad, the property continues to be regarded as his or her main residence (and therefore exempt from CGT) if he or she was employed abroad under a contract of employment and all the employment duties were performed overseas. The property must be the individual's main residence both **before** and **after** the overseas employment. The condition requiring the property to be the owner's only or main residence after working abroad is treated as satisfied if the owner is unable to resume residence because the terms of his or her new employment require him or her to work elsewhere (s 223(3B)(b) TCGA 1992). The final period of ownership is treated as actual occupation for these purposes, irrespective of physical presence at the property.

14.4.5 Periods spent working elsewhere in UK

A period of up to four years during which the owner's employment necessitated him or her living elsewhere in the UK is also a qualifying period. A period (or periods in total) that exceeds four years is covered to the extent of four years. Again, it is normally necessary that the period be followed by a period of occupation, but s 223(3B)(b) applies if the individual cannot resume occupation because his or her current employment prevents this. Again, the final 36 months of ownership (in future, the final 18 months) is treated as actual occupation for these purposes.

14.4.6 Other qualifying periods

A further period of absence (for any reason) of up to three years can be treated as qualifying for exemption, provided the period is both preceded and succeeded by a period of actual occupation. The final 36 months of ownership is treated as actual occupation for these purposes (18 months from 2014–15 onwards).

14.4.7 Summary

Table 14.1 may help in computing the position for a property where contracts are exchanged in 2013–14 or during 2014–15. The exempt gain is (X) + (Y).

14.4.8 Dependent relatives

(s 226 TCGA 1992)

In addition to the main residence exemption, an individual may qualify for exemption in respect of a property occupied by a dependent relative as his or her main residence provided the property was so occupied before 6 April 1988. To qualify for this exemption, the property must have been occupied by the dependent relative rent free, and without any other consideration.

A widowed mother (or mother-in-law) is automatically regarded as a dependent relative. In other situations, the relative is regarded as dependent only if prevented by old age or infirmity from maintaining him or herself. The exemption is not available for a property acquired after 5 April 1988, even if the property is a replacement for another property previously occupied by a dependent relative.

In some cases, it may be appropriate to form a settlement with the trustees owning the property occupied by the dependent relative as the trustees may still qualify for exemption in respect of a property occupied by a beneficiary as his or her main residence (see 31.4.11).

Table 14.1 – Computation of exempt gain on main residence

Number of complete months since 31 March 1982 when the property was actually occupied as the owner's main residence. See 14.1.2	(A)
The lesser of 18 months or such part of the last 18 months which does not already fall within A. The period was 36 months for 2013–14 and earlier years. See 14.4.3.	(B)
Months spent working abroad when the property was not occupied as the individual's main residence provided that the individual resumed residence after his or her overseas employment ceased or would have done so if he or she had not been required to take up employment elsewhere in the UK, excluding any period which already falls to be included in B above. See 14.4.4	(C)
Number of months spent living elsewhere because the individual's employment required him or her to live in another part of the UK (subject to a maximum of 48 months). Again, exclude any period already included in B.	
Note, an entry is appropriate here only if the individual resumed occupation of the property at the end of the period, or did not do so and that period fell within the final 36 months. See 14.4.5	(D)
Any further period of absence which was both preceded and succeeded by the individual occupying the property as his or her main residence (subject to a maximum of 36 months). Again exclude any period already included in B. See 14.4.6	(E)
Apply the following fraction to the overall gain which arose on the disposal of the property: $$\text{Overall gain} \times \frac{A + B + C + D + E}{\text{Months of ownership since 31 March 1982}}$$	(X)
A further exemption may also be due where the property has been let during any of the periods of absence. The additional exemption is the lesser of X or £40,000. See 14.2.3	(Y)

14.5 NEW RULES FOR NON-RESIDENTS

FA 2015 has introduced a charge on non-resident persons who realise a capital gain from the disposal of a residential property in the UK (see 13.20).

14.5.1 Reporting the gain and payment of tax

On a disposal of a UK residential property after 5 April 2015, a non-resident person will need to report the disposal to HMRC online by completing a new NRCGT return and he will usually have to pay the CGT due within 30 days of completion of the sale. However, non-residents who already file a UK self-assessment return will have the option of deferring payment of the CGT until their normal end of year tax payment date.

Non-resident vendors who file SA tax returns still need to report the disposal on the NRCGT return within 30 days of sale. They are required to file a nil return on a relevant disposal even if no CGT is due.

14.5.2 Main residence exemption

It is possible for a non-resident individual to have a main residence in the UK. FA 2015 provides that with effect from 2015–16, a property may be an individual's main residence only if it is in the country in which he or his spouse is resident, or if he or his spouse occupy the property for at least 90 days during the tax year concerned.

The fact that a property may not be treated as being occupied as the owner's main residence for a tax year will not always give rise to a tax charge on sale. For example, the year may be a period of absence during which the owner is working abroad (see 14.4.4). Where a property has been an individual's main residence, the last 18 months of ownership will be exempt (see 14.4.3) and this means that no tax will be payable on a sale which takes place before 6 October 2016.

14.6 PASSING ON THE FAMILY HOME – CGT CONSIDERATIONS

One of the main concerns that people have nowadays (as far as taxation is concerned, anyway) is the way in which their property will pass to their heirs. The IHT issues are dealt with in Chapter 30. A gift of property in an estate planning exercise would give rise to a CGT liability were it not covered by the main residence exemption. However, there is another aspect. Many IHT mitigation schemes have, as one of their consequences, the outcome that the donor's children end up owning an interest in the family home that is not covered by the main residence exemption. To that extent, the family might have saved IHT only at the cost of taking on a long-term CGT liability that will crystallise when the property is sold.

14.7 ANTI-AVOIDANCE PROVISIONS

Bear in mind the restriction on the main residence exemption where hold-over relief has been obtained on a previous disposal (see 33.14).

14.8 STAMP DUTY LAND TAX

CGT is, unfortunately, not the only tax to be considered when purchasing a new main residence – stamp duty land tax (SDLT) is a major consideration. We look at stamp duty in greater depth in Chapter 36.

15

THE TAX CALCULATION

Table 15.1 – Rates of tax on various types of income for 2014–15

Rates of tax on	Non-savings income	Savings income	UK dividends and tax credits
Starting rate for savings £0–£2,880	N/A	10%*	10%
Basic rate £0–£31,865	20%	20%	10%
Higher rate £31,865– £150,000	40%	40%[#]	32.5%[#]
Additional rate – all remaining taxable income	45%	45%	37.5%

* If your non-savings income is above this limit (after deducting personal allowances) then this starting rate is not applicable

[#] Savings and dividend income is treated as the top slice of income

---

Tax notes

Individuals are subject to a 45% tax rate on taxable non-dividend income above £150,000 per year. A 37.5% dividend tax rate applies where total taxable income is over £150,000 a year. Savings and dividend income forms the top slice of income after gains, with dividends forming the highest part.

WORKING OUT YOUR TAX FOR 2014–15

If you file your 2014–15 SA return online, HMRC will work out your tax for you. It will also do this if you submit a paper return by 31 October 2015. This chapter should help you to follow such HMRC calculations.

Example – Tax calculation

Z has the following income and gains for the tax year ended 5 April 2015

	Income	Tax	
Salary	£45,000	£8,322.00	(figures taken from P60)
Private medical	£780		(figure taken from P11D)
Bank interest	£750 (net)	£187.50	
Dividends	£1200 (net)	£133.33	
Property income	£500		
Capital gain	£12,000		

In addition Z had paid £50 a month (grossed up) into his personal pension plan and had donated £20 (net) on his Visa card to Comic Relief during the tax year.

The tax calculation would look as follows:

	Income £	Tax £
Earned income		
Earnings per P60 and P11D	45,780.00	8,322.00
Total earned income	45,780.00	8,322.00
	£	£
Investment income		
UK land and property	500.00	
UK savings	937.50	187.50
UK dividends	1,333.33	133.33
Total investment income	2,770.83	320.83
Total income		
Total earned income	45,780.00	8,322.00
Total investment income	2,770.83	320.83
Total income	48,550.83	8,642.83
Taxable income		
Total income	48,550	8,642.83
Basic allowance	£9,440	
Taxable income	39,110	8,642.83
Basic rate band adjustments*		
Basic rate band	31,865	
Pension payments	600	
Gift Aid and charitable payments	25	
Extended basic rate	32,490	

* The basic rate band is extended by grossed up payments which are made net of basic rate tax (eg pension and Gift Aid payments). This method ensures that where appropriate income tax relief is given only for higher rate tax purposes.

Tax payable	£		£
Income other than dividends			
Basic rate	32,490	@20%	6,498.00
Higher rate	5,287	@40%	2,114.80
Dividends			
Higher rate on dividends	1,333	@32.5%	433.23
			9,046.03

	£
Income tax after allowances and reliefs	9,046.03
Less: Tax credits	(133.33)
Income tax due	8,912.70
Tax deducted at source	(8,509.50)
Total income tax	403.20
Capital gains tax	
(£12,000) − (£11,000) = £1,000@28%	280.00
Total tax due for 2014–15	683.20

Once you have arrived at the net tax due figure, consider:

(1) Do you have payments on account to make? See 2.1.8.
(2) Has any of the tax liability for this year already been included in a notice of coding? See 4.2.
(3) Do you owe tax for an earlier year which should have been collected via the PAYE code for this tax year? See 4.2.

For more examples in respect of individuals with different circumstances and personal allowances, refer to Chapter 12.

HMRC might have sent you a tax calculation guide and notes on the guide. The HMRC form often seems akin to a 16-page Sudoko puzzle. The form gets the right results but only by using arcane methods which seem counter-intuitive. Using the above calculation for your own figures should give you a ready reckoner to see if you have under- or overpaid tax.

Common sense

Once you have completed your tax calculation you need to find out how the liability or tax refund arose. If you have only income from earnings, the tax paid under PAYE should more or less equal the tax liability. If it doesn't, your tax code is wrong and probably needs adjusting. One common area is incorrect benefits-in-kind. A quick cross reference of your P11D with your end of year tax code should highlight any discrepancies.

Tax notes

Initial reaction to a tax refund is positive and to a tax liability the opposite. However, another view of a tax refund is thatw HMRC has been holding your money and paying you no interest for over a year; likewise, a tax liability may indicate good deferral planning by yourself or your tax adviser.

15.1 SOME POINTS TO LOOK OUT FOR

Bank and building society interest

(1) If you are not sure from your statements how much interest you received, ask your bank for an end of year certificate. They will in any case supply these details to HMRC.

(2) Remember to gross up net payments received to get to the taxable amount.

Tax notes

If you have bank interest taxable at the higher rate, the additional tax liability will be equal (subject to small rounding differences) to the tax already deducted by the bank or society, ie 20%.

Dividends

(3) Tax credits on your dividends and unit trust income are not refundable, ie the credit is a notional credit. The effect of adding the tax credit to the dividend, computing tax at 32.5% or 42.5% thereon, and then deducting the tax credit, is that the higher rate tax comes to 25% or 30.5% of the actual dividend received.

(4) Do not include equalisation as part of your dividends from unit trusts.

(5) If you received dividends from overseas companies and you did not have a 10% shareholding in the overseas company, you could include these dividends with your UK dividends. You could then get a 10% tax credit. This system was amended with effect from 22 April 2009. The availability of tax credits was extended to include offshore funds (provided that distributions from the fund are not treated as interest) and, to some investors with shareholdings of 10% or more. The conditions for obtaining relief for >10% shareholdings are that the payer company is an offshore fund; or the payer company is resident only in a qualifying territory (broadly those with which the UK has signed tax information exchange agreements) at the time the distribution is made; or, if the relevant distribution is one of a series as part of a scheme, each of the companies in the chain is

similarly resident only in a qualifying territory – if the last condition is not satisfied, then the scheme must not be a scheme to obtain a tax advantage. Bear in mind that some countries levy a 15% withholding tax on dividends and you could get a credit for this higher amount by completing the *Foreign* pages.

Tax notes

If you have other income in excess of £31,865 (after allowances), then any additional dividend income will be taxed at an effective rate of 25% of the dividend received. However, if you have other income in excess of £150,000, then any additional dividend income will be taxed at an effective rate of 30.5% of the dividend received.

Insurance bonds

(6) Gains on UK policies are paid subject to a 20% (basic rate) notional tax credit. The notional tax credit only applies to policies taken out with UK resident insurers or with foreign insurers who have been subject to a comparable EEA tax charge. Otherwise, the policy gain will have been paid gross.

Offshore roll-up funds

(7) The gains on offshore roll-up funds are offshore income gains, and are chargeable to income tax rather than CGT. Do not deduct your CGT annual exemption.

Pension contributions

(8) Personal pension payments will have been made net of basic rate tax and relief is given by extending the basic rate tax band by the gross amount of these payments. The HMRC tax calculation guide requires you to enter the 'grossed-up' amount.

(9) Contributions to Free Standing AVC payments will also have been paid net of basic rate tax.

(10) Retirement annuity contributions may have been paid gross. It will depend on the arrangement set up by the insurance company concerned.

Deductions from your income

(11) The self-assessment tax return form requires you to enter the net amount of Gift Aid payments. You are entitled to gross up the amounts that you pay and claim higher rate relief.

(12) Remember some reliefs, such as EIS and donations to charities can be carried back from the current year (see 11.9.2).

Generally

(13) Interest and penalties are not taxed and you cannot treat them as a tax credit in your calculation.

(14) Gains, dividends, and then savings, form the top slice of your income in deciding the tax rates to apply.

(15) See 28.3.4 re top-slicing on gains from insurance bonds.

(16) Talk to HMRC about what underpayments have been included in your tax code from the tax year for which you are preparing the calculation and also for previous years.

(17) Compare this year's tax calculation with last year. HMRC will!

(18) Use the above calculation as a financial health check. If you are paying higher rate tax on investment income are you using tax-free investments to the maximum? Is it worth transferring assets to a spouse or civil partner if they pay tax at a lower rate?

Tax notes

Don't believe the hype – tax is taxing!

16

COMPUTATION OF BUSINESS PROFITS AND CAPITAL ALLOWANCES

This chapter contains the following sections:

(1) Computation of trading profits
(2) Capital allowances
(3) Pre-trading expenditure
(4) Post-cessation receipts
(5) Post-cessation expenses
(6) Rules for specific trades and professions

The calculation of business profits and accounting principles applies not only to self-employed individuals, but carries over to other areas where accounts are required, for example companies, partnerships and landlords. The changes in law over recent years have, for better or worse, brought taxable profits more into line with accounting profits calculated by reference to generally accepted accountancy principles.

16.1 COMPUTATION OF TRADING PROFITS

16.1.1 The accounts profit is generally the starting point

Most tax computations start with the words 'Profits per accounts' and then consist of a number of special adjustments to those accounts, which are required by tax legislation and case law.

16.1.2 What types of accounts are required?

The nature and complexity of accounts should be governed by the business. An individual in business as a window-cleaner can keep his or her accounts as simple as possible. Moreover, HMRC allows certain 'short-cuts'. For example, if you use your car for business and have not registered for VAT, you can generally use the approved mileage allowance rates designed for employees (see 4.4.12) and merely claim, say, 4,000 miles at the appropriate rate rather than keep all the motoring bills and claim capital allowances. Larger businesses require more complex accounting.

The following text covers the rules that govern the tax treatment of income and expenses and deals with adjustments to accounts that are required for tax purposes. For example, a set of accounts prepared for commercial reasons may include a provision for wear and tear to a building. Such a provision needs to be 'added back' (as no tax relief is available for depreciation as such, relief is due only via the capital allowances system).

See 2.4 on the types of adjustments that have been identified by HMRC in 'enabling letters' sent to self-employed individuals. These letters reflect common shortcomings in accounts received by HMRC.

16.1.3 Accounts should be on the 'accruals basis'

HMRC's view is that accounts should normally be prepared to reflect a trader's earnings for a year rather than just the cash received. For example, the accounts should include debtors, ie bills that have been issued but not paid by the year end. Similarly, the accounts should include work in progress.

16.1.4 Sound commercial accountancy principles

The Master of the Rolls stated in *Gallagher* v *Jones* [1993] STC 537, CA:

> Subject to any express or implied statutory rule . . . the ordinary way to ascertain the profits or losses of a business is to apply accepted principles of commercial accountancy. That is the very purpose for which such principles are formulated. As has often been pointed out, such principles are not static: they may be modified, refined and elaborated over time as circumstances change and accounting insights sharpen. But as long as such principles remain current and generally accepted they provide the surest answer.

Accountancy principles are constantly being refined and are published by the Accounting Standards Board (ASB) as Financial Reporting Standards (FRS). In particular, FRS18 brought together and updated a number of statements on accounting policies. Some FRSs are mandatory only for businesses of a certain size; others apply more generally. Smaller businesses that do not require an audit are governed by the regularly updated Financial Reporting Standard for Smaller Entities (FRSSE).

Key concepts for accountants include the 'going concern' concept, the need for consistency and the accruals principle whereby income and the expenses related to earning it are matched. Until recently, the concept of prudence was also regarded as a fundamental principle, ie that income and profits should not be anticipated. However, accountants now place increasing weight on accounts showing a 'realistic' position, rather than an approach that might be regarded as excessively prudent.

16.1.5 Expenditure that is specifically disallowed

(ss 33–35 and 45 ITTOIA 2005)

As mentioned above, certain types of expenditure are disallowed for tax purposes, by statute, although it may be sound accounting practice to deduct such costs in a trader's accounts. See Table 16.1 for a summary based on HMRC's tax return guide. The rest of this section looks more closely at specific types of business expenses.

Capital expenditure

(s 33 ITTOIA 2005)

The acquisition of a capital asset is not a cost that may be deducted in arriving at profits for tax purposes. This may seem obvious where an asset such as a building is acquired, but the definition of capital expenditure goes a long way beyond the acquisition of tangible assets. The generally accepted definition was given by Lord Cave in *British Insulated and Helsby Cables Ltd* v *Atherton* (1925) 10 TC 155 in which he stated:

> when an expenditure is made ... with a view to bringing into existence an asset or an advantage for the enduring benefit of a trade there is very good reason (in the absence of special circumstances leading to the opposite conclusion) for treating such expenditure as properly attributable not to revenue but to capital.

The acquisition of, for example goodwill, is capital expenditure. Less obviously, a lump sum payment to secure release from an onerous liability (eg a lease at a high rent or a fixed rate loan) is also regarded as capital expenditure.

Entertaining

(ss 45–46 ITTOIA 2005)

Any expenses relating to entertaining customers or suppliers that are included in a set of accounts normally need to be added back. There is a modest exemption that may apply where the entertaining is provided by an hotelier, restaurateur or someone else who provides entertainment in the ordinary course of his or her trade. Staff entertainment is also an allowable expense, but the individual employee may be assessed on a benefit-in-kind.

Gifts to customers, etc

(ss45, 47 ITTOIA 2005)

The cost of gifts to customers and to potential customers and introducers is also disallowed unless the gift carries a conspicuous advertisement and is neither food, drink, tobacco nor a voucher exchangeable for such goods, nor an item that costs more than £50 per recipient per year.

Table 16.1 – HMRC Summary of allowable and non-allowable business expenses (based on HMRC tax return guide)

	Allowable	*Not allowable*
Basic costs	Light, heat and power; telephone; insurance; stationery and postage; business rates and rent; advertising; protective clothing; repairs; replacement loose tools (unless capital allowances claimed instead); transport of goods to customers or materials from suppliers; subcontractors	Private and personal expenses; non-business part of running costs of premises used only partly for business; own insurance; ordinary, everyday clothing even if bought specially for business use; parking and other fines; buying, altering or improving fixed assets; depreciation or losses on sale of fixed assets
Employee costs	Employees' wages and salaries; employers' NIC; redundancy payments; pension contributions on employees' behalf; employees' expenses and benefits	Own wages or salary and drawings from the business; own pension payments and other benefits; own NIC
Finance costs	Interest on loans and overdraft used solely for business purposes; costs of arranging such finance	Repayment of loan or overdrafts (as opposed to the interest)
Professional	Accountancy fees; preparation of ordinary business costs agreement; debt recovery (if debt is for a taxable receipt); renewing leases of less than 50 years (where no premium is paid); defending business appeals against business rates	Costs of settling tax disputes; legal costs of buying fixed assets (treated as part of the cost of fixed asset); costs and fines or penalties for breaking the law

Travel	Travel on business to meet customers, suppliers, etc; travel between business premises; accommodation and reasonable cost of meals on overnight business trips; vehicle running expenses (less proportion of private use)	Travel between home and place of business (unless agreed with HMRC that your home is your base); costs of buying vehicles (but capital allowances can be claimed); meals (except on overnight business trips)
Bad debts	Irrecoverable debts written off, if taxed when they arose; recovery costs; provisions against specific doubtful debts; debts recovered later should be shown in box 15 on page SEF1of the self-assessment return	General bad debts reserve; debts not taxed when they arose, eg because they relate to sale of a fixed asset
Subscriptions	Payments to certain professional bodies (See www.hmrc.gov.uk/list3/list3.pdf for a list of approved bodies)	Payments to political parties; most payments to clubs, charities or churches
Entertaining	Costs of entertaining staff; gifts (not food or drink) up to £50 per person per year that advertise your business	All other entertaining and hospitality
VAT	Any VAT that is not recoverable is an allowable expense. This does not include any input VAT paid on capital items, or other amounts not allowable for tax purposes. However, input VAT can be included in the cost of items on which a claim can be made for capital allowances.	
	Where allowable expenses net of recoverable input VAT are shown, the turnover should be shown on the same basis, ie net of output VAT charged. Alternatively, you may prefer to show receipts and allowable expenses including VAT and the net payment to HMRC as an expense or the net repayment as a taxable receipt.	

Illegal payments

(s 55 ITTOIA 2005)

Illegal payments such as broibes are disallowed. This also applies to payments made in response to threats, menaces, blackmail and other forms of extortion. This disallowance covers payments made both inside and outside the UK. The Bribery Act 2010 has greatly extended the definition of what constitutes bribery for these (and other) purposes. The Act came into force on 1 July 2011, following the issue of detailed guidance by the Government.

Lease rentals on expensive cars

(s 48 ITTOIA 2005)

The amount that can be deducted for tax purposes may be subject to a restriction. This restriction is a flat rate disallowance of 15% of relevant payments for cars with CO_2 emissions exceeding 130g/km. There is no restriction for cars with lesser emissions.

Expenditure under leases that commenced before 6 April 2009 continue to be subject to the 'old rules' until the end of the lease. Under these rules, the amount disallowed is the following proportion of the lease rentals:

$$\frac{1}{2} \times \frac{(\text{Cost of car} - £12,000)}{\text{Cost of car}}$$

Provisions for bad debts

(s 35 ITTOIA 2005)

A general provision against bad debts is not allowable, but provisions against specific debts are an allowable deduction for tax purposes provided it can be shown the amount is a reasonable provision (see 16.1.8).

Remuneration not paid within nine months of year end

(s 36 ITTOIA 2005)

Bonus payments to employees may be made after the end of a year. If they clearly relate to a period of account, it would be normal for the trader's accounts to include a provision. However, this provision is allowable only if the remuneration is actually paid within nine months of the year end.

Pension contributions for employees

(s 196 FA 2004)

A deduction is due only if the contribution is paid during the course of the trader's year, whether to an approved or unapproved scheme. In some circumstances, large contributions may be subject to the spreading provisions in s 197. Large contributions may be spread over a period of up to four years. This spreading applies where the contribution is more than 210% of the contribution paid in the previous chargeable period and exceeds 110% of the contribution paid in that previous period by at least £500,000.

Pension contributions for the trader him or herself are not an allowable deduction in computing profits, although relief is available as a deduction from the profits taxable on him or her (see 26.1 for details of the method of dealing with personal pension contributions).

Expenditure not wholly for trade purposes

(s 34 ITTOIA 2005)

In practice, s 34 imposes a double test:

The expenditure must be incurred for the purposes of the trade

Powell v *Jackman* 2004 STC 645 concerned the expenses of a self-employed milkman who had his office at home but collected milk from a depot 26 miles away. He claimed that his travel to the depot was business travel from the base of his business operations but the High Court held this could not be justified on the facts and that his base of operation (place of work) was the area that constituted his round. The travel costs were incurred in getting to his place of work rather than in carrying on his business operations and were not allowable. As Lord Denning put it in a previous case, the cost of getting to one's place of work 'is a living expense as distinct from a business expense'. This case can be distinguished from *Horton* v *Young* 49 TC 60 where the Court of Appeal held that the base of operations for a self-employed bricklayer was his home.

> **Tax notes**
>
> It is, essentially, a matter of fact as to whether the base of the business is a trader's home.

The expenditure must be incurred wholly and exclusively for trade

The 'wholly and exclusively' test means that expenses incurred partly for trade purposes and partly for personal reasons are not allowable. For example, the cost of black dresses worn in court by a female barrister was disallowed on the grounds that the expenditure had a dual purpose (warmth and decency as well as the need to dress for court), as was the cost of meals incurred by a self-employed carpenter when he was working away from home.

Where an expense is incurred for mixed purposes the whole amount is disallowed; this rules out relief where an individual travels abroad mainly to have a holiday but carries out some work while there. However, where it can be shown that an additional cost was incurred wholly for business reasons, a deduction may be due for this. Consequently, if a person uses part of his or her home for business, the extra heat and light bills are an allowable expense for tax purposes. It should be noted that HMRC's Employment Income Manual, at EIM01476, suggests a guideline rate of £4 pw for employers reimbursing employees working from home and, in practice, HMRC has said that it will accept claims at this guideline rate from self-employed individuals also, without further enquiry. This is not a maximum; higher amounts can of course be claimed where there is evidence to justify them.

In practice, quite a number of expenses are apportioned between private (not allowable) and business (allowable) use. Phone bills and car expenses are two particular examples that arise often.

Arguments often arise where expenses relate to the preservation of a trader's reputation as HMRC will generally assume that the expenditure was at least partly incurred for personal reasons. In *McKnight* v *Sheppard HL* 1999 STC 669, a stockbroker incurred legal expenses in defending charges brought by the London Stock Exchange. He was found guilty of gross misconduct and suspended from trading. Because a suspension would have resulted in the destruction of his business, he appealed and his suspension was reduced to a fine. He was allowed tax relief for his legal expenses because these had been incurred wholly and exclusively for the purposes of the trade, but the fines imposed were disallowed. See also the recent case of *Raynor* v *HMRC* TC01649 which went the other way.

Arguments will also arise where the expense relates to an activity that is regarded by HMRC as a hobby. However, this is a question of fact, as illustrated by a case involving expenditure by a coach company on motor rallying. It was held that this was an allowable expense even though the owner of the business was a motor sports enthusiast and he drove the company cars. See *McQueen* v *HMRC* SpC 601.

Payments of reverse premiums

(s 99 ITTOIA 2005)

Relief is due to a builder or developer who pays a reverse premium to induce a tenant to take a lease. However, no relief is due to a tenant who pays a reverse premium in order to be released from an onerous lease.

Sums recoverable from insurance policy, etc

(s 106 ITTOIA 2005)

Where a trader can get back from an insurance company the money that he or she has paid out, there is no deduction due for the expenditure. The same treatment applies where a trader has been indemnified against a particular cost.

Patent royalties and other annual payments

Certain annual payments (eg patent royalties) generally need to be paid net of basic rate tax. The payments are not deductible in arriving at profits of the trade or profession, although higher rate tax relief is available when computing the payer's liability.

16.1.6 Other expenditure where adjustments may be required

interest

Relief for interest payments on qualifying loans taken by partners are given against the partner's general income (see 11.4). Interest paid by a sole trader or partnership may be deducted in arriving at the business's taxable profits provided it passes the 'wholly and exclusively' test (see above). See *Dixon* v *HMRC*, 2006 SpC 531 concerning the apportionment of interest where the loan was partly used to buy the flat over the trader's shop.

Problems may arise where overdraft interest is shown as a deduction in a set of accounts and the proprietor's capital account is overdrawn. HMRC is likely to argue that the interest (or, at any rate, part of it) was not incurred for business purposes, but to finance drawings. If you find yourself in this situation you should take advice from an accountant.

Cost of raising business finance

(s 58 ITTOIA 2005)

There are often certain costs in raising long-term finance, and a statutory deduction is available provided the costs:

- were incurred wholly and exclusively for the purposes of obtaining loan finance, providing security or repaying a loan; and
- represented expenditure on professional fees, commissions, advertising, printing or other incidental expenses in relation to raising finance.

In some cases a deduction will be available even though the expenditure fails and the loan finance is not in fact obtained.

Plant and machinery lease rentals

The way that lease rentals are treated depends on the type of lease. If it is an 'operating lease', ie a lease for a period that is less than the asset's anticipated useful life, it is normal for rentals to be deducted in arriving at the profits for the period to which the rentals refer. In practice, most leasing agreements provide for rentals to be payable in advance. So, if on 1 December a trader pays lease rentals of £12,000, which cover a period of six months, and he or she makes up accounts to the following

31 March, the amount deducted in arriving at the profits for the year ended 31 March will be:

$$\frac{4 \text{ months}}{6 \text{ months}} \times £12,000 = £8,000$$

A different accounting treatment is required where a trader pays rentals under a 'finance lease', ie a lease agreement under which the trader acquires almost all the benefits of outright ownership. HMRC's view is that the amount that should be deducted is that charged in the trader's accounts in accordance with SSAP 21 (ie the relevant Statement of Standard Accounting Practice that governs the accounting treatment of such leases).

The above provisions do not apply to 'long funding' leases; essentially, leases for periods of at least seven years (these provisions may also apply to certain leases for periods of between five and seven years where the lease is not a finance lease). FA2006 introduced rules that changed the taxation treatment of long funding leases of plant and machinery, which had previously been treated under the rules for finance leases or operating leases. The broad effect of these changes is that a lessee will be able to claim capital allowances as if he or she had bought the asset he or she is leasing. These capital allowances will be computed on the 'straight line' basis. In addition, he or she will be able to claim relief for the financing charges contained in the lease as if they were interest. The legislation also provides that a lessor and lessee may jointly elect for other post-31 March 2006 leases to be dealt with in this way.

Hire purchase

Where equipment is acquired under an HP contract, its cost counts as capital expenditure (and in most cases capital allowances will be available). The 'interest' element is apportioned over the contract term and relief is given for the amount of interest that relates to the accounting period concerned.

Example – Adjustments for HP contracts

A trader acquires a computer under a three-year HP agreement. The cost of the computer was £12,000, but the trader pays 36 monthly HP payments of £420.

The interest payable over the three years totals £3,120. This would normally be allocated roughly as follows:

Year 1:   £1,715
Year 2:   £1,040
Year 3:   £365

This type of allocation reflects the amount of the HP 'loan' outstanding during each year.

Legal and professional expenses

When HMRC examines a trader's business accounts, it normally asks for an analysis of any substantial amounts relating to legal and professional expenses. Legal costs in connection with the acquisition of capital assets are disallowable as capital expenditure, as are legal costs in connection with renewing a lease of more than 50 years. In contrast, legal costs incurred to protect a capital asset are generally allowable as a revenue expense.

Tax notes

Professional costs incurred in connection with tax appeals are not allowable on the grounds that such costs relate to tax on profits rather than an expense incurred in earning profits. However, in practice the costs of preparing and agreeing tax computations are usually allowed.

16.1.7 Relief for premiums

(ss 60, 287 ITTOIA 2005)

A trader may be required to make a lump sum payment to a landlord to obtain a lease. Where the lease is for a period of less than 50 years, part of the lump sum may be treated as income in the landlord's hands (see 8.3) and the trader may claim a deduction for this amount as if it were rent payable over the period of his or her lease. The part taxed in the landlord's hands is 100% of the premium less 2% for each complete year of the lease other than the first year.

There is no relief if the lease is for more than 50 years or if the premium is paid to someone other than the landlord because such a third party (eg an outgoing tenant) is not subject to income tax on income from the property.

Sometimes the lease will require a tenant to have certain building work carried out that will increase the value of the landlord's interest in the property. The landlord's UK property income should indicate the notional premium in this regard (see 8.3.4). Where this applies, the tenant can claim a deduction just as if he or she had been required to pay a premium in cash. However, the notional premium is generally far less than the actual cost of carrying out the work concerned.

Example – Treatment of premiums

B pays a premium of £40,000 for a lease of ten years. Of this sum, 82% (ie £32,800) is taxed in the landlord's hands as rental income for the year in which the premium is payable (see 8.3).

B can claim a deduction in his accounts for the ten years as if he had paid rent of £3,280 pa. If it were not for s 60, the expenditure would be treated as capital expenditure and would attract no relief.

16.1.8 Provision for bad or doubtful debts

HMRC has explained its approach with regard to provisions for bad or doubtful debts. Its interpretation is that a trader may be entitled to a deduction provided the following circumstances are satisfied:

- the debt existed at the balance sheet date; and
- before the accounts were finalised, the company's trader/directors discovered that the debtor's financial position at that date was such that the debt was unlikely to be paid.

HMRC has stated that a common example of this is where a debtor at the balance sheet date goes into administration or liquidation shortly after that date and before the date on which the trader approves the financial statements. Where the administration or liquidation commences after the balance sheet date, its occurrence before the accounts were finalised normally sheds light on the debtor's financial position at the balance sheet date. If the period between the balance sheet date and approval of the accounts is short, it is unlikely that a debtor would have gone from financial good health to insolvency in that period. In these circumstances it would normally be reasonable for the trader to regard the debt as doubtful. The acceptable amount of provision would depend on the information available.

HMRC contrasts this with a situation where a debtor is a habitually slow payer and there are no grounds to believe his or her financial position has changed. In such a case, HMRC argues that the length of time a debt has been outstanding is not in itself a sufficient reason to regard it as doubtful.

16.1.9 Provisions against liability to pay sums after year end

This is an aspect of a trader's accounts to which HMRC pays particular attention. It needs to be satisfied that relief is not sought for expenditure that will be incurred only in the future. Consequently, HMRC will almost certainly withhold relief unless the liability arose before the year end. For example, in the past it was not generally possible to secure a deduction for redundancy costs unless the necessary redundancy notices were served by the end of the trader's accounting period. Similarly, HMRC will often argue that a provision for an amount that may be due to a client for professional negligence is not allowable unless the client's claim has been admitted by the year end.

HMRC's approach may be challenged where the accounts comply with generally accepted accountancy principles, but you should seek professional advice if sizeable amounts of tax are at issue.

HMRC's rather restrictive approach was challenged successfully in *Johnston* v *Britannia Airways Ltd* [1994] STC 763. Civil Aviation Authority rules required each aeroplane to have a certificate of airworthiness. This would not be issued unless each engine was overhauled every 17,000 flying hours, which, in Britannia's case, meant every three to five years. Accordingly, a provision for the overhaul costs was made in each year's accounts based on the average cost of the overhaul per hour flown and the number of hours flown in the period.

HMRC took the view that the correct treatment was to make no provision before the cost of the overhaul was incurred, to capitalise the overhaul cost when incurred and then to write it off gradually over the period up to the next overhaul. The Special Commissioners found that the accruals method used by Britannia gave the most accurate picture of the airline's profits and was more effective in matching costs with revenue than the 'capitalise and amortise' method favoured by HMRC. Furthermore, the company's method was in accordance with ordinary principles of commercial accountancy. Accordingly, since there was nothing in statute or case law to contradict it, the company's appeal succeeded. This decision was upheld by the High Court.

Bear in mind that accountancy principles are being refined and updated constantly and FRS12 now sets out 'best practice' on provisions for sums payable after the year end. HMRC will resist an accounting treatment that does not comply with FRS12. The *Britannia Airways* decision has since been overtaken by changes in generally accepted accountancy principles.

There are sometimes circumstances where a payment will almost certainly be required in the future, although the precise amount has yet to be ascertained. For example, an insurance broker who may be required to refund commission to an insurance company if clients allow policies to lapse. HMRC has accepted that a provision may be allowable in these circumstances provided it is arrived at scientifically by reference to past experience. A 'rough and ready' general provision is not allowable.

16.1.10 Valuation of stock and work in progress

A trader's accounts should include his or her stock in hand at the accounts year end. Individual items of stock should be valued at the lower of cost or net realisable value. Cost should normally include a proportion of overheads.

Similarly, work in progress should be valued at the year end on the same basis. Where the accounts relate to a profession, the traditional view has been that it is not necessary to include in the cost the time value of work put in by the sole proprietor or partner, since this represents the proprietor's profit rather than a cost incurred in carrying on the profession. However, see below on UITF 40.

The treatment of long-term work in progress can involve complex issues and should be discussed with your accountant.

16.1.11 UITF 40

Where the accounts relate to a profession or other service provider, the traditional approach was changed by the ASB's guidance note on revenue recognition (UITF Abstract 40 published in March 2005), which required accountants to adopt a different method of revenue recognition for accounting periods ending on or after 22 June 2005. The traditional method was for work on unbilled services to be accounted for as work in progress (ie at the lower of cost or realisable value). Instead, UITF 40 generally requires that revenue be recognised as the services are provided and shown on the trader's balance sheet under the general heading of debtors. The difference between the two methods of accounting is that the UITF 40 method recognises profit earlier. The taxable profits of a business will normally be based on its accounting profit (subject to specific adjustments) and so the application of UITF 40 will generally mean that a business has higher taxable profits.

16.1.12 Withdrawal of 'cash basis' practice for professions

Until the late 1990s, relatively large businesses were able to prepare accounts purely on a cash receipts basis without taking into account income from unpaid invoices or the value of work in progress. The cash basis was widely used by barristers, solicitors, surveyors, actuaries, doctors and accountants, supported by a HMRC statement of practice that allowed such businesses to use this method subject to conditions that profits were computed on the earnings basis for the first three fiscal years and thereafter could be accounted on a purely cash basis. The cash basis also applied to expenses.

This cash basis was abolished by FA 1999. Businesses have had to use the earnings basis for accounting periods starting on or after 6 April 1999.

Barristers (in Scotland, advocates) have always been regarded as a 'special case'.

16.1.13 Use of 'true and fair view' approach

The 'true and fair view' approach to computing taxable profits and losses is intended merely to ensure that profits are calculated in accordance with appropriate accounting standards and that time is not wasted on immaterial amounts. HMRC has confirmed that sole traders and partnerships do not need to have an audit even though their taxable profits must now be based on accounts that would comply with the true and fair view recognised for audited accounts.

Guidance on the application of accounting principles for traders who were formerly on the cash basis is contained in the Consultative Committee of Accountancy Bodies (CCAB) guidance note on the application of UITF 40, found on HMRC's website at www.hmrc.gov. uk/manuals/bimmanual/BIM74270.htm.

16.1.14 Miscellaneous matters

Own consumption

Any manufactured items or stock that is taken out of the business for the proprietor's own use, or for members of his or her family and friends, should be treated as sales at market value. The same also applies where the proprietor has provided business services to family and/or friends. See box 59 of the full self-employment form.

This rule was previously based on *Sharkey* v *Werhner* 936 TC 275, but was put on a statutory basis by FA 2008, in chapter 11A, ITTOIA 2005, with effect from 12 March 2008.

Payments under the Business Start-up Scheme

(s 207 ITTOIA 2005)

Where a trader has received a payment under a Business Start-up Scheme it should be included in his or her computation of trading profits, in box 29 of the short form or box 74 of the full self-employment form.

Class 4 NIC

No deduction is due for the trader's liability for Class 4 NIC (see 23.4) in arriving at the trader's taxable profits.

Gifts in kind to charities

(ss 70 and 108 ITTOIA 2005)

Relief can be claimed by traders who donate computers or other equipment to charities. Relief is also due for the employer costs of staff seconded to educational establishments.

Flood defence expenditure

FA 2015 introduced a specific tax deduction for businesses that make contributions to flood and coastal erosion risk management projects on or after 1 January 2015.

16.2 CAPITAL ALLOWANCES

16.2.1 Introduction

A trader is entitled to capital allowances on plant and machinery used in the trade. Up to 2010–11, limited allowances were available on commercial buildings located in an enterprise zone, agricultural buildings, industrial buildings and hotels, although these allowances have been fully withdrawn from April 2011.

Allowances may also be claimed for expenditure on know-how and scientific research expenditure. All these are dealt with differently, and various rates of initial and annual allowances are given.

Capital allowances are treated like any other business expense. The allowances are computed on the current year basis, but once again with special rules for the first tax year. Allowances are due only if claimed within 12 months of the filing date for the relevant SA return.

As with much of UK tax law, successive Finance Acts have overlaid one another during the past 50 years and can make it difficult to see the wood for the trees. The main issues are addressed below.

16.2.2 What is plant and machinery?

Despite the introduction of specific legislation in 1994, the definition of 'plant and machinery' remains unclear. The statutory definition focuses mainly on what is *not* plant because it forms part of a building, and HMRC's practices and interpretation are still based largely on decisions handed down by the courts. The earliest judicial definition was provided in *Yarmouth* v *France* (1887) 19 QBD 647, in which Lindley LJ stated:

> . . . in its ordinary sense, it includes whatever apparatus is used by a businessman for carrying on his business – not his stock-in-trade, which he buys or makes for sale, but all goods or chattels, fixed or movable, live or dead, which he keeps for permanent employment in his business . . .

Some items are clearly within this definition (eg typewriters, dictating machines, telephone equipment, computers, manufacturing equipment, vans and other motor vehicles). What is less obvious is that a building may contain items that are plant and machinery. In some cases the plant will have become part of the building (eg a lift). Also, there may be structures that are items of plant (eg a dry dock or a grain silo, or a mezzanine floor put into a factory to create storage space). Capital allowances are also due on building work needed to enable plant and machinery to be installed (eg if a floor has to be strengthened to install a computer).

You should take professional advice if you acquire a building or adapt premises to meet the requirements of your trade to ensure that you obtain HMRC's agreement on the full amount eligible for capital allowances.

16.2.3 Expenditure treated as incurred in a period

(s 5 CAA 2001)

Expenditure is deemed to be incurred in a period if a trader enters into an unconditional contract; it is not necessary that the trader should actually have paid for the item or brought it into use by his or her year end. There is an exception for plant and machinery acquired under an HP contract where entitlement to allowances arises only when the plant is actually brought into use.

16.2.4 Assets brought into use part way through year

(s 56 CAA 2001)

An asset acquired towards the end of a trader's accounting period still attracts full writing down allowances at the appropriate rate, unless the trade has not been going for 12 months. In such a case, the allowance may be scaled down.

Example – Scaled down allowance

> *U* commences trading on 5 October 2013. On 5 April 2014 he acquires plant and machinery for £60,000. He makes up his first accounts for the six months ended 5 April 2014. Ignoring the annual investment allowance (see below), the capital allowances due to him for 2013–14 on this expenditure would be:
>
> $$\frac{6}{12} \times 18\% \times £60,000, \text{ ie } £5,400$$

16.2.5 Allowances for plant and machinery: the 'main pool'

(ss 11–15 CAA 2001)

Plant and machinery qualifies for an 18% writing-down allowance. The allowance is based on the balance of the 'pool' of expenditure at the year end. The pool's opening balance represents the cost of plant brought forward from previous years, less capital allowances already received. A trader receives writing-down allowances based on the opening balance plus the cost of additional plant acquired during the year, less any disposal proceeds.

16.2.6 Small balances can be written off

(s 56A CAA 2001)

The pool may be fully written off if it goes down to £1,000 or less.

16.2.7 Annual investment allowance

From 6 April 2010 to 5 April 2012, the annual investment allowance (AIA) at 100% applied to the first £100,000 of expenditure on plant and machinery. It was reduced to £25,000 for 2012–13 and then increased to

£250,000 for 2013–14. The allowance was further increased to £500,000 for the two years 2014–15 and 2015–16.

Example – Writing-down allowances

> S and T are in partnership. In their year to 31 March 2013 they had acquired plant and machinery at a cost of £30,000 and received capital allowances of £6,000. During their year ended 31 March 2014, they sell some of this plant for £20,000 and buy new plant for £50,000. In the year ended 31 March 2015, the partnership buys plant and machinery for £520,000. S and T's pool would be as follows:
>
> | | £ |
> |---|---:|
> | Written-down value brought forward at 1 April 2013 | 24,000 |
> | Additions during year ended 31 March 2014 | 50,000 |
> | | 74,000 |
> | Less: disposal proceeds | (20,000) |
> | | 54,000 |
> | Less: annual investment allowance | (50,000) |
> | | 4,000 |
> | Less: writing-down allowance (18%) | (720) |
> | Written-down value brought forward at 1 April 2014 | 3,280 |
> | Additions during year ended 31 March 2015 | 520,000 |
> | | 523,280 |
> | Less: annual investment allowance | (500,000) |
> | | 23,280 |
> | Less: writing-down allowance (18%) | (4,190) |
> | Written-down value carried forward | 19,090 |

Where qualifying expenditure in a period exceeds the AIA limit, a taxpayer may choose which expenditure to allocate the allowance against. Where some also qualifies for other 100% allowances (such as enhanced capital allowances for energy-efficient equipment), it makes sense to allocate the AIA against expenditure that qualifies for lower allowances, particularly integral features, which only attract allowances at 8%. Purchases are only relieved once.

Each individual business is eligible for relief. Where an individual owns more than one business, each business may be eligible for the AIA, although there are rules to prevent artificial fragmentation of businesses, abusive multiple claims and artificial use of unused allowances.

16.2.8 Reduced rate of WDA for integral features

The 18% writing-down allowance is reduced to 8% for expenditure on plant consisting of fixtures that are integral to a building (unless the fixtures qualify as energy-saving or water-saving equipment, see 16.2.12

and 16.2.13 below). However, the 100% AIA for expenditure on plant (see 16.2.7 above) may be allocated against integral features.
   Integral features (see s 33A(5) CAA 2001) include:

- electrical systems (including lighting systems);
- cold water systems;
- space or water heating systems, powered systems of ventilation, air cooling or air purification and any floor or ceiling comprised in such systems;
- lifts, escalators and moving walkways;
- external solar shading;

Post 5 April 2008 expenditure on integral features that does not attract the AIA is kept in a separate 'special rate' pool. From April 2012, allowances on the main pool are given at 18% and on the special rate pool at 8%.

Replacement/restoration expenditure

(s 33B CAA 2001)

Beware expenditure on replacement/restoration expenditure. Expenditure incurred over a 12-month period which represents more than 50% of the cost of replacing an integral feature will be capital and will fall into the 8% pool. Maintenance expenditure is normally treated as revenue expenditure, but s 33A(3) dictates that it is expenditure on an integral feature and not eligible as a revenue expense. A quote will need to be obtained for the replacement of a feature at the same time as getting it repaired.

16.2.9 Assets kept separate from the pool

Certain assets are kept separate from the pool. One particular category is assets used partly for the purposes of the trade and partly for other purposes. For example, a van used by a sole trader for 40% business and 60% private motoring is deemed to form a separate pool. The trader is entitled to 'scaled down' allowances, ie he or she would receive 40% of the full writing-down allowance and 40% of any balancing allowance.
   'Short-life' assets (see below) are also pooled separately.
   'Long-life' assets (16.2.11), integral features (16.2.8) and expenditure on thermal insulation are also kept separate in a 'special rate pool' where the rate of writing down allowances is 8%.
   Cars with emissions of more than 130g/km attract only 8% WDA.

16.2.10 Short-life assets

(ss 83–84 CAA 2001)

Where no expenditure is added to the pool, the writing-down allowances that the trader receives are likely to get smaller and smaller. For example, a trader invests expenditure of £100,000 on plant in Year 1 (which is 2011–12). He does not acquire any other plant and machinery for five years. His writing-down allowance in Year 1 will be £20,000 (ie 20% of £100,000); £14,400 in Year 2 (ie 18% of the residual £80,000); and so on. By the end of Year 5, the written-down value will be £36,170, but the equipment itself may be worn out and have a scrap value of only £2,000. To cover this type of situation, the legislation allows for a trader to designate certain assets as short-life assets. The cost of these assets is kept in a separate pool and a balancing allowance (or charge) arises on a sale within nine years (ie the eighth anniversary of the end of the chargeable period in which the qualifying expenditure was incurred, or, if the qualifying expenditure was incurred in different chargeable periods, the first chargeable period in which any of the qualifying expenditure was incurred) or on the assets being scrapped by then. If an asset is not sold within that period, the asset's written-down value is transferred to the general pool. For expenditure incurred before 6 April 2011, the cut-off period is four years rather than eight years.

(1) In the above example, if the plant were actually scrapped at the start of Year 5 and the trader received no scrap value at all, he would receive a balancing allowance of £44,110.
(2) Again using the same basic facts, if the plant and machinery were still in use at the end of Year 9, the written-down value of £16,354 would be transferred to the trader's pool of other plant.

The following cannot be short-life assets:

- cars;
- assets used partly for non-trade purposes;
- assets originally acquired for non-trade purposes (eg assets acquired before the trade commenced);
- ships;
- certain assets leased out in the course of a trade.

An election must be made for an asset to be treated as a short-life asset. This needs to be submitted to HMRC within two years of the accounting period in which the asset is acquired. HMRC will require sufficient information to be able to identify the assets at a later stage (see SP1/86).

16.2.11 Long-life assets

(ss 90–104 CAA 2001)

An LLA has an expected working life of 25 or more years. Where a trader incurs expenditure of more than £100,000 on an LLA, capital allowances are available at a rate of 8%.

Some categories of expenditure are specifically excluded from the general definition. Thus LLAs do not include any machinery or plant that is a fixture in, or is used in, a dwelling-house, retail shop, showroom, hotel or office or for ancillary purposes. Also, there are specific exclusions for motor or hire cars.

Expenditure on LLAs is segregated into the special rate pool, qualifying for writing-down allowances at 8%. This categorisation of an asset as being an LLA is irrevocable and it cannot later be reclassified as non-LLA, for instance when the remaining useful life drops below 25 years. The LLA rules do not apply where second-hand plant is purchased from a person who qualified for full writing-down allowances.

16.2.12 100% allowance for energy-saving and environmentally friendly equipment

(ss 45A–45E CAA 2001)

Expenditure on designated energy-saving technologies and products qualifies for 100% first-year allowances. The qualifying items are set out in a list issued by the government (ss 45A–45C CAA 2001): see https://etl.decc.gov.uk/etl/site.html.

A 100% FYA is also available for expenditure on equipment for refuelling vehicles with natural gas or hydrogen fuel, and for expenditure on new, zero-emission goods vehicles. 100% FYA was due for 2014–15 on expenditure on cars with lower than 96g/km CO_2 emissions. For 2015–16, the limit is 76g/km.

16.2.13 Expenditure on water technologies

Businesses are able to claim 100% FYAs for expenditure on designated plant and machinery to reduce water use and improve water quality. The designated technology classes include:

- meters and monitoring equipment;
- flow controllers;
- leakage detection;
- efficient toilets;
- efficient taps.

Qualifying technologies and products can be found at https://etl.decc.gov.uk/etl/site.html.

16.2.14 100% first-year allowances for refurbishing business premises in disadvantaged areas

This relief applies to expenditure incurred up to 10 April 2017. It gives relief for the costs of renovating business property that had been empty for at least a year in designated 'disadvantaged areas'.

The capital costs of such renovations attract a 100% first year allowance. The FYA is subject to a clawback on a disposal within seven years. The allowance (also referred to as Business Premises Renovation Allowance or BPRA) is not available for premises used for:

- farming;
- fisheries;
- aquaculture;
- manufacture of substitute milk products or synthetic fibres;
- shipbuilding;
- steel or coal industries.

It cannot be claimed for renovation expenditure on a residential property, nor for the costs of acquiring land, extending business premises or developing land next to the business premises.

Since April 2014, BPRA has been available only for the actual costs of construction and building work, and for certain specified activities such as architectural and surveying services. Additional associated costs (such as project management services) can also qualify for relief, but this is limited to 5% of the specified qualifying costs.

16.2.15 Expenditure on landlord's fixtures

(s 172 CAA 2001)

Tenants are often required to install plant within a building, such as lifts and air conditioning. Where such items become part of a building they constitute landlord's fixtures. This means that the items of plant do not 'belong' to the tenant and as such would not qualify for capital allowances under the normal rules. The legislation deals with this potential anomaly by specifically providing that a tenant who incurs expenditure on such plant can receive allowances, but is subject to a balancing charge on the expiry or surrender of his or her lease, according to the plant's market value at that time. There are complex provisions dealing with situations where more than one person incurs expenditure on the same fixture or where expenditure is incurred by an equipment lessor.

As noted above, the rate of writing-down allowance on features integral to a building was reduced to 8% from April 2012.

16.2.16 Acquisition of second-hand buildings

(ss 172–204 CAA 2001)

There are anti-avoidance provisions which:

- prevent allowances being given on fixtures as plant and machinery and under other categories such as enterprise zones or scientific research;

- limit allowances given on fixtures as plant in total to the fixtures' original cost;
- treat a fixture as sold at its tax written-down value if it is sold for less than that value to accelerate allowances (other than where the disposal is for good commercial reasons and is not part of a tax avoidance scheme).

16.2.17 Special rules for claiming capital allowances on fixtures

For second-hand buildings containing fixtures, purchased from 1 April 2012 by companies or from 6 April 2012 by unincorporated businesses, the purchaser and seller must agree a value for the fixtures purchased with the building within two years of the date of purchase by one of three methods:

- a joint election by the seller and purchaser under ss198/199 CAA 2001;
- either party referring the matter to a First-tier Tribunal for independent determination;
- the seller providing written confirmation within two years of the sale of the disposal value applied to those fixtures.

While the seller and purchaser must agree a value for the fixtures within two years of the purchase of the building, there is no time limit on the purchaser pooling the second-hand fixtures; this can be done at any time before the purchaser sells the building.

For second-hand buildings containing fixtures purchased from April 2014, the seller must have already claimed capital allowances on the fixtures in order for the purchaser to be eligible for capital allowances.

Spacial rules cover the interaction between the fixtures rules and business premises renovation allowances (BPRA), which are 100% allowances that can be claimed on conversion or renovation of unused buildings in disadvantaged areas (see 16.2.14). These are clawed back by HMRC if the building is sold within seven years of the BPRA claim. If a taxpayer loses BPRA by selling a building within seven years, the purchaser will be entitled to claim capital allowances under the fixtures rules to the extent that BPRA has been clawed back.

16.2.18 Buildings located in an enterprise zone

(ss 298–299 CAA 2001)

Qualifying expenditure on a commercial building located in an enterprise zone could in the past qualify for a 100% initial allowance. A 'commercial building' was defined as a building or structure, other than an industrial building or hotel, used for the purposes of a trade, profession or vocation or as an office. The definition specifically excluded a building wholly or partly used as a dwelling-house.

16.2.19 Expenditure on know-how

(s 452 CAA 2001)

Expenditure on acquiring know-how for use in a trade attracts capital allowances. 'Know-how' means any industrial information and techniques of assistance in manufacturing or processing goods or materials, or working or searching for mineral deposits, or that may be relevant to agricultural, forestry or fishing operations. Allowances are given on 'qualifying expenditure', which is the aggregate of any capital expenditure on know-how during the basis period, together with any unused balance of expenditure brought forward from the previous basis period and less any disposal value for know-how that has been sold.

Writing-down allowances are given at the rate of 25%.

16.2.20 Expenditure on research and development

(s 437 CAA 2001)

Certain capital expenditure incurred by a trader on research and development related to a trade attracts a 100% allowance. Research and development in relation to a trade includes research:

- that may lead to or facilitate an extension of trade; or
- of a medical nature that has a special relation to the welfare of workers employed in particular industries.

16.3 PRE-TRADING EXPENDITURE

(s 57 ITTOIA 2005)

A person may incur expenditure before starting to trade such as:

- rent for business premises;
- rates, insurance, heating and lighting;
- advertising, wages or other payments to employees;
- bank charges and interest;
- lease rentals on plant and machinery and office equipment;
- accountancy fees.

Expenditure qualifies for relief only if it is incurred within seven years of the date trade is commenced. The expense is treated as an ordinary trading expense incurred on the day the trader starts business.

Pre-trading capital expenditure that qualifies for capital allowances is also treated as having been incurred at the date trade is commenced.

16.4 POST-CESSATION RECEIPTS

(ss 242–243 ITTOIA 2005)

Where a person has been assessed on the cash basis (see 16.1.12), special rules apply if the trade or profession is discontinued. Subsequent receipts are normally taxed as income for the year in which they come in, although an election may be made for the post-cessation receipts to be treated as arising in the year of discontinuance.

Expenses may be deducted in so far as they were incurred wholly and exclusively for business and are not otherwise allowable. For example, a solicitor who had post-cessation receipts could deduct premiums paid on a professional indemnity policy where the cover related to the period after the solicitor had ceased to carry on his or her profession.

A similar charge may arise where a change occurs in the treatment of a trader's profits so that the cash basis ceases to apply and his or her profits are assessed on the earnings basis. Amounts received from customers that relate to invoices issued when the business was dealt with on the cash basis are treated as post-cessation receipts.

16.5 POST-CESSATION EXPENSES

(s 250 ITTOIA 2005)

Expenditure may qualify for tax relief if it is incurred within seven years of a business ceasing. The following types of expenditure may qualify for this relief:

- the costs of remedying defective work done, goods supplied, or services rendered while the trade or profession was continuing and damages paid by the taxpayer in respect of such defective work, goods or services whether awarded by a court or agreed during negotiations on a claim;
- insurance premiums paid to insure against the above costs;
- legal and other professional expenses incurred in connection with the above costs;
- debts owed to the business that have been taken into account in computing the profits or gains of the trade or profession before discontinuance but that have subsequently become bad;
- the costs of collecting debts that have been taken into account in computing the profits of the trade before discontinuance.

The amount of the relief will be reduced by any expense allowed as a deduction in the final accounting period that remains unpaid at the end of the year of assessment in which the new relief is given.

Expenditure that qualifies for the relief will be set against income and capital gains of the year of assessment in which the expense is paid. Where there is insufficient income or capital gains to cover the expenditure, the unrelieved expenditure of that year cannot be carried forward under the relief arrangements against future income or capital gains. However, the unrelieved expenditure will still be available to be carried forward under the existing rules and set against subsequent post-cessation receipts from the trade or profession.

> **Tax notes**
>
> The legislation requires a formal claim to be made within 22 months of the end of the year of assessment in which the expense is paid.

16.6 RULES FOR SPECIFIC TRADES AND PROFESSIONS

16.6.1 Barristers

General information

Since 1999, barristers have been required to produce accounts on an earnings (accruals) basis (see also 16.1.3).

Readers may refer to a Bar Council publication, *Taxation and Retirement Benefits Handbook,* available at www.barcouncil.org.uk. Among other things, this handbook gives detailed guidance on the amounts to be included in respect of disputed fees.

Accounts on a cash basis

(s 160 ITTOIA 2005)

Whereas a person carrying on a profession must normally submit accounts on an accruals basis, and include work-in-progress (see 16.1.12), barristers going into practice have been allowed to remain on the cash basis until the seventh anniversary of the start of their practice. They then have to change to the earnings basis and meet the catch-up charge (Chapter 17, Part 2 ITTOIA 2005) at that time (or elect to spread the catch up charge over the following ten years).

It is possible for a barrister to change to preparing accounts on the accruals basis, including work-in-progress, during the initial seven-year period, but he or she cannot then change his or her mind and revert to the cash basis, and must prepare accounts on the accruals basis thereafter. This decision will depend on a number of factors, including his or her marginal rate of income tax and the reliability of future profit projections.

The special cash basis for barristers is not available for individuals who start to practice in 2013–14 or after. They can adopt the cash basis outlined in 7.1.5 if the conditions are satisfied.

16.6.2 Doctors

Medical practices are independent contractors to the NHS, and proprietors (GPs and non-GPs) are treated for tax and national insurance purposes as self-employed individuals, either in business on their own, or in partnership.

Practice expenses claims

GPs and non-GP proprietors are entitled to make annual claims for income tax purposes in respect of any expenditure that has been incurred personally (ie not reimbursed by the practice) and is incurred wholly and exclusively for the purpose of the medical practice. The claims should be based on the accounting year-end of the partnership accounts.

These claims usually include the following items:

- motor expenses;
- home and mobile telephone;
- use of home/study allowance;
- employment costs of spouse or civil partner;
- courses and conferences;
- books and journals;
- computer costs;
- locum insurance premiums;
- professional subscriptions.

Capital allowances can also be claimed on any capital items such as cars, computers, medical equipment and surgery fittings.

Tax relief on personal loans

(ss 398–399 ITA 2007)

Interest paid on personal loans taken out by GPs to introduce capital into the partnership either to purchase a share in the partnership; to contribute money to the partnership, used wholly for the purposes of the trade or profession carried on by the partnership; to advance money to the partnership that is so used, and repaying a previous loan which qualified for this relief, attracts tax relief when claimed on the GP's personal tax return.

Surgery premises

It was previously possible to claim capital allowances on the cost of plant and machinery comprised within the surgery building. However, many of the items previously qualifying for capital allowances will now fall into the integral features category (s 33A CAA 2001) and join the '8% special rate pool' (see 16.2). The integral features listed are:

- lifts, escalators and moving walkways;
- electrical and cold water systems;
- space or water heating systems;
- powered systems of ventilation;
- air cooling or air purification (including any floors or ceilings comprised in the system);
- external solar shading.

16.6.3 Farmers

There are several tax provisions that are specific to farmers.

All farming a single trade

(s 9 ITTOIA 2005)

The legislation specifically provides that all farming activities carried on by an individual within the UK are treated as a single trade. However, where an individual is a sole trader and also a partner in a farming partnership, the two activities are regarded as separate and distinct trades for tax purposes.

What counts as farming income?

'Farming' is defined within the statute. For tax purposes, it can be said to be the occupation of land in the UK wholly or mainly for the purposes of husbandry. Although there has always been the inclusion of items that should strictly not be taxed as farm income, HMRC has generally not sought to tax small amounts separately. Wayleaves, income from grazing and income from coppice cultivation are examples of types of income that would generally be included as farming income.

Where farmers engage in ancillary activities (eg providing B&B accommodation or self-catering facilities for holidaymakers), HMRC normally regards the resulting profits as forming part of a separate business unless they are relatively modest, in which case they may be included in the profits of the farming business for administrative convenience.

Farmhouse

It was normal practice for many years to claim that one-third of the farmhouse expenses were an allowable expense in computing the farm's trading profits. HMRC has since moved away from this practice and has emphasised that regard should be had to the actual usage of the farmhouse (see HMRC business income manual at BIM55250).

Valuation of stock

As with any business, an annual stock take and valuation exercise is required. If you are involved with the accounts for a farming business then the HMRC helpsheet IR232 sets out the principles to be applied and provides some guidance.

Herd basis

(Chapter 8, Part 2 ITTOIA 2005)

The effect of a herd basis election is that the herd is treated as a fixed asset. The original cost of the herd and any additions are excluded in arriving at the farm's profit for tax purposes. If the whole herd (or a substantial part of it) is disposed of, the proceeds are not treated as a trading receipt. Advice should be sought from an accountant about the mechanics of the herd basis and the potential effect of compensation payments for compulsory slaughter of animals for disease control purposes.

Single payment system

Many farm production subsidies were replaced by the single payment system from 2005 onwards. Rather than focusing on production subsidies, the single payment system is based on the farming land available to the farmer which triggers a 'payment entitlement'. All payments are chargeable to income tax but the basis of charge will depend on the circumstances under which they are received. For example, while it is usual for active farmers to be taxed on the payment as part of their farming income, a landowner does not have to actively farm the land to receive a payment under the scheme: payments are made where the land is simply kept in good agricultural and environmental condition. In such circumstances, this is still treated as trading income unless it is clear that the land is being used for leisure purposes (keeping pets, horses, etc): in the latter case any payment received is taxed as non-trading miscellaneous income.

17

CAPITAL GAINS TAX AND BUSINESS TRANSACTIONS

This chapter contains the following sections:

(1) Loans to private businesses
(2) Losses on unquoted shares
(3) Relief for replacement of business assets
(4) Hold-over relief for gifts of business property
(5) Partnerships and capital gains
(6) Transfer of a business to a company
(7) Entrepreneurs' relief
(8) Earn-outs
(9) Gifts of shares to all-employee share trusts
(10) Gifts and sales to certain employee trusts

17.1 LOANS TO PRIVATE BUSINESSES

A common type of transaction is a loan to a sole trader or partnership (an 'unincorporated business') or to a private company. Almost as common are situations where a person gives a guarantee to a bank, etc, that makes a loan to a business. This section deals with the CGT position if a loan becomes written off, or a person is required to make a payment under a bank guarantee that he or she has given.

17.1.1 Loans to unincorporated businesses

(s 253 TCGA 1992)

A CGT loss may be deemed to accrue to the lender if HMRC is satisfied that a loan has become irrecoverable. There are conditions that need to be fulfilled, ie the borrower must:

- not be the lender's spouse or civil partner;
- be resident in the UK;
- have used the loan wholly for the purposes of a trade carried on by him or her. The trade must not have consisted of (or included) the lending of money.

When a claim is submitted, HMRC must satisfy itself that any outstanding amount of the loan is irrecoverable and that the lender has not assigned or waived his or her right to recover the loan.

A claim must be made within four years of the end of the accounting period for a company, or tax year for an individual, in which the loan becomes irrecoverable (s 253(4A)).

The allowable loss is restricted to the amount of the loan that is irrecoverable, ie there is no indexation relief (only relevant if the lender is a company) in these circumstances.

> **Tax notes**
>
> A claim for a loss on a loan must be made within four years of the end of the tax year in which the loan becomes irrecoverable.

17.1.2 Loans to companies

(s 253 TCGA 1992)

Similar provisions apply where a person has made a loan to a company that proves to be irrecoverable. The principal conditions that need to be satisfied are:

- the company must be UK resident;
- it must be a trading company;
- the lender must not be a company that is a member of the same group of companies.

In all other respects, relief normally applies exactly as described in 17.1.1.

Loan notes and debentures

(s 254 TCGA 1992)

Another complication may apply to a loss on a loan that constitutes a 'debt on a security', which is a special type of loan. In broad terms, the loan is usually evidenced by a debenture deed and is transferable. A typical example is loan stock.

If a loan falls into this category, it is necessary to ascertain whether it also falls into another sub-class, ie a qualifying corporate bond (QCB, see 13.4.2). No loss relief is available on a disposal of a QCB. However, losses on other debts on securities continue to attract relief under the general principle that a debt is not a chargeable asset in the hands of the original creditor.

17.1.3 Payments under loan guarantees

(s 253(1)(c)TCGA 1992)

Instead of lending money to a relative or friend or his or her private company, a person might have given a guarantee to a bank, etc. Similarly, a company director might have had to give personal guarantees in respect of bank loans to his or her company.

Where the borrower cannot repay the loan, the bank will call on the guarantor to pay the amount due. In these circumstances, the guarantor may be able to claim a CGT loss as if he or she had made a loan that was irrecoverable. The following conditions must be satisfied for relief to be claimed:

- payment has been made under a guarantee;
- the payment arises from a formal calling in of the guarantee – a voluntary payment attracts no relief;
- the original loan met the requirements listed in 17.1.1;
- the amount paid under the guarantee cannot be recovered either from the borrower or from a co-guarantor.

17.2 LOSSES ON UNQUOTED SHARES

(Chapter 6, Part 4 ITA 2007)

From time to time, an individual may invest in a private company, either as a working director/shareholder or perhaps as a 'passive' investor with a minority shareholding. Investments may also be made in companies that, while they are technically public companies as defined by the Companies Act 2006, are not quoted companies.

17.2.1 Special relief for subscribers

A loss may arise on a disposal of shares in such a company. If the investor acquired existing shares by purchasing them, the loss is a normal CGT loss and the only way it can be relieved is as set out in 13.1.3. However, if he or she acquired the shares by subscribing for new shares, it may be possible to obtain income tax relief for the loss. Subject to certain conditions, the capital loss may be offset against his or her income for the year in which the loss is realised.

The following conditions must be satisfied:

(1) The loss must arise from one of the following:
    (a) a sale made at arm's length for full consideration (this rules out a sale to a connected person); or
    (b) a disposal that takes place when the company is wound up; or
    (c) a deemed disposal where the shares have become of negligible value.

(2) There are also conditions that attach to the company itself. In particular:

  (a) the company must not have been a quoted company at the date the individual subscribed for the shares and there must be no arrangements for the company to cease to be unquoted or to become a subsidiary of another company. If any class of shares in the company is quoted, this rules out relief even though the loss might have arisen on another class of share that was not quoted;

  (b) the company must be a trading company, or the holding company of a trading group, at the date of disposal or it must have ceased to have been a trading company not more than three years before the date of disposal and it must not have been an investment company, an excluded company or a non-trading company since the cessation;

  (c) the company's trade must not have consisted wholly or mainly of dealing in shares, securities, land, trades or commodity futures;

  (d) for investments made on or after 6 April 1998, the company must have met the conditions necessary to qualify for EIS relief: see 25.4;

  (e) the company's trade must have been carried out on a commercial basis.

17.2.2 Relief also available for subscriber's spouse

The spouse or civil partner of a person who subscribed for shares may also claim relief where he or she has acquired the shares in question through an *inter vivos* transfer from his or her spouse or civil partner. Shares acquired on a spouse's death do *not* entitle the survivor to relief on a subsequent disposal.

17.2.3 Nature of relief

The loss is calculated according to normal CGT principles. If the loss is eligible for relief, the individual may elect, by the first anniversary of the normal self-assessment filing date for the year of the loss, for it to be set against his or her taxable income for either the year of the loss or the preceding year. For example, if an individual realises an allowable loss in 2014–15, he or she has until 31 January 2017 to make the relevant claims. Either claim may be made independently of the other. Where he or she has losses that are available for relief and is also entitled to relief for trading losses, he or she can choose which losses should be relieved in priority to the others.

Any part of the capital loss that is not relieved can be carried forward for offset against future capital gains in the normal way.

17.2.4 Shares acquired by exercising a share option

If a person acquired shares by exercising a share option, and was taxed under the employment income legislation, his or her CGT acquisition cost may be much higher than anticipated (see 13.10.3). An unexpected CGT loss may therefore arise when the shares are disposed of. If the other conditions are satisfied, the person can get income tax relief (see Chapter 7).

17.3 RELIEF FOR REPLACEMENT OF BUSINESS ASSETS

(ss 152–160 TCGA 1992)

'Roll-over' relief may be available where a person sells an asset used by him or her in a trade (or in certain circumstances, by his or her family company) and reinvests in replacement assets used for business purposes.

17.3.1 Nature of roll-over relief

A gain is said to be rolled over in that it is not charged to tax, but is deducted from the person's acquisition cost of the new assets.

Example – Roll-over relief

L sells a farm for £450,000. His capital gain is £200,000. He starts up a new business and invests £500,000 in a warehouse. By claiming roll-over relief, he avoids having to pay tax on the gain of £200,000 until the new asset is disposed of. The acquisition cost of his warehouse is reduced as follows:

	£
Actual cost	500,000
Less: rolled-over gain	(200,000)
Deemed acquisition cost	300,000

The relief is really a form of deferment since a larger gain will arise on a subsequent disposal of the replacement asset.

17.3.2 Conditions that need to be satisfied

The asset disposed of must have been used in a business and must have fallen into one of the following categories:

- land and buildings;
- fixed plant and machinery;
- ships;

- goodwill (but not goodwill purchased by companies after 31 March 2002: see 18.6);
- milk and potato quotas;
- aircraft;
- hovercraft, satellites and spacecraft;
- Lloyd's syndicate rights ('capacity');
- ewe and suckler cow premium quotas and fish quota.

The replacement asset must also fall into one of these categories (but not necessarily the same category as the assets disposed of).

The replacement asset must normally be acquired within a period starting one year before and ending three years after the date of the disposal of the original asset. The time limit can be extended (at HMRC's discretion) if it was not possible to replace the original asset within three years because of circumstances outside the person's control.

Example – Full relief available only where all the sale proceeds are reinvested
s 152(3)–(11) TCGA 1992

> Using the same figures as in 17.3.1, *L* sells his farm for £450,000, making the same capital gain of £200,000. He starts up a business but invests only £400,000 in the new warehouse. The part of the £450,000 disposal consideration for the farm that is not applied in acquiring the warehouse is £50,000. This is less than the gain that arose on the disposal of the farm and therefore, only the balance of the gain may be rolled over. The warehouse's acquisition value is reduced by £150,000, with £50,000 becoming chargeable immediately.

17.3.3 Old assets not used for business throughout ownership

If the old asset was not used in the trading business throughout the period of ownership, s 152 applies to a proportionate part of the asset concerned.

Example – Old assets

> In March 2015, *M* sold a warehouse at a gain of £50,000. It had originally been bought in March 2005 but had been used in his trade only since March 2007. The amount of gain that can be rolled over into the purchase of a new asset is calculated as follows:
>
> Chargeable gain £50,000 $\times \dfrac{\text{Period of trading use of old asset}}{\text{Period of ownership}}$
>
> This equals £50,000 $\times$ $8/10$, ie £40,000. The balance of £10,000 (£50,000 − £40,000) was a chargeable gain (before entrepreneurs' relief) of 2014–15.

17.3.4 Treatment where replacement assets are wasting assets

(s 154 TCGA 1992)

The roll-over relief is modified where the replacement expenditure consists of the purchase of a wasting asset (ie with an expected useful life of less than 50 years) or an asset that will become a wasting asset within ten years. Plant and machinery is always considered to have a useful life of less than 50 years. Furthermore, the acquisition of a lease with less than 60 years to run also constitutes the acquisition of a wasting asset. Paradoxically, the goodwill of a business is not regarded as a wasting asset.

The capital gain in these circumstances is not deferred indefinitely, but becomes chargeable on the first of the following occasions:

- the disposal of the replacement asset; or
- the asset ceasing to be used in the business; or
- the expiry of ten years.

Examples – Roll-over relief on wasting assets

(1) N sells a factory and reinvests in a 59-year lease of a warehouse that he uses in his business. In Year 6 the warehouse is let as an investment property. The rolled-over gain becomes chargeable in Year 6.

(2) O also rolls over into a 59-year lease. He is still using the property after ten years, but because it has become a wasting asset within that period, the rolled-over gain becomes chargeable in Year 10.

17.3.5 Reinvestment in non-wasting assets

If the person acquires new non-wasting replacement assets during the ten years, the capital gain that was originally held over on the purchase of the wasting assets can be transferred and rolled over into the base cost of the new replacement assets. Assume in example (1) above that N had bought the goodwill of a business in Year 5. He could transfer his roll-over relief claim to the new asset. No gain would then become chargeable in Year 6 when he lets the warehouse.

17.3.6 Furnished holiday lettings

A property acquired for letting as furnished holiday accommodation (see 8.5) may qualify for roll-over relief; gains from the disposal of such properties may be rolled over.

17.3.7 Assets used by partnership

(SP D11)

Roll-over relief can be secured where the replacement assets are used by a partnership in which the owner is a partner.

17.3.8 Assets used by family company

(s 157 TCGA 1992)

Relief can be obtained where an individual disposes of a property, etc, used by his or her 'personal trading company', but only if the replacement asset is acquired by him or her and is used by the same company. A company is an individual's personal trading company if he or she personally owns at least 5% of the voting shares.

He or she need not be a director of the company – indeed, the person need not even be employed by it. Also, roll-over relief is not lost because he or she has charged the company rent.

17.3.9 Assets owned by employee or office-holder

An employee or office-holder may claim roll-over relief where he or she disposes of an asset used in the employment. This condition may apply to, for example, a sub-postmaster who has an 'office' for tax purposes, but who generally owns the sub-post office premises. For details, see SP 5/86.

There are circumstances where these provisions can mean that a director of a family company who has sold an asset used by one company and bought new assets used by another family company is entitled to roll-over relief: this is a difficult area where professional advice is essential.

In addition, ESC D22 provides that expenditure on improvements to existing assets may be treated as expenditure incurred in acquiring other assets for the purposes of the relief. ESC D24 provides that it is possible to ignore a delay in taking an asset into use, where this arises out of the completion of improvements to the asset, and ESC D25 provides that where the proceeds from the disposal of an 'old' asset are used in acquiring a further interest in an asset already in use in the trade, the further interest can be treated as a 'new' asset taken into use for the purposes of the trade.

17.4 HOLD-OVER RELIEF FOR GIFTS OF BUSINESS PROPERTY

(s 165 TCGA 1992)

17.4.1 Background and nature of hold-over relief

At one time, a UK-resident individual could transfer any asset to another UK-resident person on a no gain/no loss basis by claiming hold-over relief.

The relief was abolished for gifts of most types of assets but the same type of relief can still be claimed on gifts of business property to a UK-resident person.

17.4.2 Definition of 'business property'

Business property is defined for these purposes as:

- an asset used by the transferor in a trade, profession or vocation (this includes properties let as furnished holiday accommodation); or
- an asset used by the transferor's personal company in a trade; or
- an asset used for a trade by a member of a trading group of which the holding company is the transferor's personal company; or
- it consists of shares in a trading company, or holding company of a trading group, which does not to any substantial extent have investment activities and is either unlisted or the trading company or holding company is the transferor's personal company.

17.4.3 Situations where hold-over relief is not available

Hold-over relief cannot be claimed in respect of a gift of shares or securities to a UK company where the gift took place after 8 November 1999. The relief can, however, still be claimed on the gift to a company of an unincorporated business. Hold-over relief is not available for transfers to settlor-interested trusts.

If the company whose shares are being gifted has substantial investment activities no hold-over relief is available. There is no hard and fast rule as to what constitutes 'substantial investment activities'. HMRC's practice is to consider the income generated, assets used in, and management time devoted to, non-trading activities. Where, in the round, at least 20% of the company's activities are non-trading, it is considered not to be a trading company.

17.4.4 **Claiming the relief**

You should obtain a copy of Helpsheet IR295, which incorporates an election that needs to be signed by the donor and donee.

17.4.5 **Relief clawed back if donee emigrates**

Where an individual holds over a gain under s 165 and becomes either resident or not ordinarily resident within six years of the end of the tax year in which the asset was transferred, then the held-over gain is deemed to have accrued to the transferee immediately before the date of migration.

17.5 PARTNERSHIPS AND CAPITAL GAINS

How CGT affects partnership transactions can at times be complex. Partners should familiarise themselves with SP D12 and take regular professional advice. The following section describes some key aspects.

17.5.1 **Partnership's acquisition value**

Although individual partners' entitlement to profits may vary over the years, the partnership's acquisition value for the firm's chargeable assets is not affected unless there are cash payments from one partner to another to acquire a greater interest in the firm, or unless assets are revalued as part of the arrangements for changes in profit-sharing.

17.5.2 **Assets held by the firm at 31 March 1982**

Where a partner disposes of an interest in a partnership asset which he or she held at 31 March 1982, his or her gain will normally be computed by reference to the value of the asset at 31 March 1982 (see 13.9.2).

Where partners have acquired interests in a partnership asset through changes in profit-sharing ratios between 31 March 1982 and 6 April 2008, they will generally have a cost computed by reference to the 31 March 1982 value plus any indexation allowance for the period from 31 March 1982 to the month in which the person making the disposal disposed of it or, if earlier, to April 1998.

See Revenue & Customs Brief 9/09.

17.5.3 **Partnership gains divisible among partners**

Where a partnership asset is sold at a capital gain (or loss), the gain is divided among the partners in accordance with their asset-sharing ratios. Each partner is personally assessable on his or her share of the gain.

The partner's actual CGT liability depends on his or her own situation, ie whether he or she has other gains for the year, has available losses, or can claim roll-over relief.

17.5.4 Revaluations and retirement and introduction of partners

Problems may arise where a partnership has substantial assets (that are chargeable assets for CGT purposes) worth more than their book value (ie the value at which they are shown in the firm's accounts). A revaluation to bring the assets' book value into line with their market value can produce a liability for individual partners if there is a reduction in their asset-sharing ratios. This commonly happens when existing partners retire or new partners are introduced.

Example – Retirement of partner

P is a partner in a five-partner firm and is entitled to 20% of the profits. He retires and his colleagues then share profits on the basis of 25% each. As part of the arrangements for his retirement, the book value of the firm's office block is increased from £150,000 to its current value of £750,000. The surplus is credited to each partner's account so that P is credited with £120,000.

P is treated as if he had realised a gain on the disposal of a one-fifth share of the building. This would be based on the £120,000 credited to his capital account. The remaining four partners are not treated as having made a disposal. Indeed, they each have made an acquisition of a 5% interest in the building for an outlay of £30,000.

Example – Introduction of partner

Q and R are partners. Their premises are included in their firm's balance sheet at £200,000 (original cost), but are actually worth £500,000. Q and R agree to admit S as an equal partner in return for his paying new capital into the firm of £700,000. They revalue the premises before admitting S as a partner, and the surplus of £300,000 is credited to their accounts. In this case, Q and R are each regarded as having made a disposal of a one-sixth interest in the premises. This is because S's new capital will go into the firm as a whole. After coming in, he effectively owns one-third of all the assets (and is responsible for one-third of the liabilities).

The former partners' ownership of the premises has been reduced from 50% to a one-third interest.

17.5.5 Retirement and introduction of partners with no revaluation of assets

There is no such problem where partners leave or come in and there is no revaluation of assets. In such a case, the remaining or incoming partners normally take over the outgoing partners' acquisition values for the firm's asset.

Example – Change of partners with no revaluation of assets

> *T* and *U* are in partnership. They own premises that have a book value of £94,000 (equal to cost in 1980). *T* retires and is replaced by *V.* The premises are not revalued. After 5 April 2008, the premises are sold for £244,000. *U* and *V* are assessed on their share of the gain.
>
> The gain is computed by reference to the premises' market value at 31 March 1982, not their value at the time that *V* became a partner. This may not apply where the partners are connected persons (eg because they are relatives), or where cash payments are made to acquire an interest in the firm. In either of these categories you should seek specialist advice.

17.6 TRANSFER OF A BUSINESS TO A COMPANY

(s 162 TCGA 1992)

Where a person transfers a business to a company (ie he or she 'incorporates' the business), there is a disposal of the assets that are transferred to the company. Not all the assets necessarily become chargeable assets for CGT purposes, but a gain may arise on assets such as land, buildings and goodwill. Fortunately, there is a relief that may cover such situations.

17.6.1 Nature of relief

The main relief applies only where a business is transferred to a company in return for an issue of shares to the former proprietor(s) of the business. Where the necessary conditions are satisfied so that s 162 relief is available, the gains that would otherwise arise on the transfer of chargeable assets are rolled over into the cost of the shares issued.

Example – Transfer of a business to a company

> *W* transfers a business to B Ltd in return for shares worth £75,000. There are capital gains of £48,000 on the assets transferred to the company. If s 162 relief applies, *W* will not have any assessable capital gain, but her

shares in B Ltd will be deemed to have an acquisition cost of £27,000 computed as follows:

	£
Market value	75,000
Less: rolled over gain	(48,000)
Base cost for CGT purposes	27,000

17.6.2 Conditions that must be satisfied

For s 162 relief to be available, all the business's assets, other than cash, must be transferred to the company. It is not acceptable for certain assets of the unincorporated business (eg trade debts) to be excluded, even though this might otherwise be advisable to save stamp duty.

Relief is available only in so far as shares are issued by the company instead of other forms of payment such as loan stock. The market value of the shares issued in return for the transfer of the business must be at least equal to the capital gains arising on the transfer of assets.

Tax notes

When transferring a business to a company, certain assets of the unincorporated business (eg trade debts) cannot be excluded, even though this might otherwise be advisable to save stamp duty.

Example – Limitations of s 162 relief

X transfers a business with a net value of £400,000 to C Ltd, a new company specially formed for the purpose. Shares in C Ltd are issued to him, and these have a value of £400,000. However, closer examination reveals that the business's value is depressed by heavy bank borrowings. Furthermore, capital gains totalling £490,000 arise on chargeable assets transferred as part of the business.

Section 162 relief would be limited to £400,000. The balance of £90,000 would be taxable in the normal way.

17.6.3 Conditions that are not required

(1) Relief is not confined to a transfer of a business to a company by a sole trader; the same relief is available where partners transfer a business currently carried on in partnership to a company.

(2) The shares that are issued need not be ordinary shares.

(3) Relief does not seem to be confined to a business that is classified as a trade. It would appear that the relevant business might, for

example, consist of letting a portfolio of properties as recently held by the Upper Tribunal in *Ramsay* v *HMRC* UKUT 0226 TCC.

(4) There is no requirement that the company should be incorporated or resident in the UK. It can be both of these things, but relief is not prejudiced just because a foreign company is involved.

17.6.4 Relief may be due on proportion of capital gains

Some relief will still be available if the business is transferred to the company in return for a mixture of shares and loan stock, or shares and cash. The formula to be used is:

$$\text{Chargeable gain} \times \frac{\text{Value of shares received}}{\text{Value of whole consideration received}}$$

17.6.5 Election to disapply this relief

It is possible to elect for s 162 relief not to apply. This might be appropriate where the disposal of individual assets to the company would qualify for entrepreneurs' relief (ER) but the subsequent disposal of the shares would not (because, for example, the company has substantial non-trading activities). The election must be made by 31 January following the filing date for the year in question, eg the election has to be made by 31 January 2014 for a business incorporated during 2011–12.

17.7 ENTREPRENEURS' RELIEF

(Chapter 3, Part 5 TCGA 1992)

There is a £10m limit for gains which may attract entrepreneurs' relief and so be taxed at only 10%. The £10m is a lifetime allowance.

17.7.1 Conditions relating to the individual

ER is normally available only if the individual has been in business, as a sole trader or as a partner, or as an officer or employee of his or her personal trading company for at least 12 months ending on the date of the relevant disposal. It is necessary for the disposal to be a material disposal of all or part of his or her interest in the business or of shares in his personal trading company (see below).

17.7.2 Only some businesses qualify

Where a business is being disposed of, it must be a trading business and not an investment business. Letting furnished holiday accommodation is a qualifying business.

17.7.3 Personal trading company

A company qualifies as an individual's personal trading company only if:

- he or she owns at least 5% of the ordinary share capital and has at least 5% of the voting rights by virtue of that holding; and
- he or she is an officer (eg director) or employee of that company; and
- the company is a trading company or the holding company of a trading group and it does not exist to any substantial extent for any non-trading purpose (this is the same as the 20% test that applies for hold-over relief purposes, as described in 17.4). An investment company that held at least 5% of the shares in a joint venture trading company was able to qualify as a trading company until 17 March 2015.
- A company that carries on business in partnership is not regarded as being a trading company by virtue of its participation in the partnership (this rule applies for disposals on or after 18 March 2015).

'Ordinary share capital' can include variable rate preference shares so professional advice should be taken where a company has more than one class of shares.

17.7.4 Transfers of goodwill to a connected company

Entrepreneurs' relief is not available for gains on certain disposals of intangible property such as goodwill which take place on or after 3 December 2014. The exclusion applies where the person making the disposal is a participator in the company or an associate of a participator.

17.7.5 Associated disposals

ER can also be claimed on gains arising from associated disposals. An associated disposal consists of the disposal by the individual of an asset he or she has owned personally but which has been used – throughout the 12 months ending on the date of the associated disposal (or the date of cessation of the business, if earlier and relevant) – in the business of a partnership of which the individual was a partner or a company that was the individual's personal trading company.

The associated disposal must take place within three years of the disposal by the individual of an interest in the partnership or company concerned (or cessation of the business of the partnership or company, whichever is the earlier). The associated disposal must also be related to the individual withdrawing from the business concerned. It is unclear precisely what this means although this condition will normally be met where the disposal takes place as part of the same arrangements under which the individual retires from the partnership or ceases to be involved in the company's business, either fully or partially.

> **Tax notes**
>
> The relief is available for a gain on the sale of land or buildings used by a partnership or an individual's personal trading company but only where the individual owner had not charged the business a market rent throughout the full period of business usage since 6 April 2008. The level of any rent charged to the business for periods of business usage before 6 April 2008 is ignored.

2015 restrictions

FA 2015 restricts relief where an associated disposal takes place on or after 18 March 2015. Entrepreneurs' relief can now apply only if the person making the disposal also significantly reduces his interest in the business. A significant reduction is where a person gives up at least 5% of a partnership's profits or where, in the case of a company, he disposes of shares which make up 5% or more of the company's ordinary share capital and which carry at least 5% of the voting rights. There must be no arrangement whereby the person's interest in the partnership or company may later be increased back again.

17.7.6 Entrepreneurs' relief where a vendor takes loan notes

Where a vendor takes Qualifying Corporate Bonds (see 13.4.2), his gain is computed as if he had made a disposal for cash but the gain is deferred until he disposes of the QCBs. In this situation, the deferred gain attracts entrepreneurs' relief.

Where a vendor takes loan notes which are not QCBs, his gain is computed as and when he disposes of the loan notes. In most situations, he will no longer meet the conditions for entrepreneurs' relief and the gain may therefore be taxed at 28%.

17.7.7 Entrepreneurs' relief and EIS investments

Where gains realised between 23 June 2010 and 2 December 2014 which would have attracted entrepreneurs' relief were deferred into EIS shares, the deferred gain which became chargeable on a disposal of the EIS investment did not then attract entrepreneurs' relief. So in many situations investors were exchanging an immediate tax charge at 10% for a deferred 28% tax. This treatment has been reversed for gains realised on or after 3 December 2014 which are deferred into qualifying EIS investments.

17.8 EARN-OUTS

An earn-out is where a person sells shares and part of the consideration is dependent on the company's subsequent performance. For example, an individual might sell his or her private company for £1m cash plus an amount based on the company achieving certain profit targets for the next three years.

The right to receive more cash if profit targets are achieved is a valuable one, but its value will not normally be the maximum sum: it depends on whether the targets are achieved. The case law *(Marren* v *Ingles)* indicates that a present (discounted) value should be ascertained and this should be included as part of the sale consideration that is taxable for the year in which the sale takes place. When the earn-out period is over, and the actual amount due under the earn-out is known, another capital gain (or loss) occurs for the year in which the entitlement is ascertained.

This has in the past meant that a person who is entitled to receive an earn-out could be taxed on sums that are never in fact received. Fortunately, the law has now changed. Provided the sale contract specifies that the earn-out consideration *must* be satisfied by the acquiring company issuing securities or debentures (eg loan notes) rather than paying cash, and provided the person entitled to the earn-out does not make an election under s 138A TCGA 1992, there is no question of anything being taxed in respect of the earn-out until the individual makes a disposal of the securities that are received in satisfaction of his or her earn-out rights.

Tax notes

Be especially careful with this. For many years, the effect of making an election under s 138A was beneficial in that it postponed the date of disposal for CGT purposes until the individual disposed of the securities received from the earn-out. The situation has now been turned upside-down: you are now automatically treated in this way unless you positively elect under the revised version of s 138A to have a CGT assessment on the initial value of the earn-out. It is possible that such a CGT assessment could be beneficial in some circumstances and in these cases the s 138A election needs to be made within 22 months of the end of the tax year in which the disposal giving rise to the earn-out takes place.

17.8.1 CGT treatment for earn-outs paid in cash

There is now also some relief for individuals who are entitled to an earn-out that can be taken in cash. Such individuals are liable to be taxed on the initial value of the earn-out but there is now a carry-back relief. This allows a vendor who has been taxed on a higher amount than is eventually received to carry back the difference as a loss. In other words, the end result is that CGT is paid only on the amount that is actually collected.

17.8.2 Earn-outs and income tax

See also 6.7 regarding a possible income tax charge on certain earn-outs.

17.9 GIFTS OF SHARES TO ALL-EMPLOYEE SHARE TRUSTS

(Schedule 7C TCGA 1992)

Where an individual transfers unquoted shares to trustees who hold them for employees under an approved all-employee share scheme (see 6.4), the individual may roll over any capital gain arising from this transfer provided he or she reinvests in chargeable assets within six months. The all-employee trust must acquire at least a 10% interest in the company. The chargeable assets into which the individual's gain is rolled over cannot consist of shares in the company concerned or a property that is exempt as the individual's main residence.

Tax notes

You will need to take professional advice if you seek to rely on this relief. But if you qualify, the roll-over relief rules are quite generous.

17.10 GIFTS AND SALES TO CERTAIN EMPLOYEE TRUSTS

(s 239 TCGA 1992)

17.10.1 Gifts to employee trusts

In certain situations, a gift (or sale at cost) of an asset by an individual to an employee trust may be treated as a disposal at cost.

The conditions which need to be satisfied are as follows:

(1) The employee trust must be for the benefit of all or most of the employees of the company concerned.

(2) No employees who are participators owning 5% or more can be eligible to benefit under the trust except on the basis that any benefits received by them will be taxable income (or would be so but for the fact that the participator is resident outside the UK).

(3) No person who is connected to a participator who owns 5% or more may benefit except on the basis that any benefits received will be taxable income.

(4) Within 12 months of the individual making his or her gift, the trustees must hold more than one half of the ordinary share capital of the company.

Tax notes

When considering any transactions with employee trusts, bear in mind the rules on disguised remuneration (see Chapter 5), which can apply even in innocent situations. You will need to take professional advice.

17.10.2 Disposals of shares to an all-employee trust

Finance Act 2014 provides an exemption for disposals of shares to a qualifying trust which benefits all employees of a company (or a group) provided certain conditions are satisfied:

- the company whose shares are under consideration must be a trading company, or the parent company of a trading group;
- the trust which acquires the shares must operate for the benefit all employees;
- the trust must have a controlling interest in the company at the end of the tax year, which it did not have at the start of that year;
- certain participators must be excluded from being beneficiaries of the trust; and
- the claimant must not previously have qualified for relief on the same company's shares.

The new relief is available for disposals which take place in a single tax year. The disposals may be made by more than one person, and can be of any number of shares. The disposals can be sales as well as gifts.

There are provisions to prevent claimants of the new relief receiving disproportionate share-related benefits from the trust.

18

TAX AND COMPANIES

This chapter contains the following sections:

(1) Corporation tax
(2) Self-assessment
(3) How 'profits' are defined
(4) Accounting periods, rates and payment of tax
(5) Loan relationships
(6) Intangible assets
(7) Companies' capital gains
(8) Dividends
(9) Losses
(10) Overseas aspects
(11) Transfer pricing rules
(12) Groups of companies
(13) Investment companies
(14) Close companies
(15) Real Estate Investment Trusts (REITs)
(16) Research and development (R&D) tax relief
(17) ECA tax credits
(18) Sale of lessor companies: anti-avoidance
(19) iXBRL and online filing
(20) Claims, elections and penalties

18.1 CORPORATION TAX

18.1.1 Corporate tax road map

The corporate tax road map is the Government's plan to make the UK a more attractive home for international business by creating a competitive and stable corporate tax system. Its principles for reform include:

- lower tax rates but fewer tax reliefs;
- avoiding unnecessary changes (for simplicity and stability);
- keeping pace with modern business practice;
- a level playing field for businesses.

18.1.2 **Who pays corporation tax?**

(ss 8–11 CTA 2009)

Corporation tax is levied on the chargeable profits of companies resident in the UK for tax purposes. A company is generally defined as meaning any body corporate or unincorporated association, but does not include a partnership, local authority or local authority association. The definition extends to authorised unit trusts, detailed provisions for which are set out in s 616 CTA 2010.

Corporation tax also extends to non-resident companies carrying on a trade in the UK through a permanent establishment. Such companies are chargeable to tax on any income attributable to the permanent establishment and on any capital gains arising on the disposal of assets used in the UK trade of the permanent establishment. Any income of a non-resident company from sources within the UK that is not charged to corporation tax is liable to income tax.

A company that was incorporated in the UK is regarded as resident here regardless of where the directors exercise their management and control. Some of the double taxation conventions negotiated with other countries override this in practice and treat a dual resident company as if it were not UK-resident.

A company that was incorporated overseas may still be regarded as resident in the UK on the basis that its central management and control is exercised in the UK. Questions relating to a foreign incorporated company's residence status are usually determined by reference to the guidelines set out in SP1/90 dated 9 January 1990 (see www.hmrc.gov. uk/manuals/intmanual/INTM120140.htm).

18.2 SELF-ASSESSMENT

(ss 5, 6 and 8 CTA 2009; s 963 CTA 2010 and Schedule18 FA 1998)

Corporation tax self-assessment is similar to the income tax self-assessment system for individuals and trustees.

Self-assessment for companies brings with it extensive record-keeping obligations.

A copy of the manual, *A Guide to Corporation Tax Self-assessment* can be obtained from HMRC's website at www.hmrc.gov.uk/ctsa/ctsaguide.pdf.

The CTSA system requires payments on account for certain companies. Where a 'large' company (as defined in 18.4.4) has taxable profits for an accounting period, and it also had such profits in the preceding year, it must make four payments on account of its expected corporation tax liability for the year. Online filing is now compulsory for almost all companies. See 18.19 for more on this.

18.3 HOW 'PROFITS' ARE DEFINED

18.3.1 Computation of profits

(ss 2–4 CTA 2009)

The income and chargeable gains of a company, collectively termed 'chargeable profits', are chargeable to corporation tax. The computation of chargeable profits can be a very complex process bearing in mind the detailed tax legislation and extensive case law. There is also a myriad of HMRC statements of practice, press releases and extra-statutory concessions that may need to be borne in mind when calculating chargeable profits on which corporation tax is payable.

18.3.2 Special computational rules for companies

Rental income

All income from UK rental activities is now treated as arising from one source and taxed along the same lines as trading profits. Any losses are relieved first against other income and gains of the same period, and any excess is available to carry forward against future property income, or may be surrendered as group relief (subject to certain restrictions).

Foreign exchange transactions

Special rules apply for foreign exchange profits and losses; professional advice should be taken if the company has significant foreign assets or borrowings in a foreign currency.

Loan relationships

Specific rules govern the treatment of loan relationships such as gilts and other fixed-interest investments. Basically, any profits on disposal of such assets are taxed as income and any losses are allowed against the company's income. If the company decides to revalue its loan relationships for accounts purposes in accordance with generally accepted accounting principles (GAAP), any increase compared with the market value at the start of the period (or the date of acquisition where the gilt, etc, was acquired during the course of the year) is taxable income; any reduction in value is an allowable loss (see 18.5).

Interest

FA 2009 introduced a regime called the worldwide debt cap that applies to all large groups for accounting periods beginning on or after 1 January

2010. A large group is defined as one having at least 250 employees or turnover of more than £50m and gross assets of more than £43m.

Under these rules, tax deductions for interest will be disallowed to UK members of the group to the extent that the 'tested amount' exceeds the 'available amount'.

The tested amount is the aggregate net finance expense of all relevant group companies (UK resident companies and non-resident companies with UK permanent establishments) that have net finance expenses for the period concerned, calculated under UK tax rules. The available amount is the worldwide group's gross consolidated finance expense (UK and non-UK). In other words, if the group's overall interest bill is £15m but UK companies have paid interest of £17.5m, broadly speaking £2.5m will be disallowed.

Capital allowances

Although depreciation is not regarded as an allowable expense for tax purposes, tax relief is given for expenditure on qualifying capital assets by means of capital allowances. The principles follow very closely those that apply to individuals (see 16.2) and therefore the main provisions are not covered in detail here. Capital allowances for a trade carried on by a company are regarded as trading expenses for the accounting period in which they arise. They are therefore taken into account in arriving at the chargeable profits or overall tax loss for the accounting period.

Capital allowances for non-trading activities are primarily deductible from the income arising from that source. Any surplus allowances may be carried forward against similar source income arising in later accounting periods or deducted from overall chargeable profits for the accounting period in which they arise.

Contributions to employee benefit trusts

Contributions attract tax relief only if an employee receives sums within nine months of the company's year end on which PAYE and NIC are charged. If this condition is not satisfied, the company receives a deduction only for the accounting period in which sums are paid out subject to PAYE and NIC. Following the introduction of new rules on disguised remuneration (see Chapter 5) from 6 April 2011, it is probable that a tax charge will arise at the time – or shortly after – a contribution has been made, if this is 'earmarked' for specific employees. Accordingly, ss 1290 to 1295 CTA 2009 have been amended to ensure that a deduction will be given in the employer's tax computation for any amounts that are subjected to tax under the new provisions in Part 7A ITEPA, for the period that the tax charge arises.

Intangible assets

The tax treatment for expenditure on, and gains from the sale of, intangible assets was introduced by FA 2002 (now in part 8 CTA 2009) (see 18.6).

Insurance policies

See 28.8 on life assurance policies held by companies.

Annual payments

(s189 CTA 2010)

Certain annual payments (termed 'charges on income') are deductible from a company's profits in arriving at the amount assessable to corporation tax. An example of such an annual payment is Gift Aid payments. The principle is that these charges on income are offset against the payer's total profits, not merely against a particular source of income with which the payment is connected.

A payment counts as a charge on income only if the following conditions are met:

- It has been made out of the company's profits brought into charge to corporation tax.
- It is a payment of money to a charity.
- It must not be in the nature of a dividend or distribution made by the company.

The basic rule is that payment must actually be made in the accounting period for it to count as a charge for that period. In certain restricted circumstances, some companies that are owned by charities are able to treat Gift Aid payments made within nine months of their year end as if they had been paid during the year.

Where the total profits for an accounting period are insufficient to absorb charges on income, excess charges in respect of payments made wholly and exclusively for the purposes of the company's trade may be carried forward and used against its future trading income. Non-trade charges may not be carried forward in this manner and no further relief is available.

Exemption for foreign dividends

Following a long period of consultation, FA 2009 introduced an exemption for foreign dividends received by a UK company on or after 1 July 2009. The dividends must satisfy one of a range of conditions. This exemption is not available to small companies unless the dividends are received from a company that is resident in a territory with which the

UK has a comprehensive double taxation agreement which includes a non-discrimination article. Anti-avoidance provisions apply to deny the exemption where one of a number of prescribed schemes has been used.

The availability of the exemption does not depend on the percentage holding in the company paying the dividend.

18.4 ACCOUNTING PERIODS, RATES AND PAYMENT OF TAX

18.4.1 Accounting periods for tax purposes

(ss 9–11 CTA 2009)

Companies pay corporation tax by reference to their accounting periods and the chargeable profit included is assessed on an actual or accruals basis. Financial years for corporation tax purposes run from 1 April to the following 31 March and tax rates are set for each financial year. The year to 31 March 2016 is called financial year 2015 and so on. Accounting periods may straddle the end of a financial year, in which case the chargeable profits are apportioned on a time basis for the purposes of determining the rate of tax to apply to the overall profit. This is only relevant, of course, if the rates of tax in the two financial years concerned are different.

An accounting period begins for corporation tax purposes when:

- the company comes within the charge to corporation tax either by becoming UK-resident or acquiring a source of income; or
- the company's previous accounting period ends without the company ceasing to be within the charge to corporation tax.

An accounting period runs on for a maximum of 12 months from its commencement. It will end earlier if the company's own accounting date falls within the 12 months and it will also end if the company:

- ceases to trade; or
- begins or ceases to be UK-resident; or
- ceases to be within the charge to corporation tax altogether.

Where accounts are made up for a period of more than 12 months, the income is usually apportioned on a time basis to the relevant accounting period. Where a more appropriate basis of apportionment is available, HMRC may apply that basis instead (see *Marshall Hus & Partners Ltd* v *Bolton* [1981] STC18). In some instances, the accounts year end may vary slightly for commercial reasons (eg where accounts are made up to the last Friday of a specified month). Provided the variation is not more than four days from the 'mean' date it is normally acceptable to treat each period of account as if it were a 12-month accounting period ending on the mean date.

18.4.2 Corporation tax rate

(s 3 CTA 2010)

The corporation tax rate is fixed for each financial year, which for these purposes starts on 1 April. The main rate of corporation tax was reduced from 21% to 20% on 1 April 2015.

18.4.3 Small companies rates and associated companies

(Part 3 CTA 2010)

A reduced corporation tax rate (known as the small companies' rate) applied to a company's profits if they did not exceed £300,000.

The relief was phased-out from 1 April 2015 when the corporation tax rate was reduced to 20%.

18.4.4 Payment of tax

Corporation tax automatically becomes due and payable nine months and one day from the end of the accounting period. Large companies must pay corporation tax by instalments. For these purposes, a 'large' company is one that has taxable profits of over £10m in the year, or profits of £1.5m for the current year *and* the preceding year. Both the £10m and the £1.5m limits are divided by the number of associated companies, in the same way that the £300,000 limit is reduced in determining eligibility for the small companies' rate. The instalment payments commence 14 days after the first six months of the year in question, and are due in four equal quarterly instalments. A company with a year end of 31 December will pay on 14 July, 14 October, 14 January and 14 April. Where a company's accounting period is less than 12 months long, the £1.5m and £10m profit limits are reduced proportionally and there may be fewer than four quarterly instalment payments.

Interest is charged on any unpaid tax due and is an allowable deduction. Interest is payable to the company on any overpayments and this interest is taxable.

18.5 LOAN RELATIONSHIPS

In broad terms, the tax treatment of profits and losses from loan relationships follows the accounting treatment. Rules introduced in FA 1996 (now found in parts 5 and 6 of CTA 2009) govern the tax treatment of items such as interest received and paid, premiums and discounts.

18.5.1 Scope of legislation

The legislation applies to all UK-resident companies and UK permanent establishments of overseas resident companies.

18.5.2 'Loan relationships'

(ss 294 and 302 CTA 2009)

The legislation refers to 'loan relationships' rather than loans, and these can arise where:

- a company is a debtor or creditor in respect of a money debt, and this debt arose as a result of a transaction for the lending of money; or
- an instrument is issued for the purpose of representing security for, or the rights of a creditor in respect of, a money debt.

Loan relationships therefore include bank loans, director's loans, gilts, inter-company accounts and debentures. Even where a money debt does not fall within the definition (eg trade creditors and debtors), the interest charged on such debts and some other items in respect of the debt fall within the regime.

18.5.3 Tax treatment

(s 297 CTA 2009)

In general, income and expenditure is taxed or allowed in the year it is credited or debited to the profit and loss account or, if appropriate, reserves. The company's accounting treatment must comply with GAAP (which means either UK GAAP or IFRS).

Banks are permitted to use an authorised mark-to-market basis where a loan relationship is brought into account in each accounting period at the fair value.

18.5.4 Taxation of corporate debt

(s 298 CTA 2009)

The tax treatment of corporate debt depends on whether the item arose from the trade. Debits and credits arising in an accounting period from loan relationships entered into for the company's trade purposes are treated as forming part of its trading profits or losses, whereas any debits and credits arising from activities outside the company's trade (or any loan relationships of a company without a trade) are aggregated in arriving at a profit or loss on non-trading loan relationships.

Where any expenditure or income arises partly from trading and partly from non-trading, it is split pro rata.

Taxation of non-trading profits and losses

(Chapter 16, Part 5 CTA 2009)

Net profits from non-trading loan relationships are taxed as non-trading profits. If there are net losses, these may be:

- offset against the company's profits chargeable to corporation tax for that accounting period; or
- surrendered as group relief to other group companies; or
- carried back against total profits arising in the 12 months prior to the accounting period in which the loss arose; or
- carried forward against all profits, other than trading profits, of the next period.

Claims must be made within two years of the accounting period in which the loss arose for the first three relief methods. No claim is required for losses carried forward under the fourth.

18.5.5 Connected parties

(Chapter 5, Part 5 CTA 2009)

Special rules apply when the two parties to the loan relationship are connected companies. A company and another party are connected for these purposes if one controls the other at any time or they are under the control of the same person, in that accounting period. A person controls a company if he, she or it has the power to secure that the affairs of the company are conducted in accordance with the person's wishes. This could be achieved by holding shares or possessing voting power in the company or could be conferred under the articles of association or other document regulating the affairs of that company or any other company.

18.5.6 Late interest

(Chapter 8, Part 5 CTA 2009)

The legislation originally provided that if two parties were connected (and in some other situations), then interest would only allowable when it was paid in the course of the year or within 12 months of the end of the accounting period unless the connected party was liable to UK corporation tax on the full amount of interest received.

This led to a general understanding that, if the connected party was an individual, trustee, non-resident company or exempt body such as a charity, the interest must actually be paid by the anniversary of the accounting reference date of the company to secure a deduction.

It then transpired that the denial of relief where interest is paid to a non-UK resident company is contrary to EU law. The anti-avoidance rule was suspended from 28 July 2008 whilst the Government took stock of the situation (see Revenue & Customs Brief 33/08).

The Government addressed this situation so that the late interest rule applied only to loans made by individuals or trustees or where a creditor company is resident in a 'non-qualifying' territory. This is broadly one that does not have a double taxation agreement with the UK with a non-discrimination article. FA 2015 now allows relief for interest to be claimed on a normal 'accruals basis' where the loan was made on or after 3 December 2014. For interest on pre 3 December 2014 loans, the accruals basis will generally apply only from 1 January 2016. But if the terms of a pre 3 December 2014 loan are substantially modified before 1 January 2016, the accruals basis will apply from the date of such modification.

18.5.7 Bad debts and waivers

(Chapter 6, Part 5 CTA 2009)

Generally, no tax relief is available for any losses arising from providing against or writing off bad debts on connected party loan relationships, and conversely no liability to tax arises on the borrower when such a debt is waived. However, tax relief may be available for bad debts on connected party loan relationships where the creditor company is in liquidation. This aspect of the legislation is extremely technical and specialist advice should be taken where material sums are involved.

When a company formally releases another company from an outstanding trade debt, the loan relationship rules will apply to both the company that owes the debt (the debtor) and the company which is owed this amount (the creditor). Where the two companies are unconnected, the debtor will be taxed on the release and the creditor will be able to obtain tax relief for the bad debt expense. However, if the two companies are connected, no tax charge will arise on the debtor and, similarly, the creditor cannot claim tax relief for the bad debt expense incurred.

18.5.8 Income tax deduction at source

For many years, companies were required to deduct and account to HMRC for income tax on payments of annual interest and other charges on income, with the exception of annual interest paid to a UK bank. A return form CT61 had to be submitted each quarter, detailing payments made and computing the income tax payable to HMRC. In arriving at the income tax liability due, any income tax suffered on income received under deduction of tax could be offset. Where the income tax suffered on income received exceeded the income tax payable on annual charges, the surplus could be carried forward to the next quarterly return. If at the end of the accounting period it had not proved possible to obtain credit against income tax payable, credit could be obtained against the corporation tax liability for the accounting period (and if there was no or insufficient corporation tax liability to offset any income tax credit, a repayment could be obtained from HMRC).

There is no longer any requirement for a company paying interest, etc, to deduct income tax provided the recipient is a UK-resident company.

A company is still required to deduct basic rate income tax where the recipient is an individual or a non-resident company.

Sometimes a company pays interest by issuing funding bonds. Basic rate tax has to be accounted for on the market value of funding bonds issued to individuals or non-resident companies.

18.6 INTANGIBLE ASSETS

The tax regime for intangible assets that has applied since 1 April 2002 was designed to:

- provide tax relief to companies for the cost of acquired intangibles;
- give relief in line with the amortisation in the company's accounts;
- treat gains on the disposal of relevant intangibles as taxable income but allow for roll-over relief where the proceeds are reinvested in new intangibles;
- provide transitional provisions that preserved the previous regime for intangibles held on 31 March 2002.

The legislation applies to intangible fixed assets as recognised under UK GAAP or IFRS. It is specifically stated to apply to goodwill and intellectual property, which includes patents, trademarks, registered designs, copyright and design rights; licensing and similar rights are also included.

Assets representing rights over real property (ie land and buildings), tangible moveable property, oil licences and financial assets are among the categories of intangibles specifically excluded from the regime.

18.6.1 Key concepts

The structure of the legislation is similar to that relating to corporate debt in that it identifies tax-effective accounting debits and credits in respect of expenditure incurred after 31 March 2002 on intangible fixed assets.

Debits that attract tax relief for expenditure and losses include all expenditure on an intangible fixed asset that is charged to the profit and loss account. This includes the amortisation of capitalised costs (or, at the taxpayer's option, 4% annually of that cost) and even abortive expenditure of realisation of an intangible fixed asset. A loss on the sale of such an asset (compared against its tax written-down value) also qualifies for relief.

Taxable credits include all receipts in respect of intangible fixed assets credited to the profit and loss account, gains over the tax written down value on disposal of the asset and the total proceeds of realisation of intangible fixed assets not carried on the balance sheet.

18.6.2 How debits and credits are given effect

Debits and credits are brought into account for corporation tax purposes as follows:

- assets held for the purposes of a trade – treated as a trading expense or receipt;
- assets held for the purposes of a property business – treated as an expense or receipt of the business;
- any other assets – the debits and credits are described as giving rise to non-trading losses and gains and aggregated. Credits are taxed while debits may be relieved against total profits, carried forward or surrendered as group relief.

18.6.3 Roll-over relief

Where the proceeds of the realisation of a chargeable intangible fixed asset are reinvested in whole or in part in the purchase of other intangible fixed assets, the legislation provides for a form of roll-over relief. Entitlement to relief is subject to certain conditions. The amount of the relief is calculated as follows:

- If the expenditure on new assets exceeds the proceeds of old assets, relief is the excess of proceeds over the indexed cost of the old asset.
- If the expenditure on new assets is less than the proceeds of old assets, relief is the excess of expenditure over the indexed cost of the old asset.

18.6.4 Pre-commencement intangible assets

It was never intended that a company should secure the tax reliefs under the intangibles regime by buying intangible assets already in existence at 31 March 2002. Therefore, where a company acquires assets from a related party (which includes fellow group companies or, in the case of a close company, participators in that company) and the vendor held or created those assets before 1 April 2002, the assets remain outside the intangible fixed assets regime from the perspective of the purchaser.

The tax treatment then depends on the nature of the asset concerned. Goodwill, for example, would fall within the capital gains rules as they apply to companies (see 18.7 below).

18.6.5 Acquisition of goodwill after 2 December 2014

A company cannot amortise goodwill or other intangible rights where they have been acquired from a connected person on or after 3 December 2014.

18.7 COMPANIES' CAPITAL GAINS

18.7.1 Computation of gains

Capital gains made by companies are included in their chargeable profits and are subject to corporation tax. CGT therefore does not apply to companies, although chargeable gains and losses are computed in accordance with the detailed provisions of CGT. The main differences between CGT and corporation tax on chargeable gains for companies are, first, that provisions that clearly apply only to individuals (eg the annual exemption) have no application as far as companies are concerned and, second, that computations of chargeable gains are prepared on an accounting period basis rather than by income tax years of assessment. Furthermore, companies remain entitled to indexation allowance. The total chargeable gains for an accounting period less a deduction for any allowable losses are brought into charge to corporation tax in the same way as any other source of income.

Capital losses can only be offset against chargeable gains; they cannot be offset against trading or other income. However, it is possible for another company in the group to treat a loss arising after 31 March 2000 as if it had realised that loss. That then allows it to offset the loss against its chargeable gains.

18.7.2 Roll-over relief

(ss 152–158 and 175 TCGA 1992)

Roll-over relief is available where the proceeds on the disposal of a qualifying asset are reinvested in other qualifying assets. It operates as a deferral of the corporation tax liability arising on the chargeable gain if the proceeds are fully reinvested in qualifying assets up to 12 months before or three years after the date of disposal.

Where the proceeds are only partly reinvested, a proportion of the gain is deferred or 'rolled over' and the balance (equivalent to the amount of proceeds not reinvested) is brought into charge. The element of gain deferred or rolled over is deducted from the new asset's base cost for capital gains purposes. This operates to increase the potential gain on the eventual sale of the new asset acquired, hence the term 'roll-over relief'.

Qualifying assets for this purpose are freehold and leasehold land and buildings, ships, aircraft and hovercraft, fixed plant and machinery, satellite space stations and spacecraft. Expenditure on an asset acquired from a group company (see 18.12) does not rank as qualifying expenditure for roll-over relief.

18.7.3 Disposals of substantial shareholdings

A gain accruing to a company on the disposal of a shareholding in another company is not taxable provided certain conditions are met. The exemption also applies to a disposal of an asset that derives its value from a substantial shareholding, including put or call options on the shares, securities that carry rights to acquire or dispose of the shares and interests in such securities.

The company making the disposal (the 'investing company') must have had a substantial shareholding in the company whose shares are being disposed of for a continuous 12-month period beginning not more than two years before the date of disposal.

A 'substantial shareholding' is one where the investing company is beneficially entitled to not less than 10% of:

- the ordinary share capital; and
- the profits available for distribution to equity holders of the company; and
- the assets available for distribution to equity holders of the company on a winding-up.

In addition, the following tests must be met throughout the period beginning with the start of the latest 12-month period by reference to which the substantial shareholdings test was met and ending immediately after the disposal.

(1) The investing company must have been a trading company or a member of a trading group. For this purpose, 'group' refers to a capital gains group but with a 51% ownership requirement. Non-trading activities must not be a substantial part of the vendor company/group's business. For this purpose, activities carried on by a group company that contribute to the trade of another member of the group qualify as trading. 'Substantial' is taken to be 20% or more.

(2) The company that has been invested in must have been a qualifying trading company. In practice this means that less than 20% of its assets consist of investments and less than 20% of its income is derived from non-trading activities.

Figure 18.1 – Exemption for disposals of substantial shareholdings

Conditions to be satisfied by the vendor company

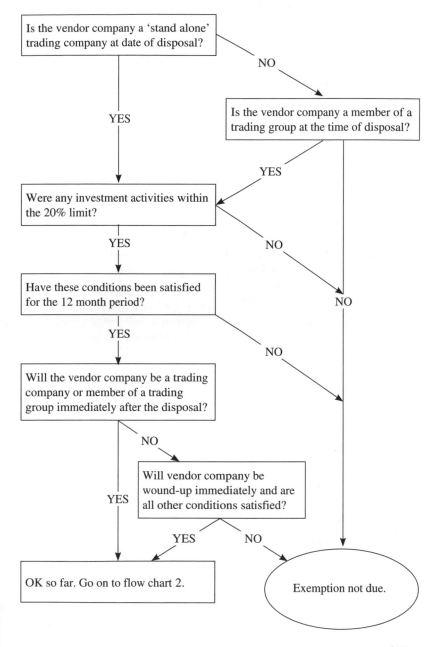

Figure 18.1 – Continued
Conditions regarding the shares which are being sold

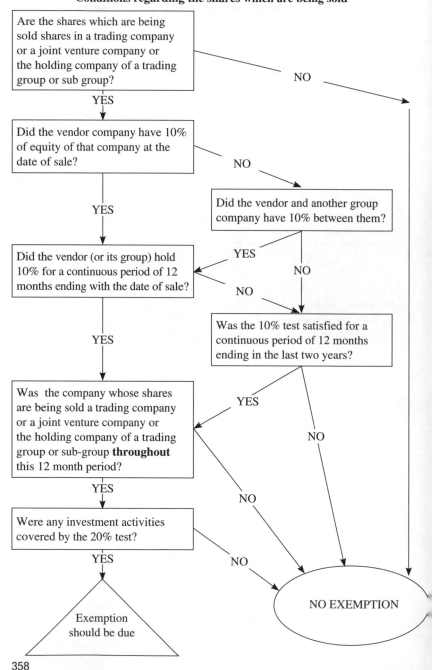

Note that this exemption can apply to disposals of shares in foreign trading companies.

In the same way that gains are exempt, losses are not normally available for offset against other chargeable gains where the substantial shareholdings conditions are met.

See the flow charts in Figure 18.1 on the main conditions that need to be satisfied. However, this relief has complex provisions and professional advice should be taken. For example, some commentaries take the view that a company can never qualify if it is liquidated immediately after selling its only subsidiary but a contrary opinion is expressed in the leading textbook (*Bramwell on Corporation Tax*) and this interpretation is reflected in the flow charts.

18.7.4 Investment trusts and REITs

Approved investment trusts are exempt from tax on capital gains. A similar exemption applies for Real Estate Investment Trusts (REITs). Both need to be quoted companies to enjoy this status.

18.8 DIVIDENDS

18.8.1 Taxation of company distributions

Company distributions are defined as any dividends, and any other distribution out of the company's assets, paid by a company in respect of shares in the company. The main exception to this is that any repayment of share capital is not regarded as a distribution of assets.

No tax deduction is available to a UK company on its making a distribution.

UK recipients of the distribution are entitled to a tax credit. This aggregate amount is described as a 'franked' payment and, as far as individuals are concerned, represents the gross equivalent of the dividend received. This amount is taxable income, but the shareholder may set the tax credit against his or her tax liability on the 'grossed-up' amount.

In most cases, dividends received from another UK company are not taxed. However, the conditions set out in the dividend exemption rules must apply. The most important condition is that the dividend does not form part of a tax avoidance scheme.

18.8.2 Advance corporation tax (abolished from 6 April 1999)

ACT was a tax that became payable when a company made distributions. This tax was then treated as a prepayment of the company's tax liability on its profits.

ACT was abolished with effect from 6 April 1999. However, if you are dealing with a company which paid substantial dividends before that date and which has not paid out a similar proportion of its post-1999 profits, you should refer to the 2007–08 edition of the *Tax Handbook* on relief for 'shadow ACT'.

18.9 LOSSES

In this section, we look first at rules on trading losses and we then cover relief for capital losses.

18.9.1 Trading losses arising in accounting period

(ss 37 and 44 CTA 2010)

When a company has a trading loss for an accounting period, it may claim that the loss arising may be offset against other profits including chargeable gains arising in that accounting period. A tax loss is computed in the same manner as taxable profits, but is restricted to losses arising from trading activities carried out on a commercial basis and with a view to realising profit.

18.9.2 Utilisation of loss relief

(ss 37 and 45 CTA 2010)

There are several ways in which a trading loss may be relieved for tax purposes apart from being offset against other profits arising in the accounting period. The loss can be carried forward to offset against trading profits from the same trade arising in succeeding accounting periods. Losses can be carried forward indefinitely in this manner for as long as the company carries on the trading activity that generated the loss. A loss may also be carried back.

Losses can be carried back and offset against profits in the 12 months immediately preceding the accounting period in which the loss was incurred.

Any trading losses carried back to a previous period can be set against any type of profits.

The company must have been carrying on the relevant trade in the earlier periods. Partial relief claims were not allowed, and relief was obtained for later years before earlier years. Relief must be obtained for the loss against other profits of the accounting period before computing the balance of the loss available for carry-back.

Tax notes

Losses can be carried back and offset against profits in the 12 months preceding the accounting period in which the loss was incurred.

18.9.3 Terminal losses

(ss 39 and 41 CTA 2010)

A trading loss arising in the accounting period in which the trade ceases may be carried back and offset against profits of the three years ending immediately before the commencement of the final period of trading.

Anti-avoidance provisions apply if the trade ceases as a result of its transfer to a person not subject to corporation tax and the transfer was part of arrangements the main purpose, or one of the main purposes, of which was to secure that terminal loss relief applied.

18.9.4 Changes in company ownership

(ss 673 to 676 CTA 2010)

There are anti-avoidance provisions designed to ensure that trading losses carried forward can only be used against future trading income from the trading activity that generated the losses. Losses may not be carried forward if:

- within any period of three years there is a change in the ownership of the company preceded or followed by a major change in the nature or conduct of the trade carried on by the company; or
- there is a change in ownership of the company at any time after the scale of activities in a trade carried on by the company has become small or negligible, and before any considerable revival in the trade.

A 'change in ownership' broadly means a change in more than 50% of the ownership of the ordinary share capital in the company. A 'major change in the nature or conduct of a trade' includes a major change in the type of property dealt in, or the services or facilities provided in the trade or in customers, outlets or markets. HMRC issued SP10/91 on some of the factors that are relevant in determining whether there has been a major change in the nature or conduct of a trade or business.

Similar anti-avoidance provisions apply for excess management expenses and other non-trading losses brought forward by a company with an investment business.

These provisions were tightened by FA 2013 with effect from 20 March 2013.

18.9.5 Foreign denominated losses

(ss 7–9 and 11–17 CTA 2010)

Where a company's primary economic activities are carried out in a currency other than sterling, it can produce its accounts and compute its profits for tax purposes in that other currency. The basic rule is that it then translates such foreign currency profits into sterling at the appropriate exchange rate for the period. If losses are carried forward or carried back, special rules apply so as to stop exchange rate fluctuations distorting loss relief claims. These rules broadly state that a loss will be converted into sterling at the rate used for conversion of the profits against which the losses are offset.

Most commonly, foreign currency losses are carried back or forward to utilise against profits in an accounting period where the profits have been calculated in the same foreign functional currency. In these circumstances the above rule will apply. However, where there has been a change in functional currency of the company so that the currency used for the period in which the loss arose is different from that used in the period the profits arose:

- the loss must first be translated at the spot rate of exchange between the two currencies;
- this loss is then translated into sterling at the rate used for conversion of the profits against which the losses are offset.

If the losses are being carried forward, the spot rate of exchange used is that operating on the first day of the period in which the functional currency changed. If the losses are being carried back the spot rate used is the one operating on the last day of the accounting period in which the old operational currency was used.

18.9.6 Capital losses

Capital losses, like capital gains, are computed in accordance with CGT rules, although the net capital gains are subject to corporation tax as part of the overall chargeable profits for the accounting period. Capital losses cannot be set against a company's other profits but they may be offset against capital gains in computing net chargeable gains. Capital losses that cannot be relieved in this way may be carried forward and offset against gains arising in subsequent accounting periods without limit. The carry-forward of capital losses is not dependent on whether the company continues to carry on its trading activity, and may be offset against gains arising on trade and non-trade assets.

18.10 OVERSEAS ASPECTS

(Part 2 TIOPA 2010)

Where a UK company has a shareholding in a foreign company, there are a number of tax provisions to be considered:

- transfer pricing (also applies to UK–UK transactions);
- controlled foreign company rules;
- double taxation relief;
- unremittable dividends;
- the regime for foreign dividends.

18.10.1 Transfer pricing

This is dealt with separately at 18.11.

18.10.2 Controlled foreign companies

A controlled foreign company or 'CFC' is one which:

- is not resident in the UK; and
- is controlled directly or indirectly by persons who are resident in the UK; and
- is subject to a 'lower level of taxation' in the territory in which it is resident.

A foreign company is treated as controlled by persons in the UK if they hold 40% of the share capital, either on their own or together with their associates.

'Lower level of taxation' means less than 75% of the tax that would be payable if the foreign company had been UK resident.

The legislation on CFCs has been in place for over 20 years. The business community has been unhappy with its complexity.

18.10.3 Fundamental reform

The Finance Act 2012 repealed the previous CFC legislation and replaced it with a new regime.

The business profits of a foreign subsidiary are now outside the scope of the new CFC regime if they meet the specified conditions set out in a 'gateway test'. The conditions define what is to be treated for the purposes of the regime as profits artificially diverted from the UK.

Safe harbours are provided for the gateway conditions covering general commercial business, incidental finance income and some sector specific rules. A foreign subsidiary can rely on these safe harbours to show that some or all of its profits are outside the regime's scope.

As an alternative to the gateway test, the regime also provides certain exemptions for CFCs. The exemptions will apply to the CFC as a whole and include an excluded territory exemption and a low profits exemption. The 'lower level of tax test', which previously formed part of the definition of a CFC, is an exemption under the new regime.

The regime includes rules for finance companies which will generally result in an effective tax rate on intra-group finance income of one-quarter of the main CT rate or full exemption in certain circumstances.

Tax notes

The CFC rules are still not straightforward and readers should obtain professional advice if they believe that they may be affected by this legislation.

18.10.4 Branch profits

An opt-in exemption regime for UK companies with foreign branches was introduced by FA 2011.

Once a company has made the necessary irrevocable election, profits arising in all of its current and future overseas branches will be permanently exempt from UK corporation tax. Should any of the branches make losses, those losses will not be available to offset against the company's profits. A transitional measure deals with those companies with branches that have realised losses in any of the six years before applying the exemption. Under this rule, a company's branch profits will become exempt as soon as the tax losses of those branches in the immediately preceding six years have been matched by profits. A special rule applies to very large losses (those over £50m).

The exemption applies to the trading profits, investment income and chargeable gains that are effectively connected to the branches concerned. Trading profits and chargeable gains are defined with reference to the relevant double tax treaty. Investment income must be genuinely connected to the business to qualify for the exemption. In other words, the economic ownership of the assets that generate the income should lie with the branch. However, the exemption is not available to a company whose business is wholly or mainly investment business.

18.10.5 Patent box

The Finance Bill 2012 introduced the patent box regime. This allows companies to elect to apply a 10% rate of corporation tax to all profits attributable to qualifying intellectual property (IP). The patent box applies to existing and new IP. It will also apply to IP which has been purchased, provided that the group has further developed the IP or the product which incorporates it. The small claims safe harbour will be limited to companies making profits with residual profits of no more than £3m.

Qualifying IP includes patents granted by the UK Intellectual Property Office (IPO) and the European Patent Office (EPO), as well as supplementary protection certificates, regulatory data protection and plant variety rights. The Government intends to extend the patent box to other EU member states which have similar examination and patentability criteria as the UK.

Key features of the new regime are as follows:

- entry into the regime is optional, to avoid placing a compliance burden on businesses that may only receive marginal benefit;
- the intention is that all patents first commercialised after 29 November 2010 qualify for inclusion, subject to specific qualification and transitional rules;
- the patent box is available for both royalty income and embedded income included in the price of the patented products;
- the intention is for the preferential rate to apply to net patent income after associated expenses (including pre-commercialisation expenses); and
- the relief is not meant to incentivise the purely passive holding of IP.

18.10.6 Double taxation relief

A UK resident company may claim a credit for foreign tax paid on income or capital gains arising from any overseas source. Credit is available against the corporation tax liability payable on the same income or gains. Relief may be due either under the provisions of a double taxation agreement between the UK and the overseas country concerned, or under the general rules for 'unilateral relief' as provided in s 2 *et seq.* TIOPA 2010. Where credit is due under a double taxation agreement, the relevant agreement takes precedence over UK domestic legislation.

For most types of income and gains, the full amount is brought into charge for the purpose of computing the corporation tax liability on chargeable profits for the accounting period. Any overseas tax suffered is then offset by way of credit against the corporation tax liability. The amount of credit available is limited to the corporation tax liability on the source of income or gain that has suffered overseas tax. No relief is due for the excess foreign tax paid.

Further relief may be available for dividends received. In addition to relief for withholding or other taxes suffered on payment of the dividend, relief may also be available for the foreign tax suffered on the profits out of which the dividend has been paid. This is known as 'underlying tax', for which relief is given automatically if the UK-recipient company controls 10% or more of the voting share capital in the overseas company paying the dividend. The dividend taxable in the UK is grossed up at the rate of underlying tax applicable to the profits out of which the dividend has been paid. This, together with any withholding and other taxes suffered on payment of the dividend, can then be offset against the corporation tax liability arising on the grossed up equivalent of the dividend received (subject to the restriction that underlying tax relief cannot exceed the corporation tax liability on the same income).

In the vast majority of cases, overseas dividends are not taxed in the UK due to the dividend exemption (section 18.3).

Where double tax relief would be lost (eg where no corporation tax liability arises for the accounting period) it is possible to obtain relief for overseas tax paid by treating the tax as an expense in computing profits of the company's trade.

18.10.7 DTR on dividends

FA 2009 retrospectively amended the double tax relief rules applicable to overseas dividends received by UK companies since 1 April 2008. These rules restrict the amount of relief available using a formula which makes reference to the corporation tax rate in force on the date the dividend is paid. Where the actual rate of UK tax paid by the recipient company is different (because, for example, the rate of corporation tax changes during the accounting period) this produces a mismatch. The FA 2009 amendment ensures that double tax relief is limited by reference to the actual corporation tax suffered on the dividend concerned.

18.10.8 Unremittable income

Where an overseas source of income is taxable on an arising basis but it is not possible to remit the income because of government actions in the overseas territory, it is possible to make a claim to defer the corporation tax liability until such time as sufficient funds are remitted to the UK to satisfy the liability. A claim under these circumstances may be made to HMRC at any time within four years of the end of the accounting period in which the income arises.

18.11 TRANSFER PRICING RULES

(Part 4 TIOPA 2010)

Transfer pricing tax rules are designed to prevent related parties that are subject to different levels of taxation from entering into uncommercial transactions which move profits into a lower level of taxation. The rules require corporation tax to be computed as if transactions had been carried out on arm's-length terms. This may result in a UK company having profits imputed to it which substantially exceed the actual profits.

The scope of the transfer pricing rules was extended from 1 April 2004 to include UK-to-UK related party transactions. Previously, these rules only applied to cross-border transactions.

The change was forced on the UK Government by European Court of Justice (ECJ) decisions. In a number of cases the ECJ decided that the UK rules were invalid because, by exempting UK-to-UK related party transactions, they were discriminatory under EC law.

This means that now, for tax purposes, all related party transactions that are not carried out on an arm's-length basis may trigger investigations and tax adjustments. However, for UK-to-UK transactions, HMRC allows a compensating reduction in the profits of the other party to the transaction (ie if costs are disallowed for one party, the corresponding income should not be taxed in the other).

18.11.1 Related parties

Related parties can be companies, individuals, partnerships and trusts where a control relationship exists (ie one party controls the other). A transaction can be anything from a normal sale of goods to the use of one party's assets or lending arrangements.

Fortunately, many small and medium-sized businesses are exempt from the rules. The exemption applies to all related parties in the same control relationship (including entities based outside the UK) and is based on their combined number of employees and turnover. Small groups, those that have not more than 50 employees and either total turnover or total assets of no more than £10m, will not need to self-assess.

Medium-sized groups, those with not more than 250 employees and either an annual turnover of less than £50m or net assets of less than £43m, should maintain records of relevant transactions. HMRC has the power to require any medium-sized business to apply an arm's-length price where there has been blatant manipulation of transaction prices leading to a significant loss of UK tax.

Businesses close to the limits should watch out for seasonal staffing increases because these count, pro rata, towards the annual limits.

If staffing limits are breached at any point during an account year, transactions during the whole account year are subject to the rules and documentation requirements.

Neither exemption applies if the transaction is with a party resident outside the UK, unless they are in a country with which the UK has a double tax treaty that includes a non-discrimination article.

18.11.2 Keeping up to date

If your business carries out transactions with related parties, the first thing to establish is whether or not the small enterprise exemption applies. If not, then you will need to identify which related party transactions may not be on an arm's-length basis and assess what records should be maintained. Only a higher level review may be needed if the medium-sized exemption applies, but detailed records and analysis will be needed if your business is part of a larger group.

18.12 GROUPS OF COMPANIES

18.12.1 Group relationships

(Part 5 CTA 2010)

There are special rules that apply to groups of companies. For corporation tax purposes, a group relationship exists between two companies if one company holds not less than 75% of the other's ordinary share capital, or if both companies are 75% subsidiaries of a third company. At one time, such companies had to be UK-resident 75% subsidiaries of a UK-resident parent company, but the rules now allow UK-resident subsidiaries of non-resident companies to constitute a group for UK tax purposes.

The definition of a 75% subsidiary was amended by FA 2009 in order to ensure that companies do not fall outside of loss relief and capital gains groups as a result of issuing certain types of preference shares to external investors such as financial institutions.

The rules that define whether companies form a group for loss relief and capital gains purposes have included provisions which require the interests of all equity holders to be taken into account in determining the interest that a parent has in its subsidiaries. These rules required loans to be taken into account where, in certain circumstances, the loan is convertible into shares. This has led to some group relief relationships being broken on the issue of loans, despite the fact that the loans may never be converted into equity. Changes were made by FA 2012 so that loan notes issued to third parties, where the notes have a right to conversion into shares in a company listed on a recognised stock exchange, will be treated as normal commercial loans and will therefore not prejudice the group position.

18.12.2 Use of losses

(ss 99–110 CTA 2010)

Where one company in a group makes a tax loss for an accounting period, it may 'surrender' that loss to a member of the group for offset against that company's taxable profits. For this purpose, losses available for surrender include charges on income to the extent that they exceed profits chargeable to corporation tax. Where the accounting periods of the surrendering and claimant companies do not coincide, the amount of loss to be surrendered is restricted on a time basis reflecting the length of the accounting periods common to both companies.

For group relief purposes, the requirement for a 75% shareholding relationship is extended so that the company owning the shares must also be beneficially entitled to 75% or more of the profits available for distribution to equity shareholders, and of assets available for distribution in a winding-up. This requirement prevents group relief being secured by the use of ordinary shares which carry limited rights to dividends, etc. See 18.12.1 on FA 2009 changes which are intended to ensure that the existence of certain types of preference shares do not create problems in this regard.

Group relief is not available for losses in an accounting period during which arrangements exist for the company to leave the group.

The legislation originally required that the company seeking to surrender a loss must be UK-resident but this requirement was successfully challenged by Marks and Spencer before the ECJ. FA 2006 introduced provisions that in theory allow group relief for a non UK-resident company's losses but such relief is dependent on various tests, which in practice are rarely satisfied. The UK's legislation was referred to the EC as a result. The FA 2013 introduced changes but it is still extremely difficult to secure relief.

18.12.3 Capital gains

(ss 171 and 175 TCGA 1992)

For capital gains purposes, chargeable assets may be transferred from one group company to another without tax consequences. Such transfers are treated as if made on a no gain/no loss basis and the recipient company will take over the assets' capital gains base cost from the transferor company. A capital gains tax group exists where at least 75% of the ordinary share capital is beneficially owned (directly or indirectly) by the principal company. This is extended to 75% subsidiaries of subsidiaries provided the subsidiary company in question is an effective 51% subsidiary of the principal company.

For roll-over relief purposes, all the trades carried on by group companies are treated as a single trade and therefore it is possible to roll over a gain made on qualifying assets by one group member against qualifying expenditure incurred by another group member within the appropriate timescale. Roll-over relief is generally available only for trading companies within a group although, by concession, relief is also available for a property-holding company where the properties are used for trading purposes by the other group members.

TCGA 1992 does not allow losses of one company in a group to be set off against gains of another group company. However, since 1 April 2000, two members of a group may jointly elect for the gain or loss arising on the disposal of an asset outside the group by one of them to be attributed to the other company. Previously, the asset had to be actually transferred to the company that wished to make use of the gain or loss.

18.12.4 Transfer of a business within a group

Where a trading activity is transferred from one group company to another, relief is available under ss 939–953 CTA 2010, to ensure that the company transferring the trade does not suffer balancing charges on assets that have qualified for capital allowances. The successor company merely takes over the tax residue for capital allowances purposes relating to those assets. Generally, all unrelieved trade losses are also transferred with the trade to the successor company.

This relief also applies where a trade is transferred to another company that is under 75% common control, even though it is not a member of a group.

18.13 INVESTMENT COMPANIES

(ss 1217–1255 CTA 2009)

A company with an investment business is able to claim relief for management expenses. A company with an investment business is a company whose business consists wholly or partly of making investments. It is possible for a company be a 'hybrid company' which undertakes both trading and investment activity, thereby taking relief for both trading costs and management expenses. The expenses of managing a UK-resident company with an investment business are deductible in computing its total profits from that investment activity for corporation tax purposes. Where management expenses exceed the company's chargeable income and gains for an accounting period, the surplus may be carried forward and treated as management expenses incurred in the next succeeding accounting period, and may continue to be carried forward until relieved. Surplus management expenses may also be surrendered as group relief from one group company to another. Expenses brought forward from previous periods are not available for surrender as group relief.

18.14 CLOSE COMPANIES

(Part 10 CTA 2010)

18.14.1 Definition

(s 439 CTA 2010)

Companies that are under the control of five or fewer persons, or are under the control of their directors, are known as 'close companies'. There are special provisions designed to ensure that such individuals cannot take undue advantage of corporation tax legislation by virtue of their positions of influence over the company's affairs.

A person controls a company if, in fact, he or she is able to exercise control directly or indirectly over its affairs by owning the greater part of its share capital, voting capital, or other capital giving entitlement to more than half the assets on a winding-up. Shareholders and certain loan creditors in a close company are known as 'participators'.

18.14.2 Loans to participators

(ss 455–464 CTA 2010)

Where a close company makes a loan or advances any money to a participator, or an associate of a participator, there is a liability to account for an amount of tax equal to 25% of the loan.

This tax falls due on the normal corporation tax due dates of the company's accounting period in which the loan is made; no tax need be paid if the loan is repaid before the tax falls due. Where the loan is repaid after the tax falls due, the repayment of tax is not due until nine months and a day after the accounting period in which the loan is actually repaid.

Regardless of when the loan was originally made, if it is wholly or partly written off or released, the borrower is treated as receiving, as part of his or her total income, an amount equal to the amount so written off, grossed up at the lower rate of income tax. While no basic or lower rate tax liability arises, there may be a further liability to higher rate tax collected via the self-assessment regime. From 24 March 2010, it is specifically provided that companies cannot obtain a corporation tax deduction on the release of such a loan.

A number of loopholes in s 455 CTA 2010 were closed by FA 2013. There is now a '30 day rule' where loans are repaid and then new loans are granted. Also s 455 can now bite where a close company makes a loan to a partnership in which a participator is a member.

18.14.3 Close investment-holding companies

(s 34 CTA 2010)

These are close companies carrying on specific investment-holding activities. For this purpose, investment-holding activities do not include carrying on a trade on a commercial basis, property holding, or holding shares in companies carrying on either of these activities. An exception to this rule is a company that exists wholly or mainly for holding property rented to connected persons.

A close investment-holding company did not qualify for the small companies' corporation tax rate. With this relief having been phased-out on 1 April 2015, it does not seem that a company being a close investment-holding company carries any disadvantages.

18.15 REAL ESTATE INVESTMENT TRUSTS (REITS)

A REIT is a listed property company that has elected for REIT status in the UK.

The broad rationale is that a REIT itself pays no corporation tax at the company level on qualifying activities. Instead, tax is payable by the shareholders on distributions received – this applies to both rental profits and capital gains.

However, a withholding tax of 20% applies to most distributions by a REIT to its investors. The main exceptions are where the investors are UK-resident companies or various exempt bodies.

Qualifying distributions received from a REIT are treated as rental income rather than dividends. This means that investors can use their personal allowances to mitigate any tax charge.

18.16 RESEARCH AND DEVELOPMENT (R&D) TAX RELIEF

Research & development tax relief is available to all companies that incur expenditure on qualifying R&D activities. The relief works by increasing the companies' tax deductible R&D costs.

18.16.1 Small and medium-sized entities

The rate of relief available to SMEs on qualifying expenditure was 225% for the period 1 April 2012–31 March 2015. The relief has been increased to 230% with effect from 1 April 2015.

Accordingly, this amounts to relief at an effective rate of 46%.

In some cases, SMEs can choose to claim a tax credit by surrendering the tax relief available on qualifying expenditure. This is typically where the company is loss-making and therefore would otherwise have merely carried forward a trading loss enhanced by the uplifted tax relief. The value of the tax credit has been increased to 33.5% by FA 2015.

An SME is defined for these purposes as a company with fewer than 500 employees and either turnover not exceeding £100m or a balance sheet total of not more than £86m. This data can be drawn from the company's statutory accounts. However, where a company is owned 25% or more by another company then a proportion of that company's data will need to be aggregated in assessing whether the limits are exceeded. There are exemptions to this rule where the ownership does not exceed 50% and is held by certain types of investors. Where the company is part of a group or under the control of another company then the consolidated data of the group needs to be taken into account.

In addition to being an SME enterprise as per the above definition, a company has also needed to meet all the following conditions:

- carry on a trade with its accounts prepared as a going concern;
- retain any intellectual property created as a result of the R&D.

18.16.2 Large companies

R&D expenditure by large companies may attract relief on 130% of the cost. Alternatively, the company may take an 'above the line' repayable credit of 11% of its qualifying expenditure.

18.16.3 Definition of research and development

The definition of R&D is set out in the *DTI Guidelines on the Meaning of Research and Development for Tax Purposes* dated 5 March 2004 and can be found on HMRC's website (www.hmrc.gov.uk/manuals/cirdmanual/cird81900.htm). The significant points covered in the guidelines are that:

- R&D for tax purposes takes place when a project seeks to achieve an advance in science or technology with activities that directly contribute to the resolution of scientific or technological uncertainty.
- Certain indirect activities related to a qualifying project also qualify.
- Activities other than qualifying indirect activities that do not directly contribute to the resolution of scientific or technological uncertainty in a project do not qualify as R&D.

The interpretation of certain areas of the DTI guidelines has been the subject of much debate between HMRC and tax advisers and in 2009 HMRC confirmed its view on production activities related to R&D whilst also announcing a change in its approach to indirect activities.

With regard to production activities it was confirmed that where the intention behind the activity is the manufacture or attempted manufacture of goods, or the delivery or attempted delivery of services, for customers, then the activity will not qualify as an R&D activity. However, where the manufacturing activity is undertaken solely to resolve technological uncertainties aimed at advancing technology then it may do so.

Indirect activities as listed in section 31 of the DTI guidelines have long been disputed by HMRC as qualifying for relief. However, in 2009 it relented and confirmed that as long as the activity was specifically identifiable as a particular part of the activity of an R&D project it could qualify. There is no effective date for this change so any corporation tax returns which are still open may be amended to reflect this.

18.16.4 Qualifying R&D costs

A claim for R&D tax relief may be made in respect of the following qualifying cost categories:

- staffing costs – including employers' NIC and pension costs but excluding benefits in kind;
- computer software;
- consumable or transformable materials;
- payments for externally provided workers – only where the payment is made to a company and the workers who are being provided are employees of that agency company;
- payments to the subjects of clinical trials;
- payments made in respect of subcontracting out an R&D activity.

Under the SME provisions, if any of the above costs are subsidised then they will not be eligible for R&D tax relief. If the subsidy is notified state aid, then the expenditure is treated as subsidised if it is or has been obtained in respect of the whole or part of the above expenditure or received in respect of any other expenditure associated with the same R&D project. Accordingly, any notified state aid subsidy in respect of the R&D project is capable of disqualifying all of the expenditure on that project.

Where the qualifying costs are met wholly or partly by a grant or subsidy which is not a notified state aid or by someone other than the company, then only the element that is subsidised will not be eligible for R&D and the remaining unsubsidised element will be eligible for R&D tax relief.

These restrictions do not apply to claims made under the large company relief provisions and therefore in such circumstances an SME may be able to make a claim under the provisions for those subsidised costs.

18.17 ECA TAX CREDITS

Loss-making companies carrying on a qualifying activity can surrender losses in exchange for a cash payment provided:

- the losses are attributable to 100% first-year allowances available on designated energy-saving or environmentally beneficial plant and machinery;
- the losses cannot be otherwise relieved by the company; and
- the qualifying expenditure was incurred on or after 1 April 2008.

The amount of the first-year tax credit that will be paid to the company is equal to 19% of the losses being surrendered, although it cannot exceed the greater of:

- the total of the company's PAYE and NIC for the chargeable period; or
- £250,000.

Any first-year tax credit will be clawed back if the qualifying plant and machinery is sold within four years of the end of the period in which the first-year tax credit was paid.

The lists for designated energy-saving or environmentally beneficial plant and machinery can be found at https://etl.decc.gov.uk/etl/site.html.

18.18 SALE OF LESSOR COMPANIES: ANTI-AVOIDANCE

Where there is a change in ownership of a company that carries on a business of leasing plant and machinery (either on its own or in partnership with other companies), a tax charge arises at the time of the sale on profits that have been earned but not yet taxed, because of the mismatch between recognition of leasing income for tax and accounting purposes.

18.19 iXBRL AND ONLINE FILING

18.19.1 iXBRL

Online filing is now mandatory for all corporation tax returns. Paper returns are no longer accepted, and online returns must (with very few exceptions) be filed using the iXBRL standard reporting language. Similarly, corporation tax must also be paid electronically.

A complete corporation tax return includes the tax computation and accounts alongside the return (CT600), so iXBRL tags in the correct form must be applied to each of these elements.

iXBRL tagging is complex, with thousands of possible tags (collectively termed the 'taxonomy' by HMRC). Any staff members who undertake it will need a good understanding of the taxonomy. In addition, if you submit your own corporation tax returns, you will need to use the facilities on the HMRC website (but these are very basic) or use specialist tax software.

To avoid the need to maintain such software and expertise in-house, you could consider asking your accountant to produce your accounts and submit CT600 for you in the correct iXBRL format. Your accountant should be able to produce accounts using their standard template for a fixed (relatively low) additional fee, which should include the time spent reviewing the iXBRL file independently of the accounts. For customised accounts, tailored to your specific requirements, it is likely that fees will increase substantially. Your accountant will then ask you to review and approve the final iXBRL document that is to be submitted with your corporation tax return.

Sets of tags (taxonomies) have been created for accounts prepared using UK GAAP (around 5,300 tags) and for accounts prepared using IFRS (up to 3,800 tags). HMRC requires full tagging of accounts. To view the taxonomies online, as well as guidance on iXBRL and online filing generally, go to www.hmrc.gov.uk/thelibrary/ct-online.htm\#4.

Submitted files may be rejected by HMRC, even after being apparently accepted by the HMRC online filing gateway at the time of submission, if there is a shortfall in the iXBRL tagging.

18.19.2 Charity returns concession

Charities required to prepare accounts under the Companies Act 2006 or the Friendly and Industrial and Provident Societies Act 1968 are also required to file their company tax return and accounts and computations online.

Therefore, as a transitional measure, HMRC will continue to accept accounts from smaller charities in PDF format although the tax computations must be filed in iXBRL format (because the free HMRC software can be used). Where no computation is required because all income and gains of the charity are exempt from tax (ie form CT600E is filed), a charity can simply attach a PDF of a letter stating so.

A smaller charity is defined as one where the combined income of the charity and any wholly owned subsidiaries does not exceed £6.5 million for the accounting period. In addition, unincorporated associations and charities that are incorporated by guarantee, shares or charter can also continue to submit accounts as a PDF with computations in iXBRL format. However, subsidiary companies of charities are required to submit returns, accounts and computations in iXBRL format. Unincorporated charities are not required to file using iXBRL.

These transitional arrangements will end when HMRC is able to provide free online filing software that is suitable for charity returns.

18.20 CLAIMS, ELECTIONS AND PENALTIES

Throughout the Taxes Acts there are various claims for relief from corporation tax that must be lodged with HMRC and, in practice, are made to the tax office dealing with the company's affairs. Unless otherwise specified by legislation, claims must be made within four years of the end of the accounting period to which they relate. The most common claims and elections are set out below, together with the time limit by which the claim or election must be made. HMRC does not generally have discretion to accept claims made after the time limit has expired for a particular claim unless the legislation (or HMRC practice) allows otherwise.

In practice, most claims are normally made in the CTSA return form CT600.

Claim	Time limit for submission	Reference
Trading losses offset against other income of accounting period	2 years	s 37 CTA 2010
Trading losses carried back	2 years	s 37 CTA 2010
Terminal loss relief	2 years	s 39 CTA 2010
Capital allowances	2 years	s 3 CAA 2001
Group relief	2 years	Chapter 4, Part 5 CTA 2010
Roll-over relief	4 years	s 152 TCGA 1992

18.20.1 Error and mistake relief claims; recovery of overpaid tax

Relief may be claimed within four years against any over-assessment to corporation tax because of an error or mistake in, or an omission from, any return or statement. No relief is due where the information was not used to form the basis of an assessment, or where the assessment was made in accordance with practice generally prevailing at the time of issue. An error or mistake claim under para 51, Schedule 18, FA 1998 (as amended by Schedule 52, FA 2009) should be made to HMRC.

Amended Schedule18 goes into much more prescriptive detail than its predecessor. The gist of the rules has, however, not changed, although prescribed circumstances are now listed at paras 51A to 51C where such claims will not be entertained. These include cases where the taxpayer knew (or ought to have known) that relief could have been claimed before a certain period expired (such as the tax return amendment window or the time limit to appeal against an assessment) but did not do so.

18.20.2 Penalties

- Failure to notify chargeability – for obligations arising on or after 1 April 2009, Schedule 41 FA 2008 introduced an amended penalty regime for failing to notify chargeability to tax, based on the same principles as those contained in Schedule 24 FA 2007 for penalising incorrect returns.

- Filing deadline – 12 months after accounting reference date – Schedule 55 FA 2009, contains details of changes to the penalty system, and has applied since 1 April 2011. In addition to the £100 penalty for submitting a return late, a penalty of £10 may be applied for each day that the failure continues during the period of 90 days beginning with the date specified in a notice given by HMRC. If a return is more than six months late, the penalty will be the higher of 5% of any liability to tax which would have been shown in the return in question, and £300. If the failure continues for more than 12 months and the taxpayer has deliberately withheld information that would enable HMRC to assess the tax due, this becomes the greater of 100% of any liability to tax which would have been shown in the return in question, and £300. If the withholding of the information is deliberate and concealed, the penalty is the greater of 100% of any liability to tax that would have been shown in the return in question, and £300. If the withholding of the information is deliberate but not concealed, the penalty is the greater of 70% of any liability to tax that would have been shown in the return, and £300. In any other case, the penalty will be the greater of 5% of any liability to tax which would have been shown in the return, and £300. Higher penalties (up to double the amount of tax due) can be charged where the withheld information concerns offshore matters.

- Error in return – tax-related penalty of between 30% and 100% of potential lost revenue.

- Failure to keep proper records – penalty currently up to £3,000.

- Failure to produce documents for an enquiry – penalty £300 plus a daily fine of up to £60.

19

FINANCING YOUR BUSINESS

This chapter contains the following sections:

(1) Financing through own resources
(2) Financing through personal borrowing
(3) Issuing additional shares (with and without tax incentives)
(4) Borrowing through the business
(5) Financing assets
(6) Cash flow management

19.1 FINANCING THROUGH OWN RESOURCES

19.1.1 Separate funding

The establishment of a partnership or the incorporation of a limited liability company allows an individual to separate and invest funds to provide capital for a business. In the case of a partnership, funds can be made available through contributions to a partner's capital account or the subscription of quotas. In the case of limited liability companies, funding can be made through subscription to newly issued share capital. The purchase of shares in a company from an existing shareholder or a partnership interest from an existing partner does not provide additional liquid funds to the company or partnership. Further capital can be subscribed as necessary to fund the growth of the business, through additional contributions to the partner's capital account, or subscription to quotas or additional share issues.

In the case of a sole trader, funds may be put into a separate business bank account but there is no formal separation of assets between the business and its owner.

The capital accounts of partners can be either interest-bearing or free of interest. The decision lies with the partners and will be reflected in the partnership deed. The payment of interest by a partnership to partners is treated as an allocation of partnership income to the specific partner and will be included as partnership income of that partner for tax purposes.

Limited liability companies do not pay interest on funds that have been subscribed as share capital. Preference shares can be used to give a recurrent and fixed dividend on an equity base, with preference dividends paid out in priority to ordinary dividends. For UK tax on income and capital gains, preference dividends are treated in the same way as other dividends.

An individual who is a shareholder in a company can provide funds to the company by way of a loan as well as, or instead of, subscribing for shares. Such loan accounts fall within the loan relationship rules and the charge in the profit and loss account for any interest charged will normally be followed for tax purposes, subject to observing the conditions applicable to connected party transactions (see 18.5.5).

19.1.2 Losses on funding a sole trader's business

Because there is no effective separation of funds paid into the business, no specific relief is given for the loss of such funds. As with partnerships, relief for losses that have arisen and resulted in the failure of a business will be given under the various specific headings of the tax legislation (see 7.7).

19.1.3 Losses on capital investments in partnerships

No specific income tax relief is given for losses of capital invested in a partnership. A partner's share of trading losses can be relieved against his or her other income (see 7.7). A capital loss may arise on an individual retiring from the firm if payment has been made to acquire the partnership interest.

19.1.4 Loss on shares

(ss 131–133 ITA 2007)

If an individual acquires shares in a company through subscribing for the shares and realises a loss on those shares, then, subject to various conditions being satisfied, the loss can be set off against the income of the individual for the year in which the loss is suffered or for the previous year. The conditions placed on this relief are given at 17.2.

A qualifying loss is calculated according to CGT principles. A claim to set the loss off against income has to be made within one year from 31 January of the year following that in which the loss arose. A loss not so used can be carried forward as a loss for CGT purposes.

Normal CGT rules apply to losses on shares in companies when the shares have not been acquired through subscribing for the shares.

19.2 FINANCING THROUGH PERSONAL BORROWING

To be able to finance a business entirely from personal resources is a rare luxury; in most cases borrowing will be required. Such borrowing can be through the business itself (see 19.4), or drawn down personally by the individual. The form of security that has to be provided as a condition of the loan being made is not significant; whether the individual obtains tax relief on the interest depends on satisfying the conditions in the tax legislation.

19.2.1 Loans to invest in partnerships

(ss 398–400 ITA 2007)

An individual can claim relief against income for interest paid on eligible loans (see 11.4). Conditions are that the loan is used:

- to purchase a share in a partnership; or
- to contribute capital to a partnership or to make an advance to a partnership where the advance is used wholly for the purposes of the trade profession or vocation carried on by the partnership; or
- to pay off another qualifying loan.

The borrower:

- must be a member of the partnership throughout the period during which the interest expense arises;
- must not have recovered any capital from the partnership since the loan has been drawn down.

19.2.2 Interest on loans to invest in companies

(ss 392–395 ITA 2007)

An individual can claim relief against income for interest paid on eligible loans (see 11.5). Conditions are that:

- the loan is used to purchase shares in a close company; or
- the loan is used by a close company for its business purposes; or
- the loan is used to pay off another loan that would have qualified for relief;
- the individual alone or with associates owns a material interest in the close company (material interest being defined as more than 5% of the ordinary share capital of the company or the right to receive more than 5% of the assets of the company on a winding-up of the company); or
- the individual holds less than 5% of the ordinary share capital but works for the greater part of the time in the management or conduct of the company or an associated company;
- the company is a qualifying company.

Status as a qualifying company depends on the activity. The close company must exist wholly or mainly:

- to carry on a trade or trades on a commercial basis;
- to make investments in land or property let commercially to unconnected parties;

- to hold shares or securities or to make loans to qualifying companies or intermediate companies that are under the control of the company (qualifying meaning that the business of the company falls under one of the two headings immediately above);
- to co-ordinate the administration of two or more qualifying companies.

Relief for interest expense on a loan can continue if the company ceases to be close at a time after the loan has been drawn down provided that the other conditions continue to be satisfied.

19.2.3 Definitions

(ss 439–441 CTA 2009)

A close company is a company that is resident in the UK or (from 2014–15) elsewhere in the EEA and which is under the control of five or fewer persons (see 18.14.1). Interests of associates are taken into account when testing.

Ordinary share capital, for these purposes, comprises all shares other than those that can participate in distributions only at a fixed rate.

19.2.4 Loans to invest in employee-controlled companies

(ss 396–397 ITA 2007)

Interest on qualifying loans drawn down to acquire shares in companies controlled by employees can also qualify for relief. The excess of an individual's holding over 10% of the shares of the company is treated as being owned by a person who is not an employee of the company when testing whether the company is employee-controlled, so this relief is likely to be of limited use when financing a business. For the conditions to be met for a qualifying loan, see 11.6.

19.3 ISSUING ADDITIONAL SHARES (WITH AND WITHOUT TAX INCENTIVES)

A limited liability company can obtain funds through the issue of additional share capital in return for cash payments. If the additional shares are placed through a rights issue, in which the share allocation is proportional to existing shareholdings, the company will only receive additional funds to the extent that the shareholders make payment for the new shares. The share subscription can be structured as an issue to new or existing shareholders, without specific tax advantages, or to qualify as an investment under the Enterprise Investment Scheme, the Venture Capital Trust scheme or the Corporate Venturing Scheme.

In all cases, the effect of the share issue in diluting the ownership interests of existing shareholders will need to be considered.

19.3.1 Share issue without tax incentives

If the share issue is not to be structured to be a qualifying investment under a tax incentive scheme:

(1) The terms and conditions of the share issue and the amount of the issue are a decision for the owner and, if applicable, the other shareholders in the company.

(2) The shares taken up in return for the new investment will be an asset for CGT purposes with the gain or loss on disposal being calculated according to the normal rules of CGT.

(3) Tax relief for interest paid on qualifying loans will be available subject to the required conditions being met (see 19.2.1 above); otherwise the issue will not attract tax relief or incentives.

Share issues to venture capitalists may be structured through venture capital trusts; see 19.3.8 below, or as an issue that does not attract tax relief in which case the above three points will apply.

19.3.2 Enterprise Investment Scheme

(Part 5 ITA 2007)

The Enterprise Investment Scheme (EIS) provides tax incentives for individuals to encourage investment in shares in companies that meet certain conditions and carry on qualifying activities. It is intended to help small, higher risk, unquoted trading companies raise start-up and expansion finance by issuing ordinary shares.

Individuals investing in companies qualifying under the EIS can claim income tax relief at a rate of 30% on the first £1m invested.

The maximum annual amount that can be raised by an individual company from EIS or Venture Capital Trust investments is £5m and the maximum limit on gross assets held by the investee company before any investment is £15m. The maximum permitted number of employees of the company is fewer than 250 (previously fewer than 50).

This section provides a summary of the conditions that have to be met for the investment to qualify and continue to qualify during the required holding period (see 25.4 for a more detailed analysis). The trade-off for the current shareholder or shareholders in the company is between the ability to access funds through the share issue (investors may not be prepared to make an investment in the absence of tax relief) and the continuing commitments (which are likely to be legally enforceable through contractual obligations required by investors) for the company to continue to comply with the conditions.

19.3.3 EIS conditions relating to the company

(ss 172–188 ITA 2007)

For EIS to apply:

(1) The issue must be of new ordinary shares in the company; the shares cannot have preference features.
(2) The company cannot have assets of more than £15m before the share issue and £16m after the issue.
(3) The company (or group of companies) must have fewer than 250 full-time employees or their equivalents at the time the shares are issued.
(4) The company must have raised no more than £5m under EIS or the Corporate Venturing Scheme or as a qualifying holding for a Venture Capital Trust (see below). If the limit is exceeded, none of the shares within the issue that causes the limit to be breached will qualify for EIS. The £5m limit was to have been £10m but had to be cut back because it would have breached EU rules.
(5) The company must be unquoted (although the shares of the company can be listed on the AIM) and there must be no arrangements under which the company can become quoted.
(6) The company cannot be under the control of another company, or another company and associated persons and there must be no arrangements under which it can come under such control.
(7) The company must not control another company unless that second company is a qualifying subsidiary (see 25.4.5 for the definition) and there must be no arrangements under which such control can be established.
(8) See also 25.4.7 on proposed changes.
(9) Most fundamentally, the company or qualifying subsidiary must be carrying on a qualifying trade (see 19.3.4).

The company will be expected to issue certificate EIS 3 to investors claiming relief, confirming that conditions have been met in respect of the issued shares. The conditions summarised above should clearly fall within the knowledge of the company's existing shareholders and/ or management who, in addition to the issue of the certificate, will be expected to give a warranty that the conditions have been met.

19.3.4 Qualifying trades

(s 192 ITA 2007)

Certain trades are excluded under s 192. The company's business must not consist to any substantial extent of any of the following:

(1) dealing in land, commodities or futures, or shares, securities or other financial instruments;

(2) dealing in goods otherwise than in the course of any ordinary trade of wholesale or retail distribution;

(3) banking, insurance (but not insurance broking), money-lending, debt-factoring, HP financing or other financial activities;

(4) oil extraction activities;

(5) leasing (except for certain short-term charters of ships) or receiving royalties or licence fees. A recent Special Commissioners case concerned a medical company called Optos, which developed eye test machines that it leased to opticians. It was held that the company was excluded from EIS relief because of this leasing;

(6) providing legal or accountancy services;

(7) providing services or facilities for any trade carried on by another person (other than a parent company) that consists to any substantial extent of activities within any of (1)–(6) above and in which a controlling interest is held by a person who also has a controlling interest in the trade carried on by the company;

(8) any of the following property-backed activities:

    (a) farming and market gardening;

    (b) forestry and timber production;

    (c) property development;

    (d) operating or managing hotels or guest houses; and

    (e) operating or managing nursing or residential care homes.

Wholesale and retail distribution trades

Wholesale and retail distribution trades qualify only if they are 'ordinary' trades. Section 193(5) states that a trade does not qualify as an ordinary trade of wholesale or retail distribution if:

- it consists to a substantial extent of dealing in goods of a kind that are collected or held as an investment; and

- a substantial proportion of those goods are held by the company for a period that is significantly longer than the period for which a vendor would reasonably be expected to hold them while endeavouring to dispose of them at their market value.

The following are taken as indications that a company's trade is a qualifying trade:

- The trader buys the goods in quantities larger than those in which he sells them.

- The trader buys and sells the goods in different markets.

- The company incurs expenses in the trade in addition to the costs of the goods, and employs people who are not connected with it.

The following are 'indications' that the trade is not a qualifying trade:

- There are purchases or sales from or to persons who are connected with the trader.

- Purchases are matched with forward sales or vice versa.
- The trader holds the goods for longer than is normal for such goods.
- The trade is carried on otherwise than at a place or places commonly used for the type of trade.
- The trader does not take physical possession of the goods.

The above are only indications and are not conclusive that a company's trade is or is not a qualifying trade, but it will be difficult to persuade HMRC that a trade qualifies if there are several indications to the contrary.

19.3.5 EIS conditions relating to the individual investor

(ss 162–171 ITA 2007)

EIS income tax relief is denied if the investor is connected with the company. This means that the individual alone or with associated parties possesses directly or indirectly more than 30% of:

- the share capital of the company or any of its subsidiaries;
- loan capital of the company or any of its subsidiaries;
- voting power in the company or any of its subsidiaries; or
- rights that would give entitlement to more than 30% of assets available for distribution to shareholders in the event of the company being wound up.

While the more-than-30% test can be monitored by the company in respect of investment or rights of an individual investor, knowledge of which persons are to be treated as associated may go beyond what the existing shareholders and/or management of the company might be expected to know.

EIS income tax relief is also denied if the individual has been previously connected with the company within the two years before the issue of the EIS shares. 'Connected' in this sense means an individual who is or was:

- a paid director of the company or any of its subsidiaries;
- an employee of the company or any of its subsidiaries;
- a partner of the company or any of its subsidiaries;
- an associate of a person falling into any of these categories.

Again, while the company can be expected to have knowledge of an individual falling into any of the categories, knowledge of the associated persons may go beyond what the existing shareholders and/or management of the company might be expected to know.

The First-tier Tribunal has held (*Thomason, Godwin & Markham* v *HMRC* [2010] UKFTT 579 TC) that a management buy-out (MBO) team was entitled to EIS relief on shares it subscribed for in the acquisition company, despite the fact that the managers had previously worked for the company whose trade was taken over.

19.3.6 EIS – withdrawal of relief

(ss 208–244 ITA 2007)

As detailed in 25.4, EIS relief is withdrawn where:

- The company redeems share capital.
- The investor receives value from the company.
- The company ceases to be a qualifying company.
- The investor becomes connected with the company (withdrawal of income tax relief).
- The investor disposes of the share within a three-year period (withdrawal of income tax relief).

With the exception of the last heading, the other grounds for the withdrawal of relief should lie within the knowledge of the company's existing shareholders and/or management.

19.3.7 Seed Enterprise Investment Scheme

This gives even greater benefits to investors (see 25.5).

Conditions which must be satisfied by the company

The scheme applies only to companies with under 25 employees and gross assets of up to £200,000, which are carrying on or preparing to carry on a genuine new trading venture that is less than two years old. The company can have a subsidiary (this is one of the improvements compared with the original proposals).

The company must not be insolvent at the time that it issues the SEIS shares.

The company must use the money raised under the SEIS share issue within three years. Enterprise Investment Scheme (EIS) and Venture Capital Scheme (VCT) money can subsequently be raised after 75% of the SEIS money has been spent.

Advance assurance as to whether a company qualifies can be obtained from HMRC.

19.3.8 Venture Capital Trusts

(Part 6, ITA 2007)

Venture Capital Trusts (VCTs) are companies that are quoted on the London Stock Exchange and derive value from investment in shares or securities. The requirements for qualification as a VCT are set out in 25.7.

The Finance Act 2012 made the following changes to VCTs, which had effect from 6 April 2012:

- an increase in the threshold for the size of qualifying company for VCTs to fewer than 250 employees (previously fewer than 50) and to the company having no more than £15m (previously £7m) of gross assets before the investment;
- an increase in the annual amount that can be invested through EIS or VCTs in an individual company to £5m (previously £2m).

At least 70% by value of the investments made by a VCT must consist of shares or securities in qualifying holdings, defined as holdings in unquoted companies that exist wholly for the purpose of carrying on one or more qualifying trades, wholly or mainly in the UK. Cash proceeds from disposals are ignored for six months when applying the 70% test. Qualifying trade is defined as for the EIS.

An individual investor in a VCT obtains income tax relief at 30% on a subscription for new ordinary shares in the VCT not exceeding £200,000.

The investor also benefits from income tax relief on dividends paid on shares in a VCT to the extent that the shares acquired each year do not exceed £200,000 in value.

The minimum period for which VCT investors must hold their shares is five years.

The trade-off for the current shareholder or shareholders in the company seeking finance is between the ability to access funds through the share issue to the VCT (investors may not be prepared to make an investment in the absence of tax relief) and the continuing commitment (which is likely to be legally enforceable through contractual obligations) for the company to continue to comply with the conditions for the relief to be obtained.

19.4 BORROWING THROUGH THE BUSINESS

As a business develops, its actual and projected cash flows and the assets it owns may allow it to borrow funds in its own right. As with other forms of borrowings discussed in this chapter, the deductibility of the interest expense depends on satisfaction of the conditions in the tax legislation and not on the form of security given for the borrowings.

19.4.1 Loans to unincorporated businesses

Interest paid by a sole trader or partnership (as opposed to a partner in a personal capacity) and incurred wholly and exclusively for the purposes of the business can be claimed as a deduction in computing the profits of the business.

A deduction for tax is also available for costs of raising finance when these costs:

(1) were incurred wholly and exclusively for the purposes of obtaining loan finance, providing security or repaying a loan; and

(2) represented expenditure on professional fees, commissions, advertising, printing or other incidental expenses in relation to raising finance.

19.4.2 Corporate loan relationships

The treatment of interest expense incurred by companies for tax is governed by the loan relationship legislation (Parts 5 and 6 of CTA 2009) (see 18.5). The legislation applies to all UK resident companies and UK permanent establishments of non-UK resident companies. Loan relationships arise when:

- a company is a debtor or creditor in respect of a money debt and the debt arose as a result of a transaction for the lending of money; or
- an instrument is issued for the purpose of representing security for, or the rights of a creditor in respect of, a money debt.

In general, the tax treatment follows the accounting treatment with the expenditure on interest being allowed in the year that it is charged to the profit and loss account of the company. The company's accounting treatment must comply with generally accepted accounting practice (GAAP) (which means either UK GAAP or IFRS).

Where interest was payable to a connected party, a 12 month rule meant that the company secured relief only when the interest was paid. However, this rule has now been abolished (see 18.5.6).

19.5 FINANCING ASSETS

As a business expands, it usually will need access to more assets. Possibilities are that the assets are financed outside the business and made available to the business or that the business itself acquires the assets.

19.5.1 Loans to purchase assets

A decision to provide an asset to a business through personal funding may result from an individual having better access to credit than the business itself. There can also be efficiencies, for instance a building needed by the business but owned by an individual offers the possibility of long-term capital appreciation and, if so, the possibility of realisation with one layer of tax rather than two if the property were owned by a limited liability company. Entrepreneurs' relief may be available to reduce the eventual gain on disposal. A property may also be a suitable investment for a self-administered pension scheme.

An asset acquired personally and let or leased to a business may attract capital allowances, depending, according to the heading under which the allowances are claimed, on the nature of the asset and demonstrating that the asset is used for a qualifying activity. Capital allowances are first set off against the income generated from the asset.

As the investor and the business are likely to be connected, care must be taken to ensure that the terms of the transaction are justifiable as arm's length, defined as being the terms that would have been agreed in the absence of such a connection.

19.5.2 Interest on loan to acquire property

Generally, interest expense on a loan drawn down by an individual for the purchase of a property to be let to a business will attract tax relief, through set-off against the rental income received.

19.5.3 Loans drawn down by a partner

(ss 388–389 ITA 2007)

A partner can claim a deduction for interest paid on a loan drawn down to finance capital expenditure on the provision of plant and machinery for the purposes of the business of the partnership. The relief is available in the year in which the loan is drawn down and the following three years.

19.5.4 Purchase of assets by business

If the business draws down a loan to finance the purchase of an asset, interest deductibility will depend on the loan relationship legislation (see 19.4.2 and 18.5).

Depreciation on fixed assets charged in the profit and loss account of a business is disallowed and added back when calculating the taxable profit. If the asset qualifies, capital expenditure will qualify for capital allowances under various headings (see 16.2). The rates of capital allowances vary and not all fixed assets will qualify for capital allowances. For tax purposes, the deductions in respect of the purchase of intangible assets generally follow the charge in the accounts of the business.

19.5.5 Leasing of assets by business

Leasing is another method for a business to obtain assets. A substantial volume of asset leasing business is written annually. In many cases, leasing is provided by the manufacturers or suppliers of assets, for example office machinery such as computer equipment and copiers, but leasing possibilities also exist for major fixed assets. The lessor is often a subsidiary of a financial institution and the cost of the lease reflects the ability to reduce taxable profits of the company itself and through group relief the profits of associated companies by the capital allowances available.

The accounting treatment of leased assets varies as to whether the lease is an operating or a financial lease. An operating lease is for a period that is less that the asset's anticipated useful life; a financial lease is written for a period that effectively equates to the expected life of an asset. When testing to determine the category of the lease transaction, an arrangement in which the net present value of the rentals is 90% or greater than the value of the asset will be treated as a finance lease.

Lease rentals under an operating lease are charged to the profit and loss account as incurred and a corresponding deduction is given when calculating taxable income of the business.

To ensure that the accounts give an accurate picture of the resources and obligations of a business, a finance-lease transaction is capitalised on the balance sheet, entries reflecting the purchase of the rights to use and enjoy the asset and the requirement to make future payments. The rental payments are apportioned between a finance charge and a reduction of the obligation to make future payments. The tax deduction in respect of payments under a finance lease is normally the amount charged to the profit and loss account in that period in respect of the finance lease. However, the tax treatment of long funding leases changed from 1 April 2006 and the lessee may now be entitled to capital allowances (see 16.1.6), but not in excess of the costs incurred (see s 33 Finance Act 2011).

If the lease is for a major asset, the lessee is usually required to enter into a contractual commitment to make good any reduction in the tax benefit to the lessor of the capital allowances on the leased asset through a change in tax legislation, including a reduction in the rates of tax.

19.5.6 Lease/buy analysis

When carrying out a lease/buy analysis to determine the optimum method of acquiring assets for the business, the cash flows under each of the two cases will have to be set out for the expected period of use of the asset, or a period of, say, five or ten years, if considered more appropriate to the circumstances and forecasting pattern of the business. The cash flows will include the tax effects, in the purchase case the reduction in tax for the interest costs and the capital allowances received on the asset and, in the lease case, the reduction in tax through the lease rental payments allowed for tax. Tax is only one consideration: the real point in preparing the cash flows is to ensure that the business will be able to meet the obligations under the chosen route. The effect on the profit and loss account of each route should also be determined so that a well informed decision can be taken.

19.5.7 Sale and leaseback

A business can seek to raise finance for current expenditure through selling an asset and leasing it back. This arrangement may be particularly useful if the business has an asset or series of assets that would fit within a specialist activity of the buyer. An example would be a business that sells a portfolio of properties to a pension fund or property company.

The tax effects of the disposal of the asset will need to be calculated in advance of the decision being taken. While the tax effect of the purchase is a matter for the purchaser, there are certain situations in which the capital allowances on the purchased asset will be restricted.

19.5.8 Hire purchase

When an asset is bought on hire purchase, the purchaser is entitled to capital allowances on the full purchase price from the beginning of the contract, although this sum is going to be paid by instalments. The interest element of the periodic payments charged to the profit and loss account is allowable as a tax deduction in the year when it is so charged.

19.6 CASH FLOW MANAGEMENT

Managing cash flow prudently for a growing business requires the owner/ managers to avoid circumstances in which tax liabilities bear heavily on cash flow. It should also involve accelerating tax deductions wherever possible. Three points are worth noting.

19.6.1 Cash basis for VAT

Using the cash basis for VAT means that the output VAT due on invoices issued to customers does not have to be accounted for to HMRC before the money has been received from the customer. The business owner should review the turnover limits to determine whether the scheme will apply.

19.6.2 Research and development

There are specific incentives to encourage research and development (see 18.16). The business owner should review activity to determine whether these incentives will apply.

19.6.3 Capital expenditure

Capital expenditure incurred by the business should be reviewed to allocate as much as possible to assets qualifying for capital allowances. Although deferred tax may have to be provided on the difference between the written down values for book and tax, it is an accounting entry and not a cash movement.

20

SHOULD YOU OPERATE THROUGH A COMPANY?

This chapter contains the following sections:

(1) Tax advantages of having a company
(2) Possible disadvantages
(3) CGT and IHT considerations
(4) Limited liability partnerships (LLPs)
(5) Transferring an existing business to a company or LLP
(6) Having a company as member of a partnership
(7) Disincorporation

20.1 TAX ADVANTAGES OF HAVING A COMPANY

20.1.1 Lower rate of tax on profits

Having a company means that a lower rate of tax will apply to retained profits. The rate of corporation tax is 20% – the same as the basic rate of income tax.

Example – Tax saving through incorporation in 2015–16

	£
Unincorporated business	
Profits	450,000
Tax and NIC	200,030
Incorporated business	£
Profits before director's remuneration	450,000
Less: director's remuneration and employers' NIC, say	(170,700)*
	279,300
Corporation tax at 20% on £279,300	55,860
Tax and NIC on director's remuneration (no PA as gross > £120,000)	59,844
Employer's NIC	20,700
Total tax and NIC on profits of £450,000	136,404
Annual saving in tax through operating via a company	63,626

Of course, some of this saving may have to be handed back as and when the retained profits are extracted from the company as dividends, which attract higher rate tax.

*£150,000 + employer's NIC

It is clear that if profits of (say) £500,000 are earned and retained by a company owned by such an individual rather than paid out to him or her as remuneration, the company will retain between £395,000 and £400,000 after corporation tax. If it used the £500,000 to pay remuneration, the position would be as follows:

	£
Available for remuneration and Employer's NIC	500,000
Employers' NIC	(60,632)
Tax and Employees' NIC (assuming no other income)	(195,847)
Retained by individual	243,521

In other words, the money available for reinvestment in the business will be increased by about 55% by leaving money in the company.

20.1.2 Other tax considerations

Timing difference

There is a useful timing difference where a business is carried on through a company in that remuneration can be deducted from the company's profits even though it is not paid (and is not taxable income of the individuals until the earlier of payment, or entitlement to receive payment, provided it does not trigger the anti-avoidance rules on disguised remuneration – see Chapter 5). Provided the remuneration is actually paid within nine months of the company's year end, the company is normally entitled to a deduction in arriving at its profits.

Example – Timing of tax payments

If a company draws up accounts to 31 March 2016, it may secure a deduction for director's remuneration of £150,000 even though the remuneration is not paid until 31 December 2016, in which case PAYE does not have to be paid over until 19 January 2017. Contrast this with an unincorporated business where tax needs to be paid on account on 31 January 2016 and on 31 July 2016, with a balancing payment on the following 31 January.

An even longer timing difference would arise if an individual takes his or her £150,000 out as a dividend on 31 December 2016. The company would have to pay corporation tax on 1 January 2017 but the individual will often not need to pay tax on his or her dividend until 31 January 2018 (depending on whether he is liable to pay instalments for 2016–17).

Pension contributions

With the introduction of the new regime for registered pension schemes, there is more of a level playing field for proprietors of unincorporated businesses and companies. There is no longer any great advantage in having a company in terms of pension provision.

Payment of remuneration may prevent personal allowances going to waste

Where an unincorporated business operates at a loss, and the individual concerned has no other private income, the benefit of his or her personal allowance is lost forever. By trading through a company, it is possible to vote remuneration equal to the personal allowance and the remuneration voted in this way will increase the amount of the company's loss that can be carried forward and set against subsequent profits.

Certain reliefs are only available to companies

Companies can qualify for R&D and ECA tax credits (see 18.16 and 18.17) and get allowances for expenditure on intangibles (see 18.6). These reliefs are not available to unincorporated businesses.

20.2 POSSIBLE DISADVANTAGES

Possible disadvantages of operating through a company include the following:

20.2.1 Extra administration

There are more statutory requirements concerning book-keeping, filing annual accounts, audit (in some cases), iXBRL filing, disclosure, etc. An unincorporated business does not normally need to file annual accounts at all, whereas a company must file accounts with Companies House and make an annual return.

20.2.2 IR35 regulations

Some companies may be caught by IR35. Income received by personal service companies may still be taxed as if it were remuneration (see 21.3).

20.2.3 Admitting future partners

If profits are retained, this may make it increasingly difficult for individuals who come up through the business to become shareholder directors. For example, if a company has 100 £1 shares in issue and retains profits after tax of £15,000 pa for ten years, each share will be worth £1,500 more at the end of the ten years than at the start of the period. For an individual to acquire a 10% shareholding, he or she must find sufficient finance to purchase shares that reflect this. The problem does not arise in the case of a partnership, since the normal procedure is to allocate past profits to partners' capital accounts and then admit a partner on the basis that he or she would share in future profits at a specified percentage.

20.2.4 Tax savings may only be a deferment

The traditional analysis has been that tax generally becomes payable by the shareholders on their share of retained profits, either when they sell their shares and realise a capital gain, or as and when they extract retained profits by taking a dividend. On this analysis, the tax saving on retained profits is often little more than a deferment of tax. This is not really the end of the story as there can be a true saving because of the difference between the 28% CGT rate (or even 10% if entrepreneurs' relief applies) and the higher rates of tax payable on income. For example, an unincorporated trader will pay tax at an effective rate of 47% on his or her earnings in the additional rate band (45% income tax and 2% NIC) – say, £100,000 for the purposes of this illustration. If £100,000 accrued to a company, the company would retain £80,000 after corporation tax.

If the trader eventually realised his or her shares, he or she might pay 28% CGT on this £80,000 and end up with around £57,600. If the gain attracted entrepreneurs' relief, he would have £72,000.

20.2.5 Increased liability for NIC

A company must pay Class 1 NIC at a single rate on all amounts above a certain level paid as remuneration. There is no reduced rate above the upper earnings limit such as applies to employees' contributions. This can give rise to a substantially increased burden for a company as compared with an unincorporated business. Comparing an unincorporated business owned by four equal partners with a company that has four 25% shareholders (and it is assumed that in both cases the individuals had income of £75,000 each), the NIC bill for 2015–16 is as follows:

Partnership			Company
	£		£
Class 2	582	Employees' Class 1 (not-contracted-out)	18,828
Class 4	14,968	Employer's contributions	36,635
	15,550		55,463

While the benefits payable to employees can be better than those received by the self-employed, the higher NIC cost can be a very expensive way of financing such benefits.

20.2.6 Work in progress

In principle, a professional firm should not include partner time in arriving at the cost of work in progress. This means the figure brought into account should be lower because of this. However, if a business is carried on by a company, time put in by a director should be included when valuing work in progress.

20.3 CGT AND IHT CONSIDERATIONS

20.3.1 Potential double charge for capital gains

Where a valuable asset is held within a company, a tax liability may arise at two stages before the shareholders can enjoy the sale proceeds. For example, if a company liable at the mainstream corporation tax rate acquired a property at a cost of £100,000, and it is sold five years later when it is worth £550,000 then there is a gain for the company of £450,000 (ignoring indexation). The company might pay tax on this capital gain at 20%. The company will have net funds available – after paying tax – of £360,000, as here:

	£
Profits for accounting purposes	450,000
Less: tax on gain (£450,000 at 20%)	90,000
	360,000

If the company is then wound up and the cash distributed to the shareholders, they are likely to have a personal CGT liability on the £360,000. The maximum CGT payable by the shareholders (ignoring the availability of entrepreneurs' relief, annual exemptions, losses, etc) would be £100,800 (ie £360,000 at 28%), giving an effective overall rate of 42.4% on the disposal and extraction of the gain.

While it is not generally good policy to have appreciating assets within a company, the extent of the extra tax payable is not as great as it was in the past. While some additional tax is likely to be payable if an appreciating asset is held within a company, this is not an argument in itself against a business operating through a company. Correctly analysed, the treatment of capital gains within a company is an argument in favour of shareholder directors holding such assets in their personal capacity rather than through a company.

20.3.2 Property owned privately but used by a company

Where a shareholder director owns a property used by his or her trading company, roll-over relief (see 17.3) should be available if he or she sells the property and buys another property for use by the same company.

If a shareholder director needs to take a loan to buy property, he or she can secure relief on the interest by charging rent. Doing this will not prejudice roll-over relief but it will mean that CGT entrepreneurs' relief may not be available on an eventual sale of the property (this relief is restricted if the individual has charged a market rent during any periods of business use after 6 April 2008).

20.3.3 Inheritance tax

Where a partner owns a property that is used by the firm, he or she will generally qualify for 50% business property relief.

Where a controlling shareholder owns a property that is used by a trading company, he or she will also qualify for 50% business property relief. But no BPR is available for non-controlling shareholders who own a property used by the company. From this point of view, it is better for the property to be owned by the company because 100% business property relief will generally be due for all holdings of unquoted shares in trading companies, controlling and non-controlling.

20.4 LIMITED LIABILITY PARTNERSHIPS (LLPs)

An option that should be borne in mind is to operate through an LLP (see 7.5). These are treated as companies for company law (and VAT) purposes but are taxed as partnerships (ie profits or losses, and gains, are attributed to each individual partner in proportion to his or her stake in the business, and taxed as his or her own income). Using an LLP means you can limit your personal liability towards customers, etc, while retaining the tax treatment that applies to partnerships.

20.5 TRANSFERRING AN EXISTING BUSINESS TO A COMPANY OR LLP

20.5.1 Transferring to a company

Some care is necessary when transferring a business to ensure that no CGT charge arises. Fortunately there is a special CGT relief intended to cover this (see 17.6). See also Chapter 36 on stamp duty. The VAT consequences should also be explored and this is an area where you will need to seek professional advice.

The timing of the transfer may be important. Bear in mind that if you were carrying on an unincorporated business, transferring it to a company may enable you to utilise your overlap relief (see 7.3.5). If your future employment income is expected to be much lower than your current self-employed profits, consider applying for a reduction in your payments on account (see 2.1.8).

If you have substantial qualifying loans used to put money into a partnership, you should take advice. But an HMRC concession will cover most situations (see 11.4.4).

See *Tax Bulletin 76*, April 2005 regarding the tax implications if HMRC challenges a sale of goodwill as being at an over-value. HMRC is likely to tax the over-value as a distribution (see 9.9.6). Furthermore, the tax on such a sale is unlikely to be acceptable given that the capital gain no longer attracts entrepreneurs' relief (see 17.7.4).

20.5.2 Transferring to an LLP

Transferring an existing unincorporated business to an LLP does not normally involve a disposal for CGT purposes or a cessation of your self-employed business for income tax purposes. Remember to keep your VAT office advised and take advice on any VAT implications of the transfer.

20.6 HAVING A COMPANY AS A MEMBER OF A PARTNERSHIP

A possible way of fine-tuning the position may be for the members of a partnership or LLP to consist of individuals and a company that is owned by them. Provided that there is a commercial basis for the company being a member (it might, for example, employ the staff), this allows for some profits to be retained as working capital rather than forming part of the taxable income of the individual partners.

This is something that you should discuss with your tax adviser. See 33.8 on FA 2014 changes to mixed partnerships.

20.7 DISINCORPORATION

Small companies can claim disincorporation relief which allows a company to transfer goodwill and land and buildings to its shareholders without corporation tax on the transfer.

The relief is available to companies with qualifying assets (goodwill and land and buildings used in the business) with a value not exceeding £150,000. The relief runs for five years from 1 April 2013.

Disincorporation relief will not cover tax liabilities for the shareholders on the distribution of these assets.

21

DEDUCTING TAX AT SOURCE AND PAYING IT OVER TO HMRC

MIKE EVANS

The chapter contains the following sections:

(1) Employers
(2) Contractors in the construction industry
(3) IR35
(4) Managed service companies (MSCs)
(5) Offshore employment intermediaries
(6) Non-resident landlord scheme
(7) Non-resident sportsmen and entertainers
(8) Other payments to non-UK resident persons

21.1 EMPLOYERS

An employer has an obligation to collect tax and national insurance contributions (NIC) and to operate the following schemes:

- Pay As You Earn (PAYE)/NIC;
- student loans;
- Construction Industry Scheme (CIS).

The employer also has responsibilities for providing HMRC with returns and information on a real-time basis.

21.1.1 Payment of PAYE to HMRC

Employers are required to withhold tax under PAYE and deduct Class 1 primary (employees') and secondary (employers') NIC and pay them over to HMRC each month. If the total PAYE and NIC deductions do not normally exceed £1,500 pm, the employer can account for the tax and NIC deductions quarterly. The £1,500 pm is inclusive of sums collected under the Student Loans Scheme. At the end of the year, the employer must give employees form P60 (by 31 May) showing the tax and NIC withheld from their earnings.

21.1.2 Earnings subject to PAYE

The payment of earnings by a UK-resident employer to directors and employees is subject to PAYE.

Earnings, in relation to employment income means any salary, wages or fees, any gratuity or other profit or incidental benefit of any kind obtained by the employee if it is money's worth, or anything else that counts as income from the employment.

The following list provides some examples of payments that are earnings and are subject to PAYE:

- salary;
- wages;
- fees;
- overtime;
- bonus;
- commission;
- pension;
- honoraria;
- pay during sickness or other absence from work;
- holiday pay;
- Christmas gifts in cash;
- employee's income tax borne by his or her employer;
- payments for the cost of travelling between the employee's home and his or her normal place of employment;
- payments for time spent in travelling;
- cash payments for meals;
- payments in lieu of benefits-in-kind;
- certain lump sum payments made on retirement or removal from employment;
- gratuities or service charges paid out by the employer.

A far more exhaustive list can be found in HMRC booklet CWG2 *Employers' Further Guide to PAYE and NIC*.

There are however certain payments from which PAYE cannot be deducted even though they are regarded as taxable income of the employment. The most common of these is known as the pecuniary liability principle. This is where an employer discharges an employee's debt. An example of this is where the employer pays for an employee's home internet service. An employer cannot deduct PAYE when making a payment to a third party. The item should therefore be reported to HMRC on Form P9D or P11D.

It must be remembered however that such payments are still earnings and therefore both employees' and employers' Class 1 NIC must be deducted and paid over to HMRC in the normal pay period.

The PAYE regulations also require employers to account for PAYE when they pay staff using 'readily convertible assets' (RCAs). There are ten classes that fall within this category:

- an asset capable of being sold or otherwise realised on a recognised investment exchange;
- an asset capable of being sold or otherwise realised on the London Bullion Market;
- an asset capable of being sold or otherwise realised on the New York Stock Exchange;
- an asset capable of being sold or otherwise realised on a market for the time being specified in PAYE regulations;
- an asset consisting in the rights of an assignee, or any other rights, in respect of a money debt that is or may become due to the employer or any other person;
- an asset consisting in property that is subject to a warehousing regime, or any right in respect of property so subject;
- an asset consisting in anything that is likely (without anything being done by the employee) to give rise to, or to become, a right enabling a person to obtain an amount or total amount of money that is likely to be similar to the expense incurred in the provision of the asset;
- an asset for which trading arrangements are in existence, or are likely to come into existence in accordance with any arrangements of another description existing when the asset is provided;
- an asset for which trading arrangements are in existence, or are likely to come into existence in accordance with any understanding existing when the asset is provided;
- an asset consisting in securities, which is not a readily convertible asset under the above, is to be treated as a readily convertible asset unless the securities are shares that are corporation tax deductible.

PAYE may also have to be accounted for on gifts of shares in the employing company or profits realised in connection with the acquisition of employment-related securities or shares (see 6.3) or where a charge arises under Part 7A ITEPA (disguised remuneration – see Chapter 5).

National insurance contributions

The PAYE and NIC rules have been largely aligned and it is now unusual for a payment or benefit to be taxable as employment income but not subject to NIC. See Chapter 23.

21.1.3 Anti-avoidance of PAYE and NIC

The PAYE legislation deals with assignments of trade debts by employers to their employees. The legislation originally referred to 'tradeable assets' and treated such assets as if they were cash payments.

The term 'tradeable assets' was subsequently replaced by 'readily convertible assets': these include the assets listed above.

If an employee becomes liable to income tax on employment income on the exercise, assignment or release of an option for shares that are readily convertible assets, these provisions require the employer to operate PAYE. Similarly, PAYE will apply if the employee is rewarded by the enhancement of a readily convertible asset that he or she already owns. PAYE must be operated on a reasonable estimate of the amount likely to be charged to tax as employment income. Comparable rules were also introduced for NIC.

21.1.4 Failure to operate PAYE

An employer who fails to operate PAYE (and/or deduct NIC) takes a substantial risk. The primary liability to account for the tax rests with the employer and the scope of PAYE does not extend simply to deducting tax from an employee's gross pay and remitting it to HMRC. Instead, an employer must remember that PAYE can also apply to all forms of casual labour, which may or may not be paid through the payroll, and to individuals otherwise considered to be self-employed (see 7.2).

Another area frequently overlooked is expenses (see 4.4) that constitute part of an employee's income from employment and accordingly fall within the scope of PAYE. While genuine business expenses incurred wholly, exclusively and necessarily in the course of an employee's duties may qualify for a tax deduction, there remain several areas where employers are required to operate PAYE and deduct NIC. These include the payment of all round sum allowances that have not been approved by HMRC in the form of a dispensation, and the payment of unauthorised or unvouched expenses. Even the payment of travel expenses may not be permitted tax free in circumstances where the place visited is deemed to be the permanent place of work. As an example, an employee living in London and permanently working on a site in Aberdeen will be taxed on all his or her expenses for travel between London and Aberdeen. This shows that special attention must be paid to such payments and the circumstances surrounding them. HMRC's booklet 490, *Employee Travel – a Tax and NIC Guide for Employers,* provides more details on the rules.

HMRC is legally obliged to seek recovery of any underpaid tax from the employer in the first instance. In limited circumstances HMRC has discretion to issue a direction that underpaid tax may be recovered from the employee. The Regulations make it clear that such a direction will only be given if the employee received payments knowing that the employer wilfully failed to deduct the amount of tax that should have been deducted or an employee received a notional payment that was not taxed, the most obvious example of which would be employee shares.

All lump sum compensation payments should be considered carefully because of HMRC's approach to the taxation of termination payments. It is wrong to assume that the first £30,000 of **every** lump sum compensation payment is exempt from income tax. Basically, if there is any contractual obligation or expectation on the part of the employee to receive a sum then HMRC is likely to take the view that the employer should have deducted tax and Class 1 NIC. HMRC looks specifically at the habitual and automatic making of payments in lieu of notice (autopilons) – see HMRC's employment income manual at www.hmrc.gov.uk/manuals/eimanual/eim12800.htm.

21.1.5 Forms P11D and P9D

An employer must file forms P11D to report benefits and expenses for all employees earning at a rate of £8,500+ pa. Directors are automatically included in this category unless they:

- are full-time working directors or directors of a not-for-profit organisation; and
- earn less than £8,500 pa; and
- do not control directly or indirectly more than 5% of the company's ordinary share capital; and
- do not have directorships in other businesses under the same control.

All benefits and expenses payments (including business expenses) must be reported, except those covered by dispensations or PAYE Settlement Agreements. The amount is the cash equivalent (see 4.4–4.9 on taxation of benefits in general).

Except where special rules apply, the cash equivalent is normally the VAT-inclusive cost to the provider. Where the special rules apply, employers are responsible for calculating the cash equivalent and entering the appropriate amount on the P11D. HMRC can supply the following P11D Working Sheets to assist you:

- living accommodation and associated benefits
- car and fuel benefits
- vans available for private use
- interest-free and low interest loans
- relocation expenses
- mileage allowance and passenger payments.

If an arrangement has been made for someone else to provide benefits to an employer's employees, the cash equivalents must be reported on P11D as though the employer itself had provided the benefits. If the provider cannot or will not give details of the benefits to the employer, the employer must make a best estimate of the cash equivalent and notify HMRC of this. The affected arrangements are where an employer has guaranteed or facilitated provision of benefits, or the benefits were part of a reciprocal arrangement with another employer.

If a third party makes any expense payments or provides benefits to an employer's employees and the employer is not involved, the third party has an obligation to notify the employees of the cash equivalent of the expense payment paid or benefit provided. The third party does not have to submit a P11D for another employer's employee and many third party providers enter into arrangements to pay the tax due through a Taxed Award Scheme (TAS). These are dealt with by HMRC's Incentive Award Unit in Manchester and guidance is available in *The Employer's Further Guide to PAYE and NIC* at Chapter 2. Unlike awards covered by PAYE Settlement Agreements (PSAs), non-cash awards and the tax paid on them under TAS arrangements remain assessable on the employee. So the employee has to enter the grossed-up value of the award and the tax paid on it on his or her tax return. Normally no further tax is due from an employee unless the provider has only entered into a basic rate TAS and the recipient of the award is liable at the higher or additional rate.

P11D returns are due for submission to HMRC by 6 July following the end of the tax year. Filing an incorrect return can result in a penalty as detailed above.

Details of taxable benefits must be supplied to employees by 6 July. Forms P9D may also be required for benefits provided to employees earning less than £8,500 pa. The deadlines for submitting returns of Classes 1A and 1B NIC must also be borne in mind (see 23.1.7–23.1.8).

21.1.6 Summary of due dates and penalties

Due dates for submission of end of year and end of quarter returns

1	Agreement of PAYE Settlement Agreement contracts	5 July
2	Expenses and benefit returns (**P9D, P11D, P11D(b)**)	6 July
3	Termination payment details, if in excess of £30,000	6 July
4	Benefits in excess of £100 provided to former employees, where not excluded from charge	6 July
5	**P46** (car) – employers must submit these forms when an employee is provided with a company car or when the employee no longer has the company car. HMRC does not accept any other car information	5 July, 5 October, 5 January, 5 April

Employers are now required to operate within the Real Time Information regime. However, some year-end returns are still required and these may be submitted online. The 2014–15 return must be filed by 19 May 2015. It is possible (but not mandatory) to file the following forms in this way: P9D, P11D, P11D(b), P12, P37, P38A, P46 (Car), WNU (works number update) and CIS300 (verification request for the Construction Industry Scheme).

Due dates for providing information to employees for tax year ended 5 April 2015

1	**P60** (Pay and tax details)	31 May 2015
2	Expenses and Benefit Returns (**P9D, P11D**)	6 July 2015
3	Termination payment details, if in excess of £30,000	6 July 2015

Due dates for payments (automatic interest applies if paid late)

		Paid by cheque (date reaches HMRC accounts office)	**Paid electronically** (cleared payment in HMRC's bank)
1	PAYE/NIC	19 April	22 April
2	Class 1A NIC	19 July	22 July
3	PAYE Settlement Agreement tax and Class 1B NIC	19 October	22 October
4	Monthly PAYE/NIC remittances	19th of each month	22nd each month
5	Quarterly PAYE/NIC remittances	19 July, 19 October, 19 January and 19 April	22 July, 22 October, 22 January and 22 April

It is mandatory for employers with 250 or more employees to make their payments electronically.
See www.hmrc.gov.uk/paye/file-or-pay/payments/deadlines.htm#1

Penalties for late payment

Penalties apply for late payment of income tax, Class 1, 1A and 1B NIC and CIS and student loan deductions collected via PAYE. There are two types of penalty. The first is based on the number of defaults (late payments) in the year as shown in Table 21.1 below. The additional penalty is independent and targets very late payments.

Table 21.1 – Late payment penalties

Number of times payments are late in the tax year	Penalty percentage	Amount to which penalty percentages apply
1	No penalty	
2–4	1%	Total amount that is paid late in the tax year (ignoring the first late payment in that tax year)
5–7	2%	
8–10	3%	
11 or more	4%	
Additional penalty		
Any number	5% penalty on each amount of tax paid more than 6 months late	Total amount that is paid late
Any number	Additional 5% penalty on each amount of tax paid more than 12 months late	

Table 21.2 – Return filing penalties

Return filing penalties	Late returns and late provision of information to employees	Failure to file online (in addition to late filing penalty)*	
		No. of employees	Penalty
1 PAYE returns and P11D(b)	Initial up to £1,200 per 50 employees, fixed monthly penalty of £100 per 50 employees or part thereof, up to 12 months, with an additional tax-geared penalty thereafter	50–249 250–399 400–499 500–599 600–699	£600 £900 £1,200 £1,500 £1,800
2 Expense and benefit returns (P11D)	Up to £300 per return **plus** up to £60 per day	700–799 800–899 900–999 1,000 or more	£2,100 £2,400 £2,700 £3,000

* Note that submitting a return on paper (even if within the deadlines) will not be treated as filing a return as most employer returns have to be filed online.

Table 21.3 – Penalties for incorrect returns

Penalties for incorrect returns	
1 PAYE and Sub-contractor returns and P11D(b)	Up to the difference between the amounts payable on the incorrect and correct returns
2 Expense and Benefit Returns (P11D, P9D)	Up to £3,000 per return

Late filing penalties

There have been a number of Tribunal decisions on the subject of what is a reasonable excuse.

- In *Kestrel Guards Limited* [2014] TC 03324, the First-tier Tribunal allowed a taxpayer's appeal against penalties imposed by HMRC in relation to eight late payments of PAYE, finding that all payments were posted first class in sufficient time to arrive on or before the due date. HMRC was unable to prove the date the payments were received and so failed to prove that the payments did not arrive on time. Additionally, the taxpayer also had a 'reasonable excuse' in that it was reasonable to believe that first class posted cheques would arrive the next day and, therefore, that the cheques would arrive on time.

- In *Providence Health Consultants Ltd* [2013] TC 02988, the First-tier Tribunal allowed a taxpayer's appeal against the imposition of late filing penalties in respect of its P35 Employer's Annual Return for 2010–11. This was on the grounds that there was a reasonable excuse for the delay because the taxpayer had reasonably relied on their agent to submit their return and as soon as they realised there was a problem, appointed a new agent who rectified matters without unreasonable delay.

- In *Howard (t/a The Albion Inn)* [2013] TC 02976 the First-tier Tribunal allowed a taxpayer's appeal against the imposition of late filing penalties in respect of its P35 and P14's Employer's Annual Return for 2009–10. This was on the grounds that there was a reasonable excuse for the delay because the taxpayer had paid for someone he knew and trusted to deal with his employers' returns and if the taxpayer had not been ill he may well have checked that the return had been filed.

- In *Littlewood Hire Ltd* [2013] TC 02975 the First-tier Tribunal allowed a taxpayer's appeal against late filing penalties in respect of its P35 Employer's Annual Return for 2011–12. It held that there was a reasonable excuse for part of the delay arising from an HMRC computer error and the taxpayer's reasonable belief that the return had been properly submitted.

21.1.7 Pensions and benefits for former employees

A return must also be made of pensions and other payments to former employees, and 'relevant benefits' taxable under Part 4 and Schedule 36 FA 2004, and s 393B ITEPA 2003. See 4.16.6 on this.

21.1.8 Collection of student loans

Student loans are the main source of funding higher education. The Student Loans Company (SLC) administers the scheme but employers are responsible for making deductions from the former student's salary and for paying over the amounts deducted to HMRC.

The system is similar to that for working tax credits in that employers will receive start and stop notifications from HMRC. The employer is not responsible for identifying employees who are liable to make these repayments or for answering questions from the employee regarding the loan. Such queries should be referred to the SLC. Only questions about the operational aspects of the scheme should be referred to HMRC.

The calculation of student loan repayments is very similar to that for NIC. The repayment percentage (currently 9%) is applied to those earnings subject to secondary Class 1 NIC. There is an annual limit of £17,335 (£1,444 pm) below which no deductions are made. This limit is non-cumulative as with NIC so an employee who earns £1,000 in one month and £2,000 in the next will only be liable to deduction in the second month. The deduction made would be as follows in respect of the latter case:

$$£2000 - £1,444 \quad = \quad £556.00$$
$$\text{Rate of deduction} \quad = \quad 9\%$$
$$\text{Student loan repaid} \quad = \quad £50.04$$

Different rules apply for student loans made for courses which started on or after 1 September 2012. An individual starts making repayments when he earns over £21,000 pa. The monthly repayments work out as follows:

Annual income	Monthly repayments
£25,000	£30
£30,000	£67
£50,000	£217

An employer should only begin to make deductions when a start notice (form SL1) is received from HMRC. This gives at least six weeks' notice before deductions should commence. Deductions should begin on the first pay day after this date.

If a new employee hands over a P45 with a 'Y' in the SL box, it means the previous employer had received a start notice. In this situation, deductions should be made as soon as possible. If the P45 is received some time after the employee has started work, no attempt should be made to deduct any arrears. If the employee completes box D (student loans) of the new form P46, you should make deductions. The employer collects student loan repayments by making deductions from the borrower's pay either calculating the deduction (as above, or using the free tool on HMRC's employer CD), or by using the Student Loan Deduction Tables. These tables are available from the Employer's Orderline, on 08457 646 646. Further information is available in HMRC leaflet E17, which is available online at www.hmrc.gov.uk/helpsheets/e17.pdf.

21.2 CONTRACTORS IN THE CONSTRUCTION INDUSTRY

HMRC regards payments made by contractors to subcontractors as a high risk area because of cash payments and what it refers to as 'dubious practices'. It is an obvious area in which tax is being lost to the Treasury. Subcontractors can now be paid:

- net after the deduction of PAYE/NIC as employees;
- net under deduction at the standard CIS deduction rate of 20%, if registered for the standard rate deduction;
- net under deduction at the higher CIS deduction rate of 30%, if not registered for the Scheme;
- gross, if registered for Gross Payment under the New Construction Industry Scheme.

Agency workers

Construction workers supplied by employment agencies or other third parties were brought within the PAYE system by FA 1998. This aligned the tax and NIC treatment of such workers, who were in the past regarded as self-employed for tax purposes but as employees for NIC purposes.

Note that this does not only apply to agencies. Companies acting as 'in-house' agencies within the construction industry that supply labour to others, and anyone else who supplies construction workers to others, fall within the legislation.

21.2.1 Payments to subcontractors in the construction industry

Where a person carries on a business that includes construction work, payments to a subcontractor in respect of 'construction operations' may be subject to deduction of tax, as outlined above.

The contractor is normally the person making the payment for 'construction operations'. A contractor is a business or other concern that pays subcontractors for construction work. Contractors may be construction companies and building firms, but may also be government departments, local authorities, and many other businesses that are normally known in the industry as 'clients'. Non-construction businesses or other concerns that spend more than £1m a year (as an average over three years) on construction work, are treated as contractors and are also covered by the scheme.

Most charities are excluded provided that they are not 'mainstream contractors' (Regulation 24 SI 2005/2045) and deemed contractors in relation to expenditure on their own premises (Regulation 22). The exclusion does not apply to premises that are let or where there is significant use by third parties.

Construction operations

'Construction operations' are defined in law in s 74 FA 2004 and HMRC guidance can be found in Appendix B of the booklet CIS340 (see www. hmrc.gov.uk/forms/cis340.pdf). As a general guide, 'construction operations' cover almost any work that is done to a permanent or temporary building or structure, a civil engineering work or installation. The work can include site preparation, alterations, dismantling, construction, repairs, decorating and demolition. Some activities on construction sites are not regarded as construction operations under the scheme, including any activity that is clearly not construction work, such as the running of a canteen, a hostel, provision of medical or safety and security services and the provision of site facilities.

Where a single contract relates to a mixture of construction and non-construction operations, all payments due under the contract are within the scheme. This is the case even if only one of the jobs is regarded as a construction operation. A typical example is where a carpet fitter is engaged to 'finish' a house, laying carpet in some rooms and wood flooring in other rooms. Unless there is a separate contract for the carpet fitting, which is not a construction operation; the scheme would have to be applied to all the works.

21.2.2 Construction Industry Scheme

The current scheme removed a lot of the administration created by the previous scheme, dispensing with CIS registration cards and exemption certificates and offering options of online checking (verification) of subcontractor tax payment status, which becomes compulsory from 6 April 2017 and online filing of monthly returns, which becomes compulsory from 6 April 2016.

The main features are:

- Contractors must check or 'verify' the payment status of new subcontractors with HMRC. This requires the contractor to provide details of the subcontractor's name, national insurance number and unique tax reference number (UTR); company name and registration number if a company subcontractor and partnership name and UTR, if a partnership.

- Most subcontractors will be paid net of the standard rate of deduction of 20%, subject to being registered for the scheme.
- Subcontractors that fail to register or fail to provide the correct information to the contractor, resulting in their details not being matched by HMRC, will suffer the higher rate of deduction of 30%.
- When asked to verify a subcontractor, HMRC will instruct the contractor or Agent of the rate of deduction or confirm gross payment.
- Three tests need to be satisfied before a subcontractor can be granted gross payment status:
  - The business test – the subcotractor needs to show that it is carrying out construction work in the UK, or supplying labour, and the business is run through a bank account.
  - The turnover test is based on net turnover, ie gross income from construction work excluding VAT and the cost of materials. Individuals need a net construction turnover of at least £30,000 in the 12 months preceding their application for gross payment.
  - Partnerships and companies can use the alternative (turnover) test currently set at £200,000, but reducing to £100,000 from 6 April 2016.
  - The compliance test requires that in the 12 months to the date of application for gross payment the subcontractor's tax affairs have been up to date and payment of all tax due from the subcontractor and the business, including subcontractor deductions, PAYE, NIC and any business tax have been made on time. It extends to the partners' and directors' affairs, where appropriate. HMRC's CIS343 fact sheet provides guidance on applying.
- The initial and annual compliance tests will focus on fewer obligations from 6 April 2016, but full details are awaited. HMRC guidance can be found on its website. HMRC police compliance by reviewing gross paid subcontractors annually and removing gross payment status if there are any significant failings at the time of the review. This is an on-going process known as the Tax Treatment Qualification Test (TTQT), under which a subcontractor's compliance obligations are kept under constant review and errors in compliance identified. These might include for example, where monthly PAYE or CIS deductions are paid late or monthly CIS returns (whether a nil return or not) are either late, or not submitted at all. Under the TTQT a computer generated letter will be issued to the subcontractor. This letter will itemise compliance failures,

and advise the subcontractor that its gross payment status will be withdrawn within 90 days from the date of the letter.

- Any subcontractor receiving this letter may appeal against the decision to withdraw gross payment status within 30 days. If no appeal is received by HMRC, then contractors who use the services of this subcontractor will be advised to withhold tax from future payments
- To appeal against the withdrawal of gross payment status, the subcontractor must have a 'reasonable excuse' as to why the compliance failures occurred. A 'reasonable excuse' can include:
  - an unavoidable or unexpected absence close to a payment or return filing date because of business commitments or domestic emergencies;
  - accidental destruction of records by fire or flood;
  - exceptional postal delays as a result of industrial action or civil disturbance;
  - sudden disruption to a business as a result of a break-in;
  - the installation of a computer system or program for payroll accounting which has hit 'unexpected teething problems'.
- HMRC has changed its approach to the cancellation of the subcontractor gross payment status since it was criticised in the *Scofield* case and will now write to subcontractors indicating the intention to cancel, but offering the opportunity to give mitigating reasons such as problems in getting paid by a contractor that resulted in non-payment of taxes.
- There is a higher rate tax deduction of 30% if a subcontractor cannot be 'matched' on the HMRC system. This rate will continue to apply until the subcontractor contacts HMRC and registers or sorts out any matching problem.
- Contractors must make a return every month to HMRC showing payments made to all subcontractors. A late return gives rise to an automatic £100 penalty, followed by a further £200 penalty if the return is two months late. If the return is over six months late, there is a further penalty of £300 or 5% of the tax shown in the return, whichever is greater. If the failure continues after the end of the period of 12 months beginning with the penalty date, where, by failing to make the return, information which would enable or assist HMRC to assess the amount payable is withheld, the penalty is determined as follows:
  - If the withholding of the information is deliberate and concealed, the penalty is the greater of 100% of any liability which would have been shown in the return in question, and £3,000.
  - If the withholding of the information is deliberate but not concealed, the penalty is the greater of 70% of any liability which would have been shown in the return in question, and £1,500.

- – In any other case, the penalty is the greater of 5% of any liability which would have been shown in the return in question, and £300.
- If the return is incomplete or incorrect, the penalty rules in Schedule 24, FA 2007 will apply to determine the amount of further penalties which may be payable. Furthermore, repeated non-compliance could affect the contractor's own right to receive payments without tax being deducted.
- Contractors must declare on their return that none of the workers listed on the return is an employee. This is called a status declaration.
- Nil returns are no longer compulsory, from 6 April 2015, but many contractors are continuing to submit nil returns, which can be done online until 6 April 2016.

The penalty regime discussed above was introduced by Schedule 55, FA 2009. The specific rules for CIS returns are in paras 8 to 13.

21.2.3 'False self-employment' in the construction industry

HMRC seeks to prevent construction workers 'falsely' claiming to be self-employed by establishing simple indicators of self-employment. Its favoured indicators are:

- the provision by the worker of the plant and equipment required to complete the job;
- the provision by the worker of the materials used in the job;
- the employment or provision of other workers.

There is a concern that genuinely self-employed workers can be caught by these basic tests even though they are properly treated as self-employed under current case law.

HMRC has said that those 'genuinely running their own businesses' are not affected, but its track record on such issues does not inspire confidence. In recent years, the trend has been for HMRC to use the strictest possible interpretation wherever possible. This is bound to cause yet more disputes in what is already a complex area of tax law.

Using VAT registration as a further test of self-employment was roundly condemned by respondents to the consultation, but HMRC has still not ruled out this idea entirely. It states that 'further consideration needs to be given' to it and to other possible indicators such as the provision of own transport and public liability insurance, submission of invoices and working for only one engager. It has completely ignored the fact that such a test would unfairly discriminate against those businesses that are too small to be VAT registered.

In addition, those affected will have the worst of both worlds, as they will be treated as employees for tax and NIC purposes, but will not be entitled to the employment law rights that normally go with that status.

The intention is that the paying company will be responsible for operating PAYE and NIC for those classified as employees for tax purposes under the new rules. The Government has stated that these rules would be brought in as soon as the construction industry had 'recovered from the current economic downturn'.

21.3 IR35

These rules use existing case law (see Chapter 7) to determine whether an individual performs services that would be taxed as employment income were it not for the fact that his or her services are provided through an intermediary such as a service company. Those caught by these rules will pay approximately the same PAYE and NIC as an individual who is an employee of the end customer.

Earlier this year, there was great excitement when it was announced that the OTS would review IR35 to see whether it could be simplified, improved, or even replaced. These hopes were however dashed in the 2011 Budget, when the Government stated that:

> . . . following the publication of the OTS review of small business tax, the Government commits to making clear improvements in the way IR35 is administered. These improvements will include setting up a dedicated helpline staffed by specialists, publishing guidance on those types of cases HMRC views as outside the scope of IR35, targeting compliance activity by restricting reviews to high risk cases and setting up an IR35 Forum which will monitor HMRC's new approach. The Government has decided to retain IR35, as abolition would put substantial revenue at risk.

HMRC has set out a nine-point plan for determining the deemed employment income tax charge for a tax year:

- *Step 1* determines that the starting point for the calculation is the total amount received by the intermediary during the tax year from relevant engagements. This figure includes any benefits-in-kind provided to the intermediary in respect of those engagements. This total amount is then reduced by 5%, which is an allowance for the intermediary's running costs.
- *Step 2* adds in any payments or benefits-in-kind received by the worker or his or her family in respect of any relevant engagements from anyone other than the intermediary, which are not otherwise taxable as employment income, but which would have been so taxable had the worker been employed by the client.

- *Step 3* deducts any amounts spent by the intermediary that could have been claimed as expenses against income tax had the worker been the client's employee and met them him or herself.
- *Step 4* allows a deduction for any capital allowances that could have been claimed by the worker had he or she been the client's employee.
- *Step 5* deducts any contributions paid by the intermediary to an approved pension scheme for the worker's benefit.
- *Step 6* deducts any employers' NIC (Classes 1 and 1A) paid by the intermediary in respect of salary or benefits-in-kind provided to the worker during the year.
- *Step 7* deducts any amount of salary and benefits-in-kind provided by the intermediary to the worker during the year, which has already been subject to income tax and Class 1 and 1A NIC (excluding any amounts that have already been deducted at Step 3). Note: if, after Step 7, the result is nil or a negative amount, there is no deemed employment income payment and no further tax or NIC is payable. If the result is positive, a deemed employment income payment must be calculated in accordance with Steps 8 and 9.
- *Step 8* allows for a deduction of the employers' NIC payable on the deemed payment. So Step 8 requires the calculation of the amount that, together with the employer's NIC due on it, equals the result of Step 7.
- *Step 9* states that the result after Step 8 is the amount of the deemed employment income payment.

Note that if the worker is within the Construction Industry Scheme (see above), it is the amount before deduction of tax under that scheme that must be brought in at Step 1 of the calculation.

Payment of tax

The tax and NIC calculated under IR35 regulations in respect of deemed payments is due for payment by 19 April following the end of the tax year. In some situations, HMRC believes that the P35 should be filed on the basis of estimates of the deemed payment and the tax and NIC due on it. See the advice published on www.hmrc.gov.uk/ir35.

Rules to be tightened up

A package of measures will be introduced to tackle avoidance through the use of personal service companies and to make the rules (IR35) easier to understand for those who are genuinely in business. This will include:

- strengthening specialist compliance teams to tackle avoidance of employment income;

- simplifying the way IR35 is administered; and
- subject to consultation, requiring office holders/controlling persons who are integral to the running of an organisation to have PAYE and NIC deducted at source by the engaging organisation (this reflects current HMRC policy).

21.4 MANAGED SERVICE COMPANIES (MSCs)

Payments received by individuals who supply their services through a MSC are subject to PAYE. Furthermore, the cost of travel from the individual's home to place of work is not a tax-free expense for workers supplied by a MSC.

This is subject to the following exclusions:

- companies providing individuals who perform professional accountancy or legal services;
- 'normal employment agencies' that do not influence or control the way in which payments to individual workers are made.

Collection of tax from directors of the managed service company

Where PAYE and NIC cannot be recovered from a MSC, HMRC may enforce the debt personally against a director of the MSC or from a person who has provided the MSC. There are also wider provisions that allow HMRC to transfer the debt to 'specified persons', ie people who 'encourage, facilitate or are otherwise actively involved in the provision of an individual's services' through a MSC.

A template to show how to calculate the deemed payment is provided by HMRC at: www.hmrc.gov.uk/ir35/index.htm

21.5 OFFSHORE EMPLOYMENT INTERMEDIARIES

Further legislation has been introduced in order to strengthen the income tax and NIC obligations of offshore employment intermediaries.

The idea is to enable HMRC to be able to more easily prove the facts in cases where PAYE and NIC have not been deducted.

There are new rules where an employee is employed by or through an offshore intermediary.

- Where there is a UK agency in the contractual chain, the UK agency is responsible for operating PAYE and NIC.
- If there is more than one UK agency in the contractual chain, the UK agency that contracts with the end client is responsible for operating PAYE and NIC.

- Where there is no UK agency in the contractual chain the client, who the employed person works for, is responsible for operating PAYE and NIC.
- There is a special rule that applies the secondary NIC obligation to a UK agency that is involved in supplying workers overseas, where the worker is in Class 1 National Insurance when working abroad.

The new legislation also simplifies the agency rules so that a worker is subject to Class 1 National Insurance and PAYE when they work through an agency and:

- the worker personally provides or is personally involved in the provision of services to the client;
- there is a contract between client and an agency under or in consequence of which the services are provided or the client provides consideration for the services, and remuneration is receivable by the worker.

The agency worker rule does not apply to those workers where it can be shown that the worker is not subject to (or has the right of) supervision, direction or control by any person.

21.6 NON-RESIDENT LANDLORD SCHEME

If you rent a property from a non-resident landlord, you have an obligation to withhold basic rate tax and pay this over to HMRC each quarter. There are two main exceptions to this rule, ie where:

- the rent paid is less than £100 pw; or
- you have received confirmation from HMRC that you may make the payment gross.

If you are paying rent to a non-resident landlord you should contact:

HMRC Centre for Non-Residents
St John's House

Example – Calculation of quarterly payment

Tax is calculated at the basic rate on the rent due in the quarter less allowable expenses. Therefore, if the rent due in the quarter to 31 December 2014 is £3,000 but during the quarter you have paid £300 out of this sum to repair a broken window, then the calculation would be as follows:

	£
Rent	3,000
Less: Allowable expenses	(300)
	2,700
Tax at 20%	540

Merton Road
Bootle
Merseyside L69 9BB.

HMRC will forward you a form to complete within 30 days of the end of each quarter, explaining how the tax is calculated and how to make a payment to the Accounts Office.

No later than 5 July following the end of each tax year you must provide a return including details of the rent paid, allowable expenses and tax deducted. Within the same time frame you should also supply the landlord with a certificate of the tax deducted. The payments are dealt with by the Centre for Non-Residents (previously FICO) at the address above.

Landlords can obtain exemption from these provisions by entering the Non-Resident Landlords Scheme. If they do so, in return for undertaking to account for tax on their rental income, they will be permitted to receive rental payments without the deduction of any tax at source.

In order to qualify, at least one of the following conditions must apply:

- the landlord's UK tax affairs are up to date; or
- he or she has not had any UK tax obligations prior to applying; or
- he or she does not expect to be liable to UK income tax for the year in which he or she applies; or
- he or she is not liable to pay UK tax because he or she is a sovereign immune (these are generally foreign heads of state, governments or government departments).

21.7 NON-RESIDENT SPORTSMEN AND ENTERTAINERS

Basic rate tax must be withheld from most payments made to non-UK resident sportsmen and women and entertainers for work performed in the UK. In addition, where benefits-in-kind are provided to them, the cost must be 'grossed up' for tax at the basic rate and accounted for. A tax voucher must be provided for each payment and the person making the payments must account for tax on a quarterly basis.

21.7.1 Payments caught by this scheme

Payments or benefits subject to these regulations include:

- prize money;
- appearance or performance fees;
- endorsement fees where the individual has appeared in the UK (whether or not his or her appearance is to promote the goods he or she is endorsing);
- payments that finance any of the above (eg commercial sponsorship).

Certain payments specifically excluded from the scheme are those:

- subject to deduction of tax;

- subject to PAYE;
- solely for the use of copyright in words or music;
- made to the Performing Rights Society;
- made to UK residents and ancillary to a performance (including the cost of hiring a venue and payments for the services of UK-resident performers appearing with a non-resident);
- that are royalties on the sale of records and tapes; and
- amounting to less than £1,000 in a tax year. This de minimis limit applies to all payments made in a tax year in connection with the same event. Furthermore, payments made by the same or connected persons must be aggregated and the £1,000 exemption applies only if the total is less than £1,000.

In practice, where sports authorities and organisations in the UK have to bid for the right to stage events such as the Olympic Games or the Champions League Cup Final, a special exemption is granted from UK tax in respect of non-resident athletes'/players' earnings from these events. Such exemption is granted on a case by case basis.

21.7.2 Special arrangements

It is possible for a payer to secure HMRC's agreement to a lower rate of withholding tax provided an application is made at least 30 days in advance. Such authorisation may be given provided that:

- the organiser can arrange that he or she is responsible for accounting for the tax; or
- the sponsor can apply for clearance on the grounds that the tax will be collected from someone else; or
- to reflect the fact that the non-resident will have certain allowable expenses or perhaps because only some members of a group are non-resident. Expenses which may be taken into account include general subsistence expenses, UK and international travelling expenses, commission, manager's and agent's fees.

21.7.3 Indirect payments also caught

The regulations provide that the withholding system should also apply to payments made to any person:

- who is under the control of the non-resident sportsman or woman or entertainer;
- who is
  - not resident in the UK; and
  - not liable to tax in a territory outside the UK where the rate of tax charged on profits exceeds 20%;
- who receives a connected payment or value transferred by a connected transfer where there is a contract or arrangement under which it is reasonable to suppose that the entertainer (or

other person connected with him or her) is, will or may become entitled to receive amounts not substantially less than the amount paid.

The High Court held that the obligation to withhold tax applied to payments made by non-resident companies, to a company owned by Andre Agassi (see *Agassi* v *Robinson* (2004) STC 610). This ruling was overturned in the Court of Appeal but was then upheld in the House of Lords.

21.7.4 Further information

See HMRC booklet FEU 50 *A Guide to Paying Foreign Entertainers*. This has recently been of considerable concern to foreign entertainers, sportspeople and their advisers. HMRC has completely changed its view regarding the basis on which the income to be subjected to UK tax is calculated. Firstly, HMRC is no longer willing to accept that an element of endorsement deals relates to passive income, but even worse, HMRC's view on the calculation of the apportionment fraction to the UK has also changed.

Instead of looking at days spent competing and preparing to compete, training and preparation is completely ignored and HMRC instead considers 'worldwide playing days', ie the days on which performers actually compete or perform. This could have the effect of halving (or worse) the denominator for a top level sports star.

The change in interpretation becomes even more disadvantageous for an individual who may only compete or perform two or three times in a typical year. Where previously, the number of days training and preparing per annum might have been over 300, based on worldwide competition and performance days, under the new interpretation, the denominator in the fraction would be only two or three. This means that if an individual plays one concert in New York and one in London, albeit he or she spends the bulk of time outside the UK practising and preparing to perform, half of all endorsement deals would be subject to UK tax.

21.8 OTHER PAYMENTS TO NON-UK RESIDENT PERSONS

21.8.1 Interest paid to non-resident lender

Tax at 20% must normally be deducted where interest is paid by a UK-resident person and the lender is not UK-resident. It may be possible for the lender to make a claim under a double taxation agreement and where such a claim has been made, HMRC may authorise payment of interest without deduction of tax.

Section 934 ITA 2007 contains provisions that enable a member of a group of companies to pay interest to another member of the group without deduction of tax provided that the overseas company trades in the UK via a permanent establishment and the payment is required to be brought into account in calculating the profits (within the meaning of s 19 CTA 2009) subject to UK tax.

21.8.2 Patent royalties paid to non-residents

Patent royalties paid to a non-resident are normally subject to deduction of basic rate tax. Companies may pay royalties without deducting tax if the recipient is a person resident in a country for which the relevant double tax treaty contains an exemption from UK tax. If it turns out that the exemption was not in fact due, the company paying the royalty will have to account for the tax that should have been withheld.

21.8.3 Copyright royalties

Copyright royalties paid to a non-resident are also normally subject to deduction of tax. Where the payment is made via a commission agent, basic rate tax must be withheld for the net amount paid on to the non-resident. The obligation to withhold tax does not apply where copyright payments are made to rights owners who are resident abroad and are not within the charge to UK income tax or corporation tax (ss 906(1)(b), 906(2) ITA 2007).

21.8.4 Purchase of British patent rights

There is an obligation for basic rate tax to be withheld where a person sells all or part of his or her patent rights and the vendor is not UK-resident. Once again, the provisions of a double taxation agreement may override this, but a person making payment for such rights must deduct tax unless he or she is authorised not to do so by HMRC.

22

OUTLINE OF VAT

TIM BUSS

This chapter contains the following sections:

(1) Introduction
(2) Legal authorities
(3) Liability to VAT
(4) Practical implications
(5) Anti-avoidance measures
(6) Special schemes
(7) Control and enforcement procedures
(8) Fraud
(9) Appeals

22.1 INTRODUCTION

The introduction of VAT was a precondition of the UK's acceptance into the then European Economic Community (EEC) which, as a result of the European Communities Act 1982, became the European Community (EC), now commonly referred to as the European Union (EU). Part of the single market philosophy is the harmonisation of taxes, particularly those that affect cross-border trading activities, a good example of this being customs duty, which is payable whenever goods enter the EU and is charged at the same rate when or wherever the goods enter the Community.

The harmonisation of VAT has been the subject of much discussion by the EC Commission, resulting in the introduction of the Single Market legislation. The rules implement a degree of harmonisation on the VAT accounting requirements for the movement of goods between member states. Further harmonisation has been agreed in respect of invoicing and the cross border supply of services.

Several EC directives are the ultimate legal authority for VAT, and they must be reflected in the national legislation of each member state. To that extent, directives have what is known as 'direct effect'. For example, if national law is not in accordance with a directive and thereby disadvantages the taxpayer, the taxpayer can argue his or her case, using the directive, in the national court, which must recognise the directive, and with the ultimate right of appeal to the European Court of Justice (ECJ).

The UK administration of VAT was given to HM Customs & Excise, which introduced a completely new system of tax enforcement to the majority of businesses and the accounting profession. Customs & Excise, which was steeped in the history of duty enforcement, brought with it its practical approach to controlling the taxpayer. For the first time, many businesses and their professional advisers had to justify, face to face with the VAT control officer, what had been declared in the VAT return and the amounts shown in the annual accounts. Customs & Excise merged with HM Inland Revenue in April 2005 to form a combined government department, HM Revenue & Customs (HMRC).

VAT is not, in principle, a tax on profits but a tax on transactions. VAT is a tax on the consumer that is collected in stages throughout the business chain and, eventually, by the business supplying the consumer, whether that be an individual, or a business that is not registered for VAT.

A business must account for VAT on its supplies ('outputs') but can deduct VAT on its expenditure ('input tax') thereby adding tax to the 'value'.

If a business fails to charge and account for VAT correctly, it must account for both the VAT and any penalties from its own resources and thereby, by default, VAT becomes a charge on profits. Put simply, the business is a tax collector.

For VAT purposes, the UK consists of England, Scotland, Wales, Northern Ireland and the Isle of Man; the Channel Islands are not included. There is an administrative agreement between the UK and Isle of Man governments contained in the Customs and Excise Agreement 1979.

22.2 LEGAL AUTHORITIES

No single piece of legislation covers the administration and collection of VAT. The VAT legislation is described briefly below.

22.2.1 The VAT Act 1994 (VATA 1994)

This consolidation Act brought together VATA 1983 and subsequent Finance Acts amending the original legislation. It deals with the administration of the tax and provides for certain aspects to be dealt with by delegated legislation.

22.2.2 VAT Regulations 1995

This consolidated 60 sets of existing regulations and amendments introduced since 1972. It deals with a wide range of administrative procedures that must be complied with, for example the detail to be shown on tax invoices, the method of recovering VAT when a VAT-registered person is not entitled to a full recovery of VAT paid to his or her suppliers, and special VAT accounting procedures for particular transactions.

22.2.3 Treasury Orders

Certain Treasury Orders describe among other things what is or is not chargeable to VAT, and give certain organisations legal authority to recover VAT that would otherwise not be recoverable. Treasury Orders are published in the *London Gazette.*

22.2.4 Public Notices, leaflets and Information Sheets

Generally, VAT public notices are not part of the law, although certain notices are published pursuant to VATA 1994 and the VAT Regulations 1995 and, thereby, become part of the law. As such they have the same status as Acts of Parliament and are legally binding on the taxpayer. For example, Notice 700 (General Guide) is principally HMRC's interpretation of the law, but the section dealing with values expressed in a foreign currency is part of the law, as is much of the Public Notice on the special VAT Retail Schemes (Notice 727).

HMRC's leaflets are not strictly part of the law, but certain leaflets explaining HMRC's requirements for particular types of transactions have legal force. This applies to relatively few of the leaflets, the vast majority being simply HMRC's interpretation of the law.

22.2.5 EC directives

All VAT law now has its roots in European Council Directive 2006/112 on the common system of value added tax, which is implemented in the UK and other EU countries through their respective national laws. This Directive replaced the Sixth VAT Directive, which dated from 1977, and consolidated other EC legislation. There are still other EC directives (the Thirteenth Directive and Directive 2008/9) dealing with traders' rights to recover VAT incurred in countries other than their own.

22.3 LIABILITY TO VAT

Unless excluded by zero rating or one of the exemptions, VAT is chargeable on transactions in the UK when the goods or services are supplied 'in the course or furtherance of any business'. Services supplied free of charge are not made in the course of business so are not subject to VAT. Supplies made outside the UK are outside the scope of UK VAT. There are complex rules for determining the place of supply and the rules differ depending on whether the supply is one of goods or services.

With effect from 1 January 2010, the default position for the place of supply of services between businesses is the country where the customer belongs. There are however a number of exceptions to this rule and professional advice should be taken if you are unsure about the place of supply of a transaction.

22.3.1 Business

(s 94 VATA 1994)

'Business' is not defined in VAT legislation, but has been widely interpreted to cover all organisations that carry on an activity in a business-like way. This has resulted in a number of organisations that do not consider themselves to be carrying on a business (eg charities) having to conform to VAT legislation and, where appropriate, register and account for VAT on their business income. In addition, the VAT legislation provides that certain organisations are deemed to be businesses (eg clubs and associations). If it can be demonstrated that an activity is a hobby, there is no requirement to charge VAT on any resulting income.

An employee's services to an employer in return for a salary meets the definition of a supply of services, but the law specifically provides that they are not in the course or furtherance of a business and so are outside the scope of VAT.

Charities

There is no automatic relief from VAT for supplies either to or by charities. A charity carrying on a business activity must register and account for VAT on its business income the same as any commercial organisation.

Certain supplies to charities are zero-rated (see 22.3.2), but these are mainly in the health and welfare area, and new commercial property used wholly for charitable non-business activities, known as 'qualifying buildings'. HMRC allows zero rating by concession where there is a small amount of business use (up to 5%) by the charity concerned.

Zero rating was extended in FA 2000 to include supplies of advertising when made to charities and all costs incurred in producing the advertising material when supplied with advertising. This includes pay-per-click advertising services on internet search engines. In addition certain goods used in connection with collecting monetary donations became zero-rated by concession from 1 April 2000.

A more generous relief from VAT for fundraising by charities was also introduced by FA 2000. This allows charities, in certain circumstances, to treat fundraising income as exempt from VAT.

Clubs and associations

(s 94(2)(a) VATA 1994)

Many local clubs and associations, including those formed by local residents, consider they are not carrying on a business, but this is not correct. The law specifically provides that the provision of benefits to members in return for a subscription or other payment is a business activity.

Certain trade and professional organisations consider they either are not in business or qualify for exemption as professional associations, and consequently have no requirement to register for VAT. Yet because they generally provide other benefits to their members and possibly non-members that are not within the exemption, they may be liable to register.

To avoid the risk of penalties all clubs, associations and similar organisations should review their activities to ensure they meet their VAT obligations at the correct time.

Admission to premises

(s 94(2)(b) VATA 1994)

Admitting persons to any premises in return for a payment is a business activity. Anyone carrying on such an activity must register and account for VAT if the income exceeds the registration threshold.

Under s 33A VATA 1994, several national museums and galleries granting free admissions are treated in the same way as local authorities and similar organisations covered. Thus, these museums and galleries can recover VAT on related costs. The museums and galleries eligible to recover VAT on costs are chosen by the Treasury. Normally free admission is a non-business activity and museums and galleries granting free admission cannot recover VAT on costs although certain national museums are permitted VAT recovery. A similar arrangement applies to Academies (schools).

22.3.2 Supplies

The application of VAT differs depending on whether there is a supply of goods or a supply of services.

A supply of goods is where title to the goods is, or is to be, transferred to another person. This includes, for example, the transfer of title in land by means of a freehold sale or a lease exceeding 21 years.

Anything that is not a supply of goods and supplied for a consideration is a supply of services. The definition is deliberately wide. For VAT to be charged on a supply, it must be a taxable supply made in the UK. This means that the supply must not fall within any of the categories of exempt supply (22.4.7). A charge to VAT arises only where consideration is present, so a free supply of services is outside the scope of VAT. Care is required, because what may appear to be free is not necessarily so in real terms (eg barter transactions) and a hidden VAT liability could arise.

Taxable supplies

These are supplies subject to VAT at either the zero, reduced (see below) or the standard rate. There is no list of standard-rated goods or services. If a particular supply is not relieved from VAT by lower rating, zero rating or exemption, and is not treated as outside the scope, then the supply is by default standard-rated.

The standard rate of VAT is currently 20%.

Zero-rated supplies

Zero-rated supplies include exports of goods to places outside the EU (s 30(6) VATA 1994). Supplies of goods to VAT registered customers in other member states are zero-rated (s 30(8) VATA 1994). Other categories of zero-rated supplies are listed in Schedule 8 VATA 1994. The current groups in Schedule 8 are:

(1) Food for human consumption and animal feeding stuffs.
(2) Sewerage services and water (but not bottled water).
(3) Books and newspapers, etc (but not downloads).
(4) Talking books and wireless sets for the blind.
(5) Construction of new dwellings and grants of major interests (freehold sale or lease over 21 years) in new dwellings and non-residential buildings converted to dwellings.
(6) The first grant of a major interest in substantially reconstructed protected buildings (applies only to dwellings). Note the major changes to this group from 1 October 2012 and transitional arrangements which apply until 30 September 2015.
(7) International services (ie making arrangements for the export of goods outside the EU or work on goods that have been imported from outside the EU for repair and will be re-exported afterwards).
(8) Transport.
(9) Caravans and houseboats.
(10) Gold.
(11) Bank notes.
(12) Drugs, medicines, aids for the handicapped, etc.
(13) Imports, exports, etc.
(14) *This group has been deleted – it was tax-free shops.*
(15) Charities (certain supplies to or by charities).
(16) Clothing and footwear (children's and protective).
(17) Emissions allowances (withdrawn from 1 November 2010).

Reduced-rate supplies

VAT is charged on certain supplies of goods and services at a reduced rate, currently 5%. The categories of goods and services to which the lower rate applies are set out in Schedule 7A VATA 1994:

- Supplies of domestic fuel and power.
- Installation of energy-saving materials.
- Grant funded installation of heating equipment or security goods or connection of gas supply.
- Women's sanitary products.
- Children's car seats.
- Residential conversions.
- Residential renovations and alterations.
- Contraceptive products.
- Welfare advice or information.
- Installation of mobility aids for the elderly.
- Smoking cessation products.
- Caravans (exceeding certain limits) from 6 April 2013.

Care is required when determining whether the zero or reduced rate applies. Only the group headings are shown above and there is extensive detail to consider.

Exempt supplies

These are supplies that are exempt from VAT by statute, ie those listed in Schedule 9 VATA 1994 (see 22.4.7). The exemption rules are, in theory, the same throughout the EU whereas zero rating is a derogation from normal EU rules. Exemption and zero rating must not be confused because the overall effect on a business is totally different. As discussed below, zero rating gives entitlement to recover VAT on underlying costs whereas exemption does not.

VAT-exempt goods and services are listed in Schedule 9 VATA 1994. The main headings are:

- Land (with a number of exceptions, and see above).
- Insurance.
- Postal services.
- Betting, gaming and lotteries.
- Finance.
- Education (when provided by eligible bodies, which include youth clubs).
- Health and welfare.
- Burial and cremation.
- Trade unions, professional bodies and other public interest bodies.
- Sports, sports competitions and physical education.

- Works of art, etc (in limited circumstances).
- Fundraising events by charities and other qualifying bodies.
- Cultural services.
- Supplies of goods where input tax cannot be recovered.
- Investment gold.
- Cost sharing (subject to conditions) from 17 July 2012.

As the headings are a general description and the rules for exemption can be complex, it is advisable to take professional advice before exempting a particular transaction.

'Outside the scope'

Certain supplies or business activities are outside the scope of VAT. For example, the supply of goods situated outside the UK, or services where the place of supply is treated as being outside the UK. There are also sundry business transactions which are not subject to VAT (eg transactions between companies in the same VAT group (see 22.4.1)).

VAT is recoverable, subject to partial exemption rules, on costs relating to supplies outside the UK (and therefore outside the scope of UK VAT) which would be taxable supplies if made in the UK.

Non-business activities are outside the scope. VAT is irrecoverable on costs relating to non-business activities. Examples of non-business activities include free supplies of services, donations, free entry to museums, etc.

22.3.3 Value of supplies

The general rules for determining the value of a supply of goods or services are to be found in VATA 1994, s 19(2) and s 19(3). There are special valuation rules. Details can be found in HMRC Notice 700, section 7.

One of the special rules relates to discounts. Where a prompt payment discount is offered to a customer, VAT has only been payable on the discounted amount, even if the discount is not taken up. This can lead to VAT being due on a lower amount than is actually paid for the goods or services.

FA 2014 has amended the rules on prompt payment discounts to ensure that VAT is accounted for on the full consideration paid by the customer.

The changes to the rules will mean that VAT will be due on the amount actually paid.

The new rules came into effect for the majority of businesses on 1 April 2015. However, for business-to-consumer supplies of telecoms and broadcasting services (where HMRC had particular concerns about VAT loss), they came into force on 1 May 2014.

22.3.4 Exports

Goods which are exported to a place outside the EU are zero-rated. This includes goods exported to the Channel Islands but not to the Isle of Man. Usually, it is only the final exporter who is allowed to zero rate his or her supply, although in certain cases zero rating is allowed one stage back from the last supply in the UK. Details can be found in HMRC Notices 703 and 704.

Exporters must be able to satisfy HMRC that the goods have been exported. Detailed records of exports must be retained. HMRC requirements are contained in Notice 703, parts of which have the force of law.

22.3.5 Imports

VAT is normally charged on the importation of goods into the UK from outside the EC. Payment of VAT is due at the time of importation, but can be deferred until the 15th day of the month following importation provided a deferment number is obtained. The VAT payable can be recovered as input tax, subject to the normal rules. Security may be required for VAT and duty payable in the form of a bank guarantee. The duty deferment scheme has been relaxed for 'approved importers'. Approved importers no longer have to provide security for the full amount of VAT deferred. Customs duties must still be fully secured. Businesses can apply to HMRC for approved importer status which will reduce bank charges as the guarantee will be either cancelled or reduced (if goods are liable to Customs duty).

22.3.6 European Community

The terms 'acquisitions' and 'despatches' replace 'imports' and 'exports' respectively for transactions with other member states. It is not necessary to make an import declaration on an acquisition of goods from a supplier in another EC country. Provided the customer gives his or her VAT registration number to the supplier, the supplier will not charge local VAT. However, VAT has to be declared to HMRC on the acquisition of goods by calculating the VAT on the amount payable and declaring the VAT in box 2 of the VAT return. The self-generated 'acquisition' VAT charge can be recovered as input tax in box 4 of the VAT return subject to the normal rules.

Subject to certain conditions (eg showing the customer's VAT number on each invoice), despatches or supplies to a customer registered for VAT in another EC country can be zero-rated. UK VAT is chargeable if the conditions cannot be met.

UK VAT is chargeable on goods provided to non-registered customers in other member states. However, where the supplier is responsible for delivery (eg mail order businesses) then distance selling rules apply. The effect of the distance selling rules is that, subject to turnover limits, suppliers have to register in the relevant customer member state and charge local VAT.

22.3.7 Commercial property

The sale of the freehold of a new commercial property ('new' meaning less than three years old) is subject to standard rate VAT. The standard rate applies to all sales of a property within three years of completion. The grant of the freehold of 'old' commercial property or the grant of a leasehold interest in new or old property is exempt from VAT, but the landlord has the right to elect to waive the exemption and charge VAT on the sale or on rental payments, commonly known as 'the option to tax'. The major advantage of making an option to tax is that a landlord can recover VAT on costs relating to an opted property. The tenant can recover VAT charged on rent provided he or she is using the property for taxable purposes.

The option to tax election is not available for certain supplies where, at the time the interest was granted, there is an intention or expectation that the land will become 'exempt land'. In broad terms, exempt land is land or buildings used wholly or mainly for non-VATable purposes. See 22.5.6.

The legislation relating to the option to tax land and/or buildings was rewritten with effect from 1 June 2008. The intention was to simplify the legislation. It is also now possible, for the first time, for taxpayers to revoke an option to tax after 20 years. A number of associated changes were also made. For example, it is now possible to revoke an option within six months after it was made (the 'cooling off period') in limited circumstances.

22.3.8 Transfers of going concerns (TOGC)

The sale of a business as a going concern is, subject to certain conditions, outside the scope of VAT. The conditions can be found in Article 5 of the VAT (Special Provisions) Order 1995 (SI 1995/1268). This area has been the subject of extensive litigation and, if there is any doubt as to whether or not a transfer of trade and/or assets qualifies as a TOGC, advice should be sought. There are also special rules when a TOGC includes property.

22.4 PRACTICAL IMPLICATIONS

The administration of VAT is by a system of VAT registration, the submission of regular VAT returns and control verification visits (known as 'assurance visits') by HMRC.

22.4.1 VAT registration

Compulsory registration

Registration is required where a business or any other organisation makes taxable supplies over a predetermined limit. The limits, which are based on gross turnover, are increased each year, generally in line with inflation. It is the person who is registered, not the business activity. Once registered, all business activities must be reflected in the VAT accounting records; for example, a solicitor VAT-registered as a sole proprietor must also include his or her farming or writing income in his or her VAT accounts.

Currently, registration is required when one of the following two conditions is satisfied:

(1) When, at the end of any month, the gross taxable turnover during the previous 12 months, on a rolling basis, exceeds £82,000. Liability to VAT registration must be notified within 30 days and registration is effective from the first of the month following the month in which a liability to notify arose. For example, where taxable turnover in the 12 months to 31 May 2015 is, say, £85,000, notification must be made within 30 days (by 30 June 2015) and registration is effective from 1 July 2015. There is no VAT liability on income received prior to the effective date of registration.

(2) As soon as there are reasonable grounds to believe the value of taxable supplies to be made within the following 30 days will exceed £82,000 notification has to be made immediately. This rule catches large transactions (eg property sales). Registration is effective from the first day of the month in which the large transaction will take place.

Only taxable turnover (ie goods or services liable to VAT at either the zero, reduced or standard rate) is taken into consideration when determining whether there is a liability to register for VAT. Income that is exempt or outside the scope of VAT is ignored for the purposes of the VAT registration threshold.

Voluntary registration

There is an entitlement to voluntarily register for VAT where the taxable turnover of the business is below the VAT registration limits. This could be an advantage to a small or expanding business as VAT on costs is recoverable and, providing the VAT charge on supplies does not reduce demand for the product, will increase profitability. Businesses based in the UK that do not make any supplies in the UK but make what would be taxable supplies overseas are entitled to register and can thereby recover VAT on UK costs.

Deregistration

A VAT registered person can apply for deregistration once annual turnover falls below £82,000.

VAT groups

Incorporated companies under common control may register as a single unit – a VAT group. All supplies between the companies in the VAT group are disregarded for VAT purposes; ie no VAT charge arises. One company is nominated as the representative member and is responsible for submitting the VAT returns and accounting for VAT on all supplies to or received from persons outside the group. There is joint and several liability on all companies within a VAT group for any VAT due to HMRC. This means HMRC can recover a debt by a member of a VAT group from any other member of the group. HMRC has extensive powers to refuse to allow VAT grouping but in practice only uses its powers where it considers there is an avoidance motive to grouping (for further comment see 22.5.5).

22.4.2 Tax invoices

A tax invoice containing specified details must be issued by a VAT-registered person in the following circumstances:

- when a standard- or reduced-rate supply is made to another taxable person;
- a supply, other than an exempt supply, is made to a person in another member state of the EU.

The details required are set out in Regulation 14 to the VAT (General) Regulations 1995. Issuing invoices by electronic means is permitted, provided the invoices are electronically signed and their authenticity and integrity can be guaranteed.

Where the value of a supply does not exceed £250, a document referred to as a 'less-detailed tax invoice' can be issued. In addition to the supplier's name, address and VAT registration number, the document need only include time of supply, description, total amount payable (including VAT) and the VAT rate in force.

22.4.3 Time of supply

VAT has to be accounted for in the VAT accounting period (22.4.4) in which the time of supply (or tax point) occurs.

The basic tax point is determined in accordance with rules set out in s 6 VATA 1994. These rules are different depending on whether the supply is goods or services (22.3.2). The basic tax point for goods is the date the goods are sent to or made available to the customer. For services, the basic tax point is the date the service is performed.

However, if an invoice is issued or any payment is received before the basic tax point, the date of issue or receipt creates a tax point that overrides the basic tax point date.

Another tax point rule allows for an invoice issued after the basic tax point to become the actual overriding tax point. This is provided the invoice is issued within 14 days of the basic tax point.

There are also rules for particular circumstances including continuous supplies of services. The tax point rules are complex and if in doubt professional advice should be sought.

22.4.4 VAT returns

Once a business is registered, VAT returns must be submitted on a regular basis. Each VAT-registered person is allocated a three-monthly VAT accounting period, but it is possible to request particular VAT periods (eg to coincide with the business's financial year). It is also possible to request monthly returns if the business regularly recovers VAT from HMRC.

Returns must be submitted, with full payment, by the end of the month following the end of the VAT accounting period. Failure to submit returns and make full payment by the due date is penalised by a default surcharge (see 22.7.2). There is an automatic seven-day extension to the due date for electronic payments. Payment of VAT by direct debit is also available (payment is taken ten days after the due date).

For VAT periods beginning on or after 1 April 2012, all businesses (subject to minor exceptions) are obliged to submit their VAT returns online. The current exceptions are some insolvent businesses and those that can satisfy HMRC that they have a religious objection to the use of electronic communications.

A recent VAT tribunal found that because of the disproportionate application of the regulations to persons who are computer illiterate due to their age or who have a disability, which makes using a computer difficult or painful, or to persons who live too remotely for a reliable internet connection, those regulations were an interference with the taxpayers' rights under the European Convention on Human Rights. So far as EU law was concerned, the tribunal found the online filing obligations to be disproportionate because they failed to provide exemptions for those unable to comply by reason of age, disability or lack of internet access. The decision has resulted in HMRC conducting a review on ways it can assist businesses having difficulty in submitting VAT returns online.

The VAT chargeable on supplies made during the period (known as 'output tax') must be declared on the VAT return. Output tax is due on all tax invoices issued during the period, irrespective of whether they have been paid. Special schemes are available to ease this particular requirement for certain classes of business, as explained in 22.6. In addition, VAT is also due on all monies received for supplies made during the period and for which a tax invoice has not been issued, for example scrap sales, vending machine income, emptying phone boxes, staff canteen sales, and certain deductions from salaries for supplies to staff.

For businesses that do not issue tax invoices (eg retailers), VAT is due on the gross taxable income received during the VAT period.

Payments on account

Businesses that normally pay more than £2.3m annually to HMRC must make monthly payments on account with a balancing payment when the three-monthly VAT return is submitted; payments must be made by electronic means. Monthly payments on account are 1/24th of the annual VAT liability. Businesses have the option of paying their actual monthly VAT liability instead of the set amount. Unfortunately, payments on account are subject to the default surcharge (see 22.7.2) and the seven-day period of grace given to taxpayers who pay their VAT liability by electronic means does not extend to businesses that have to pay on account.

22.4.5 **VAT recovery**

VAT-registered businesses may offset any VAT paid to suppliers (known as 'input tax') against the output tax declared, subject to the following conditions:

- goods/services have been supplied to and have been, or will be, used by the business to make taxable supplies;
- documentary evidence of the supply received, ie a tax invoice, is obtained and retained.

If there is no tax invoice or other documentary evidence, HMRC will normally refuse claims for input tax. However, HMRC has discretion and may accept other evidence of VAT paid.

Supplies of zero-rated and reduced-rated goods or services are taxable supplies with an entitlement to recover VAT on related costs, whereas there is no such entitlement in respect of exempt supplies.

VAT is recoverable on the purchase of a motor car used wholly for business purposes. In practice, this means the car must not be available for private use. HMRC interprets 'wholly for business purposes' strictly, and in practice most businesses, with the exception of car leasing companies, cannot recover the VAT.

VAT is recoverable on buying road fuel for business purposes, but unless business mileage is logged, VAT on private use of the fuel has to be declared using the scale charges laid down. The amount of VAT to be declared depends on the engine size and type of vehicle. VAT chargeable on private use of fuel is based on the vehicle's CO_2 emissions.

The rules were amended with effect from 1 March 2000 to allow for the sale of items to be treated as exempt where input tax deduction on the purchase of the item had previously been blocked. This follows an ECJ decision against the Italian Government in favour of an appeal made by a taxpayer.

VAT is not normally recoverable on business entertainment expenses but it can be recovered on the cost of entertaining overseas customers (provided the entertaining is of a reasonable kind and scale). In addition, VAT on goods or services received by the VAT-registered person and used for either a non-business activity or private use is not recoverable as input tax.

Many people believe that merely because a VAT-registered person pays an invoice, there is an automatic entitlement to recover the VAT shown on it. This belief is not correct and recovery of VAT that is not input tax may give rise to penalties. Where assets are purchased and used for both business and private (non-business) purposes, taxpayers should normally apportion input tax at source between business and non-business use. An alternative approach, known as *Lennartz* accounting, allowed VAT to be recovered in full at the time of purchase, with output tax to be accounted for on non-business use over a set number of years, however recent EU case law has curtailed the use of this approach. *Lennartz* is no longer available for corporate bodies or charities and similar organisations and can no longer be used to apportion VAT incurred on land and property purchases.

The recovery of VAT by businesses that make both taxable and exempt supplies is described in 22.4.7.

Bad debt relief

A claim for bad debt relief may be made for any debt that is more than six months old. Businesses that have not paid for supplies within six months of the due date for payment will have to repay the input tax to HMRC automatically and regardless of whether the supplier has made a bad debt relief claim.

Once a debt is six months old and providing the VAT has previously been accounted for to HMRC, the debt may be written off by being entered in a Refund for Bad Debt Account (ie not written off in the accounting sense, as for corporation tax). The VAT is recovered by including the sum in Box 4 (input tax recovery). Any payment received after the claim has been made is VAT inclusive and the VAT element must be repaid to HMRC. VAT bad debt relief is not available for businesses that use either a retail scheme or the cash accounting scheme; as such relief is automatically built into such schemes.

22.4.6 Time limit for refund claims

Claims for refunds of overpaid VAT are now limited to a period of four years. The time limit was three years until April 2009. HMRC's power to issue assessments for underdeclared VAT is also limited to the same period. However, there is a 20-year limit in cases of fraud. It should be noted that there is currently a series of challenges to the way the three-year cap was introduced in 1996, ie relating to the lack of a proper transitional period following a decision from the ECJ in the case of *Marks & Spencer.* A number of recent cases have been won by taxpayers at both tribunal and court level and there could be a further reference to the European Court in future.

22.4.7 Partial exemption

A business that makes both exempt and taxable supplies is known as 'partly exempt' and is generally unable to recover all VAT paid to its suppliers. Partly exempt businesses have to adopt a method of calculating recoverable VAT. The only method which can be used without HMRC's written approval is the standard method. This method apportions VAT incurred in the ratio of taxable to total income, eg if 50% of income is taxable then 50% of VAT on costs which are not directly related to taxable or exempt supplies, ie general overheads, can be recovered.

Partial exemption calculations are normally carried out on a provisional basis on quarterly or monthly VAT returns, with a set annual adjustment taking place at the end of the partial exemption year, where the calculations from all four quarters (or twelve months) are consolidated, a percentage calculated for the year, and adjustments to input tax, either under or over, are accounted for on the VAT return.

If any other method of calculating recoverable VAT is required the method has to be negotiated with and agreed in writing by HMRC. Methods other than the standard method are known as special methods. Businesses submitting applications for special methods are required to declare that the proposed special method is fair and reasonable.

If the VAT on costs relating, directly and indirectly, to the exempt activities (known as 'exempt input tax') is below prescribed limits (known as 'de minimis limits'), all the VAT incurred is recoverable in full. The current limits are that the exempt input tax must not exceed £625 pm on average and 50% of the total input tax incurred. This means that a business can incur approximately £7,500 of VAT per annum on costs that relate to its exempt activities without having to restrict its recovery of input tax (provided the 50% qualification is not breached). Once the exempt input tax limit is exceeded in any VAT year (the VAT year ends in March, April or May depending on the business's VAT return period), all the relevant VAT is irrecoverable, ie the £625 pcm is not an automatic entitlement.

There are other minor limits that apply in particular circumstances. The rules are complex and it is advisable to obtain professional advice. Full details may be found in the VAT Regulations 1995 (SI No 2518), Regulations 99–111 and VAT Notice 706.

One situation where partial exemption can arise, which has been of particular significance recently, is where house builders let dwellings before selling them. Many house builders can recover all their input tax because the sale or first grant of a 'major interest' in a dwelling is standard-rated for VAT purposes. The letting of a dwelling, in contrast, is an exempt supply. HMRC VAT Information Sheet 07/08 (September 2008) explains the issues and implications.

22.4.8 Capital goods scheme

Certain capital expenditure used for partly exempt purposes and for non-business use is also subject to adjustments under the capital goods scheme. Under the scheme, adjustments are made to take account of any change in the extent to which the asset is put to a taxable use. All businesses are required to maintain records of any capital items described below.

The scheme applies to:

- the purchase of single items of computer equipment costing £50,000 or more (adjustments must be carried out over a period of five years);
- taxable land and property purchases, civil engineering works, property extensions and refurbishments, each where the value is at least £250,000 (adjustments must be carried out over a period of ten years);
- ships and aircraft costing £50,000 or more.

22.5 ANTI-AVOIDANCE MEASURES

Several anti-avoidance measures are available to HMRC. These include the following.

22.5.1 Business splitting

Where a business activity has been divided among a number of legal entities (eg a series of partnerships with a partner common to all) and the reason for splitting the business is to avoid accounting for VAT, HMRC may issue a direction informing all the businesses that they are registered as a single unit (see 22.4.1) and that VAT must be accounted for on all taxable income. The direction can only take effect from a current or future date.

HMRC is not obliged to prove the division was for VAT avoidance; it can treat connected businesses as one entity for VAT purposes, whether or not there is genuine commercial reason for the division.

22.5.2 Sales to connected parties

Where a VAT-registered business supplies goods or services at below market value to a connected party that is not entitled to a full recovery of input tax, HMRC may direct at any time, during the three years following the supply, that VAT is accounted for on the open market value.

22.5.3 Self supplies, etc

In certain circumstances, an output VAT charge will arise on normal business activities that are not supplies made to third parties, ie a VAT charge arises on business expenditure (usually referred to as 'self supplies'). The value of such supplies is taken into consideration when determining a liability to register for VAT; the more important ones are described below. The reasons behind such a liability are both anti-avoidance and to reduce possible trade distortion.

Reverse charges

Since 1 January 2010, the scope of reverse charges has been greatly widened and most B2B (business to business) services purchased from overseas persons give rise to an output tax liability on the recipient. The services are deemed to be both supplied and received by the UK organisation, ie there is an output tax liability, and the VAT may also be recovered under the normal rules (restricted if partly exempt). Exceptions to this general rule are listed in Schedule 4A VATA 1994 and include services related to land, passenger transport, restaurant and catering services, hire of goods, telecom and broadcasting services and, from 1 January 2011, supplies of admissions to cultural, artistic, sporting, scientific, educational and entertainment services, including fairs and exhibitions. Local VAT may be charged on the exceptions and the reverse charge does not have to be applied to these services (whether or not local VAT is charged).

Services purchased from abroad on a B2C (business to non-business customer) basis are generally taxed in the country where the service provider belongs. Again, exceptions to this are listed in Schedule 4A VATA 1994. The exceptions will include from 1 January 2015 the supply of e-services which will be taxed in the country of the customer rather than the supplier.

HMRC has also introduced the reverse charge as an anti-avoidance measure on certain B2B specified goods and services, eg mobile phones, computer chips and trading in emissions allowances. Full details are in HMRC Notice 735. The measures mean suppliers will not charge VAT (customers will apply the reverse charge), thereby reducing the scope for VAT fraud.

Joint and several liability

The VAT legislation provides that VAT-registered purchasers of certain goods can be held jointly and severally liable for any VAT unpaid in the supply chain. This is provided the purchaser has reasonable grounds for suspecting VAT would be unpaid. This measure was first applied to mobile phones and computer chips but now applies to electronic equipment used by individuals for leisure, amusement or entertainment purposes.

22.5.4 Transfer of a business to a partly exempt VAT group

Where the assets of a business are transferred to another person who intends to use them to carry on the same kind of business as the vendor, the transaction is not subject to a VAT charge (22.3.8). However, where a partly exempt VAT group (ie a VAT group that is not entitled to a full recovery of input tax) acquires assets in these circumstances, there is a deemed taxable supply by the VAT group and output tax must be accounted for on its VAT return. There are a number of conditions that may reduce the amount of this charge. This is a complex area, and professional advice should be sought. The corresponding input tax will be restricted by whatever method has been agreed with the local VAT office.

22.5.5 Group registration

HMRC can, in exceptional circumstances, direct that VAT be charged on intra-group supplies, which are normally disregarded for VAT purposes. In addition, it can treat an associated company as part of a VAT group retrospectively from a particular date or remove a VAT group member from that group with effect from a particular date.

These powers are used only where the group structure will result in a loss of tax revenue; they are designed to have effect only in cases involving VAT avoidance. See statement of practice SP6/1996 which gives examples of proposed structures where the powers will be used.

HMRC is also able to remove companies that are no longer eligible from a VAT group and also has the power to remove companies where it appears to be necessary for the protection of the revenue.

Overseas companies are not eligible to be included in VAT groups unless they have a branch or substantial business establishment in the UK.

22.5.6 Option to tax commercial property

The option to tax the grant of freehold or leasehold interests in commercial property is not available in certain circumstances if the purchaser or tenant does not use the property wholly or mainly for taxable purposes. This is to counter avoidance by businesses which are not entitled to recover all or any of the input tax they incur on purchase or major construction work on land and property.

Landlords and vendors of commercial property must enquire about a tenant's or purchaser's legal relationship with the vendor, the financing arrangements and likely use of the property as, if the option is disapplied, this may affect the landlord's or vendor's right to recover VAT on related costs. Indemnity clauses may therefore need to be inserted into leases and agreements. A full discussion of these anti-avoidance provisions is beyond the scope of this book; those entering into property transactions should seek professional advice, as this is a complex area and the cost of 'getting it wrong' may be considerable.

22.5.7 Disclosure of VAT schemes

Users of tax avoidance schemes designated by HMRC are required to notify HMRC (on the relevant VAT return) that the scheme has been used in the period concerned. HMRC has published a list of the designated schemes which includes schemes relating to land and property, value shifting arrangements, various cash-flow saving schemes where goods are supplied on approval or sale or return, and credit card or cash handling services provided as an intermediary for a retailer. The list is updated from time to time, to include new arrangements that have come to HMRC's attention.

Smaller businesses do not need to report the use of designated schemes. Smaller businesses are those with a turnover below £600,000 in the year immediately preceding the VAT accounting period that triggers notification, or where the turnover in the immediately preceding VAT accounting period is less than £50,000 (monthly returns) or £150,000 (quarterly returns).

Businesses which have a turnover above £10m in the year immediately preceding the VAT accounting period that triggers notification, or where the turnover in the immediately preceding VAT accounting period is less than £833,334 (monthly returns) or £2.5m (quarterly returns) are required to report the use of any scheme where the main purpose is to save VAT and the scheme arrangements include a published list of specific provisions known as 'hallmarks'. These include agreements to share tax savings with another party or adviser, where contingency fees will be paid and where consideration for a supply is given by a loan or by subscription for shares between connected parties.

Businesses that are currently considering putting VAT saving arrangements in place should take professional advice and consider the most current list of designated schemes and hallmarks published by HMRC. Full details can be found in Public Notice 700/8.

22.6 SPECIAL SCHEMES

Several special schemes are either designed to simplify accounting for VAT or reduce the VAT liability.

22.6.1 Flat-rate scheme for small businesses

A flat-rate scheme is available for VAT-registered small businesses. A business can use the scheme where its taxable turnover in the next year is expected to be £150,000 or less and its total business income is expected to be £187,500 or less. A business that elects to use the flat-rate scheme will simply account for VAT at a flat-rate percentage of its turnover rather than on every single transaction. The flat-rate percentage applied depends on the trade sector of the business concerned, and is calculated to include relief for input tax. It is not possible to use cash accounting (see 22.6.4) with a flat-rate scheme, but the flat-rate scheme in any case has its own cash basis. HMRC has published full details of the scheme in VAT Notice 733.

22.6.2 Retail schemes

These are special schemes used by retailers, ie businesses that sell, hire or repair goods direct to the general public rather than to other VAT-registered businesses and are in trade classification Groups 24 (Retail Division) and 28 (Miscellaneous Services). Generally the schemes are for those businesses which deal direct with the public on a cash basis and who do not normally issue tax invoices.

Use of retail schemes is however restricted. Taxpayers are only allowed to use a retail scheme when normal VAT accounting is not possible. Further information on specific schemes can be found in notices:

- 727/2 Bespoke retail schemes
- 727/3 How to work the Point of Sale scheme
- 727/4 How to work the Apportionment schemes
- 727/5 How to work the Direct Calculation schemes.

As retailers normally account for VAT on receipt of payment, retail schemes provide automatic bad debt relief, although retailers must account for VAT on all credit sales at the time of sale.

22.6.3 Second-hand schemes

The second-hand scheme allows suppliers to charge and account for VAT on the profit, if any, as opposed to the full selling price, provided the goods have not been acquired with VAT thereon. The scheme is currently available for sales of the following:

- supplies of works of art, antiques and collectors' items;
- supplies of motor vehicles;

- supplies of second-hand goods;
- any supply of goods through an agent acting in his or her own name.

Special stock recording and records are required.

Dealers in low-value, high-volume goods have difficulty maintaining the detailed records required, so may use a simplified VAT accounting method, 'Global Accounting'. Under this method, 'eligible businesses' can account for VAT on the difference between total purchases and sales in each tax period rather than on individual items.

22.6.4 Cash accounting

The general principle is that VAT must be accounted for on all tax invoices issued, whether or not the customer/client has paid for the supply. Businesses that cannot use a retail scheme and have a turnover of less than £1.35m pa excluding VAT (since 1 April 2007; previously the limit was £600,000), may use the cash accounting scheme, provided certain conditions are satisfied. The conditions are laid down in regulations as described in HMRC Notice 731, which in this respect has the force of law. Output VAT is not due until payment has been received but, similarly, input tax on purchases/expenses cannot be recovered until the supplier has been paid and a receipt obtained. Once a business has joined the scheme it may continue to use it until the annual value of its taxable supplies (including the disposal of stock and capital assets, but excluding VAT), reaches £1.6m. If this figure is exceeded, the business will have to leave the scheme at the end of its current VAT period and use the normal method of accounting in future.

22.6.5 Annual accounting

To avoid having to submit returns quarterly, businesses with an annual turnover not exceeding £1.35m (excluding VAT) may be authorised, in writing, by HMRC to use the annual accounting scheme. Nine monthly payments or three quarterly payments, in either case based on the previous year's VAT liability, are made by direct debit and a final, balancing payment is made with the VAT return at the end of the second month following the allocated VAT year.

The annual accounting scheme can be combined with the flat-rate scheme, under which a business can account for VAT as a flat-rate percentage of its turnover. The applicable percentage depends on the business sector concerned. A business can apply to join the flat-rate scheme if its taxable turnover in the next year will be £150,000 or less and its total business income will not exceed £230,000.

22.6.6 Tour operators' margin scheme

This scheme must be used by any VAT-registered business that supplies packaged travel/accommodation services. As the name implies, VAT is accountable on the margin, if any, on the taxable element of the package. Special record keeping and an annual calculation are required.

22.6.7 Agricultural flat-rate scheme

This is a special scheme under which farmers and other agricultural businesses need not register and submit VAT returns in order to recover VAT on overhead expenses, etc. Instead, the farmer charges VAT at a nominal 4% on all his or her supplies that he or she retains (in lieu of input tax). The recipient is entitled to recover the charge as input tax under the normal rules. The scheme requires authorisation by HMRC and is not applicable to all farmers: farmers who would benefit by more than £3,000 pa compared with being VAT registered are not entitled to join the scheme.

22.7 CONTROL AND ENFORCEMENT PROCEDURES

22.7.1 VAT visits

HMRC officers regularly visit VAT-registered businesses to verify the returns submitted. Their powers are extensive and include the right to see any documents, accounts, etc relating to the business activities, and to inspect (but not search) the business premises. The frequency of visits depends on a number of factors such as business size, types of business activity and compliance history. Visits can range from half a day every few years for smaller business to several weeks a year for multinationals.

Where errors are discovered, the visiting officer will raise an assessment for any VAT previously underdeclared and, where appropriate, impose penalty and interest charges (see 22.7.2). It is therefore advisable to have all assessments independently reviewed.

22.7.2 Penalties

HMRC may impose a number of penalties, automatically and arbitrarily, for failure to comply with the many complex VAT regulations. The penalty provisions were introduced with a view to improving compliance and reducing the amount of VAT outstanding at any one time.

HMRC is currently in the process of modernising and harmonising its penalties for all taxes, including VAT. New provisions have recently been introduced in respect of late registration, incorrect VAT returns and voluntary disclosures, while further changes to the penalties affecting late VAT returns are expected in the near future.

Broadly speaking, the new penalties are based on behaviour and degrees of culpability. For the purposes of calculating a penalty, an error or failure is deemed to be:

- 'careless' if it is due to the taxpayer's failure to take reasonable care;
- 'deliberate but not concealed' if it was deliberate but the taxpayer does not make arrangements to conceal it;
- 'deliberate and concealed' if it is deliberate and the taxpayer makes arrangements to conceal it, eg by submitting false evidence to support an error or failure.

HMRC can waive penalties if the taxpayer can show that they had a reasonable excuse for failing to comply with the VAT rules. However, HMRC regards most errors as, at minimum, 'careless', so the potential for incurring a penalty is high.

Late registration

(Schedule 41 FA 2008)

The current penalty system for the belated notification of a liability to register for VAT was introduced with effect from 1 April 2010.

The standard penalties are as follows:

- a deliberate or concealed act or failure – up to 100% of the potential lost revenue;
- a deliberate but not concealed act or failure – up to 70% of the lost revenue;
- for other cases – up to 30% of the lost revenue.

Late payments

(s 59 VATA 1994)

If one payment is submitted late in any 12-month period, HMRC issues a Surcharge Liability Notice to notify the VAT-registered person that payments submitted late during the following 12 months will be subject to a default surcharge of the specified percentage (see below) or £30, whichever is greater.

If a payment is submitted late during the 12-month surcharge period, a 2% penalty is imposed and the surcharge period extended for a further 12 months. The surcharge rises for each successive late payment during the surcharge period; for the second, to 5%; for the third, to 10%; and for the fourth and any further defaults, to the maximum of 15%. If payments have been submitted by the due dates for a full 12 months after the last penalty was imposed, the business is removed from the default surcharge regime and the cycle starts again.

HMRC will generally waive the surcharge where it is assessable at the 2% or 5% rates and below a minimum amount of £400. However, the Surcharge Liability Notice period will be extended to 12 months from the date of the default, and any following defaults in that period remain liable to surcharges.

Businesses may appeal against the imposition of a surcharge on the grounds that they had a reasonable excuse for the default – either by asking HMRC to review the decision, or appealing to a tribunal.

In the 2010 *Enersys* case, a large energy company, operating non-standard tax periods, had misunderstood the due date of its VAT return and submitted the return and payment just one day late, resulting in a surcharge of over £130,000. The First-tier Tribunal ruled that the penalty should be withdrawn, stating that no reasonable court or tribunal would impose such a high penalty for an error of this kind. The *Enersys* decision does not, however, set out clearly quantifiable limits to decide where the line should be drawn between a fair surcharge and an excessive one.

This is the first time that a tribunal has quashed a default surcharge on the grounds of proportionality. However, HMRC has not changed its system following the decision. Despite this, a business that has incurred substantial surcharges in similar circumstances should consider asking HMRC to reconsider the surcharge in the light of the *Enersys* decision.

A new penalty regime, which is to replace the current surcharge system for late VAT returns, was announced in the 2010 Budget. So far, no firm implementation date has been announced, but the new system is expected to introduce separate penalties for late submission and late payment of VAT returns, plus additional penalties if the return remains outstanding at six or 12 months past its due date.

Penalties for incorrect returns or claims

(Schedule 24 FA 2007)

A new penalty regime, relating to incorrect returns for income tax, corporation tax, PAYE, NIC and VAT, came into force on 1 April 2008 in respect of documents relating to tax periods starting on or after that date. No-one will however be liable to a penalty under the new regime in respect of a tax period for which a return is required to be made before 1 April 2009.

Under the new regime the penalties are as follows:

- for careless action – up to 30% of the potential lost revenue;
- for deliberate but not concealed action – up to 70% of the potential lost revenue;
- for deliberate and concealed action – up to 100% of the potential lost revenue.

HMRC has the power to conditionally suspend a penalty for a careless error for up to two years.

Voluntary disclosures

Errors in VAT returns may be corrected on a subsequent VAT return, subject to the following limits:

- where the turnover in Box 6 of the VAT return is less than £5m, the greater of £10,000 or 1% of that turnover;
- where the turnover in Box 6 of the VAT return is £5m or more, £50,000.

Errors where the net tax exceeds these thresholds must be specifically disclosed to HMRC in writing. (The limit applicable to VAT periods beginning before 1 July 2008 was £2,000.) Where the error has resulted in an underpayment of VAT, HMRC may charge interest on this type of voluntary disclosure.

HMRC may decide not to impose a penalty, provided it is satisfied that the disclosure is voluntary and unprompted. HMRC also has the power to reduce penalties in the case of an unprompted disclosure of a deliberate error. Once an attempt to arrange an assurance visit is made by an officer, HMRC normally considers the point of voluntary disclosure to have passed.

Interest

(s 74 VATA 1994)

An interest charge is imposed on assessments for additional tax issued by VAT visiting officers. The interest rate is the prescribed rate as enacted by Treasury order and is not deductible for income or corporation tax. HMRC has stated that interest may not be imposed where there is no overall loss of revenue, for example where a supplier has failed to charge VAT to a customer who would have been entitled to recover the VAT charge. HMRC has indicated that each case will be decided on its merits, but that officers have been made aware of the need to consider whether there has been a loss of revenue.

It should be noted that, in some circumstances, interest is payable from HMRC to the taxpayer where VAT has been overpaid or under-recovered due to an official error. The legislation currently provides for the payment of simple interest only on sums refunded by HMRC. There are several (direct tax and indirect tax) cases currently going to appeal on the question of whether EU law requires compound interest to be paid. This is a very complex area, and an analysis of the relevant case law is worthy of a book of its own, so it will not be addressed further here.

Other penalties

There are other penalty provisions which may be levied for various failures and inaccuracies. A discussion of these is beyond the scope of this book: however, they include failure to keep or produce records, unauthorised issue of a tax invoice (by non-registered persons), failure to notify use of certain avoidance schemes, failure to comply with the duties of senior accounting officers, incorrect issue of certificates to support zero-rating and inaccuracies in or failure to submit EC Sales Lists.

22.8 FRAUD

There are two forms of fraud in VAT law: civil and criminal.

22.8.1 Civil

(s 60 VATA 1994)

The civil penalties for dishonesty under s 60 have been largely superseded by the new penalties for incorrect declarations and failure to comply with VAT obligations. These civil fraud provisions will, however, remain in effect with respect to dishonest conduct which does not relate to an inaccuracy in a document or a failure to notify HMRC of an underassessment by HMRC.

If, after an investigation, HMRC is satisfied there has been an element of dishonesty, it may seek to impose a civil fraud penalty of 100% of the tax involved. If there has been full co-operation by the taxpayer, HMRC, or (on appeal) a VAT tribunal, may reduce the penalty by whatever percentage is considered reasonable.

22.8.2 Criminal

(s 72 VATA 1994)

The more serious cases are dealt with under the criminal law with a fine or imprisonment, or both. In these cases HMRC must use the criminal rules of evidence, etc and prove beyond reasonable doubt that a fraud has been committed deliberately. HMRC may accept a financial settlement in lieu of criminal proceedings.

22.9 APPEALS

22.9.1 **VAT tribunals**

There is a right of appeal to an independent Tribunal on a number of matters, including:

- assessments considered to be incorrect or not issued to the Commissioners' best judgement;
- liability rulings by HMRC in respect of a specified supply;
- penalties, other than the interest charged for errors, if there is a reasonable excuse for the error. (The law does not define 'reasonable excuse' but does state that insufficiency of funds or reliance on another is not a reasonable excuse.)
- the amount of the reduction, if any, of a penalty for civil fraud where the taxpayer considers he or she has provided full co-operation with the investigating officers.

In April 2009 a single tax appeal system was introduced for VAT and direct taxes, comprising a First-tier Tribunal and an Upper Tribunal. The First-tier Tribunal will hear most tax appeals; the Upper Tribunal will hear appeals against the decisions of the First-tier tribunal and may also hear some first instance appeals.

The details of appeal procedures are outside the scope of this book. However, the procedure for lodging an appeal to a tribunal (which must be made within 30 days of the appealable decision) is straightforward. It is prudent to obtain professional advice before appealing and it is advisable to be represented at the tribunal hearing, which in many ways resembles a court hearing, although less formal.

A First-tier Tribunal decision may be appealed against to the Upper Tribunal on a point of law and, in some circumstances, an appeal may be referred to the ECJ for a ruling.

Where a dispute arises over an issue that does not constitute an appealable decision (eg unreasonable delays by HMRC or refusal to apply a concessionary VAT treatment), the taxpayer cannot appeal to the tribunal. The matter can however be pursued through one of the following channels:

- complaining to HMRC, either to the officer involved or the Regional Complaints Unit;
- complaining to the independent Adjudicator;
- complaining to a Member of Parliament;
- an application to the High Court for a judicial review.

22.9.2 Departmental reviews

(ss 83A–83G VATA 1994)

Many disputes are settled by negotiation with HMRC by formally requesting a departmental review of the disputed ruling/assessment within the 30-day time limit. This allows discussions to continue without the loss of the right to appeal to the tribunal.

The review is carried out by a review officer who was not previously involved in the disputed decision. Unless it agrees a longer review period with the taxpayer, HMRC must complete the review within 45 days. A review is not compulsory and the taxpayer is entitled to appeal to tribunal without requesting a departmental review first.

23

NATIONAL INSURANCE CONTRIBUTIONS

This chapter contains the following sections:

(1) Class 1 contribution
(2) Class 2 contribution
(3) Class 3 contribution
(4) Class 4 contribution

Where rates are quoted, they are the 2015–16 rates; these and the 2014–15 rates can be found in Table 23.1.

23.1 CLASS 1 CONTRIBUTION

23.1.1 Introduction

Employed individuals are liable for Class 1 NIC unless they are under 16 or have reached pensionable age. Secondary contributions are paid by employers (see 23.1.7).

No contribution is payable unless the employee earns £155 pw, although entitlement to benefits starts for earnings in excess of £112. If he or she earns more than £155, contributions are calculated at 12% on the excess over £155 on earnings of up to £815pw (eg on weekly earnings of £179 the employee NIC is £179 − £155 = £24 × 12% = £2.88). A lower rate of 10.6% contributions is payable on earnings below the upper earnings limit if the employee is contracted out of the State Second Pension (S2P).

An additional 2% charge is imposed on all earnings above the upper earnings limit.

Women who married on or before 6 April 1977 and have chosen to pay a reduced rate are subject to pay NIC at only 5.85%. This right is lost if the woman is divorced, but is not lost if she is widowed. Women in this situation still have to pay the 2% on earnings in excess of £815 pw.

Contributions are assessed by reference to the normal earnings period which will usually be either weekly or monthly. If the employee is paid on a different schedule (eg fortnightly), contributions are calculated on the corresponding figures for whatever other period is covered by the payment to him or her.

An individual's liability to NIC is not affected by a previous period of unemployment during the year. Each 'earnings period' is looked at in isolation and there is no principle that corresponds to the cumulative method used for income tax where a tax year is looked at as a whole. There is an exception to this for company directors (see 23.1.3), but this is basically an anti-avoidance provision.

HMRC's National Insurance Contributions Office (NICO) administers NIC, statutory sick pay (SSP) and statutory maternity pay (SMP).

Most NIC, SSP and SMP appeals can be heard by an independent tribunal in the same way as tax appeals. Note, however, that appeals on contracting-out pensions issues and Working Families' Tax Credits (WFTC) are not heard by the tax tribunals.

23.1.2 Deferment

An individual who has more than one job and total earnings likely to exceed the upper limit may apply for deferment. The result is that NICO can authorise certain employers not to withhold contributions from his or her remuneration (form CA 2700). The deferment application is made on form CA72A. Ideally, this form should be submitted before the start of a tax year for which deferment is sought. Deferment will not usually be granted for a tax year unless NICO has received the application form by 14 February before the start of the year. NICO is also reluctant to grant deferment for a year in which the individual will reach pensionable age. Where a deferment application is made, the individual cannot choose which earnings should be subject to deduction of NIC. In addition, NICO will always defer contributions at the non-contracted out rate if any of the employments is not contracted out.

The position is reviewed after the end of a tax year. If an individual has not had the anticipated level of earnings from a particular employment and thus the liability for the year has not been satisfied, NICO will apply for payment of the balance. This falls due for payment within 28 days of its making such a demand.

Where the employee's contributions exceed the maximum for the year, there is still an entitlement to a repayment of contributions withheld from the remuneration, even if the individual has not applied for deferment.

Where deferment is granted, the second employer should deduct 2% contributions from all earnings above the earnings threshold and not just the upper earnings limit. A similar principle applies if someone is employed and also has profits from self-employment. In this situation, there will generally be a residual 2% on all profits above the lower profits limit.

23.1.3 Company directors

Remuneration paid to a company director is normally assessed for NIC as if it arose on an annual basis. Therefore, a large lump sum payment of fees or a bonus early in the year could attract the maximum annual contributions, rather than just the contributions limit for one week or one month.

Regulation 6A of the Social Security (Contributions) Regulations (SSCR) 1979 ensures that the earnings period is annual but it is possible to make payments on account. When the last payment is made to the director in the tax year, the employer is required to reassess the NIC due on the total earnings for the tax year on an annual, or pro rata annual, earnings period, as appropriate. To qualify for these arrangements, the following three conditions must be satisfied:

• the director agrees to NIC being assessed this way;
• he or she normally receives his or her earnings in a regular pattern; and
• those payments normally exceed the lower earnings limit for the pay period.

Directors (and officers) may also be held liable for secondary contributions where the employer has failed to pay NIC on time and the failure appears to be attributable to fraud or neglect by the culpable officers.

23.1.4 Definition of earnings

'Earnings' for NIC purposes includes all cash remuneration. Contributions are also payable on sick pay, holiday pay, etc. The NIC definition of 'earnings' is quite different from that used for income tax purposes. For example, NIC is assessed on an individual's pay before pension contributions and before any charitable donations made under a payroll deduction scheme. There are also special rules for tips, service charges and troncs.

Where an employer settles an employee's pecuniary liability, the sum paid is treated as earnings for NIC purposes even though it is not pay for PAYE purposes. Previously, only certain types of benefits-in-kind that could easily be converted into cash were liable to NIC. For example, premium bonds and National Savings Certificates are regarded as earnings for NIC purposes because they can be encashed if the holder surrenders them. The definition of earnings for NIC purposes also covers all benefits-in-kind that are taxed as employment income (see 23.1.8).

Non-cash vouchers are also treated as earnings with the following exceptions (see 4.4):

• transport vouchers where the employee earns less than £8,500;
• transport vouchers for the disabled;
• transport vouchers for the armed forces;
• vouchers exchangeable for the use of sports or recreational facilities;

- vouchers associated with long service awards;
- vouchers in respect of staff functions (less than £150 per person);
- vouchers exchangeable for meals provided on employer's premises or at a staff canteen;
- incentive awards up to £150 pa per donor;
- childcare vouchers for children up to age 16.

NIC was not previously due on employer's contributions to an EFRBS (employer funded retirement benefit scheme) established specifically for an individual director or employee, however, after introducing new Part 7A ITEPA 2003 dealing with 'disguised remuneration' (see Chapter 5), the Government brought forward equivalent NIC provisions.

In *R & C Commrs* v *Forde and McHugh Ltd* [2014] UKSC 14, the Supreme Court ruled on the meaning of 'earnings' for Class 1 NIC purposes. It decided that a transfer to a retirement benefit scheme was not a payment of earnings to or for the benefit of an employee.

Share options

No NIC arises on the grant or exercise of approved share options, unless the shares are readily convertible assets and the event gives rise to an income tax charge, for example, where an EMI option is exercised at below the market value at the time of grant.

There is no NIC liability on the grant of an unapproved option.

The exercise of unapproved options over shares that are 'readily convertible assets' attracts NIC. The charge arises on the same amount as is chargeable to tax (see 6.4.2), ie it is based on the amount the shares would realise if sold on the day the option is exercised less any sum paid for the grant of the option and/or its exercise.

No NIC liability arises on the exercise of a non-approved option over shares that are not readily convertible assets at the time of exercise.

Employers and employees can jointly elect for employees to bear the employers' NIC or reimburse the employer for the NIC. The elections cover securities options, conditional awards such as long-term incentive plans, cash cancellation payments made to give up a security option or restricted and convertible securities and post-acquisition gains from restricted or convertible securities.

Income tax relief will be available to the employee equal to the amount of the secondary NIC borne by the employee under the terms of the election.

Dividends

In the normal course of business, NIC ought not to arise where a director receives a dividend, or interest on a loan made to the company, or rent for a property used by the company. However, following the tribunal decision in *PA Holdings Ltd* v *HMRC* [2009] UKFTT 95(TC), it was established that in certain circumstances, payments that are treated as distributions and not taxable as earnings can still be subject to NIC.

23.1.5 Problem areas

One major problem area concerns directors' drawings. HMRC takes the view that where a director arranges for a personal liability to be settled by the employer and charged to his or her drawings account, the payment constitutes earnings for NIC purposes unless the drawings account is in credit.

Example – Directors' drawings

A has a drawings account with his company which is £60 in credit. The company pays a personal bill for A of £100 and debits his drawings account with £100, thus turning the credit balance into an overdrawn balance of £40.

HRMC often takes the view that £60 of the payment of the £100 bill is a repayment of a loan and attracts no NIC, but the balance of £40 is a payment of earnings and the grossed up amount is subject to NIC.

Another problem area surrounds tips paid to employees. Tips are exempt from Class 1 NIC if one of two conditions is satisfied:

- they are not paid, directly or indirectly, to the employee by the employer and do not comprise or represent monies previously paid to the employer by a customer;
- they are not allocated, directly or indirectly, to the employee by the employer.

Therefore, NIC is due on tips paid through a tronc if the employer decides, directly or indirectly through another person, who should receive what amount by way of tips. Thus, to avoid any charge, an independent troncmaster should be appointed who genuinely decides which employees are to receive a payment and the amount of such a payment. Only in this way is it possible to ensure that the employer does not allocate the payments.

23.1.6 Loans from the employer

HRMC accepts that if an individual arranges for a loan from his or her employer that is used to settle a personal liability, there is no NIC liability unless (and until) the employer writes off the loan. Considerable care should be taken when dealing with any documentation and the structure of such arrangements to minimise liability.

23.1.7 Employer's NIC

In addition to the 'primary' contributions paid by the employee, employers are required to pay 'secondary' contributions. There is no ceiling on the amount of an employee's earnings that attracts secondary contributions. No liability for secondary contributions can arise unless there is a liability for primary contributions, except when an employee with other employments has a deferment form CA 2700 or is a pensioner (Table C or S). The rate of employer's contributions is 13.8% (there is a 3.4% rebate on earnings up to £770 pw where the employee is contracted-out).

An employee can agree to pay his or her employer's NIC on profits from the exercise of non-approved share options. The NIC borne by the employee is then deducted in arriving at his or her ITEPA 2003 income (see 6.2.2). HMRC has published model agreements under which an employee can agree to pay the employer's NIC on his or her share option (see www.hmrc.gov.uk/shareschemes).

£2,000 rebate

A new Class 1A NIC employment allowance of £2,000 was introduced on 6 April 2014. This removes the first £2,000 from the NI bill of all businesses.

Benefits in kind

Employers are also liable for Class 1A NIC where the employee receives benefits-in-kind (see 23.1.8).

For company cars, the cash equivalent used for income tax purposes is treated as if it were additional earnings subject to secondary contributions. A further charge may arise if the employee is provided with fuel for private mileage, with the Class 1A charge again being based on the scale benefit used for income tax purposes.

The Class 1A NIC charge on cars also extends to unremunerated employees and directors. Where a director or employee is provided with a car which attracts a car benefit charge, but no other earnings are paid, the car itself is treated as a relevant payment of earnings for the purposes of identifying the secondary contributor.

NIC has been aligned with HMRC's treatment of income tax in the operation of PAYE Settlement Agreements (PSAs). This means that Class 1B NIC is payable on PSAs and is payable at the same time as the tax (19 October). Class 1B NIC is currently payable at 13.8% on the total value of:

- all items covered by the PSA that would give rise to a Class 1 or 1A liability, and
- the tax payable by the employer under the PSA.

Relief from employer's NIC

From 6 April 2015 employers are no longer be liable for Class 1 secondary NICs on earnings paid up to the Upper Earnings Limit to any employee under the age of 21 unless they are earning more than the NIC upper earnings threshold.

23.1.8 Class 1A NIC

Class 1A NIC now applies to most benefits-in-kind and the payment date of Class 1A NIC is 19 July after the end of the year of assessment. The Class 1A liability is an employer's charge only and is a tax-deductible expense. The charge is not payable by employees or directors.

The amount of the charge is normally equivalent to the highest rate of employer's secondary Class 1 NIC, which is currently 13.8%.

Class 1A NIC is not charged if:

- Class 1 NIC is already due (eg on expense payments);
- the expense payment or benefit-in-kind is covered by a P11D dispensation, extra-statutory concession or specific exemption;
- the expenses payment or benefit-in-kind is included in a PSA (where Class 1B NIC will be payable instead); or
- the benefit-in-kind is provided to an employee earning at a rate (inclusive of benefits) of less than £8,500 pa.

To reduce reporting requirements, HMRC has announced an exemption from income tax and NIC for the following:

- tools and equipment provided for work use where there may be a small amount of private use in the home, workplace or elsewhere;
- qualifying beneficial loans;
- general welfare counselling (but not private medical treatment or consultation); and
- refreshments provided by employers.

Class 1A NIC reports are merged with the existing forms P11D.

23.2 CLASS 2 CONTRIBUTION

23.2.1 Introduction

A self-employed individual is liable to Class 2 NIC of £2.80 pw unless his or her earnings are less than £5,965 pa and he or she has applied for a Certificate of Exemption. HMRC has recently concluded that contributions should be paid by 'sleeping partners' and other individuals who carry on a business without being actively involved such as limited partners in partnerships governed by the Limited Partnership Act 1907

– see HMRC statement of 4 April 2013. A penalty can be charged if he or she has not notified NICO within three months of taking up self-employment.

The Class 2 NIC for share fishermen is £3.40 pw and for volunteer development workers is £5.60 pw.

The Government is to simplify the administrative process for collecting NICs for the self-employed.

From April 2016, Class 2 NICs will be collected through self-assessment alongside income tax and Class 4 NICs.

23.2.2 Earnings from employment and self-employment

Where an individual has income from both employment and self-employment, both Class 1 and 2 NIC is payable unless he or she applies for deferment. The maximum he or she may pay for any year is an amount equal to the maximum Class 1 primary contributions on 53 weeks' earnings. A repayment may be claimed if he or she has paid a mixture of Class 1 and 2 NIC in excess of this amount. Payments of Class 2 NIC fall due on 31 January and 31 July, at the same time as the self-assessment tax payments.

23.2.3 Small earnings exemption

It used to be possible to avoid paying Class 2 NIC by applying in advance for the small earnings exemption. The limit for the small earnings exemption for 2014–15 was £5,885.

Earnings for this purpose are measured by reference to actual earnings for the tax year. For example, if a trader makes up accounts to 30 September, the small earnings exemption is available only if his or her earnings for 2014–15 are less than £5,965 when computed as follows:

$^{6}/_{12} \times$ profits for the year ended 30 September 2014
$^{6}/_{12} \times$ profits for the year ended 30 September 2015

An individual may apply for repayment if Class 2 NIC has been overpaid. The repayment claim must normally be made between 6 April and 31 January following the end of the tax year and thus the deadline for making a repayment claim for 2014–15 will be 31 January 2016.

The small earnings exemption was abolished for 2015–16 but there is now a small profits threshold of £5,965 and a self-employed person can elect not to pay contributions where his profits are below this amount.

A false economy?

In general, choosing not to pay Class 2 NIC could prove a false economy as entitlement to benefits such as pensions and sick pay may be affected.

23.3 CLASS 3 CONTRIBUTION

This is a type of voluntary contribution. A person who is neither employed nor self-employed (or whose earnings fall below the exemption) may pay voluntary Class 3 NIC to secure the state retirement pension and certain bereavement payments. The weekly rate is set at £14.10 for 2015–16.

The Government has introduced lump sum Class 3A contributions so that existing pensioners may increase their State pension by up to £25 pw. This will start in October 2015.

23.4 CLASS 4 CONTRIBUTION

This is payable by self-employed individuals according to the level of their profits as determined for income tax purposes. For 2015–16, Class 4 NIC is levied at the rate of 9% of trading profits between £8,060 and £42,385. Earnings in excess of the upper profits limit attract Class 4 NIC at the rate of 2%.

Where an individual pays interest on a business loan or has suffered trading losses, such amounts may be set against his or her earnings for the purposes of assessing liability for Class 4 NIC. This situation applies even where the losses have been relieved for income tax purposes by way of offset against his or her other income.

International issues surrounding NIC are outside the scope of this book. However, EC regulations can apply. HMRC has published guidance on this which can be found at www.hmrc.gov.uk/nic/work/new-rules.htm

Class 4 contributions are payable for the whole of the year in which the individual attains 65 (unless his or her birthday is 6 April).

Table 23.1 – National insurance contributions

Item	2013–14	2014–15	2015–16
Lower earnings limit, primary class 1	£109 per week	£111 per week	£112 per week
Upper earnings limit, primary class 1	£797 per week	£805 per week	£815 per week
Primary threshold	£149 per week	£153 per week	£155 per week
Secondary threshold	£148 per week	£153 per week	£155 per week
Employees' primary class 1 rate	12% of £149.01 to £797 per week; 2% above £797 per week	12% of £153.01 to £805 per week; 2% above £805 per week	12% of £155 to £815 per week; 2% above £815 per week
Employees' contracted-out rebate	1.4%	1.4%	1.4%
Married women's reduced rate	5.85% of £149 to £797 per week; 2% above £797	5.85% of £155 to £805 per week; 2% above £805	5.85% of £155 to £815 per week; 2% above £815
Employers' secondary Class 1 rate	13.8% on earnings above £149 per week	13.8% on earnings above £153 per week	13.8% on earnings above £155 per week
Employers' contracted-out rebate, salary-related schemes	3.4%	3.4%	3.4%
Class 2 rate	£2.70 per week	£2.75 per week	£2.80 per week
Class 2 small earnings exception	£5,725 per year	£5,885 per year	Abolished
Special Class 2 rate for share fishermen	£3.35 per week	£3.40 per week	£3.45 per week
Special Class 2 rate for volunteer development workers	£5.45 per week	£5.55 per week	£5.60 per week
Class 3 rate	£13.55 per week	£13.90 per week	£14.10 per week
Class 4 rate	9% of £7,755 to £41,450 per year; 2% above £41,450 per year	9% of £7,956 to £41,865 per year; 2% above £41,865 per year	9% of £8,060 to £42,385 per year; 2% above £42,385 per year
Class 4 lower profits limit	£7,755 per year	£7,956 per year	£8,060 per year
Class 4 upper profits limit	£41,450 per year	£41,865 per year	£42,385 per year

24

WEALTH PLANNING BY MANAGING YOUR FINANCIAL AFFAIRS

This chapter contains the following sections:

(1) Your family and personal financial planning
(2) Managing your investments
(3) Tax-deductible investments
(4) Some special situations
(5) Planning for retirement
(6) Taking your retirement benefits
(7) Helping the next generation
(8) Estate planning

24.1 YOUR FAMILY AND PERSONAL FINANCIAL PLANNING

There are important personal financial planning issues to be addressed. These may include selecting a suitable type of mortgage, making sure you claim all that is due to you from child tax credits, tax implications of marriage and civil partnership (and separation and divorce), protecting your dependants by taking out life assurance, funding school and university education, providing help to elderly dependent relatives and assisting your children in buying their first home. Looking further ahead, there are longer-term matters that need to be kept in mind, for example the way in which your (and possibly your spouse or civil partner's) Will should be drawn up. IHT planning also needs to be considered.

24.1.1 House purchase

When you buy a home, there are several types of mortgage available. For interest-only loans take advice about which investment vehicle is utilised to pay the outstanding mortgage at the end of the term. For instance, an option is to open an ISA and use this type of tax privileged savings to build up capital so you can clear the mortgage in due course.

Some mortgages involve an offset arrangement so that an allowance is made for a credit balance on your current account and you are charged interest only on your net indebtedness to the bank. These offset mortgages can be a way of saving interest, which far exceeds the amounts that you would retain after tax if you had a conventional mortgage and earned interest on temporary cash surpluses and the money that you would otherwise put on deposit. You should, however, be aware of the danger of actually increasing your indebtedness if you overspend, especially if you are locked into a comparatively unfavourable interest rate.

If you are lucky, you may have a tracker mortgage where interest is currently being charged at comparatively low rates. Make the most of it because it will not last. Even if you have a normal mortgage, the rate of interest will often be very low compared with past years. Try to put the difference to one side rather than use it to cover your monthly outgoings as sooner or later interest rates may go back up.

24.1.2 Pay down debt before making long-term investments

If you receive a bonus, a gift or an inheritance, it will probably make more sense to use it to clear expensive debt than to make investments. For example, clearing credit card debt may save you from paying 15% interest – you would need to make 25% or maybe 30% pa on investments to get an equivalent return.

24.1.3 If you and your partner are not married

UK tax legislation does not currently recognise common law marriages, although the extension of some rights to long-term partners is under consideration. If your partner has not made a Will, you may have no rights under the intestacy rules. The tax legislation may also be stacked against you because the CGT exemption for transfers between spouses and civil partners will not be available and neither will the IHT exemption for transfers of assets to your partner. The absence of such relief could seriously damage your wealth if you and your partner have substantial assets.

If your partner is a foreign national, bear in mind that the intestacy rules that would apply on his or her death may be quite different from the rules that apply here.

All in all, there is a lot to be said in favour of marriage from a financial point of view. However, there may be other considerations (see below).

Tax notes

Tax legislation does not recognise common law marriages, so the CGT exemption for transfers between spouses and civil partners is not available and neither is there an IHT exemption for transfers of assets to your partner.

24.1.4 Marriage

There are several important tax considerations that arise in connection with marriage.

Capital gains tax

Bear in mind that if, for instance, you transfer shares or other chargeable assets to your fiancé(e) at less than market value, you are deemed to have made a disposal at market value and a capital gain may therefore arise. From this point of view, it may be better to delay matters until after you marry as no capital gain arises on transfers between spouses or civil partners who are living together. However, if you are thinking of transferring an asset on which a capital *loss* would arise, it may be best to crystallise this loss by making the transfer before you marry.

Something else to bear in mind is the position if each of you already owns your own home. Basically, you have two years' grace to resolve the position, but at the end of that time only one property can qualify as your main residence (see 14.2.6). The property concerned may be a new home or one of you may move into the other's existing home.

Inheritance tax

No IHT arises on transfers of assets by one spouse to another unless the transferor is UK-domiciled and the transferee is not (see 30.5.1).

24.1.5 Civil partners

The rules for same-sex relationships are governed by the Civil Partnership Act 2004.

The most notable benefits of the Act are that registered civil partners benefit from spouse exemption for IHT and CGT. These benefits are, however, tempered by the fact that civil partners are also subject to the same anti-avoidance provisions that affect married couples (see 33.5 on transfers of assets overseas and 33.6 on the settlement provisions).

Couples entering into a civil partnership will generally need advice on the following:

- private residence (a couple can have only one main residence for CGT purposes);
- pension planning;
- IHT and estate planning.

Civil partners who own businesses or who have a significant shareholding in a company should talk to their tax and financial advisers before registering as civil partners.

24.1.6 Pre-nuptial agreements

Divorce lawyers say that there is no certainty that the UK courts will pay any attention to pre-nuptial agreements, although recent case law has indicated that these are increasingly being given weight provided that the wealthier spouse has made full disclosure of his or her assets and given the other party a proper opportunity to consider matters and take advice. Simply thrusting a bit of paper in front of your fiancé(e) the day before the marriage will not meet these tests.

> **Tax notes**
>
> Divorce lawyers say there is no guarantee that UK courts will pay any attention to pre-nuptial agreements in all cases.

24.1.7 Child tax credits

Remember you have to claim your entitlement, and you should bear in mind that claims cannot be backdated by more than three months (see 12.7.1).

24.1.8 Life assurance

You may well have some death in service cover through your employer's pension scheme, or your personal pension plan will produce a lump sum in the event of your untimely death. Remember, you will need to nominate a beneficiary, who will be paid at the discretion of the scheme trustees, in order to prevent the proceeds from falling into your estate.

However, this is unlikely to be sufficient if you have a young family. Consider taking out term insurance or family income cover, which provides a series of capital sums on death, if the death occurs during a specified period. The sums payable are known as 'family income benefit'. Remember to have the policies written in trust so they would not attract IHT if you and your spouse or civil partner were to die in quick succession.

24.1.9 Funding school fees and higher education

Your children's school may run a prepayment scheme that effectively gives you a tax-free return on money you deposit with the school. Ask the bursar about this.

If grandparents or other relatives are able to help, advantage could be taken of your children's tax allowances. One way is for your relatives to set up trusts, utilising part of their nil rate band for IHT, and for the trustees to distribute income to your children. This money could then be used to pay school fees.

Bear in mind that this will not work if you make a trust for your own children, as any income that is paid out before they attain age 18 will be treated as if it were your income. Where relatives cannot assist, matters are more difficult but not necessarily impossible. You should start saving as early as possible and take full advantage of privileged investments such as NISAs and qualifying insurance policies. Take advice from a specialist.

If your son or daughter is over 18, you may be able to save tax by assigning insurance bonds for him or her to cash in and use to cover university costs. A gift of such a bond does not trigger a tax charge (see 28.3.1). No tax will be payable on encashment unless your son or daughter is liable for higher or additional rate tax at that time.

Investigate the possibility of buying a property for your son or daughter to occupy while at university. They may be able to let spare rooms to fellow students and the rent can then cover some of your costs. Remember that you will have to pay tax on any net rental income you receive. If the house or flat is bought in your children's name, they may be able to claim CGT main residence exemption when the property is sold (see 14.1).

Another approach would be to set up a trust to hold the property with the trustees making the property available to your adult child for them to use as their main residence (see 31.4.11) because the CGT exemption can also be available in these circumstances. If you are a trustee, you will have some measure of control over what happens to the property after that particular child has finished his or her course.

24.1.10 Saving for retirement

It's never too early to start making provision for retirement. A pension contribution that you make when you are 30 will benefit from tax free growth for 30 years, a contribution that you make when you are 62 will not grow to anything like the same extent.

24.1.11 Separation and divorce

You may need to make the best of an event that you would rather had not arisen, the break-up of your marriage or civil partnership. First, there is only one situation in which any tax relief for maintenance payments is available: to qualify, you or your ex-spouse or former civil partner must have been born before 6 April 1935 and be separated or divorced or had your civil partnership dissolved and you must be making the payments under a court order.

The payments must be for the maintenance of your ex-spouse or former civil partner (provided he or she has not remarried or entered into a new civil partnership) or for your children who are aged under 21).

In these extremely limited circumstances, for the tax year 2015–16, relief for maintenance payments can reduce your tax bill by the lower of 10% of £3,220 (£322) (where you make maintenance payments of £3,220 pa or more) or 10% of the amount you have actually paid (where you make maintenance payments of less than £3,220 pa).

You cannot claim a tax reduction for any voluntary payments that you may make for a child, ex-spouse or former civil partner.

So far as CGT is concerned, you could find yourself in a Catch 22. The legislation provides that spouses or civil partners are connected persons for CGT purposes until the marriage comes to an end. The marriage comes to an end when there is a decree absolute, not a decree nisi. However, the exemption for transfers between spouses and civil partners applies only if you are living together. You may therefore find yourself in a situation where a CGT charge may arise because you are required to transfer assets to your spouse or civil partner as part of your divorce settlement.

It is possible to get round this problem if you plan ahead. The basic rule that transfers between spouses are not subject to CGT applies to transfers made during a tax year in which you have been living together at some time. Thus, if you and your spouse or civil partner separated on, say, 10 April 2015, a transfer of assets between you will not give rise to a CGT charge provided the transfer is made before 6 April 2016.

Tax notes

Taking financial and legal advice if you become separated is a difficult issue but, as in most situations, the earlier you seek expert advice the more likely it is that tax liabilities can be minimised – benefiting both parties when it comes to a financial settlement.

24.1.12 Buying a second home

There are some tax issues with buying a second home.

If you are going to let it out when you do not want to use it yourself, it might make sense to take out a mortgage because at least part of the interest that you pay will then attract income tax relief (by deduction when calculating your rental profit).

If you create a trust to hold your second home, you may be able to achieve a more flexible situation. In due course, when your children have grown up, the trustees might allow one of them to use the property as his or her main residence and this could save tax when the property is eventually sold as the trustees may then escape CGT on part of their capital gain because of the main residence exemption (see 31.4.11).

The property may be overseas. If so, think twice about having an overseas company own the property because this can, in some situations, expose you to an income tax charge. If lawyers or other professionals in the country concerned recommend that you buy through a local company, it may be best for the property to be registered in the name of the company but held by that company on trust for you and your spouse or civil partner – this is a matter where you need specialist advice, both in the UK and in the jurisdiction where the property is located.

24.1.13 Utilise the savings income nil rate band

There is a nil rate for the first £5,000 savings income for individuals whose other income is covered by their personal allowance (see 9.1). Don't let this go to waste. Think about lending money to your spouse or student children if the resulting income will fall within this band.

24.1.14 Take advantage of the new personal savings allowance

Basic rate taxpayers will have a £1,000 annual allowance for 2016–17. Higher rate taxpayers have a £500 allowance. Use it.

24.1.15 Providing for dependants

Disabled children

You may have a disabled child or grandchild. If so, consider making provision for him or her; perhaps by creating a trust (see 31.7).

Elderly dependants

Many readers will be making a contribution towards the support of elderly parents or other relatives. Unfortunately, successive Chancellors have significantly reduced the scope for obtaining assistance towards these costs through tax relief: it was once possible to transfer income via a deed of covenant and claim an income tax allowance for dependent relatives, but these reliefs have been abolished.

One possibility for securing tax relief is where it is necessary to purchase a property that is used by the relative as his or her home. There is no tax relief for a mortgage taken out for this purpose and CGT exemption is not available if you own the property yourself (unless you owned it before 5 April 1988). It may, however, be possible to secure CGT exemption in due course if you follow a fairly involved route, using a trust. IHT could be a problem here if the property is worth more than £325,000 or if you have previously made chargeable transfers and a gift into trust takes you over the £325,000 nil rate band.

Talk this through with a specialist tax adviser to see if a trust would fit with your objectives and makes sense in your particular circumstances.

24.1.16 Helping your adult children to make investments

If you can afford it, it may make sense for you to give or lend your adult children the money so that they can use their quota of tax exempt and tax privileged investments such as ISAs or even pensions.

Another option offering more control to the parent is to set up a family investment company. Such companies can be used in a similar way to a family trust with the parents gifting some shares in the company but retaining large enough share holdings (over 50% combined) to keep control of it. This gives the parents control over the way the investments are managed and when cash distributions are made, while putting income in the hands of their children. It can also be a tax-efficient method of investing in equities for the long term as companies do not suffer tax on dividends received from other companies – allowing income to be accumulated and reinvested without an income tax or corporation tax charge.

A family investment company is a complex vehicle and using one should only be contemplated after taking expert advice.

24.1.17 Giving to charity

There are many ways of getting tax relief for gifts to charities. Gift Aid means that the charity will get a tax rebate of nearly one third of what you give and you will receive higher tax relief at your highest marginal rate (which could be 45%) (see 11.9). Gift Aid donations made between 6 April 2015 and 31 January 2016 (or the date that you file your 2014–15 tax return if that is earlier) may be 'related back' to 2014–15. This could be beneficial if your top rate for 2014–15 is higher than that for 2015–16.

If you have quoted securities that you bought for a fraction of the current price, it may be better to give these to charity rather than draw down on your cash – you will save the CGT that you would have paid if you had sold the shares and you will get income tax relief at your top rate. See 11.10–11.11 on the income tax reliefs for gifts of quoted securities and land, as well as the anti-avoidance measures that have recently been introduced.

Some readers may be able to set up charitable trusts of their own. This can make financial sense if you are prepared to put in capital of (say) £100,000 or make regular Gift Aid payments of £20,000 or £25,000 pa.

Watch out for the rules on 'tainted donations' though, where you enter into arrangements to obtain an advantage from a charity, as under the new rules it is the donor who will be penalised rather than the charity.

Notwithstanding this, as part of a wider package of measures to encourage charitable giving, the benefit limit for donations over £10,000 has been increased. The current rule that any benefits to the donor must not exceed 5% of the donation remains but the upper limit has been increased from £500 to £2,500. This enables charities to thank their larger donors in a more generous way, without disqualifying the donation from Gift Aid.

Tax notes

If you have quoted securities that you bought for a fraction of the current price, it may be better to give these to charity to avoid paying the CGT – and get income tax relief.

24.1.18 Increasing disposable income in retirement

There are many ways of increasing your retirement income. For example, you can invest in an insurance bond and make 5% annual withdrawals (as a deemed return of capital) to use as income. No tax is charged on such withdrawals although they are taken into account in determining any tax charge on encashment of the policy. You may also invest in National Savings certificates, premium bonds and NISAs. See Chapter 24 on tax reliefs. If all else fails, you might consider using some of your capital to buy an annuity but hopefully you will be able to postpone such a radical step as it is by its nature irrevocable.

One issue to consider in this context is that income-producing investments can reduce the available age allowance. An investment bond does not produce regular income year on year, but when it is surrendered any gain accrued then counts as notional income, subject to a notional 20% tax credit for UK bonds, which should mean that basic rate taxpayers have no further tax to pay. There will be tax leakage within the fund though, which generally means growth is likely to be more limited than in unit trusts or open-ended investment company shares (OEICS). The term, tax rate and your attitude to risk will determine which is the most suitable option for you – this will often be a combination of investments.

Withdrawals from the bond are not assessed as income for age allowance purposes. In addition an income stream taken from NISAs and National Savings will not be taken into consideration when assessing eligibility for age allowance.

Another option is the use of the CGT annual exemption (£11,100 for 2015–16) to reduce tax liabilities and (if appropriate in terms of risk and performance) lower yield unit trusts or OEICS.

Remember not to look only at one tax. For example, a wealthy individual has pension income taxable at 40%. He puts all his shares into his (much younger) wife's name so that the dividends are declared on her return and do not attract higher rate tax. This works fine but when he dies she is left with a potential CGT charge if she sells the shares. It might have been better if they had stayed in his name so that most of the exposure to CGT would have disappeared on his death.

24.1.19 Funding grandchildren's school and further education costs

If you are able to do so, you will make a tremendous contribution to your children's financial position by relieving them of some of the costs of educating your grandchildren.

Regular gifts out of surplus income qualify for IHT exemption (see 30.5.2).

Setting up a settlement for your grandchildren with funds less than the nil rate band (£325,000) can still be tax-efficient. Putting capital into such a trust will be a chargeable transfer for IHT purposes, but the immediate tax charge will be nil and there should be no further IHT charge on your death provided you survive seven years (see 30.6 on this). In addition, there should be no IHT charges within the trust for the first ten years and on the ten-year anniversary, only if the value exceeds the nil rate band at the time. The trustees will have to pay income tax at 50% on income that they receive but part or all of this tax (probably most of it) can be reclaimed on behalf of your grandchildren as and when income is paid out for their benefit (see 31.5.7).

24.1.20 Passing on capital to children

If you are having a prosperous retirement, it may be that you should turn your attention to IHT planning. You should consider making PETs and chargeable transfers that are covered by your £325,000 nil rate band and utilising any other available IHT exemptions. This is covered in more detail at 24.7.

24.2 MANAGING YOUR INVESTMENTS

24.2.1 General strategy

All investments involve a degree of risk. Investments that are apparently risk-free, such as keeping money on deposit, run the risk that they will not keep up with inflation. The reality is that people who concentrate all their financial resources on any one investment automatically run some risks, albeit the nature of the risk varies according to the nature of the investments and the way they are funded.

Investments based on borrowings are inherently more risky: if you have taken a 100% mortgage to buy an investment property you are going to be under financial pressure if the tenant moves out and the property remains vacant. If you cannot cover the interest costs, you will have to liquidate your investment even though you would have preferred to wait until the property market had picked up.

There are probably higher short-term risks with stock market investments. Don't assume that past performance is a guarantee to what will happen in the future, especially in the near future. All markets fluctuate in value daily. Stock markets tend to overshoot. They are just as liable to respond to good news by surging ahead and becoming 'over bought' as to over react to bad news or a period of uncertainty.

If you have known financial commitments (eg a tax liability falling due for payment on 31 January 2016 or your mortgage has to be redeemed in two years' time) then you should set aside funds to cover these and invest the funds conservatively. Most sound investments will make money for you in the long term but it's much more risky to take a bet on the level of the stock market in 15 months' or two years' time. The long-term trend may be positive but the markets could give you a bumpy ride in between.

The same applies if there are things that could happen in the next few years, eg if you can foresee being made redundant.

As retirement approaches, you may need to be able to draw on savings in the foreseeable future. This means that you are less able to sit tight and ride out the fluctuations of the markets.

It is therefore important to keep tax planning in perspective. In general, investment considerations should dictate your investment policy. Naturally, these vary according to an individual's perspective, whether it be age, need for short-term and medium-term liquidity, income requirements, the degree of acceptable risk, expectations for future inflation levels, perception of the economic climate, etc. Tax planning must fit in around such considerations. However, there are some simple steps that can help you to reduce the tax payable on your investment income and gains.

24.2.2 Selecting investments that suit your requirements

Investments have varying tax treatments and this variation needs to be taken into account. For example, advisers often say that you should try to arrange matters so that both you and your spouse or civil partner use up your CGT annual exemption every year but as always it will depend on your individual circumstances. You should take independent financial advice.

Here are our thoughts on certain types of investment and the objectives they are likely to meet:

Objective	*Type of investment*
Tax-free returns	Certain index linked and fixed-interest National Savings certificates (see 25.2)
	ISAs (see 25.1)
	VCT investments (see 25.7)
Use annual exemptions and brought-forward CGT losses	Quoted shares
	Unit trusts/OEICs
	Investment trust shares

	Collective funds
Avoid internal tax*	Unit trusts/OEICs
	Investment trusts
	Offshore insurance bonds (see 28.4)
Avoid paying tax on switching between specialised funds	Insurance bonds (see 28.2)
Avoid paying tax until encashment	Roll-up funds (see 10.7) insurance bonds (28.2)
Deferring taxable income	Roll-up funds
	Insurance bonds
Avoid two-tier CGT**	Unit trusts/OEICs
	Investment trusts/shares
	REITs (see 27.6)
Reducing tax by making investments also known as 'tax reducers'	VCTs (see 25.7)
	SEIS investments (see 25.5)
	EIS investments (see 25.4)
	Pension schemes (see 26.1)
IHT savings	Unquoted shares (see 30.8.2)
	AIM shares

* Investments are subject to internal tax where the fund is liable for tax (eg corporation tax) that is separate from the tax payable by the investor and which cannot be reclaimed by him or her.
** Investments attract a two-tier tax charge where tax is charged on income and gains realised by the fund and the investor is subject to a separate tax charge, usually on realising his or her investment.

Property investments

Chapter 26 looks at some of the differences in the tax treatment various types of property investments.

24.2.3 Further analysis

Selecting an appropriate investment involves a great deal more than just the 'tick box' approach that the above table may suggest. This is partly because some of the objectives run in opposite directions. For example, investing in a VCT may give you tax-free dividends but it is also a more risky investment.

Similarly, it may well be desirable (all other things being equal) to avoid a fund that is subject to an internal tax charge but this drawback may be less than it looks. If you hold shares and unit trusts that are likely to produce capital gains, and you are subject to 40% or 45% income tax, an investment in an insurance company may have its plus points.

A lot depends on circumstances. If you are giving £5,000 to be set aside for your newly arrived grandson to use when he gets to age 18, it may well be best to invest in a broadly based unit trust or other managed investment rather than, for example, using the money to buy shares in one particular company.

It is important to know what you are getting. If you are buying units in an offshore fund, you need to know whether it has reporting status because profits realised on the sale of reporting funds are taxed in a different way.

Similarly, if you invest in an investment vehicle known as a structured product issued by a bank that gives you (say) 75% of the increase in the FTSE100 index over the next five years or a minimum 10% return if the index goes down, you need to know how any profit will be taxed. The tax treatment of these bonds means the return may be taxed either as a gain or as income, depending on the structure, and it is important to know which will apply, and plan accordingly.

You should consult an IFA or other investment specialist on these types of issues.

24.2.4 Managing investments to take account of your personal situation

In the next section of this chapter, we look at ways in which you may be able to fine-tune your investments by taking full advantage of opportunities that arise from your own (and your family's) circumstances.

24.2.5 Take full advantage of tax-efficient investments

Investments in an ISA are not charged to tax in your hands (though charges can arise in some instances within the funds held) (see 25.1), so if possible you should open ISAs for yourself and your spouse or civil partner. National Savings certificates and Friendly Society tax exempt policies also offer a safe and tax-free return, albeit at a relatively low interest rate.

Also consider taking out a personal pension plan for a non-working spouse or partner.

24.2.6 Use all your family's allowances

There is generally scope for planning both in relation to income tax and CGT.

ISAs

The tax-free income and capital growth available through use of an ISA make it one of the most important vehicles for family investment. Ensuring that the annual ISA allowances of both spouses are used (£15,240 for 2015–16) is important and don't forget that adult children can also invest through an ISA. It may even make sense for you to lend cash to your adult children so that they can make tax-efficient investments in ISAs (see 25.1).

For children aged under 18, there is a junior ISA with an annual investment limit of £4,080, which can all be invested in stocks and shares or in a cash deposit. The invested funds will be locked in until the child reaches the age of 18 and both parents and other relatives can pay in funds but, unlike the child trust fund (CTF), the Government makes no contributions to the savings.

Deposit interest

Spouses and civil partners each have their own personal allowances and each spouse or civil partner's income is taxed completely separately. If your spouse or civil partner has little or no income, or is liable only at 20% whereas you have to pay 40% or 45% tax, there may be advantages in transferring income to him or her. A fairly straightforward way of doing this is to hold bank deposit accounts and other investments in your joint names. The basic rule is that where investments are held in this way, half of the resulting income is taxed on each spouse or civil partner.

Sterling is exempt from CGT (and from the gift with reservation of benefit tracing rules see 30.7) so partners can gift cash of any amount. This will be a potentially exempt transfer for IHT purposes, chargeable if you die within seven years, but you may be able to use the annual and normal expenditure out of income exemptions to exempt much of the value of the gift.

If you open a bank account in your minor child's name, the interest is treated as your income for tax purposes only if the total income arising from such potential gifts exceeds £100 pa per child (see 33.6.4), so there may be some limited opportunity for achieving tax-free savings. Note that this rule does not apply to the junior ISA (see above) making them particularly tax-efficient for parents.

Capital gains tax

Your spouse or civil partner will have his or her own £11,100 CGT annual exemption and you should look for ways of using this each year where your combined gains exceed a single allowance. This could be achieved by transferring investments (transfers between spouses and civil partners are deemed to take place on a no gain/no loss basis) in order to put your spouse or civil partner in a position to realise a gain on a sale to a third party which you would otherwise have had to pay tax on (see 29.1.1).

This is often appropriate where a gain has built up on quoted securities. A judicious transfer of stocks and shares that show a paper gain can save significant amounts of tax even if the transfer takes place shortly before the securities are sold. But take care: HMRC often looks very closely at the paperwork on such inter-spouse transfers and you must show that beneficial ownership of the securities actually passed to your spouse or civil partner before a firm of stockbrokers was instructed to sell the shares. All other things being equal (which they seldom are), it is generally best to allow at least a few days, but better still, a couple of months, to elapse between the transfer of the shares to your spouse or civil partner and the sale by him or her.

There may sometimes be scope for using your children's annual CGT exemption as the £100 limit for income tax purposes does not apply for capital gains. Bear in mind that this is more difficult since a gift of shares, etc, to anyone other than your spouse or civil partner is normally treated as a disposal that is deemed to take place for CGT purposes at market value. However, if you hold shares in unquoted trading companies and you can see an opportunity coming up whereby you could realise those shares at a large gain, it may be worth transferring part of your shareholding to your children. Because the shares are in unquoted trading companies, it may be possible to 'hold over' any capital gain so that your child (or other relation or friend) takes over the shares at your original acquisition value (see 17.5). This means that you will have no capital gain. The recipient will have a gain on disposal of the difference between your acquisition value and the sale proceeds, which may be covered in whole or in part by the annual exemption or losses available when the asset is disposed of.

When there is an opportunity to take up an attractive share issue, consideration should be given to subscribing in your child's name as well as your own.

For CGT planning generally, see Chapter 29.

Tax notes

When there is an opportunity to take up an attractive share issue, consideration should be given to subscribing in your child's name as well as your own.

Long-term planning

You may even take out a personal pension plan for a minor child and contribute up to £2,880 (£3,600 gross) pa – but bear in mind that this is a much more long-term savings plan. (Based on current legislation benefits cannot be taken before age 55.)

24.3 TAX-DEDUCTIBLE INVESTMENTS

There are three types of investment that attract income tax relief on investment; pension contributions; investments under the EIS; and investments in VCTs.

24.3.1 Pension contributions

We return to pension contributions because the tax situation is so attractive. There is no other type of investment where you can gain tax relief when you pay money in, enjoy the benefits of a fund that pays no tax on its income and gains and take part of the fund as a tax-free lump sum. The last aspect is one of the most important; contributions to pension schemes allow a person effectively to convert taxable income into a tax-free capital sum. Bear in mind, however, that there are restrictions on the amount that can be contributed to registered pension schemes and which can obtain tax relief (see 26.4 for details).

Personal pensions

An individual is allowed to make a payment of up to £3,600 pa even if he or she does not work and so has no earnings. If he or she is employed, this limit is reduced by any contributions into an occupational scheme. The pension payments are made net of basic rate tax even if the individual has no taxable income.

Pension contributions generally

If you have employment or trading income, you can make contributions to a registered pension scheme equal to those earnings (subject to a limit of £40,000 pa, plus any unused relief (up to £40,000 pa) in the preceding three tax years). Subject to the 'wholly and exclusively' rule your employer could (if it were so inclined) make contributions which exceed your earnings (subject to the same limits). See 26.1.4 on this. For individuals who own their own company, this is a particularly tax-efficient way to extract value from the company: it avoids an immediate income tax charge on the individual, avoids any national insurance contributions that would be payable by the individual and the company if the money was paid out as a salary and the company gets corporation tax relief on the contribution.

24.3.2 Investments under the Enterprise Investment Scheme

Wealthy individuals should consider making selective investments under the EIS. It is now possible to invest up to £1m pa under this scheme. Investors are entitled to 30% income tax relief and may also be able to claim CGT deferral relief (see 25.4). Any capital gain arising on a disposal of the EIS shares after three years is totally tax free, albeit deferred gains come back into charge when the EIS shares are disposed of. You may be able to 'carry back' 2015–16 EIS investments to 2014–15 and secure tax relief against that year.

The Government has also made the EIS more attractive in other ways. Many of the restrictions and anti-avoidance rules have been abolished. It is now possible for an investor to become a paid director and take a full part in the management of the company. If you have gains in excess of the entrepreneurs' relief allowance of £10m, or you have made gains in the last few years that you would like to 'roll over', you may be able to obtain CGT deferral relief by investing further amounts under the EIS.

Remember that one of the requirements for EIS investors to qualify for the 30% income tax relief is that they must not hold more than 30% of the equity, but you do not need to meet this rule if you are investing in an EIS company only in order to secure CGT deferral relief (see 25.4).

24.3.3 New Seed Enterprise Investment Scheme

See 25.6 on this new scheme which gives 50% income tax relief.

24.3.4 Venture Capital Trusts

An individual is allowed to invest up to £200,000 pa in VCTs – although note that these can be relatively high-risk investments. There are significant tax advantages in that if you subscribe for new VCT shares you are entitled to income tax relief at 30%, although there is no longer any CGT deferral relief. In addition, the dividends you receive from your investment and any capital gain when you eventually dispose of it (after the end of the five-year clawback period) can be tax free (see 25.7).

24.4 SOME SPECIAL SITUATIONS

24.4.1 Securing tax relief for losses on investments

If you are nursing losses on investments in shares and unit trusts (OEICs), and you have realised gains on other investments during the current tax year (eg on the sale of a property that you have been letting), it may make sense to crystallise the losses, unless you hope that the investments will in time recover much of their value and you do not want to dispose of them altogether. It is still possible to consider transfers between spouses or civil partners to crystallise loses, however s 16A TCGA 1992 is a targeted anti-avoidance rule aimed at restricting allowable losses for those realising capital losses, where tax avoidance is a motive, and it may enable HMRC to attack such sales as artificial transactions entered into solely for tax avoidance, especially if the purchasing spouse or civil partner subsequently transfers the shares to the original owner.

Basically, s 16A is very widely drafted and would appear to catch even completely innocent transactions. In effect, it will be up to HMRC whether it takes the point, on a case by case basis. As a general rule of thumb, if the parties genuinely suffer the economic consequences of the transactions they each enter into, then the rule is unlikely to apply.

If you are the main beneficiary under the Will of someone who has died in the past few months, it may be possible to reduce the IHT on your inheritance. If the executors sell quoted securities within 12 months of the death, and the proceeds are less than their value at the date of death ('probate value'), it may be possible to have the IHT recalculated so that it is charged only on the lower value (see 30.11.3).

24.4.2 Planning for specific situations

Your circumstances may be special because of your residence or domicile status or your plans for the future.

For example, it may be that you plan to work overseas for a few years and will therefore cease to be UK resident. In such a case, it makes sense to defer taxable income until after you have ceased to be resident as this means no tax will arise provided it is not UK source income, and is not 'deferred' employment income that relates to a year when you were UK resident. A possible way of doing this is to invest in offshore roll-up funds, rather than bank deposit accounts, with a view to cashing in the roll-up investments after you have ceased to be a resident.

If you are about to return to the UK, having been resident abroad, then you should take advice on any investment bonds and insurance policies issued by foreign insurance companies (see 28.4). If you have been non-resident for a minimum of five tax years there may be merit in realising capital gains before you resume UK residence (see 34.5.4).

Your circumstances may be special in another way: if you have suffered 'miscellaneous income' losses in the past, look out for ways of realising miscellaneous income. The point is that such losses brought forward from previous years may only be set against miscellaneous income but the income does not have to arise from the same source (see 10.8).

24.4.3 Property investments

Investments in real estate tend to be longer-term investments. For that reason, the tax planning considerations also tend to be long term in nature.

One planning point is relevant at the time you acquire an investment property. Interest on a qualifying loan may be set against any UK rental income. The planning point is therefore very simple: you should normally borrow at the outset unless you are quite sure that you will not need to borrow money to finance your property investments later on. Even if you do have sufficient capital, it may be best to borrow to make property investments and use your spare capital for other purposes. For example, it would not be good tax planning to use your capital to purchase an investment property and at the same time take a long-term non-qualifying loan to finance school fees.

Do not plan for one tax in isolation. If you let part of your home, or if you let your home for a period while you are living elsewhere, check on the CGT implications (see 14.4.3). There are reliefs and extra-statutory concessions, but you must be very careful not to put your extremely valuable main residence exemption into jeopardy.

If you do let part of your home, bear in mind the special rent-a-room relief (see 8.4) that may mean rental income of up to £4,250 is exempt from tax.

It may make sense to form a company to hold property investments. The company is subject to corporation tax at only 20% on its rental income. But once again take advice on the long-term implications if capital gains are likely to arise when properties are sold. The VAT implications of property investment are also complex (see 22.3.7). This is an area where you need to take professional advice as there are special rules (eg option to tax and capital goods scheme) that are not straightforward. There are opportunities to save VAT, but also numerous pitfalls.

Bear in mind SDLT, both on purchasing a property and on transferring it to a company (see Chapter 36).

24.4.4 Qualifying loans for company directors

If you work full time for a close company in a managerial capacity or hold more than 5% of the shares, and you wish to purchase more shares, you may be able to raise a qualifying loan (see 11.5). The interest attracts tax relief at your top rate and there is no upper limit.

24.4.5 Plan ahead when buying a private company

If you purchase the whole of the share capital of a private trading company and things do not go to plan, you are not normally due income tax relief for any loss. You may be able to get a loss allowed for CGT purposes, but capital losses may be set only against capital gains, not against income, and therefore it may be some years before you get effective relief.

There may be a way around this if you follow certain steps when you acquire the company. You should speak to your accountant, but basically what will be involved is for you to form a new company, subscribe cash for new shares in that company and have the company acquire the shares in the private trading company. At the end of the day, your position will be almost exactly the same, except that you will hold shares in a company with a wholly owned subsidiary rather than hold shares in the subsidiary itself. What is important is that by dealing with matters in this way, you will be entitled to relief under s131 ITA 2007 on any capital loss (see 17.2), ie you will be able to set the loss against your income for the year of loss or the preceding tax year.

If you need to raise equity from outside investors, see if you can structure your company in a way that qualifies under the Enterprise Investment Scheme if possible – see 25.4. Also consider Venture Capital Trusts as a potential source of equity investment (see 25.7).

If you are in the process of buying or setting up a business, we suggest that you read Chapter 19 as part of your preparation for a discussion with your professional advisers.

24.4.6 Will you be affected by the cap on tax reliefs?

See 11.14 on this. You may need to take advice if you have reliefs that exceed £50,000.

24.4.7 Long-term planning for foreign domiciliaries

There are planning possibilities if you have foreign domicile (see Chapter 35) or indeed if part of your family has always been based overseas.

24.5 PLANNING FOR RETIREMENT

We all need to put serious thought into providing for our retirement. There are many things to be considered and this section can only highlight possibilities and direct you to the relevant parts of this book.

The obvious way of planning for retirement is to make contributions to a registered pension scheme (see 26.1).

You may wish to increase your State pension by making Class 3A lump sum contributions when they become available in October 2015. See 23.3.

If you are employed by someone else, first find out if there is an occupational pension scheme that you can join; otherwise consider making contributions into a personal pension scheme. Take full advantage of approved share schemes in order to accumulate capital for your retirement (see Chapter 6).

If you own and run a trading company, you should ensure that the company sets up the most beneficial scheme possible for both you and your spouse or civil partner (assuming he or she also works for the company). There is also CGT to be considered. Putting money into an executive pension scheme may mean that you can effectively make investments in a wider class of assets without your company undertaking substantial investment activities in its own right.

If you run your own unincorporated business, there are several retirement planning opportunities available to you. These could include direct investments into commercial property, equities, fixed interest securities or contributions into a personal pension plan. You need to take professional advice on the options available to you, to find the best 'fit' for your circumstances.

If your spouse or civil partner does not work, fund a stakeholder pension scheme for him or her. Annual contributions can be made of £2,880 (£3,600 after the addition of tax relief).

Looking at another aspect of retirement planning: if your work requires you to occupy job-related accommodation, and you don't own a home of your own, you should probably buy a property and nominate it as your main residence for CGT purposes (see 14.3).

Tax notes

If your work requires you to occupy job-related accommodation and you don't own a home of your own, you should probably buy a property and nominate it as your main residence for CGT purposes.

24.6 TAKING YOUR RETIREMENT BENEFITS

The FA 2014 and the Pension Schemes Act 2015 have revolutionised the way in which people can take their benefits from registered pension schemes.

From 6 April 2015, anyone over the age of 55 who has a 'defined contribution' pension can choose to withdraw as much money as they like from their pension pot. As HMRC points out, the options previously available for people to access their pension are still there, and so nobody has to change their plans if they don't want to do so.

There are now three main ways for people to access their pension, and they can choose any combination:

- Lifetime annuity – as before, you can use some or all of your pension pot to buy an annuity. You can take a tax-free lump sum of up to 25% of your pension pot at the time that you take your annuity.
- Flexi-access drawdown – another option which is still open to you is for you to put part of your pension pot into a drawdown fund, and take payments from this fund whenever you choose. There are now no limits on how much or how little you can take each year. You can take a tax-free lump sum of 25% of the value of your pension pot when you first put money into a drawdown fund

- Lump sum payment – since 6 April 2015, you are allowed to withdraw money directly from your pension pot without having to buy an annuity or put the fund into drawdown. 25% of these withdrawals will normally be tax-free.

See further at 26.2.8.

You should take professional advice on the way in which you should take your retirement benefits.

24.6.1 Pension wise

The Government has arranged for impartial advice to be made available by the Citizen's Advice Bureau and the Pensions Advisory Service. For details, go to www.pensionwise.gov.uk.

24.6.2 Other tax issues

You may also need advice on the tax treatment of funds that would be paid out on your death, before and after age 75.

Some people may wish to explore the tax treatment of their selling an annuity that started before 6 April 2015.

24.7 HELPING THE NEXT GENERATION

Once again, the purpose of this part of the chapter is to get you thinking about possible issues and to refer you on to other parts of this book.

There are all sorts of ways in which you may help your children. These may include loans or gifts to help with house purchases. You could give the £200 per month to invest in Help to Buy ISAs (see 25.1.4). Why not investigate the possibility of having your spare after-tax income taken into account if your son or daughter has an offset mortgage? They will still pay the same amount each month but by entering into this arrangement you could help them to clear their mortgage after 15 or 16 years rather than the full term, and if properly documented, the gift is likely to qualify for the IHT normal expenditure out of income exemption.

Another situation where you might help is by making gifts or loans to fund retraining if they embark on a new career. We have already covered tax aspects of helping your children by covering part of the costs of school fees, etc. Another way in which you may wish to assist the next generation is by setting them up in business or passing on your family business – see Chapter 32 on this.

If your children work for your family company, you will want to ensure that they can also benefit fully from your company pension scheme. If they work for an unincorporated family business, you should encourage them to make regular contributions to a pension scheme.

One very important way of helping the next generation is to establish one or more family settlements (see Chapter 31).

24.8 ESTATE PLANNING

Inheritance tax planning is a complex technical area (see Chapter 30), but in general a person should:

- make a Will as dying intestate will mean that the intestacy rules will govern the way that your estate will be distributed and these rules may not coincide with your wishes (see 30.14);
- if you already have a Will, get it reviewed if it has not been since the IHT changes in 2006 (see 30.5.1). It is in any case good practice to review your Will regularly, because your assets and aspirations will change over time;
- use the annual exemptions as far as possible (see 30.6);
- preserve and maximise business property and agricultural reliefs;
- if you receive an inheritance, consider making exempt transfers by a deed of variation;
- make potentially exempt transfers that escape IHT after the donor has survived seven years; and
- fund insurance policies written in trust so as to provide cash to meet IHT payable on death.

Making a trust can be an excellent way of putting capital outside your estate without relinquishing all control over the way that the capital is used (especially if you appoint yourself as one of the trustees); see Chapter 31 on trusts in general. You need to bear in mind the GWR (gift with reservation) rules (see 30.7) but with appropriate planning these rules need not apply if you are a potential beneficiary of a trust created by your spouse. There is also an exception from the GWR rule where a person gives an interest in a property to someone who also occupies the property and certain other conditions are satisfied (see 30.7).

See Chapter 32 on passing on the family business.

25

TAX EFFICIENT INVESTMENT

This chapter contains the following sections:

Investments providing a tax exempt return

(1) Individual savings accounts (ISAs)
(2) National Savings investments
(3) Friendly society investments

Investments qualifying for tax deductions

(4) Enterprise Investment Scheme (EIS)
(5) Seed Enterprise Investment Scheme (SEIS)
(6) Social investment tax relief
(7) Venture capital trusts (VCTs)
(8) Social venture capital trusts

INVESTMENTS PROVIDING A TAX EXEMPT RETURN

25.1 INDIVIDUAL SAVINGS ACCOUNTS (ISAs)

ISAs are tax efficient savings vehicles and can be held in either cash or stocks and shares. The tax efficient status of such accounts means that they should be the starting point for any individuals considering saving in a tax-free environment.

UK tax residents can now save up to £15,240 each year within ISAs (Individual Savings Accounts, introduced by FA2014).

25.1.1 Transfers of shares into an ISA

It is possible to transfer shares received from an approved profit-sharing scheme (see 6.2) or from an approved savings-related share option scheme (see 6.4) into an ISA. The market value of shares transferred into the ISA counts towards the annual limit, but no CGT is payable on the transfer. The transfer must take place within three years of the shares being appropriated in the case of a profit-sharing scheme and within 90 days of acquisition under a savings-related share option scheme.

It is not possible to transfer other shares into an ISA, for example, shares acquired under a public offer.

25.1.2 Withdrawals

It is possible to make withdrawals from an ISA at any time without loss of tax relief, but it has not been possible to return sums to an ISA. The Government plans to change this from Autumn 2015 so that individuals can replace cash withdrawn from an ISA later in the year that a withdrawal takes place.

25.1.3 Consequences if rules are broken

If the rules are broken within a cash ISA, the provider must withhold 20% tax and the individual must include the interest on his or her self-assessment return and pay any higher rate tax due. An individual who has knowingly broken the rules may also be liable for a penalty.

25.1.4 Help to Buy ISA

These will be introduced later in 2015. A first time home buyer can save up to £200 every month and the Government will add 25% on top. A person can also save an additional £1,000 when he first opens the ISA.

The minimum that you will need to have saved in order to qualify for the bonus is £1,600, and the maximum the Government will contribute is £3,000 (if you have saved a total of £12,000).

The Help to Buy ISA will be available through banks and building societies and rates will be set by them in the normal way.

You cannot contribute to a cash ISA and a Help to Buy ISA in the same tax year.

25.2 NATIONAL SAVINGS INVESTMENTS

25.2.1 National Savings certificates

(s 692 ITTOIA 2005)

These certificates pay an accumulating rate of interest over a two, three or five-year period. All returns are tax free. Index-linked certificates accumulate at a rate related to the RPI. A bonus is payable if they are held for either a three or five year period. Similar tax-free benefits can be obtained from premium bonds and children's bonus bonds.

25.3 FRIENDLY SOCIETY INVESTMENTS

Friendly societies issue qualifying insurance policies and there is no tax charge for investors when such policies mature. In this respect the position is no different from policies issued by insurance companies. The difference lies in the way friendly societies are treated favourably for tax purposes in that they are not normally subject to tax on life assurance business; this has generally enabled them to produce attractive returns.

Friendly society policies are essentially a long-term investment (minimum ten years). The maximum premiums are very low: the maximum permitted is £270 pa (or £300 if paid monthly). Some societies do permit a lump sum investment to be made to cover a full ten-year plan. Most of the larger friendly societies are governed by the same investment regulations as life assurance companies. All investment income and capital gains within the fund are free of all UK tax, which enhances the rate of return.

INVESTMENTS QUALIFYING FOR TAX DEDUCTION

25.4 ENTERPRISE INVESTMENT SCHEME (EIS)

(Part 5 ITA 2007)

The enterprise investment scheme (EIS) is intended to provide a targeted incentive for new equity investment in unquoted trading companies and to encourage outside investors to introduce finance and expertise to a company. The reliefs allow minority investors to secure 30% income tax relief in addition to CGT deferral relief, which could be worth up to another 28% of the amount invested.

Individuals can secure EIS CGT deferral relief even if they do not qualify for the income tax relief (eg because they take a controlling stake in the company). Trustees can also use the EIS to secure CGT deferral relief but are not eligible for the income tax relief.

25.4.1 Summary of main aspects

Tax relief is due only if an individual subscribes for new shares in a qualifying company (see 25.4.3) which satisfies the gross asset test (see 25.4.6).

Income tax relief

Income tax relief may be given at 30% on the amount invested up to a maximum of £1m this relief is forfeited if there is a disposal within three years.

There is a 'carry back' facility which allows all or part of the cost of shares acquired in one tax year to be treated as though those shares had been acquired in the preceding tax year. Relief is then given against the income tax liability of that preceding year rather than against the tax year in which those shares were acquired. This is subject to the overriding limit for relief for each year.

CGT reliefs

Shares that attract the 30% income tax relief are exempt from CGT, provided all the relevant qualifying conditions continue to be met throughout the relevant period.

Where EIS shares are sold at a loss, relief is available either against capital gains or against the individual's income by virtue of s 131 ITA 2007 (see 17.2) but this will not normally give additional relief where the investment has qualified for EIS CGT deferral relief.

Conditions to be satisfied

Income tax relief is not available if the individual has – or is entitled to acquire – an interest in the company that exceeds 30%, but CGT deferral relief may still be available in these circumstances.

Income tax relief is also not available to an individual who had such an interest in the company at any time in the two years prior to the issue of the shares. This does not prevent a connected investor from qualifying for the CGT deferral relief.

There is a ceiling for investment by individuals who qualify for income tax relief under the EIS of £1m. An individual can make a claim to treat any EIS investment as having been made in the previous tax year, thereby allowing up to £2m (currently) of income tax relieved investment in EIS companies in 2015–16. £1m would attract tax relief in the current tax year and £1m would be treated as if invested in 2014–15.

Further details on the EIS can be found at www.hmrc.gov.uk/eis.

Certificate EIS 3

An investor must obtain a certificate EIS 3 from the company before claiming either type of EIS relief.

25.4.2 Conditions to be satisfied for relief to be available

Subscription for new shares in a qualifying company

Neither EIS income tax relief nor EIS CGT deferral relief are available unless an individual subscribes for shares. The shares must be ordinary shares with no preferential rights and a minimum investment of at least £500 is required. The company must be a qualifying company.

25.4.3 Qualifying companies

A qualifying company can be a UK-resident or non-resident company, but it must be an unquoted company that:

(1) has a permanent establishment in the UK; and
(2) has a qualifying trade or be the parent of a group of companies where the business of the group does not consist, wholly or substantially, in the carrying on of non-qualifying activities. A qualifying trade is one which is conducted on a commercial basis with a view to the realisation of profits and does not consist wholly or substantially of one or more of the prescribed 'excluded' activities.

Groups

A group's activities must be considered as a whole, rather than on a company-by-company basis. HMRC has confirmed that relief will not be withdrawn where any non-qualifying activities do not form a substantial part of the group's activities as a whole. In practice, 'substantial' is understood to mean 20% or more.

Company must be unquoted

A company does not qualify if any of its shares or securities are dealt in on the London Stock Exchange. The fact that a company's shares are dealt in on AIM does not disqualify it, but the gross asset test will rule out many AIM companies (see 25.4.6).

Other conditions

There are other conditions, all of which need to be satisfied, if a company is to be a qualifying company:

- The company should be less than 12 years old except where the money raised by the EIS issue will be used to fund a substantial change in the company' activities.
- It must not control another company apart from a qualifying subsidiary, either on its own or together with a connected person, and there must not be any arrangements in place under which the issuing company can acquire such control.
- It must not itself be under the control of another company, or of another company and persons connected with it, and again there must be no arrangements in place whereby such a company may acquire control of the issuing company.

- There must be no arrangements for the company to become quoted.
- It must not be reasonable to assume that the company would be treated as an 'enterprise in difficulty' for the purposes of the European Commission's Rescue and Restructuring Guidelines.
- The company must have fewer than 250 full-time, or full-time equivalent, employees at the time the EIS shares are issued. The limit will be 499 employees for 'knowledge intensive companies'.
- There is a £5m annual limit to the amount that may be raised by an EIS share issue.

25.4.4 Meaning of 'qualifying trade'

This is covered at 19.3.4. Certain asset-based or low-risk trades are excluded, as are investment businesses. Feed-in tariff businesses are also to be excluded.

25.4.5 Definition of 'qualifying subsidiary'

(s 191 ITA 2007)

A qualifying subsidiary is one in which the issuing company or one of its subsidiaries holds at least 51% of the share capital. In addition, the company must meet one of the following tests:

- it must be carrying on a qualifying trade; or
- it must exist to hold and manage a property used by the parent company, or by a fellow 51% subsidiary, for qualifying trade purposes; or
- it must be dormant.

However, a subsidiary needs to be a 90% subsidiary if it is to be the company that uses the EIS money.

25.4.6 Gross asset test

EIS reliefs are available only where the company has gross assets of less than £15m before and no more than £16m after the EIS share issue.

25.4.7 Proposed new rules

The Government stated in March 2015 that two new rules would be introduced:

- All investors will need to be independent from the EIS company at the time of the first share issue.
- A £15m cap will apply for all venture capital investments in a single company (£20m for a knowledge intensive company).

25.4.8 Reliefs available to an EIS investor

There are two types of relief: income tax and CGT deferral relief (see 25.4.1). They are separate, and either can be claimed without the other. An individual who invests, say, £100,000 can claim both reliefs by reference to the same £100,000 invested. Trustees can only claim the CGT relief.

25.4.9 Income tax relief

An investor is entitled to the lower of the income tax payable by him or her and relief at 30% on the amount invested up to a limit of £1m. For this purpose, his or her tax liability is calculated without regard to any reliefs given as a reduction expressed in terms of tax.

His or her tax liability is also computed without regard to double taxation credits and basic rate tax deducted at source on annual payments.

25.4.10 Other conditions for income tax relief

Individual must not be connected with the company

The legislation provides that an individual may be treated as connected with the issuing company, and therefore not entitled to EIS income tax relief, if he or she directly or indirectly possesses or is entitled to acquire more than 30% of the:

- issued ordinary share capital of the company, or any of its subsidiaries;
- loan capital and issued share capital of the company or any subsidiary; or
- voting power in the company or any subsidiary.

A connected individual can still be eligible for CGT deferral relief.

An individual is also regarded as being connected with the issuing company if he or she directly or indirectly possesses, or is entitled to acquire such rights as would, in the event of the winding-up of the company (or any of its subsidiaries), mean he or she is entitled to receive more than 30% of the assets available for distribution to the company's equity holders.

Rights of 'associates' need to be taken into account. For these purposes, 'associate' means business partner, spouse or civil partner, parent, grandparent, great-grandparent etc, child, grandchild, great-grandchild etc and certain family trusts. The necessity to take account of partners' interests was confirmed by the decision in *Cook* v *Billings & others*.

An individual is also regarded as connected with the company if he or she possesses any loan capital in a subsidiary of the company.

Finally, if an investor receives a loan from a third party that would not have been made but for the EIS investment, he or she is disqualified. This also applies where a bank makes a loan that is secured on the EIS shares.

An individual is also deemed to be connected with the company if he or she is:

- a paid director of the issuing company or any of its subsidiaries; or
- an employee of the issuing company or any of its subsidiaries; or
- a partner of the issuing company or any subsidiary; or
- an associate of someone who is a director, employee or partner of the issuing company, or any of its subsidiaries.

An individual is disqualified if he or she falls into any of the above categories during the two years prior to the date the EIS shares are issued. Furthermore, he or she will not qualify for EIS relief if he or she is connected with the issuing company at the time the shares are issued, unless the individual is a business angel who qualified for EIS relief on his or her original investment and is now acquiring additional shares and is connected only because he or she is a paid director.

25.4.11 CGT deferral relief

(Schedule 5B TCGA 1992)

This relief involves a concept of deferred gain. Basically, an individual who has realised a gain may secure deferral relief if he or she invests in the EIS during the period beginning one year before and ending three years after the disposal giving rise to the chargeable gain. CGT deferral relief can be claimed even where the investor is 'connected' with the company (see 25.4.10).

However, the deferred gain is separately identified and will come back into charge when certain events happen (see 25.4.18).

Example – EIS CGT deferral relief

N sold quoted shares for £65,000 in December 2013. The shares were originally purchased in January 2004 for £10,000. In July 2014, N invested £55,000 in ordinary shares in an EIS company. The CGT position for 2013–14 would then be as follows:

	£
Proceeds	65,000
Less: Cost	(10,000)
Gain	55,000
Less: EIS CGT deferral relief	44,100
Net chargeable gain for 2013–14	10,900

Note: Although N invested £55,000, it is possible for him to claim CGT deferral relief of only £44,100 so as to avoid wasting the annual exemption for 2013–14. See 17.7.5 regarding the interaction of EIS deferral and entrepreneurs' relief and transitional considerations.

25.4.12 Withdrawal of relief where company redeems share capital

All EIS investors lose a proportion of their relief if at any time during the investor's relevant period the company repays, redeems or repurchases any of its share capital which belongs to any member other than:

(1) the qualifying individual in question; or
(2) another EIS investor who thereby loses relief under the disposal of shares rule;
(3) the total relief withdrawn from EIS investors is the greater of:
    (a) the amount receivable by the non-EIS investor; or
    (b) the nominal value of the share capital in question.

The relief so lost is apportioned between the EIS investors in proportion to the amounts of the investments that have previously qualified for relief.

25.4.13 Withdrawal of relief where value is received from the company

Relief is withdrawn to the extent that an investor receives value from the company within three years of making his or her investment. An investor is regarded as having received value where the company:

- repays, redeems or repurchases any part of his or her holding of its share capital or securities, or makes any payment to him or her for the cancellation of rights;
- repays any debt to him or her (other than a debt incurred by the company on or after the date on which he or she subscribed for the shares that are the subject of EIS relief);
- pays him or her for the cancellation of any debt owed to him or her other than an ordinary trade debt, ie a debt incurred for a supply of goods or services on normal trade credit terms. The legislation specifically provides that normal trade credit does not allow for payment to be left outstanding for a period that exceeds six months; or
- releases or waives any liability of his or hers to the company (the liability is deemed to have been waived if the liability is outstanding for more than 12 months) or discharges or undertakes to discharge any liability of his or hers to a third person.

Further, he or she is regarded as having received value where the company:
(a) makes a loan or advance to him or her if this includes the situation where the individual becomes indebted to the company other than by an ordinary trade debt;
(b) provides a benefit or facility for him or her;
(c) transfers an asset to him or her for no consideration or for consideration less than market value;

(d) acquires an asset from him or her for consideration exceeding market value; or

(e) makes any other payment to him or her except:

    (i) one that represents payment or reimbursement of allowable expenditure;

    (ii) interest at a commercial rate on a loan from the individual;

    (iii) dividends representing a normal return on investment;

    (iv) payment for a supply of goods by the individual to the company (provided the price does not exceed the goods' market value);

    (v) reasonable and necessary remuneration for services rendered to the company where the income is taxed as trading income (this does not cover remuneration for secretarial or managerial services).

However, any receipt of insignificant value can be ignored. A receipt is of insignificant value if it is not more than £1,000 or, if more is insignificant in relation to the amount subscribed by the investor for the relevant shares.

25.4.14 Withdrawal of relief where company ceases to be a qualifying company

EIS relief is withdrawn completely where any of the following events occurs during the three-year relevant period:

- the company issues shares that are not fully paid up;
- the company ceases to exist wholly for a qualifying trade purpose;
- the company comes under the control of another company, or of another company and persons connected with it;
- arrangements come into being whereby another company could acquire control.

25.4.15 Clawback of income tax relief where investor becomes connected with the company

EIS income tax relief (but not CGT deferral relief) is withdrawn completely where an investor becomes connected with the company during his or her relevant period (three years from the date that his or her shares are issued).

Definition of 'connected'

An individual is regarded as becoming connected with the company if he or she is:

- the owner (directly or indirectly) of more than 30% of the company's voting shares, its issued ordinary share capital, or its loan capital and issued share capital taken together;
- the owner of rights entitling him or her to more than 30% of the company's assets available for distribution to equity holders;

- entitled to acquire more than 30% of the company's voting shares, its issued share capital, or its share and loan capital taken together;
- entitled to acquire rights entitling him or her to more than 30% of the company's assets available for distribution to the company's equity holders;
- the associate of a person who owns or is entitled to acquire more than a 30% interest;
- the owner of any loan capital in a subsidiary of the company;
- an employee of the company;
- a partner of the company;
- an associate of an employee or a partner of the company; or
- a director of the company – unless he or she receives only 'necessary and reasonable' remuneration; reimbursement of expenses incurred wholly and necessarily in the performance of his or her duties; normal commercial returns on funds lent or normal commercial dividends on shares held; reasonable and commercial rents from property occupied by the company; or payment for the supply of goods not exceeding market value.

25.4.16 Withdrawal of income tax relief on disposal within three years

If a disposal takes place within three years, and the disposal is not to the investor's spouse or civil partner, relief is withdrawn. If the disposal is anything other than a sale to an unconnected party at an arm's length price, EIS income tax relief is withdrawn completely. Where the disposal is on an arm's length basis, relief is withdrawn only on the sale consideration received by the investor, as a proportion of the original investment.

The grant of an option during the relevant period may be treated as a disposal, ie where the exercise of the option would bind the grantor to purchase any of the EIS shares, or the investor to sell any of the EIS shares.

25.4.17 Loss relief on arm's length disposal at less than cost

Where a loss arises on disposal or the company goes into liquidation within the three-year period, further income tax/CGT relief may be due to the investor. In a case where the investor receives no payment under the liquidation, the net amount of his or her investment may qualify as a capital loss.

Example – EIS income tax relief

O invests £80,000 under the EIS. She receives income tax relief at 20% of £80,000, ie £16,000. If the entire investment has to be written off, she will be entitled to a capital loss of £64,000. This loss may be set against O's income or relieved against capital gains.

25.4.18 Clawback of CGT deferral relief

A gain that has been deferred is brought back into charge if any of the following events happens:

(1) the investor disposes of the shares other than to his or her spouse or civil partner and the deferred gain is not rolled forward into a new EIS investment within one year before and three years after the sale;
(2) the investor (or, where there has been a transfer between spouses, his or her spouse or civil partner) ceases to be UK resident at any time within three years of the issue of the EIS shares;
(3) the company ceases to be a qualifying company for EIS purposes within three years of the issue of the shares, or within three years of the date that it starts trading if this happens later.

The rule in (2) above does not apply if an individual temporarily becomes non-resident because of his or her employment, and he or she returns to the UK within three years still owning the shares.

Example – Withdrawal of CGT deferral relief

During the year 2009–10, P realised a capital gain of £60,000. She made an investment into an EIS company of £55,000 in August 2011. Her other income was sufficient to warrant full EIS relief.

For 2012–13 P receives EIS relief of £55,000 × 30% = £16,500. She could also elect to defer her 2009–10 gains of £49,900 (£60,000 less the annual exemption £10,100). This would defer a potential CGT liability of £8,982.

In May 2014 P decides to emigrate. This causes the deferred gain of £49,900 to be reinstated as if it were a 2014–15 capital gain.

The gain is then taxed at 28%. If P was aware, in August 2011, that emigration in 2014 was an option, it would have been cheaper not to defer her 2009–10 gain, and pay CGT at only 18%.

25.4.19 Taper relief and entrepreneurs' relief

Where a capital gain arising between 6 April 1998 and 5 April 2008 has been reduced by taper relief and the gain is deferred by an EIS investment, the gain clawed back on disposal is the original gain (ie there could be no further accrual of the taper relief holding period during the period the EIS shares are held). A different rule applies for entrepreneurs' relief where an EIS investment is made on or after 3 December 2014 (see 17.7.7).

25.4.20 Disposal after three years of shares that qualified for EIS income tax relief

Once shares that qualify for the 30% income tax relief have been held for three years, there is no clawback of relief on a disposal of the shares.

Furthermore, these shares are an exempt asset for CGT purposes so that no CGT will be payable on any gain on the shares. However, a loss realised on the disposal of the shares after the three-year period may still attract either income tax or CGT relief. Again, the loss is calculated as the difference between the net of tax cost and the disposal proceeds (see 25.4.17).

CGT may still be payable on disposal to the extent that CGT deferral relief has been obtained (see 25.4.17), even though any capital gain arising on the EIS shares themselves may be exempt.

25.5 SEED ENTERPRISE INVESTMENT SCHEME (SEIS)

The Seed Enterprise Investment Scheme (SEIS) was introduced by FA 2012. The main features of the scheme are as follows:

- Investors, including directors, can receive initial tax relief of 50% on investments up to £100,000.
- Investors are also eligible for a CGT exemption for any gains on SEIS shares.
- CGT exemption is available for half of the gains which are reinvested in SEIS investments in 2014–15.

25.5.1 Eligible investors

Past but not current employees can make investments under the SEIS.

An investor can make an investment which qualifies for SEIS relief, become a director and take a salary.

An individual does not qualify if the investment takes their share of the company's equity beyond 30%.

25.6 SOCIAL INVESTMENT TAX RELIEF

Individuals who make qualifying investments into qualifying social enterprises in 2014–15 or 2015–16 are entitled to claim relief in the form of an income tax reduction equal to 30% of the amount invested. This is the same as the rate for EIS and VCT.

The relief is designed to encourage investment by individuals in qualifying social enterprises. Social enterprises are businesses with social objectives that trade in a variety of sectors including employment, healthcare, sport and leisure.

The maximum investment eligible for income tax relief by an individual is £1m.

The investor must not be an employee, partner, trustee or paid director of the social enterprise or hold over 30% of the share/loan capital or voting rights. The enterprise must have fewer than 500 employees and an asset value of not more than £15m before the investment and not more than £16m after the investment.

The maximum investment that an eligible social enterprise can receive over three years is £275,000. However, it is proposed that this limit will be increased to £15m.

25.7 VENTURE CAPITAL TRUSTS (VCTs)

(Part 6 ITA 2007)

25.7.1 Qualifying trusts

Venture capital trusts (VCTs) are companies broadly similar to investment trusts. The monetary and employee limits for VCT (and EIS) qualifying companies have been relaxed from 6 April 2012 – see 19.3.2 for details. The main conditions for approval are that, in its most recent accounting period, as well as the period in which application for approval is made, the VCT meets the following requirements:

- its ordinary share capital has been or will be admitted on any EU regulated market (prior to April 2010, the condition was that shares should be quoted on the London Stock Exchange);
- it has not, or will not, retain more than 15% of the income that it derived or derives from shares or securities;
- its income must be, or have been, derived wholly or mainly from shares or securities;
- at least 70% by value of its investments has been, or will be, represented by shares or securities in qualifying holdings (see below). Securities can include medium-term loans for a period of at least five years;
- the VCT's qualifying holdings must contain at least 70% eligible shares, but these may include shares which carry certain preferential rights to dividends; and
- no holding in any one company represents more than 15% of the VCT's investments.

A VCT may be given provisional approval if HMRC is satisfied that the 70% requirements will be met within three years and the other conditions will be met in the current or next accounting period. If the trust fails to meet the conditions within these time periods, provisional approval is withdrawn.

Qualifying holdings

'Qualifying holdings' are holdings in unquoted companies that exist wholly for the purpose of carrying on wholly or mainly in the UK one or more qualifying trades (defined as for the EIS).

VCTs may count annual investments of up to £1m in total in any one qualifying unquoted trading company as a qualifying holding. The unquoted company's gross assets must not exceed £15m before and £16m immediately after the VCT's investment.

If a VCT holds shares in a qualifying company which subsequently becomes quoted, any shares or securities in that company will continue to be treated as qualifying for a period of five years from the time at which the company became quoted.

The rules that govern the types of companies in which VCTs may invest are very similar to the EIS rules (see 25.4).

It is permissible for a VCT to exchange its shares in an unquoted company for shares in a new holding company where that holding company has a 100% interest in the original company and the share exchange is being carried out to facilitate a flotation. In broad terms, the VCT may treat its shares in the new holding company as a qualifying investment provided the VCT has the same interest in the holding company and the VCT's shares in the original company were a qualifying investment.

Similarly, where a VCT holds convertible loan stock or preference shares, and it exercises its conversion rights, the resulting shareholding can be a qualifying investment.

Mergers and liquidations

The legislation specifically provides for a VCT to retain its approved status where it merged with another VCT. The legislation also allows VCTs to maintain approved status during a winding-up. These provisions mean that investors do not forfeit their tax reliefs simply because of a merger or the appointment of a liquidator.

25.7.2 Income tax reliefs

There are two kinds of income tax relief available for investments in VCTs:

(1) Individuals aged 18 or over are exempt from income tax on dividends from ordinary shares in VCTs to the extent that the shares acquired each year do not exceed £200,000 in value. This relief can be withheld if HMRC can show that the VCT shares were acquired in order to avoid tax (eg where they were acquired shortly before the VCT paid a dividend and sold shortly afterwards).

(2) Individuals aged 18 or over who subscribe for new ordinary shares in VCTs are, in addition, entitled to claim income tax relief at 30%, subject to a limit on the amount subscribed in any one year of £200,000. This relief on investment will be withdrawn unless the shares are held for at least five years.

25.7.3 CGT reliefs

At one time, there was a CGT deferral relief for investors but this was abolished from 6 April 2004.

25.7.4 FA 2014 changes

FA 2014 prevents VCTs from returning capital subscribed by investors within three years of the end of the accounting period in which the shares were issued.

The Chancellor indicated in his 2013 Budget that the Government was concerned that particular forms of share buy-back and reinvestment offered by VCTs were not in keeping with the spirit of the legislation. Following a technical consultation which ran between July and September 2013, questions were also raised about the use of share premium accounts to return capital to investors.

FA 2014 now prevents VCTs from returning capital to investors within three years of the end of the accounting period in which the shares were issued.

Distributions made from realised profits are not affected by these provisions.

FA 2014 also restricts VCT income tax relief where the investments are conditionally linked to any form of buy-back, or the investment has been made within six months of a disposal in shares of the same VCT.

These changes took effect from 6 April 2014 and are intended to ensure that the VCT tax reliefs operate in a fair and sustainable way.

The Government has made procedural changes to allow investors to subscribe for VCT shares via nominees.

25.8 SOCIAL VENTURE CAPITAL TRUSTS

The Government announced in March 2015 that a new category of privileged investment, Social VCTs, would be introduced once permission for State Aid has been obtained from the EU. Investors will receive 30% income tax relief for making such an investment. They will pay no tax on dividends from Social VCTs and any gain on disposal will be exempt from capital gains tax.

26

PENSIONS

PAUL CULLEN

This chapter contains the following sections:

Registered pension schemes

(1) The current tax regime
(2) Retirement benefits under the present regime
(3) Pension scheme investments
(4) Tax relief for contributions
(5) Recent changes
(6) Auto enrolment and qualifying workplace pensions

Other retirement benefit schemes

(7) Unapproved schemes
(8) Transfers from UK pension schemes into a QROPS

State benefits

(9) State pension benefits
(10) Contracting out

Glossary of terms and abbreviations

REGISTERED PENSION SCHEMES

26.1 THE CURRENT TAX REGIME

On 6 April 2006 ('A' Day), a new, unified, pensions tax regime came into force replacing the existing pension tax regimes. The rules affect pension scheme savers in all types of pension schemes, employers and the pension industry, together with financial advisers.

26.1.1 Pension scheme registration

On 'A' Day the whole concept of approved pension schemes and discretionary approval was replaced with the concept of registration.

To benefit from all tax privileges, a pension scheme must be registered with HMRC. All schemes are automatically registered unless they elect to be non-registered. De-registration results in a tax charge of 40% on the value of the scheme assets with the lump sum payable at retirement no longer being tax-free.

Tax notes

No tax benefits can be enjoyed until a scheme is registered. This could be important for company year-end tax planning.

26.1.2 Statutory lifetime allowance (SLA)

Limits on retirement benefits were replaced by a single statutory lifetime allowance (SLA) covering the amount of tax-privileged pension saving. The SLA was set at £1.8m for 2010–11 and 2011–12, but was reduced to £1.5m from 2012–13. Following changes announced by the Government in the 2012 Autumn Statement the SLA has been reduced to £1.25m from tax year 2014–15.

The Chancellor announced in his March 2015 Budget that the SLA will fall again from 6 April 2016 to £1m. It will also become index-linked in line with the Consumer Price Index from 2018 onwards (ie go up and down in line with the CPI).

The value of pension benefits, whatever the type of pension scheme, is tested against the individual's lifetime allowance whenever a benefit crystallisation event (BCE) occurs. BCEs include vesting of a policy, taking a tax-free cash lump sum, death and purchase of an annuity.

Under a defined benefit scheme, the pension is valued for the purposes of the SLA on a 20:1 basis. If the pension started before 'A' Day and was already in payment then this is valued by a factor of 25:1. This is applied to the annual payment when the first BCE on or after 'A' Day occurs.

Where the income is related to a pension income drawdown arrangement in place prior to 6 April 2006 then the 25:1 factor is applied to the maximum permitted annual income at the most recent review of the member's fund.

Any excess over the SLA that is taken as income attracts a recovery charge of 25%. This is charged to the member and deducted by the scheme. The additional pension income arising from the excess is taxed at the marginal rates prevailing at the time. Alternatively, the excess can be taken as a lump sum in which case the recovery charge will be 55% (regardless of the member's tax position).

26.1.3 **Annual allowance (AA)**

There are no limits on pension contributions although there is an annual allowance (AA) – an effective cap on the amount which can qualify for tax relief.

The AA had increased to £255,000 for 2010–11 and was expected to remain at this level until 2015–16. However, the coalition Government was reluctant to implement the complex restrictions on pensions tax relief for high earners designed by the previous administration that were to come into force on 6 April 2011 and instead reduced the annual allowance to £50,000 with effect from 6 April 2011. The AA was also amended again in the 2012 Autumn Statement and is reduced further still to £40,000 from the 2014–15 tax year.

The £10,000 annual allowance!

For those utilising the new 'flexible' rules from 5 April 2015 care needs to be taken as this may result in your annual allowance being reduced to £10,000 – known as the money purchase annual allowance (MPAA). This would happen in the follow circumstances:

- Uncrystallised fund pension lump sum (UFPLS) – where a pension scheme member accesses their pension fund via an UFPLS.
- Capped drawdown income (above the cap) – for those in capped drawdown, as of 5 April 2015, this may continue. If a member decides to take an income in excess of their cap then the MPAA would apply. This said, the scheme itself may not allow a payment in excess of the cap to be paid anyway.
- Starting flexible drawdown income – it is possible to designate funds for flexi-drawdown which will not trigger the MPAA at that point. Once income starts to be taken from a flexi-drawdown plan the MPAA will apply (see also below).
- Existing flexible drawdown – members in flexible drawdown before 6 April 2015 will be treated as having accessed 'flexibility' on 6 April 2015 as their drawdown income becomes 'flexi-accessed' from this date onwards.
- Drawing an income payment from a scheme pension (with 12 or less members) or from a flexible annuity.

The MPAA will not be triggered in the following instances:

- taking tax-free cash and no income;
- taking income via capped drawdown set up prior to 5 April 2015 providing the drawdown limits are not exceeded;
- accessing a pension as a 'small pot' due to it being worth less than £10,000;
- drawing pension income as an annuity or scheme pension (other than outlined above).

Tax relief is currently available on a member's contributions of up to 100% of relevant earnings, or the annual allowance if lower, or £3,600 if earnings are less than £3,600.

In a defined benefit scheme, it is not the actual contributions paid into the scheme but is instead the capital value of the member's pension at the end of the pension input period (PIP) – the 'closing value' – *less* the value of the member's pension at the start of the PIP (the 'opening value'), revalued by the CPI, that is tested against the AA. A factor of 16:1 is applied to the increase in benefit – after allowing for CPI revaluation – in order to calculate the capital value. Therefore a member within a defined benefit scheme would be able to accrue additional benefits of up to £2,500 (£40,000 divided by 16) for 2015–16 without exceeding the annual allowance.

An exemption may apply for a tax year in which an individual becomes entitled to a lump sum from a defined benefit scheme because of serious ill health.

An individual's inputs to a pension scheme are not tested against the annual allowance in the tax year in which he or she dies.

Pension input period (PIP)

The annual allowance is tested against the total level of pension contributions made in a particular pension input period (PIP) that ends in the relevant tax year. As input periods are not necessarily aligned to the timing of tax years the annual allowance is not (as one might intuitively expect) tested against the total pension contributions made in any particular tax year.

The rules governing the length of the first PIP differ slightly depending on whether it commenced before or after 5 April 2011. Both will start on the date that the first relievable pension contribution is made. A first PIP that commenced on or before 5 April 2011 will last for a year and one day whereas a first PIP commencing after 5 April 2011 will end automatically on the 5 April of the same tax year (unless a nomination is made for it to end on a different date). The nomination for an end date after the 5 April can be made after the 5 April but the nominated end date cannot be a date before the nomination is actually made. The nominated date can be any date within 12 months of the start date of the PIP.

Pension schemes will have a scheme input period which will be specific to the particular type of scheme, although a pension arrangement can have only one PIP ending in any given tax year. The starting period will typically begin either on the first payment after 'A' Day or for defined benefit schemes, the date that benefits start to accrue. The pension input period will end one year after the period started.

Input periods can be changed by the member, or the scheme administrator, within a money purchase scheme. Changing input periods within a money purchase scheme may represent a planning opportunity for some individuals to make higher pension contributions above the annual allowance in a short period of time. If an individual had changed his or her input period during tax year 2013–14, then with careful planning he or she could have contributed up to £100,000 (£50,000 × 2) plus any unused relief (capped at £50,000 pa) for 2010–11, 2011–12 and 2012–13.

Employer pension contributions and spreading

Corporation tax relief is potentially available without limit on all employer contributions provided that they meet the 'wholly and exclusively' test. HMRC will determine whether a payment is appropriate in each case. Employers will also need to take into account the relevant annual allowance when considering making a larger contribution.

The employer's tax relief may have to be spread over a period of years if the contribution is over £500,000 or they represent an increase of 210% over the previous years' contributions.

Three-year 'carry forward' rules

An individual can carry forward any annual allowance that was not used during the previous three tax years into the current tax year to give him or her an increased annual allowance.

1. The individual must use the current year's annual allowance first then the three previous years' unused allowances in order of oldest first (ie 2012–13 then 2013–14 then 2014–15 and so on).
2. They must have been a member of a registered pension scheme to have any unused annual allowance to carry forward from an earlier tax year. They do not however need to have paid into the pension during that year, so in effect could have the entire year's allowance available to carry forward.

Example

David has been a member of a registered pension scheme for several years and has made contributions as follows:

	Annual allowance	Total contributions paid	Carry forward amount
2012–13	£50,000	£55,000	£0
2013–14	£50,000	£30,000	£20,000
2014–15	£40,000	£25,000	£15,000
2015–16	£40,000	£20,000	£20,000

By using 'carry forward' David still has an available allowance for the 2015–16 tax year of £55,000 which could be used prior to 5 April 2016.

Tax notes

Even though there may be an increased annual allowance, tax relief is still only available on contributions of up to 100% of earnings in a tax year.

26.1.4 Transitional rules

The 'A' Day rules apply to all pension savings after 6 April 2006. However, under transitional provisions, all rights built up before April 2006 could be protected by electing for appropriate protection. This applied to pension benefits that exceeded the SLA at 6 April 2006, or could be expected to exceed it after 6 April 2006, and tax-free cash sums, which may be greater than 25% of the value of the pension fund. There were two ways to protect a member's pre-6 April 2006 fund.

Primary protection (PP)

Primary protection was only available to those individuals whose fund value at 6 April 2006 exceeded £1.5m. Future contributions could be made, and any growth on the fund up to the increase in the SLA each year was protected from tax charges. However, should the fund grow at a faster rate than the SLA, a tax charge would be payable on the funds over this level.

Those people who registered for primary protection were also able to protect any tax-free entitlement over £375,000 (£1.5m × 25%). They will be able to take the amount of their pre-6 April 2006 lump sum rights increased in line with the increase in the standard lifetime allowance.

Enhanced protection (EP)

This allowed protection of funds even if they were below the SLA at 6 April 2006. This protection effectively required the individual to stop funding his or her pension, and accruing further pensionable service. However, a small level of accrual was allowed and this is described within the 'relevant benefit accrual' rules.

Providing enhanced protection had been elected for and any benefit accrual is within the rules, any benefits coming in to payment after 5 April 2006 will normally be exempt from the SLA, whatever the value. For an occupational scheme member who elected for enhanced protection who has earmarked funds within the pension scheme, it will require the benefits to be tested within the scheme under the old rules. If a surplus exists in the fund then this must be returned to the company and taxed at 35%.

It was also possible to protect any tax-free cash entitlement in excess of £375,000, at 5 April 2006, through enhanced protection. Under this option, the tax-free cash is protected as a percentage of an individual's overall pension benefits. Therefore, unlike primary protection, the entitlement can increase at a faster rate than the SLA with no penalties being applied. For individuals in defined benefit schemes who have opted for enhanced protection, while benefits accrued after 5 April 2012 will not trigger an end to protection, they may still trigger an AA charge if the deemed inputs in a year exceed the AA limit for that year.

If enhanced protection was elected for and future pension contributions or accruals occur, then it is possible to revert to primary protection *only* if it has also been elected for, otherwise the position will automatically revert to 'no protection'. Protection from the recovery charge is determined by the pre-6 April 2006 pension value, or the prevailing SLA for those whose pension value did not exceed £1.5m. The deadline for electing for transitional protection was 5 April 2009.

The new regime which came into force on 6 April 2012 (ie SLA reducing to £1.5m) included a right for individuals to opt for protection ('fixed protection') of the £1.8m current lifetime limit in a similar way as enhanced protection operated from 'A' Day.

Tax payment administration

In a defined contribution pension scheme, any tax charge which is payable on retirement will be paid to HMRC by the administrators of the scheme and the fund value reduced accordingly. The remaining fund value will then be used to provide benefits for the individual on retirement.

With defined benefit pension schemes, the situation is slightly different. The tax charge due at retirement is computed on the basis that the value of the pension rights is equal to 20 times the annual pension.

Tax notes

- It is not possible to switch from primary protection to enhanced protection – or vice versa – at any time, although those individuals who are registered for both are able to relinquish EP in order to benefit from PP.
- The deadline for applying for transitional protection expired on 5 April 2009.

26.2 RETIREMENT BENEFITS UNDER THE PRESENT REGIME

26.2.1 The 2014 Budget announcement

The 2014 Budget announcement outlined some major changes to pensions, in particular in regards to how savers can draw benefits from defined contribution plans. These new changes came into full effect from 6 April 2015.

26.2.2 Minimum retirement age

The tax-free cash lump sum can be taken at any time after age 55. An income can also be taken from age 55 but can be deferred until a later date.

Those with certain existing contractual rights to draw a pension earlier than age 55 may have that right protected. There is special protection for members of those approved schemes in existence before April 2006 with low normal retirement ages, such as those for sports people. The minimum retirement age also does not apply to 'unregistered' arrangements such as EFRBS. In those cases, retirement will continue to be a question of fact.

It is not necessary for a member to leave employment in order to access an employer's occupational pension. Members of occupational pension schemes may, where the scheme rules allow it, continue working for the same employer whilst drawing retirement benefits.

26.2.3 Lump sum payments on death

From 6 April 2015 there are some major changes to the way in which benefits are paid from annuities and drawdown pensions upon death.

This in part is formed by a reduction in the level of tax paid on death benefits but also added flexibility in terms of who the beneficiary is – the Government has removed the restriction that this has to be a 'dependant'.

The tables below outline the old and new rules.

Table 26.1 – For those with unused pension funds or in drawdown

Death before 75:		
Form of benefit passed on	*Original rules*	*New rules*
Lump sum	Tax free if passed on prior to tax-free cash or income having been taken	Tax free
	55% tax applied if passed on once in income drawdown (ie after taking tax-free cash and/ or income)	
Income	Taxed as income*	Taxed as income if taken via an annuity* (Only available to dependants)
		Or
		Tax free via an annuity or income drawdown (either option can be chosen by any beneficiary)

Death after 75:		
Form of benefit passed on	*Original rules*	*New rules*
Lump sum	Subject to 55% tax	Subject to 45% tax for payments made in 2015–16
		Taxed as income* for payments made from 6 April 2016
Income	Taxed as income via annuity or income drawdown*	Taxed as income via an annuity* (see below)
		Or
		Taxed as income via income drawdown* (either option can be chosen by any beneficiary)

*Based on the beneficiary's income tax rate.

Table 26.2 – For those who have purchased an annuity

Death before 75:		
Form of benefit passed on	*Original rules*	*New rules*
Lump sum (where value protection has been chosen)	Subject to 55% tax	Tax free
Income (where a joint life or guaranteed period has been chosen)	Income is taxable* (see below)	Tax free
Death after 75:		
Form of benefit passed on	*Original rules*	*New rules*
Lump sum (where value protection has been chosen)	Subject to 55% tax	Subject to 55% tax for payments made before 6 April 2015
		Subject to 45% tax for payments made in 2015–16
		Taxed as income* for payments made from 6 April 2016
Income (where a joint life or guaranteed period has been chosen)	Income is taxable* (see below)	Income is taxable* (see below)

*Based on the beneficiary's income tax rate.

There is still a two-year rule on tax-free lump sum payments from pensions where the member dies under the age of 75. These must be paid out within two years of the scheme administrator being notified of the death of the member. Any payment made outside this time would be subject to a tax charge at 45%

26.2.4 Tax-free lump sums

The maximum amount of pension commencement lump sum (tax-free cash) that can be paid from all pension schemes – except those with either enhanced, primary or fixed protection – is now a quarter of the value of the benefits subject to an overall maximum of a quarter of the SLA (2015–16 on £1.25m × 25% = £312,500). However, for members of occupational schemes before 6 April 2006, who were entitled to a tax-free lump sum of more than 25% in respect of their service before 'A' Day, it is possible for their entitlement to higher tax-free cash to be protected, provided they remain in the same pension scheme. However, any transfer away from the scheme (unless part of a bulk transfer) could result in the higher entitlement being lost.

Members of post-1987 AVC schemes, FSAVC schemes and appropriate personal pension plans can now also take tax-free cash from these arrangements. This has introduced an extra degree of flexibility, because previous rules did not allow this.

26.2.5 Retirement income now

The most radical (and most welcomed) change is the removal of the requirement to buy an annuity or indeed be restricted to any drawdown limits when taking benefits from a defined contribution scheme.

Subject to the rules of the pension scheme permitting, individuals after reaching the age of 55 will have no limit to the amount they decide to draw from their pension fund in any one year.

This new 'flexibility' provides great scope for financial planning and control in retirement. It also brings with it considerable risk as the possibility of spending your entire pension pot too early in retirement is now a genuine concern. There will be those who will prefer to have 'the cash' but a very important note here is that while the option to take tax-free cash will remain this is still going to be limited to 25% of the fund value (up to the SLA), therefore any other withdrawal taken from the pension fund will be treated as income and taxable at the individual's marginal rate of income tax in the year of the withdrawal.

While the temptation to draw a large amount from your pension after the age of 55 may be appealing to some, the tax implications of doing this and the longer-term impact of using your pension too quickly is something that must not be ignored and specialist advice should be sought.

26.2.6 Retirement income under the old rules

There were previously three ways in which income could be paid to an individual on retirement: as secured income; as unsecured income; and as an alternatively secured pension. This changed from 2011–12, with unsecured and alternatively secured pensions in effect disappearing.

Secured income

A secured income is a pension income in retirement that is promised to be paid until death. There are two forms of secured pensions – annuities and scheme pensions – both types will be treated as income for tax purposes.

An annuity is an income stream purchased from an insurance provider using the pension fund at retirement. An annuity could be considered as longevity insurance as it will continue to be paid until death, whenever that may happen.

Where annuities are purchased via money purchase type pension plans, the individual should use the open market option. The annuity market is competitive and this option will help to ensure that the most competitive annuity is purchased for the individual's personal requirements.

Many features can be built into an annuity. These include payment frequency, payment increases, spouse or civil partner's pension and pension guarantees. Depending upon the level and whether an individual selects a spouse or civil partner's pension or guarantee, the options chosen will effectively determine the death benefit position of the annuity.

In a defined benefit pension a scheme pension will be provided. This can either be paid to the member out of the scheme assets or the scheme can purchase an annuity to secure the income for the member. Death benefit options may be determined by the pension scheme rules or may offer flexibility.

Unsecured income

The alternative to securing benefits under secured income was to take income directly from the pension fund by means of income drawdown. Unsecured income could only continue until the age of 75, or 77 for those reaching 75 on or after 22 June 2010, and has effectively disappeared as an option from 6 April 2011. Alternatively, there were 'third way' products which are effectively temporary annuities offering end of term guarantees. Third way products are outside the scope of this book and are not discussed further here.

Annual income could be taken of up to a maximum of 120% of the annual income payable from a single level annuity rate determined by the Government Actuary's Department (GAD) table. There was no minimum level of income set. Income levels could vary up to the limit and had to be reviewed every five years.

Alternatively secured pension (ASP)

Before April 2006, the main option for the majority of pensioners was to secure their income from age 75 using an annuity. The 2006 rules introduced the alternatively secured pension (ASP). This was an alternative to purchasing an annuity as it allowed unsecured income to be drawn from age 75 (or 77, if reaching age 75 on or after 22 June 2010 and before 6 April 2011), but with different rules from those that applied before age 75/77 (unsecured income).

Alternatively secured pensions could not start before age 75 (or 77, if reaching age 75 on or after 22 June 2010 but before 6 April 2011), and unless benefits were crystallised before age 75 into an unsecured pension arrangement, the tax-free lump sum was lost.

The income limits under ASP were different from the unsecured pension income rules:

- A minimum pension income requirement was introduced: 55% of the single life GAD rate at age 75.
- The maximum pension income requirement was increased to 90% of the single life GAD rate at age 75.

Once income withdrawal had commenced under ASP, the upper income limit had to be reviewed every year, although the pension was always calculated based on the individual being age 75, regardless of their actual age.

The death benefit rules while an individual was in ASP are as follows:

- Where an individual died with dependants, the remaining drawdown fund had to be used to provide survivors' pensions.
- If an individual died with no dependants, the remaining fund could be gifted to a charity tax-free.
- The payment of any remaining pension fund, other than to a charity, was classified as an unauthorised payment and therefore attracted unauthorised payment tax charges. In many cases the total reallocation charges amounted to 70% (40% unauthorised payment charge + 15% unauthorised payments surcharge + 15% scheme sanction charge).

Scheme pensions

Scheme pensions were another option for those aged 75 and over. These were normally (apart from defined benefit schemes) only offered by a SIPP or small, self-administered scheme (SSAS) and are effectively annuities paid out of scheme funds. The benefit was that more income could be drawn than with an ASP and the income level could be reviewed in line with actual mortality rates. This was considered a good option for those who did not want their pension to die with them or wished to use their pension income for IHT planning.

Changes to the annuities and drawdown rules from 6 April 2011

As pension annuity rates declined, the requirement that individuals with personal or group personal pensions (defined contribution schemes) had to buy an annuity or take an ASP at age 75 was increasingly regarded as a disincentive to fund a pension. This was particularly the case as any unused part of the pension fund is liable to IHT should the individual die after age 75 but before an annuity is purchased (IHT can also apply on earlier deaths if an annuity was deliberately delayed).

As explained above, since April 2006, individuals have already been able to take an unsecured pension (drawdown arrangement) up to age 75 and an alternatively secured pension (ASP) from age 75 rather than buy an annuity. The amount that an individual could draw down was based on a percentage of a single life conventional annuity that the fund would buy as calculated by the Government Actuary's Department (GAD).

Changes in 2011 introduced the concept of 'capped drawdown' and 'flexible drawdown'. Under capped drawdown the maximum income was still linked to GAD annuity rates, with the maximum income being 100% of GAD. However, if an individual could show that they had annual pension income (a total of all pension income apart from drawdown amounts) in excess of £20,000, they could opt for flexible drawdown under this option. This gave significant flexibility to better funded pensioners.

The Autumn Statement 2012 stated that legislation would be introduced in the Finance Bill 2013 to increase the maximum GAD limits for capped drawdown from 100% back to 120% with effect from March 2013.

March 2014 Budget

To offer some transitional flexibility before the full rule changes outlined above came into effect on 6 April 2015, once again the rules surrounding drawdown were amended.

Two significant changes were introduced with effect from 27 March 2014:

- The drawdown limit went up to 150%.
- The minimum income requirement (MIR) to qualify for flexible drawdown reduced from £20,000 pa to £12,000 pa.

26.2.7 Trivial commutation

Previously in cases when an individual had a small level of pension benefits the rules allowed them to be paid off as a lump sum as opposed to drawing a small pension for life – this was known as a trivial commutation lump sum.

The rules were that for full commutation all benefits must be taken at the same time, and the total amount of all of the individual's pensions was not more than 1% of the SLA currently in force. One quarter could be paid tax-free with the rest paid as a lump sum, which was subject to income tax at the individual's marginal rate. The triviality rules cannot be used before age 60, or after age 75.

New rules from 6 April 2015

From 6 April 2015, trivial commutation at retirement is no longer available under defined contribution (DC) pensions. That is unless the 12-month commutation period started before 6 April 2015.

The introduction of 'uncrystallised funds pension lump sums' (UFPLS) provides an alternative method for taking all funds under a DC arrangement as a lump sum (albeit taxed).

Trivial commutation is still possible for final salary/defined denefits (DB) schemes after 5 April 2015. If there are AVCs (or any other) money purchase arrangements under the same scheme these need to be taken into account when testing the DB member's total pension savings against the £30,000 commutation limit.

The minimum age for taking a trivial commutation lump sum has reduced from age 60 to 55, or a protected low pension age if the individual has one under the scheme. Also benefits may be taken earlier than this if the member is in ill-health.

Small pots

The minimum age for taking a small pension pot as a taxed lump sum, from either an occupational or non-occupational pension scheme, has also reduced from age 60 to 55 (or a protected low pension age if applicable) and benefits may be taken earlier if the member is in ill-health.

Up to three small non-occupational pensions (personal pension plans, etc) can be commuted under small pots payments. However there is no limit on the number of occupational pensions that can be taken under small pots. To allow the payment of small pot commutation, the following conditions need to be fulfilled:

- The member has reach the minimum retirement age of 55.
- Each pension payment received does not exceed £10,000.
- The payment extinguishes all member benefit entitlements within the scheme.

Accessing a 'small pot' does not trigger the money purchase annual allowance (MPAA).

The first 25% of the lump sum will be tax-free, with the balance being taxed as pension income in the year received.

26.2.8 Recycling of lump sums

Where an individual takes a pre-commencement lump sum (tax-free lump sum) from a pension and then deliberately reinvests this within another pension scheme this may be considered as recycling and pension tax law has had specific rules in place to prevent this since April 2006.

Recycling applies when the reinvestment is pre-planned, and in the following circumstances:

- where the individual has received a pre-commencement lump sum (PCLS), which, when added to any other PCLS received in the previous 12-month period, exceeds 1% of the lifetime allowance (up until 5 April 2015) or £7,500 from 6 April 2015); and
- because of the payment of the PCLS, the amount of the contribution paid to a pension scheme is significantly greater than would otherwise be the case. This is defined as where the amount of the additional contributions are more than 30% of the contributions that might have been expected; and
- the cumulative amount of the additional contributions to the registered scheme exceeds 30% of the PCLS.

If recycling is deemed to apply, the PCLS will be considered an unauthorised payment and a tax charge of up to 70% could apply.

26.3 PENSION SCHEME INVESTMENTS

26.3.1 General rules for scheme investments

A single set of investment rules now applies to all registered pension schemes. This effectively means that, in theory, it is possible to invest in almost any kind of asset, including residential property and connected party transactions. However, to avoid investment abuse HMRC also introduced tax charges if pensions schemes invest in 'taxable property'. All investments must be made on a commercial basis. It is considered unlikely that all pension companies will accept the full range of investments in their schemes, and a wider choice of investments will only be made available by specialist pension companies operating either SIPP or SSAS arrangements.

Loans to members, people or other entities connected to members are unauthorised payments and will be taxed accordingly. From 'A' Day, any registered pension scheme is permitted to make a loan to an unconnected third party, or in the case of SSAS to the sponsoring employer (scheme lending is limited to a maximum of 50% of the net SSAS fund).

There are specific rules applying to loans made to sponsoring employers:

- the loan must be secured through a first charge on an asset at least equivalent in value to the loan plus interest;

- the minimum interest rate must be no less than 1% above the base lending rates of the leading high street clearing banks;
- the loan term must not be longer than five years; and
- the loan must be repaid through regular, at least annual, instalments of capital and interest.

Any investment entered into before 'A' Day is normally subject to the rules then in force and is not affected by the new rules. However, where a change takes place after 5 April 2006 to the terms of a loan made by the scheme before 6 April 2006, the whole loan is subject to the new rules. Scheme borrowing is limited to 50% of the value of the scheme assets and must be secured.

26.3.2 Prohibited investments

FA 2006 contains provisions relating to 'taxable property' (ie assets previously described as 'prohibited assets').

Taxable property consists of any of the following:

- residential property (whether in the UK or overseas);
- chattels (ie tangible moveable property) other than gold bullion.

A registered pension scheme is not debarred from investing in taxable property but, where it does so, it and the members of the scheme are subject to punitive tax charges. In addition, the pension scheme could face de-registration if it invests in any prohibited investment, which in addition to the punitive tax charges applied, would also mean that the scheme loses all the tax privileges associated with a registered scheme, for all of its assets.

There are exceptions for certain types of residential property that might be acquired as an investment (eg a nursing home).

Great care should be taken before a scheme invests in property that may constitute residential property and advice from a specialist will be required.

26.3.3 Pension investment strategies

Pension strategies by their very nature are long-term and therefore even small enhancements can have a big effect at retirement.

Individuals with money purchase type arrangements (stakeholder, personal pensions, self-invested personal pensions) should carefully consider the underlying investment strategy employed within their pension plan. Future investment performance is a determinant of future fund value at retirement and individuals should seek to assess the suitability of their underlying strategy particularly in relation to their objectives and personal attitude to investment risk.

The investment choices for most money purchase pension plans will be linked to collective investment funds and typically the pension provider will offer a flexible range to suit different risk profiles. As with all investments some managers will perform more consistently than others and assessing the long-term consistency of performance of an underlying manager is an important consideration.

Individuals within money purchase type schemes should also seek to adjust their asset allocation to a more cautious position when approaching annuity purchase, particularly when within five years of that date. Any equity-focused investment strategy has the potential risk of a sudden fall in value within five years of retirement and therefore by adjusting the allocation to a more cautious position the value of the retirement fund can be protected. Those intending to take an unsecured pension will remain invested for a longer time – and possibly until death under the new rules. However if they are likely to purchase an annuity in the future they should still assess their likely investment term prior to annuity purchase to ensure they are not exposed to excess volatility.

Pension investors with a longer time frame until retirement should consider carefully before making major changes to the asset allocation of their fund as this may crystallise a loss by moving out of an asset class when prices are low. Where possible advice should be sought. It is nevertheless still important to review the performance of individual investments to ensure investment managers are meeting expectations. Understanding your pension investment strategy and risk levels being taken is very important and pension investors would be well advised to remind themselves of the longer-term principles of developing an appropriate asset-allocation pension investment strategy and implementing a suitable review process to monitor this.

> **Tax notes**
>
> A registered pension scheme is not debarred from investing in taxable property but, where it does so, it and the members of the scheme are subject to punitive tax charges.

26.4 TAX RELIEF FOR CONTRIBUTIONS

Employer contributions are always paid gross.

Contributions by a member into a registered scheme will normally be net of basic rate tax, ie a payment to an insurance company of £1,000 is treated as a payment of £1,250 from which £250 has been deducted. The insurance company recovers this £250 from HMRC.

In many occupational schemes (but not group personal pensions), pension contributions are deducted in full from pay prior to income tax being applied. As a result the member receives relief at his or her highest marginal rate immediately.

There is one other situation where a member's contributions may still be made in full, which is where the payment is in respect of an old retirement annuity policy and the insurance company has not established an arrangement for payments to be made net of tax relief.

26.5 RECENT CHANGES

26.5.1 The main changes

The coalition Government simplified the former Government's planned restrictions to pension tax relief from 2011–12. However, for some simpler does not mean more generous: for many individuals, the options for making tax-efficient pension contributions were more restricted.

26.5.2 Tax relief on contributions from 2011–12

From 2011–12, the maximum amount that can be paid into an approved pension scheme by (or on behalf of) an individual in a tax year without penalty – the annual allowance (AA) – was reduced from £255,000 to £50,000 and, more recently, to £40,0000 (subject to the usual limit of 100% of the individual's relevant earnings for the year if lower). Contributions made by or on behalf of individuals that are in excess of this amount trigger an AA charge.

Tax relief on pension contributions continues to be available at the individual's marginal income tax rate. However, the charge arising if the AA is exceeded is at the full marginal rate of relief that an individual would otherwise have benefitted from – ie no tax relief will be available on excess contributions.

26.5.3 2012–13 and 2013–14: lower lifetime allowance

When the SLA was introduced in April 2006, individuals with large pension pots were able to protect themselves from the excess charge on their pension funds. Individuals whose funds already exceeded the LTA could apply for 'primary' protection and individuals with smaller funds could opt for 'enhanced' protection on the basis that their fund would grow over time (even though they would be blocked from making new contributions to it). See 26.1.4 for more details.

These protections continue after 5 April 2012. However, for individuals in defined benefit schemes who have opted for enhanced protection, while benefits accrued after 5 April 2012 (provided these benefits are not deemed to be relevant benefits accruals) would not trigger an end to protection, they may still trigger an AA charge if the deemed inputs in a year exceed the annual limit.

The 2012 changes included a right for individuals to opt for protection ('fixed protection') of the £1.8m current lifetime limit in a similar way as enhanced protection operated from 'A' Day:

- It was not necessary for an individual's fund to exceed £1.5m at 5 April 2012 for the fixed protection election to be made; but

- protection will end if further contributions are made by the individual after 5 April 2012 (including where individuals in defined benefit schemes accrue further pension benefits in the current scheme or under a new scheme in excess of the limits currently available to those claiming enhanced protection under the 'A' Day rules).

Fixed protection was not available to any individual already holding enhanced or primary protection. HMRC must have received the completed applications for fixed protection before 5 April 2012.

26.5.4 Reduction in annual allowance

As previously mentioned, FA 2013 reduced the annual allowance from £50,000 to £40,000 and also reduce the standard lifetime allowance (SLA) from £1.5m to £1.25m from the 2014–15 tax year.

A charge under the SLA rules will continue to arise at the time the pension vests and will remain at 55% of the excess used for a lump sum entitlement and 25% of the excess used for the pension entitlement.

The charge may also arise at other later 'benefit crystallisation events' for individuals who opt to take a drawdown pension – in particular on reaching age 75.

Fixed protection 2014 (FP14)

Individuals who did not already have enhanced, primary or fixed protection (2012) would be able to register for fixed protection (2014) which will entitle them to a personal lifetime allowance of the greater of £1.5m and the SLA.

Individuals with large pension pots – those already in excess of £1.25m – or who think that they will be prior to retirement age should take advice on their personal options as there are likely to be many situations where opting for fixed protection will be a sensible way of protecting the future growth of pension funds from a possible charge.

There are rules for maintaining fixed protection (2014) as follows:

- Individuals in defined contribution (money purchase) pension schemes must make no further contributions nor have any made on their behalf to the scheme on or after 5 April 2014.
- Those in defined benefits schemes must not accrue further benefits above a relevant percentage from 5 April 2014. The relevant percentage is broadly defined as either the annual rate specified in the scheme rules (as of 11 December 2012) for the revaluation of accrued rights or the Consumer Price Index (if no rate is specified).

Where an individual dies before 6 April 2014 but lump sum death benefits are not paid until on or after 6 April 2014, the lump sum death benefit will be measured against the SLA at the time of death.

Those with existing primary or enhanced (A-day) protection but who do not have lump sum protection will still retain a right to a lump sum of 25% of £1.5m.

In addition to fixed protection (2014) an individual protection regime was also introduced that unlike fixed protection (2014) would not restrict future contributions or benefit accrual.

Individual protection 2014

Those with pension funds in excess of £1.25m on 5 April 2014 who do not already have 'primary protection' will be able to apply for 'individual protection' (IP). It is possible to apply for both FP14 and IP in which case FP14 will take precedence

It is also possible for those with fixed protection 2012 (FP12) or 'enhanced protection' to apply for IP, when again the earlier protection will take precedence.

IP14 will allow a person with pension savings of between £1.25m and £1.5m (as at 5 April 2014) to protect that amount from a lifetime allowance charge. If the pension value at 5 April 2014 is in excess of £1.5m then the protection is capped at £1.5m. The limit is set as a monetary amount and referred to as the person's protected lifetime allowance. Importantly this will not increase in the future, so if the SLA subsequently exceeds the amount of the IP, the IP will cease and their benefits will be tested against the SLA instead.

The main difference with IP is that the person can still make or have contributions made to their pension without losing the protection. If the fund value however exceeds the protected level when tested against the lifetime allowance they will bear the same lifetime allowance charge on the excess – 55% if taken as a lump sum and 25% if taken as income.

It has been possible to apply for IP 2014 since August 2014 using form APSS240, which will need to be completed, and individuals will have until 6 April 2017 to apply.

It is anticipated that there will be some form of protection that will be available to protect those affected by the further decrease in the SLA from £1.25m to £1m from April 2016. However at the time of writing details on what this will look like are not yet available.

26.6 AUTO ENROLMENT AND QUALIFYING WORKPLACE PENSIONS

The Labour Government introduced stakeholder pensions in 2001 in an attempt to make it easier for individuals to save for their retirement. The introduction of stakeholder pensions has heralded a generally lower and more transparent charging system, however still too few people are saving for their retirement. The Labour administration's response to this was to introduce auto enrolment in the March 2010 Budget. This measure was then confirmed at the Emergency Budget in June 2010 and took effect from April 2012.

Qualifying workplace pensions are effectively personal type pensions run on an occupational basis and administered by employers and need to meet certain criteria in respect of charges, contribution levels and compliance.

UK employers are required to automatically enrol those employees aged between 22 and state pension age who earn more than £10,000 (for 2015–16) into a 'qualifying' workplace pension scheme from October 2012. If an existing current company scheme does not meet the qualifying criteria (or the employer does not operate one) then it is possible to be enrolled into a simple, low-cost national pension scheme such as the National Employment Savings Trust (NEST).

There are a number of other solutions that could be considered as well but these are outside the scope of this book.

The ultimate goal is for employees to contribute 4% of their earnings, employers 3% and a further 1% via tax relief to give a total overall minimum contribution rate of 8%.

Starting with the largest employers in October 2012, the auto enrolment scheme was rolled out to all employers with 250 or more (as at April 2012) staff by February 2014. For employers with fewer than 250 staff the planned staging dates were to be between April 2014 and 2018. The Regulator will write to all employers around 12 months before their start date so that they know when to automatically enrol their eligible employees. Three months before the employer's start date the Regulator will write again to remind them of their new duties and the need to register.

Employers with more than one payroll will start automatic enrolment for all their payrolls at the same time, on the start date of their largest payroll. In addition to the automatic enrolment of all eligible employees, employees aged between 16 and 22, and earning more than the threshold, will be able to opt into the scheme, as will any employees earning less than the threshold.

Employees will need to pay a personal contribution on which tax relief (based on a percentage of qualifying earnings) will be given but they can opt out of the scheme: employers will be required to make a contribution. The minimum contributions for employees and employers are to be phased in as follows:

Date	Employee (including basic rate tax relief)	Employer
October 2012 to September 2017	1%	1%
October 2017 to September 2018	3%	2%
From October 2018	5%	3%

Auto enrolment may require a significant change for employers and they will need to be aware of these proposals and more importantly their responsibilities and duties under the rules.

OTHER RETIREMENT BENEFIT SCHEMES

26.7 UNAPPROVED SCHEMES

Unapproved (now unregistered) occupational pension schemes were introduced to allow employers the flexibility to provide benefits for those employees who had earnings in excess of the salary cap. However, their use is not restricted to such employees and they may be used to provide benefits in excess of the normal two-thirds maximum pension benefit or to provide greater benefits for those with less than 20 years' service.

26.7.1 Eligibility

Any person in receipt of employment income is eligible for an unregistered scheme. There is no requirement that the employee is also a member of a registered scheme.

26.7.2 Types of plan

Such schemes may be funded (ie contributions set aside to fund the promised benefits) or unfunded (ie at retirement the benefits will be paid by the company out of current income or investments). A funded scheme was traditionally called a FURBS (funded unapproved retirement benefits scheme) but both funded and unfunded retirement benefit schemes are now known as EFRBS (employer funded retirement benefit schemes). There is no requirement that funded schemes are established under trust, but this is commonly the case.

26.7.3 Contributions

Where a scheme was funded, the employer used to obtain tax relief on the contributions as a normal business expense and the employee was taxed on such contributions as if they were earnings. This ceased to be the case from 'A' Day. Contributions between 6 April 2006 and 5 April 2011 attracted no tax relief for the employer until the employee drew his or her benefits and the employee paid no tax until he or she drew the benefits.

The landscape has now completely changed for funded schemes; the introduction of the disguised remuneration rules (see Chapter 5) has meant that, where an amount is 'earmarked' for an employee, or the employee is given a benefit such as a loan or the use of a trust asset, a tax charge will arise under Part 7A ITEPA 2003 and the employer will be able to claim a deduction in the accounts to the extent that sums have been subjected to a Part 7A charge. A tax charge could already have arisen between 9 December 2010 and 5 April 2011 under the transitional provisions in certain circumstances.

There are continuing protections for sums placed in trust prior to 6 April 2006 (which were taxed up-front), but generally, the Part 7A charge will take precedence over a charge under s 394 ITEPA, which will then only apply to any excess.

In an unfunded scheme, there has never been a charge to tax on any reserves set up to provide for future benefits. Equally, the employer will not obtain any tax relief until the funds are provided and benefits are actually paid. 'Quasi' unfunded schemes (ie where the employer has secured payment of the future liabilities under the scheme against an asset or has earmarked funds with which to pay future liabilities) will be caught by the new Part 7A charge. Genuinely unfunded schemes will not.

26.7.4 Taxation of scheme investments

Unapproved schemes do not benefit from 'gross roll-up'. In the past, the trustees of a FURBS paid tax only at basic rate on investment income. For onshore trusts, from 6 April 2006, income and capital gains became subject to the rate applicable to trusts, ie currently 45% on income other than dividends, and 37.5% on UK dividends. From 6 April 2008 to 22 June 2010, capital gains in a pre-'A' Day EFRBS were subject to 18% CGT. This increased to 28% from 23 June 2010. Offshore EFRBS are taxed according to the normal rules for offshore trusts.

There are transitional rules in paras 56–58, schedule 36 FA 2004 which continue the existing treatment for FURBS where no new contributions have been made after 5 April 2006, and which ensure that where the contributions were taxed on the employee when they were made, they are not also taxed when benefits are paid from the scheme under the post-'A' Day EFRBS rules. If contributions have been made post-6 April 2006, tax charges will arise on the part of the fund relating to the post-'A' Day contributions. The Part 7A provisions make similar allowance for pre-6 April 2006 amounts.

26.7.5 Benefits

The scheme must be set up to provide relevant benefits, but there are no set limits on the benefits that can be provided. Pensions from unregistered schemes, whether funded or unfunded, are subject to income tax as earned income.

Where a scheme with UK resident trustees was funded before 'A' Day, that part of the fund may be used to provide a tax-free lump sum on retirement. Where an offshore scheme was funded prior to 'A' Day, the tax-free amount will usually be the aggregate of the employer contributions before 6 April 2006. Any lump sum in excess of these limits is taxable in the normal way.

> **Tax notes**
>
> Where a scheme with UK resident trustees was funded before 'A' Day, that part of the fund may be taken as a tax-free lump sum on retirement.

In the March 2010 Budget, the then Chancellor announced that anti-avoidance was to be introduced from 6 April 2011 to prevent tax avoidance using 'employee trusts'. This was reiterated in the June Budget and the Chancellor made it clear that the planned anti-avoidance legislation would apply to both EBTs and EFRBS. It became clear, when the draft legislation on disguised remuneration was released on 9 December 2010, that these rules will cause these structures to become very much less attractive.

26.8 TRANSFERS FROM UK PENSION SCHEMES INTO A QROPS

For individuals who are working abroad and/or are going to retire overseas, transferring into a qualifying recognised overseas pension scheme (QROPS) can have advantages once the individuals have established five complete tax years of non-residence in the UK. However, such an early switch carries high risks for individuals since if the QROPS ceases to qualify (see below), there will be penalty tax charges. One must also remember the increasing difficulty of establishing non-UK residence, reflected by current case law. Until such time as a statutory residence test is introduced, uncertainty will remain the order of the day, unless the individual has clearly made a complete and total break with the UK.

26.8.1 Advantages once you have completed five tax years of non-UK residence

One of the key advantages of a QROPS once you have completed five tax years of non-UK residence is that the fund can grow beyond the statutory lifetime limit imposed in the UK (£1.25m from 2015–16).

HMRC has recently made it clear that it believes any payment or investments that would be unauthorised under a UK scheme would also be liable to charges under a QROPS, regardless of whether the five-year limit is passed. It should therefore be assumed that benefits and allowable investments will broadly mirror UK rules and expert tax and financial advice should be sought in all cases.

When it comes to taking benefits, the advantages of a QROPS will vary depending on the jurisdiction in which it is established but have previously included:

- the opportunity to take 30% of the whole pension fund in cash (compared to previous 25% of the statutory lifetime limit for UK pensions);
- income limits in draw down are determined by the QROPS jurisdiction and scheme rules, so could be significantly more attractive than the previous limits applied to UK schemes;
- lump sum death benefits may be taxed at lower rates if the country the individual has retired to does not tax such benefits or only taxes them at low rates;
- depending on the local tax rules in the country to which the individual has retired, there may also be scope for trust planning to pass pension wealth down to the next generation rather than to a surviving spouse or civil partner.

The above said, given the new rules on UK registered pensions from 6 April 2015 which will allow significantly more flexibility in terms of how pension funds are accessed this may make the perceived benefits of using a QROPS less attractive when the risks of such plans are considered.

The Government also said in the March 2014 Budget announcement that it will be consulting on ways to give equivalent treatment to qualifying non-UK pension schemes (QNUPS) and UK registered pension schemes to remove the opportunity to avoid inheritance tax.

A the time of writing there were some concerns that previously qualifying QROPS plans would no longer qualify due to the most recent UK pension changes. Although the extent of this is unclear it does highlight the potential risks of these arrangements due to government 'tinkering' with tax and pension rules over time.

26.8.2 Qualifying rules

Firstly, the scheme must be either an occupational pension scheme or personal pension scheme regulated by the appropriate government regulator in the country in which the scheme is administered (this need not be the same country to which the individual retires). Secondly, the scheme must be open to persons resident in the country in which it is established and:

- tax relief is not available on contributions made by the employee and/or employer; or
- it is liable to tax on income and gains; or
- all or most of the benefits paid out are subject to taxation.

In addition, the scheme must be established in the EU, Norway, Iceland, Liechtenstein or one of the many countries with which the UK has a double taxation treaty. This requirement means that HMRC should be able to impose tax penalties on the fund via the local tax authorities for any breach of the qualifying rules.

The other limits on QROPS are that at least 70% of funds must be used to provide pension income and that retirement benefits cannot be paid earlier than under a UK registered scheme. These requirements do not fall away after five years' non-UK residence.

In addition to these rules, if the QROPS makes any payments or investments while the individual is resident in the UK or before five complete tax years of non-UK residence have been established that would breach the standard UK pension scheme rules, it must report them to the UK authorities and the relevant UK tax penalty charges will be applied. For this reason, QROPS providers effectively operate two types of fund, one that mirrors the UK rules for the first five tax years and, once the five years of non-UK residence have been established, another that follows the more advantageous investment rules of the local jurisdiction.

HMRC regularly updates a list of overseas pension schemes that meet the QROPS tests (available on its website) but not all approved schemes are listed, as scheme operators can choose whether or not to appear on the list. HMRC also regularly reviews jurisdictions to decide whether abuse is occurring; it famously dis-approved all the schemes in Singapore in 2010, and recently, anti-avoidance has been included in Finance Act 2011 to prevent a potential abuse of the treaty between the UK and Hong Kong, which would have meant that no tax was payable on the QROPS pension.

26.8.3 Finance Act 2013 and QROPS

Changes in legislation were introduced by FA 2013 to strengthen reporting requirements and powers of exclusion relating to the QROPS regime. The Government also announced that where the country or territory in which a QROPS is established makes legislation or changes to a pension scheme to provide tax advantages that are not intended or available under the QROPS rules, the Government will act to exclude the relevant types of pension scheme in those countries or territories from being QROPS.

26.8.4 Retiring abroad

In practice, it is best to regard a QROPS as a conduit to switch a UK pension into a more flexible overseas vehicle after the individual has left the UK for good. Given the five-year rule and the fact that a person's intentions may change after retirement (many expats return to the UK after spending some time in retirement overseas), transferring into a QROPS before leaving the UK or in the early years after leaving could prove to be an expensive mistake in the longer term. It should also be remembered that, particularly on retirement, it can be difficult to establish non-UK residence so great care should be taken to confirm the five-year non-UK residence test has been met before the advantages of a QROPS can be realised.

Even then, the long arm of HMRC could still impose penalties (via the local tax authorities). So, although a QROPS can have advantages, it will never provide a route to total flexibility. If you are considering such a transfer, it is vital that you seek advice from an independent financial adviser.

STATE BENEFITS

26.9 STATE PENSION BENEFITS

Currently the state provides a number of pension benefits with a range of eligibility conditions and contribution requirements. There are also additional means-tested benefits payable in retirement, which are beyond the scope of this book.

The main state pension benefits in place at the moment are outlined briefly below but it is important to highlight that with effect from 6 April 2016 a new 'single tier' state pension is to be introduced to replace the current somewhat complicated system.

26.9.1 New single-tier state pension from 6 April 2016

You will get the new state pension if you are eligible and are either a man born after 6 April 1951 or a woman born after 6 April 1953.

The full new state pension will be no less than £148.40 per week (the actual amount being set in Autumn 2015).

You will usually need ten qualifying years of NI record to be eligible for any state pension and 35 qualifying years to receive the full new state pension.

The amount you receive will be based on your total NI record and will include the period before 6 April 2016.

Your NI record before 6 April 2016 is used to calculate your 'starting amount'. This will count towards your new state pension.

Your starting amount will be the higher of either:

- the amount you would get under the current state pension rules (which includes basic state pension and additional state pension), or
- the amount you would get if the new state pension had been in place at the start of your working life.

Your starting amount will include a deduction if you were contracted out.

If your starting amount is less than the full new state pension then you may be able to get more state pension by adding more qualifying years on your NI record after 5 April 2016 (until you reach the full new state pension amount or reach state pension age – whichever is first).

26.9.2 The basic state pension

The basic state pension is the first part of the Government's pension provision. Individuals will be eligible for all or a part, providing they have a sufficient national insurance contribution record. Individuals with earnings above or equal to the lower earnings level (LEL) in any year will be credited with a year's qualifying record for the purposes of the basic state pension. There are also special dispensations for carers (home responsibilities protection).

With effect from 6 April 2010, both men and women have needed 30 years of qualifying national insurance records to be entitled to the full basic state pension.

The state pension age has started to equalise (from April 2010) in stages and by 2019–20 the state retirement age will be 65 for both sexes. The state pension age for both men and women will then rise from 65 to 66 by April 2020 and is proposed to rise again to 67 by April 2028.

The Government has abolished the statutory retirement age, so that employers cannot automatically dismiss employees on attaining age 65.

The value of the basic state pension has in the past been linked to increases in inflation (RPI) each year in April. This level of increases has not been considered fair by many pensioners as average wages have typically risen at a higher rate and therefore the long-term value of the basic state pension has been gradually eroded. The Government has confirmed that it will re-link pensions to average earnings from April 2011. Old age pensions will also be protected by a new 'triple lock' which will guarantee every year a rise in the basic state pension in line with earnings, prices or a 2.5% increase, whichever is greater. The triple lock does not apply to SERPS or S2P.

In 2015–16 the full basic state pension for a single person is £115.95 per week.

26.9.3 State Earnings Related Pension Scheme (SERPS)

SERPS was introduced in 1978 and provides a pension that is based on earnings between the lower and upper earnings limits (for 2015–16, £5,824 and £42,380 pa, respectively). People who are self-employed have neither contributed towards, nor will benefit from, SERPS.

Benefit accrual under SERPS ended in April 2002 with the introduction of the state second pension (S2P) but benefits already accrued continue to be calculated in accordance with the rules at that date.

SERPS provides a pension at state retirement age expressed as a percentage of band earnings. For those retiring now the percentage is currently 20%, with those retiring before then receiving a higher percentage up to a maximum of 25% of band earnings. Band earnings are based on an average over the whole of your working life.

26.9.4 State second pension (S2P)

S2P was introduced on 6 April 2002. Like SERPS, which it replaced, S2P is based on NI contributions made by employers and employees. However, S2P provides better benefits than SERPS for low and moderate earners.

Aside from providing an additional state pension for the employed, S2P gives an additional state pension based on earnings of £15,300 (2015–16) to those:

- employed and earning over the lower earnings limit of £5,824 in the 2015 to 2016 tax year;
- looking after children under 12 and claiming Child Benefit;
- caring for a sick or disabled person more than 20 hours a week and claiming Carer's Credit;
- working as a registered foster carer and claiming Carer's Credit;
- receiving certain other benefits due to illness or disability.

You are not eligible if you are:

- employed and earning less than £5,824 per year;
- self-employed;
- unemployed;
- in full-time training.

Before 6 April 2010, earnings were divided into three bands rather than the single 'band earnings' used to calculate SERPS. In addition to the lower and upper earnings limits, there was a 'low earnings threshold' broadly equal to half of national average earnings and a second earnings threshold.

State pension forecast

To obtain an illustration of potential state pension benefits and state second pension entitlement at state pension age individuals should obtain a forecast by completing the Department of Work and Pensions form BR19 or an online application directly on the DWP website (www.thepensionservice.gov.uk).

26.10 CONTRACTING OUT

Individuals were previously able to leave the state second pension by 'contracting out'. For any year where the individual has been contracted out they will forgo their second state pension benefits at retirement for that particular tax year. Individuals were also previously able to contract out of SERPS.

There are three ways in which an employee could be contracted out. These are:

- contracting out via a personal pension;
- membership of a contracted-out money purchase pension scheme (COMPS); or
- membership of an occupational scheme providing a guaranteed minimum pension (GMP)* – unavailable since 6 April 1997 – or an occupational scheme that satisfies a 'Reference Scheme' test.

It was possible to leave S2P provided appropriate provision was made to replace the S2P benefits with a suitable approved alternative. To encourage this, individuals and employers who contract out in this way receive benefits in the form of reduced NIC charges and/or a direct payment into an individual's personal pension scheme.

26.10.1 Contracting out is no longer an option

The Pensions Act 2008 brought an end to contracting out both through contracted out money purchase schemes and via personal type pensions (stakeholder and personal pension) from April 2012.

---

* This method of contracting out involved an occupational pension scheme providing a guaranteed minimum level of pension equivalent to that provided by SERPS. Both the employer and the employee benefited from a reduced level of NIC, but the employer had to be prepared to provide the pension scheme with sufficient funds to enable it to meet the guarantee. No further GMPs can accrue for periods after 5 April 1997.

Glossary of terms and abbreviations

'A' Day	6 April 2006
AA	Annual allowance
Annuity	Income stream purchased from an insurance provider
ASP	Alternatively secured pension
AVC	Additional voluntary contribution
BCE	Benefit crystallisation event
CPI	Consumer Price Index
DC	Defined contributions
EFRBS	Employer funded retirement benefit schemes
EP	Enhanced protection
FSAVC	Free-standing additional voluntary contribution
FURBS	Funded unapproved retirement benefits scheme
GAD rate	Government Actuary's Department (GAD) table
LEL	Lower earnings level
Minimum retirement age	55
MIR	Minimum income requirement
MPAA	Money purchase annual allowance
PCLS	Pre-commencement lump sum
PIP	Pension input period
PP	Primary protection
QROPS	Qualifying recognised overseas pension scheme
S2P	State second pension
Secured income	Pension income that is promised to be paid until death
SERPS	State Earnings Related Pension Scheme
SIPP	Self-invested personal pension
SLA	Statutory lifetime allowance
SSAS	Small self-administered scheme
State pension forecast	Available online at www.thepensionservice.gov.uk
UFPLS	Uncrystallised fund pension lump sum

27

INVESTING IN REAL ESTATE

This chapter contains the following sections:

(1) 'Buy to let' investments
(2) Private investment companies
(3) Limited liability partnerships (LLPs)
(4) Investing surplus funds within a trading company
(5) Using an offshore company to buy UK residential property
(6) Buying overseas property
(7) Quoted property companies
(8) Property funds offered by insurance companies
(9) Pension funds

27.1 'BUY TO LET' INVESTMENTS

The subject of rental property is covered in general in Chapter 8.

The attraction of buying properties for letting is that the business should produce a reasonable return provided that the gearing (financing by loans) is not excessive, void periods are kept to a minimum and the properties are properly maintained. Problems arise from unexpectedly long periods without a tenant and the fact that it is often necessary to refurbish the property substantially after a tenant moves out. It may be time-consuming and difficult to manage a portfolio of investment properties, particularly if they are let on short leases or the properties require a lot of maintenance and are a long way from one another. Letting properties can require a lot of business and management skills and the ability to think ahead.

27.1.1 Relief for interest

The decision whether to borrow and invest in a second property involves two factors: interest rates and tax relief. A loan to invest in a rental property will attract tax relief but most financial institutions will then charge a significantly higher rate of interest. A loan to purchase your main residence or a remortgage of your main residence does not normally attract tax relief but will attract a competitive interest rate from the bank or building society. However, relief for interest is governed by the way that the borrowed money is used, not by the way the loan is secured. Relief should therefore be available for interest on a loan that is secured by way of a remortgage of your home but is used to buy an investment property.

> **Tax notes**
>
> When considering any investment, you need to look at how you will fund the transaction and what you think you will gain at the end of that transaction. Borrowing money to buy investment properties makes no sense if the interest charges are likely to exceed the rental income and future capital gains on the disposal of the properties. But if you can get tax relief for the interest, it is more likely that the benefits will outweigh the costs.

27.1.2 Increasing your gearing

It is not always necessary to take loans out when you purchase properties. We have explained at 8.2.12 that it may be possible to obtain tax relief for interest if you take fresh loans later on that are used to fund your property business.

27.1.3 No IHT business property relief

Letting properties is a business but it is not normally the sort of business which will qualify for business property relief.

27.2 PRIVATE INVESTMENT COMPANIES

In this section, we look at UK and foreign investment companies.

27.2.1 UK investment companies

A UK investment company has certain pros and cons.

Pros

- An individual can raise qualifying loans if the borrowings are used to finance the purchase of shares or the making of a loan to a UK close company that exists to manage property investments. It is necessary that the individual holds a material interest in the company (either on his or her own or in conjunction with his or her associates) – see 11.5. Usually, where the individual and his or her immediate family hold all the shares and this condition is clearly satisfied, interest on such a loan may be set against the individual's general income. Relief is not confined to income from the company but may be restricted if the individual 'recovers' capital from the company (see 11.5.5).

- The investment company may pay corporation tax at only 20% whereas an individual who lets properties may well be subject to 40% or 45% tax because of the level of his or her other income.
- It will be easier for an individual to either put shares into his or her children's names from the outset, or to transfer shares to his or her children later on, than it would be if he or she needed to transfer a part interest in an investment property owned personally.
- When the company sells the properties, it will be liable for corporation tax on its gains at 20% as opposed to the personal tax rate of 28%. Also, these gains are computed with relief for indexation (see 13.12).

Cons

- When the individual draws money from the company, this will generally involve his or her taking remuneration or interest or a dividend. The receipt of such income may attract higher rate tax.
- When the shareholders realise a capital gain on disposing of their shares (on a sale or a winding-up), they will also be liable for CGT (in addition to the corporation tax liability the company may have on any property disposal gain – the 'two tier CGT charge').

> **Tax notes**
>
> In general, before you put any property in a company, consider the exit route. A buyer will be interested in the asset, ie the house, but may not be so keen to buy shares in a private company.

In general, the two tier CGT charge means that it is not likely to be beneficial for most landlords to operate through an investment company. Nevertheless, if you have an existing investment company and it has unrelieved losses, it may make sense for you to put an investment property into the company to generate more rental income and so use up these losses.

Putting investment properties into a company will normally result in an SDLT charge (see Chapter 36).

27.2.2 Foreign investment companies

Until FA 2014 was enacted, a UK individual could not raise a qualifying loan to finance the purchase of shares in a non-UK resident company or to make a loan to such a company. It is now possible to get relief for interest where the company is not resident in the UK but is resident elsewhere in the EEA (see 11.5).

A non-UK resident company that receives rents from UK properties will generally be subject to basic rate income tax.

It will not be subject to tax on capital gains but the shareholders may be taxed under s 13 TCGA 1992 (see 33.18) where the company would be a close company if it were UK resident and the shareholder and his or her associates hold an interest in the company that amounts to at least 10%. This charge now also applies to foreign domiciled individuals.

In practice, it may be difficult to show that an investment company owned by UK-resident individuals is not resident here for tax purposes (see Chapter 35).

27.3 LIMITED LIABILITY PARTNERSHIPS (LLPs)

An LLP is a type of body corporate (company) that has a transparent tax treatment for some purposes. For property investment LLPs, this is subject to the proviso that the properties are used in the commercial letting business of the LLP.

There is no relief where an individual borrows personally to finance the purchase of an interest in an investment LLP (see 11.4). However, interest on borrowings taken by the LLP is an expense in computing the LLP's rental income for tax purposes.

An individual member's share of the income received by an LLP (computed in the normal way and after deducting loan interest) is taxed as if he or she had received that income personally.

When an investment property is sold by an LLP, the gain is divided among the members. Those members who are individuals or trustees may enjoy the benefit of the annual exemption. Non-resident members are not subject to UK CGT on their share of the LLP's capital gains.

No further income tax or capital gains tax is payable when members withdraw profits or the LLP is wound up.

A member's share in an LLP that carries on a property letting business will not qualify for IHT business property relief.

Tax notes

Both LLPs and UK limited companies have annual Companies House filing obligations, which need to be met to keep the entity in good standing. More information can be found at the Companies House website (www.companieshouse.gov.uk) or by calling 0303 1234 500.

27.4 INVESTING SURPLUS FUNDS WITHIN A TRADING COMPANY

Many people operate a business through a limited company and, as the business prospers, start to make investments by using the company's surplus funds. This may involve direct investment in real estate or indirect investment via the purchase of quoted shares or other investments.

This may have adverse tax consequences in the long-term. See 17.7 on the way in which HMRC can withhold entrepreneurs' relief where a company has substantial investment activities. Entitlement to business property relief (see 30.8) will also be affected.

27.5 USING AN OFFSHORE COMPANY TO BUY UK RESIDENTIAL PROPERTY

It is very common for non-resident investors to hold UK property, especially residential property. However, FA 2013 has introduced two major changes which will often make this unattractive.

27.5.1 Capital gains tax for non-residents

There is now a potential liability for capital gains tax which can be charged on a sale of residential property for more than £2m. This tax may be charged at 28% on disposals made after 5 April 2013. The disposal may consist of a sale by the company or a sale of shares in the company.

The gain which may be charged under these provisions will generally be limited to the appreciation in value over the value at 5 April 2013.

The £2m threshold was reduced to £1m from 1 April 2015 and will be further reduced to £500,000 with effect from 1 April 2016.

Furthermore, legislation was introduced by FA 2015 to charge capital gains tax on gains made by non-residents disposing of UK residential property (see 34.6.8).

27.5.2 Principal exemptions

Certain companies and other non-natural persons are exempt from this charge. These are companies, etc engaged in

- property development;
- renting properties on a commercial basis to unconnected persons;
- carrying on a trade;
- holding a property for occupation by employees who hold less than 5% of the shares in the company itself or in the holding company of the group in which the property-owning company is a member.

27.5.3 Other exemptions

There are two exemptions which can apply even where the occupant is connected with the company:

- The charge does not apply to a farmhouse if the company is engaged in carrying on a trade of farming.
- The charge does not apply if a company owns an historic house that is open to the public or provides access to the dwelling as part of its services (eg as a wedding venue) with the intention of being open for at least 28 days per annum.

The company's activities in the historic house must be commercial and with a profit-seeking motive, even if that profit does not cover the full costs of the house. Also, access must be to a significant part of the property.

27.5.4 Charities

A charity which owns residential property is not liable for CGT.

27.5.5 Annual tax on enveloped dwellings

This started as an annual tax for residential properties worth more than £2m which are owned by non-natural persons such as companies (also called the annual residential property tax). The same exemptions apply as for the capital gains tax charge on non-residents (see above). For further details, see 36.4. Note that the £2m threshold was reduced to £1m by FA 2015 and it is going to be futher reduced to £500,000.

27.6 BUYING PROPERTY OVERSEAS

There are several aspects to be considered here.

27.6.1 Holiday homes

Many people buy a holiday home with a view to letting it out for a few weeks and occupying it themselves for the rest of the year. A proportion of the interest on a loan used to buy the property can be claimed as a deduction in arriving at your taxable income from such lettings.

The Government has recently relaxed the rules on benefits in kind (see 4.8.6) but there are still many traps for the unwary in holding such investments through a company.

27.6.2 Furnished holiday lettings

If you buy an investment property in the European Economic Area, and it qualifies as furnished holiday accommodation (see 8.5.1), you may be able to set any loss against other income. Subject to the normal time limits, you may also be able to claim such relief for past years. You may also claim roll-over relief (see 17.4).

While furnished holiday lettings (FHL) in the UK and other EEA countries will continue to qualify for the special tax reliefs available for FHL, the qualifying conditions have altered from April 2011 onwards.

In particular, it is now more difficult for a property to qualify as a holiday letting – it has to be available for commercial letting as holiday accommodation for 210 days a year (previously 140 days) and actually let for 105 days (previously 70 days). However, to cater for fluctuations in lettings from year to year, it is possible for owners to elect for continuation of a qualifying holiday letting to cover a break of one or two years where the letting thresholds are not reached.

FHL owners who may struggle to meet the new letting thresholds will have to decide whether or not to retain the property for personal use and/or hold it as an investment or take steps to ensure that the property is available and actually let for the appropriate periods (by advertising more widely etc).

27.6.3 Relief for financing costs

A UK individual may create a special purpose vehicle (SPV) to acquire overseas investment properties, eg by forming a UK or EEA limited company to make investments in overseas property. If the company is a close company, as will normally be the case, and the individual has a material interest (see 11.5), he or she can raise a qualifying loan to finance the investment by either subscribing for shares or making loans to the close company. The interest on such loans can be relieved against the individual's other income.

27.6.4 The company will be liable for tax on capital gains

Holding overseas property in this way will mean that the UK company may have a tax liability as and when it eventually realises the investment. There may then be a further CGT charge on getting money out of the company. However, there may be ways of minimising this if you plan sufficiently far ahead. One possibility is to hold each overseas investment in a separate SPV with a view to eventually selling shares in that company rather than having the company sell its property. It is not quite as simple as this because you may well need to be able to deal with a possible objection by a UK purchaser that this will leave him or her with a latent tax liability if he or she ever wishes to take the property out of the company. There are ways of squaring the circle and you should consult a specialist at the outset rather than only as and when you are ready to divest.

27.6.5 Using an overseas company

An overseas company may often be treated in the same way as a UK company. If the company is centrally managed and controlled in the UK it will be treated as resident here (see 18.1). Even if you manage to surmount this obstacle, you may still suffer tax on a disposal of the property if s13 TCGA 1992 applies (see 33.19).

27.6.6 Make the SPV a limited liability partnership instead?

Another way of organising matters is to form a limited liability partnership to hold overseas property. The LLP could be a UK LLP or, if you were acquiring a US property, a Delaware LLP. The tax treatment is likely to be as follows:

* Interest relief against rental income provided that the borrowings are taken out by the LLP.
* Capital gains on a disposal of a property (but only a single charge, not a two-tier charge as described at 27.2.1 above).

27.7 QUOTED PROPERTY COMPANIES

27.7.1 UK quoted shares

Shares in a quoted UK property company have the following tax treatment:

* No relief for interest on loans used to buy shares unless, exceptionally, the quoted company is a close company and the individual either has a material interest or works full-time in the management of the company's business (see 11.5).
* The company pays corporation tax on rental income and capital gains.
* A shareholder pays tax in the normal way on dividends (see 9.8).
* An individual who realises a capital gain on a disposal of shares is subject to CGT if he or she is resident in the UK.

27.7.2 Real estate investment trusts

REITs are quoted collective vehicles for investment in rental property. They were introduced in the UK in 2007 but have been available in other countries for a number of years.

Investments into REITs are broadly the same as making direct property investments. No tax is charged at the company level. Tax is instead payable by the shareholders – this applies to both rental profits and capital gains.

However, a withholding tax of 20% will apply to most distributions by a REIT to its investors. The main exceptions are UK-resident companies and various exempt bodies.

Qualifying distributions received from a REIT are treated as rental income rather than dividends. They are known as Property Income Distributions (PIDs).

27.7.3 Non-resident companies

Where a company is not resident in the UK (even though it may be quoted in London), the tax treatment is as follows:

- UK rental income is subject to tax at basic rate;
- capital gains are not normally taxed at the company level;
- distributions of income are taxed as dividends: these may attract a 10% credit (see 9.10);
- a shareholder will not normally be subject to tax on the company's capital gains: the only circumstance where this can apply is where the foreign company is a close company and the UK resident individual has a 10% or greater interest;
- a capital gain may arise for a UK shareholder on realising his or her investment.

27.8 PROPERTY FUNDS OFFERED BY INSURANCE COMPANIES

Most insurance companies offer unitised funds that include funds invested in property. These funds pay corporation tax at 20% on rental income and realised capital gains.

The tax treatment of individuals who take out investment bonds that are invested in such funds is set out at 28.2.

27.9 PENSION FUNDS

See 26.3.2 on the fact that residential property investments are a taxable asset for pension schemes, ie what were formerly called 'prohibited assets'.

Other property investments and, in particular, investments in quoted property companies and REITs are regarded as normal investments.

28

LIFE ASSURANCE

This chapter contains the following sections:

(1) Introduction
(2) Qualifying and non-qualifying policies
(3) Taxation of life policy proceeds
(4) Foreign life policies
(5) Annuities
(6) Income protection
(7) Pre-owned assets charge
(8) Life policies held by companies
(9) Life policies in trust affected by the FA 2006 IHT changes
(10) Discounted gift schemes

28.1 INTRODUCTION

A life assurance policy is simply the evidence of a contract between the individual policyholder and the life assurance company. The general principle is that the company is the collecting house for pooled investments and mortality risks, offering benefits directly to policyholders based on personal contracts. Life assurance policies can be used for a variety of purposes ranging from pure self -protection to a tax-advantaged way to invest.

Life assurance policies can be classified in a number of ways, but the most common practical classification reflects the nature of the benefits provided under the policy and the periods for which they are provided. Types of policy are:

- whole of life policies, where the sum assured is payable on the death of the life assured, whenever that occurs;
- term policies, where the sum assured is payable on death during the policy term only; and
- endowment policies, where the underlying investment value is payable at the end of the policy term and the sum assured is paid out on death during the term.

Each type of policy has its own characteristics in terms of the blend of life assurance protection and potential investment return. Term policies for a relatively short period are most likely to offer the highest sum assured for each pound of premium while, towards the other end of the spectrum, an endowment policy will have a greater investment element.

An important characteristic of life assurance policies is that they do not produce income as such, but are essentially medium- or long-term accumulators. While a policy is held intact, the income and gains arising from the underlying investments held by the life company are taxed in the hands of the life company itself at 20%. In general, a tax liability only arises for the policyholder when he or she receives payment under the policy.

This chapter deals with the tax consequences of the policyholder paying premiums or receiving benefits under a life assurance policy issued by a UK company or a foreign insurer operating through a branch in the UK (although foreign life policies are covered briefly at 28.4).

Over the years many changes have been made to this complex and technical area.

28.1.1 The company's tax position

The taxation of life companies is complex, but broadly speaking, in respect of their life assurance business, companies are generally taxed on the excess of their investment income and realised capital gains over management expenses (the 'I-E' basis). For proprietary companies there is a formula to determine the proportions of the company's income and gains that should be allocated to policyholders and shareholders, respectively. Since 1 April 2003, the tax rate charged on the policyholder share of all life fund income has been 20%. The company's profits attributable to shareholders are also now subject to corporation tax at 20%.

Registered friendly societies are in a different position, being exempt from corporation tax in respect of tax-exempt life or endowment business. This is life and endowment business where total premiums under contracts do not exceed £270 pa, or £300 if paid monthly (a limit unchanged since 6 April 1995). Policies that can be written on the tax-exempt basis are generally qualifying policies provided they satisfy a 'minimum sum assured' test. Such policies can give tax-free proceeds even to higher rate taxpayers (see 25.3), but non-qualifying friendly society policies are taxable at basic and higher rates. The remainder of this chapter does not deal specifically with friendly society business.

28.2 QUALIFYING AND NON-QUALIFYING POLICIES

Although there is no differentiation between qualifying and non-qualifying policies in respect of taxation of the income and gains from the underlying assets in the life company's hands, the distinction does have a major impact on the tax position of the individual policyholder. Each of the three types of policy already identified (whole of life, endowment and term assurance) is capable of being a qualifying or non-qualifying policy depending on its initial design and the way in which it is dealt with once in force.

28.2.1 Qualifying policies

These are policies that satisfy the conditions set out in Schedule 15 ICTA 1988, and do not fall foul of the various anti-avoidance provisions. The main features of the qualifying rules are as follows.

Premiums

- These must be payable for a period of ten years or more (though term assurances may be written for shorter periods) and must be payable annually or more frequently; and
- must be fairly evenly spread so that premiums payable in any one period of 12 months are neither more than twice the amount of premiums paid in any other 12-month period, nor more than one-eighth of the total amount of premiums payable over the first ten years (in the case of whole of life policies) or over the term of the policy (in the case of an endowment).

Premiums payable for an exceptional risk of death are left out of account for these purposes as are premiums payable for exceptional risk of a critical illness (see 28.3.8). However, these premium rules mean that 'single premium' policies used for lump sum investments are not qualifying policies (see 28.2.2).

An annual limit of £3,600 applies from 6 April 2013. This limit does not apply to policies already in existence at 21 March 2012. Transitional provisions apply to policies issued between 21 March 2012 and 5 April 2013.

The sum assured

- This for an endowment policy, must not be less than 75% of the total premiums payable during the term of the policy. This percentage is reduced by 2% for each year by which the insured individual's age exceeds 55 years at the issue of the policy;
- for a whole of life policy, must not be less than 75% of the total premiums payable if death were to occur at age 75;
- for a term policy that has no surrender value and ends before the insured individual's 75th birthday, need not satisfy any minimum requirement.

Benefits

- These may include the right to participate in profits, the right to benefits arising because of disability or the right to a return of premiums on death under a certain specified age (not exceeding 16 years); but
- may not include any other benefits of a capital nature.

The rules for certain special types of policy may vary from those referred to above, for example, mortgage protection policies, family income policies and industrial assurances.

Life assurers usually submit standard policy wordings to HMRC so that they can be certified as satisfying the qualifying rules (pre-certification). Policies in those standard forms can then be marketed as 'qualifying'.

Where a policy contains options by which the policyholder may, for example, increase the sum assured or the premium, or extend the policy term, these options are tested at the outset to ensure that, however any options are exercised, the policy will still satisfy the qualifying rules.

28.2.2 Insurance bonds and other non-qualifying policies

Non-qualifying policies are all other life policies not satisfying the qualifying rules, and those that, although they might have satisfied the qualifying rules at the outset, have been changed in some way such that they no longer satisfy those rules.

The most significant category of policies that are non-qualifying is single premium investment contracts (usually referred to as insurance or investment 'bonds'). These are written as whole of life contracts and provide for only a small amount of life cover, being primarily investment vehicles.

28.2.3 Taxation of premiums

(ss 266 et seq and Schedule 14 ICTA 1988)

No specific tax relief is available to an individual in respect of premiums paid under a non-qualifying life assurance policy. Similarly, there is no specific relief for premiums paid under qualifying policies issued in respect of contracts made after 13 March 1984. However, where qualifying policies issued before that date were still in force, Life Assurance Premium Relief (LAPR) was available until 2014–15 at the rate of 12.5% on premiums up to the greater of £1,500 or one-sixth of total income.

This relief was abolished with effect from 6 April 2015.

28.3 TAXATION OF LIFE POLICY PROCEEDS

(ss 461–546 ITTOIA 2005)

In view of life policies' position as income accumulators, where liability for gains and income in respect of the underlying assets is dealt with by taxing the life company, the usual income tax principles are inappropriate to life policy taxation. Accordingly, the tax regime that applies to the individual policyholder has been specifically constructed for the purpose. It caters separately for qualifying and non-qualifying policies and for mortality and investment profits realised from policies.

It is first necessary to determine if any particular action constitutes a 'chargeable event' in respect of the policy. If it does not, no income tax consequence arises under the life policy regime from that action. If it does, it is then necessary to calculate the 'gain', to determine the rate of tax applicable to the gain and to determine who is liable to pay the resulting tax.

Despite references to 'chargeable events' and 'gains', it is the income tax regime that applies to life policies (for the CGT position, see 28.3.10). For the taxation of personal portfolio bonds, see 28.3.11.

28.3.1 Chargeable events

Non-qualifying policy

(s 484 ITTOIA 2005)

For a non-qualifying policy such as an insurance bond, the chargeable events are broadly:

- the death of the life assured;
- the maturity of the policy;
- the total surrender of the policy;
- the assignment of the policy for money or money's worth; and
- excesses arising on partial surrenders or partial assignments in any policy year.

No chargeable event occurs where an assignment takes place by way of security for a debt (or on the discharge of the security). Similarly, an assignment between spouses or civil partners who are living together is not a chargeable event.

Qualifying policy

For qualifying policies, there are exemptions from the rules on chargeable events.

Three consequences of the chargeable event rules are that:

(1) the gift (ie assignment of the whole policy with no consideration) of qualifying or non-qualifying policies is not a chargeable event and so triggers no income tax consequences;
(2) there is no chargeable event on the death of the life assured under, or on the maturity of, a qualifying policy where all due premiums were paid prior to the event in question;
(3) there is no chargeable event on the assignment for value or surrender (in whole or part) of a qualifying policy where premiums have been paid for the first ten years (or three-quarters of the term for an endowment policy).

Where there is no chargeable event in respect of a life policy, there is no income tax charge under the specific life policy tax regime, irrespective of the tax position of the individual policyholder. In particular, points (2) and (3) above illustrate the main current advantage of qualifying policies – ie their ability to provide tax-free proceeds to individual policyholders.

28.3.2 Calculating life policy gains

(s 491 ITTOIA 2005)

Broadly speaking, where the chargeable event is either a maturity, total surrender or an assignment for consideration, the chargeable gain is the investment profit made under the policy. This is calculated by reference to the value of the benefits being received as a result of the chargeable event, plus the amount of any relevant capital payments previously received under the policy (ie any sum or other benefit of a capital nature, other than one paid as a result of an individual's disability), less the amount paid by way of premiums and any taxable gains as a result of previous partial surrenders.

This principle of charging tax only on investment gains also applies where the chargeable event is the death of the life assured. The exclusion of mortality profit from the taxable gain is achieved by using the policy's surrender value immediately before death instead of the value of the benefits being received under the policy.

A policy capable of paying benefits on more than one death could have the considerable disadvantage that, on a death, lump sums paid on previous deaths were taken into account when calculating the 'investment gain' under the policy. This result was not intended and FA 2003 confirmed this to be the case (both for the future and the past), subject to certain conditions.

See 10.9 regarding commission rebates.

28.3.3 Partial surrenders

(ss 498–508 ITTOIA 2005)

A chargeable event occurs when a policyholder surrenders part of the policy (often referred to as making 'withdrawals' from the policy). Partial surrenders include the surrender of a right to a bonus. They also include loans to a policyholder made by (or by arrangement with) the insurance company, unless the policyholder's policy is a qualifying policy and the loan bears a commercial rate of interest, or the loan is made to a full time employee of the insurer for the purposes of a house purchase or improvement.

At the end of each policy year, the policy attracts an allowable payment of 5% of the total premium then paid under the policy. This allowance is then set against the value of any partial surrenders made up to that date. If the value of those partial surrenders exceeds the current cumulative net total of allowable payments, a chargeable event occurs; if the net total of allowable payments is equal to or exceeds cumulative withdrawals, no chargeable event occurs. Allowable payments are given up to 100% of the total premiums paid so that, for a single premium investment bond, the allowances are given at the rate of 5% for 20 years, ie a policyholder can take his or her allowable payment tax free every year for a 20-year period or in separate years spread over a longer period, so long as the cumulative allowable payments total for the relevant policy year is not exceeded. For instance, a policyholder who withdrew nothing in years one and two could withdraw up to 15% in year three.

Once an 'excess' (ie an occasion on which the cumulative partial surrenders exceed the cumulative allowances) has occurred, the cumulative withdrawals and allowances up to that date are considered to have been used and the process of accumulating allowances and withdrawals starts afresh (subject to the '100% of premiums' limit that applies to the allowances).

Example – Cumulation of allowances and withdrawals

X invests £10,000 in a single premium investment bond; £1,200 is withdrawn after four policy years, a further £4,500 after six policy years and £1,000 after eight policy years.

Policy years	A Cumulative allowable payments £	B Partial surrender (C – A) £	C Cumulative surrender between £	D Taxable gain £
1	500 (1 × 500)	0	0	0
2	1,000 (2 × 500)	0	0	0
3	1,500 (3 × 500)	0	0	0
4	2,000 (4 × 500)	1,200	1,200	0
5	2,500 (5 × 500)	0	1,200	0
6	3,000 (6 × 500)	4,500	5,700	2,700
7	500 (1 × 500)	0	0	0
8	1,000 (2 × 500)	1,000	1,000	0
9	1,500 (3 × 500)	0	1,000	0
10	2,000 (4 × 500)	0	1,000	0

Note: (1) A chargeable event occurs only when C exceeds A.

(2) The value of the policy is irrelevant to these calculations so that it is possible to have a taxable gain under a policy at a time when the policy itself is worth less than the premiums paid. When the final chargeable event occurs under the policy (ie death, maturity, final surrender or assignment for value), the total profit on the policy is brought into account. The profit is the final proceeds (excluding any mortality profit where the event is death), plus previous partial surrenders, less premiums paid and any taxable gains from previous partial withdrawals.

ZURICH TAX HANDBOOK

Example – Total surrender after partial surrenders

> Using the example immediately above, if the policy were totally surrendered at the end of the tenth policy year for £10,400, the taxable gain on that final encashment would be as follows:
>
> $$£10,400 + £1,200 + £4,500 + £1,000 - (£10,000 + £2,700) = £4,400$$
>
> Note: If, on final termination, the 'gain' calculated in this way is a negative figure, it may be deducted from taxable income for the purposes of higher rate tax only (see 28.3.4).

Get professional advice

A recent case has drawn attention to the dangers attached to making part withdrawals without first getting professional advice.

Mr Lobler came to the UK for work purposes. He sold his house in the Netherlands and invested the proceeds and further borrowings in life insurance policies. He subsequently made several withdrawals of funds from the policies in order to repay a loan and fund the purchase and renovation of a house. Mr Lobler did not take independent advice when he withdrew the funds and on the withdrawal forms he elected as his surrender option 'partial surrender across all policies from specific funds'. Mr Lobler assumed that because he had withdrawn no more than what he had paid for the policies, no taxable gain would arise and therefore he made no mention of the withdrawals in his tax returns.

HMRC amended Mr Lobler's tax returns to include his income arising from the withdrawals from the insurance policies, with each withdrawal producing a deemed gain. This meant that he had a substantial tax charge representing an effective tax rate of 779% on actual income generated by the policy. If instead Mr Lobler had opted for a full surrender of some policies, his tax charge would have been much lower.

Mr Lobler appealed but the First Tax Tribunal held in favour of HMRC. On an appeal to the Upper Tribunal, it was held that he could rectify his mistake.

This case drew attention to the complex (and many would say unfair) tax regime governing part surrenders of life insurance policies which the Upper Tribunal described as being 'unintuitive, unexpected and surprising for . . . most policyholders'.

Partial assignments of policies

FA 2001 clarified the position on partial assignments of policies (eg where spouses or civil partners jointly own a policy and want to transfer it to one of them only, such as on divorce) so that:

556

(1) partial assignments for no consideration are not chargeable events (but note that HMRC believes that assignment on divorce will almost invariably be for consideration); and

(2) any tax liability will fall on the person whose interest in the policy is reducing.

28.3.4 Taxing gains on chargeable events

(s 491 ITTOIA 2005)

In the majority of cases where the policyholder owns the policy for his or her own absolute benefit, the gain is treated as the top slice of his or her income and is taxed appropriately.

However, because the income and gains attributable to the policy's underlying assets have already been taxed in the hands of the life company, life policy gains are not chargeable to income tax at the basic rate. This applies to both qualifying and non-qualifying policies. Despite the fact that the gain is treated as having already suffered tax as if it were income from savings, there is no grossing up of the gain for higher rate tax purposes.

Accordingly, for an individual paying tax at the additional rate, the maximum rate of tax payable on life policy gains at present is 25% (45% less 20%). An individual whose income (including the gain) is taxable at the basic rate only will have no further income tax liability on the policy gain. Non-taxpayers will not be able to make any reclaim in respect of the notional credit for tax paid by the life company.

If the individual realises a loss under the policy, that loss is only available as a deduction from taxable income for the purposes of higher rate tax. Furthermore, the loss is only eligible for such relief to the extent of amounts charged as income in respect of previous chargeable events. FA 2004 contained anti-avoidance legislation that prevents loss relief for deficiencies on 'second-hand' insurance bonds.

Top-slicing

In view of the fact that the gain will have arisen over a period of years, the legislation recognises that it would be harsh to treat the total gain as part of the taxpayer's income in the year of receipt. A measure of relief is afforded by a process known as 'top-slicing'.

Top-slicing first requires calculation of the 'appropriate fraction' of the gain, more usually referred to as the 'slice'. Where the chargeable event in question is death, maturity, total encashment or assignment for value, the slice is calculated by dividing the gain by the number of complete policy years for which the policy has been in force. Where the chargeable event is caused by a partial surrender, the gain is divided by the number of complete policy years since the last excess caused by a partial surrender (or by the number of years for which the policy has been in force where the chargeable event is the first excess).

The slice (and not the whole of the gain) is treated as the top part of the policyholder's income, and the average rate of tax applicable to the slice (less the basic rate) is calculated. That tax rate will then apply to the whole of the gain to determine the total income tax liability on the gain. The result is that relief is given to individuals whose other income would mean that they pay tax at no more than the basic rate, but who would be taken into the higher rates of tax if the whole of the gain were added to their income.

Example – No tax on the gain

A invests £20,000 in a single premium investment bond in May 2011 and cashes it in after five years for £27,500. The gain is therefore £7,500 and the 'slice' is £1,500 (£7,500 divided by 5).

	£
Taxable income (excluding policy gain)	25,000
'Slice'	1,500
Taxable income	26,500

The tax rate applicable to the 'slice' is therefore 20% less 20% = 0%.

Example – Slice falling into basic and higher rate bands

B invests £12,000 in a single premium investment bond in May 2011. After five years she cashes it in for £17,000. The gain is £5,000 and the slice is £1,000 (£5,000 divided by 5). In that year her other taxable income after reliefs is £31,510.

Tax calculation on gain:	£
Taxable income + 'slice'	32,510
Tax applicable to slice	
On £500 (ie £31,510 to £32,010) at 0% (20% − 20%)	Nil
On £500 (ie £32,011 to £32,511) at 20% (40% − 20%)	100
Total tax on slice	100

Average rate on slice

$$\frac{100}{1000} \times 100 = \%$$

The tax payable is £5,000 × 10% = £500.

To illustrate the effect of top-slicing, if it had not been available the calculations would have been:

Tax applicable to the gain	£
On £500 at 0% (20%)	Nil
On £4,500 at 20% (40% − 20%)	900
Tax payable	900

Notes:

(1) The whole gain (without top-slicing) is counted as income in determining whether any age allowance or entitlement to children's tax credit should be reduced.

(2) There is no top-slicing where the taxpayer is a company.

(3) For top-slicing purposes, total income is computed without reference to amounts chargeable in respect of loss of office or lease premiums chargeable as rent.

(4) The examples given in this chapter assume no reliefs or amounts as mentioned in (3).

Age allowance for over 65s

If an individual is entitled to the age allowance, the gain on a life policy can reduce (or even eliminate) that additional allowance. Top-slicing relief does not apply in respect of this reduction of the additional allowance. See 12.2.1 for an example of how age related allowances can be reduced.

Tax credits

The gain on a life policy can affect entitlement to tax credits and, as for age allowance, top-slicing relief does not apply.

28.3.5 Two policy gains in one tax year

Where an individual has two policies with chargeable gains in a tax year, tax is calculated as if the gains arose under only one policy, with a slice equal to the sum of the individual slices. Thus, if two policies are surrendered in the same tax year, one with a gain of £10,000 (having been in force for five years) and one with a gain of £24,000 (having been in force for eight years), tax on the gains is calculated as if one policy had been surrendered, yielding a gain of £34,000 and with a slice of £5,000 (£10,000/5 + £24,000/8).

This approach can have the effect of increasing or decreasing the total tax payable (compared with disposing of the policies in separate tax years) depending on the individual's tax position and the performance of the relevant policies.

28.3.6 Persons liable for the charge

Where a policy is held by an individual for his or her own benefit, the tax charge falls on that individual. The same applies to an individual where the policy is held as security for a debt owed by the individual.

If the policy is held in trust, the charge falls on the settlor, who can recover the tax paid from the trustees. If a policy is held by a trust created by a settlor who has since died, it was possible that gains realised by trustees in these circumstances might escape tax altogether in view of the impossibility of taxing somebody who has not been alive in the appropriate year of assessment. Although somewhat anomalous, this has been very useful where an individual owned a policy that would not come to an end on his or her death (eg a joint life policy paying out on the second death). By declaring a suitable trust of the policy in his or her Will, the individual might have been able to put future gains realised under the policy outside the income tax net.

FA 1998 included provisions to counter this by enabling the trustees, or perhaps even the trust's beneficiaries, to be taxed where the settlor is dead (or not UK-resident at the time of the chargeable event). These rules do not apply where the settlor died before 17 March 1998 and the policy is not 'enhanced' after that date.

HMRC has recently clarified that where a policy is held on a bare trust for a minor, any chargeable event is taxed as arising to the minor. For example, if a grandparent assigns a policy to a grandchild but it has to be held by the parents until the child reaches age 18, any chargeable event gain would be taxable on the minor. However, where parents gift policies to their own minor children, the normal settlement rules apply and the parent would be taxable on any chargeable event gain arising before the child reaches age 18.

Where the policy is held by a company, or on a trust created by – or as security for a debt owed by – a company, the charge falls on the company (the company has the right to recover the tax paid from the trustees where the policy is held on trust). If a policy is assigned by way of gift, chargeable excesses arising during that policy year, but prior to the assignment are taxed on the assignor. Future gains are taxed on the new beneficial owner. This can allow some scope for tax planning, eg where one spouse assigns a policy to the other spouse or civil partner, who is subject to a lower rate of tax, and he or she then surrenders the policy.

28.3.7 Timing of the taxation of gains

Where the chargeable event is death, maturity, total surrender or assignment for value, the gain is treated as arising at the time of that event.

Excesses arising from partial surrenders, on the other hand, are generally only regarded as arising at the end of the policy year in which the excess occurs. Accordingly, if the policy was taken out in June 2008 and an excess occurs as a result of a partial surrender in February 2014, the gain resulting from that partial surrender is treated as arising in June 2014 and so is taxable in 2014–15.

28.3.8 Critical illness policies

For a number of years it has been possible to include critical illness or 'dread disease' benefits in a variety of policies. In general, such a benefit pays a capital sum if the insured individual is diagnosed as suffering from any of the specified 'dread diseases or events'. The diseases or events specified vary from company to company, but usually include heart attack, stroke, cancer and heart by-pass surgery.

It is understood that HMRC accepts that the payment of a benefit on the happening of a dread disease is not a chargeable event, so that this benefit is paid free of tax under the life policy tax regime. With critical illness plans, you have to survive a number of days before benefits are payable (the industry average is 28 days) also known as 'survival plans'.

28.3.9 Chargeable event certificates

(s 552 ICTA 1988)

When a chargeable event occurs, the life assurance company is required to provide HMRC with a chargeable event certificate that gives the policyholder's name and address, the nature and date of the chargeable event and information required for computing the gain, where the gain exceeds the threshold (set at half the basic rate tax band). Life companies also have to supply policyholders with chargeable event certificates to enable them to include the gains in their SA returns. The certificates also have to include information about the chargeable event and the gain produced.

28.3.10 Capital gains tax and life policies

(s 210 TCGA 1992)

If the policy is disposed of by a person who is not the original beneficial owner, and the policy at any time prior to that disposal changed hands for money or money's worth, the policy will be an asset potentially liable to CGT. The potential for double taxation (income tax and CGT) is resolved by s 37 TCGA 1992, which provides, broadly, that money or money's worth charged to income tax will be taken into account and excluded from the CGT calculations.

FA (No.1) 2010 included anti-avoidance which prevents capital losses arising in addition to income tax losses as a result of the interaction of these provisions.

Where a life policy is subject to the CGT regime, the occasion of the payment of the sum(s) assured and the surrender of the policy are treated as disposals.

28.3.11 Personal portfolio bonds

These are policies usually, but not exclusively, written offshore where the benefits due under the policy are (or may be) closely linked with the value of a portfolio of assets personal to the policyholder.

Since 6 April 1999 such policies have suffered a specific additional charge on a deemed gain of 15% of the total premiums paid to the end of each policy year and deemed gains from previous policy years. This charge does not apply to 'managed portfolio bonds', ie those that do not allow personalisation by restricting the policy investment to pooled assets generally available to investors.

28.4 FOREIGN LIFE POLICIES

(s 476 ITTOIA 2005)

In general, policies issued in respect of contracts made after 17 November 1983 cannot be 'qualifying' unless they are issued by a UK insurance company or the UK branch of a foreign insurer. Before that date, foreign policies could be qualifying policies if they satisfied the normal qualifying rules.

Other ways in which the life policy tax regime gives a different tax treatment for foreign policies are as follows:

(1) The gain calculated on a chargeable event is reduced by reference to the amount of time, during the life of the policy, that the policyholder was not UK resident.

(2) In calculating the 'appropriate fraction' for top-slicing purposes, any complete years during which the policyholder was not UK resident are excluded.

(3) Taxable gains arising under such policies are charged to basic rate as well as higher rate tax, as appropriate, as the life company has paid no underlying tax to 'frank' a notional tax credit. An exception to this applies where the insurer is taxed on the investment income and gains accruing for the policyholder's benefit at a rate of not less than 20%. In such cases, the policy gains will not be liable to basic rate UK income tax. This exception will apply only to policies issued by EU or EEA insurers.

FA 1998 included a framework requiring certain categories of foreign life companies to appoint a fiscal representative in the UK to be responsible for reporting gains on life policies to HMRC in accordance with s 552 ICTA 1988 (see 28.3.9).

At one time there was an advantage in holding offshore insurance bonds through a non-UK resident company but FA 2006 contained provisions that enabled HMRC to tax profits from the surrender of such policies under s 721 ITA 2007 (see 33.5) from 5 December 2005.

Gains arising from foreign policies are taxed as miscellaneous income. This means that a UK resident policyholder is taxed on the arising basis even if he or she is domiciled overseas (the remittance basis does not apply).

28.5 ANNUITIES

(ss 422–426 ITTOIA 2005)

An annuity is an arrangement under which one person agrees to pay another a sum of money for a known period, or a period to be determined by some specified contingency.

Annuities may be immediate (ie the payment will start straightaway) or deferred (where payments will start at some predetermined point in the future). Many annuities are established to continue for the lifetime of the annuitant, but temporary annuities cease at the end of a fixed period or on the annuitant's death, whichever comes earlier. Annuities may be effected on the lives of two or more individuals and, for example, continue until the death of the survivor. Annuities may be paid monthly, quarterly or annually, and may be of a fixed amount or subject to some sort of index-linking. Annuities may also be written with a guaranteed minimum period so as to reduce the loss that might otherwise be suffered by an individual who dies shortly after purchasing an annuity.

There are five main types of annuity:

(1) Purchased life annuities, where an individual pays a lump sum to an insurance company in return for the annuity.
(2) Annuities received as a gift (eg at one time it was common for testators to direct that annuities be paid out of their estates).
(3) Annuities paid as part of the purchase price of a business or by continuing members of a partnership to a former partner who has retired.
(4) Compulsory purchase annuities, for example, those purchased out of pension funds.
(5) Immediate needs annuities.

For the annuitant, a purchased life annuity attracts a special relief in that amounts received are treated in part as a return of the money paid for by the annuity (the capital element) and in part as interest on that purchase price. The capital element of each payment is calculated by reference to actuarial tables and is not taxable. This tax exemption applies even where the annuitant lives long enough for the capital element of the annuity payments he or she has received to exceed the original purchase price of the annuity. Other types of annuity do not receive this favourable treatment in respect of the capital element of annuity payments.

Purchased life annuities are also subject to an income tax regime similar to that applying to life policies (see 28.3.4). Chargeable events for life annuities are total surrender, assignment for money or money's worth and 'excesses' (calculated in much the same way as for life policy partial surrenders).

Where a gain arises on a chargeable event, the gain is not charged to basic rate tax where the company offering the annuity has been taxed in the UK. A notional tax credit is given in respect of tax paid by the life company on the income and gains of its general annuity fund.

For CGT purposes, deferred annuities are also treated in a similar way to life policies, with the effect that no chargeable gain accrues on the disposal of such a contract except where the person making the disposal is not the original beneficial owner and the annuity at any time changed hands for money or money's worth.

28.5.1 Immediate needs annuities

In general, payments under a policy which qualified as an immediate needs annuity when it was taken out, which are made to a registered care provider and are for the care of the person protected under the policy, are not taxable income of the insured person.

28.6 INCOME PROTECTION

28.6.1 Introduction

Income protection insurance plans (also known as permanent health insurance) provide a replacement income for an individual who is unable to work through illness or disability. Contracts are usually available to those aged between 16 and 60 but terminate on the insured individual reaching his or her normal retirement date.

Once the disability or illness arises, benefits commence on expiry of a deferred period, typically between one and 12 months, selected by the policyholder. The longer the deferred period, the fewer claims the insurer will expect to pay and so the lower the premium will be per £ of benefit.

Income protection contracts can be written as life assurance policies – typically as non-qualifying policies to avoid the provision of substantial sums assured payable on death. If structured as a life policy, payment of disability benefits is not treated as a surrender of rights for the purposes of life policy taxation.

28.6.2 Tax consequences

If an individual effects an income protection contract for him or herself, premiums are not deductible for tax purposes. If an employer effects a policy on an employee to enable the employer to continue to pay the employee's salary during a period of disability or illness, or if the policy covers a revenue loss during such a period, the employer may be able to claim the premiums as a business expense.

Benefits from most individually owned income protection policies are tax-free.

If the contract is effected by an employer to maintain the employee's salary during the period of illness or disability, the income is taxable in the individual's hands, in the same way as salary would have been.

28.7 PRE-OWNED ASSETS CHARGE

A problem may arise where individuals have taken out a policy that is written in trust so the proceeds on death would be paid to their business partners/fellow shareholders but the individual remains entitled to the amount paid out on the maturity of the policy. This type of arrangement may be wholly commercial and yet still be caught by the FA 2004 legislation (see 33.8), which imposes a charge on an annual benefit that will normally be a rate equal to the official rate at the valuation date, currently 4% of the capital involved (in this context, the surrender value of the policy).

The pre-owned assets legislation is extremely complex and this is an area where you should seek advice from a specialist.

28.8 LIFE POLICIES HELD BY COMPANIES

There are circumstances in which a company can own a life policy. For example, it may do so on the life of a director or other key executive to provide the company with compensation for the death of that individual. Similarly, policies may be taken out in order to provide funds to repay loans.

In general, if a company buys term assurance for a short period (usually not more than five years), which does not acquire a surrender value and is used solely to provide protection against the loss of profits resulting from the death of a key person, the premiums are tax deductible and the proceeds taxable in the hands of the company.

If, on the other hand, the policy is for a longer term, may acquire a surrender value, is effected for a capital purpose, or where the life assured has a material shareholding in the company, the premiums are not tax-deductible but the proceeds are unlikely to be charged to corporation tax in the company's hands, other than by virtue of the life assurance chargeable event rules.

Since 14 March 1989 policies owned by companies (or held on trusts created by a company, or held as security for a debt owed by the company) cannot be qualifying policies – irrespective of their compliance with the qualifying rules. The only exception to this denial of qualifying status is where policies are used to secure company debts incurred in purchasing land to be occupied by the company for the purposes of its trade (or in constructing, extending or improving buildings occupied in that way). Broadly speaking, provided the policy has been used for this purpose since its inception, the chargeable gain will only be the amount by which the policy proceeds exceed the lowest amount of the loan that has been secured by the policy.

28.9 LIFE POLICIES IN TRUST AFFECTED BY THE FA 2006 IHT CHANGES

The 2006 Budget changed the way in which many trusts are taxed. The main change was bringing the IHT treatment of most interest in possession trusts into line with the regime that was previously confined to discretionary trusts. This means the creation of such trusts will normally be taxed as a chargeable lifetime transfer whereas such gifts were previously treated as potentially exempt transfers (PETs), which attracted IHT only if the donor died within seven years.

Interest in possession trusts had historically been used for protection policies written in trust, principally because of the flexibility that this type of trust provides. However, the change in rules means a more complex and potentially more highly taxed regime for policies now written in these types of trust.

For any protection plan written in an interest in possession trust after 22 March 2006, the premiums will potentially be subject to an immediate IHT tax charge of 20% (taxed as a chargeable lifetime transfer, see 30.2). The trust itself will be subject to a periodic charge on the value of the trust assets every ten years (maximum 6%) and there will also be an exit charge on any capital distributions from the trust (see 31.4.23).

However, most regular premium plans written into interest in possession trusts should escape these tax charges. If the premiums are below £3,000 pa, they will be exempted by the annual IHT exemption. For premiums above this level, providing they are regular and meet the relevant conditions (see 30.5.2), they should be exempted from the tax charge, as 'normal expenditure out of income'. Where neither of these situations arises there will be no immediate tax charge provided they (together with other transfers made by the settlor in the previous seven years) do not exceed the IHT nil rate band (currently £325,000).

Protection policies established in trust before 22 March 2006 will not normally be caught by the new IHT regime, however care should be taken when any changes are made to these policies.

Absolute trusts or, to use their proper name, bare trusts, continue to fall within the PET rules and therefore do not attract tax as a chargeable lifetime transfer. Clearly, there will now be a temptation to write more policies under bare trusts. However, the disadvantage of these types of trust is that, by definition, it is extremely difficult to change the beneficiary and, should an individual's personal circumstances change in the future, they may be left with a policy written in trust that is no longer appropriate.

28.10 DISCOUNTED GIFT SCHEMES

A discounted gift scheme involves a gift of an investment bond (see 28.2.2) where certain rights are retained, typically the right to take annual withdrawals. For example, a couple aged 70 may give a bond valued at £100,000 to their children whilst retaining the right to take 5% pa for the rest of their lives. In such a situation, the gift is not £100,000 but the discounted value of the right to receive what value is left in the bond when the couple have both died.

HMRC published a technical note on discounted gift schemes on 1 May 2007 (although it should be noted that the valuation rate of interest has changed since then). See also the decision in *Executors of Mrs Marjorie Bower* v *HMRC.*

See also *Revenue & Customs Brief 22/13* and the December 2013 issue of *HMRC Trusts & Estates Newsletter,* both of which deal with valuation issues.

29

CAPITAL GAINS TAX PLANNING

This chapter contains the following sections:

(1) Make use of annual exemptions for both spouses/civil partners
(2) Realise gains to avoid wasting the annual exemption
(3) Make sure you get relief for capital losses
(4) Use the basic rate band
(5) Save tax by making gifts to relatives
(6) Reinvestment relief
(7) Claim roll-over relief on furnished holiday accommodation
(8) Make the most of entrepreneurs' relief
(9) Selling the family company

29.1 MAKE USE OF ANNUAL EXEMPTIONS FOR BOTH SPOUSES/CIVIL PARTNERS

29.1.1 Inter-spouse transfers can be a way of saving tax

Each individual is allowed to realise capital gains of £11,100 in 2015–16 before he or she becomes liable for CGT. This applies to both spouses and civil partners – each partner is entitled to his or her own annual exemption. However, there are no provisions under which any unused amount may be transferred to the other spouse or partner.

Example – Inter-spouse/civil partner transfers

If *A* has gains of £8,000 and his wife *B* has gains of £16,000, the position is as follows:

	A	B
	£	
Gains	8,000	16,000
Less: exemption	(11,100)	(11,100)
Taxable	Nil	4,900

There is often a way of avoiding this type of mismatch. If *B* had transferred * assets to *A* and he then sold them, she could effectively transfer her gain to him. A transfer between spouses does not count as a disposal for tax purposes and *A* would take over *B*'s base cost. So, with a little forethought, the position could have been:

	A	B
	£	
Gains	12,000	12,000
Less: exemption	(11,100)	(11,100)
Taxable	900	900

*It is important to ensure that any such transfer is genuine, outright and unconditional.

29.2 REALISE GAINS TO AVOID WASTING THE ANNUAL EXEMPTION

Any unused annual exemption cannot be carried forward for use in a future tax year. Dealing costs may be a disincentive but, provided you expect to sell shares, etc, at some time, it can make sense to 'top up' any net gains to make full use of the exemption each year.

The rules for matching sales and purchases within a 30-day period before and after a transaction mean that 'bed and breakfast' transactions will not achieve this. However, you may be able to realise gains and then have your ISA buy the same shares (ie 'bed and ISA'). Alternatively, your spouse, civil partner or family trust could buy the shares.

29.3 MAKE SURE YOU GET RELIEF FOR CAPITAL LOSSES

Capital losses for previous years attach to each spouse or civil partner separately and can be set only against that spouse or civil partner's gain. However, it may be possible to save tax by transferring an asset between spouses or civil partners before it is sold to an outsider. Again, it is important to ensure that any such transfer is outright and unconditional so that the individual receiving the asset has complete freedom to sell or retain the asset as he or she sees fit.

Example – Relief for capital losses

If C's wife D has losses of £35,000 and C has an asset that has appreciated by £50,400, it will make sense for him to transfer it to D so that she can then choose to sell it. Instead of the position being like this:

	£
C's gains	50,400
Less: exemption	(11,100)
Taxable	39,300

the position could be:

	£
D's gains	50,400
Less: capital losses	(35,000)
	15,400
Less: exemption	(11,100)
Taxable	4,300

Of course, the ideal position would be achieved by C transferring part of the asset to D, so that they eventually make a joint disposal, use D's losses and take full advantage of both of their annual exemptions.

29.3.1 Negligible value claims

You may have made an investment in the past that has gone badly. Indeed, you may have written it off in your own mind but, if you have not sold it, the loss is normally only a paper loss that is not allowable for CGT purposes. There is however an exception to this rule: you may be able to establish an allowable loss even though there has been no disposal. If HMRC can be persuaded that the asset has become of 'negligible value' (ie virtually worthless), you can claim a loss (see 13.5.9). In practice, HMRC issues lists of quoted shares that have been suspended and are recognised to be of negligible value: you can view the list online at www. hmrc.gov.uk/cgt/negvalist.htm. It may also be possible to establish losses on unquoted shares and other investments, by negotiation with HMRC.

In some situations, it may be best to defer making a negligible value claim. If you have made capital gains that are covered by the annual exemption you will waste part of your CGT loss by making a negligible value claim for that year.

29.3.2 Review your holdings

If you find yourself holding shares that have failed to live up to your expectations when you purchased them, or worse, made a loss, consider selling these shares to crystallise a loss to offset against your capital gains. By taking positive action before the end of the tax year, you may be able to save on your CGT bill and recoup in part the loss you suffered on a disappointing investment. However, if you have already made capital gains in the same tax year that are covered by the annual exemption there will be no point in crystallising a loss, only to see it wasted.

An experienced stockbroker, IFA or investment adviser working in conjunction with a good accountant should be able to more than cover their professional fees with proactive advice.

29.4 USE THE BASIC RATE BAND

Remember that where a taxable gain falls within an individual's basic rate band for the year it is liable to tax at 18% rather than 28% (which is charged once the band is exceeded) – see 13.1.4. It should also be remembered that it is the extended basic rate band that is taken into account for these purposes – see Chapter 15 for illustrations of when the basic rate band is extended. So, for example, an individual making taxable capital gains that take him or her over the basic rate band for the year, may wish to make additional pension contributions in that year or an additional Gift Aid payment to obtain further tax relief.

Example

Jane has taxable income of £30,000 for 2015–16 (after allowances) and realises chargeable gains of £25,000 in the year. Her capital gains tax position would be as follows:

Gain	£25,000	
Less annual exemption	£11,100	
Taxable gain	£13,900	
Tax at 18% (£31,785 − £30,000) =	£1,785 × 18% =	£321.30
Tax at 28%	£12,115 × 28% =	£3,392.20
Total		£3,713.50

However, if Jane were to make a personal pension contribution in the year of £10,000 this would reduce her tax liability as follows:

Basic rate band extended by grossed up contribution (£10,000 × 100/80 = £12,500): £12,500 + £31,785 = £44,285)

Taxable gain £13,900
Tax at 18% (£43,900 − £30,000): £13,900 × 18% = £2,502

The tax saving to Jane is £1,211.50. The net result is that a total contribution to her pension fund (including the basic rate tax relief added by the Government) is £12,500 but this has only effectively cost Jane £8,788.50 (£10,000 − £1,211.50) giving her nearly 30% tax relief on the gross contribution.

For married couples, where one spouse or civil partner is a basic rate taxpayer and the other a higher rate taxpayer, and it is clear that total chargeable gains for a year will exceed both annual exemptions, it makes sense for transfers of assets to be made such that the taxable gains arise in the hands of the basic rate taxpayer. This will save the couple 10% on the taxable gain up to the limit of the lower income spouse or civil partner's basic rate band for the year.

29.5 SAVE TAX BY MAKING GIFTS TO RELATIVES

If you are planning to sell shares in unquoted companies it may be possible to save tax.

Example – Sale of unquoted shares

G who is an additional rate taxpayer holds a block of shares in a private trading company. G does not qualify for enterpreneurs' relief. He has reached broad agreement with a potential purchaser to sell his shares for £1,000 each in October 2015, which will produce a gain of £750 per share.

If G so wishes, he could transfer some shares to his son H (a higher rate taxpayer) to enable him to use his annual exemption, ie G could give H 15 shares in the company and claim hold-over relief. No capital gain need arise for G on his gift to H who would then dispose of the shares to the ultimate purchaser. H's capital gain would then be as follows:

	£
Capital gain: 15 × £750 =	11,250
Less: annual exemption	(11,100)
Taxable at 28%	150

The overall effect is that G's family saves tax of £3,108.

If G had four children, he could make similar gifts to all of them and save up to £12,432 by using their annual exemptions and even greater savings could be achieved by using their basis rate tax bands. As always, it is important to ensure that any such transfer is genuine, outright and unconditional.

Gifts of listed shares and securities

It is sometimes possible to achieve a similar saving by transferring shares that do not attract s 165 hold-over relief, for example shares in a quoted trading company where the owner has less than 5% of the voting shares, or shares in a private investment company. But you have to plan some way ahead.

It is also possible to claim hold-over relief under a different part of the legislation where you make a chargeable transfer for IHT purposes, normally on your putting assets into a trust (see 13.6, 31.4.23 and 31.5). (Bear in mind that neither s 165 or s 260 relief is available if the trust is a settlor-interested trust, see 33.6.) If the trustees subsequently appoint property in favour of the trust beneficiaries (eg your children, grandchildren, etc), they can make a similar hold-over election to avoid any CGT charge on them. The overall effect will be that the trust beneficiaries will have taken the property that you put into trust at a value equal to your original acquisition cost.

You will need to take professional advice. In particular, bear in mind that if transfers into trusts take your cumulative transfers over the nil rate band (at present £325,000), you may have to pay IHT at the rate of 20% on the excess (see 30.2, 30.10 and 31.4.23). And do not try to do all this in rapid succession because HMRC may well attack the transactions as a preordained scheme (see 33.19 on *Ramsay*).

29.6 REINVESTMENT RELIEF

Relief from CGT is available where disposal proceeds are reinvested in a company qualifying for the EIS. The original gain is frozen until the EIS shares are sold. Any further gain made on the qualifying EIS shares may be exempt provided they have been held for a minimum period of three years and certain qualifying conditions continue to be met. Income tax relief can also be available on such investments. Although EIS investments remain higher risk than many other investment choices, there are now a wide range of sector options available in this maturing market.

Remember that any decisions that affect your investments and realising gains and losses should only be taken after seeking expert advice from an Independent Financial Adviser and should take into account the impact of the proposed transactions on your investment strategy as well as any possible tax advantages.

In principle, the EIS company can be wholly-owned but that will mean that no income tax relief will be available (see 25.4.10). An investor who is connected with the EIS company can still be eligible for the CGT deferral relief.

29.7 CLAIM ROLL-OVER RELIEF ON FURNISHED HOLIDAY ACCOMMODATION

Where a person has realised a capital gain on the disposal of a business, or has sold a property used by a firm in which they are a partner, the gain may be rolled-over (see 17.3). This normally involves the person continuing to be in business. However, if the individual does not wish to carry on trading, roll-over relief may still be available. A particular type of property investment qualifies in this way because where a property is acquired for letting as furnished holiday accommodation and is let sufficiently as furnished holiday accommodation to meet the qualifying tests, the owner is deemed to have acquired an asset for a trade and roll-over relief may therefore be obtained.

Two points are of particular interest:

- The property does not need be located at the seaside. A property in, for example, Central London could qualify provided it is let for at least part of the year on a short-term basis (see 8.5 and 17.3.6).
- Roll-over relief may be obtained provided the property has been let as furnished holiday accommodation for a period. If the property is subsequently let for a longer-term or used for some other purpose (eg as a second home) the relief is not normally withdrawn. The one exception to this is if the owner had acquired a leasehold interest in the property and the lease had less than 60 years to run at the time it was acquired. Taking such a property out of use as furnished holiday accommodation means that the deferred gain would become chargeable (see 17.3.4).

29.8 MAKE THE MOST OF ENTREPRENEURS' RELIEF

Entrepreneurs' relief is available on capital gains of up to a lifetime limit of £10m of gains. The tax rate is 10% rather than 18% or 28% so the relief is potentially worth a maximum of £1.8m. In principle, both spouses or civil partners, and other family members, can each qualify for relief on up to £10m of gains.

A gain on the sale of a property let as furnished holiday accommodation should, in principle, qualify for entrepreneurs' relief.

Conditions

The following conditions must be satisfied for the 12 months ending with the date of sale:

- The vendor must either be an individual who is employed by his or her personal trading company or, in certain circumstances, the trustees of a life interest trust where the life tenant is employed by the company and personally holds at least 5% of the shares in the company. This means that an individual who has retired completely may not qualify.
- A company is an individual's personal trading company only if he or she holds at least 5% of the shares and those shares give him or her at least 5% of the voting rights. Relief is therefore not available if the individual holds only 4.999% of the ordinary shares, even if he or she has more than 5% of the voting rights due to other holdings.

A gain on an associated disposal may also attract relief. Such a disposal may include the sale of a property used by the individual's personal company but the relief will be restricted where he or she has charged the company rent post-6 April 2008 (see 17.7.5).

29.9 SELLING THE FAMILY COMPANY

The sale of a family company may involve complex tax issues. Much will depend on the facts and circumstances. However, the vendors' advisers should generally address the following points.

29.9.1 Get clearance or you may end up paying income tax rather than CGT

It is advisable to obtain advance clearance from HMRC that it accepts that s 682 ITA 2007 does not apply in relation to the sale (see 33.3). If s 682 were applicable, the vendors might have to pay higher rate income tax rather than 28% CGT (or 10% where entrepreneurs' relief is available).

Another situation where vendors may have to pay income tax rather than capital gains tax is where they hold employment-related securities (see 6.6). Bear in mind that the tax liability will often then fall on the company but if the company obtains a deduction under Chapter 2, Part 12, CTA 2009 (see 18.3.2) the extra tax cost may be rather less than one would expect.

29.9.2 Checklist

Relevant questions include:

(1) Should the company make large pension contributions for the benefit of shareholder directors? This will lead to a reduction in the sale price and to a corresponding reduction in CGT. However, be careful: there is a subtle difference between having your company pay pension contributions and requiring the purchaser to make such contributions. See *HMRC* v *Collins* [2009] EWHC 284 on this. It is also important for the individual to consider whether such contributions will cause him or her to exceed the annual allowance, and the effect an annual allowance charge will have on the owner's overall tax position.

(2) Should shareholder directors receive termination payments (possibly exempt up to £30,000)? Again, this will lead to a reduction both in the sale price and the shareholders' CGT.

(3) If the purchaser really wants some specific parts of the company's business, would it make better sense for the company to sell those business operations rather than for the shareholders to sell their shares? Could the company secure roll-over relief (see 18.7.2)?

(4) If the company is a holding company, would it make better sense for it to sell its trading subsidiary? A crucially important aspect here is whether such a sale would qualify for the Substantial Shareholding Exemption (see 18.7.3).

(5) Does any member of the shareholder's family have substantial unrelieved capital losses? If so, consider gifts of shares to him or her before the sale.

(6) Are any of the shareholders long term non-UK resident? Look for ways of taking full advantage of their not being liable for CGT.

(7) Are any of the shareholders themselves companies? If so, a pre-sale dividend may be attractive.

(8) Will the purchaser want to acquire premises that are used by the company but owned by some of the shareholders in their personal capacity? What are the CGT implications? Those shareholders may not be able to secure roll-over relief in the future as the relief is limited to situations where the old and new assets are used by the same company (see 17.3.8). However, it may be that shareholders who are directors or employees are able to claim roll-over relief under a different head by reinvesting in assets to be used by another personal trading company (see 17.3.9).

(9) Will entrepreneurs' relief be available for some or all of the shareholders?

(10) If there is a 'mix' of types of consideration on offer (eg cash, loan notes, preference shares, ordinary shares, warrants, rights to an earn-out, etc), is it more appropriate for some vendors to take their entitlement in a particular form?

    (a) For example, if loan notes are offered, this can allow can CGT be deferred by shareholders simply by not selling them or seeking an early redemption (but see 29.9.4 on loan note issues).

    (b) Alternatively, an ambitious shareholder who has been offered a senior position by the purchaser might accept a share for share exchange if this will mean that he or she has a 5% stake in the acquiring company and should therefore qualify for entrepreneurs' relief on a future sale. This would especially make sense where the sale of the shares in the existing company would not use up a substantial part of the £10m relief.

    (c) Conversely, elderly shareholders may take loan notes on the basis that they intend to retain them for the rest of their lives (in which case the potential CGT liability will disappear) or they may take preference shares in the acquiring company on the grounds that these shares should continue to attract business property relief.

(11) To what extent is it practical for the vendors to plough their proceeds back into a new company and defer tax using the CGT

deferral relief available for investments in companies qualifying under the Enterprise Investment Scheme?

29.9.3 Vendors temporarily non-UK resident

If you are selling your shares while you are non-UK resident but you expect to resume residence in the UK within five years of your departure, you may end up being liable for capital gains tax (see 13.3.2).

29.9.4 Treatment of loan notes

Questions regularly arise concerning the tax treatment of loan notes issued by a company that takes over a family company.

The first point to bear in mind is that the vendor's advisers should seek clearance under s 138 TCGA 1992 to ensure the exchange of shares in company A for loan notes issued by company B will not be a disposal for CGT purposes. HMRC will normally give such clearance provided it is satisfied that the transaction is being entered into for bona fide commercial reasons and is not part of a CGT avoidance scheme. This in turn means that no CGT charge will normally arise until the loan note holder disposes of his or her loan notes, either by redeeming them or by selling or giving them away.

A second issue concerns the tax treatment of loan notes that are qualifying corporate bonds (QCBs) which are eventually realised at less than their face value. This can leave the loan note holders with a tax charge based on the value of the loan notes at the time of the share exchange. In practice, vendors of private companies should think hard about accepting loan notes unless they are guaranteed by a bank. You should seek professional advice if you hold loan notes that are QCBs and the company that issued them is likely to default on its obligations.

Finally, bear in mind that it may be possible to secure s 165 hold-over relief on gifts of loan notes that are not QCBs. This may allow you to achieve similar savings after the sale to those that can arise from gifts of shares before a sale of the family company (see 29.4 above). Section 165 relief is available where the securities (ie the loan notes in the purchasing company) are not quoted and the relief can therefore apply even though the shares of the company are quoted (provided it is a trading company).

30

INHERITANCE TAX AND INDIVIDUALS

This chapter contains the following sections:

(1)   Who is subject to IHT?
(2)   When may a charge arise?
(3)   Transfers of value
(4)   Certain gifts are not transfers of value
(5)   Exempt transfers
(6)   Potentially exempt transfers
(7)   Reservation of benefit
(8)   Business property
(9)   Agricultural property and woodlands
(10) Computation of tax payable on lifetime transfers
(11) Tax payable on death
(12) Life assurance and pension policies
(13) Heritage property
(14) Planning: the first step

30.1   WHO IS SUBJECT TO IHT?

As a general principle, a UK-domiciled individual is subject to IHT on all property owned by him or her, whether located in the UK or overseas. By contrast, a person of foreign domicile is subject to IHT only on property sited in the UK. There are however various specific exceptions to this. For example, UK unit trusts and open-ended investment companies (OEICs) held by non-UK domiciled individuals are excluded from any IHT charge. Also, transfers of exempt gilts are excluded from any IHT charge if the transferor is not resident or ordinarily resident in the UK even though he or she may be domiciled in the UK. Foreign currency accounts with UK banks are not regarded as UK assets if the account holder is neither resident nor domiciled in the UK. (See Chapters 34 and 35 on domicile, residence, etc.)

   Section 267 IHTA 1984 contains a special rule that applies for IHT purposes whereby an individual will be deemed to be UK-domiciled for a tax year if he or she has been resident in the UK during 17 out of the 20 tax years that end with the current tax year. Because residence for an entire tax year is not required, only residence *in* a tax year, this period can be as little as 15 years and 2 days.

Example – Deemed domicile

> A became UK resident on 5 April 2001 and resides in the UK continuously thereafter. He will become deemed domiciled for IHT purposes on 6 April 2016.
>
> He could however leave the UK on 5 April 2016 and avoid becoming deemed domiciled, provided he remains outside of the UK for four complete years of assessment, ie he could not return until 6 April 2020. If he did return then and resided again in the UK continuously, he would not be deemed to be domiciled here for IHT purposes until 6 April 2036.

Acquisition of deemed domicile in the UK for IHT purposes does not impact on domicile status under general law for other tax purposes.

This rule also applies so that a deemed domiciled, long-term UK resident will be treated as retaining his or her deemed domicile for IHT for three calendar years after leaving the UK for good.

Example – Deemed domicile

> B is domiciled in Australia, but has resided in the UK for the past 30 years. If she decides to return home to Australia permanently on 9 December 2013, her UK deemed domicile for IHT purposes will persist until 5 April 2017.

The deemed domicile rule may in some circumstances be overruled by provisions contained in a few of the UK's older double taxation agreements, dating back to Estate Duty days, ie pre-1974 (basically, those with India, Pakistan, Italy and France). The exemption generally only applies on death, not to chargeable lifetime transfers.

30.1.1 Nil rate band

The first £325,000 of chargeable transfers (the nil rate band) is free of IHT. The nil rate band is expected to remain at £325,000 until 5 April 2016.

There are circumstances where an additional amount can be claimed in respect of a spouse's unused nil rate band (see 30.11.8).

30.2 WHEN MAY A CHARGE ARISE?

IHT can apply in the following circumstances:

- on a chargeable lifetime transfer (CLT), ie a gift to anyone other than an individual, including gifts to most trusts;
- on an individual's death (including further tax to pay on chargeable or potentially exempt lifetime transfers made within the preceding seven years).

A lifetime gift to an individual or to some favoured trusts is regarded as a potentially exempt transfer (PET), unless exempt under some specific provision such as the spouse exemption, gifts on the occasion of marriage, etc. Gifts into most trusts, to a company, and some transfers by close companies and trustees are all chargeable transfers.

Trusts post-FA 2006

A person who had an interest in possession under a trust or settlement at 22 March 2006 is normally regarded as if he or she were entitled to the capital. When the beneficiary dies, the trust property's full value is treated as part of his or her estate for IHT purposes (see 31.4.15). The position is quite different where an individual first acquired his or her interest in possession after that date (see 31.4.17). In general, the capital in such trusts will not be subject to IHT on the death of the individual who has the interest in possession but instead the trust will be subject to the ten-year periodic charge applicable to relevant property trusts (see 31.5.15). There are, however, special rules that cover an individual who acquires an interest in possession on the death of his or her spouse or civil partner at any time after 22 March 2006, or where the interest in possession arose before 6 October 2008 and replaced an interest in possession held by someone else at 22 March 2006 and, in those cases, the trust property is still treated as forming part of the beneficiary's estate on death.

Figure 30.1 indicates the circumstances under which a gift may be a chargeable transfer for IHT purposes.

30.3 TRANSFERS OF VALUE

30.3.1 Not all transfers are gifts

(s 3 IHTA 1984)

The legislation refers to transfers and dispositions rather than gifts. The reason for this is that all gifts are transfers of value, but not all transfers of value are gifts. For example, where an individual deliberately sells an asset at less than market value he or she may not be making a gift, but he or she is certainly making a transfer of value. Similarly, deliberately omitting to exercise a right can be a transfer of value, but this is not a gift in the normal sense of the word. To give a third example, a transfer can even involve property not owned by the person since the IHT legislation deems a person to make a gift for IHT purposes if his or her 'qualifying' (ie treated as forming part of his or her estate) interest in possession under a trust comes to an end.

Figure 30.1 – Is a gift a chargeable transfer?

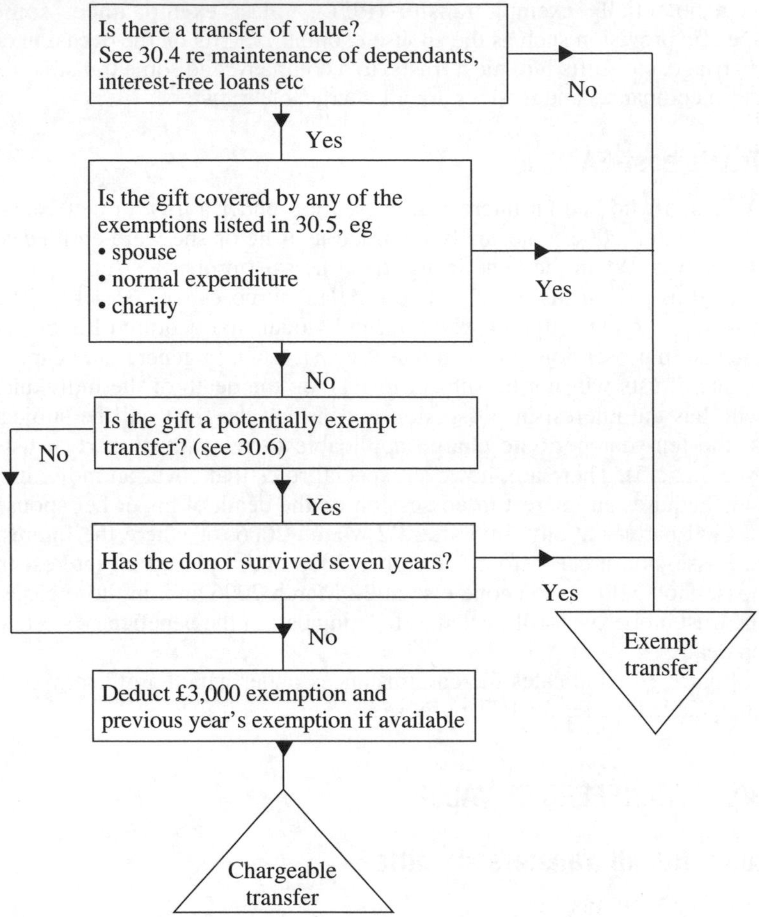

Is there a transfer of value?
See 30.4 re maintenance of dependants, interest-free loans etc

→ No

↓ Yes

Is the gift covered by any of the exemptions listed in 30.5, eg
• spouse
• normal expenditure
• charity

→ Yes

↓ No

Is the gift a potentially exempt transfer? (see 30.6)

No ←

↓ Yes

Has the donor survived seven years?

→ Yes

↓ No

Exempt transfer

Deduct £3,000 exemption and previous year's exemption if available

Chargeable transfer

30.3.2 **There must be gratuitous intent**

(s 10 IHTA 1984)

IHT does not normally apply to a gift unless there is an element of 'bounty', ie there is a deliberate intention to make a gift. An unintentional loss of value (eg a loss made on a bad business deal) is not subject to IHT because there was no intention to pass value to another person.

30.3.3 How a transfer is measured

(s 3 IHTA 1984)

The amount of any transfer of value is determined by the reduction in value of the donor's wealth. This is not necessarily the same as the increase in the recipient's wealth.

Example

> *C* owns 51 out of 100 shares in a company. He has control because he has the majority of the shares. If he were to give two shares to his son, he would relinquish control of the company and his remaining 49 shares might be worth considerably less because of this. The two shares given to his son might not be worth very much in isolation, and the son might not have acquired a very valuable asset, but *C*'s estate would have decreased in value by the difference between the value of a 51% shareholding and that of a 49% shareholding, which could be a substantial amount.

30.4 CERTAIN GIFTS ARE NOT TRANSFERS OF VALUE

Certain gifts and other transactions are not regarded as transfers of value, so the issue of whether they are chargeable transfers simply does not arise. These include:

- maintenance of dependants, family, etc;
- waivers of dividends;
- waivers of remuneration;
- interest-free loans;
- disclaimers of legacies;
- deeds of variation;
- transfers involving trusts where the settlor has retained powers of appointment.

30.4.1 Maintenance of dependants, family, etc

(s 11 IHTA 1984)

The legislation specifically provides that the following lifetime payments are not transfers of value:

- payments for the maintenance of a current or former spouse or civil partner;
- payments for the maintenance, education or training of a child or stepchild under age 18;

- payments made to maintain a child aged over 18 who is in full-time education or training;
- reasonable provision for the care or maintenance of a dependent relative, ie the individual's relative who is incapacitated by old age or infirmity from maintaining him or herself, or the individual's mother or father, or his or her spouse or civil partner's mother or father.

30.4.2 Waivers of dividends

(s 15 IHTA 1984)

A waiver of a dividend by a company or an individual is not regarded as a transfer of value provided certain conditions are satisfied:

- The dividend must be waived by deed.
- The deed must not be executed more than 12 months before the right to the dividend has accrued.
- The deed waiving the dividend must be executed before any legal entitlement to the dividend arises.

The relief applies only to the waiver of dividends on shares and not to any other form of receipt such as debenture interest. The position is slightly different for interim and final dividends as the point in time at which entitlement may arise can be different.

Interim dividends

A shareholder has no enforceable right to payment before the date on which a board resolution has declared that a dividend shall be payable. However, the directors can declare an interim dividend that is payable immediately without having to first seek shareholders' approval. Therefore, a deed waiving a dividend should be executed in good time before any board resolution is passed.

Final dividends

A company may declare a dividend without stipulating any date for payment. In such circumstances, the declaration of the dividend creates an immediate debt and it is therefore too late to execute a waiver.

In other cases where a final dividend is declared as being payable at a later date, a shareholder may waive his or her entitlement provided he or she does so before the due date for payment.

In practice, a final dividend will require the shareholders' approval and an individual shareholder may therefore waive a dividend provided the deed is executed within 12 months before the company's annual meeting.

30.4.3 Waivers of remuneration

(s 14 IHTA 1984)

There is a specific provision whereby a waiver of remuneration does not constitute a transfer of value. Remuneration for these purposes does not include pensions. In practice, HMRC accept that remuneration is not subject to income tax if it is formally waived and the employer's assessable profits are adjusted accordingly to disallow a deduction for the sum waived.

It would be advisable to check in advance with HMRC that this treatment will apply in your particular circumstances, especially where substantial amounts are involved.

30.4.4 Interest-free loans

The grant of an interest-free loan repayable on demand is not a transfer of value (because the loan can be called in at any time and thus there is no discounting of the value of the right to repayment in the lender's estate).

This treatment does not apply in a situation where a loan is made for a specific period, with the lender having no legal right to call for repayment before that time. The grant of such a loan might well be a transfer of value, with HMRC seeking to assess the transfer as the difference between the loan amount and its present market value if it were to be assigned. For loans between individuals, this is only an issue if the lender dies whilst the loan is outstanding, or if he or she dies within seven years of making the loan. The transfer of value on making the loan will be a PET. If the full value has been repaid to the donor's estate prior to death within seven years, you may be left with a 'failed PET' (the original loan) in the cumulation, which the double charges regulations fail to relieve.

30.4.5 Disclaimer of legacies

(s 142(1) IHTA 1984)

If a person becomes entitled to property under a Will or an intestacy or under a trust (eg on a life tenant's death), he or she may disclaim entitlement. Such a disclaimer is normally effective for IHT purposes and is not treated as a transfer of value provided that:

- no payment or other consideration is given for the disclaimer; and
- the person has not already accepted his or her entitlement, either expressly or by implication.

30.4.6 Deeds of variation

(s 142(2) IHTA 1984)

A deed of variation may be entered into where a person has died leaving property to his or her beneficiaries, and the beneficiaries (for whatever reason; generally to distribute the estate among the family in the most tax efficient manner) elect to vary the legacies, the effect being to redirect property. Where the necessary conditions are fulfilled, the revised disposition is treated as having taken place on the deceased person's death. Once again, a person who gives up an entitlement is not treated as making a transfer of value.

The following conditions need to be satisfied:

- The deed of variation must be executed within two years of the death
- It must be in writing and must specifically refer to the provisions of the Will, etc that are to be varied
- It must be signed by the person who would otherwise have, and anyone else who might have, benefited (in practice, this may cause issues where the Will contains legacies for minor beneficiaries, as their interests must be protected)
- Only one deed of variation in respect of each particular piece of property can be effective for IHT purposes
- No payment or other consideration may pass between beneficiaries to induce them to enter into the deed of variation (except that a variation is permitted that consists of an exchange of inheritances and a cash adjustment)
- Where the deed refers to the relevant legislation, there is no need for a formal election to be submitted to HMRC.

The Government has introduced a consultation on deeds of variation. HMRC probably thinks that the tax treatment can be overgenerous. The first round of the consultation runs until October 2015.

30.4.7 Powers of appointment over settled property

(ss 5(2), 47A, 55A, 272 IHTA 1984)

Powers of appointment are not treated as being part of an individual's estate for IHT purposes.

The applicable legislation was introduced following the decision in *IRC* v *Melville* CA [2001] STC 1297. This case concerned an individual who transferred property to a new discretionary settlement but had power to direct the trustees to return the property to him after three months. The Court of Appeal held that the chargeable transfer was only a modest amount as the settlor had retained a valuable right. Although this worked to the advantage of the taxpayer in *Melville,* it had caused concern for settlors who had retained such powers, particularly individuals who had created settlements while domiciled abroad (see 33.17.2). However, if the settlor retains an interest – rather than merely a power of appointment – in the trust, this will constitute a gift with reservation (see 30.7).

30.5 EXEMPT TRANSFERS

Even if a transfer takes place, it will not attract IHT if it is an exempt transfer. The full list of exempt transfers is as follows:

- gifts to spouse or civil partner (s 18);
- normal expenditure out of income (s 21);
- £250 small gifts exemption (s 20);
- annual £3,000 exemption (s 19);
- gifts in consideration of marriage or civil partnership (s 22);
- gifts to charities or registered clubs (s 23);
- gifts for national purposes (s 25, Schedule 3);
- gifts to political parties (s 24);
- gifts to housing associations (s 24A);
- certain transfers to employee trusts (ss 13, 28);
- compensation paid to former prisoners of war and Holocaust victims (ESC F20 and s 64 FA 2006);
- maintenance funds for historic buildings (s 27, Schedule 4);
- death on active service (s 154).

30.5.1 Gifts to spouse or civil partner

(s 18 IHTA 1984)

There is normally an unlimited exemption for transfers between spouses or civil partners. For this purpose, a couple is regarded as married or in civil partnership until a decree absolute has been obtained. The exemption covers outright gifts, legacies and a transfer of property on death to a trust under which the survivor has an interest in possession.

The exemption is restricted where a UK-domiciled spouse makes transfers to a foreign domiciled spouse. In this situation, the exemption is limited to £325,000 and this exempt amount is then reduced by all past transfers to that or any previous spouse. However, the 'deemed domicile' rule (see 30.1) applies for all IHT purposes except where expressly excluded. Consequently, a gift by a UK-domiciled individual to a spouse who has a foreign domicile, but who is treated as UK-domiciled for IHT purposes under the 17-year rule, qualifies for the unlimited exemption. Gifts from a non-UK domiciliary to a UK domiciled spouse or civil partner attract unlimited exemption, as do gifts of UK situs assets between two non-UK domiciled spouses or civil partners (non-UK situs assets of such individuals are excluded property).

As from 6 April 2013, it is possible for a spouse or civil partner who is domiciled outside the UK to elect to be treated as UK-domiciled for IHT purposes to get the benefit of unlimited IHT-free transfers from his or her spouse (including for testamentary dispositions). Such an election continues to apply unless or until the electing individual ceased to be resident in the UK for a period of more than three years.

30.5.2 Spouse exemption and settled property

In the past, the spouse exemption has also applied to settled property in which a surviving spouse has an interest in possession. This could arise in one of two situations. First, the deceased might have been the life tenant of a settlement and his or her spouse might have been entitled to a succeeding life interest on his or her death. Alternatively, the deceased might have drawn his or her Will so as to create a Will trust under which the surviving spouse had an interest in possession.

Spouse exemption applies in both cases where the deceased died before 22 March 2006. For an individual who died on or after that date, the spouse exemption is still available in respect of a transfer under a Will trust. But where the trust is a lifetime trust, spouse exemption is now generally available only where the deceased either held a transitional serial interest (TSI) with a general power to appoint the interest to the survivor by Will (creating an immediate post-death interest), or held his or her interest at 22 March 2006 and the survivor takes a life interest on his or her spouse's death.

30.5.3 Normal expenditure out of income

(s 21 IHTA 1984)

A lifetime gift is exempt if it is shown that the gift was made as part of the donor's normal expenditure and is made out of surplus income. The legislation requires that the gift should be normal, ie the donor had a habit of making such gifts. The legislation also requires that taking one year with another, taking into account all normal transfers of value made by the donor, the gifts must have left the donor with sufficient income to maintain his or her normal standard of living.

Gifts that take the form of payments under deed of covenant or the payment of premiums on life assurance policies written in trust frequently qualify as exempt because of this rule. However, there is specific anti-avoidance rule to prevent abuse where the payment of the premiums is an associated operation with the purchase of an annuity by the donor. The capital repayment portion of any annuity payment the donor receives is not included as income for these purposes; however, surplus income which has been held on deposit may be.

30.5.4 £250 small gifts exemption

(s 20 IHTA 1984)

Any number of individual gifts of up to £250 in any one tax year are exempt. If an individual wished to, he or she could make 100 separate gifts of £250 at a time. However, if more than £250 was paid to any one person over the course of the tax year, it would need to be brought into account in full, subject to the availability of the £3,000 annual exemption. It is however important to remember that it is not possible to claim both exemptions. Where a payment of (say) £3,250 (or even of £300) was made to an individual in a year, then in that case, the £250 exemption would not be available at all and only the £3,000 annual exemption could be set against the payment.

30.5.5 Annual £3,000 exemption

(s 19 IHTA 1984)

This exemption is available to cover part of a larger gift. The exemption is £3,000 for each tax year. Furthermore, each spouse or civil partner has separate annual exemptions. There are detailed rules prescribed in s 19 setting out the order in which the exemption is to be used where a number of transfers take place on the same day and where a potentially exempt transfer becomes chargeable on death within seven years. However, HMRC now regards s 19(3A) as overridden by s 3A(1)(b), and will allocate the IHT annual exemption to transfers of value in chronological order, irrespective of whether the transfers would, disregarding the annual exemption, be immediately chargeable or potentially exempt. This means that if a potentially exempt transfer precedes an immediately chargeable transfer in the same tax year, the available annual exemption will be allocated to the potentially exempt transfer in priority to the immediately chargeable transfers, and unless the transferor dies within seven years of a potentially exempt transfer any annual exemption allocated to it will be wasted.

If the full £3,000 is not used in a given year, the balance can be carried forward for one year only and is then allowable only if the exemption for the second year is fully utilised.

Example – Carry forward

Situation 1	£	£
Gifts made in Year 1		1,000
Balance of exemption carried forward to Year 2		2,000
Gifts made in Year 2		4,000
Annual exemption for Year 2	3,000	
Part of unused exemption for Year 1	1,000	(4,000)
Chargeable gifts		Nil

The balance of exemption from Year 1 of £1,000 is lost completely if it cannot be used in Year 2.

Situation 2	£	£
Year 1 as in Situation 1 – unused exemption		2,000
Exemption for Year 2	3,000	
Gifts in Year 2	2,000	
Balance of Year 2 exemption to be carried forward to Year 3	1,000	

The balance of the Year 1 exemption of £2,000 is lost completely and may not be carried forward to Year 3.

30.5.6 Gifts in consideration of marriage

(s 22 IHTA 1984)

Gifts made to the bride or groom in consideration of their marriage or civil partnership, are exempt up to the following amounts:

Gifts made by:	Maximum exemption
Each parent	£5,000
Grandparents (or great grandparents)	£2,500
Bride or groom	£2,500
Any other person	£1,000

Parents may make gifts to either party to the marriage: their exemption is not restricted to gifts made to their own child but covers gifts made to both parties rather than £5,000 total for each recipient. This means that in relation to the groom, for example, the bride's parents may each give up to £5,000. Gifts should be made so that they are conditional upon the marriage taking place.

30.5.7 Gifts to charities and registered clubs

(s 23 IHTA 1984)

Gifts to charities established in the UK are exempt regardless of the amount. A charity may be established or registered in the UK even though it carries out its work overseas, and the exemption covers gifts to such charities. It has previously been the case that donations made to a foreign charity established abroad do not qualify but following the 2009 ECJ decision in *Persche,* Finance Act (No.1) 2010 extended the relief to charities established in the EU, Norway and Iceland.

Registered sports clubs were added to this exemption in 2010. In the case of any property which is given to a registered club, the relief will not apply if any part of the gifted property may be used other than for:

- the purposes of the club in question;
- the purposes of another registered club;
- the purposes of the governing body of an eligible sport for the purposes of which the club in question exists; or
- charitable purposes.

A reduced rate of IHT is to apply for deaths occurring on or after 6 April 2012 where 10% or more of a deceased's net estate (after the deduction of all IHT exemptions, reliefs and the nil rate band) is left to charity. In such cases, the current rate of 40% will be reduced to 36%.

30.5.8 Gifts for national purposes

(s 25 IHTA 1984)

Gifts to certain national bodies are totally exempt. These include colleges and universities, the National Trust, the National Gallery, the British Museum and other galleries and museums run by local authorities or universities.

30.5.9 Gifts to political parties

(s 24 IHTA 1984)

Gifts to 'qualifying political parties' are exempt only if certain conditions are satisfied. A political party qualifies if it had at least two MPs returned at the last general election, or if it had at least one MP and more than 150,000 votes were cast for its candidates.

30.5.10 Gifts to housing associations

(s 24A IHTA 1984)

Gifts of UK land to registered housing associations are exempt.

30.5.11 Certain transfers to employee trusts

(ss 13, 28 IHTA 1984)

Transfers by a close company to an employee trust, or where an individual transfers shares in a company to an employee trust may be exempt provided the following conditions are satisfied:

(1) The trust's beneficiaries include all or most of the persons employed by, or holding office with, the company.

(2) The trust deed must not permit any of the trust property to be applied at any time for the benefit of:

(a) a participator in the company (ie a person who holds a 5% or greater interest);

(b) any person who has been a participator at any time during the ten years prior to the transfer;

(c) any person connected with a participator or former participator.

The exclusions above do not apply if a participator, etc, can only receive benefits on which income tax will be charged (or would be charged if the participator was UK resident).

A further restriction applies where an individual makes a transfer of shares to an employee trust.

Within one year of the transfer:

(a) the trustees must hold more than 50% of the company's ordinary share capital and have voting control on all questions that affect the company as a whole; and

(b) the trustees' control must not be fettered by some other provision or agreement between the shareholders.

30.5.12 *Ex-gratia* payments to POWs

There is an exemption for compensation and *ex-gratia* payments made to former prisoners of war by the Japanese Government. This has been extended to cover compensation received by prisoners of war from the German Government. Ask for a copy of ESC F20.

30.5.13 Holocaust compensation

(s 64 FA 2006)

Compensation paid to Holocaust victims or their families is exempt.

30.6 POTENTIALLY EXEMPT TRANSFERS

(s 3A IHTA 1984)

30.6.1 Definition of potentially exempt transfer (PET)

Irrevocable gifts made during an individual's lifetime may, provided certain conditions are satisfied, be PETs. These gifts become exempt only if the donor survives seven years. If he or she dies during that period, the PET becomes a chargeable transfer. The tax payable depends on the IHT rates in force at the date of death. The donee is liable to pay the tax.

The main conditions to be satisfied for a gift to be a PET are that the gift is made to:

- an individual; or
- (for transfers up to 21 March 2006) a trust under which an individual has an interest in possession; or
- a trust for the disabled (see 31.7); or
- a trust for a bereaved minor out of an immediate post-death interest (see 31.6). Note that from 22 March 2006, a lifetime trust qualifies as an accumulation and maintenance trust only if it existed at 21 March 2006 and the beneficiaries will become absolutely entitled to the trust capital on attaining age 18 – this is a new condition and transfers to trusts before that date might well have constituted PETs even though the beneficiaries did not have an entitlement to anything other than income before age 25.

A gift that is subject to a reservation of benefit (see 30.7) cannot be a PET. Furthermore, a gift to a discretionary or (after 21 March 2006) an interest in possession trust is a CLT.

There is a quirk in the operation of the legislation where a PET is made between a chargeable transfer and death more than seven years later, for example:

2005: gift into discretionary trust equal to nil rate-band
2007: potentially exempt transfer on establishing an A&M trust
2013: death of donor.

If the potentially exempt transfer (PET) had not been made, the nil rate-band would have been available in full on death as death occurs more than seven years after the chargeable transfer. However, the PET was made and becomes chargeable on the donor's death within seven years of making it. In looking at the amount of IHT chargeable on the PET, it is necessary to take into account the fact that the nil-rate band was used on the chargeable transfer made within the previous seven years.

This means that the review period in seeking to establish the history of chargeable transfers can be extended back as far as 14 years.

30.6.2 Taper relief

(s 7 IHTA 1984)

Where an individual makes a PET or CLT and dies within the seven-year period, taper relief may reduce the amount of tax payable. The tax payable on the transfer that has become chargeable is reduced so that only a proportion is charged. The proportion is as follows:

Years between gift and death	Percentage of full charge
Three to four	80
Four to five	60
Five to six	40
Six to seven	20

Taper relief cannot reduce the tax on a lifetime chargeable transfer below the tax payable at the time the transfer was made. If a gift falls within the nil rate band, the taper relief is of no real benefit and does not reduce the tax that arises on other property that passes on the donor's death.

30.7 RESERVATION OF BENEFIT

(ss 102, 102ZA, 102A, 102B, 102C and Schedule 20 FA 1986)

30.7.1 Introduction

Property that has been given away may still be deemed to form part of a deceased person's estate unless:

- possession and enjoyment of the property was bona fide assumed by the donee; and
- the property was enjoyed virtually to the entire exclusion of the donor and of any benefit to him or her by contract or otherwise.

The reference to the property being enjoyed 'virtually to the entire exclusion' of the donor means that for all practical purposes this is an 'all or nothing' test. HMRC's view is that the exception is intended to cover trivial benefits such as might arise where, for example, the donor of a picture enjoyed the chance to view it when making occasional visits to the donee's home. HMRC has provided guidance on benefits it considers to be de minimis. The later pre-owned asset tax rules on de minimis benefits are broadly the same.

The Act refers to a benefit reserved 'by contract or otherwise' and this is meant to refer to arrangements that are not legally binding but amount to an honourable understanding. This may arise where a person gifts away a house but remains in occupation. A reservation of benefit would arise even if there were no legal tenancy and the donee could, in law, require the donor to vacate the property at any time.

For the purposes of the gift with reservation (GWR) legislation, property includes property bought with the proceeds of the original gift. However, HMRC has confirmed that there is no such tracing where the original gift was cash (unless the cash is settled, in which case the tracing provisions in para 5, Schedule 20 may take precedence).

30.7.2 Start date

The GWR rules apply to gifts made on or after 18 March 1986. Where a gift or transfer was made before that date, and the donor reserved a benefit, the gift is effective for IHT purposes and the capital does not form part of that person's estate.

30.7.3 Two cases where the taxpayer succeeded (and the Government changed the rules)

The rules on gifts of land and buildings were tightened up in FA 1999 to block the type of arrangements upheld by the House of Lords in *IRC* v *Ingram* [1999] STC 37. Here, the late Lady Ingram carved out a 20-year lease that entitled her to occupy the property rent free and then gave away the freehold. It was decided that this did not constitute a gift with reservation, but the law was amended with effect from 9 March 1999 to block this loophole.

The Court of Appeal held in *IRC* v *Eversden* [2003] STC 822 that the reservation of benefit rules did not apply where a wife transferred property into a trust under which her husband had an interest in possession even though that interest subsequently came to an end and the settlor was then able to benefit. The point was that the original transfer (gift into settlement) was covered by the spouse exemption and the GWR rules were therefore not applicable. The subsequent termination of the spouse's interest in possession was not caught by the GWR rules because it was a transfer of value and not a gift (the GWR legislation applies only to gifts). However, this loophole was closed with effect from 20 June 2003.

30.7.4 Retrospective legislation

FA 2004 contained legislation on pre-owned assets that imposed an income tax liability from 6 April 2005 on many people who had used (entirely lawful) ways of sidestepping the GWR rules in the past. If Lady Ingram were still alive, she might well be caught by this legislation. These provisions can catch transactions that took place as long ago as 18 March 1986. See 33.8 for more details.

30.7.5 Recent GWR case

In *Buzzoni & others* v *HMRC* [2012] UKUT 360 (TCC), Mrs Kahmi held a lease on a flat in central London. In 1997 she granted a rent-free underlease to O Limited. On the same day, she transferred the underlease to a newly-created settlement where the beneficiaries were her two sons. The underlease contained an obligation to pay a service charge which at the time of Mrs Kahmi's death in 2008 was £9,000 per annum.

The Upper Tribunal held that this was a GWR. There was a clear benefit to Mrs Kahmi as the settlement took over the liability to pay the service charge. The requirement that the property must be enjoyed by the donee to the virtual exclusion of the donor was not satisfied.

The decision was, however, overruled by the Court of Appeal. The Court held that there cannot be a GWR unless the donees have suffered some detriment in their enjoyment of the property given to them.

30.7.6 Three specific exemptions to the GWR rule

Donor pays a market rent

FA 1986 specifically provides that occupation of property or use of chattels does not count as a benefit provided the donor pays a market rent.

Benefit enjoyed after major change in circumstances

The legislation also provides that a benefit enjoyed by a donor occupying property can be ignored where there is an unforeseen change in the donor's circumstances, financial or otherwise, after the gift has been made and the occupation represents 'reasonable provision' by the donee for the care and maintenance of the donor.

Co-ownership

FA 1999 introduced a further exemption whereby an individual who transfers an interest in a residence to another individual who also occupies the property is not regarded as reserving a benefit provided that he or she continues to meet his or her share of all the expenses and outgoings. This can be a very important let-out where, for example, parents wish to give a half-share in the family home to children who live with them. However, relief is not limited to situations where only a half share has been gifted. A donor can give (say) a 60% or 70% interest in the property to a donee who then owns only (say) 30% or 40% of the property provided the donor meets at least his or her share of the normal property expenses and outgoings. It could however cause problems if in future a co-owner marries (for instance) and sets up home with his or her new spouse. Once the donee no longer occupies the property, if the original donor is still in occupation, then there will be a GWR at that point.

You should take expert advice before taking action that relies on this let-out, as the tax cost of getting it wrong may be severe.

30.7.7 Position where reservation of benefit ceases

Where a person makes a gift and initially reserves a benefit, but then relinquishes that reservation, he or she is normally treated as making a

PET at the time he or she gives up the reserved benefit. The amount of the PET is governed by the donated property's market value at that time.

Example – Giving up reservation of benefit

> A gave away property worth £150,000 in July 2001 but reserved a benefit. The benefit was relinquished in July 2010 when the property was worth £220,000. A dies in October 2012.
>
> If no benefit had been reserved, the gift would have been completely exempt by August 2008 (ie seven years after the gift), but because a benefit was retained until July 2010 the seven-year period starts only from that date. The full £220,000 (ie the value at July 2010 when the reservation of benefit was released) would form part of A's estate for IHT purposes, with no tapering of the IHT charge, since death occurred less than three years afterwards.

30.7.8 Settlements and trusts

The same applies where a person has sought to reserve only the possibility of a benefit, for example, where he or she has created a settlement and he or she is a potential beneficiary. It is HMRC's opinion that a benefit is reserved where the settlor creates a discretionary trust and is a member of the class of potential beneficiaries. This would also apply where the trust clauses are such that the settlor may later be added to the class of potential beneficiaries during his or her lifetime.

Unless para 7, Schedule 20 FA 1986 applies, it will be a question of fact whether enjoyment, by or benefit to, the donor's spouse or civil partner is a benefit to the donor. Where spouses or civil partners are living together it will be difficult to avoid any benefit received or actual enjoyment of property, by the spouse or civil partner, from being shared by the donor, and thus being a GWR in relation to the donor, particularly as benefits by associated operations can be taken into account.

In contrast to this, HMRC has confirmed that no reservation of benefit arises where a person creates a settlement and is only a contingent or default beneficiary. This may apply, for example, where property is put into trust for the settlor's children but the property would revert to the settlor in the event of the children dying or becoming bankrupt.

HMRC has confirmed that a settlor may be a trustee of a settlement created by him or herself without this constituting a reservation of benefit. Care should be taken over charging for the settlor's services as a trustee though, and it is recommended that professional advice is obtained for all matters where the GWR rules might apply, as they are notoriously complex. Where the settled property includes shares in a family company, the settlor/trustee may also be a director of the company and may be permitted under the trust deed to retain his or her remuneration provided it is reasonable in relation to the services rendered.

30.8 BUSINESS PROPERTY

(ss 103–114 IHTA 1984)

30.8.1 Basic requirements

A special deduction is given against the value of business property where the following conditions are satisfied:

(1) The property must have been owned during the previous two years or have been inherited from a spouse or civil partner and, when the spouse's period of ownership is taken into account, the combined period of ownership of the property, or any replacement property, exceeds two years out of the last five.
(2) The property must not be subject to a binding contract for sale.

Where replacement property has been acquired, relief is limited to that which would have been available on the original qualifying property. (See 30.11.13 on replacement property.)

30.8.2 Rates of business property relief (BPR)

(s 103 IHTA 1984)

Unincorporated businesses

A sole proprietor's interest in his or her business qualifies for a 100% deduction, as does a partner's interest in his or her firm.

A 50% deduction is available for an asset owned personally by a partner but used by his or her firm.

Shares and debentures

Business relief is available on shares only where the company concerned is a trading company or the holding company of a trading group. The 100% relief is available on:

- unquoted ordinary or preference shares in a trading company; and
- other securities (eg debentures) in an unquoted company which gave the donor voting control of the company.

AIM shares are treated as unquoted.

Where a company's shares are quoted, 50% relief is due if (and only if) the person making the capital transfer had voting control before the transfer.

A 50% deduction is available where a controlling shareholder transfers an asset used by his or her trading company, or where such an asset passes on his or her death.

Figure 30.2 – Is there reservation of benefit?

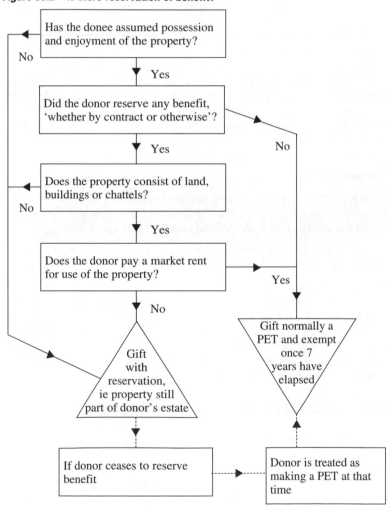

30.8.3 Businesses that do not qualify

Business relief is not normally available where the business carried on consists wholly or mainly of dealing in securities, stocks or shares, land or buildings or in holding or making investments.

HMRC takes the view that this may preclude BPR where shares in trading companies are held within a LLP.

Furnished holiday properties

HMRC has recently changed its stance on properties which are let as furnished holiday lettings. BPR will only be given where HMRC is satisfied that the owner or his or her agent provided substantial services to holidaymakers 'on and off the premises'. (See 8.5 for an update on furnished holiday lettings.) In *Pawson* v *HMRC* [2013] UKUT 050 (TCC), the Court held that BPR was not due. The logic of Mr Justice Henderson's judgment seems to mean that BPR will be due only where the charges for additional services exceed the charges which related to the provision of the accommodation. This approach was followed in *Green* [2015] TC 04427.

Excepted assets

Where a transfer involves shares, business relief may be restricted if the company owns investments. The legislation refers to such investments as 'excepted assets', which are defined as assets that are neither:

- used wholly or mainly for the purposes of the business, nor
- required for the future use of the business.

Where a company has subsidiaries, it is necessary to look at the group situation (ie shares in subsidiaries may have to be treated as excepted assets if the subsidiaries are investment companies).

Other examples of assets that may be excepted assets are cash balances in excess of monies required to fund working capital and property used personally by the shareholders. The CIOT, STEP and the ICAEW have recently issued technical guidance on this.

30.9 AGRICULTURAL PROPERTY AND WOODLANDS

(ss 115–124B IHTA 1984)

Agricultural property relief (APR) has historically been available on the agricultural value of farmland in the UK, Channel Islands or Isle of Man. From 22 April 2009, it also became available for land in other countries which belong to the European Economic Area.

30.9.1 Land occupied by the transferor

A 100% deduction is available where the individual has occupied farmland for the two years prior to the transfer date. Where a farm has been sold and another acquired, the replacement farm normally qualifies for APR provided the owner has occupied the two farms for a combined period of at least two years in the last five years. APR is also available for land owned by an individual but occupied by a firm of which he or she is a partner or a company of which he or she is the controlling shareholder for the two years preceding the transfer date, or two out of the preceding five years where replacement property is involved. Where replacement property has been acquired, relief is limited to that which would have been available on the original qualifying property. (See 30.11.13 on replacement property.)

30.9.2 Relief for other land

A 100% deduction is also available on land not occupied by the owner provided he or she has (or had) the legal right to regain vacant possession within a period not exceeding 12 months. To qualify under this head, the individual must normally have owned the land for at least seven years.

30.9.3 Relief for tenanted farmland

A 100% deduction is available for farmland let on a tenancy granted on or after 1 September 1995 where the owner cannot obtain vacant possession within 12 months. This would generally be the case where the land is let under an agricultural tenancy. Once again, the land must normally have been owned for seven years.

The 100% deduction is also available for a tenancy over property in Scotland acquired on or after 1 September 1995 by right of succession.

A 50% deduction is available for land which is let under a tenancy granted before 1 September 1995.

30.9.4 Farmhouses

Farmhouses can attract APR.

A farmhouse need not be owned by the same person as is carrying on the farming business – see *HMRC* v *Joseph Nicholas Hanson* [2013] UKUT 224 (TCC).

30.9.5 Woodlands

(ss 125–130 IHTA 1984)

The tax treatment of UK woodlands is largely beneficial as business relief is normally available after two years of ownership. In very unusual circumstances where business relief is not available, alternative relief may be due under s 125 after five years of ownership.

30.10 COMPUTATION OF TAX PAYABLE ON LIFETIME TRANSFERS

In practice, IHT is likely only to be paid during a person's lifetime for chargeable transfers made by him or her to a trust. The tax payable is calculated as follows:

Initial calculation

Chargeable transfers made during the preceding seven years		A
Add	Amount of chargeable transfer	B
		C
Deduct	Nil rate band	D
		E
	IHT thereon at 20%	X
Deduct	IHT on a notional transfer of A minus D as if it took place at the same time	Y
	IHT payable in respect of the chargeable transfer	Z

Position if the donor dies within three years

Chargeable transfers made during the previous seven years		A
Add	PETs caught by the seven-year rule	B
		C
Add	amount of chargeable transfer	D
		E
Deduct	Nil rate band	F
		G
	IHT thereon at 40%	H
Deduct	IHT at 40% on a notional transfer of C minus F	I
		J

The donee is liable to pay additional IHT of J minus the amount Z above already paid.

Position if the donor dies during years 4–7

The above will be liable for additional IHT computed as J above, but subject to the IHT on PETs caught by the seven-year rule being reduced by taper relief (see 30.6.2).

30.11 TAX PAYABLE ON DEATH

30.11.1 Normal basis of computation

The charge on death is normally computed as shown in the flowchart in Figure 30.3. The IHT will be the tax on the figure in Box 6 minus the tax payable on a normal transfer equal to the amount in Box 4 as if the notional transfer took place immediately before the death. Some taper relief may be due on the PETs caught by the seven-year rule (see 30.6.2). Lifetime transfers use up the nil rate band first, with any balance being deducted from the chargeable transfer on death. However, special reliefs may be available.

30.11.2 Death on active service

(s 154 IHTA 1984)

Since World War II, death duty legislation has contained an exemption for a person who dies from wounds suffered while on active service. The exemption applies to the estates of those killed in the Falklands conflict and the Gulf War, and of members of the RUC killed by terrorists in Northern Ireland. The relief can only be granted by HMRC on receipt of a certificate from the appropriate MoD issuing department; the family of the deceased will need to apply to the MoD and the certificate is then forwarded direct to HMRC. HMRC has no discretion in operating this relief and can only do so once it is in possession of the appropriate certificate.

The exemption may well apply more often than people think. Death does not have to be immediate, nor need the wound be the only cause of death. The High Court held in 1978 that the exemption was owed to the estate of the fourth Duke of Westminster because serious wounds that he had suffered in 1944 contributed to his death in 1967.

30.11.3 Debts that may be disallowed

(s 103 FA 1986)

There is a general rule that debts are not deductible where the deceased has made a capital transfer to a person who subsequently made a loan back to the deceased. This rule applies only to loans made after 18 March 1986, but there is no such time limit on the capital transfers. A debt may be disallowed because the deceased had made a capital transfer to the lender even though that capital transfer took place long before 18 March 1986. It is also of no help that the loan was made on normal commercial terms and a market rate of interest was payable.

Figure 30.3 – Charge on death computation

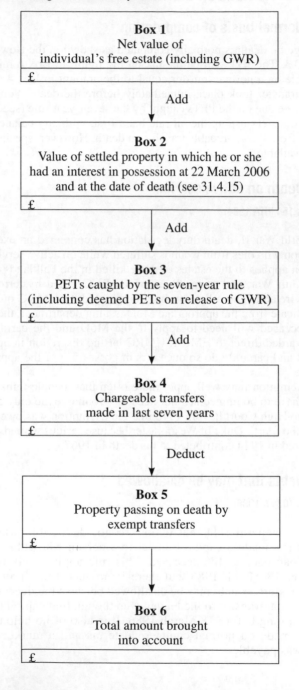

Box 1

Net value of
individual's free estate (including GWR)

£

Add

Box 2

Value of settled property in which he or she
had an interest in possession at 22 March 2006
and at the date of death (see 31.4.15)

£

Add

Box 3

PETs caught by the seven-year rule
(including deemed PETs on release of GWR)

£

Add

Box 4

Chargeable transfers
made in last seven years

£

Deduct

Box 5

Property passing on death by
exempt transfers

£

Box 6

Total amount brought
into account

£

This legislation was successfully invoked by HMRC to deny a deduction for a debt incurred by a widower where the debt arose from his buying an interest in the matrimonial home from his late wife's executors. He had given his wife her interest in the property eight years before her death – see *Phizackerley* v *HMRC* (SpC 591). This seems a very harsh decision, especially as s 103 would not have been in point if Mr Phizackerley had died first and his wife had incurred a similar debt in buying a similar interest in the property from his executors.

30.11.4 Debts and liabilities

The FA 2013 introduced major changes which apply in relation to chargeable transfers made from 17 July 2013.

Liabilities which are not settled in full

A deduction for a debt or liability will be allowed only to the extent that the creditor receives payment unless it can be shown that:

- there is a commercial reason for the liability not being settled; and
- the liability is not left unpaid as part of arrangements to get a tax advantage.

Liabilities incurred for the acquisition of excluded property

No deduction will be allowed for a liability incurred for the acquisition of excluded property except that relief may be due if:

- the excluded property has been sold and replaced with UK assets; or
- the liability exceeds the value of the excluded property (and certain other conditions are satisfied).

FA 2014 has extended this to cover situations where borrowed money has been put into foreign currency UK bank accounts by individuals who are neither resident nor domiciled in the UK.

Liabilities incurred for the acquisition of property which qualifies for BPR or APR

Where a liability has been incurred in order to acquire assets on which a relief such as BPR, APR or woodlands relief is due, the liability will reduce the value of those assets that can qualify for relief. A liability may be deducted from the deceased's assets which do not qualify for BPR or APR only to the extent that the liability exceeds the value of the business or agricultural property. However, this treatment does not apply to liabilities which were already in existence at 5 April 2013.

30.11.5 Sales of quoted securities at a loss

(ss 178–189 IHTA 1984)

Relief is given where quoted securities or unit trusts are sold at a loss within 12 months of death. Where shares are suspended, s 186B permits similar relief to be claimed by reference to the shares' value when they return from suspension. If the shares are cancelled, s 186A treats them as having been disposed of for a nominal value of £1, enabling a claim to be made. It is not possible to pick and choose: the relief is confined to the amount of any overall loss. Executors must, in effect, elect that the total proceeds of any sales should be substituted for the value at date of death. The time limit for making a claim under this section is due to be reduced to four years from the end of the 12 months following the date of death (para 9, Schedule 51, FA 2009), but the date for this change is yet to be appointed.

Example – Sale of quoted securities at a loss

> B died on 1 October 2014. His estate included a portfolio worth £70,000. The executors have to sell all of the securities in December 2014 and realise an overall loss of £25,000. The estate can be reduced by this amount so that, in effect, only £45,000 is taken into account.
>
> The overall loss of £25,000 may have been made up of a gain of £5,000 and losses of £30,000. Relief is, however, limited to the net figure.

30.11.6 Relief restricted where executors purchase quoted securities

Furthermore, the relief is restricted where at any time during the period beginning on the date of the death in question and ending two months after the date of the last sale is made, the executors repurchase quoted securities.

Example – Restriction of relief on quoted securities

> C died on 2 January 2014. His executors also sell securities for £45,000 in December 2014 at a £25,000 loss. On 10 January 2015, they reinvest £10,000 in new securities. The £25,000 loss cannot be claimed in full, it has to be reduced by
>
> $$\frac{10,000}{45,000} \times £25,000 = £5,556$$

30.11.7 **Sales of land at a loss**

(ss190–198 IHTA 1984)

Relief is due where land and buildings are sold at a loss within four years of death provided the loss is at least £1,000 or 5% of probate value (whichever is less). The net proceeds are substituted for the value at the date of death and the IHT is recomputed. This relief will be denied where the property is sold to a beneficiary (or his or her spouse, civil partner, child or remoter issue) where the interest sold is the same as the beneficiary's original interest. The relief does, however, apply if the purchaser's entitlement is less than the interest sold (eg the sale of the whole property to a beneficiary, who was entitled to only a half share of the property).

Again, it is not possible to pick and choose: the relief is confined to the amount of any overall loss. Executors must, in effect, elect that the total proceeds of any sales should be substituted for the value at date of death. The only sales not taken into account in this way are sales in the fourth year for more than the date of death value, and sales excluded from the relief.

Note that there is no equivalent relief where the deceased held shares in a company that owned land which was subsequently sold at a lower value.

30.11.8 **Using the balance of the nil rate band of a former spouse or civil partner**

Section 8A provides that where an individual dies on or after 9 October 2007, he or she may also be entitled to an additional nil rate band amount based on the proportion of his or her spouse or civil partner's nil rate band which remained unused on the earlier death of that spouse or civil partner.

The additional relief has to be claimed.

The maximum relief is an amount equal to the full nil rate band at the rate in force at the time of the second death (in other words, a person who has been bereaved twice cannot claim the full unused nil rate band in respect of both his or her previous spouses or civil partners).

There is no time limit and the relief may therefore be claimed for cases where the spouse had died under the estate duty regime before the introduction of IHT on 26 March 1974.

There is also no restriction by reference to the size of the spouse's estate or domicile status. In principle, the additional nil rate band can be claimed in respect of a spouse or civil partner who had no assets at all on his or her death. Even the situation where both spouses are non-UK domiciled may attract this relief, where there is a UK chargeable estate (ie UK situs assets). There could be a restriction if a UK domiciled spouse or civil partner had died in 2012–13 or an earlier year and he or she had a non-UK domiciled spouse, because only £55,000 of property passing to the spouse would have been exempt with the balance being chargeable; the relief would therefore be limited to the proportion of the nil rate band unused on the first death.

Care needs to be taken if the Will contains a survivorship clause as this may prevent the nil rate band from being transferred. Advice should always be taken when drafting Wills to ensure they are tax efficient.

30.11.9 Legitim: special rules for Scotland

(s 147 IHTA 1984)

Scottish law provides that a person must leave a set part of his or her moveable estate to his or her children: their entitlement is called 'legitim'. If a person makes a Will that does not take account of this, the children can have it set aside. In practice, children often decide to renounce their right to legitim; especially where a person's Will bequeaths all his or her property to the surviving spouse or civil partner. The legislation provides that children who renounce their entitlement within two years of the death are not treated as making a chargeable transfer and the property is treated as passing to the survivor in accordance with the Will.

The deed renouncing the rights must satisfy the provisions as to variations: see 30.4.6.

Practical problems arise where minor children are involved. The IHT legislation provides that children under age 18 (at the date of death) may renounce their entitlement within two years of attaining age 18 without this constituting a chargeable transfer by them. The property is then treated (for IHT purposes) as passing to the survivor in accordance with the Will. As a child under age 18 does not have the legal capacity to renounce his or her entitlement, the executors have a difficult choice: they can either account for IHT on the basis that the child takes his or her entitlement or on the assumption that the child will renounce his or her rights on reaching age18.

Position where executors assume legitim rights are taken

IHT will have to be paid to the extent that the property that passes to the children exceeds the nil rate band. When each child attains 18, he or she may elect to renounce his or her rights so that the surviving spouse or civil partner benefits. The spouse exemption will then mean that no tax should have been paid. HMRC will then repay the IHT paid and pay repayment interest.

Position where executors assume that legitim will be renounced

No IHT will be paid in the first instance. However, if it turns out that one of the children decides not to renounce his or her entitlement, IHT on the death is recomputed and the tax payable attracts interest from the date it should have been paid.

30.11.10 Rate of IHT where there are charitable bequests

Where individuals leave at least 10% of their estates chargeable to inheritance tax to charity, the remaining chargeable estate will be taxed at only 36%, rather than 40%. The nil rate band for inheritance tax will remain at £325,000 until 2015; from 6 April 2015, the nil rate band will rise each tax year in line with the consumer price index.

30.11.11 Quick succession relief

(s 141 IHTA 1984)

Suppose a person has recently inherited property from someone else. If he or she was to die and the full rate of IHT applied, the same property would have been subject to IHT twice within a relatively short period of time.

Quick succession relief is intended to alleviate this. The relief works by giving credit for a proportion of the tax charged on the first occasion against the tax payable on the second death. The proportion is set out below:

Both deaths occur:	Proportion:
within one year	100%
within two years	80%
within three years	60%
within four years	40%
within five years	20%

Example – Quick succession relief

D inherited property worth £150,000 in October 2010. IHT was paid on that estate at an average rate of 25%, so the grossed-up amount was £200,000 (£150,000 × 100/75) and the tax suffered was £50,000. D dies in August 2013. The maximum amount on which quick succession relief can be claimed is:

$$\frac{150,000}{200,000} \times £50,000 = £37,500$$

This has to be reduced to 60% of £37,500 (ie £22,500) as three complete years have elapsed. The relief is not affected by the fact that property has been sold or given away before the second death takes place.

30.11.12 Treatment of gifts caught by seven-year rule

(s 113A IHTA 1984)

Tax on a PET that becomes a chargeable transfer because of the transferor's death is payable by the recipient of the gift. Business relief is available on a PET that becomes a chargeable transfer only if the conditions in 30.8 are satisfied both at the time of the gift and at the time of death.

Examples – Business relief on PETs

(1) *E* owns all the shares in a family company. He gives his son *F* a 24% shareholding. Three years later, the company is sold and F receives cash for his shares. One year after that *E* dies.

Business relief will not normally be available as the necessary conditions are not satisfied by the donee at the time of *E*'s death. If *F* had reinvested the proceeds in another private company, business relief might have been available after all.

(2) The basic position is as in (1) (ie *E*'s gift to *F* of a 24% shareholding). This time, *F* retains his shares, but by the time *E* dies the shares are quoted. No relief is due as *F* does not control the company and his shares are quoted shares.

(3) The basic position is as in (1), but *F* retains the shares and they are still unquoted at the time of *E*'s death. The shares attract the 100% relief and this is not lost even if *F* disposes of the shares shortly after *E*'s death.

30.11.13 Replacement property

(s 107 IHTA 1984)

Where a donee has disposed of business property, but acquires replacement property, the PET may still attract business relief provided the replacement property is acquired within three years of the disposal. Similar rules apply for agricultural property.

30.11.14 Reduction in value

Where the value at the date of death of property transferred within the previous seven years by a PET is lower than the value at date of gift, the chargeable transfer is based on the value at death. However, the value of the property at the time of the gift still counts towards the deceased's cumulative chargeable transfers.

30.11.15 Acceptance of property in lieu of IHT

HMRC has power to accept certain types of property in satisfaction of IHT liabilities. Such property includes pictures, prints, books, manuscripts, works of art, scientific objects and other items regarded as being of national, scientific, artistic and historic interest. HMRC has to clear such arrangements with Heritage ministers and in practice only property regarded as of 'pre-eminent interest' is accepted.

Taxpayers who own such items, that have been acknowledged as being first rate, can find out more about these arrangements by obtaining a copy of *Capital Taxation and The National Heritage* (CTNH) from: www.hmrc.gov.uk/government/publications

30.11.16 Double taxation agreements

The UK has only a handful of tax treaties that cover inheritance tax. There are treaties with France, India, Italy, Netherlands, Pakistan, Ireland, South Africa, Sweden, Switzerland and the USA.

Where no double taxation arrangement exists, unilateral relief will normally be available by way of a foreign tax credit against the UK IHT charge.

30.11.17 Payment of IHT by instalments

It is possible to defer payment of IHT on certain types of property. IHT on assets that attract 50% BPR or APR, or IHT payable on other business/agricultural property because the two-year period of ownership is not satisfied, can be paid by instalments over ten years, with interest being charged only on instalments that are paid late. IHT on other land and buildings can also be paid by instalments but interest is charged from the normal due date.

Outstanding instalments generally become payable as and when the property is sold.

30.12 LIFE ASSURANCE AND PENSION POLICIES

30.12.1 Life assurance

Life assurance is one of the best ways of providing for the payment of IHT, but the tax treatment of policies needs to be watched carefully. The following is only a summary of a complex area and is not intended to be a substitute for taking independent professional advice.

30.12.2 Death of policyholder

A life assurance policy beneficially owned by the deceased is property subject to IHT in the same way as any other property owned by him or her.

30.12.3 Gifts of policies

Gifts of policies may generally be made in two ways:

- writing the policy in trust or making a subsequent declaration of trust;
- assignment of the policy.

In either case, subsequent premiums may be paid:

- by the donor direct;
- by the beneficiary out of cash gifts from the donor;
- by the beneficiary out of his or her own resources;
- by a combination of the above.

In general, if the gift is an outright gift to an individual or a trust for the disabled, it will constitute a PET and will only be taxable if the donor dies within seven years of making the gift. Gifts to other trusts such as discretionary trusts may attract lifetime IHT.

If any of the usual IHT exemptions applies (see 30.5), neither the gift of the policy nor any gifts of premiums that have been made will be taxable, for example:

(1) The gift of the premium or policy falls within the annual exemption – currently £3,000 (note that if the policy is a qualifying policy and premiums are payable net of life assurance relief, it is the net premium that constitutes the gift; if the premiums are paid gross, it is the gross premium that constitutes the gift).
(2) The premiums come within the donor's normal expenditure out of income exemption (note that this applies to payment of premiums, not to the gift of an existing policy).
(3) The gifts fall within the marriage settlement exemption.
(4) The gifts fall within the small gifts exemption – outright gifts of not more than £250 per donee (eg a premium on a policy written in trust for the absolute benefit of a child).
(5) Policies written by either spouse or civil partner for the absolute benefit of the other.

If none of the exemptions applies, IHT may be payable in respect of the gift of the policy or the payment of subsequent premiums (unless they fall within the nil rate band). However, payment of premiums on policies written under interest in possession trusts before 22 March 2006 will often constitute PETs under transitional provisions contained in FA 2006, provided there are no increases in premiums paid after that date which were not allowed for within the policy terms as they then stood.

If IHT is payable, the chargeable transfers are the premiums paid by the donor; or, if a gift of an existing policy is made by assignment or declaration of trust, the chargeable transfer is generally the greater of the total gross premiums paid or the policy's market value (usually the surrender value).

If cash gifts have been made to enable the premiums to be paid by the beneficiary, the amount of the cash gifts will usually be PETs. The proceeds of the policy on death, maturity or surrender will not be subject to IHT in the hands of the recipient of the assignment or a beneficiary having an interest in possession in the trusts.

30.12.4 Life of another policies ('pur autre vie')

On the death of the life assured the proceeds are totally free of IHT. Clearly they do not form part of the life assured's estate, as the policy is not owned by him or her. The surrender value will, however, be potentially chargeable in the policyholder's estate if he or she dies before the life assured.

If the donor makes cash gifts to the policyholder to help him or her pay the premiums, the cash gifts will be taxable for the donor, unless the exemptions mentioned above apply, but the proceeds will be free of IHT in the policyholder's hands, provided he or she survives the life assured.

30.12.5 Use of policies

Life assurance policies can be used in two main ways in IHT planning:

- as a vehicle for making gifts to beneficiaries; and
- to create a fund for the eventual payment of the tax.

Thus they may help to both minimise the amount of tax payable and offer a means of paying any unavoidable liability whenever it arises.

30.12.6 IHT and pension plans

Although the legislation does not permit a policyholder to alienate his or her right to a retirement pension, it is possible to assign any death benefits provided under retirement annuity or personal pension plans, whether provided as a sum assured or as a return of the retirement fund. The IHT rules are broadly similar to those applicable to life policy assignments except that:

- discretionary trusts of these assignable benefits will not be subject to the usual IHT charging regime of ten-yearly and exit charges provided the benefits are distributed within two years of the individual's death;

- the right to a pension is not treated as giving rise to an interest in possession in the pension fund;
- the gift of a 'return of fund' death benefit will usually be regarded as having no value, provided the individual is in good health at the time of the gift. Similarly, subsequent contributions to the pension will be treated as being attributable to the provision of the pension benefits and not the death benefit, provided the individual is in good health at the time the contribution is made;
- an IHT charge no longer arises on the death after age 77 of a person who has an alternatively secured pension, as these rules have now been abolished. Instead a pensions tax charge arises (see 26.2.3).

Occupational schemes are usually written under discretionary trusts and also achieve the same IHT exemptions on payment of contributions and distribution of benefits.

30.13 HERITAGE PROPERTY

It is possible to claim exemption for transfers of qualifying heritage assets, for example chattels of museum quality, land of outstanding natural beauty or of historic or scientific interest, and buildings and amenity land deemed to be of outstanding historic or architectural interest. The exemption is currently conditional on the new owner undertaking to maintain and preserve the asset and to provide reasonable public access to it. It is no longer possible to restrict access by requiring an appointment with the asset's owner.

The rules for defining qualifying chattels were made more restrictive by FA 1998. There used to be no time limit for claiming heritage tax exemptions, but now a claim for exemption normally has to be made within two years of the date of the relevant chargeable event. Furthermore, transfers do not qualify for the special exemption previously available for gifts and bequests to certain non-profit making bodies.

30.14 PLANNING: THE FIRST STEP

Planning for IHT is something that many people would rather not think about. The first step should be to sit down and work out the value of your estate: it is something that your next of kin may already have done if you've ever argued! If the net value of your estate is close to the IHT threshold, then perhaps the time has come to talk with your financial or tax adviser to discuss ways in which you can ensure the people you would like to benefit from your estate are provided for.

If you not have a Will, this should be the starting point for any planning. Bear in mind that if you do not have a Will, your assets will pass as set out in Figure 30.4. Do not assume all your assets will automatically pass to your spouse or civil partner. They will not, unless you have written a Will to provide that they do.

If you have a Will, you should review it regularly *and* ensure that you have taken advantage of all available IHT reliefs; especially given the changes introduced by FA 2006 and the possibility of future legislative change.

Figure 30.4 – What happens if a person dies without making a valid Will?

When a person dies without making a valid Will, he or she is said to have died 'intestate'. His or her estate then passes as follows:

If he or she was married or in a civil partnership and had children, grandchildren or great grandchildren

- Spouse or civil partner gets everything up to £250,000 and all personal chattels.
- Anything over and above this (the 'residue') is divided into two:
  - half goes in trust for children to get on attaining age 18, or on their marriage if earlier;
  - half goes to the spouse or civil partner.

If he or she was married or in a civil partnership but had no children:

- Spouse or civil partner gets everything.

If he or she was married or in a civil partnership but had no parents or siblings or nephews or nieces

- Spouse or civil partner takes the whole estate.

If he or she was not married or in a civil partnership, and had children

- Estate goes to children at age 18 or on their earlier marriage. If a child has predeceased and had children, those children take his or her share *per stirpes*.

Note

A person who was dependent on the deceased may make a claim for provision out of an estate even though he or she is not a named beneficiary under a Will or is not entitled to benefit under the intestacy provisions.

31

THE TAXATION OF TRUSTS

This chapter covers the taxation of trusts under the following headings:

(1) When are trustees liable to pay income tax?
(2) When are trustees liable for UK capital gains tax (CGT)?
(3) Bare trusts
(4) Fixed-interest trusts
(5) Discretionary trusts
(6) Accumulation and maintenance trusts
(7) Trusts for the disabled
(8) Protective trusts
(9) Trusts for the most vulnerable
(10) Charitable trusts
(11) Miscellaneous aspects
(12) Executors and personal representatives
(13) Some planning points

31.1 WHEN ARE TRUSTEES LIABLE TO PAY INCOME TAX?

(ss 474, 475 and 812 ITA 2007)

31.1.1 General rules

UK resident trusts are liable to pay income tax on both UK and overseas income; trusts that are not UK resident are liable only in respect of UK source income.

Trustees are not entitled to personal allowances. In the main, trustees are liable for tax at the basic or lower rate, of 20%. Trustees of discretionary and accumulation trusts are subject to additional tax (the rate applicable to trusts). The rate is 45% for non-dividend income and 37.5% for dividend income and has been so since 2013–14.

A 'basic rate band' applies since 6 April 2005. This is £1,000 and is split pro rata among existing settlements made by the same settlor since 1978 (see 31.5.2).

A non-resident trust is subject to tax on UK income under s 812 ITA 2007.

The offshore trustees will be subject to UK tax on UK trust income on the arising basis.

617

Where the settlor or his or her spouse, or civil partner, or unmarried, minor children can benefit, the trust income will be deemed to be that of the settlor for tax purposes (see 33.6) but any income received by the trustees still needs to be reported in the trust return.

If an offshore trust is settlor interested, the income is treated as that of the settlor for all purposes of the taxes acts, subject to the settlor's right of recovery as against the trustees. The remittance basis (under s 648 ITTOIA 2005) may be available to a non-domiciled settlor in respect of non-UK income, subject to a charge if funds are later remitted to the UK whether to the settlor or any other beneficiary.

31.1.2 Trusts and self-assessment

The same general rules apply to trustees as they do to individuals under self-assessment (SA). If a trust has UK chargeable income and gains, then the trustees have to file a self-assessment form (Form SA900) by 31 October for paper returns or 31 January for online filing (HMRC does not provide software to file form SA900 online, so proprietary software will be needed), following the relevant tax year.

31.1.3 Rules for determining the residence status of a trust

A single set of rules applies for determining the income tax and CGT residence of a trust:

- If all the trustees are UK resident, the trust is UK resident.
- If none of the trustees is UK resident, the trust is not UK resident.
- If only some of the trustees are UK resident, and the settlor was not domiciled or ordinarily resident or resident in the UK at the time that the trust was created, the trust is not UK resident.

Where a non-UK resident trustee acts as a trustee in the course of a business carried on through a branch, agency or permanent establishment in the UK, he, she or it will be treated as UK resident.

31.2 WHEN ARE TRUSTEES LIABLE FOR UK CAPITAL GAINS TAX (CGT)?

(ss 2 and 69 TCGA 1992)

31.2.1 General rules

Trustees are subject to CGT only if the trust is resident in the UK, or if they realise capital gains from the disposal of assets used by them in carrying on a business in the UK through a branch or permanent establishment. In general, therefore, trustees are responsible for reporting gains and paying tax.

31.2.2 Annual exemption

(Schedule 1 TCGA 1992)

For a number of years the annual CGT exemption available to trustees has been half the individual amount, for example for 2014–15, the exemption is £5,500 (half of £11,000).

Where a settlor has created a number of settlements since 6 June 1978, the annual exemption is shared equally between them. The minimum annual exemption for each settlement is currently £1,100 (ie one-tenth of the £11,000 individual annual exemption for 2014–15). An unused part of the exemption for one settlement cannot be used by another settlement.

Consequently, if a person created three trusts in 1975 and four in 1989, the 2014–15 exemption for the 1975 trusts would be £5,500 each, and the four trusts created after 6 June 1978 would each have an exemption of £1,375. If all seven trusts had been created after 6 June 1978, each would have an annual exemption of £1,100.

31.2.3 Entrepreneurs' relief

Where an individual has not used up his or her maximum relief, trustees of a trust in which he or she is a life tenant can use the balance of the ER lifetime allowance to cover gains realised from the trustees' sale of all or part of the life tenant's trust interest in an unincorporated business or trust holding of shares in the life tenant's personal trading company (ie a company where the life tenant is a director and he or she holds at least 5% of the shares and voting rights in his or her own right). It is necessary for the trustees to have owned the asset for at least 12 months.

The trustees may also be able to claim ER on gains realised from associated disposals, ie sales by the trustees of land and buildings that were used by the unincorporated business or by the life tenant's personal trading company. Relief will not normally be available where the trustees have charged a full market rent for periods after 5 April 2008.

31.3 BARE TRUSTS

A bare trust is one where trustees hold property on behalf of a beneficiary who is absolutely entitled to that property, or would be absolutely entitled if he or she were not a minor and therefore unable to give a valid receipt. Income and capital gains received by trustees of a bare trust belong to the beneficiary and he or she is required to report income and gains in his or her own return and to account to HMRC for the full amount of tax due.

The trustees normally have no liability to tax and no requirement to complete trust tax returns.

Under self-assessment, bare trustees cannot deduct tax from income arising to them. Any income received gross by the trustees must be paid gross to the beneficiaries. The only exception to this rule is that UK resident trustees may be required, under the non-resident landlord scheme, to deduct and account for tax on the rental income of beneficiaries whose usual place of abode is outside the UK (see 33.7).

31.4 FIXED-INTEREST TRUSTS

A fixed interest trust is one where a beneficiary is entitled to receive income as it arises, either during his or her lifetime or for a specific period. A simple type of fixed interest trust would be where the beneficiary (the life tenant) is entitled to receive all the income during his or her lifetime with the trust coming to an end on his or her death, perhaps with the capital then passing to his or her children absolutely.

There may also be a situation where a life tenant is entitled to receive a proportion of the trust income, say half, with the other half being held on different types of trust. It is also possible to have an entitlement to income (an interest in possession) for a specific period, so that a trust under which someone had a right to all of the income for a fixed period of ten years would be a fixed interest trust until the end of that period.

31.4.1 Settlor-interested settlements are subject to a special tax treatment

The following analysis is on the basis that the settlor, and his or her spouse or civil partner, or minor unmarried children are excluded from benefiting. See 33.6.2 on the tax position where the settlor can benefit.

A previously non-settlor interested trust can become settlor-interested where the settlor marries, enters a civil partnership, or has children and such relatives have not been excluded from benefiting under the terms of the trust, because in the past there have been no such persons.

31.4.2 Income tax

Where property is held on fixed interest trusts, income tax is charged on the trustees at the following rates:

- dividend income at 10%;
- all other income at 20% (basic/lower rate).

As mentioned above there is no deduction for personal allowances, but if a trust owns investment properties on which an entitlement to capital allowances arises, such allowances may be set against the trustees' income in the same way as for individuals. Similarly, if the trustees carry on a trade, any losses arising may be relieved against other income. Subject to this, the trustees will either suffer tax at source or be assessed to tax on all untaxed income arising to them.

31.4.3 Ascertaining the beneficiary's income

It will not generally be possible for the trustees to pay over to a beneficiary with a fixed interest the full amount of the income left after tax. Inevitably, there will be some expenses (eg bank charges, interest, professional fees, etc) that are properly charged to income, and there may also be the trustees' own fees. Such expenses may not be deducted in arriving at the trustees' taxable income, but they need to be taken into account in determining the amount of the beneficiary's income. See 31.11.2 regarding an HMRC statement on expenses that may be taken into account in this way.

In broad terms, the proper procedure is to ascertain the trustees' taxable income for the year. The tax paid by the trustees for the year should then be deducted, and a further deduction made for expenses that are properly charged against income. The net amount must then be 'grossed up' at the appropriate rate and this is the amount the beneficiary will need to declare on his or her tax return.

Example – Tax treatment of income from a fixed interest trust

The trustees of a fixed interest trust have taxable deposit interest of £20,000 for 2014–15. They pay tax of £4,000 (20%). There are expenses of £1,700 that are properly chargeable against the income. The balance belongs to the life tenant, whose gross income will be ascertained as follows:

	£
Trustees' taxable income	20,000
Less: basic rate tax	(4,000)
	16,000
Less: expenses	(1,700)
	14,300
£14,300 grossed up at the lower rate (20%)	17,875

This income forms part of the life tenant's income for the year whether or not it is actually paid out to him or her. If the life tenant is subject to higher rate tax, he or she must pay the difference between his or her highest rate and the rate paid by the trustees.

31.4.4 Dividend income

(ss13, 481 ITA 2007)

It is necessary to distinguish UK dividends from income from other sources. Dividend income is taxable at 10% as opposed to the 20% charge on other income. Trustees' expenses are set first against UK dividend income, so as to minimise the restriction of the tax deemed to be withheld from the trust income.

31.4.5 Tax deduction certificates

For fixed interest trusts a tax deduction certificate (Form R185 (trust income)) should be completed by the trustees or their professional advisers, showing the appropriate gross, tax and net figures in respect of the beneficiary's income. It is necessary to show the different types of income separately on the certificate. If the trust has received foreign dividends it will also be necessary to advise the beneficiary (or his or her tax adviser) of the overseas tax deducted on those dividends.

31.4.6 Income mandated to a beneficiary

Trustees sometimes take the view that it is simpler to mandate dividends and other income to the beneficiary so that such income does not pass through the trustees' hands. This does not alter the fact that the trustees are still the legal owners of the assets that produce the income.

Although this income can be entered directly in the beneficiary's personal tax return, care should be taken to ensure that it is entered in the correct section for trust income so as to avoid any confusion with the beneficiary's personal income. Where this is done, HMRC will assess the beneficiary rather than the trustees.

If the trustees incur expenses, these may not be deducted (as in 31.4.3); this applies even where the beneficiary reimburses the trustees for such expenses later on.

Tax notes

Since 22 March 2006, trusts can be life interest trusts for income and capital gains purposes, but relevant property trusts for inheritance tax purposes. Accordingly, it may be sensible to appoint a flexible or revocable life interest from an existing discretionary trust, with no IHT impact, and mandate the relevant income to the beneficiary, in order for the income to be treated as that of the beneficiary and taxed at their marginal rates, rather than at the rate applicable to trusts which is 37.5% (dividends) and 45% (other income).

31.4.7 Beneficiary's exempt income

It is sometimes possible for UK-resident trustees to take advantage of a beneficiary's tax exemption to avoid paying tax that he or she would then have to claim back. For example, where a beneficiary is entitled to all the income of the trust and he or she is resident outside the UK, the trustees can agree with HMRC that the income that arises outside the UK (and any other income that is exempt for a non-resident, for example, interest from exempt gilts: see 34.6.3) should not be taxed in the trustees' hands.

This treatment is not normally available where a non-resident beneficiary is entitled to only a proportion of the trustees' income.

Tax notes

Where, under the terms of a settlement, income from foreign dividends belongs to, and is paid to, a beneficiary resident and domiciled abroad, that income cannot be assessed on trustees who are resident in the UK (*Williams* v *Singer* [1921] 1 AC 65; 7 TC 387 HL). If however there is no identifiable beneficiary in respect of income arising and accumulated abroad, a UK resident trustee is assessable in respect of that income (*Kelly* v *Rogers* [1935] 2 KB 446; 19 TC 692, CA).

Where a beneficiary is entitled to all the income of the trust and is resident outside the UK, the trustees can agree with HMRC that the income that arises outside the UK should not be taxed in the trustees' hands.

31.4.8 Where taxable income is not income for trust purposes

Difficulties can arise where the trustees receive something that constitutes income for tax, but not for trust, purposes. For example, if trustees of a fixed-interest trust receive a lump sum premium that is taxable income from property (see 8.3); this is not income that belongs to the life tenant. Similarly, a distribution such as may arise on a company buying back its own shares may be income for income tax purposes (see 9.9.7), but is capital for trust purposes. In both these situations, the trustees must pay tax on such deemed income at the trust rates, and the amounts must be excluded when calculating the life tenant's income for tax purposes.

Section 482 ITA 2007 provides that trustees of fixed interest trusts are subject to the trust rate on any amounts that are taxed as if they were income but are not income of the life tenant for trust purposes. These provisions, however, still do not mean that the income is deemed to be that of the life tenant. The types of payment which are taxable at the trust rates are as follows:

(1) A payment which is made to the trustees or to which the trustees are entitled, and which is made by way of qualifying distribution

by a company on the redemption, repayment or purchase of shares in the company or on the purchase of rights to acquire such shares.

(2) Accrued income profits treated as made by the trustees under ss 628(5) or 630(2) ITA 2007.

(3) Income treated as arising to the trustees under regulation 17 of the Offshore Funds (Tax) Regulations 2009 (SI 2009/3001).

(4) Income which the trustees are treated as receiving under ss 68(2) or 71(4) FA 1989 (which relate to employee share ownership trusts).

(5) A sum to which Chapter 4, Part 3, ITTOIA 2005 (which provides for certain amounts to be treated as receipts of a property business) applies.

(6) A profit in relation to which the trustees are liable for income tax under s 429 ITTOIA 2005 (profits from deeply discounted securities).

(7) A gain in relation to which the trustees are liable for income, tax under s 467 ITTOIA 2005 (gains from contracts for life insurance etc), other than a gain to which subsection (7) of that section applies.

(8) A profit or gain in relation to which the trustees are liable for income tax under s 554 ITTOIA 2005 (transactions in deposits).

(9) A profit or gain in relation to which the trustees are liable for income tax under s 557 ITTOIA 2005 (disposals of futures and options), and which does not meet any of conditions A to C in s 568 ITTOIA 2005.

(10) Proceeds in relation to which the trustees are liable for income tax under s 573 ITTOIA 2005 (sales of foreign dividend coupons).

(11) Income treated as arising to the trustees under Chapter 3 of Part 13 of ITA 2007 (tax avoidance: transactions in land).

31.4.9 Exempt receipts that are income for trust purposes

The converse may happen. For example, a trustee may receive income in the form of a tax repayment supplement that is exempt. This will still constitute income for trust law purposes and the life tenant will generally be entitled to receive the full amount, but it is not taxable income of the beneficiary.

The treatment of dividends arising from demergers (see 9.8.8) also gave rise to concern, but a test case involving the ICI demerger established that such receipts by trustees were generally capital rather than income from the point of view of trust law, so in this particular case the treatment for trust law and taxation will normally be the same. It is important to take professional advice where significant sums of money are involved as HMRC distinguishes between different types of demergers.

31.4.10 Capital gains tax

Capital gains realised by UK resident trustees are taxed at 28% (unless ER is due). No further CGT (or income tax) liability normally arises on the trustees distributing cash to a beneficiary after they had realised a capital gain by selling an asset. Since 23 June 2010, trust gains have been chargeable at a flat rate of 28% (subject to the availability of ER).

31.4.11 Exemption for property occupied by a beneficiary

(s 225 TCGA 1992)

There is an exemption for trustees in respect of a property owned by them, but occupied by a beneficiary as his or her main residence (provided he or she is entitled to do so under the terms of the trust deed). The beneficiary may not also claim exemption for a property owned by him or her personally. Where an individual has more than one residence, and it is desired to elect that a property owned by trustees be treated as his or her main residence, a joint notice must be given by the trustees and that individual.

Anti-avoidance legislation, which came into force from December 2003 (see 33.14), restricts main residence exemption where hold-over relief has been claimed on the transfer of the property to the trust.

31.4.12 Disposals of business assets

ER may be claimed for gains arising from the sale of an interest in an unincorporated business or from the sale of shares in the eligible beneficiary's personal company. ER may also be claimed on gains arising from disposals of assets used by the business/personal company where the disposal is associated with a disposal of an interest in an unincorporated business or of shares in the beneficiary's personal company. (See further at 31.2.3.)

31.4.13 Liability may also arise on deemed disposals

A capital gain may arise on a deemed disposal such as where the trustees distribute assets to a beneficiary, or where a beneficiary becomes absolutely entitled to capital under the terms of a trust. Hold-over relief is only available in a pre-22 March 2006 (or other 'qualifying') fixed interest trust if the disposal involves business property (see 17.4).

31.4.14 Transfer of capital losses to a trust beneficiary

Where a beneficiary becomes absolutely entitled to settled property, losses realised in the past by the trustees do not pass across. Furthermore, if a loss arises for the trustees on an asset passing across to the beneficiary, he or she may use this only against a capital gain that he or she may subsequently realise on a disposal of that asset.

31.4.15 Death of the life tenant

(s 73 TCGA 1992)

There is one type of deemed disposal that does not give rise to a CGT charge. Where an interest in possession ceases on a death, the assets are treated as having been disposed of and reacquired at their value at that date, but there is no chargeable gain for the trustees. This does not apply where the trustees hold assets that were subject to a hold-over claim by the settlor at the time he or she transferred the assets to the trustees.

31.4.16 Inheritance tax

(s 49 IHTA 1984)

Where a beneficiary has an interest in possession, and he or she had that interest at 22 March 2006, or it is a transitional serial interest (TSI) or an immediate post-death interest (IPDI) (collectively referred to in this text as 'qualifying' interests in possession), he or she is treated for IHT purposes as if he or she owned the trust capital. On death, the value of the trust capital is brought into account as part of the individual's estate and IHT is charged accordingly. The trustees are, however, responsible for paying the IHT on the proportion of the tax attributable to the trust property.

Example – IHT liability on a pre-22 March 2006 fixed interest trust

A dies on 1 May 2013 owning property in his personal capacity worth £205,000 (this is called his 'free estate') and he was also the life tenant of a trust that had a capital value of £350,000. The total IHT payable is:

	£
Free estate	205,000
Trust	350,000
	555,000
Less: nil rate band for 2013–14	(325,000)
	230,000
IHT thereon at 40%	92,000

IHT is payable as follows:

$$\text{Executors} \; \frac{205{,}000}{555{,}000} \times 92{,}000 = 33{,}982$$

$$\text{Trustees} \; \frac{350{,}000}{555{,}000} \times 92{,}000 = 58{,}018$$

31.4.17 Fixed interest trusts where the interest in possession did not exist at 22 March 2006

FA 2006 introduced a new IHT regime for such trusts (see 31.4.23). An IHT charge will not normally arise on the death of the life tenant but the trustees will be subject to a periodic charge.

31.4.18 Exemption where settled property reverts to settlor

(s 54 IHTA 1984)

The treatment described in 31.4.16 does not apply where the trust assets pass back to the settlor on the death of the life tenant who held his or her interest at 22 March 2006. No IHT charge arises on the property that reverts to the settlor. There is a similar exemption where property reverts to the settlor's spouse or his or her civil partner, but this is conditional on the spouse or civil partner being domiciled in the UK.

For post-22 March 2006 interests, the reverter to settlor exemption only applies if the trust is a disabled person's trust or a TSI and the property reverts to the settlor or his or her spouse or civil partner. If the trust is an IPDI, the exemption may be available if the property reverts to the settlor's UK domiciled spouse.

The reverter to settlor exemption does not apply if the settlor (or his or her spouse or civil partner) has purchased a reversionary interest.

31.4.19 Exempt pre-13 November 1974 Will trusts

(Para 2, Schedule 6 IHTA 1984)

These are trusts created by the Will of a person who died before 13 November 1974 and left property in trust on the following terms:

- his or her surviving spouse was entitled to an interest in possession;
- the surviving spouse was not entitled to demand that the capital should be paid out to him or her.

These trusts are exempt from the normal charge that arises when the surviving spouse's interest in possession comes to an end. The reason for this is that before 13 November 1974, estate duty was levied on an individual's death even if he or she left property in trust for his or her spouse. However, the estate duty legislation then provided an exemption on the death of the surviving spouse and this has been carried over to IHT.

Will trusts that came into being after 12 November 1974 are treated differently because of the exemption that applies for IHT purposes where property passes to a surviving spouse. Property held in a post-12 November 1974 Will trust is subject to IHT on the life tenant's death.

31.4.20 No charge where life tenant of qualifying settlement becomes absolutely entitled to trust property

(s 53(2) IHTA 1984)

There are no IHT implications where a life tenant (or any other beneficiary entitled to an interest in possession) who held his or her interest at 22 March 2006 (or is entitled to a post-22 March 2006 qualifying life interest) becomes absolutely entitled to the trust property. This is because the beneficiary is already regarded for IHT purposes as if he or she owns the capital concerned. All that has happened is that the beneficiary's interest has been enlarged and, while this may have CGT consequences, it does not give rise to an IHT charge.

Prior to 12 March 2008, no tax charge arose where a person's qualifying interest in possession ended and he or she became entitled to another interest in possession in the trust property, so long as the new interest was in the whole of the capital in which the first interest subsisted. From 12 March 2008, this exemption is restricted so that it only applies where the individual's new interest is a disabled person's interest or a transitional serial interest, ie in very limited circumstances.

Tax notes

There are no IHT implications where a life tenant who held his or her interest at 22 March 2006 (or is entitled to a post-22 March 2006 qualifying life interest) becomes absolutely entitled to the trust property because he or she is already regarded for IHT purposes as owning the capital concerned. However, if the value of the new interest is less than the value of the old interest (for instance, if a beneficiary with an entitlement to the whole of the income from a £1m fund becomes absolutely entitled to £500,000 of capital on attaining (say) age 35, with another beneficiary gaining absolute entitlement to the remaining £500,000) then tax will be chargeable on the difference.

31.4.21 If interest in possession ends during a person's lifetime

(ss 3A, 23 and 52 IHTA 1984)

Where a beneficiary's interest in possession comes to an end during his or her lifetime, and it was either a qualifying interest in possession (an IPDI, TSI or disabled person's interest) *or* was an interest within s 5(1B) (ie an IIP to which a UK domiciled individual became beneficially entitled on or after 9 December 2009 as a result of a disposition within s 10 IHTA) and he or she does not personally become entitled to the trust property, he or she is treated as making a transfer of value. The transfer is normally either a PET (see 30.6) or a chargeable lifetime transfer (CLT), according to what happens as a result of the interest in possession coming to an end. If, however, an individual's spouse or civil partner becomes absolutely entitled on the termination of his or her interest in possession, the transfer will normally be an exempt transfer because of the spouse exemption (see 30.5.1).

Section 5(1B) was inserted by s 53 FA (No.1) 2010 as an anti-avoidance provision to prevent planning whereby an individual *A,* paid the settlor full value to create the settlement (so that s 10 applied and neither the settlor nor the life tenant had made a transfer of value) with a life interest to *A* and remainder to *B* (a family member). *B* would also have had to pay full value for his or her interest and then the trust capital could have passed to *B* tax free on *A*'s death. Section 5(1B) prevents this from working by treating such interests owned by UK domiciliaries as qualifying interests in possession, which means that the value of the trust fund would be treated as forming part of *A*'s estate on his or her death, with IHT charges arising accordingly.

Until 5 October 2008, spouse exemption was also available if the spouse or civil partner acquired an interest in possession following the lifetime termination of a pre-22 March 2006 interest in possession, as opposed to acquiring the trust property absolutely. The interest thus created was a TSI and the trust property will be treated as being part of the spouse or civil partner's estate on his or her death.

Potentially exempt transfers (PETs)

If the effect of the beneficiary's interest coming to an end is that:

- another individual becomes entitled to an interest in possession; or
- another person becomes absolutely entitled to the trust property; or
- the trust becomes a disabled person's trust, or
- the trust becomes a trust for a bereaved minor when an IPDI ends,

then the person whose interest in possession has terminated is treated as having made a PET. In such instances, IHT is charged if (and only if) the person dies within the following seven years. If this should happen, the trustees are liable to pay the IHT unless the settled property passes to a beneficiary through his or her becoming absolutely entitled on the termination of the interest in possession. In such a situation the person who becomes absolutely entitled is liable to pay any such IHT.

Exempt transfers

Occasionally, the effect of a person's interest in possession coming to an end is that his or her spouse becomes entitled to an interest in possession. Where this happens, the person whose interest in possession has come to an end is treated as having made an exempt transfer. This treatment also applies if a trust becomes a charitable trust as a result of a beneficiary's interest in possession coming to an end.

Chargeable lifetime transfers (CLTs)

Where a person's interest in possession comes to an end and the trust thereby becomes a relevant property trust, he or she is treated as having made a CLT. If his or her cumulative CLTs bring him or her over the nil rate band, IHT is payable right away at the lifetime rate of 20%. If he or she should then die within three years, the rate increases to 40% (see 30.11); with tapering if death occurs in years four to seven.

31.4.22 How a transfer of value is computed on lifetime transfers

The legislation contains an anomaly. Where an individual makes a gift in his or her personal capacity, the transfer of value is deemed to be the amount by which his or her estate is reduced in value (see 30.6.2). This rule does not apply where a person's interest in possession comes to an end because, in this case, the amount of the transfer of value is taken as the value of the property in which the interest in possession has terminated.

Example – Calculation of value of lifetime transfer

B owns 90% of a company in his personal capacity and is the life tenant of a trust that owns the remaining 10%. The value of a 100% shareholding in the company is worth £500,000. The value of a 90% shareholding is £450,000, but a 10% shareholding valued in isolation is worth only £20,000. If *B* had made a gift of 10% out of his personal shareholding, his transfer of value would be taken to be:

	£
Value of a 100% shareholding	500,000
Less: value of remaining 90% shareholding (taking his own shares and the trust together)	(450,000)
Reduction in value of his estate	50,000

However, if *B* surrenders his life interest in the trust so that his interest in possession comes to an end, the value transferred is taken as £20,000.

31.4.23 Different regime for fixed interest trusts created after 21 March 2006

FA 2006 introduced a new regime for lifetime trusts where an interest in possession came into existence on or after 22 March 2006. The rules do not apply where before 6 October 2008 a new interest in possession replaced an interest in possession held at 22 March 2006 (see 31.4.24 below).

New fixed interest trusts and existing trusts where an interest in possession has been created on or after 22 March 2006 are normally subject to the IHT regime that was formerly confined to discretionary trusts (see 31.5 below), ie the creation of such a trust will be a CLT for IHT and the trust will be subject to the periodic charge (see 31.5.13) and the exit charge (see 31.5.19). On the other hand, no IHT charge will normally arise on the termination of an interest in possession, whether on death or during the beneficiary's lifetime (contrast the treatment of qualifying trusts and interests within s 5(1B) described in 31.4.21 above).

Where a fixed interest trust is caught by the FA 2006 provisions, there will not be a CGT disposal and re-acquisition at the date of the life tenant's death (see 31.4.15). On the other hand, CGT hold-over relief may be available under s 260 TCGA 1992 (see 31.6.2) when property is put into a UK trust or comes out of the trust to a UK resident beneficiary.

31.4.24 Some situations where the pre-22 March 2006 treatment continues to apply

The regime does not apply where:

- An individual acquired an interest in possession before 6 October 2008 that replaced an interest in possession held by another individual at 22 March 2006 (the previous 5 April 2008 deadline was extended by six months by FA 2008).
- The trust is created as part of arrangements dealing with a relationship breakdown.
- An interest in possession trust was in being at 22 March 2006 to hold life policies and money is only added to the trust by additional premiums being paid.
- The trust is for the benefit of a disabled person (see 31.7 for definition). In this case, the let-out can apply both to lifetime trusts and trusts created on death.
- An individual who is in the early stages of a degenerative disease creates a settlement under which he or she has a life interest.
- A trust is created on death (by Will or intestacy) for the benefit of the deceased's minor child and the child will become absolutely entitled at age 18.
- Life interest trusts are created on death (by Will or intestacy).
- The life tenant is the deceased's widow or widower – spouse exemption is available (see 30.5.1).

31.5 DISCRETIONARY TRUSTS

In contrast to a fixed interest trust, a discretionary trust is one where the trustees can control the way in which income and capital are used. In most cases, the trustees have power to accumulate income, in which case it may be retained by them either with a view to its being paid out in later years or as an addition to the trust capital.

In other cases, the trustees have no legal right to accumulate income, but the trust is regarded as discretionary because no beneficiary has a fixed entitlement (ie the trustees must distribute the income, but they can choose how it is distributed and which particular beneficiary should receive it).

31.5.1 Special tax treatment for certain trusts

The following analysis is on the basis that the settlor and spouse are excluded from benefiting under the settlement. The tax treatment where a settlor can benefit is covered in more detail at 33.15 but it should be noted that trustees of discretionary trusts are currently liable for 45% tax on non-dividend income, and 37.5% tax on dividend income (subject to the £1,000 nil rate band).

If the settlor is able to reclaim tax, because of allowances or reliefs he or she would otherwise not have been able to access, or because his or her effective tax rate is lower than that of the trustees, the repayment belongs to the trustees. Currently, a settlor has a right to reclaim tax due to be paid on trust income from the trustees but conversely, if he or she receives a repayment of tax in respect of an 'allowance or relief' in relation to trust income, this must be repaid to the trustees. Section 7 FA (No.3) 2010 amends s 646 ITTOIA 2005 so that it requires that any tax repayment received by a settlor, in relation to trust income, must be repaid to the trustees, including where the settlor's marginal tax rate is lower than that of the trust, but the Government has confirmed that such payments to the trustees will be disregarded for IHT purposes.

Employee share ownership trusts may be exempt from the rate applicable to trusts (see 31.5.2 below) on certain types of income.

Since 23 June 2010, all onshore trusts have been liable to CGT at a flat rate of 28% (18% between 6 April 2008 and 22 June 2010).

31.5.2 Rate applicable to trusts

(ss 9, 479 ITA 2007)

Subject to the £1,000 basic rate band (see below), trustees of discretionary trusts are liable for tax on income that is not dividend income at 45%. (This is called 'the rate applicable to trusts' although, as we have seen, it is not applicable to all trusts.)

Where part of the trust income is subject to a fixed-interest trust and the balance is held on a discretionary trust, the trust rate is charged only on the income held on discretionary trusts.

Exception for the first £1,000 of trust income (basic rate band)

(ss 491 and 492 ITA 2007)

There is an exception for the first £1,000 of the trustees' income subject to the rate applicable to trusts, which instead is taxable at the basic rate (currently 20%) or the dividend ordinary rate (10%) and only the balance over the threshold is taxed at the rate applicable to trusts. The relief is set against income bearing a higher rate of tax in priority to that bearing a lower rate, so dividends will be treated as the highest part of trust income for these purposes. Any income which is already charged at reduced rates (eg because it is covered by trust expenses) is not included in the first £1,000 for the purpose of this relief. So income which is received net of tax, and falls within this band, does not bear any further tax.

The band is modified if the settlor of the relevant settlement has made one or more other current (ie in existence at the date of measurement) settlements. In that case, references to £1,000 are to be read as references to either £200, or if greater, 'the settlor's threshold amount'. The settlor's threshold amount is the amount calculated by dividing £1,000 by the number of current settlements (including the relevant settlement) made by the settlor. If there is more than one settlor, the fraction of the £1,000 is taken in relation to the settlor who has made the most settlements. The restriction applies irrespective of when the settlements were made or where they may be resident.

Calculation of the tax payable

In most cases, the trustees suffer basic rate tax at source and then pay additional tax to bring the total up to the required amount.

Notional income

Certain types of income are capital profits under trust law, for example:

- premiums treated as rent (see 8.3);
- profits on sale of certificates of deposit (see 10.6);
- gains from disposals of offshore funds (see 10.7).

Income which falls into one of the above categories is still subject to the rate applicable to trusts (ie 45%).

Accrued income scheme

Income taxed under the accrued income scheme is also taxed at the rate applicable to trusts (regardless of whether the trust is a fixed-interest or discretionary trust).

31.5.3 Computing the trustees' liability to the rate applicable to trusts

The trustees' liability for basic and lower rate taxes on income from savings is calculated in exactly the same way as for trustees of fixed interest trusts. A separate computation is then required for the purposes of the rates applicable to trusts (also called the 'special trust rates').

Expenses paid out of net income are 'grossed up' at the appropriate lower or dividend rate and the resulting amount is then deducted. Expenses are allowable expenses if they are expenses of the trustees, properly chargeable to income (ignoring the express terms of the settlement). Examples of such expenses are:

- bank charges;
- interest that does not qualify for tax relief;
- the costs of administering the trust;
- charges made by professional trustees;
- deficits on properties where the deficiency cannot be relieved against other UK property income.

Costs such as premiums on an insurance policy (excluding fire insurance), or property expenses such as the cost of maintenance or insurance of a property or charges made for collecting rents, cannot be included directly as a deduction in computing liability for additional rate tax. Expenses are set off first against basic rate/savings income with any balance being set against dividend income.

Example – Calculating the additional tax on discretionary trusts for 2014–15

A discretionary trust receives income from savings of £15,000 in 2014–15 which has suffered basic rate tax. It has no other income. Expenses that are not allowable in computing income for basic rate tax purposes, but are properly chargeable to income, amount to £960. The trustees' liability for tax at the trust rate for 2014–15 is computed as follows:

	£
Income from savings	15,000
Less: expenses – grossed up: £960 $\times$ $^{100}/_{80}$	(1,200)
	13,800
Less amount not subject to the rate applicable to trusts	(1,000)
	12,800
Tax charged at trust rate (45%) (before deducting basic rate tax)	5,760

31.5.4 Special rate on dividend income

Trustees of discretionary trusts are taxed on dividend income at 37.5%. Dividends received from UK companies carry a 10% tax credit.

Example – Calculating the additional tax on dividend income for 2014–15

A discretionary trust receives cash dividend income of £9,000 in a tax year. The trustees' tax liability on that income is computed is follows:

	£
Cash dividend received	9,000
Tax credit (10/90)	1,000
Taxable income	10,000
Rate applicable to trusts (37.5%)	3,750
Less: tax credit	(1,000)
Tax payable	2,750

Furthermore, when the trustees distribute income to beneficiaries, they will be required to pay additional tax unless the distribution can be shown to have come out of a 'pool' that has suffered the rate applicable to trusts.

Example – Situation where dividend income distributed between beneficiaries

In the above example, the trustees had dividend income of £9,000 on which they paid tax of £2,750, leaving them with £6,250. If they distribute the whole of this income to the beneficiaries, the trustees will have to pay further tax. The calculation is complicated and is as follows:

	£
Maximum distribution	4,950
Tax thereon (£9,000 × 45%)	4,050
Gross income for beneficiary	900

This income is regarded as having suffered 45% tax. The trustees then pay tax of £1,300 over to HMRC so that they have paid a total of £4,050 ie:

	£
Tax payable on the dividend	2,750
Tax payable on the distribution to bring payment up to tax of 45% of £9,000	1,300
	4,050

Tax Bulletin 71 (June 2004), covers all this in detail (albeit at historic rates), as does HMRC's Trusts manual (www.hmrc.gov.uk/manuals/tsemmanual/TSEM3010.htm).

31.5.5 Income distributions in excess of trustees' taxable income

(ss 493 and 494 ITA 2007)

There may be situations where trustees make distributions in excess of their taxable income. Such distributions also give rise to a liability for the trustees to account for tax at the rate applicable to trusts. There are several situations in which such a liability can arise:

- A trust may have income on which income tax does not have to be paid. If such income is paid out to a beneficiary as an income distribution, the trustees must account for tax at the rate applicable to trusts.
- Similarly, trustees may make a payment of an income nature that is subject to tax as income in the hands of the beneficiary even though it comes out of the trust capital. In practice, HMRC would not normally assess such distributions unless they were made regularly.

If the income is fully distributed each year and foreign securities are held, there will be an additional liability to tax when the foreign income is distributed to beneficiaries. The liability is equal to the credit allowed against basic rate tax for double taxation relief.

31.5.6 Tax returns

One tax return (form SA900) is now completed whether the trust is fixed-interest or discretionary. There are supplementary forms to be completed for various types of income, for capital gains, and where the trust is a non-resident or charitable trust.

> **Tax notes**
>
> HMRC provides a tax calculation guide for trusts and estates, but as the calculation layout is Byzantine in its complexity, the form is generally not used.

Tax deduction certificates

Where payments are made to beneficiaries during a particular tax year, a tax deduction certificate form R185 should be completed by the trustees or their professional advisers, showing the appropriate gross, tax and net figures.

31.5.7 The beneficiary's position

A beneficiary needs to include on his or her tax return the grossed up amount of any income distributed to him or her by the trustees during the tax year. Since the trustees are subject to the additional rate, the beneficiary's income is treated as net of tax withheld at the rate applicable to trusts.

31.5.8 Accumulated income subsequently distributed as capital

A distribution of capital that represents income that has been accumulated is not normally taxable income for the beneficiary. Such a distribution is treated as a capital distribution, although this presupposes that the trustees have power to accumulate income. In cases where they have no such power, any distributions will remain as income.

31.5.9 Capital gains tax

The rate for trustees and personal representatives is 28%.

As with a fixed-interest trust, no further CGT (or income tax) liability will normally arise when trustees of a UK resident trust distribute cash to a beneficiary, after they have realised a capital gain by selling an asset, albeit an IHT liability may arise.

31.5.10 Exemption for property occupied by beneficiary

(s 225 TCGA 1992)

The courts have held that trustees of discretionary trusts are entitled to this exemption where they permit a beneficiary to occupy a property as his or her main residence under the terms of the trust, even though the trust deed did not confer a right for him or her to require the trustees to provide such a property (but see SP 10/79). HMRC will resist allowing this exemption where the trustees do not have a power to allow a beneficiary to occupy a property. However such a power need not be contained in the trust deed, for example it may be a power given to the trustees under the Trustee Act 2000. The anti-avoidance provisions in ss 169B–169G TCGA 1992 may apply where hold-over relief is claimed on a transfer of a property to the trustees (see 33.15).

31.5.11 Entrepreneurs' relief

This relief is not available to trustees of discretionary settlements unless there is an interest in possession in part of the trust property, in which case the rules for such interests will apply in relation to that part of the fund.

31.5.12 Deemed disposals/hold-over relief

(s 71 TCGA 1992)

A capital gain may arise on a deemed disposal such as where the trustees distribute assets to a beneficiary, or where a beneficiary becomes absolutely entitled to capital under the terms of a trust. Hold-over relief is normally available under s 260 TCGA 1992 where a disposal of the property arises on a capital distribution to a UK resident beneficiary (see 13.6 on s 260 relief).

31.5.13 Inheritance tax

(ss 64 and 65 IHTA 1984)

By definition, no beneficiary has an interest in possession in a discretionary trust and it follows that the trust capital is not treated as forming part of his or her estate. Therefore, no IHT charge arises on his or her death.

To make up for the absence of such a charge, the legislation imposes a lower charge every ten years (the periodic charge). The theory is that a generation is approximately 30 years and the tax charged on three separate occasions by reason of the periodic charge will approximate to the tax payable on property passing down to the next generation.

There is also an exit charge that applies where property leaves a discretionary trust. Until 22 March 2006, the exit charge also arose if the trust became a fixed interest trust. There are different rules for discretionary trusts created before and after 26 March 1974.

31.5.14 Trusts created after 26 March 1974

Periodic charge (ss 64–69 IHTA 1984)

The periodic charge arises on the tenth anniversary of the creation of the trust and on every subsequent tenth anniversary. The maximum rate is currently 6% (ie 0.6% pa), computed as follows:

Tax payable at lifetime rate (20%) × 30%.

The computation is actually more complex and involves the following process:

Amount of CLTs made by settlor in the seven years prior to creation of the trust	A
Value of trust property at tenth anniversary	B
Add A and B	C
Deduct nil rate band at date of charge	(D)
	E

The next step is to compute the IHT payable on E and on A – D. The tax payable by the trustees on the periodic charge is 30% of the difference.

Example – Periodic charge

C created a discretionary trust in June 2005. She had previously made CLTs of £194,000. In June 2015 the trust is worth £160,000. The periodic charge is therefore computed as follows:

		£
Amount of previous CLTs	(A)	194,000
Value of trust property in June 2015	(B)	160,000
	(C)	354,000
Deduct 2015–16 nil rate band	(D)	325,000
	(E)	29,000
IHT on E		5,800
Less: IHT at lifetime rates on A–D		Nil
		5,800

The periodic charge is 30% of £5,800, ie £1,740.

31.5.15 Trusts created before 26 March 1974

This type of trust is simpler in that there cannot have been any CLTs made by the settlor before the creation of the trust. The computation is therefore:

Value of trust property at tenth anniversary	X
Deduct nil rate band	(Y)
	Z
IHT at lifetime rates on Z	w

The periodic charge is 30% of this amount.

31.5.16 Position where trustees have made capital distributions during the preceding ten years

Where the trustees have made a capital distribution within the previous ten years or property has otherwise ceased to be held upon discretionary trusts (eg by reason of a beneficiary becoming entitled to an interest in possession), the capital distribution value must also be brought into account in arriving at the periodic charge. The computation is as follows:

The sum of any CLTs made by the settlor in the seven years prior to creation of the trust and capital distributions since last periodic charge	A
Value of trust property at tenth anniversary	B
Add A and B	C
Deduct current nil rate band	(D)
	E

The next step is to compute the IHT payable on E and on A – D. The tax payable by the trustees on the period charge is 30% of the difference.

31.5.17 Treatment of undistributed income

HMRC accepts that undistributed income that has not been accumulated should be excluded in arriving at the value of the trust capital at the tenth anniversary. The reason for this is that such income remains income held for the benefit of beneficiaries and is not capital.

Where income has been formally accumulated, it must be brought into account for the purposes of the periodic charge. However, such accumulated income is treated as if it were additional capital added to the trust at the date the trustees resolved to accumulate it.

31.5.18 The exit charge (also known as the 'proportionate charge')

The way in which the exit charge is computed varies according to whether capital leaves a discretionary trust within the first ten years or only after there has been a periodic charge.

31.5.19 Exit charge during first ten years

(s 68 IHTA 1984)

The position here is that a notional rate of tax should be computed. This is the average rate of IHT that would have been payable had the settlor made a CLT at the time he or she created the trust equal to the trust property's value at that time.

Example – Exit charge during the first ten years

> D created a trust in February 2005 and the original trust property was worth £500,000. A capital distribution is made in December 2014. The notional entry charge would be computed as follows:
>
> | | £ |
> |---|---|
> | Value of trust property in February 2005 | 500,000 |
> | *Less:* nil rate band at time of distribution | (325,000) |
> | | 175,000 |
> | £175,000 at 20% = | £35,000 |
>
> $$\text{Effective rate} = \frac{35,000}{500,000} = 7\%$$

The recalculated entry charge would therefore be taken as 7% and the tax payable is a proportion of this rate. The proportion is determined by the number of complete quarters during which the property has been relevant property before ceasing to be so. In this case, the exit charge occurred after the trust had existed for nine years and eight months, the charge would therefore be at the rate of:

$$7\% \times \frac{39}{40} \times 30\% = 2.0475\%$$

31.5.20 Exit charge after a periodic charge

(s 69 IHTA 1984)

The position here is that the charge applies only to the property that leaves the discretionary trust, with the proportion being determined by the following formula:

$$\frac{\text{Number of complete quarters since the last periodic charge}}{40}$$

A distribution during the first quarter following the ten-year charge is entirely free of IHT. The tax rate charged is normally fixed by the effective rate charged on the previous periodic charge. Once again, however, the effective rate is calculated by using the rates (including the nil rate band) in force at the time the exit charge arises. Thus, the notional effective rate may be slightly lower than the effective rate of IHT that actually applied on the last periodic charge.

31.6 ACCUMULATION AND MAINTENANCE TRUSTS

(ss 71, 71A–71H IHTA 1984)

An accumulation and maintenance trust is a special form of discretionary trust that has been set up for a stated class of beneficiaries. The following conditions needed to be satisfied up to 22 March 2006:

(1) One or more beneficiaries would become entitled to an interest in possession in the trust property on attaining a specified age that could not exceed age 25.
(2) Until one of the beneficiaries became beneficially entitled, the trust income had to be held on a discretionary basis with income

being applied only for the maintenance, education or benefit of the beneficiaries or accumulated for their benefit.

(3) The trust could have a life of not more than 25 years or it had to be a trust for the benefit of grandchildren of a common grandparent.

From 22 March 2006, a trust can normally be an accumulation and maintenance trust only if the trust existed at 21 March 2006 and the beneficiaries will become absolutely entitled to the settled property at age 18. The trustees had until 5 April 2008 to vary an existing trust so that it satisfied this condition. If the trust is a Will trust for bereaved minor children of the deceased (s 71A IHTA 1984), it can qualify as a favoured trust provided that the beneficiaries will become absolutely entitled by the time they attain age 18. Grandparents can no longer settle tax favoured accumulation settlements for their grandchildren.

'18–25' (s 71D IHTA 1984) trusts provide a half-way house for families concerned that children should not have access to capital at age 18. It is possible to restrict access to capital until age 25, but with an IHT cost (maximum 4.2%) between ages 18 and 25.

If existing accumulation and maintenance settlements were not varied before 6 April 2008, and did not fall within either the s 71A or s 71D rules, then they will have become relevant property (ie discretionary) trusts on that date.

31.6.1 Taxation

The same rules apply, and the same returns and certificates need to be completed, for income tax and CGT as for discretionary trusts. There are, however, different rules for CGT hold-over relief and IHT.

31.6.2 Hold-over relief for trustees

(s 260 TCGA 1992)

Where trustees dispose of assets to a beneficiary, there may be a CGT charge. Section 260 hold-over relief will now generally be available. There is however an anomaly where the trustees hold indivisible assets: the case of *Crowe* v *Appleby* concerned a situation where beneficiaries became entitled to an undivided share in trust property on the deaths of the initial beneficiaries. The Court of Appeal decided that since the trust fund was realty, the beneficiaries could not direct the trustees how to deal with it nor could they call for the immediate payment of their respective shares or interfere with the due exercise by the trustees of their power to postpone sale, and thus could not be said to have become absolutely entitled to their shares. This is thought also to be the case where the trustees hold other indivisible assets, such as paintings or antiques or shares in private companies.

The principle in *Crowe* v *Appleby* has been applied in connection with the Schedule 20, FA 2006 trust changes to deny holdover where for instance there are several minor beneficiaries, who each become absolutely entitled to their share of the trust assets on reaching (say) the age of 18. For CGT purposes only, where a trust fund consists of land held in undivided shares under a single settlement, and those shares vest absolutely in different beneficiaries on different dates, none of the beneficiaries becomes absolutely entitled for CGT purposes to his or her share until all the shares have vested absolutely, except where there is an earlier sale of the land or earlier appropriation of specific property to an absolutely vested share. The rule in *Crowe* v *Appleby* does not however apply to IHT, so there is in that circumstance, no coterminous CGT and IHT event on which to claim holdover until the final child attains age 18.

31.6.3 IHT privileges

An accumulation and maintenance, or bereaved minors', trust that satisfies the conditions imposed by FA 2006 (ie the beneficiaries become absolutely entitled on attaining age 18) is not subject to the periodic charge described at 31.5.14. Furthermore, there is no exit charge on a beneficiary becoming entitled to an interest in possession under the trust or becoming absolutely entitled to trust property.

31.6.4 Pre-22 March 2006 trusts which were modified before 6 April 2008

An accumulation and maintenance trust which does not meet these requirements will normally attract an exit charge on the beneficiary becoming absolutely entitled.

Example – An accumulation and maintenance trust coming to an end in 2015

An accumulation and maintenance settlement set up on 5 April 2005 came to an end on 6 April 2015 on the beneficiary attaining age 25. The settlement was worth £400,000.

The basic rate of the exit charge is ascertained as follows:

- Take the tax rate as described in 31.5.15.
- Reduce this rate for the part of the ten-year period ending in April 2015 that falls before 6 April 2008, ie 12/40ths: this reduces the rate on exit to 2.6225%.

Pre-22 March 2006 trusts that do not meet the FA 2006 rules, but were modified prior to 5 April 2008 so that they fall within s 71D IHTA 1984, attract an IHT exit charge when the beneficiaries become absolutely entitled at age 25. However, provided that the beneficiaries become absolutely entitled no later than at age 25, this charge is limited to seven-tenths of the exit charge that would otherwise arise, ie the maximum rate of the exit charge is 4.2%. The charge did not arise at all on beneficiaries who became absolutely entitled before 6 April 2008, and only took effect from 6 April 2008, meaning that beneficiaries between 18 and 25 years old at that time would not incur the full seven years' charge. For example, *L* is the beneficiary of an '18–25' trust set up in 2006. She was 21 on 26 March 2009, and became entitled to trust capital on attaining age 25 on 26 March 2013. The IHT charge only applied between 6 April 2009 and 26 March 2013, ie for 15 complete quarters and so will be a maximum 2.25%.

31.7 TRUSTS FOR THE DISABLED

(Schedule 1 TCGA 1992; ss 74 and 89, 89A, 89B IHTA 1984)

A trust for a disabled person is a type of discretionary trust that enjoys certain tax privileges. The trustees are entitled to the full CGT exemption that applies for individuals and there is no liability for IHT periodic and exit charges.

Under ss 89 and 89A there is special treatment for trusts for disabled people, where there is no interest in possession (IIP), but which meet certain income and capital conditions (not the same as s 34 FA 2005 dealing with 'vulnerable beneficiaries'). Where the conditions are met, the disabled beneficiary is deemed to have an IIP. The test is the condition of the disabled person when the property is settled.

Section 89A extends this to self-settlements where the disabled person can satisfy HMRC that he or she has a condition likely to lead to serious disability. Broadly speaking the trusts must ensure that during his or her lifetime, the disabled person is the only beneficiary able to receive benefits from the trust; ie the conditions are narrower than those of s 89.

Sections 89(5) and (6) extended the definition of disabled person with regarded to property provided after 22 March 2006 to persons who would be entitled to the statutory allowances but for being in certain accommodation or being not resident in the UK.

Section 89B defines a 'disabled person's interest' as including not merely the deemed IIP in ss 89 and 89A, but also where a severely disabled person becomes beneficially entitled to an actual IIP on or after 22 March 2006. It is also considered to extend to actual IIPs where the trust would meet the tests but for the existence of the IIP. Where an actual IIP subsists, s 72 TCGA 1992 also applies, giving a tax-free uplift on the death of the beneficiary.

A disabled person is one who, at the time the trust was created, was:

- incapable by reason of mental disorder within the meaning of the Mental Health Act 1983 of administering his or her property or managing his or her affairs; or
- in receipt of an attendance allowance under s 64 Social Security Contributions and Benefits Act 1992; or
- in receipt of a disability living allowance under s 71 of the 1992 Act.

The two conditions that need to be satisfied are as follows:

- not less than half of the property within the trust should be applied for the benefit of the beneficiary concerned; and
- the person should be entitled to not less than 50% of the income arising from the trust property (this condition is regarded as satisfied where the trust provides that no income may be applied for the benefit of any other person).

Income is deemed to be applied for the benefit of a person where it is held by the trustees for that person on protective trusts.

31.8 PROTECTIVE TRUSTS

(s 88 IHTA 1984)

This is a term under s 33 Trustee Act 1925. A protective trust is one under which a person (known as the principal beneficiary) is entitled to an IIP in the trust unless he or she forfeits his or her interest, for example, by assigning it or by becoming bankrupt. Protective trusts are normally worded so that if a principal beneficiary forfeits his or her interest, the trust property is held on discretionary trusts for a class of beneficiaries that includes the principal beneficiary.

31.8.1 IHT position where principal beneficiary dies

The periodic charge does not apply while property is held on protective trusts just because the principal beneficiary has forfeited his or her interest under a trust where he or she had an interest in possession before 22 March 2006 or which met one of the conditions set out in 31.4.24. However, an IHT charge arises on the beneficiary's death. The charge varies according to whether he or she forfeited his or her interest before or after 12 April 1978. Where the interest was forfeited before 12 April 1978, the calculation of the tax on his or her eventual death was governed by ss 70(3)–70(10) IHTA 1984.

Where the interest is forfeited after that date, the trustees are subject to a charge on the principal beneficiary's death as if he or she had an interest in possession at the date of his or her death.

31.9 TRUSTS FOR THE MOST VULNERABLE

(ss 34 and 35 FA 2005)

This special tax regime has applied since 6 April 2004.
   A trust can qualify for this treatment only if it has either:

- a disabled beneficiary and; if any of the property is applied:
- for the benefit of a beneficiary, it is applied: for the benefit of the disabled person, and either:
  - the disabled person is entitled to all the income (if there is any) arising from the trust property or
  - no such income may be applied for the benefit of any other person; or
- it has beneficiaries who are under 18 and have lost at least one of their parents, or who are incapable of managing their affairs because of mental disorder, or who are in receipt of attendance allowance or of a disability living allowance at the middle or highest rate.

The trustees must make an election (by 31 January 2016 for 2013–14). Once the election has been made, it applies until the beneficiary ceases to be a vulnerable person (eg by attaining age 18), or the trustees no longer hold the settled property for the benefit of that individual, or the trust is wound-up. The broad effect of the relief is that the tax on the trustees' income and gains is limited to the tax that would have been payable if those income and gains had been personal income and gains of the vulnerable person.

31.10 CHARITABLE TRUSTS

Provided property is held for charitable purposes only, income and capital gains received by the trustees are normally exempt from tax.

Exemption from income tax

(Part 10 ITA 2007)

There is total exemption from income tax for all income other than trading profits. The exemption is dependent on income being applied for charitable purposes.

Exemption from CGT

(s 256 TCGA 1992)

There is also total exemption from CGT provided the charitable trust applies the capital gains for charitable purposes.

31.10.1 Application for charitable purposes

(s 540 ITA 2007)

A charity's exemption from tax may be restricted where income is not applied for charitable purposes. A charitable trust's non-exempt amount for any tax year is the lesser of its 'non-charitable expenditure' for that year; and its 'attributable income and gains'. This is the sum of the income for the tax year which would otherwise be exempt from income tax as a result of any exemptions and the capital gains which would otherwise be exempt under s 256 TCGA 1992.

'Qualifying expenditure' for these purposes means expenditure actually made during the year for charitable purposes and commitments for such expenditure entered into during the year.

Payments made to bodies outside the UK count as qualifying expenditure only to the extent that the charity can show that it has taken such steps that are reasonable in the circumstances to ensure the payments will be applied for charitable purposes. Expenditure for charitable purposes also includes reasonable administrative and fund-raising expenses.

Non-qualifying expenditure includes, for example, political activities, trading expenses and excessive administration costs. Furthermore, the legislation specifically mentions certain types of investments or loans that are to be regarded as not being qualifying expenditure. This is intended to catch investments in a company controlled by a connected person (eg the settlor) or loans to such a company. Indirect arrangements may also be caught such as where a charity makes loans or investments used as security for borrowings by a connected person. Where a charitable trust makes a payment to another connected charitable trust, this does not count as application of the income for charitable purposes unless the trust that receives the payment actually applies it for charitable purposes.

31.10.2 IHT position

Property held on charitable trusts is exempt from periodic and exit charges. If the property is held on temporary charitable trusts, a charge arises on those charitable trusts coming to an end with tax being charged under s 70 IHTA 1984.

31.11 MISCELLANEOUS ASPECTS

31.11.1 Trusts with sub funds

Where a trust has a number of separate sub funds, it may be possible for the trustees to elect that a sub fund should be treated as if it were a separate trust. This could be advantageous if a sub fund has trustees who are not resident in the UK. It is necessary that the sub fund's beneficiaries are not beneficiaries under the rest of the trust. An election will need to be made by 31 January 2015 for a sub fund to be treated as a separate trust for 2012–13. Making the election will mean that the trust will be treated as if it had made a CGT disposal of the assets held within the sub fund on the first day of the year in which the election takes effect.

31.11.2 Trust management expenses (TMEs)

HMRC has published a statement of practice, which indicates that many expenses incurred by trustees should be charged against capital rather than income. HMRC guidance on TMEs was issued on 31 January 2006 and is incorporated into the trusts manual at TSEM8000–8920. The professional bodies raised a number of issues with the guidance and some aspects were called into question by *Trustees of the Peter Clay Discretionary Trust* v *HMRC*. As a result, HMRC has had to substantially rewrite its guidance in the TSEM (see update on 31 March 2011 and www.hmrc.gov.uk/trusts/income-tax/reliefs-deductions.htm – also the tax return helpsheet HS392).

31.12 EXECUTORS AND PERSONAL REPRESENTATIVES

31.12.1 Being a personal representative

When a person dies leaving a valid Will, his or her assets vest in his or her executors. If he or she does not leave a Will, and so dies intestate, it is normally necessary for letters of administration to be obtained and the person who acts in this way (the 'administrator' or 'administratrix' if female) is treated for most legal purposes as if he or she or she were an executor. The term 'personal representative' covers both executors and administrators.

Personal representatives (PRs) of a deceased person are treated as a single body of persons so that there is no tax implication if an executor retires or dies. The estate is treated as a single entity for tax purposes. You may find it useful to access HMRC's guide dealing with a number of issues for the newly bereaved at www.hmrc.gov.uk/bereavement/index.htm. Also, see the Capital Taxes Office's glossary (www.hmrc.gov.uk/cto/glossary.htm).

See 31.12.7 where the deceased was not domiciled in the UK, or was not resident in the UK, at the date of death.

Tax notes

HMRC publishes a useful guide for the newly bereaved on its website at www.hmrc.gov.uk/bereavement/index.htm. There is also an online glossary at www.hmrc.gov.uk/cto/glossary.htm.

31.12.2 Income tax

(s 40 TMA 1970)

The deceased's PRs are liable to pay tax on income received by the deceased up to the date of his or her death.

The tax is assessed in exactly the same way as if the individual were still alive, ie all the normal allowances and reliefs are due. The only difference is that the PRs are responsible for settling the tax (they are also entitled to any repayments). PRs are subject to the normal time limits, ie four years after the end of the tax year concerned.

Quite separately, PRs are also charged to tax on income received by them following the death. No personal allowances are given. During the administration period, dividends are taxed at 10%, and other income at the basic rate. There is no higher rate or RAT liability for the PRs. Although there are instances where income has to be apportioned pre- and post-death for legal purposes, for tax purposes any income received after a person's death is treated as income of the estate.

Where assets devolve on trust, under the terms of the Will, the executors become trustees upon the completion of the administration period. Depending on the type of trust, the trustees may become chargeable to additional rate income tax first on the balance of accumulated income at that date and secondly on receipt of subsequent income. There is no date fixed by law to determine the completion of the administration period, but it is generally agreed that it is the date on which the residue is ascertained.

31.12.3 Beneficiary's position

(Chapter 6, Part 6 ITTOIA 2005)

A beneficiary of a Will may receive an annuity. This income is taxable for the year in which it is payable unless, as a matter of fact, the annuity is paid out of capital in which case it is income for the year in which it is paid. Beneficiaries of specific legacies are normally entitled from the date of death to the income that arises on the property they have inherited. Other beneficiaries will be entitled to the residue, either through a limited interest (eg a life tenant entitled to income arising from the residuary estate) or by an absolute entitlement. During the administration period, sums paid to a beneficiary are normally treated as income for the year of payment.

Where income that has accrued to the date of death is treated as capital of the estate for IHT purposes and as residuary income, there is higher rate tax relief available to beneficiaries. (See SA107, page TN5 'special situations'.)

31.12.4 **Capital gains tax**

(ss 3, 62 TCGA 1992)

PRs are liable at 28%. They are entitled to the full annual exemption due to an individual for the year of death and the following two tax years.

In computing capital gains, assets held by the deceased at the date of his or her death are deemed to be acquired by the PRs at their market value at that date (the probate value). The probate value may need to be adjusted where securities are sold at a loss within 12 months of the death and relief from IHT has been claimed (see 30.11.3). A similar rule applies where land is sold within four years of death at a loss and the sale proceeds are substituted for the probate value. Assets transferred to beneficiaries, either during the course of or on the completion of the administration period of an estate, do not give rise to a chargeable gain because the beneficiary is regarded as having acquired the asset him or herself, at the date of the person's death and at the probate value.

Certain expenses incurred by the PRs in establishing legal title to assets are allowed in computing gains on the sale of the assets (see SP2/04).

The PRs of an estate in the course of administration are not entitled to an annual exemption if they realise capital gains after two full tax years have elapsed since the date of death. If, however, upon completion of the administration period, the assets devolve upon a Will trust, the trustees will then become entitled to their own CGT exemption.

Losses made by the PRs during the administration period, and not used, are not available to be transferred to residuary beneficiaries with absolute interests or trustees of a trust established by the Will that takes effect on the administration of the estate being completed.

31.12.5 **Property owned by the estate, but used by beneficiary as main residence**

HMRC treats the beneficiary's main residence exemption (see 31.4.11) as applying where PRs dispose of a property that has been used by a beneficiary of the estate as his or her only or main residence both before and after the deceased's death and he or she is entitled to at least 75% of the proceeds when the estate has been administered (see ESC D5 and HMRC capital gains manual, CG65470).

31.12.6 **Deeds of variation**

Where the terms of a Will have been varied by a deed of variation (also known as a deed of family arrangement), there are important consequences so far as IHT is concerned (see 30.4.6). Basically, the revised way in which property passes to beneficiaries is read back into the Will and effectively treated as something done by the testator so far as

IHT is concerned. However, the House of Lords held in *Marshall* v *Kerr* [1994] STC 813 that where the variation creates a trust, the person(s) who relinquish their original entitlement under the Will are treated as the settlor(s) for CGT purposes.

The income tax treatment is also less favourable than the IHT treatment. Even where the deed specifically provides that all income is to be paid to a beneficiary named in the deed, this has no effect for income tax purposes for income that arose before the deed's execution. If payments have been made to the original beneficiary or beneficiaries named in the Will, they remain liable for any higher rate tax on such income that arose at a time when they were entitled to it. Furthermore, a person who gives up an entitlement under a Will by executing such a deed is treated as a settlor for income tax purposes.

Section 472 ITA 2007 and s 68C TCGA 1992 put the income tax and CGT position described above onto a statutory basis.

Tax notes

A person who gives up an entitlement under a Will by executing a deed of variation is treated as a settlor for income tax and CGT purposes.

31.12.7 Acting as a personal representative for a foreign person

(s 834 ITA 2007 and s 62(3) TCGA 1992)

The fact that one or more of the PRs is UK resident can mean that the estate is subject to UK tax. However, they are not subject to income tax on non-UK income if the deceased person was not domiciled in the UK. Furthermore, they are not subject to capital gains tax if the deceased was neither resident nor ordinarily resident in the UK at the date of death (except to the extent that capital gains are realised from disposals of UK assets that had been used in a trade which the deceased had carried on in this country). Even where neither of these exemptions applies, the PRs may not be regarded as UK resident where the deceased was not resident, ordinarily resident or domiciled in the UK at the time of his or her death.

31.13 SOME PLANNING POINTS

The following are just some of the important tax planning points that arise regularly in relation to trusts and estates.

31.13.1 Settlor-interested trusts

Would there be a significant income tax saving if steps were taken to ensure that the trust was no longer regarded as a settlor-interested trust? It might be, for example, that the trust deed provides for income to be paid to *A* but that income is treated as taxable income of the settlor (*B*) because he or she has a reversionary interest. If *A* is not subject to higher rate tax, there would be an immediate saving if the trust were varied or *B* took some other action to disclaim his or her reversionary interest (eg he or she could settle that reversionary interest on trust for his or her adult children).

31.13.2 Is it better to create a discretionary or a fixed interest trust?

It all depends! A discretionary trust has often been more appropriate where there are elderly beneficiaries as the settled property does not form part of their estate on death. The IHT exposure under the regime for discretionary trusts (see 31.5.13–31.5.20) has always been much less than it would be for a fixed interest trust. The differences are now less given the changes brought about by FA 2006 and where the fixed interest trust was created on or after 22 March 2006, the IHT treatment will now generally be the same as that which applies to a discretionary trust (see 31.4.23). For new trusts, the deciding factors are really the settlor's wish (or otherwise) to provide a beneficiary with a fixed right to income.

The CGT position is that the settlor can generally secure hold-over relief (see 13.6) for gains on transferring assets to the trustees of most fixed interest trusts created on or after 22 March 2006 and discretionary settlements. Exceptions where hold-over relief is not available are where a fixed interest trust is not caught by the FA 2006 changes (see 31.4.24) or where the trust is a settlor-interested trust or the trust is not resident in the UK.

From an income tax point of view, the position is largely neutral. A discretionary trust currently pays tax at 45% and 37.5% (see 31.5.2) but, if the trustees make distributions to beneficiaries who are not liable for tax or who are basic rate taxpayers, the beneficiaries can make repayment claims. A fixed interest trust pays income tax at 10% on dividends and at the 20% basic rate on other income but the life tenant has to include this income on his or her tax return and, if he or she is a higher or additional rate taxpayer, pay further tax, which brings the combined tax rate up to 40% or 45% (and 32.5% or 37.5% for dividends).

From the point of view of filling in forms, life is much more straightforward for the trustees of a fixed interest trust.

31.13.3 Would it save tax if a discretionary trust were converted into a fixed interest trust?

From an income tax perspective, the important thing is that income is regularly distributed to beneficiaries who are able to recover some or all of the tax. Creating an interest in possession could have a similar effect in that the trustees would not be required to pay tax at the rate applicable to trusts so that less tax would be withheld in the first place.

Tax notes

Given that the rate of income tax applicable to trusts is 45%, it will probably make sense to convert smaller discretionary trusts into fixed interest trusts ('smaller' in this context meaning a trust with less than £20,000 income).

31.13.4 Should assets be transferred to beneficiaries on a no gain/no loss basis?

This may be a good idea if the beneficiaries are able to use their annual exemptions to cover gains arising on the sale of the assets, or if they can utilise capital losses, or indeed if they plan to retain the assets. However, trustees need to be careful as they can be liable for tax on a held-over gain which becomes a chargeable gain if the beneficiary ceases to be resident (see 13.6).

Entitlement to entrepreneurs' relief (ER) on a subsequent sale by a beneficiary is available only if the beneficiary meets the conditions for ER. Thus in cases where the trustees would qualify for ER but the beneficiaries are not likely to qualify in future, the effect of claiming hold-over relief may be to exchange a 10% tax rate for a 28% rate.

Some thought should be given to the beneficiary's position if his main residence is being transferred to him and a gain arises because the property was previously let as an investment. A hold-over election by the trustees will mean that the beneficiary cannot benefit from main residence exemption on a subsequent sale (see 14.2.1 and 33.14).

31.13.5 Should a UK trust be exported?

Making a UK trust into a non-resident trust can precipitate a CGT exit charge (see 33.17). Also, it may not achieve very much if the settlor is going to be taxed on capital gains made by the non-resident trustees in the future (see 32.15). It may, however, make sense if the settlor has died or is elderly.

31.13.6 Should a discretionary trust be converted into a fixed interest trust before or after the IHT ten-year periodic charge?

It makes no difference. The changes in FA 2006 mean that there will be an exit charge only if capital is distributed outright as opposed to the trustees creating an interest in possession. Where the trustees create an interest in possession on or after 22 March 2006, the trust remains subject to the relevant property regime (see 31.5.13).

31.13.7 Should a discretionary trust make capital distributions before or after the ten-year charge?

There is no general rule here but the way in which the exit charge is computed means that the time that assets cease to be held on discretionary trusts can make a significant difference to the total tax payable (see 31.5.18–31.5.20).

31.13.8 Executors should take care

Suppose that the residuary legatees include a non-resident beneficiary or a charity that is exempt from CGT. If the executors sell a property they will be liable for CGT on any increase in value over probate value and the beneficiaries will receive their share of the amount left after tax. The beneficiaries cannot reclaim that tax. If the executors appropriate the property to the beneficiaries, the executors will have no capital gain. The beneficiaries will then be deemed to have acquired the property at probate value. Any gain on a sale will then be their gain, ie a non-taxable gain if the beneficiary is not subject to CGT.

32

PASSING ON YOUR FAMILY BUSINESS

This chapter contains the following sections:

(1) Basic strategy
(2) Setting up adult children in business
(3) Bringing an adult child into partnership
(4) Bringing an adult child into the family company
(5) Outright gifts of shares
(6) Why trusts are still often a suitable vehicle
(7) Demergers

32.1 BASIC STRATEGY

The most appropriate strategy will depend on your personal circumstances, objectives and the way that your assets are comprised. However, some principles recur time and time again when advising clients:

- The proper use of insurance policies and pension schemes can help to protect the family from any IHT charge that may arise in the short to medium term.
- Maximise the benefit of business property relief (BPR) and the facility to pay tax by instalments. Think twice about taking any action that would jeopardise these valuable reliefs.
- Draw up a Will in the most tax efficient way that is compatible with what the individual wishes to happen to his or her assets on death.
- The individual should take steps to secure his or her financial independence before making any substantial gifts.
- It may be better not to make outright gifts, especially while the individual is still making up his or her mind how to pass on the business. In some cases, the individual may prefer to set up his or her children in business on their own account, possibly by lending them money. In other cases he or she may prefer to bring them into the business as partners.
- Look for ways of making gifts that will not involve substantial CGT liabilities.
- All other things being equal, it is best for the individual to make gifts sooner rather than later, especially if the business is growing in value.
- The individual will generally wish to retain some measure of control.

32.1.1 Proper use of insurance policies and pension schemes

For an individual in his or her 40s, who is still building up a business, it may be advisable to take out substantial joint survivor life insurance, which would pay out on the second death. Such policies should be written in trust so that the proceeds will not form part of the estate (see 30.12.3). Similarly, it will normally be advisable for the death benefits payable under a pension scheme to be subject to discretionary trusts so that they do not form part of the estate and no IHT charge is payable on them. The maximum amount payable as a death in service benefit from a company scheme is generally four times final remuneration and this would provide the family with the necessary liquidity in the event of an untimely death.

32.1.2 Maximise the benefit of BPR

Provided that it has been owned for at least two years, a trading business carried on by an individual as a sole trader or as a partner attracts 100% BPR. This relief is also due on shares in an unquoted trading company. There are also situations where 100% agricultural property relief is due on property that does not qualify for BPR. See 30.8 and 30.9 on BPR and agricultural property relief generally.

There are many situations where these reliefs can be lost or restricted. For example, giving shares in an unquoted trading company to a spouse or civil partner means that the person receiving the shares will have to hold them for two years before he or she qualifies for BPR (the position is different if he or she inherits the shares).

Bear in mind that 50% BPR is available to a controlling shareholder who owns a property that is used by his or her trading company, but no relief is due to minority shareholders. Once again, this rule means that BPR could be lost if a 51% shareholder were to transfer 2% of his or her shares to a spouse or civil partner.

Another potential trap applies if the individual has entered into buy/sell agreements with other shareholders. By entering into such an agreement, BPR may be forfeited because the shares will be subject to a binding contract for sale (see 30.8.1). Cross options are a better way of achieving the same commercial objectives without losing BPR.

Certain businesses do not qualify for either BPR or APR, eg a property investment business (see 30.8.3). However, such a business may still qualify for payment of IHT by instalments over ten years (see 30.11.16).

32.1.3 Draw up a Will in a tax-efficient way

Property left to a spouse or civil partner is exempt from IHT (unless the donor is domiciled in the UK and the donee spouse or civil partner is non-UK domiciled where only the limited £325,000 exemption currently applies). This exemption applies both to property passing to the survivor absolutely and to property left in a Will trust under which he or she has a life interest.

Tax notes

Even if someone forgets to draft a will and dies intestate all is not lost. In HMRC's words: 'You can change a person's will after their death, as long as any beneficiaries left worse off by the changes agree. If there's no will the law decides who inherits. You can make changes to the inheritance in the same way as if there's a will. . . . You can change a will to reduce the amount of inheritance or capital gains tax payable.'

It would make sense from a tax perspective for assets that do not qualify for BPR to be left in a Will in such a way that the spouse/civil partner exemption applies. For example, the individual may have investment properties that do not qualify for BPR. One possibility would be for such assets to be left to the survivor and for him or her to then make gifts to the next generation. These may be outright gifts to individuals or gifts to a trust for bereaved minors given that gifts to other trusts may involve a lifetime IHT charge (see 31.4.23) although gifts that are covered by the survivor's nil rate band are still a viable option. There must be no arrangements or expectation that the survivor will make such gifts (s 29A IHTA 1984). No IHT will be payable on the survivor's death provided he or she does not die within seven years of making the gifts.

Where an individual owns assets that qualify for BPR, such as shares in a family company, it may be more appropriate for them to pass into a discretionary Will trust. This is because the assets will not then form part of the survivor's estate and so be vulnerable to IHT on his or her death if the business assets have been sold and the proceeds reinvested in other assets.

Tax notes

There can even be situations where a family can benefit from BPR twice. In many cases where shares in a family company have been left to a Will trust, it will pay for the survivor to buy the shares from the trustees, perhaps borrowing against other (non-relieved) assets to do so. You should consult a specialist on this but if you can arrange matters properly the survivor will qualify for BPR once he or she has owned the property for two years and the IHT exposure on other assets will be reduced by the borrowings secured against them.

32.1.4 Securing financial independence before making substantial gifts

A person who owns a business or shares in a private trading company would be well advised to create or ensure a separate source of income before giving away part of that business, etc. The creation and funding of a pension scheme should be a priority. Moreover, the fact that the company's profits are reduced by pension contributions may be a helpful factor in agreeing a low value for shares that are subsequently given away by the individual.

32.1.5 Would a loan be a better idea?

When the next generation are still in their 20s, parents may prefer to set them up in business on their own account rather than bringing them into the family firm. This may involve the individual making loans in a personal capacity, which will be entirely appropriate from a personal perspective but not particularly attractive from a tax point of view. Loans will not attract BPR if the lender were to die. Additionally, if the loan goes bad, the lender will not be entitled to income tax relief (but may qualify for CGT relief (see 17.1)).

Another possibility is for the family company to make a loan to the children but this may have income tax or corporation tax consequences (see for example 18.14.2 and s 455 CTA 2010). A half-way house that could work well in the right circumstances would be for the family company to inject working capital by subscribing for preference shares in a company formed by the child to carry on a business venture.

Yet another compromise is for the family company to establish a subsidiary that will carry on the son or daughter's new business. We go into these issues in more detail at 32.2.

32.1.6 Gifts that do not involve CGT

It does not make sense to give away assets to save IHT if the gift creates a substantial liability to CGT at 28%. It is therefore necessary to be selective about what is given to the next generation. There may be certain assets that would not give rise to a substantial CGT charge if given away, perhaps because they have been acquired relatively recently or are not standing at a substantial gain. Alternatively, it may be possible to rely on s 165 hold-over relief to avoid CGT being payable on gifts of business property and shares in unquoted trading companies. See 17.4 on hold-over relief.

32.1.7 Make gifts sooner rather than later

For many people, it is a question of competing priorities. They are anxious not to give away control of the business too early. This is understandable given the way in which the economic climate, personal relationships and the income and capital that they need can change so quickly. On the other hand, the sooner wealth is passed down to the next generation, the greater the potential saving in IHT. One reason for this is the seven-year rule for IHT (see 30.6). Also, in many cases the value of the business is likely to take off (perhaps a stock market flotation is planned in the next two or three years) and the amount taxed on a PET becoming a chargeable transfer on the donor's death is limited to the market value at the date of the gift.

32.1.8 Now may be a good time to make gifts

Given that company values are generally depressed in the current economic climate, now could prove to be an especially good time to make gifts, ie whilst values are low. If you can afford to make gifts now, the recovery in value which is expected to take place in the future will not form part of your estate for IHT purposes.

32.2 SETTING UP ADULT CHILDREN IN BUSINESS

As we have already touched upon, this may or may not involve bringing your son or daughter into the family firm. There are many situations where a son or daughter's business skills and mind-set mean that it makes more sense for him or her to set up his or her own business. But time and again, the problem is that he or she needs working capital.

32.2.1 Financing the child's unincorporated business

We have already covered the implications of a wealthy individual making a personal loan (see 32.1.5).

An alternative, which has much to commend it from a tax point of view, is for the adult child to form an LLP (see 7.5) and transfer his or her business to it. The parent could then become a member of the LLP in return for injecting capital. The parent need not be given any involvement in the management of the business or, indeed, in any share of the profits except for an amount corresponding to the interest that he or she would have received from making a loan.

The parent's interest in the LLP should rank as business property for IHT.

If the child's venture is unsuccessful, the parent's share of the LLP's trading losses can be set against his or her other taxable income (see 7.7), subject to the limitation on loss relief for non-active partners.

32.2.2 Financing the child's limited company

It may be that the child has already established a company. The business may have gone well to start with but now needs more substantial working capital.

One possibility is for a parent to give a bank guarantee for the company's borrowings. From a personal perspective, this seems to be the easiest option but often gives rise to major problems if and when the bank calls on the father or mother to honour the guarantee. This simply reflects the fact that most people who give guarantees never really face up to the possibility of having to part with money until it actually happens.

Where a person gives such a guarantee, is required to pay up and has lost the money, he or she can qualify for CGT relief (see 17.1). However, this is of no real benefit unless the person has capital gains.

In many cases, a more appropriate way of structuring the transactions would be for the parent to subscribe for new ordinary shares in his or her child's company (these can be non-voting shares if required, but remember, in that case, no entrepreneurs' relief would be due on an eventual sale). If the company's business fails, the parent will then be able to claim a capital loss on his or her shares and will generally be able to use this loss by setting it against his or her taxable income (see 17.2).

32.3 BRINGING AN ADULT CHILD INTO PARTNERSHIP

Moving on to another situation, suppose that the parent wishes to admit his or her son or daughter into partnership.

The section in Chapter 17 on partnerships and CGT (17.5) will be required reading in such a situation. However, the CGT aspects are manageable, especially as any deemed disposal of assets by the parent can normally be held-over under s 165 TCGA 1992 (see 17.4).

From a non-tax point of view, it may be a good idea for the new partnership to be an LLP as this will give the parties the benefit of limited liability given that a new and less experienced partner may make misjudgements that could damage the business.

It may also be advisable for certain assets (eg property) to be excluded from the partnership or LLP, with the parent continuing to own them in his or her personal capacity. Assets retained by a partner but used in the business will then attract only 50% BPR but it may be preferable to accept a lower rate of BPR rather than put those assets at risk.

32.4 BRINGING AN ADULT CHILD INTO THE FAMILY COMPANY

A son or daughter can become a director of the company without becoming a substantial shareholder (indeed, subject to the company's articles of association, he or she may not need to hold any shares at all).

In some situations, it may be advisable for the adult child to be a director of a subsidiary, especially where he or she is mainly involved in running the business of that subsidiary. He or she can always be appointed to the board of the parent company later, when it has become clear that the business relationship is going to work out as expected.

32.5 OUTRIGHT GIFTS OF SHARES

Sooner or later, the issue is likely to arise that the next generation who are involved in the business feel that they should own some of the equity.

The transfer of shares to an adult child ought not to fall within the employment related securities provisions (see Chapter 6) but the relevant legislation is drafted in such wide terms that the possibility should not be ignored. It is therefore always advisable to take professional advice in this situation.

If a parent transfers shares, he or she will be making a disposal for CGT purposes but hold-over relief should cover this (see 17.4) provided that the company does not have substantial investment activities.

32.6 WHY TRUSTS ARE STILL OFTEN A SUITABLE VEHICLE

32.6.1 Practical considerations

As we have already mentioned, many proprietors do not wish to relinquish control. This is one area where trusts are especially useful, particularly where the nil rate band or business property relief mean that little or no IHT is payable on their creation. For example, suppose that a parent who owns all the shares in a company wishes to give a 30% stake to each of his son and daughter. Making an outright gift will mean that he or she will then be a minority shareholder and his or her children will be able to outvote him or her on important business decisions. If he or she instead puts 60% of the shares into a trust for the benefit of the adult children, and he or she and/or his or her professional advisers are the trustees, the children can be given the desired stake in the equity without ceding control to them.

Trusts can also have important non-tax benefits. Suppose you and your son are in a partnership but you own the premises. You are planning to retire. You also have a daughter. You want to treat the children equally but you are not completely sure about your new son-in-law. You may therefore decide to put the premises into a trust for your two children so that your daughter may have an income without this affecting your son's security of tenure. This may be a more satisfactory compromise than giving the premises to your two children at the present time. This might, for example, lead to conflict if your daughter wishes to sell her half-share and your son cannot raise the capital to buy her out. Problems could also arise on an outright gift if your daughter goes through a divorce. Of course, the really important thing is to choose the right trustees.

Another situation where a trust comes into its own is if you want to divest yourself of shares, and so start the seven-year period running, but you are not sure how your children will work out. Perhaps your eldest son works in the company and you want to see how he shapes up before passing over control. Putting shares into a discretionary trust may be a very good way of reconciling conflicting objectives.

32.6.2 Tax issues around trusts

It is important to bear in mind the gifts with reservation legislation (see 30.7). Putting shares or other property into trust will not start the seven-year period running unless you are wholly excluded from benefiting under the trust.

An IHT charge may arise on a gift of shares into a trust if the property gifted does not qualify for business property relief (see 30.8) and the settlor's cumulative chargeable transfers exceed the nil rate band (see 30.10). On the other hand, CGT hold-over relief will generally be available, provided that the settlor, his or her spouse or civil partner, and the settlor's minor, unmarried children are excluded from benefiting under the trust (see 13.6).

32.6.3 An alternative to trusts

Some wealthy families are forming family limited partnerships or family investment companies. Typically, these structures allow older family members to retain control whilst the next generation participate in income and capital growth. There can be complications with using a partnership structure because of the FSA legislation which requires investment managers to be authorised. Going down this route may well be appropriate if your family's business assets do not qualify for IHT business property relief but you need to take specialist advice on this as it is very much a 'bespoke solution'. Another option is to use a family investment company (see 24.1.16) – once again, this is a bespoke solution and you will need to take professional advice to ensure that it meets your needs and fits your specific family circumstances.

32.7 DEMERGERS

It quite often happens that the founder's children carve out a niche for themselves in a particular section of the business. For example, a company may consist of three hotels and a daughter may run one of those hotels and have little to do with the others. It is possible for the daughter to carry out a demerger (see 9.8.8). This will involve the daughter in an exchange of her shares in the present company for 100% of the shares in a new company, which will own the hotel that she runs.

Another way of facilitating a parting of the ways may be for your company to buy back some of its shares (see 9.9.8).

The detailed aspects of such transactions are beyond the scope of this book. You should consult an accountant or solicitor if you wish to break up your family business in this way and pass part of that business down to the next generation.

33

ANTI-AVOIDANCE

This chapter contains the following sections:

Income tax

Capital gains tax

Inheritance tax

General

INCOME TAX

33.1 INTEREST INCOME

33.1.1 Background

The Taxes Acts contain extensive legislation that is designed to prevent the conversion of taxable income into capital.

33.1.2 Sale of loan stock with right to purchase

(ss 581, 922, 923, 925 ITA 2007)

At one time it was possible to enjoy the benefit of income in a capital form that was not subject to tax by selling loan stock or other interest-bearing securities and retaining a right to repurchase them. For example, a person holding £1m 3½% War Loan stock could sell the stock to a charity for £400,000 cum-interest while retaining the right to repurchase the stock once it had gone ex-interest for, say, £385,000 – an overall profit of £15,000. He or she had to forgo the income of £17,500 but that was taxable and worth less than £15,000. The charity, meanwhile, got the income free of tax.

There is now specific legislation designed to catch such arrangements. Using the above example, the legislation on repo contracts means that the person would be subject to income tax on the £15,000 profit or 'differential'.

33.1.3 Sale of right to income

(ss 443–452G ITTOIA 2005)

A variation on the above scheme worked for a number of years. It was common for individuals to sell to a charity or other exempt body the right to receive interest payments for a specified period of time, while retaining legal ownership of the securities themselves. This is now caught by ss 443–452G ITTOIA 2005. If the loan stock is a UK security, the arising income is assessed on the vendor. If it is a foreign loan stock, the sale proceeds are assessable as if they were income.

33.1.4 Manufactured dividends

Manufactured payments arise during a stock loan or repo transaction. They involve the person who currently holds the securities paying over to the original owner an amount equal to dividends or interest received. Individuals could deduct such payments from their total income for tax purposes. FA 2002 introduced anti-avoidance provisions, now in ss 573–577 ITA 2007, to counter perceived abuses. This is a specialised area and those affected will no doubt already be aware of the changes and should have taken professional advice.

33.2 TRANSACTIONS IN LAND

(s 756 ITA 2007)

33.2.1 Introduction

Section 756 is intended to prevent tax avoidance by persons concerned with land or development of land. It may apply where a capital gain is realised and one of the following conditions applies:

(1) The gain arises from UK land (or some other asset deriving its value from land) and the land was acquired with the sole or main object of realising a gain.
(2) The gain arises from the disposal of UK land held as trading stock.
(3) The gain arises from a disposal of UK land that has been developed with the sole or main object of realising a gain on its disposal.

Where s 756 applies, all or part of the capital gain is charged as income.

The definition of land includes buildings and assets deriving their value from land (eg options). Consequently, s 756 could apply if a person received a lump sum for assigning the benefit of an option.

33.2.2 Exemption

There is an exemption from s 756 for gains that arise on the disposal of an individual's principal private residence. This exemption continues to be available even where the CGT exemption is not due because the property was acquired with a view to realising a gain (see 14.2.4).

33.2.3 Sales of shares

Section 756 may also apply where a person disposes of shares in a land-owning company. If a non-resident individual were to dispose of, say, a controlling shareholding in a company that itself owned a valuable UK property, he or she might be subject to income tax on the whole of his or her capital gain.

There is a let-out in the case of a land-owning company that holds land as trading stock (ie a company that is a builder or developer or deals in land as a trade). No liability arises under s 756 on a sale of shares in such a company, provided the land held by the company is disposed of in the normal course of its trade and a full commercial profit from that land is received by the company.

Despite this let-out, s 756 may still be a problem on a sale of a land-owning company since the company may be an investment company (in which case it will not hold the land as trading stock).

33.2.4 Clearance procedure

It is possible to apply for advance clearance from HMRC that s 756 will not apply to a particular disposal. This clearance may be sought either for a sale of land or of shares in a land-owning company. The legislation requires the applicant to supply full written particulars to HMRC who must then give a decision within 30 days. Once clearance is given, HMRC cannot subsequently charge tax under s 756 unless the clearance application was invalid because it did not accurately set out all the facts.

33.3 TRANSACTIONS IN SECURITIES

(ss 682–713 ITA 2007; ss 731–751 CTA 2010)

33.3.1 Introduction

Legislation was introduced in 1960 to enable HMRC to counteract tax advantages obtained by transactions in securities. At the time, CGT did not exist, and following its introduction in 1965, the differential between rates of tax on income and rates of tax on gains was considerable (as it is today), therefore supplying a huge incentive for taxpayers to seek to realise gains rather than income. The legislation was often applied by HMRC to prevent tax savings being achieved because a right to income has been converted into a capital gain. The provisions were less frequently used during periods when the incentive to realise gains was less, but in recent years, there have been four cases involving individuals, demonstrating that HMRC is taking a new interest in these rules as a tool in its arsenal. An example of the type of transaction that may be caught in this way is where a person sells shares with a right to repurchase them for a lower amount after a dividend has been received by the purchaser. The legislation also applies to more devious types of transactions where the tax advantage is less obvious at first sight.

33.3.2 Conditions to be satisfied before legislation can apply

For s 682 (s 731 for companies) to apply, the following conditions need be satisfied:

- there must be one or more transactions in securities to which the person is a party; and
- a person must have obtained, or be in a position to obtain, a tax advantage; and

- one of the prescribed circumstances set out in s 685 must have occurred.

If the legislation does apply, an income tax (or corporation tax) assessment may be made to counteract the tax advantage.

33.3.3 The term 'transactions in securities'

This term is widely defined to include transactions of whatever description relating to securities. It includes in particular:

- the purchase, sale or exchange of securities;
- the issuing of new securities;
- alteration of rights attaching to securities.

'Securities' is, in turn, defined as including shares and loan stock.

33.3.4 Tax advantage

In general, a tax advantage is deemed to arise if there is any increased relief, or repayment of tax, arising from transactions in securities, or if the transactions result in a reduction in the amount of tax that would otherwise be assessed. The courts have taken the view that a tax advantage may arise wherever HMRC can show that an amount received in a non-taxable form could have been received in a way that would have given rise to an income tax liability. Going back to the example given in 33.3.1, HMRC would say that a tax advantage arises when a person sells shares and has a right to buy back at a lower price after a dividend has been paid because he or she could simply have retained the shares and received the dividend.

Tax notes

A tax advantage is deemed to arise if a transaction in securities results in a reduction in the amount of tax that would otherwise be assessed.

See the relatively recent case of *Trevor G Lloyd* v *HMRC* SpC 672 on the meaning of 'tax advantage'. Other relevant, recent, cases include *Snell* (2008 – SpC 699), *Ebsworth* (2009 – TC 00152) and *Grogan* (2009 – TC 00187).

33.3.5 The 'new' rules

FA (No.1) 2010 fundamentally rewrote the transactions in securities rules.

The current legislation for individuals is a targeted anti-avoidance provision aimed at transactions in securities of close companies, which are made with the intention of obtaining a tax advantage. In addition, the legislation now applies to non-UK resident companies that would have been close if they had been UK resident (s 713). The rules do not apply where, as a result of the transaction, there has been a fundamental change (at least 75%) in ownership.

Section 682 ITA 2007 (s 731 for companies) now provides an overview of the chapter. Section 683 (s 732 for companies) explains what each of the following sections deals with. Section 684 identifies the individuals (s 733 for companies) liable to counteraction of a tax advantage, where the person is a party to a transaction where the circumstances are covered by s 685 but not excluded by s 686. For companies, the foregoing analysis of circumstances C and D (see the 'old' rules above) remains relevant.

Section 685 sets out new conditions where a person is in receipt of consideration in connection with a distribution by, or assets of, a close company:

- Condition A is that, as a result of the transaction in securities or any one or more of the transactions in securities, the person receives relevant consideration in connection with the distribution, transfer or realisation of assets of a close company, or the application of assets of a close company in discharge of liabilities, or the direct or indirect transfer of assets of one close company to another close company, and does not pay or bear income tax on the consideration (apart from under these provisions).
- Condition B is that the person receives relevant consideration in connection with the transaction in securities or any one or more of the transactions in securities, or two or more close companies are involved in the transaction or transactions in securities concerned, and the person does not pay or bear income tax on the consideration (apart from under these provisions).

'Relevant consideration' means consideration which:

- is or represents the value of assets that are available for distribution by way of dividend by the company, or
- is or represents the value of assets which would have been so available apart from anything done by the company, or
- is received in respect of future receipts of the company, or
- is or represents the value of trading stock of the company.

33.3.6 Exemption for fundamental changes in ownership

A person is not caught by these rules if, immediately before the transaction in securities, the person holds shares or an interest in shares in the close company, and there is a fundamental change of ownership of the close company.

There is a fundamental change of ownership of the close company if as a result of the transaction in securities, the following conditions are met, and continue to be met for a period of two years.

Condition A is that at least 75% of the ordinary share capital of the close company is held beneficially by a person who is not connected with the original owner and has not been so connected within the period of two years ending with the day on which the transaction in securities takes place, or persons none of whom is so connected or has been so connected within that period.

Condition B is that shares in the close company held by that person or persons carry an entitlement to at least 75% of the distributions which may be made by the company.

Condition C is that shares so held carry at least 75% of the total voting rights in the close company.

33.3.7 Exemption for bona fide commercial transactions

Previously, if there was a transaction in securities and the prescribed circumstances applied, a taxpayer might still have avoided assessment if he, she or it could show that the transactions were carried out for bona fide commercial reasons or in the ordinary course of making or managing investments, and that none of them had as one of their main objects the obtaining of a tax advantage. This provision has been removed for individuals, as a result of the FA (No.1) 2010 changes, but is retained for companies in s 734 CTA 2010.

33.3.8 Clearances

Section 701 ITA 2007 (s 748 for companies; see also SP3/80) provides a procedure whereby a person can give details of the proposed transactions to HMRC and request clearance that the Board will not apply s 682.

Once a written application has been made under s 701, HMRC has 30 days in which to request more particulars, which must then be provided within 30 days.

HMRC must give a decision either within 30 days of receiving the original application or within 30 days of receiving the further particulars.

Where HMRC has notified someone that it is satisfied that s 682 should not apply, it may not subsequently change its mind. Where information given in the application is incomplete or inaccurate, any clearance given by HMRC may be void.

33.3.9 Situations where clearance should be sought

It is standard practice for vendors or their advisers to seek clearance under s 701 where a private company is being sold for a substantial amount. Quite apart from anything else, the vendor would otherwise be at the mercy of the purchaser who might extract an abnormal dividend and thus bring s 682 into consideration.

It is also advisable to seek clearance under s 701 where a company is liquidated, the reserves are extracted in a capital form and it is intended that the company's business should be carried on by a new company owned by the current shareholders.

33.4 B SHARE SCHEMES

FA 2015 contains anti-avoidance provisions aimed at the use of special share schemes (sometimes referred to as B share schemes).

These schemes consist of an issue to shareholders of B shares which carry the right to a cash dividend or to conversion into ordinary shares. These shares often also carry the right to redemption. The issue of these shares effectively allow a shareholder to receive the same value whilst choosing the most attractive tax treatment, paying:

- income tax on a cash dividend;
- no tax on conversion into ordinary shares until there is a disposal of those shares;
- capital gains tax on the amount paid out on the redemption of the shares.

From 6 April 2015, all amounts received by shareholders will be taxed as dividends.

33.5 TRANSFER OF ASSETS ABROAD

Legislation was introduced in 1936 to prevent tax savings for UK-resident and ordinarily resident individuals arising from their transferring assets overseas. The legislation refers to avoidance of income tax. Capital tax avoidance is not subject to counteraction by ss 714–723 ITA 2007, although separate anti-avoidance legislation also exists for CGT.

33.5.1 Where the individual or spouse can benefit

Section 714 applies where a UK-resident has made a transfer of assets and either he or she or his or her spouse or civil partner may benefit as a result of it. He or she is deemed to meet this test if he or she has 'power to enjoy' income that arises overseas. Power to enjoy income exists in the following circumstances:

- The income accrues for his or her benefit.
- The receipt of the income increases the value to him or her of any assets held by him or her or for his or her benefit.

- He or she may become entitled to enjoy the income in the future.
- He or she is able in any way whatsoever, and whether directly or indirectly, to control the way the income is used.

Where s 714 applies, the transferor or his or her spouse or civil partner is assessed on the income as it arises, even if it is not actually paid out to them.

33.5.2 Exemption for bona fide transactions

Section 737 ITA 2007 contains a clearance procedure. Under the original rules, the individual used to have to show to HMRC's satisfaction that:

- the purpose of avoiding tax was not one of the purposes for which the transfer of assets was carried out; or
- the transfer of assets, and any associated operations, were bona fide commercial transactions and not designed for tax avoidance.

In *Carvill* v *IRC* SpC 233, the Special Commissioners held that the test was a subjective, and not an objective, one. The taxpayer also succeeded in the case of *Beneficiary* v *IRC* where a Japanese individual who was not resident in the UK established an offshore trust for the benefit of his daughter who was not capable of managing her own finances (this was a case where HMRC sought tax under s 732 ITA 2007 (see 33.5.5 below) rather than s 714).

Unfortunately, many of the successes achieved by taxpayers have been reversed by legislation introduced in FA 2006. The requirements for exemption have been reinforced in relation to income arising on or after 5 December 2005 and the exemption is now dependent upon HMRC or, on appeal, the First-tier Tribunal, being satisfied that one of two conditions are satisfied. These conditions are:

- it would not be reasonable to infer from all the circumstances of the case that avoiding tax was the purpose, or one of the purposes, for which the relevant transactions were effected;
- all the relevant transactions were genuine commercial transactions and it would not be reasonable to infer from all the circumstances of the case that any one or more of those transactions was more than incidentally designed for the purpose of avoiding tax.

A relevant transaction is a commercial transaction only if it is effected in the course of a trade or business or with a view to setting up a business.

A transaction is commercial only if it is made on arm's length terms and is a transaction that would have been entered into by independent persons dealing at arm's length, eg a loan will not be commercial even if it carries a commercial rate of interest if no arm's length lender would have made a loan of that amount.

Section 737 ITA 2007 specifies that the intentions and purposes of professional advisers may be taken into account as well as the transferor's own objectives. This is likely to make the test more 'objective', ie it is not sufficient to look at the transferor's intentions in a subjective way.

In practice, it is always going to be extremely difficult to satisfy HMRC that the re-stated conditions are satisfied.

33.5.3 New EU exemption

A new exemption was introduced by FA 2013 which came into force with retrospective effect from 6 April 2012. The exemption applies where EU treaty freedoms are engaged. It focuses on whether the transaction is genuine in nature and whether it serves the purpose of the freedoms. Business transactions are not regarded as genuine unless they are on arm's-length terms and, in the case of transactions for the purposes of a business establishment, give rise to income attributable to economically significant activity that takes place overseas.

These provisions provide exemption for genuine commercial business activities that take place overseas. Transactions that do not involve commercial activities but are nevertheless genuine transactions protected by the single market are also exempt.

There is a further element to this test which enables HMRC to examine each transaction and make an apportionment where appropriate between the part of a transaction which is genuine and the part which is not. Only income attributable to the non-genuine (artificial) part of the transaction is liable to tax.

33.5.4 Transfer of assets by non-residents

HMRC's view has always been that s 714 ITA 2007 could apply to income arising from a transfer of assets made by an individual at a time when he or she was not UK-resident. The House of Lords found against HMRC on this in *IRC* v *Willoughby* [1997] STC 995, but FA 1997 restored the position to what HMRC always believed to be the case in relation to income arising on or after 26 November 1996.

33.5.5 Assessment of income caught by s 714 ITA 2007

Income caught by s 714 is normally taxed as miscellaneous investment income. Where it is UK dividend income or other income that has borne tax at source, relief is given for such tax and the assessment will be for higher rate tax purposes only.

33.5.6 Liability of non-transferors

(s 732 ITA 2007)

A person may not be assessed under s 714 unless he or she, or his or her spouse or civil partner, has made a transfer of assets. However, a

UK-ordinarily resident individual may be assessed under s 732 if he or she receives a benefit from a transfer made by another person. This applies particularly to beneficiaries of non-resident settlements created by someone other than the individual and/or his or her spouse or civil partner. It is also arguable that s 732 might apply to a person who had made a transfer of assets but was not 'caught' by s 714, perhaps because he or she was not resident at the time of the transfer.

In contrast to s 714, a liability may arise under s 732 only when the individual concerned receives a benefit. 'Benefit' is not specifically defined, although the legislation states it includes a payment of any kind. It is understood that HMRC regards an interest-free loan or the provision of accommodation as constituting a benefit.

This is an area where professional advice is essential.

33.5.7 Matching income with benefits

The legislation allows benefits to be matched with income received in either earlier or later years.

Example – Matching benefits

An overseas trust receives income of £10,000 in 1994–95. In 2002–03 a capital payment of £100,000 is made to a UK-resident and ordinarily resident individual. In the year 2012–13, the trustees received further income of £120,000. If s 732 applies, the individual will be taxed as follows:

	£
2002–03	10,000
2012–13	90,000

33.5.8 An interest-free loan may constitute a benefit

The High Court decided in January 2000 in *Billingham* v *Cooper* [2000] STC 122 that an interest-free loan that was repayable on demand gave rise to a benefit equal to interest at the 'official rate'.

33.5.9 Assessment under s 732

Where income is taxed under s 732, there is no credit for any UK tax suffered at source. This can give rise to double taxation. Thus, going back to the previous example, if the trustees' income represented interest from UK companies, the total tax suffered would really be as follows:

	£
Tax at source on interest: £100,000 $\times$ $^{20}/_{80}$ =	25,000
Tax charged on beneficiary under s 732 =	40,000
	65,000

33.5.10 Clearances

Once again, it is possible to obtain clearance from HMRC that s 732 should not apply because the transfer of assets concerned was not carried out for tax avoidance purposes.

33.5.11 Foreign domiciliaries

Where the income arising to the non-resident trust or company is foreign source income, no liability arises for a foreign-domiciled individual who elects for the remittance basis to apply, except to the extent that he or she remits such income to the UK. However, the individual may need to pay a £30,000 (or in some cases, £90,000) remittance basis charge to obtain the benefit of the remittance basis (see 35.2).

33.5.12 Reporting income taxable under s 714 or s 732

Question 5 on page 2 of the tax return asks, among other things:

> Have you, or could you have, received (directly or indirectly) income, or received a capital payment or benefit, from a person abroad as a result of any transfer of assets?

If you tick the 'yes box', you will be required to complete the Foreign pages. See question 46.

Other overseas income and gains

41	Gains on disposals of holdings in offshore funds (excluding the amounts entered in box 13) and discretionary income from non-resident trusts – *enter the amount of the gain or payment*	44	Number of years
42	If you have received a benefit from a person abroad, enter the value or payment received – *if you are omitting income from this section because you are claiming an exemption, see box 46*	45	Tax treated as paid – *read page FN 17 of the notes*
43	Gains on foreign life insurance policies, etc. (excluding the amounts entered in box 13) – *enter the amount of the gain*	46	If you have omitted income from boxes 11, 13 and 42 because you are claiming an exemption in relation to a transfer of assets, enter the total amount omitted (and give full details in the 'Any other information' box on your tax return)

Extracts from HMRC notes to the tax return

The notes to the Foreign pages state:

Where:

- you have transferred, or taken any part in the transfer of assets, as a result of which income has become payable to a person abroad, or

- someone else has transferred, or taken part in the transfer of assets, as a result of which income has become payable to a person abroad, and you have received a benefit as a result of the relevant transactions
- then Help Sheet 262 will help you decide if any income should be included on the *foreign pages*. A person abroad includes an individual, the trustees of a settlement, a company, or any other person.

(In notes to previous years' tax returns, HMRC stated that 'benefits' include, for example, loans at less than a commercial rate of interest and the occupation or use of property at less than a commercial rent, the value of the benefit being the difference between the commercial rate of interest or rental and any amount actually paid by you.)

HS262: How do you qualify for an exemption from charge on income or benefits?

Income or benefits may be excluded from charge under these provisions if you can show from all the circumstances of the case that the purpose of avoiding liability to taxation was not the purpose, or one of the purposes, for which the relevant transactions, or any of them, were effected. But if you omit income for this reason from boxes 11, 13 and 42, you must enter the total amount of income you have omitted in box 46, and provide relevant details and an explanation in the 'Any other information' box on your tax return, including details of the assets transferred and any associated operations, the persons abroad concerned, the circumstances of the relevant transactions and the basis of your claim to exclusion.

Source: HMRC

33.6 TRUST INCOME TAXED ON THE SETTLOR

33.6.1 Introduction

There are several provisions under which income on property that belongs to trustees may be taxed as if it were income that belonged to the settlor.

33.6.2 Trust where settlor may benefit

(s 624 ITTOIA 2005)

Legislation may catch income that arises to a trust under which the settlor or his or her spouse or civil partner may benefit (a 'settlor-interested trust'). The legislation provides that the settlor should be treated as capable of benefiting where he or she may benefit in any circumstances whatsoever except in one of the following exceptional cases:

- The bankruptcy of a person who is beneficially entitled under the settlement.

- The death under age 25 of a person who would be beneficially entitled to the trust property on attaining that age.
- In the case of a marriage settlement, the death of both parties to the marriage and of all or any of the children of the marriage.

HMRC interprets this legislation rather literally. For example, if a person creates a trust for the benefit of his or her son, and the trust deed states that the property should revert to the settlor if the son dies before age 35, HMRC takes the view that s 624 applies because the let-out applies only where property reverts on the death of someone before he or she attains age 25.

Sometimes the trust deed is silent on a matter. For example, a person creates a trust for the benefit of his or her three children and the deed makes no reference to the capital coming back to the settlor. In such circumstances, HMRC is apt to say that the property could revert to the settlor if all his or her children died and they left no children of their own. To avoid this kind of argument, it is normal for a trust to contain a clause that provides the capital shall in no circumstances whatsoever come back to the settlor but shall be held for the benefit of, say, a charity in the event that all the named beneficiaries die before the capital is distributed (the charity is often referred to as the 'longstop' beneficiary).

HMRC does not take the view that a person has reserved the benefit simply because his or her spouse or civil partner may benefit after his or her death as his or her survivor. On the other hand, cases have actually arisen where the settlor and his or her spouse were excluded but HMRC said that s 624 should apply because the settlor's current marriage might come to an end and he or she might marry or enter into civil partnership with someone who *could* benefit. Once again, it is best to make sure that the trust deed excludes such an interpretation by expressly providing that any present or future spouse or civil partner of the settlor should be excluded from all benefit, except after the settlor's death.

Where a settlor's spouse or civil partner can benefit, during the settlor's lifetime, the settlor is assessed on the trust income.

FA 2000 introduced a concession, now in s 628 ITTOIA 2005, for UK settlements. Where a settlor is not totally excluded but one of the beneficiaries under the trust is a charity, income arising after 5 April 2000 that is actually paid out to the charity will not be assessable on the settlor under s 624.

33.6.3 Settlements where the property given is just a right to income

(s 624 ITTOIA 2005)

The legislation contains a very wide definition of 'settlement'. It can even apply to an outright gift where the property given is 'wholly or substantially' a right to income. It can also apply where there is no gift at all but there are arrangements that amount to a settlement, such as might apply where an individual lets someone else subscribe for shares in a new company.

HMRC's arguments do seem to have a certain 'seasonality'. In the early 1990s, Inspectors often tried to apply these provisions where an individual had admitted his or her spouse into partnership. The argument was that this was uncommercial and the partnership's profits should be assessed on the spouse who contributed most to the business (and invariably paid tax at a higher rate). But as HMRC met dogged resistance from tax accountants these arguments largely ceased, albeit without HMRC ever conceding that the principle was incorrect.

In 2003, these arguments resurfaced in the context of small companies. HMRC argued that where one spouse was the main contributor to the company's profits, s 624 allowed HMRC to treat dividends paid to the other spouse as the first spouse's income. HMRC said tax avoidance arose from 'income-splitting'.

HMRC set out its views in the April 2003 and February 2004 editions of *Tax Bulletin (nos. 64 and 69 – see also IRInt.258)*. The February 2004 edition contains examples of circumstances where HMRC believed that s 624 was applicable. HMRC initially succeeded before the High Court in *Jones* v *Garnett* (often referred to as the *Arctic Systems Limited* case) but lost before the Court of Appeal and the House of Lords. The Government intended to reverse the decision of the House of Lords by bringing in specific legislation to counter 'income-splitting'. This was to feature in FA 2009 and take effect from 2009–10, but this proposal was deferred indefinitely following representations by professional bodies, accountants and advisers and it remains to be seen to what extent it will be revived under the new administration.

Also, bear in mind s 624 if you are entering into a dividend waiver. Again, see the *Tax Bulletin* articles for guidance on HMRC's position.

Section 836 ITA 2007 contains a specific provision regarding jointly-owned shares in private companies. The gist of this provision is that if s 624 were considered applicable, the normal rule that governs dividends from shares which are jointly owned by husband and wife is disapplied.

33.6.4 Settlements on minor children

(s 629 ITTOIA 2005)

Where a person gives capital to his or her minor children, the resulting income may be taxed as if it belonged to the parent. This treatment applies where the following three conditions are satisfied:

- The child is a minor.
- The child is unmarried (and not in a registered civil partnership).
- The income exceeds £100 per tax year for each child.

Similarly when a person makes a settlement under which his or her minor children may benefit, income distributed to the children before they attain age 18 is treated as the settlor's income (subject to the £100 *de minimis* exemption). This applies even where he or she is separated or divorced and the children live with his or her former spouse or civil partner.

For s 629 purposes, 'child' includes an adopted child and an illegitimate child. Again, HMRC interprets this legislation strictly and has even been known to tax a grandfather who set up a trust for his daughter's (illegitimate) child whom he subsequently adopted and brought up as his own.

There are two circumstances where s 629 does not apply:

- where the child has married;
- where the settlor is not resident in the UK.

The legislation does not stop here. Any capital payments made to the children are also caught so far as the capital payments may be matched with accumulated income within the trust. Since the trustees will normally pay tax at 45% (37.5% on dividends), this may mean that the settlor can claim a tax refund. However amendments to s 646 ITTOIA 2005 in FA (No.1) 2010 mean that the settlor must repay any tax repaid to him or her by HMRC, to the trustees.

Tax notes

HMRC has been known to tax a grandfather who set up a trust for his daughter's (illegitimate) child whom he subsequently adopted and brought up as his own.

33.6.5 Capital payments to settlor

(s 633 ITTOIA 2005)

Section 633 may apply to enable HMRC to charge tax on income received by the trustees of the settlement under which the settlor and his or her spouse or civil partner are totally excluded from benefit, in situations where the trustees of the settlement have accumulated income and make a capital payment to the settlor. The capital payment is then treated as if it were income for the year in which the payment was made provided there is sufficient undistributed income.

If only part of the capital payment can be 'matched', the balance is matched with income for subsequent years (up to a maximum of ten), and amounts matched in this way are then taxable on the settlor for those years.

Example – Matching of capital payments

In 2003–04 *A* received a capital payment of £50,000. The trustees had undistributed income for that year of £20,000 and £12,000 brought forward from 1999–2000. The trustees made no further capital payments but in 2006–07 and 2014–15 they have undistributed income of £10,000 and £8,000 (after tax). The following amounts are taxable under s 633:

			£
2003–04	£32,000[1] grossed up	=	48,484
2006–07	£10,000[2] grossed up	=	16,667
2014–15	£8,000[3] grossed up	=	14,545

[1] including the balance of the undistributed income available at the end of 1999–00 grossed up for 34% tax.
[2] grossed up for 40% tax
[3] grossed up for 45% tax

Section 633 can also apply to capital payments from non-resident trusts. The tax payable may be greater in such cases because the undistributed income might not have suffered tax at the rate applicable to trusts.

33.6.6 Income may be matched with capital payments made in previous 12 years

Undistributed income can be identified with past capital payments for up to 12 years. The only way to get round this is for the whole of the capital sum to be repaid by the settlor, but even doing this does not affect the position for past years and the year in which the capital sum is repaid.

33.6.7 Loans may also be caught

A loan from the trustees to the settlor or spouse may be treated under s 633 as if it were a capital payment. Furthermore, the repayment of a loan made by the settlor to the trust can also be treated as a capital payment.

Example – treatment of loans

In 1999–00 B made a £150,000 loan to a trust she had created. The trustees repaid the loan in full during 2006–07. At that time, the trustees had undistributed income of £45,000 (ie this was the net income retained after 40% tax). B was taxed under s 677 ICTA 1988 (now s 633) on £45,000 grossed up at 40%, ie £75,000.

If the trustees had undistributed income of £30,000 for 2008–09 and £85,000 for 2014–15 (in both cases after tax), assessments would be made on £30,000 grossed up for 2008–09 and £75,000 grossed up for the year 2014–15.

33.6.8 Payments by companies connected with trustees

A liability could also arise under s 633 if a company connected with the trustees makes a capital payment to the settlor. Three conditions must be met:

(1) The trustees must have undistributed income.
(2) There must be 'associated payments' by the trustees to the company. An associated payment may include a capital payment (eg a subscription for shares) or the transfer of assets at an undervalue by the trustees to the company.
(3) The company must make a capital payment to the settlor, or make a loan to him or her or repay a loan made by the settlor to the company. For loans, this must occur within five years of the associated payment taking place.

33.7 TRANSACTIONS INVOLVING LOANS OR CREDIT

(ss 809CZA–809CZC ITA 2007 for individuals; ss 777–779 CTA 2010 for companies)

Specific legislation exists to prevent any tax avoidance that could otherwise arise if a person who was liable to pay non-allowable interest found a way of converting his, her or its liability to pay interest into some other payment that was tax deductible. Sections 809CZA–809CZC and ss 777–779 may apply where a transaction is effected with reference to money-lending. It can apply whether the transaction is between the lender and borrower or involves other persons connected with them.

(1) Section 809CZB (s 778 for companies) states that if the transaction provides for payment of any annuity or other annual payment it shall be treated as interest for all purposes of the Taxes Acts.
(2) Section 809CZC (s 779 for companies) states that if the borrower agrees to sell or transfer to the lender any securities or other property carrying a right to income, the borrower may be charged income tax on an amount equal to the income that arises from the property before the borrower repays the loan.
(3) Section 809CZC(4) (s 779(4) for companies) refers to income being assigned, surrendered, waived or forgone and states that the person who has assigned, surrendered, etc may be charged to tax on the amount of income assigned, surrendered, etc.

In theory, ss 809CZA–809CZC and ss 777–779 could apply to interest-free loans. HMRC has given some degree of comfort in that it has said that in the straightforward situation where one person lends money to another and then waives the interest, and there is no further transaction linked in any way to the arrangements, this anti-avoidance will not be invoked. There has been some concern in the past that these rules could apply where, for example, a client deposited a large lump sum with his, her or its accountant on the basis that the accountant would not pay interest but would reduce his or her accountancy fees by the amount of interest that would have been paid at commercial rates on the client's deposit. It is possible to read s 809CZC(5) (or s 779(5)) as permitting HMRC to make an assessment in this way even though the type of transactions described are somewhat different from those envisaged when the legislation was enacted.

33.8 PRE-OWNED ASSETS

The Government announced in December 2003 that it proposed to impose an annual income tax charge from 2005–06 where individuals had transferred assets but continued to enjoy benefits. It justified this charge as being aimed at individuals who had used artificial schemes to avoid the IHT legislation that catches gifts with reservation of benefit (see Chapter 30). The relevant Press Release stated that the effect of these artificial structures was that 'people have been removing assets from their taxable estates but continuing to enjoy all the benefits of ownership'. In practice, most of these schemes were intended to save IHT on the family home.

The legislation is in Schedule 15, FA 2004. A number of representations were made on the unfairness of such a charge where the transactions were entered into many years ago. The Government took some (but in reality very few) of these representations on board. After considerable discussion with professional bodies and advisers, HMRC also issued detailed guidance, which can be found at M05/2006 and www.hmrc.gov. uk/poa/poa_guidance.htm.

The charge does not apply in any of the following situations where:

- the benefit enjoyed by the donor is worth less than £5,000 a year;
- the benefit enjoyed by the donor is 'consistent with' an interest retained by him or her (eg where an individual gives a 50% interest in his or her home to a child living with him or her, and continues to pay – as a minimum – the expenses relating to the property retained, so in this example, at least 50%);
- the transfer was a gift that took place before 18 March 1986 (the date that the GWR rule for IHT was introduced);
- the property has been transferred to the donor's spouse;
- the transfer was a sale at market value and the purchase price has been paid in full;
- the transfer was effected by a deed of variation as permitted under the IHT legislation;
- any enjoyment of the property that has been given away is no more than incidental (HMRC has said that it regards 'incidental'

enjoyment to fall within the same guidelines as that for GWR, which can be found in IRInt1001 (*Tax Bulletin 9,* November 1993));

- the asset given away is an intangible asset (eg an insurance policy) and the benefits retained by the donor are of a very limited nature;
- the donor was not domiciled in the UK (or deemed to be domiciled under the 17-year rule) at the time that he or she made the transfer and the property concerned is foreign property.

Furthermore, it was possible to make a special election by 31 January following the year of assessment in which the charge would first apply whereby the donor would renounce the IHT benefits in return for being exempt from the income tax charge. Where this election has been made, the property concerned will be treated as caught by the GWR rule.

33.8.1 Charge on occupation of a property

The charge may apply whenever a person occupies land and buildings that he or she does not own. The essential test is whether or not he or she owned the property or provided funds for its purchase, directly or otherwise, after 17 March 1986. If none of the reliefs and exemptions applies (see above) the calculation of the tax payable will be based on the rental value of the property.

33.8.2 Charge on use of chattels

Very similar rules can apply in respect of chattels (eg, works of art, cars, boats, etc). In this case the charge will be calculated by reference to the value of the chattel using a notional interest rate.

33.8.3 Trusts

The above charging provisions do not apply if land or chattels have been placed in an interest-in-possession trust for the benefit of either the taxpayer or his or her or her spouse or civil partner. However, there are separate rules for settlements where the settlor retains an interest in the property of the settlement and s 624 ITTOIA 2005 would apply (but not if it applies merely by reason of his or her spouse or civil partner retaining an interest under the trust). The charge is calculated by applying a notional interest rate to the value of settlement property in which the taxpayer has retained an interest.

Where the settlor suffers a capital gains or income tax charge under the existing settlement rules, the tax paid can be offset against this new liability. Nevertheless, there will be many circumstances were the taxpayer is being taxed twice in respect of the same source.

The pre-owned asset rules and their interaction with the GWR provisions are extremely complex, and a full discussion is outside the scope of this book. In October 2010, HMRC updated section 5 of its pre-owned assets guidance in relation to lifetime 'double trust/home loan' plans, adding the following note:

> Where the loan is only repayable at a time after the life tenant's death, HMRC is now of the view that these schemes are also caught as gifts with reservation. Further guidance, including the consequences for the pre-owned assets charge, will be issued shortly.

Unfortunately, the promised further guidance has not yet been issued.

Currently, all 'double trust' cases where the original owner of the house has died are being held pending a test case, but in the meantime, where significant sums are at stake, HMRC's view should be resisted as there are a number of technical reasons why HMRC's new stance may prove incorrect.

This is an area where professional advice is essential, not least because the charge generally applies because you have previously undertaken some form of IHT planning, which may need to be unwound or at least revisited, in order to keep the tax bill to a minimum.

33.9 PARTNERSHIPS

Finance Act 2014 has introduced a number of anti-avoidance provisions.

33.9.1 Disguised employment

Members of UK LLPs may be classified as employees if the following three conditions are satisfied:

(1) the reward for their performance of services as a member of the LLP is fixed rather than a share of the LLP's profits, or the reward is variable but not by reference to the LLP's profits; and
(2) they have no significant say in the running of the business; and
(3) they have no significant money invested in the business.

This provision in FA 2014 does not apply to general partnerships or to LLPs formed overseas. However, this simply reflects the fact that the UK LLP legislation previously contained a specific provision that all members of UK LLPs were to be treated as self-employed. An individual who is a member of a Jersey LLP and who is caught by the above tests can still expect to have his self-employed status attacked by HMRC.

33.9.2 Mixed partnerships

A mixed partnership is a partnership or LLP where not all the members are individuals. This would apply, for example, if some of the members were companies or trustees.

Allocations of partnership profits and losses can be adjusted by HMRC in two situations:

(1) Where a member which is not an individual is allocated more profits than is reasonable at the expense of an individual and he has power to enjoy the profits of that member. This could apply where excessive profits are allocated to a company which is owned and managed by the individual partners.

(2) Where an individual is allocated partnership losses which would normally belong to a corporate partner

There are complex provisions to ensure that individuals cannot side-step these provisions by organising a series of partnerships. There are also provisions which can apply if an individual ceases to be a partner but continues to have power to enjoy profits allocated to a corporate partner or a partner which is a trustee.

33.9.3 Transfers of assets and income streams

FA 2014 contains wide-ranging provisions which apply where individuals transfer assets or income streams to companies which are members of the same partnership (or a connected partnership). These provisions can bite even in cases where the individuals and corporate partners are not members of the partnership at the same time.

Where an income stream is transferred for a lump sum, the amount credited to the individual partners may be treated as income.

CAPITAL GAINS TAX

33.10 BED AND BREAKFAST TRANSACTIONS

For disposals of shares by individuals or trustees on or after 17 March 1998, any shares of the same class and in the same company that are sold and then repurchased within a 30-day period will be matched so that the gain or loss that would otherwise have arisen by reference to shares already held will not be realised. This blocks a widely used way in which individuals used to realise losses and then buy back the same shares on the following day. It would appear that, in some circumstances, it is still possible to circumvent this rule by one spouse or civil partner selling and the other purchasing the same securities, provided s 16A TCGA 1992 is not triggered (see below).

33.10.1 Capital losses targeted anti-avoidance

Section 16A TCGA 1992 is a targeted anti-avoidance rule aimed restricting allowable losses for those realising capital losses, where tax avoidance is a motive, and it may enable HMRC to attack such sales as artificial transactions entered into solely for tax avoidance, especially if the purchasing spouse subsequently transfers the shares to the original owner. Basically, s 16A is very widely drafted and would appear to catch even completely innocent transactions. This legislation was one of the first rules to instigate a furore about 'taxing by legislation and un-taxing by concession' which has attended so much of the tax legislation introduced by the recent Labour administration. In effect, it will be up to HMRC whether it takes the point, on a case by case basis. This is clearly unsatisfactory, but as a general rule of thumb, if the parties genuinely suffer the economic consequences of the transactions they each enter into, then the rule is unlikely to apply.

33.11 DISPOSALS BY A SERIES OF TRANSACTIONS

33.11.1 Basic principle behind the legislation

(s 19 TCGA 1992)

There are certain assets that are worth more in total than the sum of their various parts. For example, a 55% shareholding in a private company will almost always be worth a great deal more than five times the value of an 11% shareholding since a 55% shareholder has control of the company. It follows from this that if there were not specific anti-avoidance legislation, a person could reduce his or her exposure to CGT on a gift to a friend or relative by transferring the asset in stages.

In fact, in certain circumstances, HMRC may look at the value transferred by a series of transactions and assess that value by each separate transaction according to an appropriate part of the total value transferred.

Tax notes

In cases where a person has reduced his or her exposure to CGT on a gift by transferring an asset in stages, HMRC may assess the value of each separate transaction as an appropriate part of the total value transferred.

33.11.2 Legislation may have wide application

The legislation can also apply in unexpected ways. Thus, if an individual with a 75% shareholding in an investment company decided to give 25% to each of his or her brother's three children and even arranged to make the gifts over a period of two (or more) years, HMRC could still apply s 19 to catch the total value transferred.

33.11.3 Circumstances that cause s 19 to apply

The following circumstances may result in HMRC applying s 19:

(1) A person disposes of assets to another person (or other persons) who falls within the definition of a connected person.
(2) There are 'linked transactions' that fall within a period of six years.
(3) The disposals have all taken place since 19 March 1985.
(4) The aggregate value transferred by the series of linked transactions is greater than the total of the values transferred by the individual transactions.

A transaction may be caught by s 19 even if it is a sale rather than a gift.

33.11.4 Section 19 can result in retrospective adjustments

If HMRC invokes s 19, it may result in assessments for previous years being reopened. For example, C may have made a gift to her father in 2007–08 of a 10% shareholding in X Ltd and the shares' value may have been agreed with HMRC as, say, £20,000. If C made a further gift to her brother of a 70% shareholding in 2014–15 and within six years of the 2007–08 gift, the position might have to be reopened. If HMRC establishes that an 80% shareholding is worth £800,000 at the time of the gift to C's brother, the effect of applying s 19 will be:

Deemed disposal proceeds on the 2007–08 gift	£100,000
Deemed disposal proceeds on the 2014–15 gift	£700,000

33.11.5 Hold-over relief may cover the position

In some circumstances, the donor may not have to pay extra tax because he or she, together with the donee, has agreed that the hold-over provisions should apply (see 13.6 and 17.4). However, hold-over relief will not always be available since the asset will not always fall within the definition of business property or the donee may not be UK-resident or a trust (see 13.6 and 17.4.3).

Professional advice is clearly essential where a person is contemplating making a series of gifts to connected persons.

33.12 TRANSFERS TO A CONNECTED PERSON

Another potential pitfall arises from special rules that govern the way market value is to be determined when assessing a gain on a transaction between connected persons (whether the transaction is a gift or a sale).

33.12.1 Some restrictions may be taken into account

(s 18 TCGA 1992)

A gift or sale at undervalue to a connected person may involve an asset over which the acquirer already has certain rights. Thus, *D* may own the freehold of a building and his daughter, *E,* may have valuable rights as a tenant. Suppose the freehold is worth £230,000 with vacant possession, but is worth only £180,000 if *E*'s lease is taken into account. When *D* sells the freehold to *E,* will the market value be taken as £230,000 or £180,000?

The legislation states that the market value shall be taken to be the asset's market value less the lower of:

- the value of the interest held by the connected person who acquires the asset; or
- the amount by which the transferor's asset would increase in value if the connected person's rights did not exist.

Consequently, *D* would be deemed to make a disposal of an asset worth £180,000.

33.12.2 Some restrictions are ignored

(s 18(7) TCGA 1992)

Certain valuable rights may have to be left out of account. One example of this is an option. Suppose the facts set out in 33.11.1 had been slightly different so that *D* had vacant possession of a property worth £230,000, but his daughter had an option under which she could acquire it for £180,000. If *D* sells the property to *E* or if she exercises her option he will receive only £180,000, but he may be assessed as if he had received £230,000.

This is because the legislation requires options to be ignored or left out of account when computing an asset's market value. Similarly, legal rights that, if exercised, would effectively destroy or impair the asset also have to be ignored. Market value is determined as if such rights did not exist.

Tax notes

Options are ignored when computing an asset's market value. Similarly, legal rights that, if exercised, would effectively destroy or impair the asset also have to be ignored.

33.13 QUALIFYING CORPORATE BONDS

(ss 116–117A TCGA 1992)

Anti-avoidance provisions took effect from 26 November 1996 concerning situations where an individual or groups of individuals disposed of their private company shares and took loan stock issued by the acquiring company as part of the sale consideration (referred to as 'rolling over' into loan stock since no capital gain normally arises until the loan stock is sold). Since 1984, legislation has made specific provision for the situation where a person received qualifying corporate bonds (QCBs) in exchange for shares. The capital gain that would have arisen had he or she taken cash rather than QCBs is calculated but held over until such time as he or she disposes of the bonds. The legislation did not however make express provision for the situation where the vendor received loan notes that were not QCBs at the time of acquisition but subsequently become QCBs before a disposal takes place. As QCBs are normally an exempt asset for CGT purposes, the legislation seemed to allow a capital gain to escape a charge altogether, which gave rise to the term 'disappearing trick'.

HMRC was sceptical that these arrangements succeeded in their objective. However, and without prejudice to litigation on past transactions, FA 1997 clarified the position.

The CGT legislation was amended so that when a loan stock has changed from a non-QCB into a QCB after 25 November 2006, the change is treated as a conversion of securities. This ensures that any gain that has been rolled over on an exchange of shares for loan stock is preserved and does not escape charge.

33.14 TRUSTS AND MAIN RESIDENCE EXEMPTION

(ss 169B–169G and 260 TCGA 1992)

Anti-avoidance legislation was introduced by FA 2004 and took effect from 10 December 2003.

33.14.1 No main residence relief for a property that has been transferred under a hold-over election

Where a property is given to a settlor-interested trust and the donor's gain is held over (see 13.6) the trustees are not able to claim exemption under s 225 TCGA 1992 (main residence exemption where a property is occupied by a beneficiary of a trust). PPR relief is also denied where the residence was acquired by the trustees subject to a hold-over election under s 260 TCGA 1992 (s 226A) and later transferred to a beneficiary who occupies the property as his or her main residence.

There is no equivalent provision preventing trustees from making a holdover election on transferring assets out of the trust to beneficiaries.

33.14.2 Transitional rules

These provisions also apply to cases where an asset was transferred to a trust under a hold-over election before 10 December 2003. However, in this situation the trustees may be able to claim the main residence exemption for part of their gain, this being calculated on a time-apportionment basis with the proportion of the gain relating to the period up to 10 December 2003 being exempt.

Example – Claiming main residence exemption

A owned a second property. On 10 December 2002, it was worth £360,000. A transferred the property to a discretionary trust on that date and made a claim for hold-over relief under s 260 TCGA 1992. Assume that the gain held over amounted to £200,000.

The property was then occupied as the main residence of one of the beneficiaries of the trust. The property is eventually sold for £400,000 on 10 December 2014.

The trustees' gain will be calculated as follows:

Proceeds		400,000
Less cost	360,000	
Held over gain	(200,000)	
		160,000
		240,000

The trustees held the property for 12 years. The period of ownership up to 10 December 2003 was exactly one year.

The trustees would be entitled to main residence exemption on one-twelfth of the gain, ie £20,000.

33.15 DEEMED DISPOSAL WHEN A TRUST CEASES TO BE UK RESIDENT

A trust is regarded as resident or non-resident in the UK for an entire tax year, there is no 'split year' concept for trusts.

A UK resident trust can cease to be resident if non-resident trustees are appointed and the ordinary administration of the trust is then carried out overseas.

In such a case, there is a deemed disposal for CGT purposes at the time that the trust ceases to be UK resident with market value being taken as the deemed disposal proceeds. As regards subsequent disposals, the trustees are deemed to have re-acquired all of their assets at market value. There is a question mark over whether such 'exit charges' are consistent with taxpayers' Community rights and free movement of capital, but as yet, no-one has been willing to fund a case on this important principle.

33.16 OFFSHORE COMPANIES

(s 13 TCGA 1992)

A person who is resident and ordinarily resident in the UK (see 34.2) may be liable for a proportion of capital gains realised by a non-resident company in which he or she has a shareholding.

Example – Possible liability for capital gains

> *K* owns all the shares in X Ltd, a company incorporated and resident in Bermuda. The company realises a capital gain by disposing of a US property that it owns. The legislation enables HMRC to assess *K* as if he made the capital gain himself. However, certain conditions need to be satisfied before HMRC can assess a capital gain in this way (see 33.16.1).

33.16.1 Conditions that need to be satisfied

First, the company must be controlled by five or fewer shareholders, or shareholder directors must between them own more than 50% of the company's shares.

Second, the individual must be resident in the UK (see 35.1 and 35.14). Since 2008–09, s 13 can apply to individuals who are resident but not domiciled in the UK.

Third, he or she, together with any persons connected with him or her for this purpose, must between them have an interest in the company of at least 25%.

33.16.2 Certain gains not assessable under s 13

The legislation is really intended to catch gains on investment assets held through an offshore company. There is therefore an exemption under s 13(5) for gains arising:

- on the disposal of foreign currency where the currency represents money in use for a trade carried on by the company outside the UK;
- from the disposal of an asset used for the purposes of economically significant activities carried on by the company through a business establishment in a territory outside the UK;

- the disposal of an asset where it can be shown that neither that disposal nor the acquisition formed part of a scheme or arrangements of which the main purpose was the evidence of liability to capital gains tax or corporation tax;
- from disposals of assets used by a UK permanent establishment of the company.

The application of s 13 can be complex, particularly the reliefs available where there have been distributions in the period prior to the gain accruing and it is recommended that professional advice is taken where this legislation may be in point

33.17 NON-RESIDENT TRUSTS

(ss 86, 87 and Schedule 5 TCGA 1992)

33.17.1 Introduction

The trustees of a trust may be resident outside the UK and the administration of the trust may be carried out overseas. Provided both these conditions are satisfied, the trust is not resident and there will not normally be any liability for the trustees so far as UK CGT is concerned. There may be a liability for either the settlor (ie the person who set up the trust) or the beneficiaries (who may include the settlor).

33.17.2 'Qualifying' trusts

(s 86 and Schedule 5 TCGA 1992)

The legislation refers to 'qualifying settlements'. In fact, they qualify for an adverse CGT treatment in that the trustees' gains are deemed to be the settlor's personal capital gains subject to the proviso that the settlor's annual exemption and any personal losses are set first against personal gains and only any excess set against the 'attributed gains'. The amount attributed to the settlor is the amount remaining after the deduction of losses. If the computation itself produces a loss, this cannot be transferred to the settlor. Unlike the s 87 charge on beneficiaries, the s 86 charge was not extended by FA 2008 to include non-UK domiciled settlors.

33.17.3 Attribution of gains – conditions

The conditions under which the trust's capital gains will be treated in this way are as follows:

(1) The settlor must be UK resident or ordinarily resident for the year concerned.

(2) The settlor must be domiciled in the UK for the year in which the trustees realise capital gains.

(3) He or she must not have died during the course of the year.

(4) The people who benefit from the trust include one of the following:

    (a) the settlor;

    (b) the settlor's spouse or civil partner;

    (c) any child (including step-children) of the settlor or of the settlor's spouse or civil partner;

    (d) the spouse or civil partner of any such child;

    (e) any grandchild of the settlor or of the settlor's spouse or civil partner;

    (f) the spouse or civil partner of any such grandchild;

    (g) a company controlled by a person or persons falling within (a) to (f) above;

    (h) a company associated with a company falling within (g) above.

33.17.4 Relief for the settlor's personal losses

It is possible for an individual who would be taxed on capital gains under s 86 to set off his or her personal CGT losses against these attributed gains, but only after setting these (and the annual exemption) against personal gains.

33.17.5 Interaction with entrepreneurs' relief

Where trustees make a disposal of qualifying business assets and a beneficiary ('the qualifying beneficiary') has an interest in possession in the whole, or the part of the trust fund comprising those assets, then entrepreneurs' relief (ER) may be due. A further condition must be met in relation to the qualifying beneficiary's personal interest in the business assets or shares concerned. See 31.2.3 for more details.

Trustees are not themselves entitled to a £10m ER allowance in the same way as individuals. Any relief given to trustees is treated as having been given to the qualifying beneficiary and serves to reduce his or her entitlement for future disposals.

Where there are two qualifying disposals made on the same day, one by the trustees and the other by an individual who is also a qualifying beneficiary of that trust, the trustees' disposal is treated as having occurred after the one made by the individual.

The effect of these provisions is to restrict an individual's relief threshold by the relief granted to trustees of a settlement of which he or she is a qualifying beneficiary.

A claim to ER must be made jointly by the trustees and the qualifying beneficiary and so it is not possible to utilise the qualifying beneficiary's lifetime limit without his or her consent.

33.17.6 Stockpiled gains in pre-March 1991 trusts

(s 97(1) TCGA 1992)

UK-resident beneficiaries may be assessed for CGT purposes under s 87 TCGA 1992 on a proportion of the trustees' pre 1998–99 capital gains ('stockpiled gains') that can be 'matched' with capital payments received.

The receipt of a benefit may count as a deemed capital payment (the rules are virtually the same as under s 732: see 33.5).

Example – Pre-19 March 1991 offshore trusts

> Trustees of an offshore trust make capital gains in 1989–90 of £200,000. In 1989–90 to 1991–92 the trustees distribute income, but their doing this does not have any CGT consequences. In 2014–15 they make a capital payment of £50,000 to *L*, who is UK-resident.
>
> *L* would be assessed as if she had personally made capital gains of £50,000 for 2014–15. The tax actually payable will depend on whether she has made other capital gains and her rate of tax.

33.17.7 UK-resident beneficiaries of settlements not caught by s 86

(ss 87, 87A–87C TCGA 1992)

Where a UK resident beneficiary receives a capital payment from a settlement that is not caught by s 86 (eg where the settlor has died, or none of the persons defined at 33.17.3 can benefit), he or she may be taxed under s 87 on stockpiled capital gains that can be matched with the capital payment. This rule has been in place since 1981 as far as settlements created by UK domiciliaries are concerned.

33.17.8 Supplementary charge

A supplementary charge may be made of 10% of the tax for each complete year between 1 December following the year in which the trustees realised the gain and the time the trustees make the capital distribution. The supplementary charge cannot exceed 60%. Since 6 April

2008, gains are matched on a LIFO basis. Prior to that, matching was on a FIFO basis. With the increase in the tax rate from 18% to 28% for trusts, the potential maximum rate on offshore trust gains has increased from 28.8% to 44.8%.

33.17.9 Settlements created by foreign domiciliaries

UK domiciliaries were made liable to tax on capital payments from trusts created by foreign domiciliaries by FA 1998. With effect from 17 March 1998, UK-resident and domiciled beneficiaries could be assessed where they received capital payments from a non-resident trust created by a foreign domiciled settlor; this applied only where payments made after 16 March 1998 could be matched with gains realised by the trustees after that date. With effect from 6 April 2008, the charge was extended to non-UK domiciled beneficiaries, the only proviso being that they were resident in the UK.

33.17.10 Beneficiary's capital losses

It is not possible for a beneficiary to offset personal CGT losses against gains attributed to him or her under s 87 TCGA 1992.

33.17.11 Foreign domiciliaries

FA 2008 brought foreign domiciliaries within the scope of s 87 in relation to capital gains realised by the trustees on or after 6 April 2008. However, there is a key difference in that if the beneficiary is a remittance basis user he or she will be subject to tax under s 87 only if he or she brings the capital payment into the UK (depending upon his or her circumstances, the foreign domiciliary may need to pay the £30,000 special charge to obtain the benefit of the remittance basis (see 35.2)). Furthermore, the trustees can elect for all gains to be computed as if the market value of the asset at 5 April 2008 were the cost.

The FA 2008 changes are wide-reaching and this is a complex area where professional advice is essential.

33.17.12 Sale of trust interest by beneficiary

(s 76 TCGA 1992)

A disposal of an interest in a non-resident trust has been a disposal of a chargeable asset for CGT purposes since 1981. On the other hand, a disposal of an interest in a UK resident trust has not normally been subject to CGT, unless it is for consideration (see Schedule 4A).

FA 1998 introduced a further rule so that if beneficiaries of UK-resident trusts dispose of their interests, and the trust has been non-resident in the past, the beneficiaries' disposal is subject to CGT.

A double tax charge is prevented where the disposal of the interest is not exempt under s 76(1) TCGA 1992, and the disposal also triggers a deemed disposal under Schedule 4A. The broad effect is to maximise the net chargeable gain or, if there is no net gain, to minimise the net allowable loss, by securing that the provision which would maximise the gain (or minimise the loss) has effect and that the other does not.

INHERITANCE TAX

33.18 PURCHASED INTERESTS IN EXCLUDED PROPERTY SETTLEMENTS

A trust created by an individual of foreign domicile settling foreign situs assets is excluded property for IHT purposes (see 35.16).

The last Labour Government discovered that this has been used for avoidance by UK domiciliaries who purchased interests under such settlements as a form of 'death-bed planning'. The definition of excluded property now excludes interests in such trusts where the interest was purchased on or after 5 December 2005 (whether the purchase was by the individual who owns the interest or by someone else).

33.18.1 Reversionary interests in relevant property

(s 81A IHTA 1984)

Section 81A, which was inserted in IHTA by FA (No.1) 2010, applies where an individual transfers property into a trust in which he or she or his or her spouse or civil partner retains a future interest. The rule also applies where an individual purchases a future interest in a trust on or after 9 December 2009.

It provides that there will be a chargeable event for IHT purposes when the future interest comes to an end and the person becomes entitled to an actual interest under the trust. If that future interest is given away before the person becomes entitled to an actual interest, it may be immediately chargeable to IHT.

33.18.2 Purchased interests in possession

Section 5(1B) IHTA 1984 (see 31.4.21) was inserted by s 53 FA (No.1) 2010. This means that where an individual purchases an interest in possession in a trust at full value, such an interest will be treated as part of the his or her estate for IHT purposes (ie as a 'qualifying' IIP). If the interest comes to an end during the purchaser's lifetime, there may be an immediate charge to IHT. This legislation has effect for interests purchased on or after 9 December 2009.

33.18.3 New avoidance scheme closed

In response to a disclosed avoidance scheme, the Government introduced anti-avoidance legislation aimed at individuals domiciled in the UK who acquire excluded property trust interests. Where such interests are acquired so that the value of the individual's estate is reduced, the reduction will be charged to IHT as an immediately chargeable transfer. The assets settled in the offshore trust will cease to be treated as excluded property and will instead become subject to the relevant property regime. The tax (including charges normally payable by the trustees) will be payable by the individual.

The provisions apply to new schemes entered into on or after 21 March 2012. They also apply to schemes or arrangements entered into before that date but only in relation to periodic and exit charges arising on or after that date.

GENERAL

33.19 *RAMSAY* PRINCIPLE

This chapter has concentrated so far on anti-avoidance legislation. There is another factor, ie case law, which has been developed by the courts that HMRC can use in much the same way as anti-avoidance legislation to counter tax avoidance schemes.

The House of Lords decided in the *Ramsay case* (*IRC* v *W T Ramsay Limited* [1981] STC 174) that it should determine the tax consequences of a 'composite transaction' (ie a series of interlinked transactions) by looking at the overall effect. Furthermore, artificial steps that had been introduced only for tax avoidance purposes could be disregarded.

In another famous case, *Furniss* v *Dawson* 1984 STC 153, taxpayers sought to avoid CGT by exchanging their shares in a UK company for shares in an Isle of Man company which on the same day (in fact immediately after lunch) sold its shares in the UK company to a third party purchaser. The House of Lords held that the interpolation of the Isle of Man company was an artificial step that could be disregarded and the UK vendors were therefore treated as if they had sold their UK company directly to the ultimate purchaser.

Broadly, the *Ramsay* doctrine was summarised in another House of Lords case as applying only in the following circumstances:

- There was a pre-ordained series of transactions in mind from the outset that were intended to produce a given result.
- Certain transactions within that series of transactions had no purpose other than tax avoidance.
- At the time that the transactions were carried out, there was no practical likelihood that the pre-planned series of transactions

would not take place in the order ordained. In that sense, some of the intermediate transactions were not contemplated as having a life independent from the pre-ordained series of transactions.

- The pre-ordained events did in fact take place.

Note that the courts have attached a great deal of importance to transactions being pre-ordained. This is not quite the same thing as pre-conceived. An individual might carry out a series of transactions with a view to ultimately selling a company to a third party. That series of transactions would be pre-conceived but would be pre-ordained only if the series of transactions were carried out with a particular purchaser in view. In one particular case, steps had been carried out with a view to a sale to a particular purchaser. That transaction fell through and the vendors eventually sold to a different person. It was held that a series of transactions started with the original purchaser in mind was not a single composite transaction and *Ramsay* therefore did not enable HMRC to strike out those individual steps that secured a tax advantage for the vendor.

The likely application of the *Ramsay* doctrine to specific transactions carried out with tax savings in mind is fraught with uncertainty. There have been several recent court decisions. At one stage, it appeared that a distinction was being drawn between commercial concepts and legal concepts, with purely legal concepts being less susceptible to *Ramsay*. However, this appears to have been a misunderstanding and recent decisions in the *Arrowtown* and *Carreras* cases indicate a very wide interpretation of the *Ramsay* doctrine.

The House of Lords has held that conditions put into contracts merely to create some uncertainty as to the final outcome should be ignored. Their Lordships held that the creation of uncertainty by the insertion of such conditions did not prevent the final outcome from being preordained. Tax statutes generally will be construed purposively, unless it is obvious that they should not be so construed (for instance in the case of a purely 'mechanical' section, stating how the gain or loss on a certain transaction is to be calculated).

The ECJ has held that a VAT avoidance scheme failed because it amounted to an 'abuse of rights'. It remains to be seen whether this will be invoked by HMRC in areas other than VAT (*Halifax plc & others* v *C&E Commissioners 2006* 2 WLR 905).

Tax notes

Any taxpayer undertaking an artificial tax scheme should bear in mind that HMRC may well attack it by invoking the *Ramsay* doctrine and that the courts have become increasingly sympathetic to such arguments.

33.20   GENERAL ANTI-ABUSE RULE (GAAR)

GAAR can apply to transactions which are entered into after FA 2013 received royal assent and operates so as to eliminate tax advantages that might otherwise accrue from those transactions.

The tests which must be satisfied for GAAR to apply are:

- Are there arrangements which give rise to a tax advantage?
- Is it reasonable to conclude that the obtaining of the tax advantage was the main purpose, or one of the main purposes, of the arrangements?
- Are the arrangements abusive?

Arrangements are abusive if they cannot reasonably be regarded as a reasonable course of action in relation to the relevant tax provisions, having regard to all the circumstances, and in particular taking into account:

- whether the substantive results of the arrangements are consistent with the principles on which the tax provisions are based and the policy objectives of those provisions;
- whether the means of achieving those results involve one or more contrived or abnormal steps; and
- whether the arrangements are intended to exploit shortcomings in the relevant tax provisions.

An indicator that arrangements are not abusive is that they accord with established practice and HMRC had indicated its acceptance of this practice at the time that the transactions were carried out.

33.21   DISCLOSURE OF TAX AVOIDANCE SCHEMES (DOTAS)

33.21.1   Basic structure of the DOTAS regulations

A tax arrangement must be disclosed when:

- it will, or might be expected to, enable any person to obtain a tax advantage;
- that tax advantage is, or might be expected to be, the main benefit or one of the main benefits of the arrangement; and
- it is a tax arrangement that falls within any description ('hallmarks') prescribed in the relevant regulations.

In most situations where a disclosure is required it must be made by the scheme 'promoter' within five days of it being marketed. However, the scheme user may need to make the disclosure where:

- the promoter is based outside the UK;
- the promoter is a lawyer and legal privilege applies; or
- there is no promoter.

The hallmarks are:

- wishing to keep the arrangements confidential from a competitor;
- wishing to keep the arrangements confidential from HMRC;
- arrangements for which a premium fee could reasonably be obtained;
- arrangements that are standardised tax products;
- arrangements that are loss schemes;
- arrangements that are certain leasing arrangements.

Upon receiving the disclosure under the disclosure regime, HMRC issues the promoter with an eight-digit scheme reference number for the disclosed scheme. By law the promoter must provide this number to each client that uses the scheme, who in turn must include the number on his or her return or form AAG4. A person who designs and implements their own scheme must disclose it within 30 days of it being implemented. The registration does not imply any judgment on the technical merits of the scheme.

33.21.2 Other DOTAS obligations and penalties

'Introducers' must disclose details of promoters – advisers who are approached by promoters of schemes with a view to introducing them to their clients will be required, on production of a notice by HMRC, to provide details of the promoters that have approached them. The maximum penalty can be £1m.

Promoters of tax schemes are required to provide quarterly lists of clients to whom they should have issued a scheme reference number.

See also the HMRC guidance at www.hmrc.gov.uk/aiu/, which is regularly updated.

> **Tax notes**
>
> It is necessary to disclose all arrangements that seek to avoid income tax, corporation tax and CGT which contain certain 'hallmarks'.

33.21.3 DOTAS extended to other taxes

The disclosure regime also applies to tax arrangements relating to SDLT where the subject matter of the arrangements is commercial property with a market value of at least £5m and further in 2008 to include residential property with a value in excess of £1m.

The main differences compared with the disclosure regime for income tax, corporation tax and capital gains tax are:

- the hallmarks are not applied to limit what is required to be disclosed, however there is a 'white list' of arrangements that are not required to be disclosed;

- promoters are not obliged to provide reference numbers to scheme users;
- some minor differences in the time limits for making disclosure.

The disclosure regime applies also to arrangements relating to NIC. Again the rules broadly mirror those for income tax, corporation tax and capital gains tax, except that the last two hallmarks do not apply. VAT is subject to a separate disclosure regime.

33.21.4 Advance payment may be required

FA 2014 provided that payment of tax can be required from taxpayers involved in planning arrangements which HMRC believes should fail as a result of principles established in related court decisions. It may also issue a notice requiring 'accelerated payments' in cases where a taxpayer has used a scheme which has been disclosed under the DOTAS regulations or has entered into transactions which HMRC counteracts under the GAAR provisions.

34

RESIDENCE STATUS

This chapter contains the following sections:

(1) Consequences of residence in the UK
(2) Various criteria for determining residence status
(3) Split year treatment
(4) Short-term residents
(5) Double taxation agreements
(6) UK income and capital gains received by non-residents
(7) Non-resident investment companies
(8) When tax should be withheld from payments to non-residents
(9) Crown servants working overseas
(10) Scotland

34.1 CONSEQUENCES OF RESIDENCE IN THE UK

The basic principle of UK taxation is that an individual may be charged tax on worldwide income and capital gains if he or she is resident in the UK. If not so resident, he or she is still liable for tax on income that arises in the UK, but not for tax on income that arises overseas, or on any capital gains wherever arising (subject to the provisions relating to temporary non-UK residence and UK property).

There is an exception to this in that an individual who is UK resident but not domiciled in the UK, may only have to pay tax on UK income and overseas income which is brought to (or 'remitted' to) the UK. The concept of domicile is different from residence (see 35.1) and this chapter proceeds on the basis that an individual has a domicile within the UK. (Technically, an individual's domicile in the UK will be within a specific country, ie England, Wales, Scotland or Northern Ireland. For the sake of expediency, this is referred to throughout this book as 'domicile within the UK', 'UK domicile', etc).

34.2 VARIOUS CRITERIA FOR DETERMINING RESIDENCE STATUS

34.2.1 Introduction

For UK taxation purposes, 'the UK' means England, Scotland, Wales and Northern Ireland. It does not include the Republic of Ireland, the Channel Islands or the Isle of Man. A person may be resident in more than one country so the fact that he or she is treated as resident in another country does not necessarily mean that he or she is not resident in the UK.

34.2.2 Onus on taxpayer to prove non-residence

In *Rumbelow* [2013] TC03022, the taxpayers appealed against amendments to self-assessments and discovery assessments relating to tax years from 2001–02 to 2004–05. A key issue was whether Mr and Mrs Rumbelow were resident in the UK for each of these years. The Tribunal decided:

- that their settled and usual abode was in the UK in 2001–02 and 2002–03, and that they had remained UK resident in those years; and
- that because the taxpayers had brought insufficient evidence as to where they were during 2003–04 and 2004–05, they had not discharged the burden of proof and were to be treated as resident for those years.

This decision contrasts with that in *Glyn* v *HMRC* TC03029 where the Tribunal found in favour of the taxpayer which succeeded because of his meticulous record-keeping. Mr Glyn moved to Monacco but retained his London home. Mrs Glyn remained UK resident as she spent more than 90 days per annum in the UK. Mr Glyn came to the UK for business reasons and sometimes stayed in the family home. He was held to have been not resident for 2005–06 despite his having spent 65 days in the UK.

34.2.3 Statutory definition of 'resident'

Somewhat surprisingly, up to FA 2013, the word 'resident' was not defined in the Taxes Acts, and up to 5 April 2013 was based on case law and HMRC practice. However, a Statutory Residence Test (SRT) applied with effect from 6 April 2013. It had been hoped that the test would be a straightforward day counting exercise, similar to those applying in other jurisdictions such as the USA, but sadly this is not the case. Instead the new legislation is quite complex and requires a series of tests to be considered. Under the new rules an individual will be treated as tax resident in the UK if he or she satisfies one of the Automatic UK Tests, or the Sufficient Ties Test, and does not satisfy one of the Automatic Overseas Tests.

In addition, the Government has abolished the general concept of ordinary residence although it has been replaced by legislation which allows short-term UK resident, foreign domiciled employees to continue to claim the remittance basis where part of their duties is carried out overseas.

34.2.4 The various tests

Automatic Overseas Tests

There are four Automatic Overseas Tests, and if an individual meets the conditions of any one of these tests he or she will automatically be treated as non-resident. These tests are as follows:

- The individual was resident in the UK for one or more of the three previous years and spent less than 16 days in the UK in the current year.
- He or she was not resident in the UK for any of the three previous tax years and spend less than 46 days in the UK in the current year.
- In the current tax year the individual leaves the UK to take up full-time work overseas, spends less than 91 days in the UK and spends less than 31 days working in the UK.
- He or she dies in the current tax year, and spent less than 46 days in the UK.

Automatic UK Tests

If an individual is unable to meet any of the Automatic Overseas Tests, there are four Automatic UK Tests to consider as follows:

- The individual spent at least 183 days in the UK during the tax year.
- That there is a period of more than 90 days, part of which falls within the tax year, when the individual has a home in the UK and no home overseas. Any home at which he or she is present for less than 30 days is disregarded.
- He or she works full time in the UK.
- He or she dies in the current tax year, having been resident in the UK in the previous three years.

Sufficient Ties Test

If an individual does not qualify as a non-resident under any of the Automatic Overseas Tests, and is not treated as resident under any of the Automatic UK Tests, it is necessary to consider the Sufficient Ties Test. This test compares the number of days spent in the UK with a number of connection factors, and varies depending on whether the individual has been UK resident in any of the three previous year, or not.

These connection factors are:

- UK resident family;
- substantive UK employment or self-employment for 40 or more days in the tax year;
- available accommodation in the UK;
- more than 90 days spent in the UK in either or both of the previous two tax years. There is a further addition to this connection for individuals who have been UK resident in any of the previous three years, and this is that they spend more time in the UK than any other country.

Table 34.1 and Figure 34.1 show the comparison.

Table 34.1 – Sufficient Ties Test

Individuals not UK resident in any of three previous years	
Number of days spent in the UK	UK resident if number of ties is at least
More than 45 but less than 91	4
More than 90 but less than 121	3
More than 120	2
Individuals UK resident in any of three previous years	
Number of days spent in the UK	UK resident if number of ties is at least
More than 15 but less than 46	4
More than 45 but less than 91	3
More than 90 but less than 121	2
More than 120	1

34.2.5 Days that are counted as UK days

Sections 831(1A) and 831(1B) ITA 2007 provided that from 6 April 2008 onwards, any day in which an individual is present in the UK at midnight is counted as a day in the UK. However, days spent in transit will not count as UK days even if the individual is present in the UK at midnight, provided that the individual does not engage in activities that are inconsistent with merely being in transit. This definition is reaffirmed in FA 2013 although there are a number of exceptions in certain circumstances to ensure that certain other days will not apply for the purposes of some of the residence tests. In particular, different rules apply to those present on a large number of days without being in the UK at midnight on those days. These rules will apply to individuals who have been resident in the UK for any of the previous three years, have at least three ties for the tax year, and are present in the UK at some point on more than 30 days, but not at midnight.

Figure 34.1 – Sufficient Ties Test

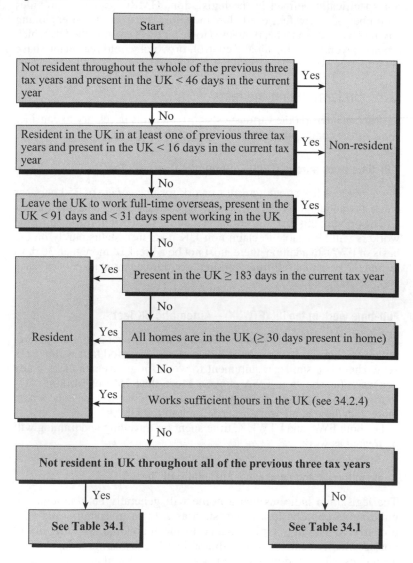

Days spent in the UK due to exceptional circumstances

Up to 60 days may be disregarded if an individual's presence in the UK is due to exceptional circumstances beyond his or her control. Although not specifically defined in the legislation, HMRC guidance provides a number of interesting examples, including a car crash, an exploding engine on a boat and a heart attack. However days spent in the UK which are *not* beyond the individual's control, or which could reasonably have been foreseen or predicted, will not be disregarded.

34.2.6 Understanding the tests

In order to interpret the various tests correctly it is necessary to consider some of the conditions more closely.

Full-time work abroad (FWA) – Automatic Overseas Test

The employee has a requirement to work for an average of 35 hours per week, but annual leave, sick leave and parenting leave can be disregarded when applying this test. Unfortunately, under the current rules, part-time workers will be unable to claim non-UK residence status purely on the basis of FWA. In addition, there must not be a break of more than 30 days during the period of full-time working, excluding annual leave, sick leave and parenting leave.

Full-time work in the UK (FTWUK) – Automatic UK Test

This test is met by employees who work in the UK over a 365-day period, without a significant break, and all or part of this period falls within a tax year. There is a similar requirement to work for an average of 35 hours per week (as shown in FWA above). More than 75% of working days in this period must be UK work days, and a UK work day is one where more than three hours work is carried out in the UK.

For both FWA and FTWUK, time spent on travelling and training will be treated as work.

Home in the UK and overseas – Automatic UK Test

The legislation indicates that a home will generally be a structure or building as opposed to a place, such as a town or country, and with a degree of stability or permanence to the individual, and that it will not necessarily continue to be a home just because an individual holds an interest in it. A property used periodically as nothing more than a holiday home will not count as a home, and HMRC has stated that 'we consider that a person's home is a place that a reasonable onlooker with a knowledge of the material facts would regard as that person's home'.

There is also a minimum presence rule which disregards any home that is occupied by the individual on less than 30 days during the tax year. For this purpose a person will be regarded as having spent a day at home if he or she is there at any point during the day.

Accommodation in the UK – Sufficient Ties Test

Accommodation will be treated as available accommodation for the purposes of this test if the individual would be able to stay there for at least a three-month period, but a casual invitation by a friend or relative would not be treated as available accommodation unless the offer would genuinely extend for a stay of at least three months, ignoring gaps of less than 16 days when it is available. Unlike the home tests, accommodation for this test will include a holiday home if this is available,

Family ties – Sufficient Ties Test

An individual is considered to have a family tie for a tax year if he or she has a relevant relationship with another person in that tax year and that other person is someone who is resident in the UK in that tax year. The individual will be treated as having a relevant relationship with another person if that other person is his or her husband, wife or civil partner (so long as they are not separated) or they are living together in that manner. This of course raises the question of how the nature of an informal relationship will be determined by HMRC.

There will also be a family tie for a tax year if the individual has a child under age 18 who is UK resident in that tax year, unless the individual sees that child on no more than 60 days in that tax year, or the part of that tax year before the child reaches the age of 18. For the purposes of this test the child will not be treated as UK resident if he or she is in full-time education, and spends less than 21 days in the UK, outside term time. Half-term breaks are however considered as term time.

34.2.7 Death in the tax year

There are special rules for establishing the residence position of individuals who die during the tax year.

A new Automatic Overseas Test is introduced, which will automatically treat the deceased as non-UK resident if:

- he or she was not resident for both immediately preceding tax years, or not resident for the preceding year and eligible for split year treatment by virtue of his or her departure from the UK in the year before that; and
- he or she spends less than 46 days in the UK in the tax year.

The first, second and third Automatic UK Tests will apply to deceased individuals, but additionally there is a fourth test if:

- the individual was resident for each of the three preceding tax years, by virtue of meeting one of the automatic UK residence tests in those years;
- assuming that he or she was not resident in the UK for the tax year, the preceding year would not have been a split year; and
- he or she had a home in the UK at the time of death.

34.3 SPLIT YEAR TREATMENT

The split year treatment allows an individual to qualify as a non-resident for part of a tax year. Prior to 6 April 2013, the split year rules were relatively straightforward, but there are now eight split year scenarios depending on the circumstances. Cases 1–3 deal with leavers and cases 4–8 with arrivers. These are:

- Case 1: starting full-time work overseas;
- Case 2: the partner of someone who starts full-time work overseas;
- Case 3: leaving the UK to live abroad;
- Case 4: starting to have a home in the UK;
- Case 5: coming to live or work full-time in the UK;
- Case 6: deals with an individual ceasing to have full-time work overseas;
- Case 7: deals with the partner of someone ceasing to have full-time work overseas; and
- Case 8: deals with an individual starting to have a home in the UK.

Where an individual's circumstances are such that he or she would fall within more than one of cases 4–8, then the following priorities apply:

(1) For individuals falling within case 6, case 6 takes priority EXCEPT where case 5 applies AND the split year date in case 5 is earlier than in case 6, in which circumstance case 5 takes priority.
(2) For individuals falling within case 7 (but not within case 6), case 7 takes priority EXCEPT where case 5 applies AND the split year date in case 5 is earlier than in case 7, in which circumstance case 5 takes priority.
(3) For individuals falling within two or more of cases 4, 5 and 8, the case with the earliest split year date takes priority.

34.4 SHORT-TERM RESIDENTS

The concept of ordinary residence has been removed from 6 April 2013 and this has the effect of restricting claims for the remittance basis to those individuals who are not domiciled in the UK.

34.4.1 Employment income

Ordinary residence was relevant to some short-term resident individuals who worked both in the UK and overseas where part, or all, of their earnings were paid offshore. These non-ordinarily resident individuals were able to claim the remittance basis on the proportion of their unremitted earnings which related to overseas workdays.

When it removed the special treatment for non-ordinarily resident individuals, the Government introduced a similar relief for short-term foreign domiciled individuals. Overseas workday relief (OWR) can be claimed by any foreign-domiciled individual who arrives in the UK after 5 April 2013.

See the Guidance Note on Overseas Workday Relief issued by HMRC in May 2013.

In fact, this treatment is more generous than the previous relief in that it is no longer just limited to individuals intending to stay for less than three years, and is available to all new residents arriving in the UK. In addition, unlike the previous rules, the relief will be available for the tax year of arrival and the two complete tax years following, regardless of whether the individual decides to buy a property in the UK or take further steps that would suggest a more permanent connection with the UK.

Table 34.2 – Basis for assessment for employment income

	Services performed			
	Wholly in UK	*Partly in UK*	*Partly abroad*	*Wholly abroad*
Non-resident	All	That part	None	None
Resident but not UK domiciled and entitled to OWD relief	All	That part	Remittances*	Remittances*
All other residents	All	All	All	All

* From 6 April 2008, all employment income is taxable on the arising basis unless a remittance basis claim is made.

Remuneration from a mixed employment (ie duties performed both within and outside the UK) is normally allocated on a working day basis. It is HMRC's practice to work to the nearest half day.

See SP1/09 on the various conditions which need to be satisfied in order that remittances to the UK out of an offshore account which contains only the income from a single employment. Interest and currency gains thereon can be matched primarily with remuneration for duties performed in the UK.

See also 35.6 on tax free subsistence and accommodation allowances which may be paid to employees who are seconded to the UK for periods not exceeding 24 months.

34.4.2 Overseas investment income

Provided that the necessary claim was made, this was taxable under the remittance basis, up to 5 April 2008. From 6 April 2008 until 5 April 2013, it is taxable on an arising basis unless a formal claim for the remittance basis is made in respect of all overseas income and capital gains. Moreover, offshore income gains from sales of non-distributor funds are always taxed on the arising basis unless the taxpayer is foreign domiciled and claiming the remittance basis. The remittance basis cannot apply for 2013–14 and subsequent years because the concept of being not ordinarily resident has been abolished.

34.4.3 Involuntary residence

(SP2/91)

HMRC accepts that where individuals are forced to spend time in the UK because of exceptional circumstances outside their control, for example, someone who was working in Libya in 2011, but who had to return to the UK prematurely following advice from the Government, would not be regarded as spending time in the UK when it was unsafe to remain in Libya. This particular concession only applied to the 91-day average test but not the 183-day test. Similarly, where an individual spends days in the UK because of becoming ill while in the UK, these may be left out of account.

These concessions do not apply where an individual returns to the UK because his or her employer has prematurely terminated his or her employment contract. Also, and more fundamentally, HMRC's concession does not affect the statutory rule that an individual is automatically treated as UK-resident if he or she spends 183 days or more in the UK during a particular tax year.

Tax notes

Concessions on residence status do not apply where an individual returns to the UK because the employer has prematurely terminated an employment contract or for the 183-day residence rule.

34.4.4 **Temporary non-residence**

An individual who leaves the UK and who:

- has been tax resident in the UK for any part of at least four out of the seven tax years immediately preceding the year of departure; and
- becomes not resident and not ordinarily resident for a period of less than five tax years; and
- owns assets before he or she leaves the UK,

remains liable to tax on any gains arising on those assets after departure from the UK. Gains made by him or her in the year of assessment in which he or she leaves the UK are chargeable for that year. Gains made after that year are chargeable in the year of assessment in which he or she resumes residence in the UK at the rates prevailing in that year. Losses are allowable on the same basis as gains are chargeable. Gains of non-resident trusts and companies may also be taxed if they would have been taxable had the individual been resident here.

Any gains made in the intervening years (ie between the tax years of departure and of return) on assets acquired by the taxpayer after becoming tax resident abroad are exempt from the charge. This exemption will not apply to assets held in a non-resident trust or closely controlled non-resident company. Special rules prevent gains on assets held before departure from escaping the charge, where gains are rolled over or otherwise deferred on the acquisition of assets during the period of absence.

It was at one point believed that certain double taxation agreements might protect a temporary non-resident from the five-year rule. Statements by HMRC cast doubt on this and the matter was put beyond doubt in FA 2005.

A similar rule was introduced in FA 2008 (now in s 832A ITTOIA 2005) in respect of relevant foreign income of temporary non-residents remitted to the UK during periods of temporary non-UK residence. FA 2013 has extended this further and other income such as profits from non-qualifying insurance bonds, gains from offshore funds, lump sum payments from pension schemes and certain dividends from close companies may now be taxed as income of the year in which the individual resumes residence in the UK.

34.5 DOUBLE TAXATION AGREEMENTS

The UK has entered into many double taxation agreements (also known as double tax treaties) with other countries. The provisions of such an agreement may override UK tax law. Specifically, the agreement may provide exemption for certain income received by a person resident overseas even though the income arises in the UK. For example, most double taxation agreements provide that a resident of the foreign country concerned may claim exemption from UK tax in connection with interest income arising in the UK.

Most double taxation agreements also make provision for the situation where an individual is resident in both the foreign country and the UK. They usually contain a clause along the following lines:

(1) If the individual has a permanent home in only one country, he or she is deemed to be resident there.
(2) If the position has not been resolved by (1), he or she is treated as resident where he or she has the centre of his or her personal and economic interests.
(3) If the above tests do not resolve the position, he or she is treated as resident in the country where he or she has a 'habitual abode'.
(4) If he or she has a habitual abode in both countries, he or she is deemed to be a resident of the country of which he or she is a national.
(5) If he or she is a national of both countries or he or she is not a national of either country; the revenue authorities of the UK and the foreign country may settle the matter by mutual agreement.

These provisions apply only for the purposes of determining residence under the agreement. They are deeming provisions and, under UK law, an individual might still be regarded as UK resident even though he or she might be treated as resident in the foreign country for the purposes of the double taxation agreement. However, the terms of a double taxation agreement override UK tax law and, if an individual is deemed to be resident in a foreign country under the agreement, his or her liability to UK tax is then computed in accordance with the other provisions of the agreement.

34.6 UK INCOME AND CAPITAL GAINS RECEIVED BY NON-RESIDENTS

A person who is not UK resident for a tax year may still be subject to tax on UK source income, but is not liable to tax on income that arises abroad. The following types of income are deemed to arise within the UK and are therefore subject to tax even where the individual is not resident there:

- employment income that relates to duties performed in the UK;
- trading profits from a branch or permanent establishment in the UK;
- rents from UK properties;
- dividends from UK companies;
- interest paid by a person who is UK-resident;
- 'annual payments' made by a UK-resident person.

Tax charged on investment income of a non-resident individual is normally limited to the tax deducted at source (s 811 ITA 2007). This does not apply to income from property in the UK or from trading in the UK through a broker or investment manager. UK investment income of non-resident trustees is specifically excluded from this limitation to tax deducted at source (s 812 ITA 2007).

The provisions of a double tax agreement or extra statutory concession may also limit the tax charged on a non-resident individual.

34.6.1 Earned income

Where an individual is non-resident, profits from a trade carried on outside the UK are not subject to UK tax. Where such a person has a branch or permanent establishment in the UK, a liability to UK tax may arise on profits earned from that UK presence. Double taxation agreement provisions may govern what type of presence in the UK is deemed to constitute a branch or permanent establishment.

Earnings from an employment will attract UK tax where the duties are performed in the UK unless exemption is available under a double taxation agreement (see 34.6.5).

Where an individual works full-time abroad under a contract of employment, the resulting income is not subject to UK tax even though the employer may be a UK company. However, a Crown employee or a member of the Armed Forces is regarded as performing the duties of his or her employment in the UK and he or she may therefore be subject to UK tax even though he or she performs all his or her duties overseas and is not resident in the UK.

Problems have arisen in recent years where an individual was granted a non-approved share option at a time when he or she was UK-resident and subject to tax under s 15 ITEPA 2003, with the option subsequently exercised after he or she ceased to be UK resident. HMRC's view is that a liability arises in these circumstances even if he or she is no longer employed by the company concerned (see *Tax Bulletin 60* (as well as articles in *Bulletins 46, 55* and *56*) October 2002 on HMRC's views on treaty relief). However, any lingering doubts were put to rest in FA 2008 with effect from 6 April 2008. The amount taxable will usually be calculated by reference to the proportion of UK residence during the option vesting period, although the provisions of some double tax treaties (e.g. UK/USA) will alternatively consider the period from the date of grant to the date of exercise.

Pensions paid by UK providers to non-UK residents are subject to tax unless the recipient can claim the benefit of a double taxation agreement (see 34.6.5).

34.6.2 Concession for bank and building society interest

In practice, certain income arising from a UK source is not subject to UK tax. In particular, bank deposit interest is not subject to deduction of UK tax at source provided the non-resident certifies he or she is not ordinarily resident in the UK (s 858 ITA 2007). HMRC will not assess such income unless the account is managed or controlled by a UK-resident agent. This also applies to interest or dividends paid gross by a building society, discounts (eg on deep discount bonds), gains on deep gain securities and interest on certificates of tax deposit.

34.6.3 Exempt gilts

Interest paid on all British Government securities is exempt from UK tax where the person who owns the security is not UK-resident (unless the interest forms part of the profits of a trade carried on in the UK).

34.6.4 Income from property

Rental income received by an individual from a UK property is subject to UK tax even if he or she is not UK-resident. A tenant who pays rent exceeding £100 pw direct to a non-resident landlord should withhold basic rate tax at source unless HMRC has authorised the rent to be paid gross under the non-resident landlord scheme. Where rent is paid to a UK agent, the tenant is not required to withhold tax at the basic rate, but the agent must then deduct tax from the net rental income.

HMRC will authorise a tenant or agent to make gross payments if the landlord has registered for self-assessment and his or her tax affairs are up to date. See www.hmrc.gov.uk/cnr/nr_landlords.htm.

> **Tax notes**
>
> Rental income received by an individual from a UK property is subject to UK tax even if he or she is not UK-resident.

34.6.5 Double taxation agreements

Where a non-UK resident individual is resident in a foreign country that has a double taxation agreement with the UK, it may be possible for certain income that would normally suffer UK tax at source to be exempted from UK tax, or subjected only to a lower rate. However it should be noted that nearly all UK double taxation agreements contain a caveat that if the remittance basis is claimed, then any relief is precluded unless the income or gain has actually been remitted to the UK, and taxed accordingly.

Remuneration for work performed in the UK

Most double taxation agreements provide an exemption from UK tax for employment income, provided that certain conditions can be satisfied. These conditions can vary from Treaty to Treaty but generally these are:

- the person who is entitled to the remuneration is present in the UK for a period not exceeding 183 days in any 12 month period; and
- the remuneration is paid by, or on behalf of, an employer who is not UK resident; and
- the remuneration is not borne by a permanent establishment or a fixed base that the employer has in the UK.

In practice, employers can agree in advance with their tax office not to apply PAYE for employees on short-term business visits to the UK if all the following conditions are met:

- the employee is resident in a country with which the UK has a double taxation agreement which contains the standard article that exempts short-term earnings in the UK;
- he or she is coming to the UK to work for a UK company or the UK branch of an overseas company;
- he or she is expected to be in the UK for no more than 183 days in any 12-month period.
- the UK company or branch is not going to bear the cost of the employee's remuneration.

See HMRC's PAYE online manual; www.hmrc.gov.uk/manuals/pommanual/PAYE82000.htm.

Pensions

Double taxation agreements generally provide for exemption from UK tax in respect of a pension paid by a UK company or pension scheme, although such a pension is normally subject to tax in the foreign country concerned.

Interest

In general, most double taxation agreements provide for a person resident in the foreign country concerned to be exempt from UK tax on interest, or it is payable at a reduced rate. If exemption applies, the company, etc that pays the interest can be given authorisation to pay it gross. In cases where tax has been fully withheld at source, the individual may be entitled to a repayment.

Dividends

A double taxation agreement usually includes a provision that a person who receives a dividend from a UK company is only taxable in the UK at a maximum rate of 15%. Such dividends will also have an attached notional dividend tax credit of 10%, but this is not refundable.

Royalties

Most double taxation agreements provide that where a royalty is received by a person resident in the foreign country concerned, the royalties shall be free from UK tax.

34.6.6 Allowances and reliefs

A British subject, or Commonwealth citizen, was previously entitled to full personal allowances for a tax year, even if he or she was not a UK resident. This entitlement was withdrawn for Commonwealth citizens from 6 April 2010, unless available under the provisions of a double taxation agreement.

Nationals of EU countries have been entitled to a full personal allowance since 1996–97. This also applies to nationals of Iceland, Norway and Liechtenstein. Allowances may also be available to residents or citizens of other countries under the terms of a double taxation agreement (eg Japan).

A non-resident person is not generally entitled to repayment supplement so it is normally important that tax should not be overpaid where this can be avoided. However, EU nationals may be entitled to such a supplement even though they are not UK-resident.

Limit on tax liability of non-residents

Chapter 1, Part 14 ITA 2007 limits the extent of the UK tax liability on non-residents so that, in general terms, it does not exceed:

- the tax due on total income less excluded income, but without relief for personal allowances, plus
- the tax deducted at source from the excluded income.

For the purposes of this section excluded income is:

- interest from UK sources (see Chapter 9);
- dividend income from UK companies (see 9.8);
- profits on the disposal of certificates of deposit (see 10.6);
- certain Social Security benefits including state pensions (see Chapter 37);

- other trading income carried out by brokers and investments managers as defined by s 817, but not Lloyd's underwriting income; and
- any other income so designated by the Treasury.

HMRC Helpsheet IR300 (www.hmrc.gov.uk/helpsheets/hs300.pdf) deals with this subject.

Bank interest

If bank interest suffers tax at source (usually because the individual has not declared his or her non-resident status to the bank) it is not exempt.

Section 811 ITA 2007 merely limits the UK tax on such income to the amount of tax which has been withheld. Unless you can make a claim under a double taxation agreement, you will be stuck.

Tax notes

If you are not resident in the UK, notify your bank so that interest need not be withheld at source. If tax is deducted, you may not be able to reclaim it.

34.6.7 Capital gains

A non-UK resident is not normally subject to CGT except where capital gains arise from the disposal of assets used by a branch or permanent establishment of a business carried on by him or her in the UK (but see 34.4.4 on the taxation of gains realised by former UK residents who are non-resident for less than five complete tax years and s 10(4) TCGA 1992 where temporary non-residents seek to rely on DTA exemption).

34.6.8 Capital gains on UK residential property

With effect from 6 April 2015 capital gains tax may be payable on UK residential property disposals by:

- non-resident individuals;
- personal representatives of non-residents who have died;
- any non-residents who are partners in a partnership that makes a property disposal;
- non-resident trustees;
- non-resident companies or funds.

For jointly owned properties each owner must notify HMRC.
The new rules apply when you dispose of:

- a UK residential property that was not your main home;
- your main home if it has been let it out, you used it for business, or you had long periods of absence (see 14.2 and 14.4);

- an interest in either of the above;
- properties in the process of being constructed or adapted for use as a dwelling;
- the right to acquire a UK residential property 'off plan'.

Change of use

If the use of the property has changed during ownership the gain is time apportioned to reflect any time that the property was not residential. For mixed residential and non-residential property you can make a fair and reasonable apportionment of the gain.

UK property not subject to capital gains tax

No capital gains tax or requirement to notify HMRC exists on disposals of non-residential property or certain types of residential property, including:

- care or nursing homes;
- purpose built student accommodation;
- building land, provided no residential building is under construction – this does not include disposals of rights to acquire UK residential property 'off plan';
- hospitals or hospices;
- military accommodation;
- prisons.

As a non-UK resident you will only get Private Residence Relief on a UK residential property for a tax year if:

- you or your spouse or civil partner were living in the UK for that tax year;
- you or your spouse or civil partner stayed overnight at the property at least 90 times in the tax year (the 90 day rule).

If you only owned the property for part of the year, the 90 days are time apportioned in line with the time you were the owner. You will also get Private Residence Relief if the total number of days spent in any UK property you own in the relevant tax year meets the 90 day rule – but you can only nominate one property for Private Residence Relief.

If you do not meet the 90 day rule you will be counted as away from the property for that tax year.

Private Residence Relief will also be available for trustees if the beneficiary is a non-UK resident and meets the 90 day rule outlined above.

Deadline for reporting and paying

You must report the disposal to HMRC within 30 days of conveyance of the property. Once you have reported the disposal, HMRC will send you an email with a payment reference and details on how to pay.

For example if you conveyed the property on 1 July 2015 you have until 31 July 2015 to report it.

Whether you are registered with HMRC for UK tax through self-assessment or not, you must report each property you dispose of after 5 April 2015 separately to HMRC. You do that using HMRC's online form.

You must give your calculations for each capital gain or loss that you report.

You must also pay the capital gains tax after conveyance of the property.

Self-assessment tax return

If you are already registered in the UK for self-assessment you will need to report the disposal within 30 days using the online form; you can pay when HMRC sends you the reference number. When you report the disposal you can elect to pay any capital gains tax you owe as part of your normal self-assessment end of year tax payment.

You must still fill in the capital gains section of your self-assessment tax return unless the gain is exempt due to Private Residence Relief.

Rate of tax

Individuals and trustees will pay tax at 28%; non-resident companies will pay tax at 20%.

34.7 NON-RESIDENT INVESTMENT COMPANIES

A non-UK resident who has significant investment income arising within the UK may take certain steps to minimise his or her UK tax liability. In particular, where he or she cannot claim the benefit of a double taxation agreement, it may be advisable for UK assets such as real estate to be held through a non-UK resident company. This means that any tax liability is confined to basic rate tax and there is no question of any higher rate liability. Care must be taken to ensure the company is not centrally managed and controlled in the UK; otherwise it will be taxed as a UK resident.

In such a case, it would still be sensible for some portfolio investments to be retained in his or her own name if he or she is a British subject or is otherwise entitled to claim a personal allowance. Sufficient personal income should arise to use such an allowance as this will be wasted if all the income arises within an offshore company.

In some cases, a non-resident landlord should form an offshore company to acquire UK properties already owned and let by him or her. The offshore company can raise a qualifying loan to purchase the properties from the individual concerned and interest payable on the loan may then be offset against the non-resident company's rental income. This is a way in which an individual who already owns a property that is not subject to a mortgage may create a situation where interest is payable on a qualifying loan that is deductible in computing UK property income.

> **Tax notes**
>
> Where a non-UK resident cannot claim the benefit of a double taxation agreement, it may be advisable for UK assets such as real estate to be held through a non-UK resident company.

34.8 WHEN TAX SHOULD BE WITHHELD FROM PAYMENTS TO NON-RESIDENTS

34.8.1 Non-resident sportsmen and entertainers

A person paying a non-UK resident sportsman or entertainer for work carried out in the UK is liable to withhold tax at basic rate and pay this over to HMRC (see 21.7), although it may be possible to agree an alternative withholding rate with HMRC.

In practice, where sports authorities and organisations in the UK have to bid for the right to stage events such as the Champions League Cup Final, a special exemption is granted from UK tax in respect of non-resident athletes'/players' earnings from these events. Such exemption is granted on a case by case basis. The FA 2013 contains a similar exemption for participants in the 2014 Commonwealth Games which will be held in Glasgow in 2014.

34.8.2 Rent payable to non-resident landlord

A person who pays rent to a non-resident landlord must withhold tax at the basic rate and account for this to HMRC unless he or she has been authorised to pay gross (see 34.6.4). This obligation arises whether the payment is made within the UK or by payment out of a bank account held overseas.

Where a UK resident pays a premium to a non-resident landlord, the same requirement to withhold tax arises.

Where a tenant has failed to withhold tax, he or she could be required to account for it to HMRC. In such circumstances, he or she may withhold sums from subsequent payments of rent to cover the amounts paid over to HMRC.

The obligation to withhold tax does not arise where the tenant pays rent to an agent in the UK. Also, HMRC would not normally pursue a tenant who had failed to deduct tax where he or she could not have known that the landlord was non-resident and nothing had happened to put him or her on notice. For more details, see 21.6.

34.8.3 Interest

A person paying interest to a non-resident individual or trust should withhold tax at the basic rate and account for this to HMRC.

34.9 CROWN SERVANTS WORKING OVERSEAS

A Crown servant is an individual who is an employee of the Crown whose remuneration is payable out of UK or Northern Ireland public revenue (ie a civil servant or member of HM Forces). The remuneration is treated as arising from work performed in the UK even though all work may actually be carried out overseas.

Crown servants may receive foreign service allowances, which are intended to represent compensation for the extra cost of having to live outside the UK in order to perform the duties of the employment. These foreign service allowances are specifically exempted from UK tax (s 299 ITEPA 2003). In practice, these foreign service allowances may include allowances for boarding school education for the Crown servant's children.

The value of any living accommodation occupied abroad is not subject to income tax as employment income. This is because Crown servants are regarded as representative occupiers required to live in the accommodation to do their job properly.

Most double taxation agreements provide an exemption from foreign tax for Crown servants living and working in the overseas country concerned.

Crown servants are allowed to take out certain tax-privileged investments such as ISAs and stakeholder pension plans even though they are not resident in the UK. A Crown servant may also be eligible to claim tax credits.

34.10 SCOTLAND

A Scottish rate of income tax will come into force from 6 April 2016. It will apply to Scottish taxpayers.

34.10.1 Definition of Scottish taxpayer

The legislation is contained in sections 80D–80F Scotland Act 1998. This provides for the status of an individual to be ascertained as follows:

- Most fundamentally, an individual must be UK resident if he is to be a Scottish taxpayer – a non-resident individual cannot be a Scottish taxpayer.
- An individual whose sole or main place of residence is in Scotland will be a Scottish taxpayer.
- Individuals who have more than one home in the UK will need to determine which has been their main residence for the longest part of the year. If this is in Scotland, the individual will be a Scottish taxpayer.
- Individuals who cannot identify a main place of residence will need to count the days that they spend in Scotland and elsewhere in the UK – if they spend more days in Scotland, they will be a Scottish taxpayer.

34.10.2 No part-year treatment

An individual who meets the definition of a Scottish taxpayer will be a Scottish taxpayer for a whole tax year.

34.10.3 Special cases

MPs representing a Scottish constituency and MEPs representing Scotland will automatically be treated as Scottish taxpayers, irrespective of where their sole or main residence is located and the number of days that they spend in and out of Scotland.

34.10.4 Guidance

HMRC published a draft guidance note on 12 June 2014. This shows how the tests are likely to be applied and sets out the records that an individual may need to keep.

35

THE INCOME AND CAPITAL GAINS OF FOREIGN DOMICILIARIES

DAVID FORD

This chapter contains the following sections:

General principles

Earned income

Investment income

Capital gains tax

Inheritance tax

Irish nationals

(19)   Irish nationals living in the UK

Recent changes

(20)   FA 2013 provisions

GENERAL PRINCIPLES

35.1   MEANING OF 'DOMICILE'

Domicile is a fundamentally different concept from residence and ordinary residence. It is not a tax concept at all, but a concept arising out of general law. It is not the same as nationality, although an individual's nationality may be one relevant factor in determining his or her domicile. The basic concept is that a person is domiciled in the country he or she regards as his or her real home. The fact that he or she may be prevented from living in that country or may need to live elsewhere because of temporary reasons (eg business and/or employment) does not necessarily mean he or she is domiciled in the country in which he or she currently resides. Under English law, an individual normally acquires his or her father's domicile at birth and retains it unless his or her father changes his own domicile before the child attains age 16. The mother's domicile will usually apply instead where a child is illegitimate or the parents divorce. The domicile acquired in this way is called the individual's 'domicile of origin'.

An individual may change his or her domicile to a 'domicile of choice'. Normally this would only occur when he or she leaves his or her country of origin and takes up permanent residence abroad with no intention of returning permanently to live in the country of origin. The domicile of origin will revive if these intentions alter and he or she decides not to make a permanent home in the new country after all. This is a question of fact; see *Allen & another (exors of Johnston)* v *HMRC,* 2006 SpC 481, where a woman who had acquired a Spanish domicile of choice was held to have retained this even though she returned to the UK to be cared for by a relative.

35.1.1   Married women

For a woman who married after 31 December 1973, the Domicile and Matrimonial Proceedings Act 1973 allows her to retain an independent domicile.

A woman married before 1 January 1974 generally acquired her husband's domicile (referred to as a 'domicile of dependency'), which continued after divorce or the husband's death, although it is possible to discard her domicile of dependency and gain a new domicile of choice (which might or might not be the same as her domicile of origin). A domicile of dependency in a jurisdiction may be discarded by a woman establishing that she no longer intends to remain permanently in that country and by her ceasing to be resident there. The mere intention is not itself sufficient: an Australian woman who had acquired a domicile of dependency in England was held to be domiciled here, despite her intention to return to Australia, because she had not ceased to be resident in England.

There may be exceptions to this rule imposed by a taxation treaty with the other state. For example, the treaty with the US treats wives as if they were married after 31 December 1973, regardless of the actual date of marriage.

35.1.2 Registration as an overseas elector

Section 835B ITA 2007 provides that where an individual registers as an overseas elector to vote in UK elections, this is not to be taken into account in determining his or her domicile status for tax purposes.

35.1.3 Remittance basis

The remittance basis means that an individual pays tax on foreign income and capital gains by reference to amounts brought into the UK. Foreign domiciliaries are eligible for this tax treatment but they have to make a claim to be taxed in this way. Up to 5 April 2008 it was only necessary to make a claim in respect of overseas investment income, as overseas earnings and capital gains were automatically taxed on a remittance basis. From 6 April 2008 the claim must cover all overseas income and capital gains, but there is a cost involved in making this claim, as personal allowances and the annual capital gains tax exemption will be forfeited. There may also be an additional £30,000 (or from 2012–13, £50,000) charge for longer term residents (see 35.2 below).

35.2 £30,000 SPECIAL CHARGE

A special annual remittance basis charge of £30,000 applies where a non-UK domiciled individual over the age of 18 elects for the remittance basis and

- he or she has been resident in the UK for seven of the preceding nine tax years; and
- his or her unremitted overseas income and capital gains are £2,000 or more.

This charge was increased to £50,000 for longer-term residents with effect from 6 April 2012 and to £90,000 for 2015–16 (see 35.3).

The special charge does not apply to minors, but years of UK residence accrue during an individual's minority, such that the remittance basis charge may apply immediately on attaining age 18, if the remittance basis is claimed.

If an individual does not elect for the remittance basis he or she will be liable for UK tax on his or her worldwide income and capital gains (see Figure 35.1).

It is open for an individual to choose the remittance basis for some tax years and not others. If the individual pays the special charge to HMRC directly from an overseas bank account, doing so will not constitute a

Figure 35.1 – Rules for non-doms from 2008–09

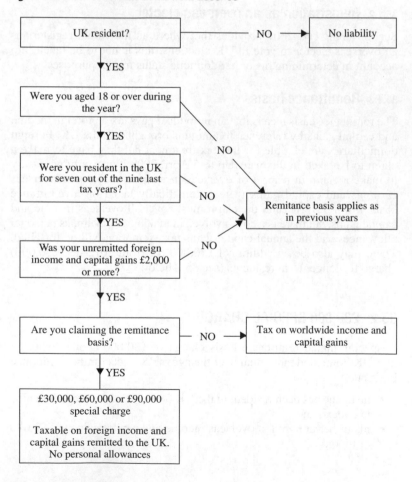

remittance. But if money is transferred into the individual's UK account to pay it this will be a remittance even if he or she then uses that money to pay the remittance basis charge.

Ideally, an individual who chooses to pay the remittance basis charge should have a small source of unremitted overseas income or gains which should be nominated for the purposes of this charge. Individuals should at all costs avoid remitting nominated funds to the UK. The income from that source need not be very much (but should be at least £1); it is not necessary that the UK tax on the nominated income should actually match the special charge.

If the individual does not nominate the income to which the remittance basis charge relates, subsequent remittances may be treated as remittances of income on the most unfavourable basis.

35.3 INCREASED SPECIAL CHARGE FOR SOME REMITTANCE BASIS USERS

In 2012–13, the Government increased the £30,000 annual charge to £50,000 for non-UK domiciliaries who have been UK resident for 12 or more years out of the last 14 year and who wish to retain access to the remittance basis. This was increased to £60,000 for 2015–16. Furthermore, the charge for an individual who has been resident in the UK for 17 of the last 20 tax years has been increased to £90,000 for 2015–16.

The £30,000 charge still applies for those who have been resident here for at least seven of the past nine tax years but fewer than 12 years. It is expected that the new charge will work in much the same way as the existing RBC, as regards minor children, nomination, etc.

35.4 WHAT CONSTITUTES A REMITTANCE?

35.4.1 General principles

A remittance arises where an individual brings money into the UK, either in cash or by transferring money to a UK bank account, or by using overseas funds to purchase an asset or a service in the UK, even if the funds themselves are paid abroad.

Overseas income and capital gains are also remitted if they are brought into the UK or enjoyed there. For example, payment of disposal proceeds into a UK bank account counts as a remittance, as does a payment into a UK bank account from an overseas bank account containing such proceeds. Less obviously, the income will be enjoyed in the UK if an individual has a large deposit account outside the UK and he or she formally secures a UK bank loan against this deposit account. However, if the money is spent outside the UK, and is not used directly or indirectly in the UK for the benefit of a relevant person, it is not deemed to have been remitted.

Payment of disposal proceeds into a bank account in the Channel Islands or Isle of Man does not constitute a remittance to the UK. An outright gift that takes place outside the UK will not normally be a remittance provided the cheque, etc is paid into an overseas bank account for the recipient. However, if the recipient is a relevant person and the funds are used in the UK for his or her benefit, or a 'gift recipient', and funds are used in the UK for the benefit of a relevant person, then a remittance will arise.

35.4.2 Constructive remittances

(ss 831–834 and 839 ITTOIA 2005)

The legislation deals with constructive remittances and states that a remittance is deemed to have occurred if an individual applies overseas income towards the satisfaction of:

- a debt (or interest thereon) for money lent to him or her in the UK;
- a debt for money lent to him or her abroad and brought to the UK;
- a loan incurred to satisfy such debts.

However, these rules were substantially amended for 2008–09 and subsequent years, see 35.4.4.

Case law also indicates that a constructive remittance is deemed to have occurred if an individual borrows from a UK bank but had his or her borrowings formally secured against money held in an overseas bank account.

The courts have held that a complex arrangement whereby money was transmitted between two South African companies, with the individual receiving a loan from one of them, constituted a constructive remittance of income because the individual had never really relinquished control of the money as it passed through various intermediaries. Since the courts are increasingly having regard for the overall consequences of a series of transactions, it would be unwise to rely on an artificial scheme that enabled an individual to enjoy sums in the UK that could be matched with overseas income.

35.4.3 Unauthorised remittances

In the Duchess of Roxburgh's case, a bank remitted untaxed overseas income by mistake. Because the bank acted contrary to its customer's instructions, it was held there was no liability under the remittance basis. HMRC has confirmed that it continues to apply this treatment after 6 April 2008 (using its discretionary powers) to allow the individual to undo his or her mistake, by reversing the transfer without unreasonable delay and in any event before the end of the tax year, for example by paying the income or gains back to the original account, so that the ordering rules at ss 809I and 809J ITA 2007 will not apply. HMRC will only use its discretion in such situations as long as there have been no relevant transactions or other benefits conferred on a relevant person in the interim. Otherwise the normal ordering rules will apply.

To take an example from HMRC's residence, domicile and remittances manual: if £20,000 is transferred in error from an overseas bank to a UK bank account and two weeks later the account owner realises the mistake and immediately transfers that £20,000 directly back to the overseas bank account, HMRC will accept that s 809I and s 809J do not apply. However if, for example, the £20,000 was spent in the UK and then £20,000 from another UK account was transferred back to the overseas account then a remittance will have occurred – s 809I and s 809J do apply.

35.4.4 Extension of the definition of 'remittance' for 2008–09 onwards

The definition of 'remittance' was extended to include bringing into the UK property that has been purchased out of overseas unremitted income. However, this does not apply to certain assets owned on 11 March 2008 or to assets acquired after that date but which were brought into the UK before 6 April 2008, or to any of the following:

- artwork brought into the UK for public display;
- personal effects, eg clothes, shoes, jewellery and watches;
- assets costing less than £1,000;
- assets brought into the UK for restoration;
- assets which are physically in the UK for less than 275 days.

A remittance may also be deemed to have occurred when a loan from a non-UK institution has been advanced in the UK and interest has been paid out of unremitted overseas income. However, this charge will not apply to mortgages already in existence on 11 March 2008 until 6 April 2028 (or the remaining period of the loan, if shorter) provided that the terms of the loan are not varied and no advances are made on or after 12 March 2008.

Tax notes

Be careful not to change the terms of an offshore mortgage in place on 11 March 2008 or using overseas income to pay the interest may in future count as a remittance.

35.4.5 Five-year rule

If a foreign domiciled individual ceases to be resident in the UK but resumes residence within five tax years, remittances made to the UK in years during which he or she was not resident may be taxed as if they were remittances made in the year that he or she returns to the UK.

35.4.6 Gifts of unremitted income after 5 April 2008

Another extension of the concept of remittance may bite where income or gains have been alienated after 5 April 2008, ie given to another person. If that person then brings the money into the UK and it is enjoyed by a relevant person, he or she is deemed to have made a remittance. Relevant persons in respect of remittances of foreign income accruing after 5 April 2008 are:

- the individual;
- the individual's spouse;
- the individual's civil partner;
- a child or grandchild of a person falling within any of the bullets above, if the child or grandchild has not reached the age of 18;
- a close company in which a person falling within any other paragraph of s 809M(2) is a participator or a company which is a 51% subsidiary of such a close company;
- a company in which a person falling within any other paragraph of s 809M(2) is a participator, and which would be a close company if it were resident in the UK, or a company which is a 51% subsidiary of such a company;
- the trustees of a settlement of which a person falling within any other paragraph of s 809M(2) is a beneficiary; or
- a body connected with such a settlement.

For these purposes, a man and woman living together as husband and wife are treated as if they were husband and wife and two people of the same sex living together as if they were civil partners of each other are treated as if they were civil partners of each other. However, there is no legislation in place to establish whether such a non-statutory relationship exists.

35.4.7 Remittances – conditions A to D

From 6 April 2008, there is a remittance of funds to the UK if either conditions A *and* B, or condition C, or condition D in s 809L ITA 2007 are met.

Condition A, (s 809L(2)) is that money or other property is brought to, or received or used in, the UK by or for the benefit of a relevant person, or a service is provided in the UK to or for the benefit of a relevant person.

Condition B is that the property, service or consideration for the service, is (wholly or in part) the income or chargeable gains, or the property, service or consideration derives (wholly or in part, and directly or indirectly) from the income or chargeable gains, and in the case of property or consideration, is property of – or consideration given by – a relevant person.

Condition B also applies where the income or chargeable gains are used outside the UK (directly or indirectly) in respect of a relevant debt, or anything deriving (wholly or in part, and directly or indirectly) from the income or chargeable gains is used outside the UK (directly or indirectly) in respect of a relevant debt.

If either condition A or condition B is not satisfied then conditions A and B together cannot be satisfied so we then have to consider conditions C (s 809L(1)(b)) and D (s 809L(1)(c)).

Turning to condition C, this requires that qualifying property of a 'gift recipient':

- is brought to, or received or used in, the UK, and is enjoyed by a relevant person;
- is consideration for a service that is enjoyed in the UK by a relevant person; or
- is used outside the UK (directly or indirectly) in respect of a relevant debt.

A gift recipient is a person, other than a relevant person, to whom the individual makes a gift of money or other property that is either income or chargeable gains of the individual, or derives (wholly or in part, and directly or indirectly) from income or chargeable gains of the individual. If a person to whom a gift is made subsequently becomes a relevant person, that person ceases to be a gift recipient.

Condition D is that property of a person other than a relevant person (apart from qualifying property of a gift recipient) is brought to, or received or used in, the UK, and is enjoyed by a relevant person, or is consideration for a service that is enjoyed in the UK by a relevant person, or is used outside the UK (directly or indirectly) in respect of a relevant debt, in circumstances where there is a connected operation. The scope of the term 'connected operation' is very wide.

35.4.8 Remittances made out of mixed funds

An individual may have a 'mixed fund', eg a bank account where the money has come from a number of sources. Section 809R ITA 2007 provides that where a mixed fund was built up out of monies from different types of income and gains, remittances of income and gains accruing post-5 April 2008 (income and gains which accrued before 6 April 2008 are still subject to the previous – non-statutory – mixed fund rules) are matched on a LIFO (last in-first out) basis with those types of income and gains in the following order:

 (1) employment income;
 (2) foreign self-employed earnings not subject to foreign tax;
 (3) relevant foreign earnings that have not suffered foreign tax;
 (4) foreign investment income that has not suffered foreign tax;
 (5) foreign capital gains that have not suffered foreign tax;
 (6) foreign self-employed earnings that have been subject to foreign tax;
 (7) relevant foreign earnings that have suffered foreign tax;
 (8) foreign investment income subject to foreign tax;
 (9) foreign capital gains on which foreign tax has been charged;
 (10) other income or capital.

35.4.9 FA 2012 reliefs for certain remittances

The FA 2012 implemented the reforms to the taxation of non-UK domiciled individuals, announced at Budget 2011. The following provisions took effect from 6 April 2012.

Remitting in order to invest

Foreign domiciliaries are now allowed to bring funds into the UK in order to invest in certain UK businesses without this constituting a taxable remittance of income or gains. The relief must be claimed in the individual's tax return.

The conditions which need to be satisfied are as follows:

- The investment is made within 45 days of the money being brought into the UK.
- The investment must take the form of the purchase of shares in a company or a loan to the company. The company need not be UK resident but, if non-resident, it must have a permanent establishment in the UK.
- The company must be a trading company.
- Companies involved in developing or letting property can qualify (this can include companies which develop or let residential property).
- A company whose trade consists of leasing is excluded.

Other key aspects

The investment may be made by the foreign domiciliary, his or her offshore company or an offshore trust.

The investor, and his or her family, may participate in the business. There is no upper limit for this relief.

Sale of the investment

When such investments are realised, the proceeds must either be reinvested or sent back overseas within 45 days. The individual is allowed to retain funds within the UK in order to buy a tax reserve certificate to cover his or her CGT liability which arises on the sale.

If there is a partial realisation, the proceeds are deemed to first consist of income and capital gains remitted at the time that the investment was made.

EARNED INCOME

35.5 FOREIGN EARNINGS

35.5.1 Introduction

Someone resident in the UK but domiciled elsewhere who is employed by a UK resident employer is usually treated in the same way as a UK domiciled individual in a similar position. The earnings from such an employment are taxed in full on the arising basis under ITEPA 2003 (for the taxation of such earnings, see Chapter 4).

Where a person domiciled outside the UK is employed by a non-UK resident employer, and he or she claims the remittance basis, the tax treatment can be fundamentally different but only if none of the duties of employment are carried out in the UK. Earnings from such an employment are called 'foreign earnings'. The tax treatment of such earnings is as set out in Table 35.1.

35.5.2 Employer's residence status need not be same as individual's domicile

It is not necessary that the employer should be resident in the same country as that in which the individual is domiciled (although this is often the case). An individual domiciled in, for example, Switzerland and employed by a company resident in the US still has foreign earnings.

35.5.3 Earnings from employer resident in the Republic of Ireland

(s 22 ITEPA 2003)

Prior to 5 April 2008, there was one exception to the general rule that foreign earnings arise from the employment of a person not domiciled in the UK in an office or employment with a non-UK resident employer. Where the employer was resident in the Republic of Ireland, the earnings were not regarded as foreign earnings. However, with effect from 6 April 2008 foreign earnings can include earnings from an employer resident in the Republic of Ireland.

Table 35.1 – Tax treatment of earnings under ITEPA 2003

UK domicile status	UK residence status	Arising basis (AB) or remittance basis (RB) claimed	Employment duties performed wholly or partly in the UK		Employment duties performed wholly outside the UK
			Duties performed in UK	Duties performed outside UK	
Domiciled within UK	R	AB	Liable	Liable	Liable
	R	AB	Liable	Liable	Liable
		RB	Liable	Liable on remittance	Liable on remittance
	NR	AB	Liable	Not liable	Not liable
Domiciled outside UK	R	AB	Liable	Liable	Liable
		RB	Liable (on AB)	Liable (on AB)	See below
	R	AB	Liable	Liable	Liable
		RB	Liable	Liable on remittance*	Liable on remittance*
	NR	AB	Liable	Not liable	Not liable

*Assuming the remittance basis claim is made.

Notes: This table is subject to any different treatment provided for under the terms of the relevant article in a double taxation agreement.

(1) Indicates the individual is liable to pay UK tax unless subject to the Seafarers Earnings Deduction.

(2) For individuals not resident in the UK, the arising basis is limited to liability to UK tax on income arising in the UK.

(3) If the individual is not domiciled in the UK and is not a short-term resident, he will be liable to UK tax on the arising basis for any earned income where the duties are performed wholly or partly in the UK. The liability to UK tax on income earned wholly outside the UK will depend on the residence status of the employer:

   (a) when the employer is non UK/foreign resident – liable on remittance basis

   (b) when the employer is UK resident – employment earnings are liable on arising basis.

(4) Overseas workday relief is available for foreign domiciled, short-term residents.

35.5.4 Short-term residents

The concept of ordinary residence was abolished with effect from 6 April 2013.

Where an individual was resident in the UK, but not ordinarily resident, it was possible to divide their earnings between those that derived from duties performed in the UK and those performed overseas.

The remuneration referable to the UK duties was always taxed on an arising basis under ITEPA 2003 but the remuneration for duties performed overseas could be taxed on the remittance basis under s 26 ITEPA 2003 for years up to 2012–13 if a remittance basis claim had been made. Typically, the earnings would be split pro rata on a time basis.

However, overseas workday relief (see 34.4.1) now provides similar treatment for the first three tax years in which a foreign domiciled individual is resident in the UK.

35.5.5 Split contracts

A different rule applies where a non-UK domiciled individual is no longer entitled to overseas workday relief.

The earnings from an employment with a foreign employer are all subject to tax in the UK on an arising basis where any of the duties are performed there. There are no provisions whereby remuneration can be split between earnings relating to work done in the UK and work performed overseas. However, if a foreign-domiciled individual has a separate contract of employment under which all of the duties are performed outside the UK, the earnings are taxed on the remittance basis under s 26 ITEPA 2003 providing that a remittance claim has been made.

An individual can take advantage of this treatment by having two separate contracts of employment, one covering duties performed in the UK and the other covering duties performed overseas. However, HMRC has announced that it will be considering dual contracts very carefully to ensure that in practice they really do relate to separate employments, and are not merely a single employment dressed up as two.

For these purposes, there have to be separate employments with distinct duties. It is not good enough merely to have contracts for carrying out the same duties in different geographical locations.

The Autumn Statement 2013 announced that legislation would be introduced so that overseas income earned by foreign domiciliaries employed under dual contracts would be taxed in the UK on the arising basis rather than the remittance basis. The Government amended these proposals after consultation and the legislation introduced by FA 2014 applies only to arrangements that are motivated by tax avoidance. There are specific let-outs:

- employments held for legal or regulatory reasons are not caught by these provisions;
- directors with less than a 5% shareholding in their employer are not subject to these rules.

Where a foreign national is given a right to tax equalisation in his or her service contract, the amount charged from the UK employment may be carefully scrutinised by HMRC. This is an area where you should take advice from a specialist.

> **Tax notes**
>
> HMRC has said that it will be considering dual contracts of employment much more carefully in future to ensure that they do indeed represent separate employments, and are not merely an artificial split of a single contract.

35.6 TRAVELLING EXPENSES

(ss 373–375 ITEPA 2003)

There are special provisions that apply to individuals of foreign domicile. Certain travel expenses paid or reimbursed by an employer are not assessable income where all the following conditions are satisfied:

- The expenses must be paid during the five-year period that begins with the date of arrival in the UK.
- The expenses must relate to a journey between the individual's usual place of abode and the place in the UK where he or she works.
- The expenses must relate to journeys made by the employee, unless he or she is in the UK for a continuous period of 60 days or more for the purposes of performing duties. In this event, the expenses of a visit by his or her spouse, civil partner or minor child will also be allowable, although there is a limit of two return journeys by any such person in a tax year.

To secure this exemption it is also necessary that the employee must not have been resident in the UK in either of the two tax years that precede the year in which he or she took up UK employment.

35.7 SUBSISTENCE ALLOWANCES FOR EMPLOYEES SECONDED TO THE UK

HMRC accepts that an employer may bear certain costs where an employee is seconded to the UK for a period where it is 'reasonable to assume' that this will not exceed 24 months.

The costs that may not be taxed under this 'detached duties relief' can include travel, subsistence and accommodation costs.

An article in *Tax Bulletin 50,* December 2000 analyses what is meant by 'secondment' and outlines circumstances in which an employee of an overseas company may actually be coming to the UK to take up a new office or employment rather than working there under a continuation of his or her existing employment contract.

The article explains that if the employer provides, for example, a flat for the seconded employee to use instead of hotels, the expenditure is not regarded as a taxable benefit provided 'the total cost of the accommodation is appropriate to the business need and is reasonable and not excessive'. Examples are given of what might not be regarded as reasonable.

35.8 'CORRESPONDING PAYMENTS'

(s 355 ITEPA 2003)

Certain payments made by an individual out of foreign earnings qualify for tax relief where they are made 'in circumstances corresponding to those in which the payments would have reduced his or her liability to income tax' had they been paid in the UK. The main type of payment that can be relieved under this heading is a contribution to an overseas pension fund (see below).

35.9 OVERSEAS PENSION FUNDS

An overseas pension fund will not normally qualify as a registered pension scheme for UK tax purposes. However, where the benefits provided by an overseas pension fund are broadly similar to those that arise from UK registered pension schemes, HMRC may regard the employer's contributions as not constituting remuneration for ITEPA 2003 purposes and any contributions made by the employee may be deducted as corresponding payments (see above). In some situations, HMRC will accord this treatment only where the individual's rights under his or her overseas pension scheme are adapted or restricted. For example, a US national who has an individual retirement plan may be required to give notice to the US administrators so as to waive his or her ability to take a lump sum in circumstances where this would not be permitted under the rules that govern UK-approved retirement benefit schemes. Some double taxation treaties (eg UK/US) also provide for relief to be given for foreign pension contributions.

35.10 SELF-EMPLOYMENT

Where an individual is resident in the UK, any earnings from a business carried on as a sole trader are taxed as self-employment income on the arising basis. This even applies in a situation where all the work is actually performed overseas. The basis for this interpretation by the courts is that a business is deemed to be carried on from where it is controlled and, in the case of a sole trader, control is located where the proprietor is resident.

A foreign-domiciled individual who is self-employed and performs a substantial amount of work overseas might wish to consider forming an offshore company which is managed and controlled overseas. In particular, if an overseas company were to be formed, employed the individual and supplied his or her services outside the UK to customers, the earnings from that employment would constitute foreign earnings. Provided no work is performed in the UK under the employment contract, interposing an offshore company in this way would mean that he or she could take full advantage of the remittance basis for earnings taxable under ss 22–26 ITEPA 2003. As always, care should be taken over where the company is centrally managed and controlled, because it will be UK resident if it is controlled here.

Tax notes

A foreign–domiciled individual who carries on self–employment and who performs a substantial amount of work overseas should consider forming an offshore company.

35.11 PARTNERSHIPS CONTROLLED OUTSIDE THE UK

Where a UK-resident but foreign domiciled individual is a partner in a firm controlled outside the UK, his or her earnings from that firm are taxed as follows:

- profits from a UK branch: as trading income on the arising basis;
- overseas profits: as foreign trading income under the remittance basis (if a remittance basis claim has been made).

35.12 PENSION BENEFITS

35.12.1 Lump sums paid under overseas pension schemes
(ESC A10)

Income tax is not charged on lump sum benefits received by an employee (or by his or her personal representatives or any dependant) from an overseas retirement benefit scheme or overseas provident fund where the employee's overseas service comprises:

- not less than 75% of his or her total service in the employment concerned; or
- the whole of the last ten years of his or her service in that employment (subject to the total service exceeding ten years); or

- not less than 50% of his or her total service in that employment, including any ten of the last 20 years, provided the total service exceeds 20 years.

If the employee's overseas service does not meet these requirements, relief from income tax is given by reducing the amount of the lump sum that would otherwise be chargeable by the same proportion as the overseas service bears to the employee's total service in that employment.

For payments from overseas EFRBS and s 615 schemes, charges can still arise. Although ESC A10 was partially withdrawn from 6 April 2011, HMRC continues to apply it to payments of lump sum relevant benefits from overseas EFRBS and s 615 ICTA 1988 schemes, where the rights to receive the benefit accrued to the employee before 6 April 2011, whenever the lump sum is paid. See Chapter 5 for the interaction of new Part 7A ITEPA with lump sum payments from overseas pensions.

35.12.2 Pensions

A non-domiciled individual who receives a pension paid by a non-UK resident person may be subject to tax under the remittance basis if this is claimed. There is no similar reduction such as that which exists for UK-domiciled individuals (see ss 573–575 ITEPA 2003), who may be taxed on only 90% of overseas pensions. If the whole pension is remitted, tax is charged on the full amount.

INVESTMENT INCOME

35.13 THE REMITTANCE BASIS FOR INVESTMENT INCOME

35.13.1 Remittance basis

Individuals who are not ordinarily resident or not domiciled in the UK can make a claim for their assessable income to be based on the amount of overseas income remitted to the UK (subject to paying the special charge, see 35.2–35.3).

35.13.2 Income arising within the Republic of Ireland

(s 269 ITTOIA 2005)

For years up to 2007–08, where a foreign-domiciled individual had income that arose within the Republic of Ireland, it was always taxed as it arose and not on the remittance basis. It was taxed on the current year basis. This distinction was abolished by FA 2008 so that Irish income can constitute overseas income and be taxed on the remittance basis.

This brings the treatment of a foreign domiciliary's Irish income into line with the treatment of capital gains arising in Ireland, which have always been taxed on a remittance basis.

35.13.3 Individual ceasing to have source of income

For years up to 2007–08, an assessment on the remittance basis could be made for a tax year only if the source of the income still existed during that year. This rule was abolished by FA 2008 with effect from 6 April 2008. This means that previously 'source-ceased' income is potentially chargeable whenever it arose. This has caused considerable concern among clients and their advisers, as many non-UK domiciliaries have accounts which, under the old rules, contained clean capital (including source-ceased income), but which under the new rules are mixed funds.

35.13.4 Relief for foreign tax

(s 18 TIOPA 2010)

Where overseas income has borne foreign tax, credit may be claimed for this against the UK tax assessed on the same income. Relief for foreign tax paid will, however, be restricted to the UK tax payable on the same income, and will only take into account the maximum foreign tax rate permitted under the terms of a double taxation treaty.

35.14 POSITION IF FOREIGN DOMICILIARY ACQUIRES UK DOMICILE

It used to be the case that where an individual who was assessable under the remittance basis acquired a UK domicile of choice, the remittance basis ceased to apply for income tax purposes and his or her overseas income was thereafter taxable only on the arising basis. No tax liability arose if he or she then remitted money that would formerly have given rise to an income tax liability under the remittance basis.

This rule ceased to apply from 6 April 2008. Where a person has been on the remittance basis, but is taxed in a year on the arising basis, he or she now remains subject to tax on bringing past years' income into the UK during a period when he or she is taxed on the arising basis, irrespective of whether or not he or she has in the meantime acquired a UK domicile.

35.15 MANAGING THE REMITTANCE BASIS

35.15.1 Maintaining separate bank accounts

Where a foreign-domiciled individual has substantial overseas income, it is normal for arrangements to be put in place so that remittances to the UK may be identified, as far as possible, with capital. The way this is normally dealt with is by arranging for him or her to have a minimum of four (but realistically, often more) separate bank accounts, as follows:

(1) The first account is capital, ie the cash actually held by the individual at the time he or she took up residence in the UK. It is normal for further sums to be paid into this bank account where the cash relates to the sale proceeds of assets sold at a loss for CGT purposes or the proceeds arise from sales of exempt assets. The bank should be instructed that any interest on this bank account should not be credited to the account, but paid to a separate income account (see below).

(2) The second account should contain the sale proceeds of assets that give rise to non-UK capital gains.

(3) A third account should be kept for income, including interest on the capital account and the capital gains account.

(4) At least one account containing a nominal amount of income or gains should be kept completely separately, and used as the 'nominated' account from which the special charge is derived. In theory, this account may contain as little as £1 of income or gains, but funds from this account must not be remitted to the UK until *all* other offshore funds have been remitted.

HMRC's residence, domicile and remittances manual sets out the information required when nominating a source of income or gains on which the remittance basis charge is to be paid. The manual states that HMRC requires the following information:

- the precise amounts of income and gains that have been nominated, (this should include the country of origin and the type and source of the income);
- the computation of the gain (if applicable);
- the exchange rates used;
- the calculation of the tax due in relation to the nominated income and gains;
- if there have been deductions for expenses or losses from either foreign income or foreign gains in arriving at the final taxable amount, full details of the amounts and nature of those expenses or losses must also be provided.

In many cases, identifying the nominated source will be simply a matter of identifying 'my bank account with XYZ Bank in Guernsey', however, there are concerns that where a client has a number of accounts with the same bank, within the same jurisdiction, stating 'my bank account with XYZ Bank in Guernsey' is not sufficient information to separately identify which account is meant, and there is a risk of 'tainting' the other accounts held at that branch so that a remittance from one of those other accounts might be treated as a remittance of nominated income or gains.

Therefore, if you have more than one account with the same bank in the same jurisdiction, when making the nomination on the SA return, you should also give sufficient information to identify the specific account, whether that is an account 'name' (eg high interest deposit account with XYZ Bank) or an account number, or some other unique identifying feature, to distinguish it from the others held with the same bank in the same territory. This does not sit well with a statement by Dave Hartnett, permanent secretary for tax, on 12 February 2008 that 'the intention is that those using the remittance basis will not be required to disclose the source of those remittances'.

Clearly, in practice, an individual may minimise his or her liability under the remittance basis by taking remittances from the capital account in (1).

In some situations, it may be sensible to go one stage further and keep two income accounts with one containing income that has not borne tax at source (eg overseas bank deposit interest) and the other income that has borne foreign tax. By organising matters in this way, remittances of income can come out of the account that contains income that has suffered foreign tax, and this will further minimise any UK tax liability.

There may also be CGT savings from having different capital gains accounts.

35.15.2 Use overseas income accounts to fund expenditure outside UK

A foreign-domiciled individual should, where possible, arrange that all possible expenditure outside the UK is funded from the income account and, where relevant, one containing income that has not borne any foreign tax at source.

CAPITAL GAINS TAX

35.16 REMITTANCE BASIS FOR CAPITAL GAINS ON FOREIGN ASSETS

35.16.1 Introduction

(ss 12 and 275 TCGA 1992)

A foreign domiciliary may be subject to CGT if he or she is either resident or ordinarily resident in the UK. Gains on UK assets are charged in the same way as gains realised by UK domiciled individuals. Gains realised on assets situated overseas by foreign domiciled remittance basis users are subject to UK CGT only if the proceeds are remitted to the UK (however the foreign domiciliary may need to pay the special charge, see 35.2–35.3).

The following rules determine whether an asset is deemed to be situated in the UK or abroad:

- Real estate and rights over such property are situated in the country where the real estate is located.
- Tangible movable property and rights over such property are situated in the country where the property is located.
- Debts are normally situated in the country where the creditor is resident.
- Stocks, shares and securities are generally situated in the country where the company maintains its principal register. Bearer shares and securities issued by a UK incorporated company were brought within the definition of UK situs assets by FA 2005.
- Goodwill is treated as situated where the trade or business is carried on.
- Patents, trademarks and designs are situated in the country where they are registered.

Tax notes

If the remittance basis has been claimed, gains realised on assets situated overseas are subject to UK CGT only if the proceeds are remitted to the UK.

35.16.2 Losses not generally allowable

(s 16(4) TCGA 1992)

For 2007–08 and earlier years, where a loss arose on an overseas asset, a person of foreign domicile could not claim a capital loss. In some situations this could give rise to hardship.

This restriction was amended, from 6 April 2008. However, if a foreign domiciliary wishes to claim such losses he or she must make an irrevocable claim under s 16ZA TCGA 1992 for the first tax year after 2007–08 that incorporates a claim for the remittance basis. Moreover, choosing this relief comes at a cost as claiming losses on overseas assets means that losses on UK assets cannot be set against past years' capital gains which are assessed on the remittance basis.

There has been confusion over the time limit for making claims. The consensus among advisers is that this is governed by s 43 TMA 1970, meaning that the time limit for making a claim for the 2011–12 tax year will be four years after the end of that year, ie by 5 April 2016. However, there is an argument that ss 42(2) and (5) reinstate the self-assessment time limit of 22 months for s 8 TMA 1970 cases (ie where a notice to complete a return has been issued).

HMRC states in the residence, domicile and remittances manual that 'The election should be made for the first year for which the remittance basis is claimed, irrespective of whether the individual has any foreign chargeable gains or overseas losses in that year. The election will usually be expected to be made within the white space in the capital gains supplementary pages of the same SA Return as the first remittance basis claim is made.' This certainly indicates that HMRC believes that where a s 8 TMA 1970 notice has been given, ss 42(2) and (5) do override the longer period in s 43(1). Therefore it would be prudent to work on the basis that this is the limit.

Tax notes

Foreign domiciliaries will need to consider whether to make a claim for loss relief on disposals of non-UK assets when the tax return for the first year in which a remittance basis claim is made post–6 April 2008 is submitted. You should seek professional advice on this.

35.16.3 Rate of CGT for foreign domiciliaries

Any UK resident non-UK domiciliary paying the remittance basis charge for a particular tax year is subject to CGT on any gains chargeable in that tax year at a rate of 28% (or 10% if the gain qualifies for entrepreneurs' relief). This is because the special charge is deemed to be the income tax or CGT payable on income or gains taxable on the arising basis, which therefore automatically exceeds the basic rate limit for the year.

35.16.4 Remittances from mixed funds

In general where a non-UK domiciliary is being taxed on the remittance basis, the tax rate applicable to a remitted gain is that in force on the date of remittance.

35.16.5 Gains arising in non-resident trusts

There are some situations where chargeable gains are treated as accruing to beneficiaries of settlements where they have been matched with capital payments. Where the capital payments are received on or after 23 June 2010, the gains are deemed to have accrued on or after that date and this means that the 28% rate normally applies.

35.16.6 How to take full advantage of the remittance basis

In some cases there may be no likelihood of the individual needing to bring the proceeds of a sale of foreign assets into the UK. In such a situation the payment of CGT is a matter of choice since he or she can control the amount of his or her chargeable gains. Where it is going to be necessary to bring money into the UK at some stage in the future, it is advisable to keep separate bank accounts as detailed above. Remitting funds to the UK and managing offshore accounts is an area where professional advice is essential, as the consequences of 'getting it wrong' can be very costly.

One account should receive the proceeds of assets that have been sold at a loss when measured for UK CGT purposes. This account may be used to fund remittances to the UK that are not going to give rise to a CGT liability. A second account should contain the sale proceeds of assets subject to foreign CGT. Remittances out of this account will give rise to a CGT assessment, but double tax relief will be due in respect of the foreign CGT that has been paid. Other sales of assets that have produced a gain, but have not been taxed in the foreign jurisdiction, should be kept in a third account, and should be remitted only as a last resort.

35.16.7 Loans secured on overseas income and gains

In the past, HMRC have not treated an individual as making a remittance where he secured loan finance on offshore assets and the loan was used to acquire UK assets.

Any foreign income or gains that were actually used to pay interest, or to repay the debt, were taxable remittances in the normal way. In the event that the security was called in then a taxable remittance would occur so far as the security comprised foreign income or gains. But apart from this, no remittance was deemed to take place.

This 'concessionary' treatment was published by HMRC in 2010 in its Residence Domicile and Remittance Basis guidance manual.

HMRC announced that from 4 August 2014 it will treat any such loans as being a constructive remittance of any foreign income or capital gains that is included in the security upon which the loan is made.

HMRC's new interpretation still means that a remittance will be deemed to occur if overseas income or gains are used to service a loan which has been used to buy UK assets. But it also means that the actual amount of any loan that is remitted to the UK will also be treated as a remittance to the extent that it is secured on unremitted foreign income or gains. This will potentially give rise to a double charge in respect of the amount of the loan used in the UK if the loan is serviced from different foreign income or gains to that used as collateral.

HMRC stated that non-domiciled individuals who have relied on the previous concession will not be assessed to tax in respect of the remittances provided they gave a written undertaking either that the foreign security had been or would be replaced by non-foreign security before 5 April 2016 or that the loan or the part that was remitted to the UK would be repaid before 5 April 2016. The undertaking has to be given by 31 December 2015 if the tax charge is to be avoided.

HMRC said that the change was made because it is became aware of 'large numbers of arrangements' which were 'not considered to be commercial and not within the intended scope of the concession'.

35.17 USE OF OFFSHORE COMPANIES AND TRUSTS

35.17.1 Offshore companies

The anti-avoidance legislation contained in s 13 TCGA 1992 (see 33.16) now applies to foreign-domiciled individuals who hold 25% or more of the share capital in overseas companies that would be close if they were UK resident. Provided that the individual is not caught by the IHT deemed domicile rule (see 30.1), it may well be advisable for him or her to create a non-resident trust and transfer shares in an existing offshore investment company to the trustees. This will create an excluded property trust, and prevent any personal tax liability arising under s 13 on the offshore company disposing of its investments.

It is also dangerous for the individual to occupy a property owned by an offshore company as HMRC may seek to assess him or her as a 'shadow director' if the provisions of ss 100A–100B ITEPA 2003 do not apply. If a trust is used to hold shares in an offshore company, which owns a UK residential property, which the non-domiciliary is to occupy, the impact of the pre-owned assets rules must also be considered

> **Tax notes**
>
> It is risky for an individual to occupy a UK property owned by an offshore company as HMRC may seek to assess him or her as a 'shadow director', unless ss 100A–100B ITEPA 2003 apply, or in some cases the pre-owned assets provisions may be triggered.

35.17.2 Offshore trusts

The formidable anti-avoidance provisions relating to offshore trusts (covered in Chapter 33) do not have the same effect where a foreign-domiciled individual is concerned.

Offshore or non-resident trusts can still be extremely tax-efficient where non-UK domiciled individuals are concerned. A settlement established by a non-UK domiciled individual after 18 March 1991 cannot be a 'qualifying settlement', however the provisions of s 86 TCGA 1992 (which charge a settlor to tax on gains realised by the trustees of his or her non-resident settlement) do not apply to non-UK domiciled settlors. The exemption from the s 86 charge applies even where the individual does not have the benefit of the remittance basis (see 35.2–35.3) for that year.

The provisions of s 87 TCGA 1992, which charge UK resident beneficiaries to tax when they receive capital payments from an offshore trust, which have been matched with gains, do apply to non-UK domiciliaries but are moderated where the beneficiary is a remittance basis user. Such an individual is taxed on capital payments only if he or she brings them into the UK.

See Figure 35.2 and Figure 35.3.

Figure 35.2 – Implications for a UK-resident user of the remittance basis having a shareholding in an offshore company

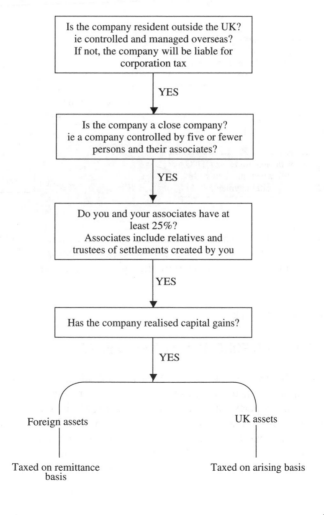

Figure 35.3 – CGT implications for a remittance basis user benefiting under an offshore trust

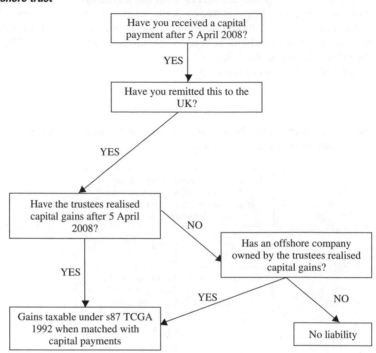

The provisions relating to offshore trusts and their interaction with the remittance basis for non-UK domiciliaries are complex. Professional advice should be taken to avoid the many potential pitfalls.

INHERITANCE TAX

35.18 UK AND FOREIGN SITUS PROPERTY

IHT may be charged on the death of an individual who is not deemed to be domiciled in the UK, but only to the extent that his or her estate consists of property situated there. No charge arises on foreign situs property as this is classified as 'excluded property'. Table 35.2 indicates the types of property that are regarded as situated in the UK.

There is a special rule for IHT whereby an individual may be deemed to be domiciled in the UK if he or she has been resident here in 17 of the

Table 35.2 – Assets chargeable to IHT

	Not chargeable	Chargeable
Channel Island property	✓	
Isle of Man property	✓	
Other foreign property	✓	
UK property	✓	✓
Bank deposits outside the UK	✓	
UK sterling bank deposits	✓	✓
UK foreign currency deposits	chargeable only if the owner is resident in the UK	
Shares in UK companies		✓
UK unit trusts and OEICs	✓	
Registered shares in foreign companies	✓	
Bearer securities	depends where the bearer certificates are held	
Debts owed by a UK resident person		✓ (normally)
Debts owed by foreign resident person	✓	

20 tax years ending with the current year. However, foreign situs assets settled by a foreign domiciliary remain excluded property even if the individual is subsequently caught by the deemed domicile rule.

IRISH NATIONALS

35.19 IRISH NATIONALS LIVING IN THE UK

An Irish national who resides in the UK is normally subject to UK tax on overseas investment income only to the extent that he or she remits such income to the UK (subject to paying the remittance basis charge where appropriate, see 35.13). Moreover, this treatment now applies to investment income received from Irish sources (the position was different for 2007–08 and earlier years).

Similarly, an Irish national who is employed by a non-resident employer, and who carries out all the duties of the employment overseas, will be able to be taxed on the remittance basis. Since 2008–09 this has also applied to employments with Irish resident employers.

RECENT CHANGES

35.20 FA 2013 PROVISIONS

The following recent changes are particularly relevant to wealthy foreign domiciled individuals who reside in the UK.

35.20.1 Capital gains tax

FA 2013 introduced a charge to capital gains tax (CGT) on both UK and non-UK resident non-natural persons (NNPs) in respect of gains accruing on the disposal of interests in high-value residential property (in excess of £2m) that are the subject of the annual tax on enveloped dwellings (ATED) – see below. For the purposes of this legislation NNPs are companies and certain collective investment schemes. Companies that are within the charge to UK corporation tax will be liable to this CGT charge in respect of such disposals rather than corporation tax, and this will apply to disposals taking place on or after 6 April 2013. For further details, see 27.5.

35.20.2 Annual tax on enveloped dwellings (ATED)

Most residential properties (dwellings) are owned directly by individuals, but in some cases a dwelling may be owned by a company (or other collective investment vehicle). In these circumstances the dwelling is said to be 'enveloped' because the ownership sits within a corporate 'wrapper' or 'envelope'. The amount of ATED is worked out using a banding system based on the value of the property, and varies from £15,000 for properties valued between £2,000,001 and £5m to £140,000 for properties valued at more than £20m. The £2m threshold was reduced to £1m from 6 April 2015 and will be futher reduced to £500,000 for 2016–17. For further details, see 36.4.

35.20.3 Spouse exemption where the donee is foreign domiciled

The Government has increased the IHT-exempt amount that a UK-domiciled individual can transfer to a non-domiciled spouse or partner from £55,000 to £325,000. In future, the increase will be linked to the prevailing nil rate band. Alongside this change it is possible for a spouse or civil partner who is domiciled outside the UK to elect to be treated as UK-domiciled for IHT purposes to get the benefit of unlimited IHT-free transfers from his or her spouse (including for testamentary dispositions). Such an election would continue to apply unless or until the electing individual ceased to be resident in the UK for a period of years. For further details, see 30.5.1.

35.20.4 Treatment of liabilities for inheritance tax purposes

IHT is normally charged on the net value of a deceased person's estate after deducting liabilities outstanding at the date of death, reliefs, exemptions and the nil-rate band. The deduction for liabilities is given for the full value due to the creditors and is not limited to the amount actually repaid after death, or restricted if the liability has been incurred to acquire property which also qualifies for a relief or is not chargeable to IHT.

Provisions have been introduced that remove the tax advantage that arises from obtaining a deduction for a liability by either not repaying the liability after death, or acquiring an asset which is not chargeable to IHT. They make arrangements which allow 'two bites at the cherry' unattractive because the estate will no longer gain the double benefit of a relief or exclusion and the deduction of a liability.

For further details, see 30.11.4.

36

STAMP TAXES

This chapter contains the following sections.

(1) Stamp Duty Reserve Tax (SDRT)
(2) Stamp Duty Land Tax (SDLT)
(3) Reliefs
(4) Annual Residential Property Tax
(5) Scotland
(6) Wales

36.1 STAMP DUTY RESERVE TAX (SDRT)

Unlike stamp duty, SDRT is a compulsory tax which applies where one person agrees with another to transfer 'chargeable securities' for consideration in money or money's worth.

36.1.1 Principles

Usually the charge to SDRT arises when the agreement is made. If the agreement is conditional the charge arises when the condition is satisfied. Tax is charged at 0.5% of the amount or value of the consideration (there is no rounding).

The charge arises irrespective of how it is documented; SDRT is a tax on transactions unlike stamp duty which is a charge on documents. Where shares are traded in de-materialised form (eg CREST on the London Stock Exchange) then SDRT only is relevant as there is no instrument capable of attracting stamp duty.

For chargeable securities of companies not traded on any exchange the due date for SDRT payment is the seventh day of the month following the month in which the charge is incurred.

36.1.2 Chargeable securities

SDRT can apply to stocks, shares and loan capital together with certain interests in the same including rights to subscribe and options, as well as units under a unit trust scheme. Most non-UK stocks are excluded but the provisions are complex, so for example shares issued by a non-UK company which are UK registered or paired with shares issued by a UK company fall within the scope of charge.

Loan capital exempted from stamp duty is also exempt from charge to SDRT, as are most units in offshore unit trusts.

36.2 STAMP DUTY LAND TAX (SDLT)

The charging provisions for land transactions were fundamentally recast in 2003 with the introduction of SDLT, a compulsory tax on a self-assessment basis. The tax is wider in scope than stamp duty, with increased financial reporting and record keeping obligations on taxpayers. Subject to transitional provisions it applies to transactions with an effective date on or after 1 December 2003.

36.2.1 Land transactions

The charging provisions operate by reference to land transactions, meaning any acquisition of a chargeable interest. The parties to any land transaction are referred to as vendor and purchaser, whether the transaction is a freehold sale, leasehold grant, surrender or assignment. It is the purchaser who is obliged to file a return and pay the tax self-assessed in it.

In most cases the effective date is completion of the transaction. The effective date might occur earlier by reason of a contract being substantially performed; this is a reference to a substantial amount of the consideration being paid or provided, in the context of a lease, any rent being paid, or the purchaser taking possession. So for example, a lessee in respect of a new lease grant might become liable to SDLT at the time of entering premises to effect tenant works in advance of actual completion.

36.2.2 Chargeable interests

SDLT is charged upon the acquisition of any 'chargeable interest', which term relates to UK real property. A chargeable interest is widely defined to include freehold and leasehold interests as well as any interest right or power over land, or the benefit of an obligation, restriction or condition affecting the value of land. The grant of an option or pre-emption right falls within the scope of charge, as would any surrender or release of rights.

The position is more complex in relation to lease variations because only a variation taking effect as, or treated as a new lease grant, or where the rent or term is reduced, is regarded as falling within the scope of charge.

36.2.3 Rates of SDLT prior to 4 December 2014

Unlike stamp duty and SDRT, SDLT is charged on the chargeable consideration for a land transaction at different rates. The rates are tiered, so that tax is payable on the entire purchase price at the rate indicated.

Table 36.1 – Rates of SDLT

Rate	Land in disadvantaged areas: residential*	Land in disadvantaged areas: non-residential*	All other land in the UK: residential	All other land in the UK: non-residential
Zero	£0–£150,000	£0–£150,000	£0–£125,000 **	£0–£150,000
1%	£150,001–£250,000	£150,001–£250,000	£125,001–£250,000 **	£150,001–£250,000
3%	£250,001–£500,000	£250,001–£500,000	£250,001–£500,000	£250,001–£500,000
4%	£500,000–£1m	Over £500,000	£500,000–£1m	Over £500,000
5%	£1m–£2m	–	£1m–£2m	–
7%	Over £2m	–	Over £2m	–

* Disadvantaged Area Relief was abolished with effect from 6 April 2013. Claims needed to have been made by 5 May 2014.

** First time buyers did not pay SDLT on residential property transactions up to £250,000 between 25 March 2010 and 24 March 2012.

In the case of non-residential property the nil rate is applicable to land transactions for chargeable consideration up to £150,000; thereafter the bands are the same, except that the highest rate is 4%.

36.2.4 Stamp duty on residential property from 4 December 2014

For exchanges and completion on residential properties on or after 4 December 2014 a new regime of stamp duty applies as shown in Table 36.2.

Table 36.2 – SDLT rates and thresholds for residential properties

Property purchase price	SDLT rate from 4 December 2014
Up to £125,000	Zero
The next £125,000 (the portion from £125,001 to £250,000)	2%
The next £675,000 (the portion from £250,001 to £925,000)	5%
The next £575,000 (the portion from £925,001 to £1.5 million)	10%
The remaining amount (the portion above £1.5 million)	12%

Under the new rules you will pay tax at graduated rates much like income tax whereas under the old rules you paid tax at the band rate within which the property price falls (see 36.2.3).

The following is an example using HMRC's online calculator.

Emma buys a property in Orpington for £277,133 (the average price of a property in the UK at the time of writing) on 7 May 2015:

Results based on SDLT rules from 4 December 2014

Effective date	Purchase price (£)	Total SDLT due (£)
07/05/2015	277,133	3,856

Breakdown of how the total amount of SDLT was calculated

Purchase price bands (£)	Percentage rate (%)	SDLT due (£)
Up to 125,000	0	0
Above 125,000 and up to 250,000	2	2,500
Above 250,000 and up to 925,000	5	1,356
Above 925,000 and up to 1,500,000	10	0
Above 1,500,000+	12	0
	Total SDLT due	3,856

As a comparison these are the results based on SDLT rules before 4 December 2014.

Purchase price (£)	Percentage rate (%)	Total SDLT due (£)
277,133	3	8,313

36.2.5 7% rate introduced by FA 2012 for expensive properties

A special rate of SDLT, 7% on residential properties valued at £2m or more, took effect from 22 March 2012.

36.2.6 Linked transactions

Linked transaction rules apply if several properties are bought as part of a single scheme, arrangement or series of transactions between the same vendor and purchaser or persons connected with either. In these circumstances the charge is based on the aggregate consideration rather than the rate otherwise applicable to each individual purchase in isolation.

Finance Act 2011 provides relief for purchasers of residential property who acquire an interest in more than one dwelling. The effect of the relief is that SDLT will be calculated on the mean consideration paid for the properties, subject to a minimum rate of 1% instead of on the aggregate consideration pursuant to the linked transaction rules.

36.2.7 Compliance

There are wide-ranging requirements relating to the filing of SDLT land transaction returns, payment, provision of information and record-keeping. The purchaser is responsible for notifying HMRC within 30 days of the effective date of a transaction and for paying the SDLT at that time. HMRC has the power to enquire into returns, to require the production of documents, to issue assessments for a failure to pay all or any SDLT, as well as to charge property in the event of a failure to pay, or underpayment. In addition to various fixed penalties interest is charged on late payment, there are also tax related penalties in certain circumstances.

HMRC may usually enquire within nine months from the last date on which a return could be made, or if later when the return was actually made. Discovery assessments may also be made no later than six years after the effective date (21 years in a case involving fraud or negligence).

36.2.8 Consideration

SDLT is chargeable on the total consideration provided, whether monetary or non-monetary. Detailed provisions provide for chargeable consideration to include any VAT, as well as the value of certain services or works. Deferred consideration is included without discount, although a payment postponement may be available. Land exchanges give rise to SDLT for both sides of the transaction, usually calculated on a market value basis. For land exchanges with an effective date on or after 24 March 2011, the Finance Act 2011 provides for the charge to be due on the greater of market value and the actual consideration paid, to prevent avoidance. As for stamp duty the assumption of indebtedness comprises chargeable consideration.

Where consideration is contingent, SDLT is payable on the basis that the amount will become payable, or that sums will continue to be payable. Where consideration is uncertain or unascertained, it should be valued at the best current estimate. Once the contingency occurs or consideration is otherwise ascertained then the purchaser will normally be obliged to file a further return, with a corresponding adjustment by way of payment or repayment of the SDLT.

There is no consideration for SDLT purposes in a number of circumstances, which include simple gifts (unless the market value rule applies as referred to below) and gifts of land where the donee agrees to pay capital gains tax or inheritance tax.

Exemption from SDLT is available for certain purchases of a property in the context of employment relocation.

36.2.9 Market value imputations

Market value may be imputed in the context of certain partnership transactions as well as transactions involving a connected company. So for example, a gift of land by an individual to a company owned by that person will give rise to SDLT based on the market value of the land so gifted.

36.2.10 Leases

The SDLT provisions in relation to leases tend to be far more onerous than was the case for stamp duty. Tax is charged on the net present value of the lease – calculated by reference to rent reserved over the entire term of the lease, discounted at a statutory rate (3.5%). The formula is available by way of an online calculator on the HMRC Stamp Taxes website.

Tax is charged at the rate of 1% of the net present value. In the case of residential property the first £125,000 of chargeable consideration is exempted (£150,000 for commercial property).

Rents are calculated by reference to the actual rents reserved in the first five years, thereafter by reference to the highest amount of rent payable in any consecutive 12-month period in the first five years. Where rents are contingent, uncertain or unascertained then a reasonable estimate is required, which should then be subject to a subsequent filing and adjustment.

There are detailed rules to cater for tenants holding over, leases for indefinite terms and rent reviews within the first five years of grant amongst others. A targeted anti-avoidance rule applicable to 'abnormal' increases in rent seeks to prevent the manipulation of rental obligations after the first five years.

36.2.11 Properties held via companies

The transfer of a property to a company owned by the transferor occasions a SDLT charge on the market value of the property.

Despite this, arrangements involving the holding of property via offshore companies have been used to avoid SDLT. To counter this, the Chancellor introduced a 15% SDLT rate for residential properties worth over £2m that were purchased after 20 March 2012 by 'non-natural persons', such as companies, trusts and Collective Investment Schemes. The £2m threshold was reduced to £500,000 with effect from 20 March 2014.

The 15% rate does not apply to properties which are:

- used as farmhouses;
- acquired for use in a trade carried on by the company;
- acquired for property development;
- acquired for letting on a commercial basis to unconnected persons.

There is also an exemption where the property is held for occupation by employees who hold less than 5% of the shares in the company itself or in the holding company of the group in which the property owning company is a member.

These exemptions are, however, dependent on the property being used in this way for three years.

36.2.12 Partnerships

Partnerships have proved to be a particularly difficult and complex area. When SDLT was first introduced transfers of partnership interests were excluded, but this changed in 2004.

Charges now potentially apply whenever a land interest is brought into or out of a partnership, (meaning any general partnership, limited partnership or limited liability partnership) or where individual partnership income profit sharing ratios change. Charges are based on the market value of the relevant proportion of the underlying land interest.

For example, if a farming partnership was formed by two individuals (who were not connected) on an equal profit share basis, with one of those partners introducing farmland and buildings, half of the value of this property would be subject to a SDLT charge.

In the case of corporate partners, a form of group relief may be applicable for certain partnership transactions where the partners have the necessary degree of connection.

A transfer of an interest in a partnership that includes an interest in land potentially attracts a SDLT charge. This rule has affected many situations where profit-sharing ratios change regularly, for example in the context of professional partnerships it is usual to change profit sharing ratios each year with potential for SDLT charges, valuation and filing obligations.

In this context several changes and simplifications have been introduced. First, a transfer of a partnership interest will now usually only trigger a charge if it comprises an interest in a property investment partnership, meaning a partnership whose sole or main activity is investing or dealing in chargeable interests.

Since 19 July 2007 a transfer of an interest in a property investment partnership it is necessary to consider the type of transfer.

'Type A transfers' continue to attract SDLT by reference to a proportion of the market value of UK land held by the partnership immediately before the transfer, namely the proportion (determined by reference to income profit entitlements) of the interest transferred. The charge arises where consideration for the transfer is given or there is a withdrawal of money or money's worth by the partner who leaves the partnership or who has a reduced interest as a result.

'Type B transfers' are more restrictive as to the scope of charge, with the important result that property acquired by a partnership subject to full SDLT is excluded when calculating relevant partnership property subject to charge on a transfer of a partnership interest.

36.2.13 Anti-avoidance

In addition to targeted rules, a general anti-avoidance rule was introduced with effect from 6 December 2006. For the rule to operate there must be a disposal by one person of a chargeable interest and an acquisition by another of it, or an interest derived from it; a number of transactions involved in connection with the disposal and acquisition; and for less SDLT to be payable than on a direct notional land transaction. There is no motive test.

The rule removes a large number of mitigation opportunities but also impacts on commercial transactions. Where it applies the purchaser is liable to SDLT on a notional transaction the consideration for which is the largest amount given or received for scheme transactions.

The rule reflects the continuing efforts of HMRC to prevent avoidance, with the threat of targeted avoidance to counter specific structures which come to its notice as a result of SDLT disclosure obligations.

36.3 RELIEFS

Each of stamp duty, SDRT and SDLT are subject to various reliefs, the more commonly encountered of which are outlined below.

36.3.1 Group relief

Exemption from stamp duty and SDLT is available for transactions between companies with the requisite degree of connection – so called 'group relief'. The required relationship is that:

- one company is the 75% subsidiary of the other; or
- both are 75% subsidiaries of a third company.

Economic tests relating to dividends and assets on a winding-up must be satisfied in addition to ownership of ordinary share capital. Non-UK companies can satisfy these tests provided they have share capital.

There are complex provisions designed to prevent avoidance in the context of exit and finance arrangements with third parties. In relation to SDLT only, targeted anti-avoidance provisions have been developed so as to deny relief if the transaction is not effected for bona fide commercial reasons, or forms part of arrangements the main or one of the main purposes of which is specified tax avoidance. In addition, withdrawal of relief can occur by reference to subsequent changes in the group relationship within, or pursuant to arrangements within, a three-year period – this rule is designed to prevent the sale of property indirectly following a group transfer.

The precise scope of such provisions can be difficult to determine: Stamp Office practice is therefore extremely relevant.

36.3.2 Reconstructions

Relief from stamp duty and SDLT is available in the context of certain reconstructions, where the whole or part of an undertaking of another company is acquired in qualifying circumstances.

For this exemption to apply, consideration must consist of or include the issue of non-redeemable shares in the acquiring company to the shareholders of the target company. The transaction must be effected for a bona fide commercial purpose not forming part of a scheme or arrangement, the main or one of the main purposes of which is the avoidance of specified taxes.

36.3.3 Acquisition relief

A reduced rate of 0.5% applies in the context of SDLT where the whole or part of the undertaking of another company is acquired in qualifying circumstances. This requires the consideration to include the issue of non-redeemable shares in the acquiring company to the target or the target shareholders.

36.3.4 Transfers of rights ('subsales')

Ever since SDLT was introduced in 2003, there has been a relief for subsales. The relief addresses the situation where a person enters into a contract to acquire land (the 'original purchaser') and then enters into a further agreement before completion that will result in a different person acquiring the land instead. Provided the original contract and the subsale are completed or substantially performed simultaneously, SDLT is only payable by the ultimate purchaser.

New rules for transfers of rights

FA 2013 has introduced the term 'transfers of rights' instead of subsales.

Different rules apply where substantial performance takes place after the date that FA 2013 received royal assent.

FA 2013 imposes a minimum consideration rule for transactions where the original purchaser and ultimate purchaser are connected or act on non-arm's-length terms. This ensures that the full price paid to the seller, under the original contract, or the price paid for the subsale if higher, is charged to SDLT.

FA 2013 has also changed the way the original contract is regarded for SDLT purposes so that the original purchaser will need to file an SDLT return and make a claim for subsale relief (previously the original purchaser's acquisition was wholly disregarded for SDLT purposes and so no SDLT return or claim for relief was needed). In addition, the original purchaser is prevented from claiming subsale relief where there is a tax avoidance motive.

36.3.5 Charities

No SDLT is payable by a charity on the purchase of a property used for the furtherance of the charity's objects or to hold as an investment the return from which will be used for the furtherance of the charity's objectives. The exemption does not apply if the involvement of the charity is part of an SDLT avoidance scheme. FA 2014 made it clear that partial relief from SDLT is available where a charity purchases property jointly with a non-charity.

36.3.6 Registered providers of social housing

A land transaction under which the purchaser is a profit-making registered provider of social housing is exempt from charge to SDLT where the funding of the transaction is assisted by public subsidy. This extension, introduced in 2009, added to an existing exemption for registered social landlords.

36.3.7 Alternative property finance

The Government's policy is to promote the UK as a leading centre for Islamic finance and it has therefore worked towards a level playing field for conventional and alternative finance structures.

Very broadly the sale of land to a financial institution and its lease back to the vendor (in other words the 'borrower'; the rent reflecting interest that would otherwise be charged on a loan) is exempted from charge to SDLT provided that the vendor is also granted a call option right (once the 'finance' is repaid the land may be reacquired).

36.4 ANNUAL RESIDENTIAL PROPERTY TAX

This tax is also called the Annual Tax on Enveloped Dwellings (ATED).

The original mischief that gave rise to the legislation was that expensive residential properties were bought by offshore companies. When the owner came to sell, he would sell the shares in the company (exempt from SDLT) instead of having the company sell the property (which would have made the purchaser liable for SDLT). The company was an 'envelope' or 'corporate wrapper' which contained the property. The vendor and purchaser usually shared the SDLT saving.

36.4.1 Outline of the tax

Annual Residential Property Tax is payable each year from 1 April 2013.

The tax is due if the property meets all the following conditions:

- it is residential property;
- it is situated in the UK;
- it was valued at more than £2m on 1 April 2012 (but see 36.4.5), or at acquisition if later; and

- it is owned, completely or partly, by a company, a partnership where one of the partners is a company or a 'collective investment vehicle', for example, a unit trust or an open ended investment company.

The amount of ATED is worked out using a banding system based on the value of your property. You need to find out which band the value of your property falls into (see Table 36.3).

> **Tax notes**
>
> The ATED threshold will be reduced to £500,000 from April 2016.

Table 36.3 – Rate bands

Property value	Annual tax 1 April to 31 March 2015
£2,000,001 to £5,000,000	£15,400
£5,000,001 to £10,000,000	£35,900
£10,000,001 to £20,000,000	£71,850
£20,000,001 and over	£143,750
Property value	Annual tax 1 April 2015 to 31 March 2016
£1,000,001 to £2,000,000	£7,000
£2,000,001 to £5,000,000	£23,350
£5,000,001 to £10,000,000	£54,450
£10,000,001 to £20,000,000	£109,050
£20,000,001 and over	£218,200

36.4.2 Principal exemptions

Certain companies and other non-natural persons are exempt from this charge. These are companies, etc engaged in:

- property development;
- renting properties on a commercial basis to unconnected persons;
- carrying on a trade;
- holding a property for occupation by employees who hold less than 5% of the shares in the company itself or in the holding company of the group in which the property-owning company is a member.

36.4.3 Other exemptions

There are two exemptions which can apply even where the occupant is connected with the company:

- The charge does not apply to a farmhouse if the company is engaged in carrying on a trade of farming.

- The charge does not apply if a company owns an historic house that is open to the public or provides access to the dwelling as part of its services (eg as a wedding venue) with the intention of being open for at least 28 days per annum.

The company's activities in the historic house must be commercial and with a profit-seeking motive, even if that profit does not cover the full costs of the house. Also, access must be to a significant part of the property.

36.4.4 Charities

A charity which owns residential property is not liable for Annual Residential Property Tax.

36.4.5 FA 2014 extends the scope of ATED

ATED was extended from 1 April 2015 to properties worth more than £1 million. From 1 April 2016, the ATED charge will be further extended to non-natural persons holding UK residential property interests valued at more than £500,000.

On 1 April 2015, a new band was introduced for interests valued from more than £1m up to £2m, with that band being subject to a charge of £7,000 in that year. From 1 April 2016, a further band will be introduced, for properties valued at more than £500,000 up to £1m, with a charge of £3,500 in that year. The charges, but not the valuation thresholds, will continue to be linked to inflation.

The valuation dates for determining the applicable ATED band will remain unchanged, meaning that the valuation on which the charge is based could be as far back as 1 April 2012, where the property was owned on that date.

Non-natural persons are broadly companies and partnerships with corporate members. Those falling into the band introduced on 1 April 2015 will have until 1 October 2015 to file their first ATED return and until 31 October 2015 to pay the charge. Thereafter the 30 April deadline will apply.

36.4.6 De-enveloping a property

HMRC has confirmed that no SDLT arises if the property is taken out of the company as a distribution *in specie* on the company being liquidated. If the company has a liability in the form of a shareholder loan, SDLT is not charged where the property is transferred to the shareholder and his debt is cancelled. See *Taxline 2014/34*.

36.5 SCOTLAND

The Scottish Parliament introduced legislation which replaced SDLT with a Land and Buildings Transactions Tax (LBTT) with effect from 1 April 2015.
The tax rates and bands for residential property transactions are as follows:

Band	Rate
Up to £145,000	–
£145,001 to £250,000	2.0%
£250,001 to £325,000	5.0%
£325,001 to £750,000	10.0%
£750,001 and over	12.0%

36.5.1 Administration of LBTT

Revenue Scotland administers LBTT, supported by Registers of Scotland.

36.5.2 Exemptions from LBTT

Schedule 1 to the LBTT Act sets out the exemptions that are available under LBTT. These include:

- Transactions for which there is no chargeable consideration. What constitutes the chargeable consideration for the purposes of a land transaction is set out in Schedule 2 to the Act. Paragraph 1 of Schedule 2 provides that the chargeable consideration is, unless otherwise provided, any consideration in money or money's worth for the transaction.
- Acquisitions by the Crown.
- Transfers of property on divorce, separation or the end of a civil partnership.
- Grants of residential leases (other than 'qualifying leases' which are due to convert to ownership under the Long Leases (Scotland) Act 2012).
- Property transferred to a person in relation to the will of a deceased person or the intestacy of a deceased person.

36.5.3 Tax reliefs from LBTT

Certain reliefs from LBTT are provided for in Schedules 3 to 16 to the LBTT Act:

- Sale and leaseback arrangements – the leaseback element is not charged to avoid double counting (Schedule 3).

- Where a developer or property trader buys a residential property in part exchange for a new residential property (Schedule 4).
- Transfers involving multiple dwellings (Schedule 5).
- Certain acquisitions by Registered Social Landlords (Schedule 6).
- Where Alternative Finance Products (Schedule 7) and Alternative Finance Investment Bonds (AFIB) (Schedule 8) are used (which includes Islamic finance transactions) to ensure that they are not taxed more than conventional loans.
- Crofting community right to buy (Schedule 9).
- Group relief which enables groups to move property between companies for commercial reasons without having to consider stamp duty land tax implications (Schedule 10).
- Certain transactions in connection with the reconstruction and acquisition of companies (Schedule 11).
- On the incorporation of limited liability partnerships (Schedule 12).
- Charities and charitable trusts, subject to certain conditions (Schedule 13).
- Where compulsory purchase orders are used by a local authority (Schedule 14).
- Land transactions resulting from compliance with planning obligations such as requiring a developer to provide affordable housing (Schedule 15).
- Transfers involving public bodies (Schedule 16).

All of these reliefs are currently available under SDLT.

36.5.4 Application of LBTT to leases

LBTT is applied to non-residential leases. Residential leases are only subject to LBTT where an ultra-long lease exceeding 175 years exists, albeit such leases will convert to ownership under the Long Leases (Scotland) Act 2012. Licences to occupy property are exempt interests, except licences that are of a description prescribed by Scottish Ministers under section 53(1) of the LBTT Act.

The chargeable consideration includes rent and other monies, such as a premium, payable over the term of the lease (Schedule 19 Part 1). The amount of tax chargeable is determined by calculating the net present value (NPV) and applying the relevant tax rates (Schedule 19 Part 2).

The taxpayer must review the amount of tax paid on every third anniversary of the lease and submit a return to the tax authority to ensure the correct tax is paid (Schedule 19 Part 4).

36.5.5 LBTT: key concepts

- A **land transaction** is the acquisition of a chargeable interest (s 3).
- A **chargeable interest** is a real right or other interest in or over land in Scotland, such as such as the ownership of a house, or the benefit of

an obligation, restriction or condition affecting the value of any such interest, right or power, which is not an exempt interest (s 4).

- A land transaction is a **chargeable transaction** (i.e. a transaction that is taxed) unless it is an **exempt** transaction or a **tax relief** is claimed (known as 'exempt from charge') (s 15).
- The **chargeable consideration** (ie the price of the transaction) in a land transaction is provided for in Schedule 2 and includes money or money's worth.
- A land transaction is **notifiable** to the Tax Authority, unless the transaction is exempt or if the chargeable consideration is less than £40,000 (s 30).
- The **effective date** of the land transaction is the date of completion of the land transaction, or another date as Scottish Ministers prescribe by regulations (s 63).
- In order to ensure that LBTT is paid, the LBTT Act makes special provision for certain scenarios:
  (1) Section 9(2) provides for the scenario in which a **contract is completed without substantial performance,** for instance when the contract is complete, but the buyer is yet to take possession of the subjects. The effective date of the land transaction is the date of completion.
  (2) Section 10(2) provides for the scenario when a **contract is substantially performed, but not completed.** For instance, when a tenant has taken possession and is paying rent, however the lease documentation has not been completed. The effective date is the date when the contract is substantially performed.
- **'Substantial performance'** is defined in s 14 of the LBTT Act as the first event of any of the following and will trigger the charge to tax irrespective of completion of the contract:
  (1) the buyer taking possession of whole or substantially the whole of the subject matter of the transaction,
  (2) when a 'substantial amount of the consideration' is paid or provided, or
  (3) an assignation or subsale or other transaction in which a third party takes possession occurs.

36.6 WALES

The Welsh Assembly plans to introduce a Land Transactions Tax to replace SDLT for Welsh properties. This will be the first Welsh tax for 800 years.

SOCIAL SECURITY BENEFITS

SUE PARR

This chapter contains the following sections:

(1) Taxable benefits
(2) Non-taxable benefits
(3) Employment and Support Allowance

37.1 TAXABLE BENEFITS

The following benefits are taxed as earned income under ITEPA 2003:

• Bereavement allowance • Certain payments of incapacity benefit • Certain payments of income support • Contributions based employment and support allowance • Industrial death benefit paid as pension • Carer's allowance • Jobseeker's allowance • The state pension • Statutory maternity pay • Statutory paternity pay • Statutory adoption pay • Statutory sick pay • Widowed parent's allowance • Widowed mother's allowance • Widow's pension

37.2 NON-TAXABLE BENEFITS

The following benefits are not taxable:

• Attendance allowance • Back to work bonus • Bereavement payment • Bereavement support payment • Child benefit (not taxed as such but there is a charge for higher rate taxpayers, see 12.7) • Child's special allowance • Christmas bonus for pensioners • Cold weather payment • Council tax benefit (administered by local authorities) • Disability living allowance • Employment rehabilitation allowance • Fares to school • Guardian's allowance • Industrial injuries benefit • Invalidity benefit • Maternity allowance • Severe disablement allowance • Employment training allowance • War orphan's pension • War widow's pension • Widow's payment • Winter fuel payment

37.2.1 Means-tested benefits

• Child tax credit • Educational maintenance allowance • Family credit • Hospital patients' travelling expenses • Housing benefit • In work credit • Income support • Social fund payments • State pension credit • Uniform and clothing grants • Working tax credit

Armed Forces compensation scheme/War disablement benefits

• Lump sum in-service compensation payments and other benefits payable under new Armed Forces Pension, Compensation and Early Departure Payments Schemes • War disablement pension, and the following allowances when paid in addition to a War disablement pension: Age allowance – Unemployability supplement (including additions for wife and family) – Invalidity allowance – Constant attendance allowance – Allowance for lowered standard of occupation – Severe disablement occupational allowance – Exceptionally severe disablement allowance – Comforts allowance – Age 80 age addition – War pensioner's mobility supplement

37.3 EMPLOYMENT AND SUPPORT ALLOWANCE

This allowance contains two elements, a means tested element and a contributory element. The means tested element is not taxable. The contributory element is taxable income.

The amount paid depends on individual circumstances. For means tested Employment and Support Allowance, household income, pension and any savings of £6,000 or more are taken into account. It also depends on the effect that any disability has on the ability to work.

37.3.1 Weekly rate during the assessment phase

The assessment phase rate is paid for the first 13 weeks of claim while a decision is made on capability for work:

- a single person aged under 25: up to £57.90 pw;
- a single person aged 25 and over: up to £73.10 pw.

37.3.2 Weekly rate during the main phase

The main phase starts from week 14 of the claim, if the assessment shows that illness or disability limits the ability to work:

- a single person in the Work Related Activity Group: up to £102.15 pw;
- a single person in the Support Group: up to £109.30 pw.

Additional amounts are paid where ESA replaces incapacity benefits and severe disablement allowance.

37.3.3 Pension income rules

Where a person receives means tested Employment and Support Allowance, any pension income is taken into account, regardless of the amount.

Where a person receives contribution-based Employment and Support Allowance and has a gross pension income of more than £85 a week, the amount of benefit payable is reduced by half of the excess.

The excess is the difference between £85 and the actual pension income. For example, for a pension income of £100, the excess is £15. The amount of Employment and Support Allowance payable is reduced by half of that, ie £7.50.

Table 37.1 – Taxable social security benefits

	2013–14	2014–15	2015–16
Retirement pension	£	£	£
single category A or B	110.15	113.10	115.95
category B (lower)	66.00	67.80	69.50
Incapacity benefit (replaced by Employment and Support Allowance from 2015–16)			
Long-term benefit	101.35	104.10	
increase for age higher	10.70	11.00	
increase for age lower	6.00	6.15	
Short-term benefit – under pension age			
lower rate	76.45	78.50	
higher rate	90.50	92.95	
Incapacity benefit			
Short-term benefit			
over pension age			
lower rate	97.25	99.90	
higher rate	101.35	104.10	
Income support			
Single/lone parent			
single, under 25, or lone parent under 18	56.80	57.35	57.90
single, 25 or over, or lone parent over 18	71.70	72.40	73.10

Table 37.1 – Continued

Couple			
both under 18	56.80	57.35	59.90
both 18 or over	112.55	113.70	114.85
Statutory sick pay			
earnings threshold	109.00	111.00	112.00
standard rate	86.70	87.55	88.45
Statutory maternity, paternity and adoption pay			
earnings threshold	109.00	111.00	112.00
lower rate	136.78	138.18	139.58
Jobseeker's allowance			
single people under 25	56.80	57.35	59.90
single people 25 and over	71.70	72.40	73.10
Widow's payment			
widowed parent's allowance	108.30	111.20	112.55
widow's pension (standard)	108.30	111.20	112.55

Table 37.2 – Non-taxable social security benefits

	2013–14	*2014–15*	*2015–16*
Attendance allowance	£	£	£
higher rate	79.15	81.30	82.30
lower rate	53.00	54.45	55.10
Child benefit			
first or only child	20.30	20.50	20.70
each subsequent child	13.40	13.55	13.70
Severe disablement allowance (replaced by Employment and Support Allowance from 2015–16)			
Basic rate	71.80	73.75	
Age-related addition			
higher rate	10.70	11.00	
Middle rate	6.00	6.15	
lower rate	6.00	6.15	
Bereavement payment			
single lump sum	2,000.00	2,000.00	2,000.00
Christmas bonus			
single annual payment	10.00	10.00	10.00

38

TAX TABLES

Table 38.1 – Rates of income tax

2015–16		
Starting rate	0%	0–5,000
Basic rate	20%	0–31,785
Higher rate	40%	31,786–150,000
Additional rate	45%	Over 150,000
2014–15	*Rate*	*Taxable income £*
Starting rate	10%	0–2,880
Basic rate	20%	0–31,865
Higher rate	40%	31,866–150,000
Additional rate	45%	Over 150,000
2013–14	*Rate*	*Taxable income £*
Starting rate	10%	0–2,790
Basic rate	20%	0–32,010
Higher rate	40%	32,011–150,000
Additional rate	45%	Over 150,000
2012–13	*Rate*	*Taxable income £*
Starting rate	10%	0–2,710
Basic rate	20%	0–34,370
Higher rate	40%	34,371–150,000
Additional rate	50%	Over 150,000
2011–12		
Starting rate	10%	0–2,560
Basic rate	20%	0–35,000
Higher rate	40%	35,001–150,000
Additional rate	50%	Over 150,000

The rates of tax applicable to dividends are 10% for income below the higher rate threshold and 32.5% for income above it for all years in Table 38.1. For 2012–13 the dividend rate is 42.5% for dividend income falling into the additional rate band. For 2013–14 onwards the additional dividend rate is 37.5%. If an individual's taxable non-savings income is above the starting rate limit then the 10% savings rate will not be applicable.

Table 38.2 – Personal allowances and reliefs (see Chapter 12)

Income tax allowances	*2011–12* £	*2012–13* £	*2013–14* £	*2014–15* £	*2015–16* £
Personal allowance1	7,475	8,105	9,440	10,000	10,600
Income limit for personal allowance	100,000	100,000	100,000	100,000	100,000
Personal allowance for people born after 5/4/1948	n/a	n/a	9,440	10,000	10,600
Personal allowance for people born between 6/4/1938 and 5/4/1948 (aged 65–75 until 2012–13)[1,2]	9,940	10,500	10,500	10,500	10,600
Personal allowance for people born before 6/4/1938 (aged over 75 until 2012–13)[1,2]	10,090	10,660	10,660	10,660	10,660
Married couple's allowance[3] either spouse born before 6/4/1935 or 75 plus	7,295	7,705	7,915	8,165	8,355
Income limit for age related allowances	24,000	25,400	26,100	27,000	27,700
Blind person's allowance	1,980	2,100	2,160	2,230	2,290

(1) The personal allowance reduces where the income is above £100,000 by £1 for every £2 above the £100,000 income limit. This reduction applies irrespective of age. For 2014–15, once income reaches £120,000, the personal allowance reduces to nil.

(2) These allowances reduce where the income is above the income limit by £1 for every £2 of income above the limit. The personal allowance for those born before 6 April 1948 (from 2013–14) can be reduced below the basic personal allowance where the income is above £100,000.

(3) Tax relief for the married couple's allowance is given at the rate of 10%.

Table 38.3 – 'Official rate' of interest for beneficial loans (see 4.7)

Average rate for year	%
2015–16	3.00
2014–15	3.25*
2013–14	4.00*
2012–13	4.00
2011–12	4.00

*The official rate of interest is set in advance by Treasury regulations for the whole of the following tax year, subject to review if necessary.

Table 38.4 – Pension contributions

Maximum contribution	2013–14 £	2014–15 £	2015–16 £
Individual – 100% of relevant earnings up to maximum of	50,000	40,000	40,000
Employer – unlimited but triggers benefit in kind if total pension contributions from both employee and employer are over	50,000	40,000	40,000
Individual's lifetime allowance	1.5m	1.25m	1.25m

Table 38.5 – Rates of capital gains tax

	2012–13	2013–14	2014–15	2015–16
Annual exemptions				
Individuals	£10,600	£10,900	£11,000	£11,100
Trusts divided by the number of trusts settled by the same settlor up to a maximum of 5 (ie minimum exemption 1/10 individual annual exemption)	£5,300	£5,450	£5,500	£5,500
Entrepreneurs' relief lifetime limit	£10m	£10m	£10m	£10m
Rates of tax				
Full rate	28%	28%	28%	28%
Entrepreneurs' rate (available on certain disposals of business assets)	10%	10%	10%	10%
Individuals				
Gain less than basic rate limit	18%	18%	18%	18%
Gain greater than basic rate limit	28%	28%	28%	28%
Trusts				
Discretionary (including accumulation and maintenance)	28%	28%	28%	28%
Interest in possession	28%	28%	28%	28%

Table 38.6 – Capital gains tax indexation allowance

	RETAIL PRICE INDEX FIGURES					
	1982	*1983*	*1984*	*1985*	*1986*	*1987*
Jan		325.9	342.6	359.8	379.7	394.5/100.0
Feb		327.3	344.0	362.9	381.1	100.4
Mar	313.4	327.9	345.1	366.1	381.6	100.6
Apr	319.7	332.5	349.7	373.9	385.3	101.8
May	322.0	333.9	351.0	375.6	386.0	101.9
June	322.9	334.7	351.9	376.4	385.8	101.9
July	320.0	336.5	351.5	375.5	384.7	101.8
Aug	323.1	338.0	354.8	376.7	385.9	102.1
Sep	322.9	339.5	355.5	376.5	387.8	102.4
Oct	324.5	340.7	357.7	377.1	388.4	102.9
Nov	326.1	341.9	358.8	378.4	391.7	103.4
Dec	325.5	342.8	358.5	378.9	393.0	103.3
	1988	*1989*	*1990*	*1991*	*1992*	*1993*
Jan	103.3	111.0	119.5	130.2	135.6	137.9
Feb	103.7	111.8	120.2	130.9	136.3	138.8
Mar	104.1	112.3	121.4	131.4	136.7	139.3
Apr	105.8	114.3	125.1	133.1	138.8	140.6
May	106.2	115.0	126.2	133.5	139.3	141.1
June	106.6	115.4	126.7	134.1	139.3	141.0
July	106.7	115.5	126.8	133.8	138.8	140.7
Aug	107.9	115.8	128.1	134.1	138.9	141.3
Sep	108.4	116.6	129.3	134.6	139.4	141.9
Oct	109.5	117.5	130.3	135.1	139.9	141.8
Nov	110.0	118.5	130.0	135.6	139.7	141.6
Dec	110.3	118.8	129.9	135.7	139.2	141.9

RETAIL PRICE INDEX FIGURES					
	1994	*1995*	*1996*	*1997*	*1998*	*1999*
Jan	141.3	146.0	150.2	154.4	159.5	163.4
Feb	142.1	146.9	150.9	155.0	160.3	163.7
Mar	142.5	147.5	151.5	155.4	160.8	164.1
Apr	144.2	149.0	152.6	156.3	162.6	165.2
May	144.7	149.6	152.9	156.9	163.5	165.6
June	144.7	149.8	153.0	157.5	163.4	165.6
July	144.0	149.1	152.4	157.5	163.0	165.1
Aug	144.7	149.9	153.1	158.5	163.7	165.5
Sep	145.0	150.6	153.8	159.3	164.4	166.2
Oct	145.2	149.8	153.8	159.5	164.5	166.5
Nov	145.3	149.8	153.9	159.6	164.4	166.7
Dec	146.0	150.7	154.4	160.0	164.4	167.3
	2000	*2001*	*2002*	*2003*	*2004*	*2005*
Jan	166.6	171.1	173.3	178.4	183.1	188.9
Feb	167.5	172.0	173.8	179.3	183.8	189.6
Mar	168.4	172.2	174.5	179.9	184.6	190.5
Apr	170.1	173.1	175.7	181.2	185.7	191.6
May	170.7	174.2	176.2	181.5	186.5	192.0
June	171.1	174.4	176.2	181.3	186.8	192.2
July	170.5	173.3	175.9	181.3	186.8	192.2
Aug	170.5	174.0	176.4	181.6	187.4	192.6
Sep	171.7	174.6	177.6	182.5	188.1	193.1
Oct	171.6	174.3	177.9	182.6	188.6	193.3
Nov	172.1	173.6	178.2	182.7	189.0	193.6
Dec	172.2	173.4	178.5	183.5	189.9	194.1

RETAIL PRICE INDEX FIGURES					
	2006	*2007*	*2008*	*2009*	*2010*	*2011*
Jan	193.4	201.6	209.8	210.1	217.9	229.0
Feb	194.2	203.1	211.4	211.4	219.2	231.3
Mar	195.0	204.4	212.1	211.3	220.7	232.5
Apr	196.5	205.4	214.0	211.5	222.8	234.4
May	197.7	206.2	215.1	212.8	223.6	235.2
June	198.5	207.3	216.8	213.4	224.1	235.2
July	198.5	206.1	216.5	213.4	223.6	234.7
Aug	199.2	207.3	217.2	214.4	224.5	236.1
Sept	200.1	208.0	218.4	215.3	225.3	237.9
Oct	200.4	208.9	217.7	216.0	225.8	238.0
Nov	201.1	209.7	216.0	216.6	226.8	238.5
Dec	202.7	210.9	212.9	218.0	228.4	239.4
	2012	*2013*	*2014*	2015		
Jan	238.0	245.8	252.6	255.4		
Feb	239.9	247.6	254.2	256.7		
Mar	240.8	248.7	254.8	257.1		
Apr	242.5	249.5	255.7	258.0		
May	242.4	250.0	255.9	258.5		
June	241.8	249.7	256.3			
Jul	242.1	249.7	256.0			
Aug	243.0	251.0	257.0			
Sept	244.2	251.9	257.6			
Oct	245.6	251.9	257.7			
Nov	245.6	252.1	257.1			
Dec	246.8	253.4	257.5			

Table 38.7 – Rates of interest on overdue tax/repayment supplement

Rates from 29 September 2009:	
For overdue income, inheritance and capital gains tax	3%
For overpaid income, inheritance and capital gains tax	0.5%

Table 38.8 – Rates of corporation tax

Financial year starting on 1 April	2012	2013	2014	2015
Full rate (see 18.4.2)	24%	23%	21%	20%
Small companies rate (see 18.4.3)	20%	20%	20%	Phased out
Small companies rate – limit	£300,000	£300,000	£300,000	
Small companies marginal rate limit	£1.5m	£1.5m	£1.5m	
Marginal rate	25%	23.75%	21.75%	
Fraction	1/100	3/400	1/400	

Table 38.9 – Rates of inheritance tax

	TRANSFERS ON DEATH	LIFETIME TRANSFERS
Cumulative chargeable transfers £	Rate on gross % age	Rate on gross % age
from 6 April 2009 – 5 April 2016		
0–325,000	nil	nil
over 325,000	40	20

For married couples and civil partners, it is possible to carry forward the proportion of the nil-rate band unused on the first death to the death of the second spouse or civil partner on or after 9 October 2007. A reduced rate of 36% applies for deaths occurring on or after 6 April 2012 where 10% or more of a deceased's net estate (after the deduction of all IHT exemptions, reliefs and the nil rate band) is left to charity. It is proposed that the nil rate band will remain at the current level until 6 April 2018.

INDEX